Gower Handbook of Quality Management

Third Edition

Gower Handbook of Quality Management

Third Edition

Edited by
MATT SEAVER

GOWER

Published by
Gower Publishing Limited
Gower House
Croft Road
Aldershot
Hants GU11 3HR
England

Gower Publishing Company
101 Cherry Street
Burlington, VT 05401–4405 USA

British Library Cataloguing in Publication Data
Gower handbook of quality management. - 3rd ed.
1. Quality control 2. Total quality management
I. Seaver, Matt II. Lock, Dennis, 1929- III. Handbook of quality management
658.5'62

ISBN 0 566 08149 0

Library of Congress Cataloging-in-Publication Data
Library of Congress Control Number: 2002106611

Printed and bound in Great Britain by MPG Books Ltd, Bodmin, Cornwall

Contents

List of Figures

List of Tables

Notes on Contributors

Trevor C. Ashton is employed by GEC ALSTHOM T&D Protection & Control Limited, Stafford. He has over twenty-five years' experience of standardization, including preparation of the full range of company standards for design, manufacture, purchasing and quality assurance in the light electronics and electromechanical field. Mr Ashton lectures for the British Standards Society, and has chaired both its Midland Region and Electronics Group, as well as serving on the management committee. He is a principal contributor to the booklet PD 3542, *The Role of Standards in Company Quality Management*, published by the British Standards Institution, and is Chairman of the British Standards Society's publications committee.

Joyce Brick is Quality Manager at the National Physical Laboratory (NPL). She joined NPL's Mathematics Division in 1961, and worked on DEUCE (Digital Electronic Computing Engine). She stayed in computing services until 1983, when she joined the staff of NATLAS (National Testing Laboratory Accreditation Scheme), where she designed and implemented a database of accredited laboratories and technical assessors, and processed applications in the fields of textiles, NDT and concrete cube testing. NATLAS and BCS (British Calibration Service) were amalgamated in 1985 to form NAMAS, and Mrs Brick became head of the Physical Testing Section in 1988. She also assumed responsibility for the accreditation of IT testing services. In 1989, she became NAMAS's quality manager, and was responsible for the implementation of its Quality Management System, which meets the requirements of European and international standards for the operation of a laboratory accreditation body. She was appointed NPL Quality Manager in 1992. Mrs Brick is Fellow of the British Computer Society, and a Member of the Institute of Quality Assurance.

Darek Celinski is a founder partner of the Kingwood Centre for Learning, Henley-on-Thames. He has extensive experience as a consultant in designing and conducting training and development for client organizations in the UK and overseas. Previously, he was with Coventry Management Training Centre (CMTC). His earlier training appointments were with the Aviation Division of Smiths Industries, The British Steel Corporation and Herbert-Ingersoll. Mr Celinski is a Fellow of the Institute of Training and Development and has written numerous articles on training and development in organizations.

Sylvia Codling has an MBA in business development from City University Business School, London, and is Senior Partner at Oak Business Developers. Her book, *Best Practice Benchmarking: The Management Guide to Successful Implementation*, was published in 1992 by Industrial Newsletters. Sylvia is on the Benchmarking Management Group of the British Quality Foundation, and is a founder member of the steering group behind the Benchmarking Centre.

Charles Corrie joined the British Standards Institution (BSI) in 1993. He has served as Secretary to ISO/TC 176/SC 2 (responsible for the development of the ISO 9001 and ISO 9004 international standards) since that time, as well as to other BSI Technical Committees. His previous work experience has included the aerospace industry (Rolls-Royce), the pressurized diecasting industry (Fry's Diecastings), and the fire protection/quality assurance certification industry (Loss Prevention Certification Board). He had formal education in mechanical engineering and business administration.

Dr Barrie Dale is Director of the UMIST Quality Management Centre. The centre is involved in four major activities: research into Total Quality Management, accommodating the Ford Motor Company Northern Regional Centre for training suppliers in total quality excellence and SPC, operating the Quality Management Multi-Company Teaching Programme (which involves, at any one time, eight industrial collaborators), and Total Quality Management consultancy, including the Q-share initiative. He is co-editor of the *International Journal of Quality and Reliability Management*, and has co-written or edited several books on quality.

Dr Pat Donnellan is a Lecturer in Industrial Engineering at the National University of Ireland, Galway, Ireland. His research interests lie in quality, safety and environmental management systems, Operations Management, and Operations Strategy. He completed his PhD in 2001 with his thesis on the integration of quality, safety and environmental management practices. Previously, he worked as a production manager in the electronics industry, and also held positions in industrial engineering, quality engineering and quality management over a sixteen-year period.

John S. Edge has over 20 years experience of the software and IT industry with 15 years in quality, project and service management. As a software consultant he advises companies seeking ISO 900 certification under the DTI's TickIT software programme. He is an ISO 900 qualified auditor and lead assessor. His specific interests include: software TickIT programme; systems and software engineering; lifecycle management; lifecycle productivity and costs; quality economics; creation of cultural change through team working; education and training programmes; and provision of effective market-driven IT services through TQM methods. Application areas include: computer aided design, telecommunications, commercial, manufacturing, off-shore and military real-time, and service management. His clients range from large multi-national organizations to very small software houses. Mr Edge has lectured and written widely on the software quality management requirements of the IT industry.

David Lascelles has his own consultancy company, David Lascelles Associates, Manchester. Previously, he was Chief Executive of Q-MAS Ltd., a Total Quality Management consultancy operating under the auspices of the UMIST Quality Management Centre. Prior to that, he was a lecturer in the Manchester School of Management at UMIST, and has held positions in sales, marketing and project management in the mechanical engineering and steel stockholding industries. His research interests include the motivational causes of quality improvement, strategic issues of TQM, and supplier development. Dr Lascelles received the 1989 European Quality Award for best European doctoral thesis on quality management, and he has written widely on quality in books and articles.

Geoffrey Leaver is Principal of G.L. Consultants, an independent consultancy specializing in quality assurance systems and quality management. Mr Leaver, who holds a master's degree in metallurgy, is a Chartered Engineer and a Lead Assessor and Fellow of the Institute of Quality Assurance. He has been involved in the technical and quality fields for over twenty years, initially in heavy engineering and fabrication, followed by quality management within the Philips Electrical Industries Group. Mr Leaver established G.L. Consultants in 1983, and as a consultant listed under the Department of Trade and Industry Support for Quality Scheme, currently offers a comprehensive service to industry and commerce covering all aspects of quality assurance and quality management.

Dennis Lock is a freelance writer. His early career began with a Higher National Certificate in Applied Physics and an appointment as an electronics engineer with the General Electric Company. His subsequent management experience has been exceptionally wide, in industries ranging from electronics to heavy machine tools and mining engineering. He is a Fellow of the Institute of Management Services, and a member of the Institute of Management. Mr Lock has carried out lecturing and consultancy assignments in the UK and overseas, and has written or edited many successful management books, mostly for Gower.

David Newton started his industrial career as an apprentice with Smiths Industries Limited, during which time he also studied for the London University external degree in Mechanical Engineering. He continued at Smiths in various appointments in quality assurance and reliability before entering academic life in 1968. He was initially a research fellow, and later a lecturer in the Department of Engineering Production at Birmingham University, particularly involved in quality assurance education, including a period as Course Director for the postgraduate course in Quality and Reliability Engineering. He left the university in 1989 to pursue a career as a freelance lecturer and consultant. He holds bachelor's and master's degrees in engineering, and is a Chartered Mechanical Engineer. He is a Fellow of the Royal Statistical Society, and of the Institute of Quality Assurance.

John Oakland is head of the European Centre for Total Quality Management, and holds the Exxon Chemical Chair in TQM at the Management Centre, University of Bradford, one of the largest business schools in Europe. Over the last ten years he has taught quality management and SPC to thousands of organizations. He has directed several large research projects on quality in Europe, funded by the British government and EC programmes, and his work has been widely acknowledged and published. Professor Oakland is the author of several books, including *Statistical Process Control* and the bestselling *Total Quality Management*, both published by Butterworth-Heinemann (Oxford). He started his career with the British Iron and Steel Research Association. He later worked for Sandoz, where he led a team engaged in research and development of production processes. He joined Bradford Management Centre in 1979, and his interests since then have centred on quality management education, training and research.

John Oxley graduated from Cambridge University, worked initially in plant design, and then plant management in the chemical industry. Subsequently, he became involved in process and plant operability and efficiency investigations, and studies into product distribution and supply chain management. He has also designed and run problem-solving courses for managers. In 1978, Mr Oxley joined the Cranfield Institute of Technology, consulting and lecturing in logistics, and specializing in the design and management of materials handling and warehousing systems. He is now a member of the academic staff, primarily involved with MSc and other courses in logistics and distribution. Mr Oxley is a chartered engineer, a member of the Institution of Mechanical Engineers, and of the Institute of Logistics and Distribution Management. He lectures widely in the UK and Europe, is an examiner for a number of professional institutions, has contributed to various logistics texts, and is co-author of *Handbook of Logistics and Distribution Management*, published by Kogan Page.

Robin Plummer is a management consultant specializing in operations, services and quality. After working for short periods in the electronics, defence and construction industries, he joined British Telecom in 1973, becoming fully involved in multi-million-pound advanced technology installations. His main responsibility was in the quality assurance of suppliers' software. Later, as part of a large consultancy team, he was seconded to Libya as senior electrical, telecommunications and building engineer on the $600 million Libyan Coaxial Cable Project, where he was held for nine months as a political detainee until his release was gained by Terry Waite. More recently, Mr Plummer has been Quality Assurance Manager for a section of British Telecom, and has been at the forefront of implementing TQM in a service environment within his own section and at the premises of dozens of suppliers. Mr Plummer has recently presented courses on TQM at Cambridge, and has provided guidance to companies across a wide spectrum of industries on a range of quality matters in his capacity as a management consultant. He is a Chartered Engineer, a member of the Institution of Electrical Engineers, a Fellow of the Institute of Quality Assurance, and a Registered Lead Assessor of quality management systems.

The late **Frank Price** was a Fellow of the Institute of Quality Assurance, and a member of the Association of Management Education and Development. He spent more than thirty years initiating and implementing quality control systems in a variety of manufacturing companies, and wrote and lectured widely on the subject. He studied statistics at Leicester College of Technology, and industrial psychology at Nottingham University. From 1957 to 1963 he was a Quality Control Manager at Pilkington, and then left to run a successful company of his own. He re-entered the world of industry when invited to set up a QC function for a new electronic enterprise, and similar assignments soon followed. Until shortly before his death, he was an independent consultant in the field of quality management and cultural change in the work organization.

Dr John G. Roche FASQ FIQA is a founder member of the Irish Quality Control Association (IQCA), now Excellence Ireland. He has been actively promoting improved quality management practices in Ireland since the 1960s. After some years in industry, he began lecturing in Dublin and moved to University College, Galway, where he developed a number of quality management programmes. He has been involved in product liability since the late 1960s. His research on product liability led to the publication of his book *Product Liability: The European Management and Quality Challenge* in 1989. He lectures part-time on quality management and product liability at National University of Ireland, Galway, Ireland.

Matt Seaver is principal of Seaver Associates, Wexford, Ireland, specializing in quality management systems, food safety and laboratory accreditation. He obtained his PhD in biochemistry in 1974 for work on the enzymes of meat. He subsequently spent a number of years in the Blood Transfusion Service in Dublin before becoming a quality manager in the babyfood industry. In 1991, after thirteen years in industry, he set up his own consultancy and training organization. Since 1992 he has been one of Ireland's expert members of ISO Technical Committee 176 (Quality Management and Quality Assurance), and has been deeply involved in the last two revisions of the ISO 9000 standards. In 2000 he co-authored *ISA 2000: The System for Occupational Health and Safety Management* with L. O'Mahony (also published by Gower). His book *Implementing ISO 9000: 2000*, based on his first-hand experience of implementing the standard and his inside knowledge of the requirements from his work with TC176, was published by Gower in 2001. The Seaver Associates Website is available at: <http://www.seaverassociates.com>.

Ray Spencer began his quality management career as Supplier Quality Manager at Rank Xerox, leading the launch of the renowned Xerox supplier capability improvement process in the UK. He later gained experience of military, professional and commercial markets as Quality Manager with STC Components, before becoming Divisional Quality Manager with Thorn EMI Ferguson. Following takeover by Thomson Consumer Electronics, he moved to Paris and led the Thomson Tubes & Displays group to ISO 9000 certification at all 15 plants in France, Poland, the USA, Mexico, Italy and Brazil. Later, as head of Thomson Multimedia Corporate Quality, Ray completed ISO 9000 certification at all 45 Thomson plants world-wide, involving 50 000 people. He then launched the Business Excellence self-assessment process to establish benchmarks and identify actions leading to world-class standards in all areas of the business. Ray is now using his experience working with progressive companies throughout Europe as principal consultant with Systex Business Solutions.

David J. Smith has spent over twenty-five years in a number of senior positions in both quality and reliability management in the telecommunications, electronics and control, and oil and gas industries. He has assisted companies of all sizes in obtaining Ministry of Defence and British Standards quality systems approvals. Mr Smith is a Fellow of the Institution of Electrical Engineers, the Institute of Quality Assurance, and the Safety and Reliability Society. He has been chairman of the Safety and Reliability Society, and edits its journal. He is best known for his many seminars and courses on reliability engineering, its contract implications and other related topics, and he has written numerous successful works on quality, reliability, maintainability and statistics.

Gordon Staples is widely experienced in quality, having worked world-wide in company-wide quality improvement, IQA/RAB Lead Auditor training, quality circles, and quality systems consultancy and training. He is now Managing Partner of Excel Partnership (UK) and President of Excel Partnership Inc., companies within the Excel group which provide consultancy and training services in quality management. Previously, he was director of a consultancy in Manchester, Training Manager for David Hutchins Associates, and Manager of Training Services for Gilbert (Europe) in London. Prior to consultancy, he worked in the gas industry, where he assessed vendors and subcontractors for both offshore and onshore supply from many industries. He also presented training courses in quality management and assessment. Earlier experience was as Quality Assurance Manager of a valve and desuperheater manufacturer (supplying the nuclear industry), and in design in the computer and machine tool industries. Mr Staples is an IQA registered Lead Assessor, and an RAB registered Quality System Lead Auditor.

Denis Walker is an independent consultant specializing in service, quality and organizational change. His previous career was with British Airways, where after holding a variety of personnel posts, he became Customer Service Manager, and ultimately Deputy General Manager, Ground Operations. He is the author of *Customer First*, published by Gower.

Preface

Anybody who has read my book on ISO 9000 will know that I have great regard for the busy manager who is trying to get a day's work done, and at the same time is expected to be leader, motivator, controller, counsellor, financial wizard and technical know-all. It is difficult to find time to gather the expertise to be all of these things and still look after the shop. When, as one of those managers, I first came across the *Gower Handbook of Quality Management*, it immediately struck me as an indispensable tool, and very soon became the one book that I referred to when issues outside my immediate competency cropped up. In editing this third edition, I have tried to maintain that practical approach while ensuring that there is adequate theoretical treatment of those topics that need it.

It is not intended to give the most comprehensive treatment available on any given topic, and probably every reader will identify some topic or sub-topic which is either not covered, or not covered in sufficient depth to rate as a definitive treatment. But I believe it gives sufficient information to enable managers to gauge the importance and usefulness of the subjects covered. I also believe that this new edition retains all the best aspects of the previous two editions, and will prove at least as useful as its predecessors. It also contains some additions and improvements that should make it even more useful.

If the previous edition was so wonderful, why was it necessary to change it? – 'If it's not broken, why fix it?' Readers of my book will also know that I regard this aphorism as a formula for stagnation: if you only fix things that are broken you deprive yourself of great opportunities for improvement. In addition, there were several chapters that had to be updated because of changes, for example, in relation to ISO 9000.

Previous editions may have appeared to lean towards engineering. I have tried to improve its applicability towards businesses in general, and most chapters should contain something of interest to everybody.

One of the problems encountered when putting together a handbook such as this is that the whole field of business management changes very rapidly. For ten years I have been involved in standards development in ISO Technical Committee 176 working groups, and I have seen at first hand how quickly ideas and approaches change as newer and better ones emerge. It is most likely that some of the references will be out of date even before publication of the handbook. I beg the reader's forbearance on this, and ask that he or she look beyond the incidental details and examine the principles involved.

The handbook is structured according to the well-known quality concept of Plan–Do–Check–Act. This has resulted in total quality management, for example, appearing quite late in the proceedings. That does not imply any downgrading of its importance. Rather, it reflects the reality that most companies will attempt to walk before they run, and will have planned and done many things before they come to the realization that they need to do something more in order to achieve real improvement.

I would like to express my immense admiration for the contributing authors, and to acknowledge the tremendous work done by them, all experts in their fields who have generously agreed to share their experience and expertise for the general improvement of quality. I would particularly like to pay tribute to Robin Plummer for the enormous amount of work he put into this revision in its early stages of preparation.

Matt Seaver
Wexford, 2002

PART 1 *Plan*

than the applying of chisels to wood. Quality makes use of statistical thinking purely as a tool of convenience, because there is no other tool as appropriate to the task as that provided by mathematical statistics. This tends to put people off: memories of the blank incomprehension occasioned by the algebra of schooldays shroud the subject in veils of mystery. It all seems too complicated, and best left to the specialist practitioners who have mastered its mysteries. Often these 'experts' themselves foster this mystification by speaking in their own esoteric tongue which is unintelligible to the rest of us. This leads us to ask what has all this fancy mathematics to do with quality in the workaday world, to which the answer is 'not much'. Maybe this is one of the reasons why quality used to be a despised discipline done by despised people, whereas nowadays, thanks in large measure to Japan on the one hand and the Ford Motor Company's quality training initiative on the other, quality is a highly respected discipline. Done by despised people.

This is one of the reasons why we in the West are, generally speaking, not as smart at quality as we could be – it is still looked upon in the corporate culture as a low-status activity of sufficient unimportance to be entrusted to low-calibre people, to those unsuited to the more rewarding and demanding jobs of financial jiggery-pokery or marketing manipulativeness. This statement is not mere opinion; it is borne out by the most cursory survey of the job advertisements in the 'quality' newspapers: see which jobs are held in highest esteem as measured by salaries offered, note where quality comes in the pecking order. In these 'quality' newspapers the prestigious positions (financial management being the most highly regarded, presumably because it is assumed that anybody who can count money correctly can also earn it for the company – a belief with no basis in reality) offer the highest pay, plus a 'quality' motor car. Note the misuse of language here. What is a 'quality' car? One which fulfils its intended purpose. So, to an itinerant window-cleaner, a fuel-thrifty Reliant Robin van with a roof-rack to carry ladders is a 'quality' car. To a successful rag-and-bone gatherer who is privately ashamed of his scavenging way of life, such a vehicle would demean his self-image, so he buys a Rolls-Royce to park on the gravel drive in front of his mansion. His is a different 'intended purpose' from the window-cleaner's.

Quality is fitness for purpose; it has nothing whatever to do with status, or grade, or class. Yet this wrong interpretation of the word is an endlessly recurring source of trouble, it causes so many misunderstandings. 'We cannot afford the luxury of quality', decrees the boss of a small outfit making modest earthenware drinking mugs. 'We are not at the Wedgwood or china porcelain end of the business.' No, but whoever buys the mugs expects them to hold the tea without leaking, expects them to fulfil their intended purpose – expects, in a word, *quality*.

Perhaps another of the reasons why we in the West are still not quite as smart about quality as we could be lies in the paradox that when it is present, quality is, in fact, invisible. What do we mean by that, *invisible*? Consider the following paraphrasing of a famous advertising jingle:

> A million housewives every day open a can … and *throw it away*!

After having emptied its contents of baked beans into the saucepan, of course. In the act of throwing the emptied can away without a second thought, these housewives are collectively paying a daily million tributes to the *quality* of the tin can which brought them something to go with their breakfast bacon – *by ignoring it*. The quality of these cans (which is to say the way they fulfil their intended purpose) is so superlatively good that it may safely be taken for granted – not once, not twice, but a million times a day. Now *that* is real quality! An invisible input. Achieved by a succession of invisible people, employed in the once-despised but lately respected calling of quality control, right back up the supply chain which ends when the emptied can is tossed absent-mindedly into the garbage bin. Achieved by the men and women in the cannery who control torrents of output streaming along the production lines at hundreds of cans per minute. At these vast output rates it is not possible to make a *little* mistake. So, very few mistakes are made. Achieved by their counterparts in the can-making plant; by those upstream in the tinplate mill; by those further back in the steel casting and rolling mill ... an unremitting application of statistical method and quality skill which culminates in an emptied can, its purpose fulfilled, being casually tossed onto the rubbish dump – by the million, and rarely does a dud appear. (When did you last see a can with its ends domed-out, blown?) The rare defectives are not counted even in parts per million; they occur as one per several million, if at all.

To sum up the foregoing:

Quality is: Giving the customer what he wants today,
at a price he is pleased to pay,
at a cost we can contain,
again, and again,and again,
and giving him something even better tomorrow.
Quality is: The degree of congruence between expectation and realization.

Or, to put this into plainer words:
The matching of what you wanted with what you got.
Expectation versus fulfilment.

Quality is: Invisible when it is good,
Impossible to ignore when it is bad.
An *invisible* input.

Quality is: NOT mathematical statistics.
Quality is: The application of simple statistical method.
Quality is: NOT status, grade or class.

Quality: Is it important?

Important? The answer to this question depends, as answers so often do, on the questioner's standpoint. Quality is relative. It is to a large extent dependent on economics, on the inexorable law of supply and demand. Whenever there is an excess of money pursuing a shortage of goods or services to spend it on, quality is of secondary importance to mere availability.

In a free market economy a famine of consumer goods is not permitted to exist for very long; market forces, in the form of entrepreneurial capitalism, respond to the imbalance of too much cash chasing too few goods. The balance is redressed. Soon there is an abundance of goods available to sop up the cash in the economy. The system overbalances in the other direction, and an excess of goods bloats the market, rival brands competing for the consumers' spending power. Now quality, which mattered not at all when things were scarce, matters more than anything else now they are plentiful. So quality is a function of supply, once sellers' markets have given way to buyers'. Of the three factors governing purchasing decisions – price, service and quality – at a time when goods were scarce, service was the be-all and end-all, 'make it ... sell it' was the order of the day. This is how things used to be in the halcyon days of Western manufacturing, before a quality revolution exploded out of the East to shatter complacency for evermore. As soon as goods became plentiful, price became the arbiter, but price wars are too costly to support for very long, so *quality* inevitably becomes the *primary purchasing determinant*, to use the language of the buying officer. This fact is borne out by formal research, as well as by general observation and historical awareness.

This economic context emphasizing the importance of quality, as it is used as a marketing competitive edge external to the manufacturing (or servicing) enterprise, is symmetrically balanced by an equal stress on the economics of quality within the enterprise. Quality is, as well as an information-gathering agency, a *discipline of thrift*, a doctrine of frugality in the use of available resources.

Resources ... what are the resources at the disposal of the manufacturer? There are four – raw materials, machinery, time and people. The 'trick' of manufacturing management is to make the best use of time and machinery, through the capabilities (or, as they are called these days, 'competencies') of people, in order to transform 100 per cent of the bought-in raw materials into saleable finished goods. Sounds simple enough. It is. But it is not easy. This conversion ratio – the proportion of raw materials entering the plant which eventually departs from the plant as finished goods (as opposed to scrap or returned products) – is a valid measure of the effectiveness of management. This must be why a good many companies are unable to quote it. The maximization of this conversion ratio is the job of quality.

You might at this point choose to step into that ancient and cloying swamp of semantics by asking that hoary old conundrum, 'Who is *responsible* for quality?' and then going on to suggest that the quality function cannot be 'responsible' for quality, since its practitioners do no more than measure it. You might then go on to suggest, as so many others before you have suggested, that since quality is not the responsibility of quality, it must therefore be the responsibility of production. Your thinking, if you have pursued this route, is now well and truly bogged down in the mire of meanings. You are now committed to a silly sectarian squabble about who is responsible for quality, and it will go on and on and you will never escape the swamp. Save your breath. *It is the process which is responsible for quality*. The job of the people in the quality department is to measure the capability of the process, to balance the see-saw on one end of which sit the customers' needs, while on the other is perched the measured capability of the process to meet those needs. The 'responsibility' for quality belongs to the process and therefore to those in whose stewardship the entire process of wealth-generation rests, whether they are called 'production' or 'quality' or whatever. They are collectively the custodians of the resources whose purpose is the generating of wealth by the adding of value, through the activity called 'work'.

Work, from an economic standpoint, is identifiable as one of two kinds:

- work which adds *value*
- work which adds *cost*.

To demonstrate this crucial difference, consider (using the following example) what research in the UK shows to be typical of manufacturing performance.

A hypothetical manufacturer buys £100's worth of components – his 'raw materials'. He processes them through his lathes and his grinders to turn them into saleable goods. He has done work which adds value. Their value is now £200. Well, it would be, but for the distressing discovery that 30 per cent of the finished goods are incorrect to specification, so these are rejected to be reworked. So only £70's worth of the original lot has achieved saleable status. It now has a value of £140. The remaining components, costing £30 but now having a *nominal* value of £60, are consigned to rework. This costs money in machine time and wages. This work is now *adding cost*. If all are salvaged, their value will still be £60, but their cost will be considerably higher. This would be a bad enough state of affairs, but there is worse: half of the 30 per cent reworked components are found to be irredeemably defective *after* the rework costs have been added. These are now scrapped. Money is now pouring down the plug-hole. All hope of any profit is lost. Company cash is added to that Danegeld which collective quality incompetence extorts from British manufacturing industry, every year to the tune of a staggering figure somewhere between £10 000 million and £20 000 million. These are statistical estimates of the awful reality; they are figures of unimpeachable pedigree, elicited by university research (Lockyer and Oakland, Bradford UMC).

The hypothetical company (Hypothetical? Don't you believe it!) which is the subject of this tale of woe might argue: 'So what! It is *our* money we are losing.' True, true yet false; it is ultimately the *nation's* wealth they are squandering through their wasteful mismanagement of the resources that society entrusts to their stewardship. Their private loss is our public loss in their frittering away of irreplaceable resources. Perhaps they seek to excuse their inexcusable misconduct by citing another of the convenient managerial cop-outs of our times and claiming 'you cannot have quality and quantity'. Again they are wrong. The truth is:

The higher the quality, the *less* it costs.

This is very obvious, when you think about it. Making duds sops up just as much machine capacity as making OK output does; thus to improve quality is to bring more productive capacity into profitable employment. You would wonder why it is necessary to state such an obvious truth. Alas, it is often necessary to do so.

So this thing we call quality – which is about satisfying the needs of the customer and doing so at an economic cost – is a subject well worthy of consideration at the highest level. Quality, used for a generation and more by Japan as a key element of manufacturing and marketing strategy, offers us the chance to create a strong competitive edge. Quality, once the Cinderella of the organization, is about to become a royal bride. Unless we get it wrong, and it becomes just another ugly sister instead. So how do we get it right?

Quality: Leadership through commitment

There is an old Chinese benediction which goes 'May you be so fortunate as to live in uninteresting times.' The idea of it is, one supposes, that the even tenor of life should never be upset by the arrival of the unexpected. There must be no surprises. It is a not inappropriate tenet of faith for anyone engaged in the supply of goods or services of specified quality – never disturb the equanimity of the customer by *surprising* him, especially by making a delivery of substandard output. This is not to confuse 'uninteresting' with 'boring'. There is no boredom to be found in consistently delivering high-quality product, but 'interest' – even shock – is generated by the delivery of the rejectable. Like the consumer who disposes of the empty can with utter disinterest (she would only find it of interest if it had failed in its purpose), the consumer has no wish to find your product 'interesting' because it is contaminated with troublesome duds. After all, what is it that you are *really* selling?

This is not a trivial question; it is central to the whole commercial thrust. Elizabeth Arden, of cosmetics fame, asked and answered this question; when someone made the observation, 'Ah, Miss Arden, I see you are selling cosmetics', she is said to have replied: 'No I am not selling cosmetics, I am selling the hope of beauty.' There is a world of difference. What is the can manufacturer selling to the cannery which puts the beans into the cans which are bought by a million consumers? Empty tin cans? Ends to be seamed onto the cans once they are filled? No, it is selling the certitude of trouble-free running to the canner who will use this product at the rate of over a thousand a minute. It is selling *peace of mind*. It is selling 'uninteresting times'.

This notion might be pushed even further by suggesting that it is in the interest of manufacturers to attend to all the interesting quality requirements of their product, in order to deprive their customers of the interesting discovery that they are not to specification. Customers will have enough problems controlling their own quality and will feel completely disinclined to add to their burden by accepting yours. Customers are people, and after all, in our mechanistic scheme of things people are generally perceived to be nuisances; this is a legacy of our rationalist and scientific culture. It is the motivation behind the millennial dream of the 'workerless factory' from which people have been exiled by automation. Trouble is, though, that the achieving and sustaining of high process and product quality is the direct result of the application of creativity, imagination, analysis, synthesis, willpower – *people* things. This is where quality leadership has its roots, in the vision of quality which is the essential precursor of its attainment.

This is not to suggest that there is no place for managerial systems and advancing technology. These are essential. But on their own they cannot be enough. The best system of quality management, ISO 9000, is a fine system. But that is *all* it is – a system, a scaffolding within which people must transform the pile of bricks it embraces into a house. Any system is all form and no content. The latter must be supplied by people. Many managers set great store by systems, and it is easy to over-systematize, to fall into the trap of assuming that because there is a system for dealing with every eventuality then every eventuality will be dealt with; disappointment and frustration sometimes ensue. Systems sometimes help us to generate the right answers to the wrong questions, whereas quality is about *asking the right questions*. Systems are concerned with administration; quality is to do with inspiration. This is the most important gift the quality function can make to the organization: a vision of success to which it is feasible to aspire, to say 'this is where we are aiming, this is our strategic goal'; and then to provide the means of achieving it, the techniques of quality, saying 'this is how we get there'. This is the tactical support.

In this way the quality function will finally free itself from the stigma of being a despised discipline. It will have earned respect. And quality, of world-class leadership, is achieved through education, which is what this handbook is all about.

Further reading

Price, Frank, *Right First Time*, Gower, Aldershot, 1984.
Price, Frank, *Right Every Time*, Gower, Aldershot, 1990.

CHAPTER 2

Statutory Considerations

*David J. Smith**

In recent years the development of health, safety and liability legislation has had a profound impact on the quality and reliability profession. The Consumer Protection Act 1987 has focused attention on the reliability, and hence the safety, of goods. Previously, the Health and Safety at Work Act 1974, together with the Control of Industrial Major Accident Hazards (CIMAH) Regulations, recently revised to COMAH (also dealt with in this chapter), have provided a similar impetus in the design of reliable process plant. Before describing the effects of the latter, it will be useful to give a brief outline of the Health and Safety Executive and the way in which it operates.

The Health and Safety Executive

The Health and Safety Executive (HSE) was set up by the UK Government under the authority of the Health and Safety at Work Act 1974. It is administered through the Department of Employment. The HSE is the executive and operational branch of the Health and Safety Commission (HSC), and it carries out the HSC's policy. The HSE is largely made up of various inspectorates, which operate within the Civil Service structure.

The Field Operations Division (FOD) is the largest operational inspectorate in the HSE. It covers many industrial and other sectors, including construction, agriculture, general manufacturing, quarries, education, health services, local government, and domestic gas safety. The FOD is managed as seven geographical divisions and the national construction division, each led by a director or head of division. Divisional staff are involved primarily in front-line activities, inspection and investigation. Each division has a sector group with the national lead for one or more industries. The resources within each division include operational groups, each with teams of inspectors carrying out work in that division. In addition, each division has access to a specialist group of engineers, scientists, medical inspectors and occupational hygiene inspectors providing expertise for the operational and sector work, as well as administrative staff to provide support for inspectors and deal with telephone enquiries/complaints.

The operator of a plant is required to establish, by using formal hazard assessment techniques, the possible ways in which the plant could fail and the nature and extent of any consequences for both the public and employees. If any of these failures is likely to cause death, multiple injury or major damage, the probability of that event must be assessed carefully in order to estimate the magnitude of the risk.

The HSE uses these hazard assessments to establish what are known as consultation zones, which are areas surrounding hazardous installations. Planning authorities are required to consult with the HSE when considering applications for development within them.

The HSE is well aware that zero risk (in other words, absolute safety) is an unrealistic objective, and in fact the law states that industrial activities shall be without risk to health, safety and welfare 'as far as is reasonably practicable'. The test of reasonable practicability ensures that the cost of reducing risk is weighed against the benefits to both public and employees (see Chapter 25).

The Health and Safety at Work Act 1974

Modern safety legislation is primarily embodied in the Health and Safety at Work Act. Although it can hardly be regarded as recent, it is extremely important and imposes responsibilities on everyone. It was drafted as enabling legislation to ensure that the health, safety and welfare of all is not adversely affected by work activities.

Section 1 of the Act sets out the general duties for every employer to ensure, as far as is reasonably practicable, the health, safety and welfare at work of all his employees.

Section 2 goes into detail as to how the employer can discharge these duties.

Section 3 establishes the duty of every employer to conduct his undertaking so as not to affect adversely the health and safety of persons not in his employment.

Section 6 of this Act is important in that it imposes strict liability in respect of articles produced for use at work, although the Consumer Protection Act extends this to all areas. It is very wide, and embraces designers, manufacturers, suppliers, hirers and employers of industrial plant and equipment. We are now dealing with criminal law: failure to observe the duties laid down in the Act is punishable by fine or imprisonment. Claims for compensation are still dealt with in civil law.

Other sections elaborate on employers' and employees' duties in various respects.

The main duties are to:

- design and construct products without risk to health or safety
- provide adequate information to the user for safe operation
- carry out research to discover and eliminate risks
- make positive tests to evaluate risks and hazards
- carry out tests to ensure that the product is inherently safe
- use safe methods of installation
- use safe (proven) substances and materials.

The main concessions are:

- It is a defence that a product has been used without regard to the relevant information supplied by the designer.
- It is a defence that the design was carried out on the basis of a written undertaking by the purchaser to take specified steps sufficient to ensure the safe use of the item.
- One's duty is restricted to matters within one's control.
- One is not required to repeat tests upon which it is reasonable to rely.

Basically, everyone concerned in the design and provision of an article is responsible for it. Directors and managers are held responsible for the designs and manufactured articles of their companies, and are expected to take steps to assure safety in their products. Employees are also responsible. The 'buck' cannot be passed in either direction.

THE IMPACT OF EUROPEAN COMMUNITY LEGISLATION

At present, EU legislation relating to health and safety at work falls into three categories:

- measures taken in pursuance of the Framework Directive 89/391/EEC, which contains basic provisions for health and safety organization at the workplace; it outlines the responsibilities of employers and workers, and is supplemented by individual directives for specific groups of workers, workplaces or substances
- measures taken in pursuance of the Framework Directive 80/1107/EEC, which is designed to protect the health and safety of workers against the risks arising from exposure to chemical, physical and biological agents at the workplace, supplemented by individual directives dealing with specific agents
- measures stemming from directives which contain provisions unconnected to the framework directives, in respect of occupational activities or specific groups at risk.

Directives dealing with occupational health and safety cover, among other aspects:

- the workplace
- use of work equipment
- use of personal protective clothing
- manual handling
- display screen equipment.

Industrial hazards

Since the 1960s, developments in the process industries have resulted in large quantities of noxious and flammable substances being stored and transmitted in locations that could, in the event of an incident, affect the public. Society is becoming increasingly aware of these hazards as a result of such incidents as:

- Flixborough (UK) 1974 – 28 deaths due to an explosion involving cyclohexane
- Beek (The Netherlands) 1975 – 14 deaths due to propylene
- Seveso (Italy) 1976 – unknown number of casualties due to a release of dioxin
- San Carlos Holiday Camp 1978 – about 150 deaths due to a propylene tanker
- Bhopal (India) 1984 – over 2000 deaths due to a release of methyl isocyanate
- Chernobyl (USSR) 1986 – unknown number of casualties due to the melt-down of a nuclear reactor
- Piper Alpha (UK) 1988 – 167 deaths due to fire on an offshore platform.

Following the Flixborough disaster, the HSC (Health and Safety Commission) set up the

Advisory Committee on Major Hazards (ACMH), which made various recommendations concerning notification of hazards.

Owing to a general lack of formal controls within the EC, a draft European Directive was issued in 1980. Delays in obtaining agreement resulted in this not being implemented until September 1984. The HSC introduced in January 1983 the Notification of Installation Handling Hazardous Substances (NIHHS) Regulations. These require the identification of hazardous installations and assessments of risks and consequences.

The EC Regulations (1984) have been implemented in the UK as the CIMAH (Control of Industrial Major Accident Hazards) Regulations 1984, and are concerned with both people and the environment, covering processes and the storage of dangerous substances. A total of 178 substances are listed, together with quantities which are notifiable. In these cases the regulations call for the preparation of a safety case, which involves a significant hazard and operability study, and a probabilistic risk assessment. The purpose of the safety case is to demonstrate either that a particular consequence is relatively minor, or that the probability of its occurrence is extremely small. It is also required to describe adequate emergency procedures in the event of an incident. The latest date for the submission of a safety case is three months prior to the bringing on site of any hazardous materials.

The CIMAH Regulations were updated to the COMAH Directive, in 1998, which is wider in scope. The main features are:

- some simplification, so that their application will be dependent on exceeding threshold quantities, and the distinction between process and storage will no longer apply
- the exclusion of explosive, chemical and waste disposal hazards at nuclear installations will be removed; the regulations will not, however, apply to offshore installations
- substances hazardous to the environment (as well as to people) will be introduced; in the first instance, these will take account of the aquatic environment
- more generic categories of substances will be introduced; the 178 substances currently named will thus reduce to 37; a spin-off is that new substances are more easily catered for by virtue of their inclusion in a generic group
- more information than before will be publicly available, including off-site emergency plans
- the HSE (the competent authority in the UK) will positively approve or reject a safety report
- the periodic update will be more frequent – three years instead of five years.

Following the offshore Piper Alpha incident in 1988 and the subsequent Cullen Inquiry, the responsibility for UK offshore safety was transferred from the Department of Energy to a newly formed department of the HSE. Equivalent requirements to the CIMAH Regulations are now being applied offshore, and safety cases are required for offshore installations.

Quantification of frequency, as well as consequence, in safety reports is now strongly favoured, and the role of human error factors in contributing to failures is attracting increasing interest. Furthermore, emphasis is also being placed on threats to the environment.

It follows that if the reliability of a particular piece of equipment is pertinent to the safety of a process or storage site, then the failure mode analysis becomes a vital part of the hazard study.

Standards and guidance

There are numerous standards and guidance documents covering hazardous equipment and so-called 'safety-related systems'. While these are not in themselves legislation, the provisions of the Health and Safety at Work Act are so wide that it is now necessary to address all relevant guidance in order to fulfil the obligation to do 'all that is reasonably practicable'.

It is not possible in a book of this nature to cover this very wide field, but the key standard at present is the IEC International Standard 61508: Functional Safety – Safety-related Systems (seven parts).

The standard deals with the safety life cycle, establishing risk levels, risk reduction measures, hardware reliability and software quality techniques. Safety integrity levels (SILs) are specified which involve placing the target reliability of safety-related systems into one of four safety integrity groups. For each group there are specific requirements in the form of configuration rules and other contributors to risk reduction and hence to safety integrity. Table 2.1 shows target figures for the four safety integrity levels, of which level 1 is the lowest and level 4 is the highest.

As an example of selecting an appropriate SIL, assume that an involuntary risk scenario (such as a customer killed by an explosion) is accepted as 10^{-5} p.a. (A). Assume that 10^{-1} of the hazardous events in question lead to fatality (B). Thus the failure rate for the hazardous event can be C = A/B = 10^{-4} p.a. Assume that a fault tree analysis indicates that the unprotected process only achieves a failure rate of 0.5×10^{-1} p.a. (D). The failure *on demand* of the safety system would need to be E = C/D = 2×10^{-3}. Consulting the right-hand column in Table 2.1 points to *level 2*.

The standard requires that reliability assessment techniques are used to demonstrate that the numerical requirements of the SIL are likely to be met, and in addition, that systematic failures are catered for by the application of qualitative measures prescribed for each SIL. The higher the SIL, the more onerous are the measures specified.

The intention is that this IEC standard should becomes an umbrella standard, and that industry groups will continue to develop specific 'second-tier' guidance such as that published by the Institution of Gas Engineers (IGE/SR/15).

Table 2.1 Safety integrity levels

Safety integrity level	*High demand rate (dangerous failures /hour)*	*Low demand rate (probability of failure on demand)*
4	>= 10^{-9} to < 10^{-8}	>= 10^{-5} to < 10^{-4}
3	>= 10^{-8} to < 10^{-7}	>= 10^{-4} to < 10^{-3}
2	>= 10^{-7} to < 10^{-6}	>= 10^{-3} to < 10^{-2}
1	>= 10^{-6} to < 10^{-5}	>= 10^{-2} to < 10^{-1}

Product liability

Product liability is the liability of a supplier, designer or manufacturer to the customer for injury or loss resulting from a defect in that product. There are reasons why it has recently become the focus of attention. The first is the publication in July 1985 of a directive by the European Community, and the second is the wave of actions under US law resulting in spectacular awards for claims involving death or injury. By 1984, sums awarded resulting from court proceedings often reached $1 000 000. Changes in the United Kingdom became inevitable, and the Consumer Protection Act reinforces the application of strict liability. It is therefore necessary to review the legal position.

THE GENERAL LAW

Contract law

This is largely governed by the Sale of Goods Act 1979, which requires that goods are of merchantable quality and are reasonably fit for the purpose intended. Privity of contract exists between the buyer and the seller, which means that only the buyer has any remedy for injury or loss, and then only against the seller, although the cascade effect of each party suing, in turn, the other would offset this. However, exclusion clauses are void for consumer contracts. This means that conditions excluding the seller from liability would be void in law. Note that a contract does not have to be in writing, and that a sale, in this context, implies the existence of a contract.

Common law

The relevant area of common law is that relating to the tort of negligence, for which damages can be awarded. Everyone has a duty of care to their neighbour, in law, and failure to exercise reasonable precautions with regard to one's skill, knowledge and the circumstances involved constitutes a breach of that care. A claim for damages for common law negligence is therefore open to anyone, and not restricted as in privity of contract. On the other hand, the onus is on the plaintiff to prove negligence, which requires proving that:

- The product was defective.
- The defect was the cause of the injury.
- This was foreseeable, and the plaintiff failed in their duty of care.

Statute law

The main Acts relevant to this area are:

Sale of Goods Act 1979

- Goods must be of merchantable quality.
- Goods must be fit for the purpose.

Unfair Contract Terms Act 1977

- Exclusion of personal injury liability is void.
- Exclusion of damage liability only if reasonable.

Consumer Protection Act 1987

- This imposes strict liability.
- It replaces the Consumer Safety Act 1978.

Health and Safety at Work Act 1974 Section 6 (see above)

In summary, the situation prior to the Consumer Protection Act 1987 involved a form of strict liability, but:

- Privity of contract excludes third parties in contract claims.
- The onus is to prove negligence, unless the loss results from a beach of contract.
- Exclusion clauses involving death and personal injury are void.

STRICT LIABILITY

Concept

The concept of strict liability hinges on the idea that liability exists for no other reason than the mere existence of a defect. No breach of contract or act of negligence is required in order to incur responsibility, and a manufacturer will be liable for compensation if his product causes injury.

Defects

A defect, for the purposes of liability, includes:

Manufacturing

- presence of impurities or foreign bodies
- fault or failure due to manufacturing or installation.

Design

- product not fit for the purpose stated
- inherent safety hazard in the design.

Documentation

- lack of necessary warnings
- inadequate or incorrect operating and maintenance instructions, resulting in a hazard.

THE CONSUMER PROTECTION ACT 1987

Background

In 1985, after nine years of discussion, the European Community adopted a directive on product liability, and member states were required to put this into effect before the end of July 1988. The English and Scottish Law Commissions each produced reports in 1977, and a Royal Commission document (The Pearson Report) was published in 1978. All of these reports recommended forms of strict liability.

The Consumer Protection Bill resulted in the Consumer Protection Act 1987, which establishes strict liability as already described above.

Provisions of the Act

The Act provides that a producer (and this includes manufacturers, those who import from outside the EC, and retailers of 'own brands') will be liable for damage caused wholly or partly by defective products, which includes goods, components and materials, but excludes unprocessed agricultural produce. 'Defective' is defined as not providing such safety as people are generally entitled to expect, taking into account the manner of marketing, instructions for use, the likely uses, and the time at which the product was supplied. The consumer must show that the defect caused the damage, but no longer has the onus of proving negligence. Defences include:

- The state of scientific and technical knowledge at the time was such that the producer could not be expected to have discovered the defect. (This is known as the 'development risks' defence.)
- The defect results from the product complying with the law.
- The producer did not supply the product.
- The defect was not present when the product was supplied by the manufacturer.
- The product was not supplied in the course of business.
- The product was in fact a component part in the manufacture of a further product, and the defect was not due to this component.

In addition, the producer's liability may be reduced by the user's contributory negligence. Further, unlike the privity limitation imposed by contract law, any consumer is covered in addition to the original purchaser.

The Act sets out a general safety requirement for consumer goods, and applies it to anyone who supplies goods which are not reasonably safe having regard to the circumstances pertaining. These include published safety standards, the cost of making goods safe, and whether or not the goods are new.

INSURANCE

The effects of product liability on insurance are:

- an increase in the number of claims
- higher premiums
- the creation of separate product liability policies
- involvement of insurance companies in defining quality and reliability standards and procedures
- contracts requiring the designer to insure the customer against genuine and frivolous consumer claims.

Some critical areas:

- **All risks** – This means only all risks specified in the policy. It is important to check that one's requirements are met by the policy.

- **Comprehensive** – Essentially means the same as the above.
- **Disclosure** – The policyholder is bound to disclose any information relevant to the risk. Failure to do so, whether asked for or not, can invalidate a claim. The test of what should be disclosed is described as 'anything the prudent insurer should know'.
- **Exclusions** – The Unfair Contract Terms Act 1977 does not apply to insurance, so one should read and negotiate accordingly. For example, defects related to design could be excluded, and this would considerably weaken a policy from the product liability standpoint.
- **Prompt notification of claims**.

Areas of cover

Premiums are usually expressed as a percentage of turnover, and cover is divided into three areas:

1 Product liability – cover against claims for personal injury or loss
2 Product guarantee – cover against the expenses of warranty/repair
3 Product recall – cover against the expenses of recall.

PRODUCT RECALL

Types of recall

A design defect causing a potential hazard to life, health or safety may become evident when a number of products are already in use. It may then become necessary to recall (for replacement or modification) a batch of items, some of which may be spread throughout the chain of distribution. The recall may vary in scope or urgency depending on whether the hazard is to life, health or merely reputation. A hazard which could reasonably be thought to endanger life, or to create a serious health hazard, should be treated as an emergency recall procedure. Where less critical risks involving minor health and safety hazards are discovered, a slightly less urgent approach may suffice. A third category, operated at the vendor's discretion, applies to defects causing little or no personal hazard and where only reputation is at risk.

If it becomes necessary to implement a recall, the extent will be determined by the nature of the defect. It might involve every user (in the worst case) or perhaps only a specific batch of items. In some cases the modification may be possible in the field, but in others physical return of the item will be required. In any case, a full evaluation of the hazard must be made and a report prepared.

Implementing the recall

One person, usually the quality manager, must be responsible for the handling of the recall, and must be directly responsible to the managing director or chief executive. The first task is to prepare, if appropriate, a hazard notice in order to warn those likely to be exposed to the risk. Circulation may involve individual customers (when traceable), the field service staff, distributors or even the news media. It will contain sufficient information to describe the nature of the hazard and the precautions to be taken. Instructions for returning the defective item can be included, preferably with a pre-paid return card. Small items can be returned with the card, whereas large ones, or products to be modified in the field, will be retained while arrangements are made.

Where products were all dispatched to known customers, a comparison of returns with output records will enable a 100 per cent check to be made on the coverage. Where products have been dispatched in batches to wholesalers or retail outlets, the task is not so easy and the quantity of returns can only be compared with a known output, perhaps by area. Individual users cannot then be traced with 100 per cent certainty. Where customers have completed and returned record cards after purchase, the effectiveness of the recall is improved.

After the recall exercise has been completed, a major investigation into the causes of the defect must be made, and the results progressed through the company's quality and reliability programme. Causes could include insufficient:

- test hours
- test coverage
- information sought on materials
- industrial engineering of the product prior to manufacture
- production testing
- field/user trials.

The environment

The Environmental Protection Act 1990 creates new obligations and codes of practice which bring about new measures to protect the environment. It has implications for most companies in all sectors of industry, including increasing awareness of the commercial benefits involved in being environmentally friendly. The Act provides a framework for the control of pollution as well as regulating waste disposal on land, noise and environmental nuisance. Supervision of the legislation is the responsibility of the Department of Environment. HM Inspectorate of Pollution regulates control measures, and advises on policy and technical matters. The National Rivers Authority and Health and Safety Executive are also responsible for enforcement in appropriate areas.

The management and control of environmental issues involves setting targets, measuring performance and dealing with non-conformances. It is thus not so different from operating a quality management system, and in many cases, will be implemented as part of a company's existing quality organization.

ISO 14001 (Environmental Management Systems – Specification with Guidance for Use) is, in content, very close to the EU Eco-Management and Audit System (EMAS) requirements. Both involve setting environmental performance objectives and targets. The principal headings of ISO 14001 are:

- **Environmental policy**
- **Planning**
  - environmental aspects
  - legal and other requirements
  - objectives and targets
  - environmental management programmes
- **Implementation and operation**
  - structure and responsibility

  - training, awareness and competence
  - communication
  - environmental management system documentation
  - document control
  - operational control
  - emergency preparedness and response
- **Checking and corrective action**
  - monitoring and measurement
  - non-conformance and corrective and preventive action
  - records
  - environmental management system audit
- **Management review**

EMAS recognizes the use of standards to meet the requirements of the regulation, and organizations using them can show (through certification) compliance with worldwide and European best practice. A 'bridging' document has been produced in the form of a CEN Report (CEN CR 12969) that identifies the few areas where EMAS requirements are covered by EN ISO 14000 standards or which are outside its scope. It also identifies where the elements are the same, if not readily apparent. These differences arise from the fact that the regulation and the standard were developed at different times and in different fora.

The similarity between many of the ISO 14001 and ISO 9001: 2000 requirements is easy to see.

The role of quality management

It has to be said that the mere practice of quality and reliability techniques alone does not release one from the obligations of the preceding legislation. Nor does it mitigate one's liability in the event of claims involving death or personal injury. Nevertheless, in view of the high cost and consequences of failure, the cost of quality and reliability efforts is nearly always repaid by a reduction in warranty and other failure-related costs.

Further reading

CEN CR 12969 – The Use of EN ISO 14001, ISO 14010, ISO 14011 and ISO 14012 for EMAS Related Purposes, European Committee for Standardization, Brussels, 1997.

ICE Standard 61508: Functional Safety of Electrical/Electronic/Programmable Electronic Safety-related Systems, International Electrotechnical Commission, Geneva, 1998.

IGE SR15: Programmable Equipment in Safety Related Applications, Institution of Gas Engineers, London, 1998.

Kelly, Patrick and Attree, Rebecca (eds), *European Product Liability*, Butterworth, London, 1992.

Miller, Christopher J., *Production Liability and Safety Encyclopaedia*, Butterworth, London, 1979 (looseleaf).

Seaver, M. and O'Mahony, L., *ISA 2000: The System for Occupational Health and Safety Management*, Gower, Aldershot, 2000.

Smith, David, J., *Reliability Maintainability and Risk*, 5th edn, Butterworth-Heinemann, Oxford, 1997.

Tromans, Stephen, *Environmental Protection Act 1990*, Sweet & Maxwell, London, 1991.

Wright, Christopher J., *Product Liability: The Law and its Implications for Risk Management*, Blackstone Press, London, 1989.

CHAPTER **3**

Product Liability and Product Safety

Dr John G. Roche

Introduction

When the EU's proposal for a strict product liability regime was published in 1976, business and producer interests expressed their fears that a US-type product liability 'crisis' would also arise in Europe. But following extensive discussions and modifications to the proposal, the 'Council Directive on the Approximation of the Laws, Regulations and Administrative Provisions of the Member States Concerning Liability for Defective Products' was adopted in July 1985. The directive has been implemented in all Member States, and has influenced product liability legislation in countries outside the EU.

The objective of the directive was to overcome divergences in national laws which 'may distort competition' and 'entail a differing degree of protection of the consumer against damage caused by a defective product to his health or property'. 'Liability without fault on the part of the producer' was regarded as 'the sole means of adequately solving the problem'.[1]

All directives bind Member States as to the objectives to be achieved, while leaving national authorities the power to choose the form and the means to be used.[2] Some Member States adhered closely to the text of the directive in implementing Acts or Decrees; others introduced special features. In addition, the product liability directive provided three derogations or options. These options allowed Member States to:

1 exclude primary agricultural products
2 include the development risk defence
3 provide a ceiling on damages caused by 'identical items with the same defect'.

In implementing legislation, five Member States (Greece, France, Luxembourg, Finland and Sweden) included primary agricultural products. But Directive 1999/34/EC, adopted in May 1999, removed option 1 and required all Member States to include primary agricultural products within the scope of the 1985 Directive with effect from December 2000.[3]

Two Member States (Finland and Luxembourg) excluded the development risk defence, while three (Germany, Portugal and Spain) provided for a financial ceiling.

The directive recognized that 'total harmonization' was not possible, but strict product liability in tort has now been introduced in all Member States.

Some legal concepts

What is strict liability? It is liability 'which does not require the plaintiff to prove that the defendant was negligent and which does not exempt the defendant from liability if he proves simply that he was not negligent'.[4]

Strict product liability is a long-established legal principle of contract law. But contract law applies only between the buyer and the seller of the product. If the buyer is injured by the product, there is a breach of contract, and the injured person can claim damages for the breach. Strict liability applies. However, if the injured person is not the purchaser, tort (negligence) law applies, and the injured party has to prove negligence on the part of the supplier or manufacturer. This requirement to prove negligence was generally recognized as a major hurdle for injured plaintiffs.

During the 1970s, there were moves towards the introduction of strict product liability in tort in a number of European countries. These national initiatives were overtaken by the Council Directive. But strict product liability is not absolute liability. Defences are available to the producer (defendant), and these are specified in the directive and in national implementing legislation.

It should be noted, however, that the directive augments but does not supplant existing legal remedies (contract or tort) available to injured parties.

While the texts of the implementing legislation in each Member State differ, the main provisions of the directive have been carried over into national legislation. The European Commission monitored the implementing process in each Member State, and endeavoured to ensure that a reasonable level of harmonization was achieved. However, producers should be aware of these differences in the Member States where their products circulate or are in use.

Under Community law, the European Court of Justice and its Court of First Instance may be called upon to resolve conflicts between the provisions of a directive and national implementing legislation. In such situations, it seems that the European Courts will interpret national law in the light of the wording and purpose of the directive in question. Consequently, the text of the directive will be used in explaining its provisions.[1]

The provisions of the directive

The major legal change is bluntly and briefly stated in Article 1: 'The producer shall be liable for damage caused by a defect in his product.' This provision, with no or minor changes, is also in the Belgian, Greek, Italian, Luxembourg and Dutch versions of the implementing legislation.

Subsequent articles give special meanings to 'producer, damage, defect and product'. Existing legal remedies remain. To succeed in a claim, the injured person is required to prove the damage, the defect and the causal relationship between defect and damage.

Article 3 regards manufacturers, raw material producers, own-branders, importers into the EC and, in special circumstances, suppliers as 'producers'. Products include all movable goods, including those used at a place of work. Damage covers death/personal injury and damage/destruction of consumer-type property, with a lower limit of 500 euros. The producer's liability lasts for ten years after the defective product was put into circulation. There is a three-year limitation on proceedings for the recovery of damages. Contributory negligence may reduce or even disallow the producer's liability.

Six defences to a claim are available to the producer in most Member States. These are listed in Article 7. As noted earlier, Finland and Luxembourg excluded the 'development risk' defence. This particular defence gave rise to much discussion and intensive lobbying while the directive was being considered. It is sometimes mistakenly called the 'state of the art' defence. 'State of the art' refers to current best practice, while the directive refers to 'the state of scientific and technical knowledge'.

What is a defective product?

The words 'defect' and 'defective' are central in the context of the strict product liability regime introduced by the directive. While both are commonly used in the quality literature, they have been given special definitions in Article 6. This associates 'defective' with a lack of expected safety. In assessing defectiveness, 'all circumstances' – which includes presentation (instructions, labels, advertising), reasonable usage expectation and the age of the product – are to be considered. As a result of this definition, the concept of 'product' needs to be broadened to cover the 'Expanded Product', which includes:

- the actual product
- labels
- packaging
- container
- installation/use instructions
- warranty documents
- sales brochures
- spare parts
- advertising material
- catalogues.

The effects of Article 6 are evident in ISO 9000: 2000, which notes that 'defect' should be used 'with extreme caution'.[5] While legal decisions are lacking, this author suggests that 'nonconformity' should replace 'defect' in quality management practice.

Developments since 1985

Industry's fears of a massive increase in claims following the adoption of the directive have not been realized. Indeed, the European Commission has had some difficulty in identifying claims made under the new liability regime.

THE FIRST REPORT 1995

Article 21 of the directive requires the Commission to present a report to the European Council on the application of the directive, and to submit appropriate proposals at five-year intervals. However, because few Member States met the implementation date of July 1988, the Commission's First Report was not produced until December 1995.[6] The report stated that the directive has contributed to an increased awareness of and emphasis on product safety without an increase in claims or in the level of insurance premiums. It concluded that no amendments to the directive were necessary at that time.

Yet unease within the European Parliament during an enquiry into bovine spongiform encephalopathy (BSE) led, in 1997, to a proposal to modify the directive by bringing primary agricultural products, including fish and game, within the scope of the directive. As noted earlier, this proposal was adopted as a directive in May 1999. Other amendments that dealt with psychological damage, the thresholds for total liability and personal property damage and time limits were proposed during discussions in the European Parliament. But these amendments were not pursued following the Commission's announcement that there would be broad consultation through a Green Paper before the second application report was produced.

A special report, produced for the European Commission in formulating its 1995 Report, noted the 'extensive programme of legislation in relation to the conditions under which products may be placed on the internal market ... There is increased regulation, increased concentration on standards, safety and quality and increased commercial and consumer pressures ... The Product Liability Directive is one aspect of this overall picture and should not be seen in isolation.'[7]

GREEN PAPER 1999

The Green Paper *Liability for Defective Products* was issued by the Commission in July 1999.[8] It had two objectives:

1 to determine the impact of the 1985 Directive on interested parties – producers, consumers, legal and insurance interests, governments and consumer associations
2 to seek reactions from interested parties to possible amendments to the 1985 Directive.

The Green Paper suggested that respondents could consider the following parameters in their replies:

1 How is the directive used in disputes?
2 Does the directive influence market entry, maintenance and withdrawal of a product?
3 What is the trend in costs, production and selling prices as a result of the directive?
4 Do differences in liability regimes in different markets require changes in production processes or additional insurance costs?
5 Does the directive affect innovation?

Section 2 sought information on the effects of the directive. It posed a series of questions dealing with the directive's impact on the internal market, on public health and safety, and on industry and the insurance sector. The Commission hoped that the second application report would reflect a further five years' experience of the directive's implementation, and also tap more sources of factual information than the 1995 Report.

Reflecting Parliamentary pressure for amendments to the directive, Section 3 of the Green Paper asked: 'Is a revision of Directive 85/374/EEC justified?' It posed questions on aspects of the directive as follows:

a Should the victim's burden of proof be eased?

b Should 'market share liability' be introduced?
c Should the 'development risk' defence be amended?
d Should the financial thresholds of 500 and 70 million euros be modified?
e Should the ten-year time limit on liability be changed?
f Should insurance cover be a requirement for producers?
g Should increased public awareness of the directive's application, including publicity for cases involving defective products, be included in any revision?
h Should supplier liability be modified to achieve prompt responses to the victim's request for information, and should others in the product supply chain be liable?
i Should real estate property come within the provisions of the directive?
j Should the directive cover other types of damage, such as non-material damage, mental suffering or damage to professional property?
k Should injunctions to bar or withdraw defective products and provisions for group/class actions be part of a revised directive?

In concluding this list of possible reforms, the Commission mentioned other issues – for example the liability of management and workers, and damage criteria – on which respondents might wish to comment with a view to legislative action.

However, the Commission emphasized that no changes were to be considered until responses to the Green Paper had been analysed.

THE SECOND REPORT 2001

The Second Report was published in January 2001 and concluded that 'it would be premature to envisage any changes to the current liability system under Directive 85/374/EEC'.[9] There are two main reasons for this conclusion:

- limited experience with regard to the application of the directive; this arises from delayed implementation in some Member States, and the continued availability of national laws or a specific national liability regime
- as in 1995, the scarce information available has not permitted the identification of any major problems with the application of the directive.

Despite the Commission's endeavours to secure information, 'the number of product liability cases seems to be relatively low' (fewer than 100 reported court cases based on the directive). However, it should be noted that the vast majority of cases are settled out of court. In addition, the Commission recognized that product safety levels have improved since 1985.

The Commission planned to set up an expert group on product liability to gather information on the application of the directive. It also proposed to launch two studies. One would assess the economic impact of introducing producer liability for development risk and of eliminating the financial limit for serial incidents. The second study would focus on the desirability of introducing a uniform product liability system in the Community.

The final sections of the report reflect the Commission's commitment to 'a high level of consumer protection against product-related risk' and noted the complementary role of Community product safety legislation. Improved consumer access to justice is seen as an issue that requires additional measures, as is environmental liability.

Other developments since 1985

Two significant EU initiatives in recent years have been the 'New Approach' to facilitate the full movement of goods throughout the EU, adopted in 1985, and the 1992 Directive on general product safety.

THE NEW APPROACH DIRECTIVES

The 'New Approach' was adopted in 1985 in an effort to facilitate the free movement of goods throughout the Community. Existing national provisions with their differing technical requirements and differing conformity assessment procedures were recognized as barriers to trade between Member States.

The New Approach focused on the essential safety and other requirements for particular products or product types, and specified the modules (methods) for assessing the conformity of products with the relevant essential requirements. The essential health and safety requirements are specified in detail in the directives which have been adopted to date.

The eight modules that may be used were initially described in a 1990 Council Decision, which was substantially amended and replaced by a 1993 Council Decision. These modules range from a declaration of conformity by the manufacturer to the testing of individual products by an independent body (a notified body). Other modules incorporate the use of EN29001 (ISO 9001), 29002 and 29003 as part of the conformity assessment procedure.[10]

CE marking is used on products or on their packaging to indicate compliance with the requirements in the relevant New Approach directive. Some directives may impose additional obligations, not just the essential requirements. Products bearing the CE mark cannot be denied access to the market of another Member State on technical grounds.

While only a limited number of New Approach directives have been adopted to date, they apply to important sectors of industry, such as construction products, machinery, medical devices, toys and motor vehicles. Their emphasis on safety and the use of the ISO 9000 standard in conformity assessment have contributed to industry's awareness of safety and the ISO 9000 standards.

The use of ISO 9000 standards in the New Approach directives has influenced the growth in ISO 9000 certificates, not just in the EU, but also in countries exporting to the EU. The references to 'statutory and regulatory requirements' in ISO 9001: 2000 reflect the increased importance of these requirements in quality management practice.

THE GENERAL PRODUCT SAFETY (GPS) DIRECTIVE

The GPS Directive (92/59/EEC) was adopted in June 1992, and has been implemented in all Member States. This directive applies only to consumer products, and its purpose is to ensure that 'products placed on the market are safe'.[11] Article 3 states: 'Producers shall be obliged to place only safe products on the market.' As in the case of the product liability directive, some terms are given special meanings. 'Producer' includes manufacturer, own-brander, reconditioner, import representative or importer and other professionals in the supply chain whose activities may affect the safety properties of the product. 'Product' covers any product intended for or likely to be used by consumers, be it new, used or reconditioned. Antiques or products to be repaired or reconditioned before use are excluded.

A 'safe product' means any product that under normal or reasonably foreseeable conditions of use does not present any risk, or only minimal risks that are acceptable and consistent with a high level of protection for the health and safety of persons. As in the case of a 'defective product', a number of points are to be taken into account in assessing a 'safe product'. These include the characteristics of the product (including its composition, packaging and instructions for assembly and maintenance), its effect on other products where it is reasonably foreseeable that it will be used with other products, its presentation (covering labelling, use and disposal instructions and 'other' information provided by the producer) and categories of consumers at serious risk when using the product, particularly children. The feasibility of obtaining higher levels of safety or the availability of other products presenting a lesser degree of risk shall not constitute grounds for considering a product to be 'unsafe' or 'dangerous'. The Expanded Product concept is equally applicable.

Producers are required to provide information which will enable consumers to assess the risks in using the product and to adopt monitoring measures, including marking of products or product batches, sample testing of products in the market, and complaint investigation. Resultant actions may involve product recall.

Producers are to keep distributors informed of such monitoring. Distributors are required to act with due care to ensure compliance, and to participate in monitoring products in the market.

The directive also requires Member States to ensure compliance, and makes provision for regulatory controls which may extend to product recall and destruction. The European Commission has a role in exchanging information and in dealing with emergency situations in Member States.

Article 8 of the GPS Directive requires Member States to inform the Commission of actions taken to deal with a product or product batch which presents a serious and immediate risk to the health and safety of consumers. On checking this information, the Commission passes it on to other Member States. This information system is now known as RAPEX.

Four years after the specified implementation date, Article 16 required the Commission to present a report on the experience acquired. On the basis of this report, the Commission was to present appropriate proposals for modification of the GPS Directive. As in the case of the Product Liability Directive, some Member States did not meet the 1994 deadline for implementation. This delayed the required report, which was not published until March 2000.[12]

The report identified so many weaknesses in the application of the 1992 Directive that it was decided to repeal it from January 2004, and to replace it with Directive 2001/95/EC.[13]

The contribution of ISO 9000 to product safety

The first version of ISO 9000 was published in 1987, and was modified in 1994 and again in 2000. ISO 9000 has become the dominant approach to quality management internationally, with certified organizations growing from 27 000 in January 1993 to 408 000 in December 2000. ISO 9000: 2000, which specifies requirements for a quality management system, begins by explaining that the requirements are specified where an organization 'needs to demonstrate its ability to consistently provide product that meets customer and applicable regulatory requirements'. A key aspect of such a management system is documentation. As described in ISO 9000: 2000:

> Documentation enables communication of intent and consistency of action. Its use contributes to
>
> a achievement of conformity to customer requirements and quality improvement
> b provision of appropriate training
> c repeatability and traceability
> d provision of objective evidence, and
> e evaluation of the effectiveness and continuing suitability of the quality management system.
>
> Generation of documentation should not be an end in itself but should be a value-adding activity.

The 2000 version of ISO 9000 reflects the changed attitude to product safety which has developed since 1985. ISO 9001: 2000 and ISO 9004: 2000 give increased prominence to product safety, statutory and regulatory requirements, product liability, risk assessment, records control, delivery and post-delivery activities, and market information.

Even though the earlier versions of ISO 9000 did not have this emphasis on considerations relevant to product safety, they did encourage a systematic approach to product quality, and contributed to the relatively low level of product liability claims in the EU since 1985.

Product liability prevention

The fact that the American pattern of product liability suits has not been experienced in Europe may breed complacency. While producers can reduce the risks of product liability claims, the claims process is externally driven, and is not under the producer's control. Just one defective product may trigger a series of claims that may ruin the producer, so producers need to be aware of the developments which have been described, and to be prepared for the one defective product which may give rise to a claim for damages.

Strict product liability and its associated general Product Safety Directive need more than an effective ISO 9000 system in place. Auditors evaluate ISO 9000 systems, but it is the courts which will ultimately examine the activities of a firm in a product liability case. It will be expected that documented procedures are being followed.

An approach which was promoted in the USA during the 1970s and which has recently received more prominence in the wake of the Bridgestone/Firestone and Ford problems is Product Liability Prevention (PLP).[14] Assuming that an ISO 9000 system is operative, PLP introduces additional considerations which emphasize product safety and which recognize that a firm must be prepared to defend a product liability claim in court.

Corporate safety policy

This clearly states top management's commitment to safe products (it could be incorporated into existing quality policy statements). The safety policy statement should be made available to all employees, internal and external, and to all suppliers. But this policy commitment also needs to be made evident by actions which support the safety policy. These include:

- the establishment of a Product Safety Committee
- the appointment of a Product Safety Co-ordinator
- the establishment of a Crisis Team.

The Product Safety Committee would consist of senior management from design, production, quality, purchasing and marketing (it may well be that these managers are members of the existing management review group). The committee's function is to implement the corporate safety policy by:

- providing overall direction for product safety activities
- ensuring a flow of relevant information between departments
- establishing information sources on developments in product liability and safety
- maintaining an up-to-date collection of product safety and liability information, applicable standards, laws, regulations and codes
- establishing audit procedures for product safety
- providing general safety awareness training for all employees
- making formal recommendations on product safety issues
- reviewing safety aspects of existing and new products, complaints and records.

While the establishment of this committee reflects top management's safety commitment, it is also necessary to appoint one member as the Product Safety Co-ordinator. This member would act as the focus for internal and external safety-related issues and information, and drive the product safety effort.

As product liability and safety crises can arise at any time, it is essential that a Crisis or Contingency Team be in place before the crisis arises. A Crisis Team could defuse or contain a threatened crisis. The team members would be drawn from the Product Safety Committee, and each member should be pre-assigned specific tasks in a potential crisis situation.

An effective ISO 9001: 2000 quality management system, supplemented by the guidelines in ISO 9004: 2000, is a sound base for PLP. But it must be recognized that certain aspects of a firm's operations will be scrutinized in detail by lawyers in a product liability case.

Design

Of all aspects which need special attention, design is the most important. As explained in a US safety handbook:

> Design is the dominant influence on product safety. Product safety starts in the mind of the product designers. It is no exaggeration to say that if all elements of manufacturing were ranked in order of their potential effect on consumer product safety, the design function would lead the list. Additionally, of course, design importantly affects subsequent decisions and practices related to materials, production, testing, processes, labelling, packaging and distribution.[15]

Designers or the design team must recognize that the product has to provide the safety which a person is entitled to expect, and that the presentation of the product, its reasonably expected use and its time of circulation are factors which will be used by the courts in assessing defectiveness. The Expanded Product concept, discussed above, should not be forgotten.

The defences of 'mandatory regulations' and 'the state of scientific and technical knowledge' require familiarity with relevant regulations and codes of practice, and the latest technology.

Design review should be an essential feature of the design process.

Materials

ISO 9001 and 9004 provide adequate requirements and guidance. But product liability introduces joint and several liability. The problems encountered by Bridgestone/Firestone and Ford illustrate what can happen when legal action arises. It is important that liability and insurance issues be discussed and agreed before a claim arises.

Labelling and instructions

Since the presentation of the product is one of the circumstances taken into account in assessing defectiveness and safety, all informative material must be designed to assist the 'safe and proper use' of the product. Warnings, which are not a substitute for safe design, should be clear, conspicuous, complete and as unambiguous as possible for the user.

Marketing and distribution

ISO 9001: 2000 requires organizations to monitor customer satisfaction. In a strict liability environment, sales/field service personnel, who are closest to the user, need to be aware of the implications for the firm's products, and the dangers of over-enthusiastic product promotion. They may hear of or observe incidents which are potentially dangerous. Rapid feedback about such incidents is crucial.

Customer complaints are another source of valuable information. Any complaints which allege personal injuries or damage should be notified immediately to the Product Safety Co-ordinator. All complaints should be recorded systematically, and action should be taken without delay to resolve the issues involved.

Sales or field service reports and complaints may indicate that a product recall is necessary to avoid personal injury or damage. The provisions of the General Product Safety (GPS) Directive may also give rise to a recall. Recall decisions would be made by the Product Safety Committee.

Records

The liability of the producer under the provisions of the Product Liability Directive lasts for ten years from the date of putting the product into circulation. So, in the case of some products, the producer may be required to provide evidence of commitment to safe products ten or more years after production. Records that show evidence of failure to remedy deficiencies can be most damaging to the producer.

Product liability insurance

A well-managed PLP programme should reduce, but does not eliminate, the risk of a product liability claim. As claims are outside the producer's control, a product liability insurance policy is the commonest form of transfer of this risk. Product liability policies have not been standardized. Careful study of the policy wording, exceptions and conditions is essential. The insurer will conduct a risk or loss control survey before a policy proposal is accepted, and may offer loss prevention services.

Response to a claim

The emphasis above has been on preventing a claim arising. But the producer cannot guarantee a 'totally safe' product, and should therefore establish a claims policy before there is a claim. The claims policy aims to provide the basis for an early settlement or a well-founded defence. The claims policy should be developed in co-operation with the insurer and with advice from the producer's legal advisers.

A claims policy should cover the following:

1 response to complaints or reports of incidents involving personal injury or damage
2 notification of insurer and legal adviser
3 claim investigation
4 settlement procedure
5 response to discovery requirements
6 further settlement effort
7 preparation for trial
8 trial.

The future

It is unlikely that the Product Liability Directive will be modified for some years. But the increased emphasis on general product safety evident in the concluding sections of the Second Report on the Product Liability Directive, in efforts to improve CE marking enforcement procedures, and particularly in the latest version of the GPS Directive, indicate that pressure to ensure that only safe products circulate in the EU will increase. The Commission's initiatives regarding access to justice for consumers could give rise to increased product liability claims.[9] A more detailed exposition of the material in the latter part of this contribution is given in the author's book, *Product Liability*.[16]

Disclaimer

This chapter reports on developments in product liability and safety since 1985, and offers the author's opinions on these developments. It is not a legal exposition.

Notes

1 'Council Directive of 25 July 1985 on the Approximation of the Laws, Regulations and Administrative Provisions of the Member States Concerning Liability for Defective Products', *Official Journal of the European Communities*, No. L210/29–33, 7 August 1985 (85/34/EEC).
2 *Serving the European Union*, Office for Official Publications of the European Communities, Luxembourg, 1996.
3 'Directive 1999/34/EC of the European Parliament and of the Council of 10 May 1999', *Official Journal of the European Communities*, No. L141/20–21, 4 June 1999.
4 *Royal Commission on Civil Liability and Compensation for Personal Injury*, HMSO, London, 1978, paragraph 1630.
5 ISO 9000: 2000, *Quality Management Systems – Fundamentals and Vocabulary*, International Organization for Standardization, Geneva 2000.
6 *First Report on the Application of Council Directive (85/374/EEC)*, COM (95)617 Final, Commission of the European Communities, Brussels, 13 December 1995.
7 *Report for the Commission of the European Communities on the Application of Directive 85/374/EEC on Liability for Defective Products*, Study Contract No. ETD/93B5-300/M1/06, Commission of the European Communities, Brussels, May 1994.
8 *Green Paper – Liability for Defective Products*, COM (1999) 396 Final, Commission of the European Communities, Brussels, 28 July 1999.
9 *Report from the Commission on the Application of Directive 85/374 on Liability for Defective Products*, COM (2000) 893 Final, Commission of the European Communities, Brussels, 31 January 2001.
10 'Council Decision of 22nd July 1993 Concerning the Modules for the Various Phases of the Conformity Assessment Procedures and the Rules for the Affixing and Use of the CE Conformity Marking, Which are Intended to be Used in the Technical Harmonisation Directives (93/465/EEC)', *Official Journal of the European Communities*, No. L220, 30 August 1992.
11 'Council Directive 92/59/EEC of 29 June 1992 on General Product Safety', *Official Journal of the European Communities*, No. L228/24–32, 11 August 1992.
12 'Commission Report to the European Parliament and the Council on the Experience Acquired in the Application of Directive 92/59/EEC on General Product Safety', COM (2000) 140 final, Commission of the European Communities, Brussels, 29 March 2000.
13 'Directive 2001/95/EC of the European Parliament and of the Council of 3 December 2001 on General Product Safety', *Official Journal of the European Communities*, No. L11/4–17, 15 January 2002.
14 Randall Goodden, 'Product Liability Prevention of Major Importance', *Quality Progress*, Vol. 3312, December 2000, ASQ, Milwaukee, WI.
15 *Handbook and Standard for Manufacturing Safer Consumer Products*, US Consumer Product Safety Commission, Washington, DC, 1975, p. 7.
16 John G. Roche, *Product Liability: The European Management and Quality Challenge*, IFS Publications, Bedford, 1989.

CHAPTER

4 *Training for Quality*

Darek Celinski

Quality is concerned with delivering, on time and at a competitive price, the goods or services that exactly satisfy the customer. Any training which helps an organization to achieve these results is, in effect, training for quality. To achieve the highest quality, everybody who works in the organization will know previously what to do, use correct methods and procedures, and be able to perform their task well and right first time. This demands the provision of planned and methodical training.

In practice, there is only one best way to organize and conduct all the training that an organization should provide for its employees. This chapter explains how, and answers questions about training which begin with the words what, why, when, where, who, and how.

Education, development and training in organizations

Training is one of three distinctly separate learning processes used in organizations. The other two are education and development.

EDUCATION

Education is a process of providing knowledge and understanding. In practice, there are two different forms of education that organizations can provide or arrange for their employees:

1 'further education', which occurs most often in the form of substantial courses of study which lead to formal and nationally recognized qualifications
2 short courses designed to provide knowledge or understanding of theories, principles and practices. Management education is an example.

DEVELOPMENT

The purpose of development is to increase the competence of people who work in organizations by extending their existing experience and building on their abilities. In practice, whether or not this produces any improvement in their competence depends on how the development is organized and conducted. The optimum benefits of development are realized when it is conducted in-company, with people working in small groups on real and carefully selected projects that are designed to produce a measurable improvement in one or more aspect of the organization's operations.

TRAINING

The third of the three learning processes discussed here, and the main subject of this chapter, is training. It is a process of instruction and practice which, when it is correctly designed and conducted, guarantees to raise the quality of the organization's products or services far above the levels obtained without training. This is the process that enables people to do work that they could not do before their training. It is also the process which enables them to do their work measurably better.

> **Training is the process of bringing employees to the desired standard of work performance by instruction and practice.**

In this definition of training, the term 'employee' means absolutely anyone who is employed by an organization. Thus, the training definition applies to every kind of training that organizations provide for their employees. This means that management training is the same process as supervisory training and all other kinds of training provided by organizations.

'The desired standard of work performance' means the standard that is desired by (and has previously been defined by) the particular employees' immediate managers and supervisors. This is how organizations make their training effective, and is the most essential requirement for raising the quality of their goods and services. This comes about because all training is based on specific requirements: that is to say that none of the training provided is needless, and the results that it is required to produce are precisely defined in advance.

THE ESSENTIAL DIFFERENCES BETWEEN THE THREE LEARNING PROCESSES

A common error of organizations nowadays is to regard the three different processes as being very similar, with little to distinguish between them. This is completely wrong, and is bound to prove unhelpful for those organizations that want to provide training which raises the quality of their products or services.

The error is unfortunate because, if the essential differences between training, education and development are not recognized, the organization will attempt to conduct all three using the same methods and procedures. Thus, instead of training being by instruction and practice, it is conducted like education, which instead of improving work performance, provides only knowledge and understanding. Instead of development being conducted so that it broadens people's experience, it too is conducted like education, so that although it provides knowledge and understanding, it fails to raise competence.

To raise the quality of an organization's products or services, it must be recognized that education, development and training are necessary to satisfy different learning needs. Each requires its own distinct methods and procedures. Each produces a different kind of improvement in the organization's human resources.

The purpose of training in organizations

The aim of training in organizations is to make those organizations measurably more successful and prosperous than they could ever be without the training. Training achieves this improvement by increasing the job performance of individuals, which results in:

- improved efficiency and productivity of sections and departments
- improvement in the quality of work produced
- a more competitive organization
- a more successful and prosperous organization.

When is training necessary?

Training should be provided only where there is a training need to be satisfied. That need exists when learning is unavoidable, so that the employee will be forced to learn to do the work by trial and error if the relevant training is not provided.

By insisting that training is provided only when learning is absolutely unavoidable, organizations ensure that what has been learned is really needed, so that it will be applied on the job and result in a recognizable improvement in work performance. This also protects organizations from wasting their time and money on providing needless training, which, of course, produces no improvement in work performance.

SITUATIONS WHERE LEARNING IS UNAVOIDABLE

If training is to improve job performance standards, it should be provided when a person or group of people is:

- newly recruited into the organization
- assessed by a supervisor or manager as needing to perform an existing job better
- given new tasks
- newly transferred to a different job or newly promoted
- required to adapt to organizational change that affects the job.

The common characteristic of these situations is that learning by the people affected is unavoidable. These people would be likely to be able to continue in their employment without being able to do whatever their changed situation requires them to learn. This signals an obvious need for training.

Where should the training take place?

There are just two kinds of environments where all training provided by organizations can take place. These are:

- off the job
- on the job.

TRAINING OFF THE JOB

Off-the-job training takes place away from the day-to-day pressures of the job, and away from the location where the job is normally performed. There are three main kinds of locations where off-the-job training is conducted:

1 the organization's own local training rooms, bays, areas and workshops
2 training centres and other locations outside the organization that belong to somebody else, for example the premises of a supplier of equipment that the organization is buying and planning to install
3 lecture rooms, which can be either inside or outside the organization.

Although systematic on-the-job training is the main and usually most effective form of training, it has to be supplemented by some off-the-job training. This is the area of training in organizations that is especially difficult to make effective. A good understanding is therefore necessary of what it can and cannot do, when it should be provided, and how it should be organized and conducted.

Training courses

Improvement in work performance is much more difficult to achieve, compared with on-the-job training, when the training provided is off the job in the form of attendance at courses.

The organizers of a training course should always state the course aims positively as 'to enable the course participants to do xyz', where xyz is a specific task or technique to be learned.

Courses without specific training objectives

The course objectives should never be expressed in terms of providing knowledge, or understanding, or appreciation of this or that practice. Unfortunately, such courses are widespread nowadays, and organizations should be warned against using them. The problem with courses which are designed to provide knowledge, understanding or appreciation is that they are not conducted by instruction and practice. The assumption is that they are conducted by instruction and practice. The assumption in such cases is that the participants will be able to make use of the knowledge gained when they return to their place of work, and thus be able to do work which they could not do previously or perform existing jobs better. In practice, there are several reasons why this never happens:

- The courses are conducted in such a way that, on their completion, no one knows whether or not the required knowledge or understanding has, in fact, been acquired.
- Even where the required knowledge or understanding has been acquired, at least 80 per cent of the newly acquired knowledge will have been forgotten by the time eight hours has elapsed after course completion, leaving little knowledge or understanding to be applied on the job.

Whatever the providers of such courses claim, therefore, organizations should be aware that sending employees to attend them is unlikely to contribute to raising the quality of their products or services.

TRAINING ON THE JOB

Training is 'on the job' when it is conducted in precisely the same environment in which employees do their job. This includes not only the same physical location, but also the same conditions and surroundings, and the same tools, equipment, materials, standards and facilities that are used when doing the actual job.

On-the-job training is unsuitable for training managers, supervisors and other employees while they are attending to the organization's clients and customers. Otherwise, it is by far the most effective form of training available to organizations, and should be used in preference to off-the-job training.

On-the-job training is so effective because, unlike off-the-job training (especially when that is conducted in a lecture room), it cannot fail to be:

- **Relevant** – Learning by doing the actual job makes the training automatically 100 per cent relevant.
- **Effective** – Learning by actually doing the job, with a great deal of practice and constant feedback about progress, produces by far the most effective conditions for learning.
- **Applied on the job** – Upon completion of training, learners continue doing the job, without interruption, at the place where they were trained. The trainee is thus not disadvantaged by the difficulties of having to transfer the learning from one environment and set of conditions to another.

Systematic on-the-job training

ON-THE-JOB LEARNING WHICH IS NOT SYSTEMATIC

If properly planned and conducted on-the-job training is not provided when learning is unavoidable, the employees learn by their own efforts – by trial and error.

Unfortunately, learning by trial and error is costly. It is a slow, inefficient and risky process that is unlikely to bring learners to the highest possible standard of work performance.

In practice, the immediate managers and supervisors will usually attempt to provide as much help as they can. One problem is that they are usually very busy people who are often away from their offices or the immediate workplace, are frequently interrupted, and have many other jobs to do that claim greater priority or urgency. Another problem is that most supervisors and managers are not trained trainers. Any training that they can provide is usually unstructured, piecemeal and incomplete.

In addition to managers and supervisors, it might be expected that more experienced colleagues could also try to help. The value of this is never very great. First of all, they are not trained trainers, so that their instruction is unlikely to be very effective. Furthermore, not all experienced colleagues are willing to take the necessary trouble. They may even be reluctant to share their 'know-how'. Even experienced colleagues may not be well informed or particularly good at their jobs, so they may teach their inexperienced colleagues bad practices that should be eliminated, not perpetuated.

There is a good deal of evidence that training by the managers, supervisors and more experienced colleagues is far from effective. This evidence is proved by the things that go wrong in organizations in the form of mistakes, misunderstandings, delays, waste, scrap, rework, customer complaints and similar failings that make organizations less competitive.

THE SYSTEMATIC ALTERNATIVE

When on-the-job training is *systematic*, it is the most effective method of bringing employees to the desired standard of performance.

In practice, organizations cannot become highly competitive and achieve high standards of efficiency, productivity and quality for their products and services without providing systematic on-the-job training in all their sections and departments. 'Systematic' means that it is planned and methodical training, conducted by *departmental trainers* who use an *instructional technique*.

DEPARTMENTAL TRAINERS

A departmental trainer is a well-experienced, non-managerial and non-supervisory employee who, upon volunteering, has been appointed by the immediate manager or supervisor to work as a part-time trainer in his or her own part of the organization. Being a part-time trainer means that the person does his or her own job when instructing is not required. The part-time trainer only switches to instructing when a need arises within the section or department.

Once officially appointed, each departmental trainer must be trained to use an instructional technique. This is essential because systematic on-the-job training achieves its high level of effectiveness only when the instructional technique is used.

WHY SYSTEMATIC ON-THE-JOB TRAINING IS MOST EFFECTIVE

There are three main reasons why systematic on-the-job training is so effective in improving quality:

1 All the training is conducted by the part-time departmental trainers who have themselves been trained to use (and actually do use) the most effective instructional technique which is the most effective training method that is available to organizations.
2 Once the departmental trainers have been appointed, all the necessary training can be provided at very short notice and, on occasions, immediately after the need for training has been identified.
3 Systematic on-the-job training is the only form of training which makes it practicable for organizations to train every employee.

An additional benefit is that time and money are saved. Time is saved because employees learn more quickly all that they need to do their jobs well. Money is saved because the total cost of providing systematic on-the-job training is only a small fraction of the value of improvements in the quantity and quality of work that result.

Who does what for training in organizations

TOP MANAGEMENT

Training is a service function. In common with all other services, it is the organization's top management who must decide the kind of service that they want training to provide. This means deciding how the function is to be organized, how many training specialists to employ, what facilities to provide, and what budgets to allow.

Top management are responsible for the overall effectiveness of training within their organizations. They cannot delegate this responsibility, but must define the improvements in efficiency, productivity and quality that they want their organizations to achieve. These objectives must be quantifiable, so that arrangements can be made to measure the improvements that training actually produces. This is because nowadays training can be provided where everybody appears to be pleased and impressed with its high quality, yet when followed up, reveals that no improvements whatsoever have resulted in efficiency, productivity and quality. It is only by checking and measuring that training is actually producing all its claimed improvements that organizations can assess the worth of the training service. Nobody can do this other than the organization's top management.

DEPARTMENTAL MANAGERS AND SUPERVISORS

It is a fundamental principle of management that managers and supervisors are responsible for training within their sections and departments. This is a responsibility which they cannot delegate. The reason for this is that it is only the managers and supervisors who know precisely what results their sections and departments are achieving and what improvements are needed.

PARTNERSHIP BETWEEN MANAGERS, SUPERVISORS AND TRAINING SPECIALISTS

Making training effective within each section and department is a partnership between managers or supervisors and the training specialists. Managers or supervisors identify the specific needs and define the results that they want training to produce within their area of control, and the training specialists provide the service to produce the results.

The four-step training cycle

Every time any training is provided, whether it is on-the-job or off-the-job training, it always follows the same four-step cycle. The roles played by managers, supervisors and the training specialist in this cycle are shown in Figure 4.1. There can never be any exception to the need for following this four-step procedure.

Even in very small organizations, where no training specialist is employed, and where the total training provided might be limited to a very occasional attendance at a training course, it is still necessary to ensure that the purpose of the training is clear, and not simply to 'provide knowledge or understanding'. The aim of training must always be to enable the person to do the required work which he or she could not do before the training. When the course has been completed, therefore, it is necessary to check that the person can in fact do the required work – not simply to ask that person for their opinion of the course value. Even when nothing relevant to the workplace has been learned on a course, its participants invariably say that it was a good course. Contrary to widely held beliefs, there is no correlation whatsoever between what participants say about a course and its real value.

It is most unfortunate for the organizations which are able to employ training specialists

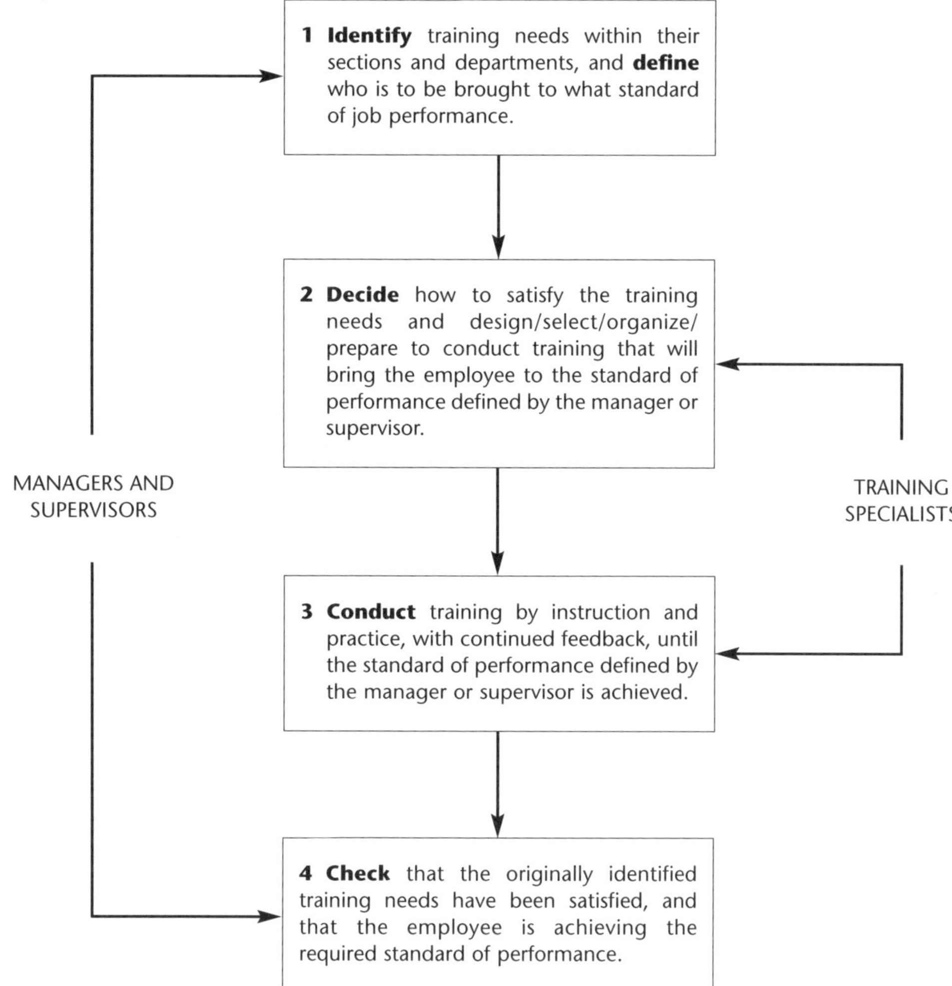

1 Identify training needs within their sections and departments, and define who is to be brought to what standard of job performance.
2 Decide how to satisfy the training needs and design/select/organize/prepare to conduct training that will bring the employee to the standard of performance defined by the manager or supervisor.
3 Conduct training by instruction and practice, with continued feedback, until the standard of performance defined by the manager or supervisor is achieved.
4 Check that the originally identified training needs have been satisfied, and that the employee is achieving the required standard of performance.
MANAGERS AND SUPERVISORS
TRAINING SPECIALISTS

Figure 4.1 Division of responsibilities between managers/supervisors and training specialists in the training cycle

that the important four-step procedure is not always followed. One reason for this is that not all people employed as training specialists appreciate that training objectives have to be stated in job performance terms, and that only the managers and supervisors have the information necessary for producing these definitions. Such training specialists usually regard their role as arranging for people to attend courses, and then checking to see how much those people liked the courses.

Another reason why the four-step procedure is not always followed is resistance by managers and supervisors to doing what the training specialists ask them to do. This is invariably due to a lack of understanding by the managers and supervisors that, without their involvement in identifying the training needs and checking their subsequent fulfilment, any training provided can do nothing towards raising the efficiency, productivity and work quality of their sections and departments.

Planning for training

RELEVANCE TO ORGANIZATIONAL FORWARD PLANS

Training can bring great benefits. The actual value of these benefits must depend on how well the training is planned and conducted. The benefits are likely to be best in those organizations which can express their training aims in terms of the standards of work performance needed to achieve the organizations' forward plans.

Planning ahead is standard management practice. Thus, at the end of each planning period (typically the financial year), an organization's top management will plan in detail for the results that they want the organization to achieve during the next 12 months. In industrial and commercial organizations, these are called the business plans, corporate plans or long-range plans, depending on the nature of the company and the period to be covered. In non-business and non-profitmaking organizations, the plans might be known by some other name, or called simply 'Plan for the year XXXX'.

In practice, whatever each of these plans might be called, they all serve the same purpose. In a successful organization, this is to set out in detail what the management have decided to do in order to ensure that the results in the new year are better than those achieved in the old. These achievements are essential for organizations that wish to survive and prosper. Thus, with these aims in view, the forward plans will define what new activities are to be introduced, what changes are to be made to existing activities, and precisely what improvements are required.

It is usual for such plans to cover every aspect of an organization's operations, broken down into every function and every section and department. Thus, practically everyone who works in the organization is involved to some degree in implementing the plan. Great amounts of learning are therefore unavoidable. This is one of the main difficulties in fulfilling these plans, and why so many organizations which fail to provide the appropriate training fail to realize their planned objectives in full.

THE TRAINING PLAN

The training plan defines how the training needs at every organizational level are to be satisfied. In order to construct this plan, it is usual that, once the business plan has been finalized, the organization's training specialist discusses the needs that arise from it. This discussion begins with the chief executive, and carries on afterwards with other members of the management team. Following these discussions, a training plan is formulated which, after approval by the chief executive, becomes the master plan for training to be provided during the ensuing year.

While preparing the master plan, it is usual that the training specialist, working down through the organization, interviews every manager and supervisor in order to help them to identify the training needs within their areas of responsibility. These discussions also help managers and supervisors to prepare their own departmental training plans.

By working to these plans, organizations ensure that no training need is overlooked, and that time and money are not wasted by providing needless training.

Figure 4.2 shows a training plan for the year 2002 in a particular branch of an insurance company. It details:

Key: V = Very good performance; L = Learn to do it; C = Change; I = Improvement; Date = by which training must be completed

Names of personnel / Jobs in the department	Provides quotations – uses rating guides	Obtains quotations from HQ (not in rating guide)	Answers enquiries from public	Refers enquiries to HQ – unable to answer	Produces urgent insurance documents (green card)	Instructs HQ to issue non-urgent documentation	Takes cash, cheques and credit cards over the counter	Reconciles cash register and does daily banking	Reimburses and reconciles petty cash	Types letters and documents			Notes
F. Carpenter	C 1 MAR	V	V	V	V	V	V	V	V	V			Branch Trainer
R. Mason	C 1 MAR	V	V	V	V	V	V	V	V	V			Retires 30 Nov.
G. Taylor	C 1 MAR	L 15 MAR	L 31 MAR	V	I 15 MAY		V	V		V			
P. Turner	C 1 MAR	V	L 30 APR	V		V	I 1 APR	L 1 MAY	V				
K. Gardener	C 1 MAR		V	L 15 APR	V		V	L 1 MAY		V			
A. Farmer	C 1 MAR		I 1 MAY	V		V	L 1 MAY	V					
W. Weaver		V	V			L 15 APR	V	L 31 MAR	V				
B. Plumber			I 15 APR	V	V	V	L 1 APR			V			
Target no. trained	5	5	8	8	5	6	8	8	4	5			

Signed: Margaret Brown **Date:** 14/12/2001

Figure 4.2 A completed training plan for a branch of an insurance company

- the individual skills (job in the department) to be addressed in training
- the names of the individuals
- their current proficiency in each of the jobs
- where training is required, and the date by which it is required
- the minimum or ideal number of staff required to be proficient in each task.

This plan can also be used as a record of progress; each module of training can be ticked off as it is delivered. In the same way, if for any reason a module cannot be delivered on schedule, it can be re-scheduled and the new date inserted on the plan.

Training policy statements

Training only achieves all of its planned objectives when it is correctly designed, organized and conducted. It is therefore necessary to ensure that all the training provided is, in fact, properly designed, organized and conducted, and that no short cuts of any kind are ever taken. This is why it is essential that, for every training scheme, the organization has a training policy statement.

The best procedure for formulating a training policy statement starts with the organization's training specialist identifying that one is needed (it might, for example, be required for induction training, or for the use of external training courses). Having identified a particular need, the training specialist discusses this with the chief executive or other authorized policy maker. After securing his or her agreement that a policy statement should be issued, the training specialist studies the relevant best practices, drafts the statement, and submits it to the policy maker for approval. Once approved, the statement becomes an authoritative document, compliance with which is mandatory throughout the organization.

By using such policy statements, organizations ensure that the correct methods and procedures are used consistently and uniformly when any kind of training is conducted. In this context, *consistently* means that every person always follows exactly the same procedure. *Uniformly* means that exactly the same procedure is followed within every section and department throughout the organization.

Figures 4.3, 4.4 and 4.5 are three examples of policy statements that have been in use over a number of years for a medium-sized engineering company, where they are still proving invaluable in helping to ensure that training produces the best possible results. Although these examples are taken from an engineering company, exactly the same procedures can, of course, be used by all other kinds of commercial and industrial organizations.

Conclusion

All the managers and supervisors, the training specialists, and anyone else with any responsibility in an organization must recognize that training is not training if it does not result in:

1 newly appointed employees being able to do the work that they could not do immediately before

I.R.I.S. plc

TRAINING POLICY STATEMENT	
Page:	1/1
Issue:	3
Date:	June 2002

Policy for the provision of training

AIM: The Company wishes to provide training that brings the greatest possible benefits. The aim of this policy is to define the responsibilities and the procedures that the Company has decided to follow in order to obtain this result.

THE POLICY IS:

1 That it is accepted that it is the training which satisfies every need arising from the Company's business plan that will bring the greatest possible benefits.

2 That after the business plan has been finalized, the training manager shall meet the chief executive to identify training needs by considering what the business plan requires, under each of the following headings:
 - 2.1 Diversification
 - 2.2 Rationalization
 - 2.3 Expansion
 - 2.4 Reduction
 - 2.5 Changes
 - 2.6 Improvements in performance/results.

3 That, based on the notes made during the meeting with the chief executive, the training manager shall draft the proposed training plan for the ensuing year which, in tabulated form, defines:
 - 3.1 Who is to be trained (with names and job titles)
 - 3.2 To enable them to do what?
 - 3.3 Who is responsible for ensuring that the training takes place
 - 3.4 Who will carry out the training
 - 3.5 Where the training will take place
 - 3.6 When the training will take place
 - 3.7 How much the training will cost.

4 That, after meeting the chief executive, the training manager shall meet each of the other five directors to identify training needs within their functions, as these arise from the business plan, by asking the following questions:
 - 4.1 What new appointments, transfers and promotions are planned?
 - 4.2 What changes in products, services, machines, equipment, working methods, etc. are planned?
 - 4.3 What improvement in the results achieved by each section and department are required by the business plan?

5 That, based on notes made during the meetings with directors, the training manager shall draft the proposed training plan for the ensuing year for each of the functions. The format shall be the same as that used in 3 above.

6 That early in December of each year, the chief executive shall organize a meeting with the five directors and the training manager to review the drafts of all the proposed training plans and, when fully satisfied, give their approval and accept full responsibility for implementing the plans.

7 That while training plans are being formulated, the training officer shall meet every company manager and supervisor to help them to complete departmental training plans for their own areas of responsibility.

8 That all directors, managers and supervisors shall monitor the effectiveness of the training provided by checking that the training needs are being satisfied and that the results specified in the business plan are being achieved (so that corrective action can be taken wherever these needs are not being satisfied).

Figure 4.3 A general policy statement
This example, developed for an engineering company, illustrates the best practices in formulating training policy statements. It also explains how to organize training so that it brings the greatest possible benefits that training can achieve.

I.R.I.S. plc

TRAINING POLICY STATEMENT	
Page:	1/1
Issue:	4
Date:	June 2002

Systematic on-the-job training

AIM: To define the responsibilities and the procedures that the Company has decided to follow for operating its systematic on-the-job training.

THE POLICY IS:

1 That systematic on-the-job training shall be provided in every section and department within the Company.

2 That 'systematic on-the-job training' means training conducted by the departmental part-time trainers at the employee's own place of work.

3 That the departmental part-time trainers use the instructional technique when instructing.

4 That the departmental trainers are part-time because they spend most of their working time doing their usual jobs, and instruct only when the need arises within their own sections and departments.

5 That the departmental part-time trainers are selected and trained in accordance with the company training policy statement (see Figure 4.5).

6 That the departmental part-time trainers remain responsible to their departmental managers and supervisors, and are subject to the same conditions of employment as the other employees within their departments.

7 That the departmental part-time trainers are paid wages and salaries that apply to their main jobs, without any additions or supplements for their instructional duties.

8 That the Company training manager is responsible for the operation of systematic on-the-job training, and checks that the employees learn at least twice as fast and achieve at least 10 per cent higher standards compared to the case where this form of training is not provided.

9 That the heads of all sections and departments co-operate with the training manager and seek specialist help and advice to ensure the full effectiveness of systematic on-the-job training within their sections and departments.

10 That the heads of all sections and departments provide adequate facilities for their departmental part-time trainers to work effectively (for example, accepting that instruction has priority over all other work of these trainers).

11 That the heads of sections and departments monitor the effectiveness of the part-time trainers working in their sections and departments, and inform the training manager whenever there is any doubt about the results achieved.

12 That heads of sections and departments maintain adequate numbers of part-time departmental trainers to cover all eventualities and inform the training manager whenever additions or replacements are required.

Note: Wherever possible, the training manager should be given four months' notice, as this is the time required to select and assemble a sufficient number of trainers and make them fully effective to run a viable in-company course.

Figure 4.4 A training policy statement for systematic on-the-job training

I.R.I.S. plc

TRAINING POLICY STATEMENT	
Page:	1/1
Issue:	6
Date:	August 2002

Policy for training departmental part-time trainers

AIM: To define the responsibilities and the procedure that the Company has decided to follow to enable the departmental part-time trainers to use an instructional technique when conducting on-the-job training within their sections or departments.

THE POLICY IS:

1 That vacancies for the departmental part-time trainers shall be advertised within the departments, and that applications to the respective managers shall be invited.

2 That the applicants shall, first of all, be given a copy of this policy statement to read, together with the policy statement headed 'Systematic on-the-job training'.

3 That every applicant who accepts the requirements laid down in these two policy statements shall be interviewed by his or her departmental manager. Every applicant shall be informed within four days whether or not the application has been successful.

4 That the preferred applicants shall be those who are well experienced in the work of the department, have no supervisory duties, are interested in training and helping their colleagues at work, and are interested in eventually becoming supervisors.

5 That the selected applicants shall be allowed by their managers to attend an in-company course in instructional technique.

6 That each course shall be run by the Company's training manager, with a total duration of 10 days arranged as follows:

– 4 consecutive days during Week 1

– 2 days during each of Weeks 2, 3 and 4.

7 That if, during the course, an applicant is unwilling or unable to comply with every requirement of the instructional technique, he or she shall not be appointed as a departmental part-time trainer.

8 That a sufficient number of courses shall be run each year to meet the needs of all the departments, planned on the understanding that the optimum number on each course is 8 participants.

9 That the departmental part-time trainers shall be encouraged by their managers to keep in touch with the members of the Training Department and seek their help and advice in constantly striving to improve their own effectiveness.

10 That the training manager and his or her staff shall monitor the effectiveness of the departmental part-time trainers and provide further training and coaching whenever this is considered necessary.

11 That the departmental part-time trainers may ask their managers, at any time, to be released from their instructional duties.

Figure 4.5 A policy statement for training departmental part-time trainers

2 an employee being able to do differently whatever must be done differently after the introduction of any kind of change that affects his or her job
3 an employee being able to do his or her own work better, following a request for such improvement by the immediate superior or manager.

In each of these cases, the improvement in job performance must be assessable by measuring performance before and after training. You cannot improve what you cannot measure.

Few organizations attempt to check or measure whether the training which they arrange actually produces any improvement. Thus, those organizations where attendance at courses is the only form of training provided cannot discover the truth – that this form of training is likely to produce any significant improvement in efficiency, productivity and the quality of goods and services. Only systematic on-the-job training can produce these improvements. Any organization that wishes to achieve must ensure that those responsible follow the requirements defined in the four-step training cycle (Figure 4.1). It has no alternative but to use formal procedures such as those detailed in Figures 4.4 and 4.5.

Further reading

Buckley, R. and Caple, J., *Theory and Practice of Training*, 4th edn, Kogan Page, London, 2000.

Evans, Bill, Reynolds, Peter and Jeffries, Dave, *Training for Total Quality Management*, 2nd edn, Kogan Page, London, 1997.

ISO 10015: 1999, *Quality Management: Guidelines for Training*, International Organization for Standardization, Geneva, 1999.

Landale, Anthony (ed.), *Gower Handbook of Training and Development*, 3rd edn, Gower, Aldershot, 1999.

CHAPTER

5 The Control of Design

R. Plummer

The product must be designed to the customer's requirements, and product realization must conform to the design.

The subject of right execution, or conformance to design, is dealt with elsewhere in this handbook. This chapter deals with ensuring that the design conforms to the customer's requirements, and that the process of design is conducted under control conditions.

Design is a process

Design is a three-stage process, consisting of:

1 inputs – the design requirements and objectives
2 creative activity – the stage of the design process in which people use their flair, initiative and inventiveness to convert the input requirements into a blueprint for later realization as a product or service
3 output – the 'blueprint'.

Design inputs

Why is it so important to get the design objectives clear at the outset?

The cost of correcting a quality defect increases exponentially with the delay incurred before the defect is corrected. The addition of each extra stage in the lifecycle of a product or service before the defect is corrected can cause up to a tenfold increase in the ultimate cost of correction.

Failing to establish the correct design objectives clearly can cause a product to be unfit for its purpose and to fail to sell well after its initial launch. It can require such extensive modification in order to make it fit for purpose as to make it uneconomical, and to necessitate its withdrawal from the market. It can cause interactive effects in a system within which the product is incorporated. This can render the entire system unfit for purpose, and even prompt the demise of a complete technology. In the 1980s, such a failure to understand design objectives resulted in the collapse of a whole telecommunications technology, but another outcome could be a catastrophic failure of some major project because the design objectives produced a component that was unfit for its implied needs. Failure to establish the true design objectives may result in a manufacturing or service specification which is far more stringent than necessary. The inevitable quality-related costs, including additional inspection, rework, disposal and so on, could be avoided simply by relaxing the manufacturing specification.

Consideration of the following input requirements is intended to eliminate such failures.

DESIGN TEAMS

A design team is a group of interested parties to the design, each of which must make a clear statement of the design inputs that it requires to be fulfilled. The group of interested parties should consist, as a minimum, of representatives of:

- the customer
- the developer
- procurement
- manufacturer
- test and evaluation
- packaging and transportation
- installation
- the overall project managers
- the quality assurance department
- design managers
- the designers themselves.

Each of the interested parties has different requirements, and therefore different inputs.

The customer's inputs may include a specification that is as limited as a bare outline of the product or service required. Alternatively, they may be as comprehensive as a full specification of the practical capability of the end product or service, complete with tolerances, choice of materials, choice of contractors to do the design work or to implement the design, cost limits, time limits, penalty clauses, and so on.

The developers of the product or service will include in their design input a statement of what is currently or historically capable of being manufactured, or of the known limits to service capability. These known limits may include simple practical hurdles, such as the limit to the human resources available for the foreseeable future.

Procurement will state what materials are available on the market, with what preferred values and tolerances, lead times to acquisition, spares availability, and so on.

The manufacturer's design input may develop, during discussion, to include advice if the design appears to be veering into territory which is unachievable or unknown in manufacturing or service provision. A well-known trap is that designers still design products and services which manufacturers or field staff cannot produce, install or maintain.

Test and evaluation departments will need to influence the nature of test and verification requirements in order to acquire the appropriate test techniques and equipment.

Packaging and transportation will need to be modified in design or made available at the appropriate time in the design product cycle.

From the project managers who are to implement the overall project (whether solely the design, or more), the design input must include a request for estimates of manning levels, logistics and equipment required, and a statement of what the natural breaks or milestones in the design project are, so that project management activities can be planned appropriately.

In its design input, the quality assurance department will provide a statement of the quality assurance activities it expects to be derived from the design project, a statement of the form that the design architecture will follow, a statement of the design methodologies which must be followed, and a statement of the form that quality assurance audits and reports will take, together with mechanisms, authorities and responsibilities for implementing corrective action.

Design managers must include in their design inputs a statement of the day-to-day supervisory techniques that they expect to employ, and the form of the outputs that they expect to have to check.

The designers themselves will request in their design input a statement of what is required to be designed.

Some of the data and logistics provided by some of the design team members will naturally be expected by others of the team. Some design inputs may come as a surprise to some team members. Some design inputs will actually conflict with other inputs, and resolution or compromise of that conflict will be necessary as a very high priority. Indeed, resolution or compromise of conflict of interest is one of the prime reasons why the design team exists at all.

An interesting conclusion to be drawn is that *all* the team members have both express and implied requirements of the design, and that no single team member, such as the customer, has an overriding say in the inputs to the design. Therefore, it is essential to consider how all of the interested parties will relate to each other.

DESIGN INTERFACES

Design interfaces can be separated into two categories: interfaces between interested parties, and interfaces between design modules. The problem to be addressed is the same in either case, and the solution is essentially the same as well.

The majority of quality defects recorded in management systems occur at the interfaces between departments. This is because managers and staff tend to think in terms of department rather than in terms of process. Consequently, each department beavers busily away, paying little or no regard to who the real customer is or the customer's requirements. In many departments, an attitude is struck, after long years of acceptance, that co-operation between departments is an impossibility, that there is no point in asking what other departments want, because nobody is listening. Not surprisingly, when a department comes to interface with other departments in the same process, the product fails to meet the customer's requirements (up to 40 per cent of the time in service industries!). Customers would have cause for concern if this kind of muddle caused a parachute to fail to open, but possibly a little difficulty in pressing their case.

The same problem – failure to communicate – is true of interfaces between design modules that are to be integrated into one overall design.

The solution to design interface problems is the same whether the interface is between interested parties or between interacting modules: how to ensure proper communication between interacting pairs. Each must have functions assigned to them. Once the functions have been chosen, the next decision concerns which other modules or parties each should interface with. The interface requirements for a given module or party constitute their inputs and outputs, and specify what must be done. As long as it complies with the interface requirements, the designer is free to do almost anything he or she wants (but see later) in order to achieve the interface requirements.

GET MARKET INTELLIGENCE

The first step is to gather market intelligence. Market intelligence can be divided into two broad categories. One category, the evolutionary design, is where a market already exists from which data on design objectives can be drawn. An example of this is the use of the newly discovered material aluminium in the fabrication of aircraft in the mid-1930s, with the transition from the Hurricane fighter, built with a tubular steel frame, to the Spitfire, built with a stressed aluminium monococque body. The parameters of flight were already well known, and the design of the Spitfire built on what already existed.

The other category, the revolutionary design, is where entirely new ground is to be broken. An example of this is the design in the early 1980s of Stored Programme Controlled (SPC) switching centres (digital telephone exchanges), where the philosophy of SPC had to be interpreted before design objectives could even be considered. Other examples were the profound electronic potentialities of high-temperature superconductors, discovered in 1987, and Internet services developed in the 1990s.

The former category, the evolutionary design, is the more normal. Experience shows that most of the significant advances in design occur from small extensions to existing and well-proven concepts.

The latter category, the revolutionary design, is the less usual and, naturally, the more difficult about which to obtain clear objectives. This is due to the far greater difficulty involved in specifying what the market is ultimately going to want, or how best to realize the potentialities of exciting new discoveries. This problem has been stated mathematically in terms of coefficients of difficulty of obtaining a precise view of the objectives to be fulfilled. Equations have been formulated and graphs drawn which assist designers in calculating the volume of design effort, and therefore of cost, probably required for a given coefficient of difficulty. This discussion agrees with common sense and experience.

Market intelligence can be gathered from different sources.

Consider first the case of objectives for evolutionary designs, which make a small advance on existing concepts. New materials, such as aluminium, allow engineers and designers to realize developments in design where an established principle has been in operation for years. Junk mail is aimed at demographic groups, for which credit ratings, income and stereotyped tastes are known or predictable. Innovative designers of junk mail merely make advances on existing design objectives in order to give their junk mail more appeal than that of their competitors. Encyclopaedias were no longer sold as complete sets, and it became more common to sell them in weekly volumes, until entire documents became available on the Internet.

In the category of objectives for revolutionary designs, the design effort might be directed at a distillation of market information to try to spot an opening requiring something that has simply never existed before. Alternatively, a designer's client may make a request for something that either does not exist or for which the solution is something of pure invention. Examples include attempts to design a forward-sweeping aircraft wing for which the equations for lift did not exist, software solutions in general and the information technology revolution in particular. Design for the client often comes in fits and starts. The erratic nature is often due to clients not knowing precisely what they want, partly because they do not know the full range of options available. The further into the design one gets, the more clients realize what they could have, and the more the design objectives are capable of being changed. The solution here is to have the maximum of consultation among the interested parties at the earliest stages of the design effort, and to feed back constantly at this crucial time. Remember how rapidly the costs of correction of quality defects increase with increased delay before action is taken. For the revolutionary design case, designers and engineers must resort in general to theoretical aspects, and climb a steep learning curve very fast. This well-known problem often results in design projects being awarded in two parts. The first part calls for a feasibility study to determine whether or not the actual design is even achievable. Once it is clear that the design is feasible, then the main design contract is awarded. Simultaneously, those involved must be aware of the problem faced by the client of the enormous diversity of possible design objectives, of which the client may be largely ignorant.

CLARIFY THE EXPRESS REQUIREMENTS

The design objectives must be ordered top-down. This means that design objectives must be ranked in the commonsense order in which they must logically be fulfilled. This seemingly obvious statement takes on importance when you realize that you have forgotten to specify stage payments on a multi-million-pound contract, and that the work-in-progress capital is going to cost you thousand of pounds in interest.

A training exercise used by the author in his presentations on design objectives has three syndicate groups. Each group plays the role of a party to the implementation of an advanced information technology project. Halfway through the groups' thinking time, the author is habitually asked: 'Can we assume this?' or 'Can we assume that?' The answer is: 'Don't assume anything. Clarify it with the other parties.'

EVALUATE THE IMPLIED REQUIREMENTS

The express requirements of a market or customer are generally more readily determined, and therefore receive more attention than the implied requirements. A few examples of implied requirements will illustrate some pitfalls to be avoided.

A woman bought a plastic bucket. On its outside was a clear and unequivocal warning not to place boiling water in the bucket, as it was not designed to withstand boiling-water temperature. Nevertheless, she poured boiling water into the bucket, which buckled, and the spilling water scalded her legs. She sued the bucket manufacturer. The magistrate threw her case out of court. Even when there is a comprehensive effort to make the limitations of a product clear, people will still abuse the stated limits.

You don't need seat belts, insurance or contraceptives until you really do need them. Design objectives are sometimes approached with a remarkably shuttered attitude: 'No. That can't possibly happen.'

Give a loaded revolver to a child, and then tell the child not to shoot itself. Murphy's Law has it that if it is allowable that an event can occur, then sooner or later it will occur. This is often cited as Sod's Law: if it can go wrong, it will!

The design objectives must include requirements that are implied by the use of the product, in that the implication can be reasonably foreseen at the time of designing.

A major Japanese industrial company employs graduate engineers as trainee designers. Part of their six years of training as designers is spent not in design at all, but in retailing. The graduates are sent to company retail outlets for two years to acquire experience of what the public wants to buy, and what they tend to bring back as unfit for purpose. After this, they spend two years in manufacturing to acquire experience of what manufacturing departments can manufacture and what they can't. Then, and only then, do they spend two years training in the function of design.

The very important principle is that the implied requirements are more difficult to determine than are the express requirements.

CLARIFY THE EXPRESS AND IMPLIED REQUIREMENTS OF RELATED LEGISLATION

The Consumer Protection Act says that the producer will be liable for damage wholly or partly caused by the product. Defences against this include the fact that the damage could not reasonably be foreseen at the time the product was designed and produced.

Health and safety legislation is taken more seriously than much other legislation. The Acts of Parliament on safety permit operatives to walk off the job rather than subject themselves to dangerous circumstances.

The implications of product liability and health and safety legislation are dealt with in other chapters. Nevertheless, they must feature in the design objectives.

CHOICE OF MARKET SECTOR

It is a business management decision to consider in which part of the market lie the requirements that the company wishes to satisfy. It is a quality management decision to ensure that the design objectives of the chosen market sector are all considered in the design process.

Consideration of design objectives must take into account the fact that there may well be an unfulfilled market niche to go for, but one that could involve a work-in-progress investment capital that is unsustainable for the company, or that the returns on investment might be doubtful or speculative or a long time coming. One large research company regularly refuses to accept design commissions on the grounds that preliminary investigation has indicated too uncertain a return on investment.

A particular part of the market may concord with the company's existing corporate image. Other parts may not. Diversification into the money markets by some companies, after the liberalization of financial services in 1987, resulted in some companies catching a cold in an area not traditionally their own. They subsequently returned to their traditional market sectors.

Other design objectives that might influence the choice of market sector include making the choice between long-life, consumer-durable or consumer-disposable products, whether they should comprise built-in obsolescence or should be state of the art, whether to design for long life coupled with high reliability (as with the nuclear industry), or disposability (as with some sealed-for-life components such as car batteries). Consideration must be given to the fact that certain sectors have market parameters that change or even oscillate with time, sometimes quite dramatically. Design objectives must reflect the potential for market changes. Is the company in the market for a swing into new tooling – for example, the changes seen in the print industry in the middle of 1980? Is the company capable of tracking changes in the degree of advancement of a particular market – for example, the far tighter tolerances demanded in ships changing from gas turbines to nuclear power? Is the company able to control more stringent processes – for example, exhaust emission control regulations? Can the company finance fluctuating commodity prices – for example, strategic metals in time of war or within cyclic markets etc? Some companies have developed a capability to adapt with staggering swiftness to market changes and to diverse customer demands. An example is traditional light engineering firms, whose set-up times for automatic machine tools ran into hours when a batch of a different product was called for. By using replacement heads for each machine tool, each head being set up for a different product, the set-up time during which the machine is not producing is limited to the time it takes to change heads, reducing set-up times from hours to tens of seconds. This is a fine example of the just-in-time approach to the management of quality in a rapidly changing environment. When due weight has been ascribed to each and all of these influences, and a decision reached about which design objectives are achievable by the company, then the company is in a position to choose its market sector. Of course, it might be that the tradition of a company already dictates the market sector. In this case, the company must choose whether to stay in its traditional sector, or to move to comply with the design objectives of a changing sector. That choice is a business management decision. The quality management decision is to ensure that whatever the market sector and whatever the degree of flux or stasis of a company's position, the design objectives are fully considered at the outset.

DESIGN PARAMETERS

The company management will decide upon a market sector. The chosen market sector will decide certain design parameters, for example certain aspects of reliability and maintainability and the extent to which the product is expected to be maintained by the user or by a service organization. Under harsh conditions of use, and where sophisticated support organizations are absent, such as in the arctic or in the desert, it is pointless driving vehicles which can only be tuned electronically or which have total dependence on one feature such as a sophisticated suspension system. The maintainer needs to be able to keep the vehicle running using simple tools and materials. The most prevalent factor keeping ambassadors' bullet-proof cars off the road in sub-Saharan countries is failure of the air conditioning system. The car is undriveable in the heat, because you can't open the windows in a bullet-proof car!

The projected life span of a product is generally thought of as proportionate to the cost of the product. A look at the total lifecycle cost to the customer of poor design shows, once again, that the lowest lifecycle costs are brought about by good design. In countries in the world where progress in design has gone by default, or is stifled as a consequence of a restrictive system, fitness for purpose is very low. Unfortunately, there is always a market for poor-quality goods because, in costing less, they are affordable by less affluent people in some nations. The lifecycle costs are high, however, because poorly designed products have a short time before replacement is inevitable.

In the case of software, one design objective to be considered is the degree of user-friendliness of the software package. User-friendliness is the extent to which the software package itself guides the user through the options available in using the package, and the choices which may be made. The degree of user-friendliness chosen by the designers will depend upon how computer-literate the intended users of the software package are. Some computer packages have several levels of user-friendliness that can be selected by users according to their knowledge and ability to use the package.

The cost-benefit of good design can be indicated by the use of standard curves (see Figure

5.1). Manufacturers' costs before sales, including the cost of design, are shown rising with increased fitness for purpose. Both manufacturers' and users' costs after sales are shown falling with increased fitness for purpose. Not surprisingly, the cost-benefit curve shows a minimum that is construed as the minimum cost per fitness for purpose. However, the indications are that users tend to be prepared to pay a total cost that rises in direct proportion to increased fitness for purpose. The cost benefit for increased fitness for purpose is therefore the optimization of the total cost curve and the straight line representing what the user is prepared to pay. This can clearly be seen to be slightly greater than the minimum cost.

FAILURE MODE EFFECT AND CRITICALITY ANALYSIS

Failure mode effect and criticality analysis (FMECA) evaluates the effect upon the overall design of a failure in any one of the identifiable failure modes of the design components, and evaluates how critically that failure will affect the design performance. Each identifiable failure mode is ascribed a probability of occurrence, and logical summation of the inclusive probabilities of occurrence of failure modes produces a figure for the reliability of the system as a whole.

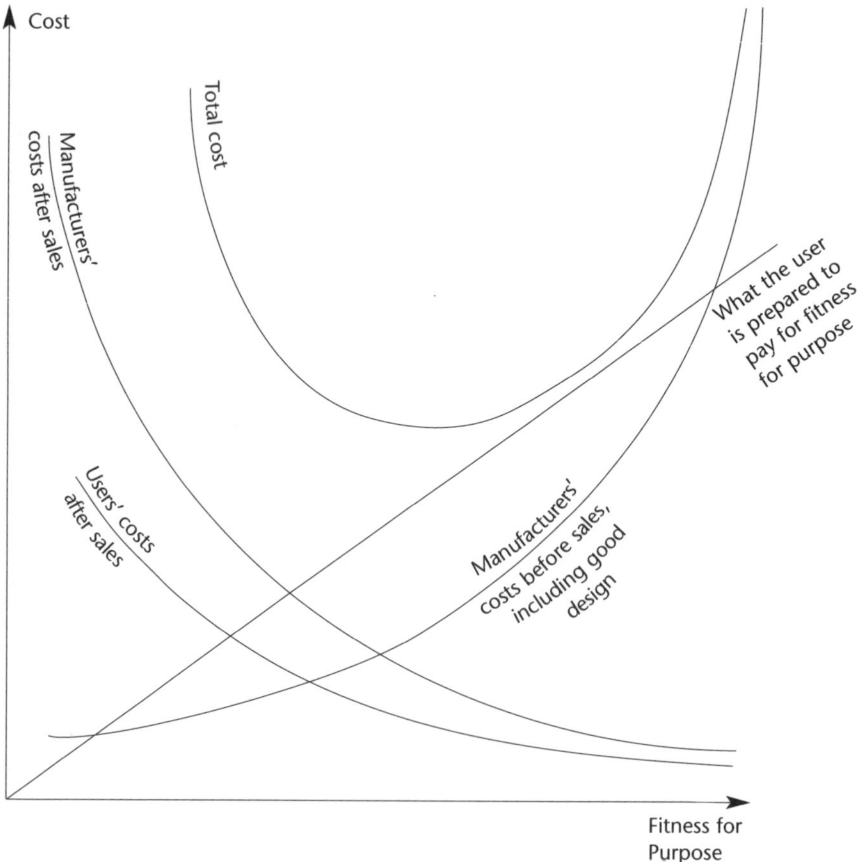

Figure 5.1 Fitness for purpose in relation to various costs

Tables of probabilities of occurrence of failure modes have been compiled to assist designers in FMECA. Probabilities for stringent applications, for instance military use, are cited in documents such as US Military Standard 217. Probabilities for less exacting requirements are quoted in British Telecom's *Handbook of Reliability Data*. Reference works compiled by acknowledged authorities in the field of reliability contain figures for the upper and lower limits of the probability of the occurrence of events, and also the most likely level of probability. The probability has even been calculated of an operator failing to operate a manually operated switch correctly.

FMECA can be justly seen as a powerful tool in assessing the extent to which a design meets certain of its design objectives.

FEEDBACK FROM PRODUCTION

Quality assurance purists will argue that quality-assured design should be right first time. So it should be. But part of the control of design (as well as of any other stage in the lifecycle of a product or service) must be a system of feedback from later stages of the lifecycle of the product. Such a system is essential to the concept of Zero Defects.

The creative activity

Once the design objectives have been determined, it is important to conduct the creative part of the design process in a way that ensures that the finished design conforms to the declared design objectives. It is also important to be able to show evidence that the design has been thus conducted. This evidence is the visible assurance of quality, or quality assurance.

DEFINITIONS

The creative activity is the part of the design process in which people use their flair, initiative and inventiveness to convert a set of requirements into a blueprint for later realization as a product or service.

Quality assurance of design is derived from first setting a boundary around the design, and then ensuring that only permitted inputs are allowed into the design and only permitted outputs are allowed out. Subject to this, the designers are allowed to do just about anything they please (but see below) within the boundary, as long as the interface requirements across the boundary (the design inputs and outputs) are complied with.

In practical terms, this is equivalent to shutting a designer in a room with all the necessary facilities and equipment, providing a statement of what needs to be designed and broadly how it is to be designed, and then only letting out of the room an output which complies with the original statement. What the designer does while in the room, what flair and initiative he or she uses, whether he or she is designing a moon rocket using a computer or an abacus, is entirely up to him.

However, in order to ensure that the things the designer does in the room meet requirements and are capable of being checked as such, there are two indispensable tools that management must apply to the creative process: the *design architecture* and the *design methodology*.

DESIGN ARCHITECTURE

A design architecture is a family tree of how the various modules within the overall design relate to each other. It is usual to depict the most significant items at the top of the tree. These are then decomposed, step by step, down to whatever level of detail is necessary to reduce the design to manageable packets of work.

The implementation of these steps, conducted from the top downwards, ensures that all the stages of design are completed in the correct order and that each stage is properly completed before proceeding to the next one. Following a design architecture in this fashion results in the realization of stepwise decomposition. Stepwise decomposition can be viewed as synonymous with the scientific method: if each step in a process is conducted correctly, then any subsequent step founded upon it will be traceable back to the origins of the process.

The topmost step in any design architecture consists of the concept of the product or service to be realized. Consider as an example a means of transport.

The first step down is a decomposition of the concept, generally into two or three major divisions, each of which is still very much an idea rather than a realization, but each of which is a standalone entity in its own right. Examples in the means of transport are the power unit, the means of transmission of power, and the rigidity (the structure).

The next step down is a decomposition of each of the two or three major divisions into practical functions that must later be realized. It is probable that some of the functions will need to interface with each other in order for each one to be able to execute its own functions. Examples are the fuel induction system, the system of conversion of energy from heat into motion within the power unit, and the control mechanism for timing and regulating the energy conversion process.

The next step down is a decomposition of the functions into blocks of practical functionality, each of which has to interface with other blocks in order for it to be able to execute its own function. Examples are the camshafts and associated equipment that open and close the valves at the correct angles in the engine's cycle.

The next step down decomposes the block into modules, each of a size that can easily be managed in terms of project or design management. Each of these modules interfaces with other modules: for example, the cam followers that interact with the camshaft and either the pushrods or the valves. The advantage of modularity is that as long as the interface requirements continue to be fulfilled, what happens inside the module in order to fulfil the interface requirements is almost irrelevant. The effect of this is that if an ingenious designer discovers a new and more efficient way of realizing the interface requirements, for example by using less energy or less software processing time, then the module can be replaced in its entirety by an updated module and no liability accrues, as long as the interface requirements continue to be fulfilled.

One remarkable aspect of stepwise decomposition and the modular approach is the surprisingly low level in the decomposition that is reached before the design team needs to commit to, for example, the type of power unit that is to be used, or the proportion of the functions of the means of transport that are to be discharged by hardware and the proportion by software, or mechanically as opposed to electronically.

Between each of the steps of the design architecture is scope for monitoring progress. The progress is monitored at the end of each step to ensure that the output from each step satisfies the requirements that were the inputs to the step. If the output does not satisfy the input requirements for that particular decomposition, then the design team must return to the inputs to that step, and design again until the output does satisfy the input requirements. If it should prove that the input requirements themselves were unreasonable or unrealizable, or diverge from the requirements, then the output of the step must be fed back to earlier and earlier stages in the architecture, until the cause of the divergence from requirements becomes clear. The cause can then be corrected. Designers and the design team should not balk at returning to steps in the decomposition which were long since written off as correct if evidence arises that an erroneous decomposition was made. Remember, not for the first time, how rapidly the costs of corrective action rise with each advancing step in the decomposition of a design.

The design architecture should exist in a clear and unequivocal written statement or graphical family tree as part of the company's declared quality management system. In a company which designs variants upon a basic theme, the design architecture will be only slightly project-dependent towards the lower steps of the architecture. Design reviews and audits can then be few in number, since the architecture will have been followed many times and will be familiar to most design team members. In a company where a wide diversity of products or services is designed, then naturally the design architecture will be project-dependent at a much earlier stage in the decomposition. In this case, design reviews and audits will need to be greater in number and more searching in order to pre-empt potential design flaws due to the lesser familiarity with the lower stages of the design architecture.

DESIGN METHODOLOGY

Design methodology is a statement of the constraints placed upon the design team. The constraints should be as few as possible, and should not be regarded as negative or repressive of the designer's natural flair and initiative. On the contrary, the design methodology is there to assist the designers by:

- relieving them of certain burdensome and unproductive decisions such as the type of metal to use, what level of personnel to request for authorization, to which particular responsible manager to delegate a defect report, which temporary software data store to use
- allowing automatic or computerized equipment relieves the designer of distracting tasks – for example, traceability, such as when part of a software refers to prescribed routines by referring to computer-generated labels (rather than to the number of the line of the software at which the prescribed routine begins, which changes as the software develops)
- guiding the designer in the use of design techniques that are part of an overall strategy within the company. Designers do brilliant work that they steadfastly refuse to document. (Yes, it still happens.) They subsequently leave the company. How much use are their piles of computer readouts to anyone if no one has a clue how or why they designed in a particular way, or how to integrate them with other piles of design data. Further, if good designs are implemented but the designers leave, then the maintenance department cannot be expected to know how to work through a design technique with which they are totally unfamiliar in order to maintain it. They might be able to, but the quality-related costs mount, as ever.

A company's design methodology should exist in a clear and unequivocal written statement, as part of the company's declared quality management system. Where the design of any step in the stepwise decomposition fails to comply with the design methodology (quite apart from failing to satisfy the design inputs to that particular step), then a defect report must be issued and the reasons for the failure discovered.

If it proves that the designer simply failed to abide by the design methodology, then the solution to the defect report should record that fact, in case any other designers fail to abide by the methodology. This gives the quality assurance department an opportunity to spot a trend of designers failing to abide by the design methodology, and thereafter seek out any weaknesses in the systematic use of the methodology. Alternatively, if it proves that design techniques have changed, and that the design methodology has not kept up to date with the changes, then the defect report will give the quality assurance department an opportunity to update the statement of methodology. It might be that a consequence of following the design methodology to the letter results in a design that was not fit for purpose. Put another way, diligent quality-assured design can produce avenues of approach which are subsequently found to be futile. The futile approaches should also be recorded when updating the design methodology, in order to prevent future designers from unwittingly wasting resources going in the same direction when the same design input arises another time. How many successive and similar designs have each been managed by a different design team, none of whose predecessors wrote down one word of what they did or why, or of the mistakes they made, in order to prevent future design teams from simply reinventing the wheel for each new design? – Another quality-related cost!

SUBCONTRACTED DESIGN

A known area of weakness in industry is the control of subcontracted design. Many contracts are let which allow the main contract holder to subcontract the design. In such cases, control of the subcontractor by the main contractor is often very poor. The biggest problem of all lies in getting the main contractor, or even the customer, to approve the various stages of design or design changes. On many occasions as an auditor, the author sees documented design procedures that state that no design or design change shall be realized until it has been approved by the contractor or the client. But this approval can take weeks, with a corresponding delay in the contract. In many contracts, the designers recognize the time delay problem and overcome it by simply putting the design into the realization phase without getting the approval. This is a nonconformity, right enough, but much more importantly, there is now a design or design change being realized without authority!

Outputs

Design output may be delivered in any acceptable form, whether it is a blueprint, a dieline drawing, a magnetic tape or disk of coordinates for drilling holes in a printed circuit board, even a model from which a full-scale product will be built.

The design output must be evaluated to ensure that it conforms in all respects to specified requirements.

There are three essential types of evaluation that can be performed on design outputs:

1 design review
2 design verification
3 design validation.

DESIGN REVIEW

Design review is the process of checking to see that all the design activities that should have been carried out have been.

It requires that all those with an interest in the design are represented at the review. Minutes of what was reviewed and what was found need to be kept.

DESIGN VERIFICATION

Design verification is the process of checking to see that the outputs of the various stages of the design meet the input requirements for that stage of design.

DESIGN VALIDATION

Design validation is the process of checking to see that the realized product or service actually meets the design objectives in full.

There are many ways to achieve these three checks. Some techniques even include aspects of one or more of the checks at the same time. Some of the techniques in use are discussed below.

Supervision

Supervision of design is basically the task of ensuring that the design architecture and methodology are being followed at all times, and assisting the designers to keep the customer requirements (the design inputs) in mind by providing someone with whom to share their ideas. Supervisors therefore need familiarity with the architecture and methodology, and must be experienced both in design and, preferably, the design in hand.

In order to ensure compliance by the designers with the architecture and the methodology, supervisors will seek evidence. Common methods of providing evidence that supervisors can check at appropriate times are checklists on which will be recorded by the designers the execution of activities which must be conducted, and also the results of those activities. In observing the checklists, supervisors must record the number of observations made, and also the number and type of deficiencies found, even if the deficiencies are put right on the spot. This latter information is important in assessing trends of deficiencies, and is a source of vital defect information that is very often lost. The layout of computer keyboards is continually under review to take into consideration the possibility of a wrong key being struck owing to its proximity to the correct key. If computer operators never reported these occurrences, believing them to be simply the result their own lack of dexterity, then no improvement would be possible, and errors would continue to be made.

Desk checks

A desk check of a piece of design is conducted by a colleague of the designer, first to ensure that a check is actually conducted, but also to eliminate witting or unwitting bias on the part of the designer who drew up the design. For this second reason, the other designer should not be engaged upon the task in question. This independence ensures impartiality in the desk check. The other designer's function is to check that the piece of design complies with its design inputs. Desk checks are milestone events in both the project management and the quality management of the design. The results of desk checks must be recorded. Deficiencies found must be included in the result, even if they are put right on the spot for the same reason as previously stated. The desk check results will form part of the quality assurance evidence of the design, and will be observed routinely by the design supervisor.

Peer group review

Peer group review is conducted by a group of the designer's peers, some or all of whom may be members of the design team. The purpose of peer group review is to check formally, at milestones in the design process, that the design output complies with the design inputs – in other words, that the designer has designed what he or she set out to design.

In general terms, a formal meeting is convened to review a stage of design. Prior to the meeting, and at a sufficient number of days' notice, all the prospective participants at the meeting are provided with a copy of the design inputs, architecture, methodology and a copy of the design output. The peers then take an appropriate length of time to compare, in isolation from one another, the design output with the design inputs. Each then logs anything that in his or her opinion constitutes a departure from the design requirements. At the peer group review meeting itself, each of the peers has an opportunity to state the features of the design they consider to be a departure from requirement. Short discussion among the peer group is permitted in order to decide whether or not it is, in fact, a departure. If a decision can be reached very quickly, then that decision is recorded and the group passes on to the next departure. If a decision as to the validity of the observation cannot be reached quickly, then the observation is recorded for the designer to take away and correct at leisure, or within a deadline set by the peer group.

The purpose of the peer group review is error detection, not error correction, and it is vital that this be borne continually in mind, otherwise the impact and brevity of peer group reviews will be lost and there is a real danger of them becoming just another talking shop.

Prototype testing

This takes a model and tests it to determine whether or not it meets the design requirements, before the main production run is started.

Final acceptance testing

In large capital projects, it is customary to run a prolonged test on the completed project to determine whether or not the final capital item meets design requirements.

Design changes

Feedback from any stage in the life of a product following design may indicate that a design change is necessary. This is part of the continuous improvement cycle. Any number of design changes is allowable according to the rules of the design company.

In quality management terms, the only requirement – and it is a very important requirement – is that any and all design changes must be communicated to all interested parties and approved by all of them, prior to being realized.

Conclusion

In conclusion, most of this chapter on quality control and quality assurance of design describes the execution of activities that appear to be quite removed from quality control and assurance. The execution of activities, sometimes thought to be 'pure' quality control or quality assurance, occupies only a small percentage of this chapter.

The conclusion to be drawn, quite correctly, from this is that the 'quality department' cannot shake a magic powder onto the design and make it a 'quality design'. Quality has to be designed in from the very beginning, not rubbed in by magic at the end. All the 'quality department' is dong is ensuring that past acquired knowledge of good ideas to be followed and of bad ideas to be avoided is brought to bear, that a commonsense, top-down approach to design is followed, and that a minimum number of checks is in place, but the checks work, are adhered to, and that the results are collated and acted upon effectively. Finally, of course, there must be evidence that all of this has taken place.

PART 2 *Do*

CHAPTER 6 *Procurement*

Matt Seaver

An organization needs to give at least the same degree of attention to purchased materials and subcontracted services as it does to the output of its own process. Surprisingly, organizations often subcontract critical products from suppliers about whom they know virtually nothing, while subjecting their own staff and processes to extraordinary controls.

The overall procurement process is shown in Figure 6.1. The degree to which a company follows this sequence of steps will depend on its particular circumstances. Some organizations will have additional controls, while smaller companies may omit some of the steps.

The word 'purchasing' implies a payment. However, there are many situations in which an organization acquires materials by means other than purchasing. For example, another company within the corporate group may supply raw materials for a process, and the recipient may have no discretion in the matter. If these materials have implications for the quality of the product or service, then their supply must nevertheless be controlled. The nature of this control will obviously be quite different, but must be adequate to protect the quality of the eventual output.

Responsibilities

As with all other aspects of quality management, responsibilities in relation to purchasing must be clearly defined. There are two principal responsibilities involved. The first relates to the quality or technical aspects of the material or service to be purchased and the capability of a potential supplier to meet requirements. This is normally the task of a quality or technical manager. The decision on whether to approve a supplier is based purely on the supplier's capability. The second responsibility relates to the actual routine purchasing activity. This involves pricing, scheduling, agreeing discounts, order size and suchlike. But this is confined to those suppliers already approved on grounds of quality and technical competence. The decision to place an order is based on purely commercial considerations, having first established the supplier's competence. In larger companies, these two functions are normally carried out by different people, whereas in a small company it may be the same person.

Define requirements

The first step in the procurement process is to identify those items, materials and services

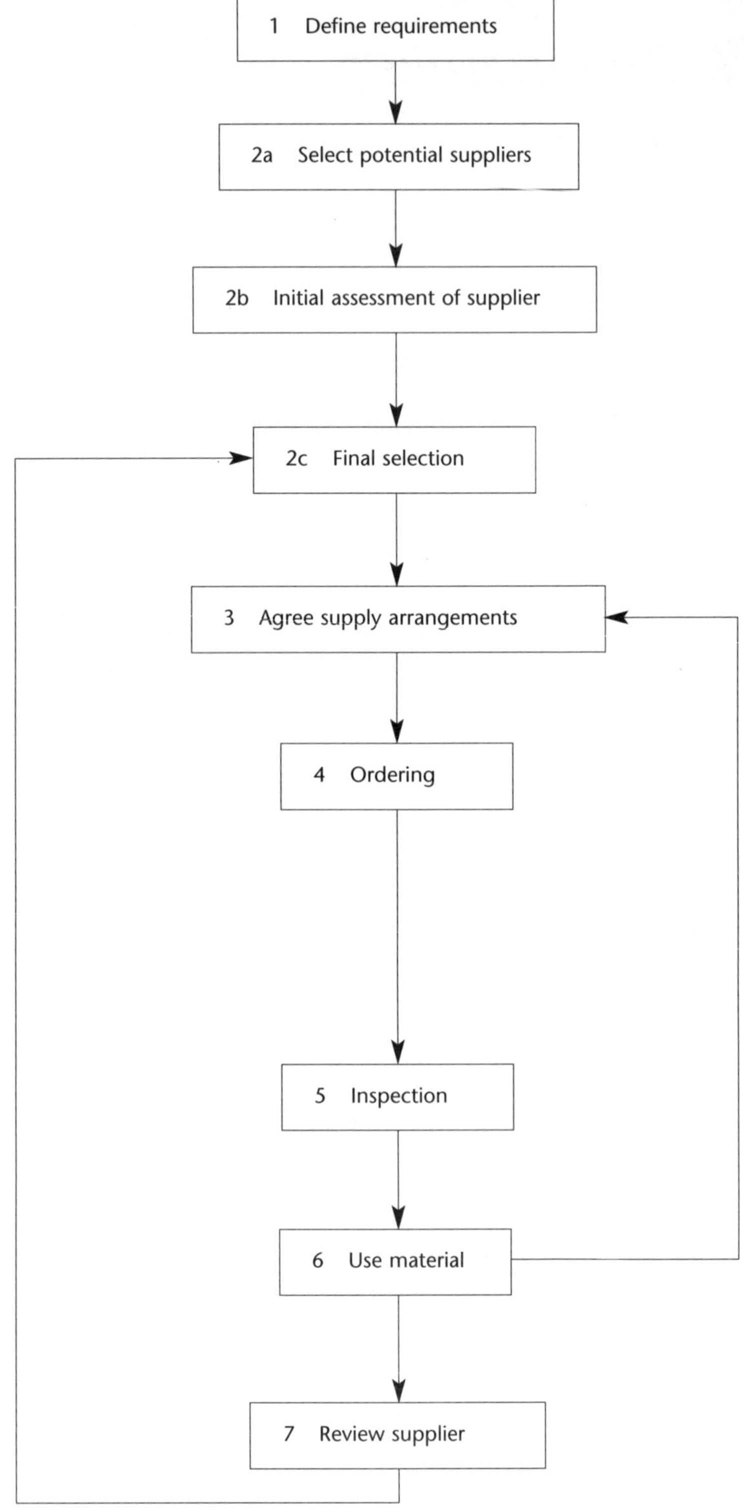

Figure 6.1 Flowchart of the purchasing process

that are to be included in the scope of the procurement controls. If its scope is confined to the requirements of, say, ISO 9001, then only those materials and services that can have an impact on the quality of the finished product or service need to be included. However, for purely commercial reasons it is highly desirable that all materials should be considered for inclusion. Thus, depending on the nature of your operation, you may decide to exclude, for example, stationery and fuel oil from the purchasing controls in the quality management system. From a strict quality point of view, ingredients or components may be excluded if it can be demonstrated that the process will correct *fully* any possible defects that might be present. This is quite unusual, however.

For each material involved, it is usually appropriate or necessary to draw up a specification.

SPECIFICATIONS

There are two main reasons why a specification is useful. Firstly, it provides the basis for agreement between you and your customer, and can prevent many disputes over basic issues. Secondly, it forms the basis for your assessment of the product or service at the end of the process.

The following are some of the issues that may be appropriate to consider when drawing up a specification for a physical product:

- physical properties
- chemical properties
- biological properties
- quality of components or materials that may be used
- functional/performance properties
- special process steps that the material must undergo
- packaging and labelling
- instructions for use/safety instructions
- storage conditions
- delivery method
- shelf life
- method of disposal.

In the case of a service (for example, a maintenance service contractor), consider the following:

- frequency of visits
- scope of work to be covered on each visit
- work to be done on each visit
- input (if any) required from the customer
- documentation to be completed and supplied to the customer
- response time
- quality of materials to be used
- exclusions.

It is important to exercise restraint when drawing up purchasing specifications. There is always a temptation to specify the highest grade of material. But this does not always result in better-quality output from the process. The specification should reflect those aspects of the material or service that can have an impact on the final output, having regard, in particular, to process capability in its widest meaning. If the specification is made stricter than is necessary, the result is an increased cost with no actual benefit.

Select suppliers

All purchases identified as critical should be purchased from reliable suppliers who have known capability to supply materials that meet requirements. The process of finding suitable suppliers can be long and complex, and it is advisable to have a formal written procedure for their selection and approval. The process may involve sending a questionnaire to a number of suppliers as a first step. The next step might be the examination of samples. Finally, it may be appropriate to visit the supplier to audit the quality management system and the process. Auditing is not essential, though clearly it is easier to assess a supplier's capability if you have seen the operation. In the absence of an audit, for example, an initial order could be replaced on the strength of the supplier's participation in an accredited quality assurance scheme or simply acting on the recommendation of somebody you trust. You would then use the trial material and assess the output from your process somewhat more carefully than normal. If you were satisfied, you could then make a decision about whether to place another trial order. In parallel with this, you would ask for supporting information about, for example, the supplier's quality management system, controls that the supplier operates, and technical details specific to the particular product. In due course, you could build up the picture that would enable you to approve the supplier.

Once identified, the capable suppliers should be listed in an Approved Suppliers list, and this should form the basis of all non-emergency purchases of the specified materials and services.

Agree supply arrangements

Defining the requirements for the product may only be part of the story. Because of the impossibility of fully demonstrating product quality by means of inspection or testing, it may be necessary to specify conditions regarding the manner in which the product is manufactured or the service delivered. This can include conditions relating to the supplier's quality management system. There has been a trend developing in recent years whereby customers insist on ISO 9001 certification for suppliers. While ISO 9001 certification is highly commendable, it is not an absolute guarantee of complete compliance with requirements. Many excellent companies supply totally reliable products through having very effective quality management systems in place, but without going down the road to certification. Some organizations fall into the trap of neglecting the real disciplines required for effective supplier control, thinking that it is sufficient to insist on ISO 9001 certification, and that this covers all possible problems that might arise in the supply of a critical item or service. Furthermore, ISO 9001 certification only covers generic good management practices; it does not guarantee that the certified company is technically competent to supply product to meet a particular specification.

Figure 6.2 shows an example of a procedure for approval of a new supplier. In this case, the responsibilities for purchasing and approval of suppliers is clearly demarcated. In smaller organizations, both tasks could be carried out by the one person, and the procedure would be correspondingly simpler.

Ordering

When placing the order, you should ensure that the requirements are stated clearly and unambiguously to guarantee that the material that will be received will be precisely what was ordered. That usually means referring to the specification. Even when the order is a regular one, the requirements should be stated or referenced each time to allow for the unexpected, such as staff changes in the supplier's organization, or cost-cutting initiatives that might result in a lower-grade material being supplied. The specification can be attached to the order, or where the specification has been agreed as part of a contract arrangement, the contract can be referenced. In the case of purchase from a catalogue, it is merely necessary to quote the item number.

Obviously, verbal orders are handled differently to written orders, but the principle is the same – the purchaser must be sure that the requirements have been communicated and understood by the supplier. It is usual to record the details of all verbal orders in some form that enables the goods inwards inspector to check them when they arrive.

Emergency purchases, when the usual approved supplies are not available, present particular problems, since shutting down the process is not normally an option, and materials must be obtained in order to continue operation. In that situation, it may be necessary to operate a less strict specification that identifies the absolute minimum requirements, possibly combined with more strict internal controls, such as increased levels of inspection.

Inspection

When the material has been delivered, it is usually necessary to check that the correct material has been delivered and that it meets the specification. The extent of checking that you carry out will depend on many factors, but primarily your confidence in the supplier. In the extreme case where you have no information about the supplier's capability but are forced by circumstances to use the material, you may carry out 100 per cent inspection or apply a formal statistical sampling scheme. As you gather more information, and as the supplier builds up a track record, you should consider reducing the level of inspection. With a lot of hard work and commitment on both sides, you could get to a situation where you do no testing, as in the case of a just-in-time relationship. (This aspect is covered in Chapter 7.) So there is no clear-cut definition of what level of inspection is appropriate for incoming materials. Ideally, a record should be kept of the receipt of all materials that have been identified as relevant to quality. Certainly, where traceability of materials through the process is an issue, the lot number should be recorded. The amount of detail recorded will depend, as always, on the circumstances.

Objective: To ensure that all suppliers of quality-critical materials and services have been properly assessed for their ability to meet requirements.

Scope: Suppliers of materials and services identified in the Controlled Materials list.

Procedure

Purchasing Officer

1 Send a copy of the New Supplier Questionnaire to the prospective supplier to be completed and returned. Attach a copy (uncontrolled) of the company specification and request agreement or comments, or a copy of the supplier's specification.
2 Pass the supplier's response to the Quality Manager.

Quality Manager

3 Assess the response, and decide whether further information is required. For example, samples may need to be tested. If none, then go to Step 9 below.
4 Inform the Purchasing Officer if further information, samples and so on are required.

Purchasing Officer

5 Request the material required by the Quality Manager.
6 Pass this on to the Quality Manager immediately it arrives.

Quality Manager

7 Assess the information received, and test any samples.
8 Decide whether to proceed with the assessment of the supplier. If necessary, instruct the Purchasing Officer to arrange an audit.
9 Make out a detailed set of requirements for the supplier, depending on the nature and criticality of the material to be purchased. This will include some or all of the following:
   a process control and finished product testing to be carried out by the supplier (number of samples, test methods)
   b controls to be exercised during manufacture, storage, transport
   c arrangements for visiting/auditing by us
   d information to accompany the deliveries (processing information, test results, certificates and so on).
10 Decide on a suitable trial period.

Purchasing Officer

11 Finalize the agreement with the supplier, based on Step 9 above, and place an appropriately sized trial order.

Quality Manager

12 At the end of the trial period decide whether to add the supplier to the List of Approved Suppliers.
13 Update the List of Approved Suppliers.

Notes

1 At the discretion of the Quality Manager, any of the above steps may be omitted or modified. However, the Quality Manager should make a brief note of the reason for this.
2 Both the Quality Manager and the Purchasing Officer must keep appropriate records of each of the steps above.

Responsibilities:

- Deciding whether the above procedure applies in any given case – Quality Manager.
- Approving each supplier – Quality Manager.
- Deciding whether to purchase from any particular approved supplier – Purchasing Officer.

Figure 6.2 Typical procedure for approval of suppliers for a reasonably large manufacturing company

Using the material

During processing, the material is usually subjected to the degree of scrutiny that will reveal any defects. It is important to have mechanisms in place to gather information about any such defects and to feed this back for immediate corrective action on the part of the supplier and for input to the later review of suppliers. Often, the person who has best insight into supplier performance is the person who actually handles the material.

Review of suppliers

The approved suppliers should be re-evaluated at defined intervals to confirm that they continue to supply goods and services to specification. It would be usual to do this annually; the correct frequency will depend on the circumstances, and senior management must decide what is appropriate. Evaluation of suppliers usually involves a group of key personnel with the information needed for the evaluation. Figure 6.3 is an example of a procedure for this review, and shows the functions usually involved. In contrast, in a small organization the review may be carried out by one person working alone. The basic task is the same, however: to review each supplier's performance, and decide whether to renew the approval for another period.

IDENTIFICATION AND TRACEABILITY

Related to the question of purchasing are the twin issues of identification and traceability. Identification refers to the assignment of some form of tag (physical or otherwise) to items of interest so that no confusion can arise over their identity. Traceability refers to the ability to discover, variously, the location, origin or destination of components or finished product. There are two principal questions that must be answered clearly by the identification tag:

1 **What is the item?** – Every material or item should be labelled with its identity unless it is obvious that it could not be anything else.
2 **To what group or lot does it belong?** – For example, from what batch was a particular sample taken?

The basic requirement is that it should be possible for anybody to determine the identity of the item without having to guess or make any assumptions.

Another type of identification which must be addressed is the status of an item or material in relation to any testing or inspection that has been carried out. When something has been inspected, its status automatically changes, since it is now known to be either conforming or nonconforming, assuming that the inspection or test has yielded a definitive result. It is important that this information is available to any potential users or handlers of the material, particularly if it does not conform to requirements.

The underlying concern here is that in the event of a subsequent problem, you can establish where different materials were used and are able to identify products in which the faulty materials were incorporated, or clients whose service may have been affected by the faulty material.

There are two situations in which traceability records would be called upon:

Objective: To ensure that all suppliers of specified purchases are assessed regularly for ability to supply quality products and services.

Scope: Suppliers, materials and services listed on the Controlled Materials.

Target duration of review: 45 minutes

Procedure

1 Prior to the review, the following *summary* information is gathered in relation to each supplier and each material supplied:

Information required	*By whom*
Conformity to specification	Quality Manager
Performance of the item in use	Production Manager
Nonconformity reports	Quality Manager
Customer complaint records	Customer Services Manager
Laboratory test results	Laboratory Manager
Physical condition of the materials on receipt	Materials Manager
Packaging in general	Production Manager
Technical support and corrective action	Quality Manager

Include in the summary a list of any suppliers you would recommend for de-listing.

2 The review is carried out by the persons listed above, chaired by the Quality Manager.

3 The group reviews each supplier, and makes one of the following decisions on each:

- renew the approval
- de-list the supplier
- continue to use the supplier for a limited period, but inform them that they must improve.

The final decision in each case is taken by the Quality Manager, *based purely on the confidence in the quality of the purchased item.* Costing is not to be taken as a factor, as this will be addressed by purchasing personnel at the time of placing the order.

4 The Quality Manager records the results of the review.

5 The Quality Manager updates the List of Approved Suppliers.

Responsibilities

- Ensuring that the review of suppliers takes place annually – Quality Manager.

Figure 6.3 Typical procedure for review of suppliers for a reasonably large manufacturing company

1 A component, ingredient or raw material is discovered to have been faulty after it has been used. All customers who received the faulty product must be traced, and the product recovered and replaced.

2 A customer reports a faulty product, and it is necessary to identify which component is the source of the problem. The product must now be traced back through all the process steps, and the various components that have been used in the product must be traced back to their intake and source. Once the full identity of the offending component has been established, it may then be necessary to trace forward again, since components from that particular faulty lot may have been incorporated into other batches of product, and the customers who received those products would then also have to be traced.

The degree to which traceability is required is usually a balance between the cost of operating the traceability system, and its value in the event of problems in the market.

References

Cali, J.F., *TQM for Purchasing Management*, McGraw-Hill, New York, 1993.
Farmer, David and van Weele, J., *Purchasing Management Handbook*, 2nd edn, Gower, Aldershot, 1995.
Syson, Russell, *Improving Purchase Performance*, Pitman, London, 1992.

CHAPTER 7

Just-in-time Supplies

B.G. Dale and D.M. Lascelles

Just-in-time (JIT) production has been hailed by commentators such as Hutchins (1988) and Voss (1987) as one of the miracles of the Japanese economic revolution. The concept of JIT is simplicity itself: the production of parts in the exact quantity required, just in time for use. It embraces not only the final user, but also all preceding stages in the supply chain, both internal and external. JIT is an idealized philosophy of zero inventory in which the elimination of waste is the central goal. The reduction of stocks means that a company can respond in a more agile manner to the demands of the marketplace. The JIT concept can be applied to both manufacturing and service situations, and to profitmaking and non-profitmaking organizations.

The attraction of JIT is obvious in terms of its positive effect on business, but it is a high-risk strategy because stocks are kept to a minimum and planning is short-term. Key requirements include short and rapid response set-up times so that it is economical to manufacture very small batches, simple material flows, effective material handling, damage-free material, no equipment breakdowns, no product nonconformities, and effective production scheduling. The ideal situation is to make one piece just in time for the next processing operation. There is a low level of contingency in the system, and failure of any part of the system can be catastrophic.

Holdsworth and Dale (1995) outline the typical characteristics of JIT as follows:

- it uses a 'pull' system of control which is characterized by Kanbans
- systems are designed for simplicity and visibility
- the aim is to promote material flow by removing any obstacles and disruptions
- it extends to suppliers, who are treated as partners
- the workforce is considered as an integral part of the process.

Quality is a key issue with JIT. This has implications for the way in which the business and supplier base is managed. Suppliers need to be educated by the customer on what is required of them. The need for a continuous process of supplier development and partnership becomes critical, otherwise a company might as well forget about JIT purchasing. Supplier development revolves around the establishment of a long-term business partnership between a company and its supplier community, to the competitive advantage of both parties.

This chapter opens by reviewing the concept of JIT, and examines the importance of total quality management (TQM) and supplier development for the effective use of JIT. Then, drawing on the findings of a number of research projects on the subject of TQM and supplier development, the chapter examines the important issues of supplier development, outlines how such a programme might be initiated, and describes its main features.

The JIT concept

JIT is concerned with the reduction and eventual elimination of waste. Hay (1984) defines waste as anything other than the minimum resources required to add value to the product. Taiichi Ohno, who is generally recognized as the 'father of JIT' due to his pioneering work at Toyota in the 1950s and 1960s, classified the waste incurred in the production process into: overproduction, waiting time at work centres, transportation, manufacturing processes, holding unnecessary inventories, unnecessary motion and producing defective goods (see Ohno and Mondon, 1978).

Ohno believes that overproduction leads to waste in other areas. To eliminate the problem, he devised the concept of just-in-time production (bringing the exact number of required units to each successive stage of production at the required time). Putting this concept into practice necessitated a radical change in production from 'push' to 'pull'. In other words, abandoning the traditional 'push' system that is based on a forecast generated at the outset, from which a production plan is developed to meet the forecast demand (the plan then drives manufacturing through the issue of work orders), and replacing it with a 'pull' system in which nothing is produced until it is needed, effectively allowing customer demand for finished goods to put components and material through the system. The result was a significant decline in inventory levels. Even after Ohno initiated the concept on a trial basis in machining and assembly work in 1952, it took almost ten years before it was adopted in all Toyota's plants (see Monden, 1998).

Once the JIT concept became established at Toyota, Ohno began extending it to subcontractors and suppliers. The Toyota JIT production system is now legendary. A critical lesson arises from the Toyota experience: a company must successfully implement JIT in-house before it attempts to extend the process to its suppliers. It is worth noting that in a number of companies products are built and shipped the same day.

By its very nature, JIT is a high-risk strategy: stocks which have traditionally acted as the 'safety net' to buffer failure and hide problems are minimized, and planning is short-term. The prime concern of JIT is to avoid interruptions to production. A company will create for itself a number of problems by adopting JIT unless the quality of parts flowing through the system is satisfactory. In the absence of 'safety' stocks, the production line will very quickly stop every time a nonconforming part is found. The effect ripples back through the previous processes, and eventually the entire production system grinds to a halt. The key issue is finding the optimum level of stocks for cost-effective production. Plant breakdowns will have the same effect. In addition, delays will be caused by a production scheduling system that is unresponsive to an environment with a planning horizon that is measured in hours rather than days and weeks. Therefore, the implementation of JIT demands a risk-minimization strategy featuring Kanban, simple material flows, single-minute exchange of die (SMED), total productive maintenance (TPM) and TQM.

The term 'Kanban' is often seen as being synonymous with JIT. Kanban – meaning 'signboard' or 'label' – is used as a communication, information and production control system in JIT. A Kanban signifying the delivery of a given quantity is attached to each container of parts as they are fed into the production system. When the parts have been used, the same label (Kanban) is returned to its origin, where it becomes an order for more parts. Kanbans are used to inform a workstation of the time to produce and withdraw parts, along with the details and quantity of parts required by the next process. For a detailed description of Kanban systems, the reader is referred to Schonberger (1982) and Billesbach (1994).

Not all Kanban systems use Kanban cards: some feature traffic-light signals. There are also similar pull-type production control systems in existence which use 'Kanban squares'; these are controlled inventory locations between manufacturing areas and processes. Between each two successive processes, inventory is held in a fixed-size container or fixed-area square in close proximity to the area producing the items held and the one consuming them. A process is not allowed to start work on an item until there is a space within the Kanban square to put the finished item after the process has been completed. In effect, the 'single bin' stock control principle has been applied to a dynamic inter-process inventory situation. However, all Kanban systems have several common characteristics: they are pull-type production control systems, they are dynamic, they are visual, the signals are easy to understand, and they facilitate rapid communication. According to authors such as Anderson (1994) and Krajewski et al. (1987), Kanban application is considered to have the most chance of success in a repetitive and stable production environment, though Li and Dale (1995) describe its successful use in an environment with fluctuating demand.

In JIT manufacture, it is essential that the layout of production processes and equipment facilitates continuous and unidirectional material flow. A parallel objective is to eliminate or at least minimize operations which do not add value to the material or cause delays (for example, inspections, transportation and storage). Therefore, material flows are a key consideration in the planning of JIT manufacture. This may require some replanning of manufacturing operations, changing the process sequence, or some redesign of the product to ensure manufacturability and to optimize production line efficiency. In some cases, this may involve rationalizing manufacturing operations so that all products follow the same standard process sequence; in others, changing the shape of flow lines. Another option may be the implementation of manufacturing cells to produce families of components (categorized by their component geometry, material, process sequence and equipment). A cellular system, using the concept of group technology, reduces the need for repeatedly transporting workpieces between departments, although attention must be given to work movements and layout within the cells to ensure their efficient operation (Burbidge, 1975). Decisions have to be made regarding manufacturing technology and automation, whether to invest in flexible or dedicated production lines. Some flexibility is also required from the labour force in terms of job rotation and in the tasks they perform. Extra production capacity may be needed to provide cover for breakdowns, and on occasions, to smooth out loading on machine groups.

Single-minute exchange of die (SMED) is the term used to describe the methodology for assisting with achieving set-ups in under 10 minutes, and was first used by Toyota in the late 1960s. The current classification of world-class companies is to have set-ups performed in 100 seconds or less. There are three stages of improvement using the SMED methodology:

1 Distinguish internal set-up (this activity can only be performed when a machine is stopped) and external set-up (this activity can be carried out while the machine is still running), and ensure that they are clearly understood and separated.
2 Shift as many as possible of the internal set-up activities to external set-up.
3 Improve the methods used in both internal and external set-ups.

Total productive maintenance (TPM) is defined by the Japan Institute of Plant Maintenance as: 'aiming to maximise the effectiveness of production equipment with a total system of preventive maintenance throughout its entire life. Involving everyone in all departments and at all levels, it motivates people for plant maintenance through small group and voluntary activities.' It is a scientific, company-wide approach in which every employee is concerned about the maintenance and the quality and efficiency of their equipment. The objective is to reduce the whole-life cost of machinery and equipment through more efficient maintenance management and as far as possible to integrate the activities of the maintenance and manufacturing departments. Teamwork is a key element of TPM.

By analysis of each piece of equipment, TPM focuses on reducing manufacturing losses and costs (the six major losses are breakdown, set-up/adjustment, speed, idling and minor stoppages, quality defects, and start-up) and establishes a system of preventive maintenance over a machine's working life. The emphasis of TPM is to improve the skills of operators in relation to machine technology, and to train and educate operators to clean, maintain and make adjustments to their machine. The training and education of operators is carried out by maintenance and engineering staff. In this way, machinery is kept at optimal operating efficiency. The 5 Ss are essential activities in TPM, and they also promote visible management:

1 **Seri** (organization) – separating out what is required from that which is not
2 **Seiton** (neatness) – arranging the required items in a tidy manner and in a clearly defined place
3 **Seiso** (cleaning) – keeping the surrounding area and equipment clean and tidy
4 **Seiketsu** (standardization) – cleaning the machinery and equipment according to laid-down standards in order to identify deterioration
5 **Shitsuke** (discipline) – following the procedures which have been laid down.

These can also be formulated as CANDO – Cleanliness, Arrangement, Neatness, Discipline, and Orderliness.

Preventive maintenance is usually associated with regular equipment inspection to diagnose impending failure, and servicing in order to reduce wear and so prevent or delay breakdowns. TPM goes beyond this. Total productive maintenance should be seen as a company-wide activity in which everyone is imbued with a collective responsibility – just like TQM.

Total quality management can be defined as the management approach of an organization, centred on quality, based on the participation of all its members and aiming at long-term success through customer satisfaction, and benefits to all members of the organization and to society. It is simply a way of managing the business to achieve a total quality organization (see Dale, 1999).

Any organization is a network of administrative and technical processes, each of which has a supplier and a customer, and where every employee is committed to continuous improvement of their part of the operation. It involves teamwork, and extends to external suppliers and customers. The concept of TQM requires a fundamental change in the way in which people approach their work. It means respecting the work of all people in the company by ensuring that the output of their work (whether it be a physical component or a piece of paper containing information) is correct before it is passed on to the next person.

TQM is an essential prerequisite for JIT. In reality, JIT has little hope of being successful unless a company has embraced the TQM ethic.

The customer–supplier relationship

The simplicity of the JIT concept belies the extreme difficulty which companies experience when attempting implementation. JIT involves cultural changes at every level within the organization and among its suppliers, and even among customers. JIT is a total concept, like TQM; therefore organizations must adopt the complete package, not just the elements they like. The supplier must be viewed as part of the manufacturing chain, so the JIT philosophy of producing small quantities of conforming product must be acceptable to them. They must not think that they are being forced to hold stocks for their customers.

Two surveys of JIT purchasing practices in the United States (Hutchins, 1986; Ansari and Modarress, 1986) revealed that companies were finding the implementation of JIT more difficult than they originally expected. Companies discovered that JIT is a regime which requires more than merely reducing the number of suppliers, renegotiating supplier contracts and tinkering with plant layout; changes in behaviour and attitudes are also required. Hutchins (1986) cites several examples of unsuccessful JIT programmes. The most frequent cause of failure was the way in which companies were perceived as treating JIT as a means of getting suppliers to hold inventories on their behalf. In many cases, relationships deteriorated as suppliers complained about new inventory practices that served only to benefit the purchaser. Ansari and Modarress (1986) identified poor supplier support, followed by inadequate understanding and commitment by top management in the customer company, as the most significant problems associated with the implementation of JIT. To minimize these problems, they recommended three steps: the education and training of suppliers; the development of long-term relationships with suppliers; and encouragement of senior managers to visit companies with successful JIT programmes. Hutchins (1986) concluded that JIT suppliers need a lot of 'hand-holding' from their customers, but in dealing with suppliers the old adversarial ways die hard.

The traditional relationship between the customer and its supplier community is an adversarial one, with the customer and suppliers having differing objectives. The focus tends to be on negative issues, and is characterized by uncertainty. Suppliers are kept at arm's length, and are provided with only the bare minimum of data on such issues as the schedule, financial information, future work programmes, product changes, and their own performance ratings. In this traditional relationship, suppliers are regarded with a certain amount of suspicion by the customer. On the other hand, the customer is seen by suppliers as not being concerned about their future business products and price-driven in contractual negotiation; quality is a secondary consideration. If a customer starts to place some emphasis on quality, the typical reaction from suppliers is: 'You can have quality, but it will cost you.' Some people have likened the relationship (if one can call it that) to a game of cat and mouse.

In the traditional relationship, if the customer has not provided feedback data on performance, the suppliers tend to believe that their performance is acceptable. Most suppliers are not encouraged to ask the customer how their product is performing in practice and how their systems and service are perceived. Lack of feedback on quality performance is a frequent complaint among suppliers. Suppliers, however, react to differing demand and prior experience of their customers. An example of this is the grading of their output to different levels according to individual customer requirements: 'This will not be accepted by Company X, but Company Y will take it.'

To protect themselves in this uneasy relationship with suppliers, the customer will employ a multiple-sourcing strategy, resulting in a large supplier base. Writers on single versus multiple sourcing cite a number of reasons to support the practice of multiple sourcing, the main ones being that it:

- provides some security in the event of strikes or catastrophes
- gives some flexibility to cater for changes in demand for the supplies
- reduces stock
- protects against a monopoly situation
- facilitates competition
- minimizes risk
- has price-related reasons (one supplier can be 'played off' against another).

A number of these reasons can be considered as defensive.

Another characteristic of the traditional relationship is that the customer does not have clearly defined responsibilities and accountability for the performance of the supplier base. It is not uncommon to find that a number of people and departments are requesting and providing information to suppliers, but no single area takes overall responsibility. The points of contact are frequently ill defined, resulting in uncoordinated data flow. In particular, the allocation of responsibilities between the purchasing and quality departments is not clear; purchasing personnel often view assistance from the quality department as interference. This results in weaknesses in the communication system and procedures used by the customer in dealing with suppliers.

Clearly, JIT requires a radically new form of customer–supplier relationship. This type of relationship is given a variety of names, including co-makership, supplier development, supply chain management, partnership sourcing, and partnership. The new relationship means working together towards a common goal. It is based on the principle that both parties can gain more benefit through co-operation than by separately pursuing their own self-interests. It means establishing a long-term business partnership with each supplier based on common aims and aspirations, mutual trust and co-operation, a desire by both parties to improve the product continuously, and to understand responsibilities clearly.

To develop a partnership type of relationship, considerable changes in behaviour and attitude are required in both the customer and supplier. Customers have to be prepared to develop plans and procedures for working with suppliers, and to commit resources to this. On the other hand, suppliers have to accept full responsibility for the quality of their shipped product, and not rely on the customer's receiving inspection to verify that the product is to specification. As a prerequisite of the new relationship, both parties have to reach an agreement on how they will work together (that is, establish the ground rules). The key issues involved in developing a partnership-type approach are examined in detail by Burnes and Dale (1998).

Barriers to supplier development

As part of a research programme to investigate the effects a major customer might have on supplier awareness and attitudes towards quality management and the methods and system employed, the authors carried out a postal questionnaire survey of the respective supplier bases of three major automotive companies, representatives from a number of the suppliers were interviewed, and time was spent with customers, observing how they operated and interacted with suppliers (Lascelles and Dale, 1988).

The findings of this research reveal that certain aspects of the customer–supplier relationship can act as a barrier to supplier development. They include poor communication and feedback, supplier complacency, misguided supplier improvement objectives, the credibility of the customer as viewed by their suppliers, and misconceptions regarding purchasing power.

POOR COMMUNICATION AND FEEDBACK

In general, communication and feedback in the supply chain is not good. Moreover, suppliers and customers often do not realize how poor they are at communicating with each other. It was found that while the majority of suppliers surveyed perceived as realistic the quality performance requirements of their customers, a substantial number of them felt that communications and feedback between customer and supplier could be improved. Furthermore, it was found that not all dissatisfied suppliers communicate their dissatisfaction to the customer – a typical outcome of what was seen to be an adversarial relationship.

Nonconformity of purchased items is often due to the customer's inability to communicate their requirements to suppliers clearly. Ishikawa (1985) claims that at least 70 per cent of the blame for nonconforming purchased items lies with the customer. It is up to the buyer to ensure the existence of a clear specification that defines the exact requirements, but this in itself is not enough to assure conformity. The supplier must be given the opportunity to understand the function of the part they have been requested to make and discuss design details, particularly with regard to the manufacturability of purchased or subcontracted items, before requirements are finalized.

Some purchasing managers and supplier quality engineers in less advanced companies seem to think that the quality performance of their suppliers can be achieved almost by remote control, and are disappointed, and often surprised, when nonconforming items are received. Several staff from the three automotive companies referred to above genuinely believed that they engaged in joint quality planning with suppliers, whereas the communication process was all one-way (from customer to supplier). Furthermore, feedback from suppliers was discouraged, either because it was ad hoc, and ignored, or was never sought in the first place. For example, in one case the purchaser merely asked the supplier if he remembered the nonconforming product he had shipped some months earlier. The purchaser then informed the supplier that the same problem had recurred, and instructed him to visit the purchaser's premises with a drill and rectify the nonconformity.

SUPPLIER COMPLACENCY

Many suppliers appear complacent about customer satisfaction with the quality of their product or service, and do not proactively seek out such information. Survey respondents were asked if they had any positive way of measuring how well their product satisfied their customers' requirements. All but two reported only reactive measures.

Examples of reactive measures include internal failure data (for example, scrap reports, nonconformity analysis), external failure data (for example, customer rejections, warranty claims), customer assessment rating and audit reports, verbal feedback from meetings with customers and requirements outlined in the customers' vendor improvement programme. It is clear that many suppliers see customer satisfaction in very simple terms – 'If the customer does not return our product, then quality and reliability must be satisfactory.' This is a short-term view which will ultimately result in lost business opportunities. Suppliers should, wherever possible, use proactive measures of customer satisfaction. These include: benchmarking, workshops, customer interviews, evaluating competitors' products, reliability analysis, value analysis and lifecycle costing, and advanced quality planning carried out in conjunction with customers.

MISGUIDED SUPPLIER IMPROVEMENT OBJECTIVES

Companies are often not sure what they want from a process of supplier improvement. Comments made indicate that some (who may be first- or second-line suppliers to a major automotive company) do not understand the fundamentals of TQM. Many have formal vendor audit programmes but no clear supplier development objectives. There also appears to be a dilution of the quality message as requirements are passed down the supply chain. For example, when faced with demands from customers for improved quality, suppliers are reacting by implementing specific tools and techniques, and, in turn, are insisting that their own suppliers use the same. Very few customers are actively involved with their suppliers in helping them to solve quality problems. Some companies are under the mistaken impression that the imposition of a particular tool or technique on their suppliers as a condition of purchase is the same as supplier development. McQuater et al. (1996) found that the use of tools and techniques without behaviour and attitude change will result in only short-lived benefits.

LACK OF CUSTOMER CREDIBILITY

A customer's lack of credibility in the eyes of its suppliers is another barrier to supplier development: suppliers need to be convinced that a customer is serious about continuous improvement, and that this is demonstrated by their behaviour and attitudes. Poor purchasing and supplies management practices – such as a competitive pricing policy, frequent supplier switches, unpredictable and inflated production schedules, last-minute change to schedules, poor engineering design/production/supplier liaison, overstringent specifications and inflexibility – in general all lead to a credibility gap in the customer–supplier relationship. It is not uncommon for a customer to talk quality and continuous improvement to its suppliers and then act quite differently by relegating quality to secondary importance behind, for example, price or meeting the production schedule. Similarly, there is little value in holding continuous improvement conferences and seminars for suppliers if the purchasing organization continues to adopt an adversarial approach to its suppliers, or is seen to accord a low priority to quality unless there is a serious nonconformity. In the words of one supplier quality assurance engineer: 'No one cares about vendor performance until the production line stops.'

Failure to respond to supplier requests for information or feedback on specification requirements, component functionality, and to provide a design failure mode and effects analysis (FMEA) and so on, is a further way in which a purchaser's credibility can be seriously undermined.

PURCHASING POWER: A MISCONCEPTION

Purchasing power is an important influence in the relationship between a customer and its supplier community. Lack of power is a commonly cited reason for the lack of success in improving supplier performance. There is little doubt that a customer's influence on its suppliers varies with its purchasing power, and that the greater this power, the more effective its supplier quality assurance activities will be.

However, companies with considerable purchasing power may well cause the supplier to improve the quality of supplied items, but this may not necessarily mean that continuous improvement becomes embedded in the supplier's organizational culture. There is a tendency for some vendors to treat powerful customers as special cases, leading to 'stratified quality assurance'. A number of companies do grade the quality of their products at different levels according to past experience of individual customer expectations: 'Company A won't accept this nonconformity, but Company B will.' This often stems from the traditional misconception that quality is an optional product attribute or extra for which the customer must pay. Such a philosophy ignores the benefits of a continuous improvement process (such as positive workforce attitudes, less waste and reduced handling costs) which will accrue to the supplier.

Starting supplier development

Before involving suppliers in an improvement process it is necessary for the customer to give attention to issues such as: the objectives of supplier development, developing a strategy to accomplish these objectives, and deciding which vendors to involve. But perhaps the first task is to carry out a critical review of the key aspects of their own operation that affect supplier performance, in order to ascertain whether the environment is conducive to a partnership style of working. These include purchase specifications, communications, training and organizational roles. The delivery of nonconforming product from a supplier can often be attributed to an ambiguous purchasing specification. Purchasing specifications are working documents used by both customer and supplier, and must be treated as such. A good specification will define precisely the characteristics of the material to be supplied. It is also important to recognize that the supplier is knowledgeable in its own field of operation, and should be given every opportunity to provide a design input to the preparation of the specification. This is a prerequisite in obtaining a supplier's continued commitment to its product after delivery to the customer. Suppliers are more likely to accept responsibility for field failures and warranty costs if they are involved in the design of the parts they are being asked to supply.

At an early stage in the formulation of a supplier development strategy, the most effective mechanism for communication and feedback must be established. Typically, purchasing, quality, engineering, design and production personnel all talk to suppliers, but with no single functional area accepting total responsibility for price, delivery and quality. The need for clear accountability is an important factor in ensuring that channels of communication between customers and suppliers are effective. Both parties must nominate a representative (or 'account executive') through whom all communications are directed. Such representatives should also be given sufficient authority to ensure that all necessary actions are carried out.

Professional supplier development processes need to be supported by well-trained personnel capable of helping suppliers achieve the objectives laid down. It is essential that purchasing staff can understand the capabilities of their suppliers' manufacturing processes and systems and have a good working knowledge of the philosophy, principles and practices of TQM. Embarking on a process of supplier development with insufficient regard to the needs of the customer's skills base is likely to result in frustration and possible eventual failure of the initiative.

The increasing complexity of the task of obtaining conforming supplies at the right time and at the right price suggests that the conventional form and organization of the purchasing management function may no longer be adequate. Traditional staff structures based on tight functional groups (such as purchasing, materials planning, supplier quality assurance and engineering) have resulted in compartmentalized and 'silo'-type attitudes to suppliers which hinder the partnership style of working. Several companies have carried out some restructuring of their purchasing, quality and engineering departments to ensure that they have the right skills in dealing with suppliers and that functional accountability and logistics are adequate for the process of supplier development.

To assist their suppliers, some major organizations have documented the fundamental requirements for the control of quality and the achievement of continuous improvement (for example, QS 9000). It is a requirement of the purchase order agreement that suppliers must ensure that their product systems and processes comply with these requirements.

For a company with many suppliers and bought-out items, it may take several years to develop an effective process of supplier development. Before starting, it is therefore essential to prioritize action in some way. One approach adopted by many companies is to concentrate on new products and new vendors. Another approach involves the use of Pareto analysis to focus priorities by ranking bought-out components and materials according to some appropriate parameter (such as gross annual spend).

One outcome of the trend to partnerships is that an increasing number of major customers are awarding contracts based on the life of a part. Strategic sourcing (that is, single or dual sourcing) is considered by many writers and practitioners to be a complementary policy to partnership. In recent years, this has led to reductions in the size of organizations' supplier bases. Organizations are thinking carefully about the number of suppliers they need and how to maintain this at an optimum level. The reduction in the supplier base results in benefits such as: less variation in the characteristics of the supplied product, increases in the amount of time supplier quality assurance and purchasing personnel can devote to vendors, improved and simplified communications, less paperwork, less transportation, less handling and inspection activity, fewer accounts to maintain, and reduced costs for both parties. Nor should it be forgotten that there are competitive advantages for the supplier in being recognized as a preferred source of supply to a primary purchaser.

It is easier to develop a long-term relationship if the suppliers are in close proximity to the customer. Consequently, a number of customers are now reversing their international sourcing strategies to develop shorter supply lines. Closeness is also a vital element in the use of just-in-time purchasing strategy.

It is worth mentioning also that it is the policy of some customers to take up to a certain proportion only of a supplier's output – the captive supplier issue. This sometimes results in dual sourcing, even though the policy is to single-source. In other cases, the opposite is true.

Having selected suitable suppliers for inclusion in the development programme, the next step is to get them involved and obtain their commitment. This entails communicating to suppliers what is required, and, based on a set of common objectives, to reach an understanding with them.

Initially, the most practical way of setting about this task is to hold presentations to outline to suppliers the new approach, the quality management system standard to be used, how suppliers' performance will be assessed, and how the assessment will be communicated to them. Presentations to suppliers can be held either on the customer's premises or at individual suppliers' sites. The best results, in terms of communication, are achieved when the chief executives of both the customer and the supplier are involved in face-to-face discussions.

Once a supplier's senior management have agreed to participate in the development programme, it is necessary for the customer to visit the supplier's factory and carry out a formal vendor approval survey. The objective of the survey is to assess the supplier's suitability as a business partner. The survey is a multidisciplinary task which, in a number of cases, involves the customer's purchasing, supplier quality assurance and engineering personnel. The survey should cover areas such as control, plant, quality systems, attitude, response, tooling, planning and handling. Some form of checklist is generally used to structure the survey.

As part of its assessment, a customer should assess the supplier's commitment to advanced quality planning. This is a joint exercise involving both customer and supplier, and concentrates on the methods by which quality is designed and manufactured into the product. Advanced quality planning commences with a joint review of the specification and classification of product characteristics. Failure mode and effects analysis and quality function deployment would also be carried out. The supplier then prepares a control plan to summarize the quality planning for significant product characteristics. This would include a description of the manufacturing operation and process flows, equipment used, control characteristics, control plans, specification limits, the use of SPC, inspection details, and corrective and preventive action methods and controls. The supplier would provide initial samples supported by data on machine and process capability on the key characteristics identified by both parties, plus test results. Following successful evaluation of initial samples, the supplier is now in a position to start a trial production run followed by volume production.

Once the customer has assessed the adequacy of the supplier's policies, systems, procedures and manufacturing methods, and the supplier is able to demonstrate the quality of his shipped product, the goods inward inspection of supplies can be reduced considerably; in some cases down to the ideal situation of direct line supply. At this point, 'preferred' or 'certified supplier' status can be conferred on the supplier in recognition of the achievement.

This assessment exercise is not necessarily confined to new suppliers; an increasing number of customers will, at regular intervals, review the adequacy of the quality assurance systems of all their suppliers. This review is carried out to assure them that conformity to the assessment awarded to the supplier's quality assurance system is being maintained; most enlightened customers are looking for improvement. The frequency with which reassessments are carried out is dependent on such factors as: the supplier's current performance; the classification awarded to the supplier; the type of item being supplied; the volume of parts being supplied; the occurrence of a fundamental change (such as management or facilities) at the supplier, and at the request of suppliers. A programme of continuing assessment will help suppliers and the purchaser to achieve quality improvements by providing a common database.

Supplier development does not end here; it is a continuous process aimed at building up an effective business relationship – a relationship which demands a greater and quicker exchange of information between both parties. A number of customers are encouraging electronic data and e-commerce interchanges with their key vendors. This exchange relates not only to quality, but also covers technical requirements and specifications, schedules, manufacturing programmes, lead times, inventory management and invoicing. Suppliers are obliged to communicate any changes to materials, processes or methods that may affect the dimensional, functional, compositional or appearance characteristics of the product. Customers are obliged to provide sufficient information and assistance to aid development of their suppliers' approach to TQM (including training where necessary). In some cases, this extends to joint problem-solving activities, with customer and supplier striving to improve the product and reduce its costs. Over the longer term, it is the total cost of doing business with a supplier which is important, not the price per piece. The end results of the long-term relationship, joint problem-solving activities and the increased level of supplier participation in the early stages of product design and development will bring about cost reductions to the mutual benefit of customer and supplier.

References and further reading

Anderson, E.J., *The Management of Manufacturing*, Addison-Wesley, New York, 1994.

Ansari, A. and Modarress, B., 'JIT Purchasing: Problems and Solutions', *Journal of Purchasing Materials Management*, 1986, Vol. 22, No. 2, pp. 11–15.

Billesbach, T.J., *Simplified Flow Control Using Kanban Signals, Production and Inventory Management*, 1994, Vol. 35, No. 2, pp. 72–5.

Burbidge, J.L., *The Introduction of Group Technology*, Heinemann, London, 1975.

Burnes, B. and Dale, B.G., *Working in Partnership*, Gower, Aldershot, 1998.

Dale, B.G. (ed.), *Managing Quality*, 3rd edn, Blackwell Publishers, Oxford, 1999.

Deming, W.E., *Quality, Productivity and Competitive Position*, MIT Press, Cambridge, MA, 1982.

Hay, E.J., 'Will the Real Just-in-time Purchasing Please Stand Up', in *Readings in Zero Inventories*, American Production and Inventory Control Society, Alexandria, VA, 1984.

Holdsworth, R. and Dale, B.G. 'A Just-in-Time Production System', *International Journal of Manufacturing Systems*, 1995, Vol. 2, No. 1, pp. 51–60.

Hutchins, D., 'Having a Hard Time with Just-in-Time', *Fortune*, 1986, pp. 56–8, 9 June.

Hutchins, D., *Just-in-Time*, Gower, Aldershot, 1988.

Imai, M., *Kaizen: The Key to Japan's Competitive Success*, Random House, New York, 1986.

Ishikawa, K., *What is Total Quality Control?: The Japanese Way*, Prentice-Hall, Englewood Cliffs, NJ, 1985.

ISO 9000: 2000, *Quality Management Systems: Fundamentals and Vocabulary*, International Organization for Standardization, Geneva, 2000.

Krajewski, L., King, B., Ritzman, L. and Wong, D., 'Kanban, MRP and Shaping the Manufacturing Environment', *Management Science*, 1987, Vol. 33, No. 1, pp. 39–57.

Lascelles, D.M. and Dale, B.G., 'A Study of the Quality Management Methods Employed by U.K. Automotive Suppliers', *Quality and Reliability Engineering International*, 1988, Vol. 4, No. 4, pp. 301–9.

Li, H. and Dale, B.G., 'The Use of Kanban in a Volatile High Variety, Low Quantity

Environment', *International Journal of Manufacturing System Design*, 1995, Vol. 2, No. 2, pp. 249–58.

Mass, R.A., *World Class Quality*, ASQ Quality Press, Milwaukee, WI, 1988.

McQuater, R.E., Dale, B.G., Boaden, R.J. and Wilcox, M., 'The Effectiveness of Quality, Management Tools and Techniques: An Examination of the Key Influences in Five Plants', *Proceedings of the Institution of Mechanical Engineers*, 1996, Vol. 210, No. B4, pp. 329–39.

Monden, Y., *Toyota Production System: An Integrated Approach to Just-in-Time,* 3rd edn, Institute of Industrial Engineers, New York, 1998.

Ohno, T. and Monden, Y., *Toyota Production System: Beyond Management of Large Scale Production*, Diamond Publishing, New York, 1978.

Schonberger, R.J., *Japanese Manufacturing Techniques*, Free Press, New York, 1982.

Sloan, D. and Weiss, S., *Supplier Improvement Process Handbook*, American Society for Quality Control, Milwaukee, WI, 1987.

Voss, C.A., *Just-in-time Manufacturing*, IFS Publications, New York, 1987.

CHAPTER

8 Process Capability

David Newton

No two manufactured items are ever exactly alike. All the dimensions and other measurable properties will vary under the influence of a large number of factors – conventionally known as 'noise' factors. Examples of these might include:

- **Internal noise** – factors that are inherent in the process itself, such as:
  - heating of machinery through use
  - wear of bearings and sliding surfaces
  - variations in properties of lubricants with time
  - variations within raw materials.
- **External noise** – due to factors external to the process, such as:
  - environment changes (temperature, humidity and so on)
  - different operators
  - different sources of raw materials
  - fluctuations in power supplies.

The objective of statistical process control (SPC) is to µnderstood and quantify this variation as a means of assessing its acceptability, and, subsequently, to compare the current state of the process with this assessed variation in order to detect the onset of any deterioration in the process. This constitutes a continuous control of the process, but it is conventionally considered as two separate but closely related aspects. The first of these is the assessment of variation, which is considered in this chapter. The second is the subsequent routine monitoring of the process using control charting methods, which is described in Chapters 18 and 19.

Note that in reading this chapter the section on 'random variation of the mean' can be omitted without affecting the understanding of the rest of the chapter, or of the following two chapters. This section does, however, describe an important aspect that should be understood, perhaps at a later stage of reading.

Assignable and unassignable causes

The variation due to 'noise' factors (as described above) is commonly said to be due to 'unassignable causes' of variation. The presumption in process capability analysis is that these factors will always be present. The individual effect of a particular variable will generally be very small. There will, however, be a very large number of individual noise variables. Some of these we may be able to identify, but there will often be very many individually very small ones that are not known in any way. Their overall effect is assumed to be additive, and this will give rise to a total level of variation that can be substantial – even to the extent that it renders the process quite incapable of manufacturing within the limits imposed upon it. Process capability studies have the objective of measuring the variation due to unassignable causes.

If the process has a stable mean value and its variation is due only to unassignable causes, it is said to be 'in control'. Being in control only implies stability. It does not imply acceptability. A process whose inherent variability due to unassignable causes is too large with respect to its specified limits can be perfectly in control and yet be producing large quantities of defective product.

The objective of a control chart is to compare samples from the current process with the results of the process capability analysis, so as to detect any departure from the in-control state. Any such departure is said to be due to an assignable cause. This may be an increase in the variability, a change in the mean level, or both. The implication here is that once the change is detected, the cause can be assigned and corrective action taken to remove the cause.

In some terminology, particularly in the automotive industry, unassignable causes are referred to as 'common causes' and assignable causes as 'special causes'.

Capability analysis

Capability analysis is the analysis undertaken to quantify the variation due to unassignable causes. The assumption usually made is that, for an in-control process, the mean level of a measured variable from the process has a mean that is absolutely stable. All the variation in the process is then measured by the variance about that stable mean value. This assumption permits a simple approach to the analysis, but can occasionally give rise to an over-optimistic view of the capability – an aspect which is explored later in this chapter in the section on 'random variation of the mean'.

MEASURING THE VARIATION

To evaluate the variation of a process, samples need to be taken of the measurement in question. It is, as always, a case of 'the bigger the sample the better', but conventionally a minimum sample of 50 observations is required. Rather than take a single block of observations from the process, it is preferable to adopt the same procedure that will be used later for control charting. In this, a series of small samples of typically 4, 5 or 6 observations is taken. The samples in each small subgroup are taken consecutively, with an interval (typically of around 50 items) between each successive group. The reasoning behind this is that estimates of the variance obtained within each group will give an estimate of the short-term variation about the mean uninfluenced by any variation in the mean itself. If the mean were absolutely stable, there would, of course, be exactly the same information about the variance in, for example, a single sample of 50 as in 10 samples of 5. The larger sample would, however, give a misleadingly large value for the variation if there had been any instability of the mean while the sample was being taken. The approach of taking a series of small 'snapshot' samples circumvents this problem, and also establishes the same procedure that will be used subsequently for control charting.

Every small subgroup that is taken will produce a small-sample estimate of the process mean, μ (as an $\bar{x}$ value), and of the process standard deviation, σ (as either a value of sample standard deviation s, or of sample range R). The calculation of these estimates is described in Chapter 17.

Example

Consider, as an example, a machining process which has a particular critical ground diameter with a nominal value of 15.00 mm. To assess the capability, samples of 15 items are taken at intervals during an assessment running of the process. The results of the first 7 samples are shown in Table 8.1. By this stage in the study it has become obvious that whatever else may be happening, the process mean is too high, as reflected by the x values being consistently well above the nominal value. The average of all these x values is 15.037, so the process was reset downwards in an attempt to correct the offset of 0.037 mm, and the analysis was then continued with the results shown in Table 8.2.

Throughout the analysis so far, the variability as revealed by the sample ranges and standard deviations does not appear to show any trends or step changes (plotting a graph will help to confirm this), so an estimate of the inherent process standard deviation can be calculated. This can be from either the s values or from the R values. (There is, of course, no need to calculate both estimates – one is sufficient, as they are both expected to give the same answer.) From the s values, the estimate of the process standard deviation, σ, is obtained from the square root of the average of the values of s^2 values:

$$\hat{\sigma} = \sqrt{1/13(0.017^2 + 0.011^2 + 0.016^2 + 0.007^2 + \ldots + 0.012^2 + 0.014^2 + 0.010^2}$$
$$= 0.0123$$

From the R values, under the assumption of the normal distribution, ranges can be converted into estimates of standard deviation by dividing by a conversation factor d_n. The same conversion can be applied to R, the average of the observed ranges. The value of the factor d_n varies with the sample size, as shown below:

Sample size (n)	2	3	4	5	6	7	8
Conversion factor d_n	1.128	1.693	2.059	2.326	2.534	2.704	2.847

Table 8.1 Measurement of process variation based on seven samples

Sample no.	*Measurements (mm)* 1	2	3	4	5	*Average* $\bar{x}$	*Range* R	*SD** s
1	15.028	15.024	15.049	15.017	15.055	15.035	0.038	0.017
2	15.030	15.034	15.027	15.030	15.054	15.035	0.027	0.011
3	15.034	15.051	15.058	15.075	15.041	15.052	0.041	0.016
4	15.038	15.033	15.042	15.023	15.035	15.034	0.019	0.007
5	15.020	15.053	15.010	15.045	15.041	15.034	0.043	0.018
6	15.040	15.037	15.038	15.038	15.041	15.039	0.004	0.002
7	15.034	15.032	15.026	15.042	15.033	15.033	0.016	0.006

Note: *SD = Standard Deviation.

Table 8.2 Measurement of process variation after adjustment

Sample no.	*Measurements (mm)* 1	2	3	4	5	*Average* $\bar{x}$	*Range* *R*	*SD** s
8	15.028	15.024	15.005	15.025	15.008	15.018	0.023	0.011
9	14.992	15.023	15.008	14.996	15.004	15.005	0.031	0.012
10	15.007	15.016	15.037	15.025	15.008	15.019	0.030	0.013
11	15.017	14.986	15.014	15.009	15.012	15.008	0.031	0.012
12	15.027	15.024	14.995	15.026	15.009	15.016	0.031	0.014
13	15.016	15.025	15.031	15.005	15.014	15.018	0.026	0.010

Note: *SD = Standard Deviation.

In this example, this gives:

$$R = \frac{(0.038 + 0.027 + 0.041 + \ldots + 0.031 + 0.031 + 0.026)}{13}$$

$$= 0.0277 \text{ and hence:}$$
$$\hat{\sigma} = 0.0277/d_5 = 0.0275/2.326 = 0.0119$$

Note that the standard deviations obtained by the two methods differ slightly. This is to be expected, as the use of d_n factors introduces another stage of estimation with its own associated variability. It is therefore always slightly preferable to calculate the estimate using the first method: namely, directly from the sample standard deviations.

MACHINE AND PROCESS CAPABILITY

As it is usually not possible to synthesize the effects of all the external noise factors during process capability analysis, the approach that is often adopted is to control these factors as tightly as possible. For example, only one operator would be used, only one batch of raw material processed, and so on, and as far as possible the process would be run with all environmental conditions held constant. This would result in a measure of variability that applies only under these somewhat idealized conditions. This is sometimes referred to as 'machine capability' rather than process capability. The more representative process capability variation will consist of the machine capability variation plus the extra element due the external noise factors.

RELATION TO SPECIFICATION TOLERANCES

Despite the growing acceptance of concepts such as the Taguchi quadratic loss function, and the related broader acceptance of continuing process improvement by reduction of variability, most products still have their measurable characteristics defined by conventional specification tolerances. One of the primary functions of process capability studies is to compare the process variation with these tolerances.

In the above example, the process standard deviation was estimated as 0.0129 mm (using the larger of the estimates). Assume that the specification limits for this dimension are 15.00 mm ± 0.05 mm. If a normal distribution is assumed, and it is also assumed that, given further samples, it will be possible to centre the process on its nominal value of 15.00 mm, the relation of the process to its specifications limits will be as shown in Figure 8.1.

The process is just contained within the specification limits, so as long as no assignable causes appear to change the mean or increase the variation, the process is capable of working to these limits. It would be judged to be a 'medium-precision' process – capable of working within limits, but needing to be controlled closely to ensure that any changes from this situation are speedily detected. This, and other situations, are categorized in broad terms as shown in Figure 8.2.

A high-precision process is one in which the variation is very small compared with the specification limits. Although the view can be taken that it would be unnecessary to apply control charting to such a process except to guard against it moving dangerously close to the specification limits, the modern way of thinking for such a process is that SPC should be applied in the usual way in the quest for process consistency as a valuable target in its own right, irrespective of the specification limits.

Conversely, a low-precision process is one in which the variation is so large that it is inherently incapable of working within the specification limits. The best that SPC can then offer is to control the mean at a value that minimizes the consequences of being outside limits. If the overall proportion outside both limits needs to be minimized, the mean would be set centrally. If, as is often the case, the rejects in one tail are more costly that those in the other, the mean would be controlled at a value closer to the less expensive tail. In any of these cases, there would be the necessity for 100 per cent inspection of the product. To improve the precision of such a process, either the variation has to be reduced, or the

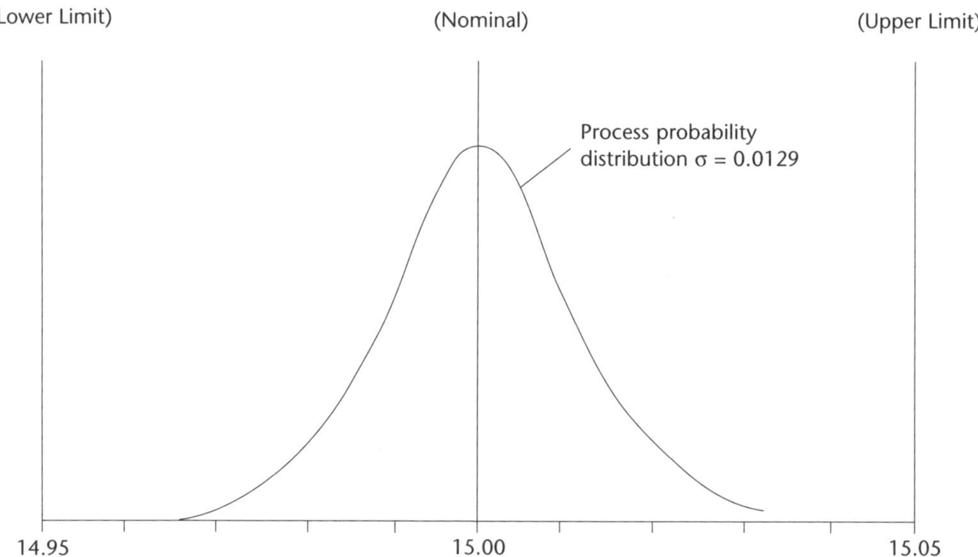

Figure 8.1 Relationship of process and specification tolerance (assuming that the process can be centred on 15.00)

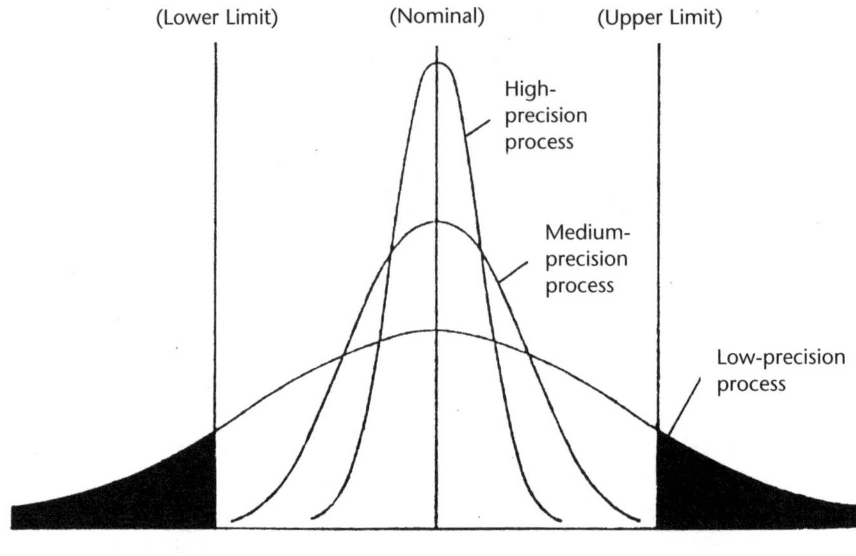

Figure 8.2 Relative precision

specification tolerances increased. The latter approach is the obvious one to adopt first. Tolerancing is often both conservative and arbitrary, and can frequently be opened for further discussion in the light of high costs of working within them. Approaches such as probabilistic tolerancing in assembly build-up can help considerably. The conventional approach of a design office in assembly tolerancing is to make the assembly tolerance the sum of the component tolerances, that is:

$T_{ASSY} = \sqrt{}(T_1 + T_2 + T_3 + \ldots \text{ and so on})$

whereas the probabilistic approach considers the low probability of randomly chosen components being on the same extreme of tolerance. A detailed description of probabilistic tolerancing is beyond the scope of this chapter, but a good starting point is an approach based on the additivity of variances, with each T being considered as a constant proportion of its individual specification limit. This gives:

$T_{ASSY} = \sqrt{}(T_1^2 + T_2^2 + T_3^2 + \ldots \text{ and so on})$

which will permit larger values for the individual component tolerances T_1, T_2, T_3, and so on.

QUANTIFYING PROCESS CAPABILITY

The idea of the 'natural tolerance' of a process is the total extent of the measurement over which it can be expected to vary. This is usually taken to be six standard deviations. This comes from the assumption of a normal distribution where (the mean) ± (three standard deviations) contains 99.73 per cent of the measurements, which is near enough to all of them for practical purposes. In practice, real processes will always depart from the assumption of normality, often to a considerable extent, but the concept of 6σ as the natural tolerance still gives a useful basis for capability assessment.

The basic measure of capability is the 'process capability index', C_P. This is given by:

$$C_P = \frac{\text{Upper limit} - \text{Lower limit}}{6\sigma} \quad \left(= \frac{\text{Specification tolerance}}{\text{Natural tolerance}} \right)$$

For a process to be considered capable, C_P should always be greater than 1. If the analysis has been strictly one of machine capability, an arbitrary 'safety factor' of at least one-third should be added to the acceptable minimum value of the index, so that C_P is 0.10/6 x 0.0129 = 1.29. This is barely adequate (and is particularly marginal if it is strictly a C_M rather than a C_P). In this case, it is possibly sufficiently close to 1.33 to permit production, but only if the process is closely monitored using control charts and further efforts are made to reduce the variation. The process is in the lower end of the medium-precision category, but the philosophy of 'never-ending improvement' requires that efforts continue to increase the value of the capability index. One of the comments occasionally heard concerning comparisons between Western and Eastern attitudes to quality is that the West talks in terms of acceptable C_P values of '1 point something' whereas the Eastern approach is to try to achieve values of 3 or more.

SETTING ACCURACY

The discussion so far has been concerned only with the precision (that is, the variation) of the process. In many processes, the mean level is capable of adjustment to any required value within the specification limits. It is still useful to quantify any error in setting the mean, and this will be particularly true in any case when the setting is not amenable to adjustment – as, for instance, in the case of a component produced in a press tool.

The setting index is denoted C_{Pk} and is given by the lower of:

$$\frac{\text{Upper specification limit} - \bar{\bar{x}}}{3\sigma} \text{ or } \frac{\bar{\bar{x}} - \text{lower specification limit}}{3\sigma}$$

This again has the requirement of exceeding 1 (if σ refers to overall process capability), or of exceeding 1.33 (if σ refers only to machine capability, in which case the index is sometimes known as C_{Mk}).

The term $\bar{\bar{x}}$ is the overall average from the process capability study (the average of the $\bar{x}$ values over a period during which they were stable). In the example, for the first seven samples the lower value of C_P is (15.05 – 15.037)/3 x 0.0129 = 0.34, which is plainly inadequate. This fact was recognized informally, and the process was reset. For the remaining samples, the new overall mean was 15.016, giving a revised C_{Pk} value of 0.88. This tells us that further adjustment is still required. After further resetting of the process in this example, further samples should be taken until there is a clear demonstration that the process is stable. As a general rule, at least 20 subgroups (or a total of at least 200 individual samples) are necessary before the capability can be viewed as fully assessed. This process merges into routine production control charting, as described in the next two chapters. It is not usually possible (or necessary) to draw a clear distinction between the end of process capability analysis and the beginning of production charting. Further, the quest for process improvement should be continued throughout the life of the process.

Note that if the process is set exactly on nominal, C_{Pk} becomes equal to C_P, so that for a process that is only marginally acceptable (as in this case), the only acceptable setting for the process mean is exactly on the nominal value. For processes of higher capability, a threshold region of acceptable settings will appear on either side of the nominal, which gives scope for setting processes liable to drift away from the limit at an initial value on the opposite side of nominal which they are drifting.

RELATIVE PRECISION INDEX

An alternative series of indices is used in British Standards. Instead of relating the index to the process standard deviation (as with C_P), the relative precision index (RPI) is the ratio

$$\frac{\text{Upper specification limit} - \text{lower specification limit}}{\bar{R}}$$

Where $\bar{R}$ is the average of the ranges of the samples. This has the problem that the index will depend on the sample size. A table of minimum values of the index is given in British Standard BS 2564, and is reproduced in Table 8.3.

Table 8.3 Minimum values of relative precision index

Sample size *n*	*Minimum value of index*
2	5.321
3	3.544
4	2.914
5	2.580
6	2.363
7	2.210
8	2.108

In the example, the RPI is 0.10/0.275 = 3.64, which is greater than the minimum for a sample of 5, and so assesses the process as capable of manufacture.

DANGERS IN CAPABILITY INDICES

All the indices described in the previous two sections give a simple assessment of the capability of the process. Inherent in this simplicity, however, is a danger of misleading results if any of the assumptions built in to the indices are not valid. They are liable to mislead if the process distribution is markedly non-normal, and are effectively meaningless if the mean value is not stable. These aspects are considered in the next two sections.

TESTING FOR NORMALITY

Once sufficient data have been gathered from a stable process – around 50 or more individual observations – it is possible to investigate the form of the probability distribution describing the data. A convenient way of doing this is by way of a probability plot on normal probability paper, as described in Chapter 17 and illustrated in Figure 17.16. Such a plot gives informal estimates of the mean and standard deviation of the process which should confirm the values obtained direct from the data. It will also test the data for normality and for outliers.

Any marked non-linearity in the plot suggests a departure from the assumption of

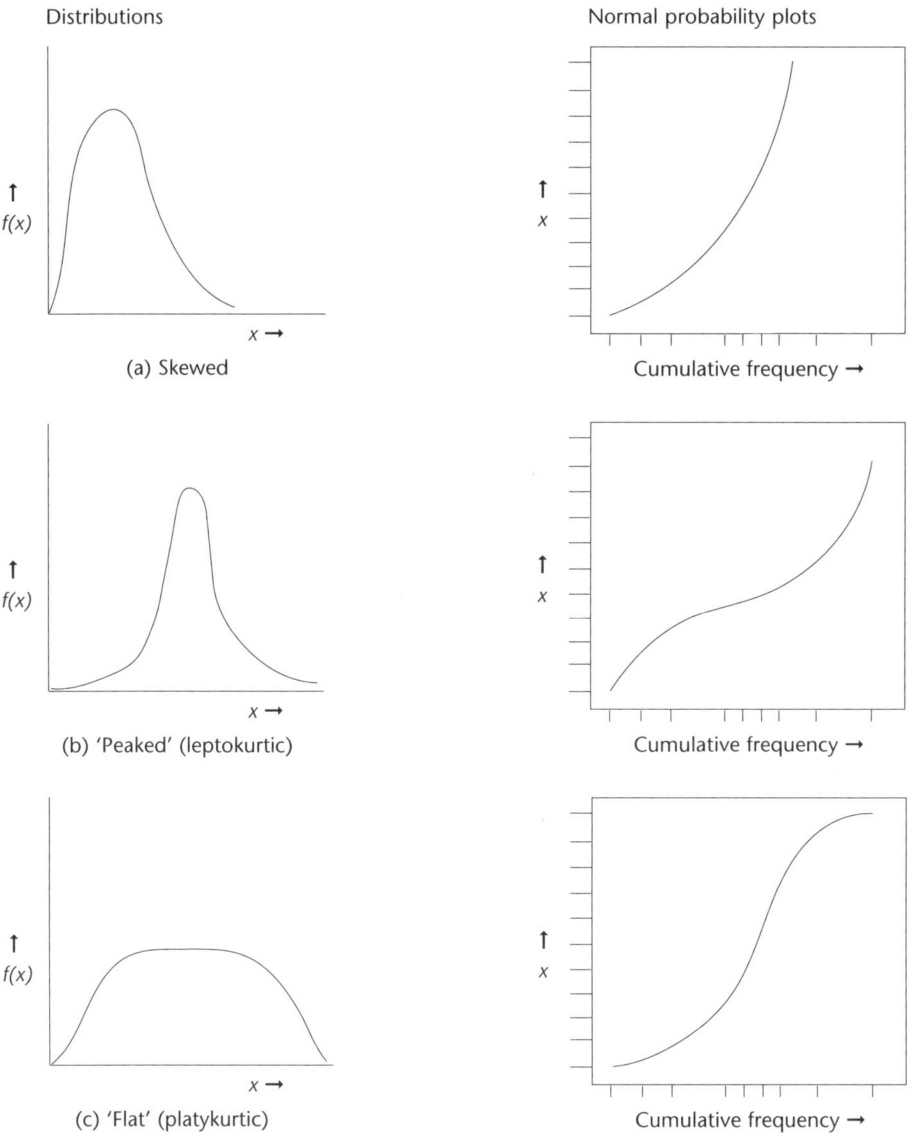

Figure 8.3 Effects of non-normality on probability plots: (a) skewed, (b) 'peaked' (leptokurtic), (c) 'flat' (platykurtic)

normality, as shown in Figure 8.3. The skewed distribution, as in Figure 8.3a, is a common occurrence. It is to be expected in the case of measurements with target value of zero, but with actual values that will always be non-negative – such things as percentages of impurities and dimensions such as surface finishes, eccentricity, ovality, parallelism, and so on. Leptokurtic and platykurtic forms can also give non-linearities, as in Figures 8.3b and 8.3c. Apparent skewness and departures from normality in terms of kurtosis can be confirmed by calculation of the appropriate coefficients, as described in Chapter 17 (see also Figures 17.4 and 17.5).

It is important to appreciate that there is nothing necessarily amiss with a process that is non-normal. There is no particular reason why the normal distribution should apply to manufacturing processes – it is simply a convenient mathematical form that is usually an adequate approximation. Its convenience comes from its properties being widely understood and extensively tabulated. In the case of a positively skewed distribution, the distribution of the logarithms of the measurements will usually be adequately close to normal, and these can be used to assess the capability.

Apart from this adaptation of the procedure for estimating process capability for skewed distributions, there is little that needs to be done in the case of non-normal distributions. The central limit theorem will, except in instances of extreme skew, make the sample averages adequately close to a normal for the usual control charting rules to apply on the averages chart. The ranges chart rules will give risks differently from those under the assumption of normality, but experience shows this to be of little importance. For extremely skewed distributions, there might be a case for operating the control chart on the logarithms of the measurements.

RANDOM VARIATION OF THE MEAN

The standard approach to process capability so far described has made the assumption that the process mean is completely stable. It frequently happens that this is not the case, and instead the mean itself is subject to small random variations (as in Figure 8.4) which are still due to unassignable causes.

The presence of such additional variation will have implications regarding both process capability (where the previous simple analysis will give over-optimistic results) and control charting. Define:

σ_0 = the standard deviation of the process about the mean (that is, what we have previously referred to simply as σ).
σ_1 = the standard deviation of the process mean about the overall process average.
σ_t = the effective total standard deviation of the process.

These are related by:

$$\sigma_t^2 = \sigma_0^2 + \sigma_1^2$$

To see whether this extra variability exists, the variation of the sample means that was observed is compared with the value it should have taken if σ_1 were zero. The standard deviation of a series of observed *x* values over a period of apparent stability in the capability data is calculated in the usual way. This is the calculated standard error, denoted σ_e. Under

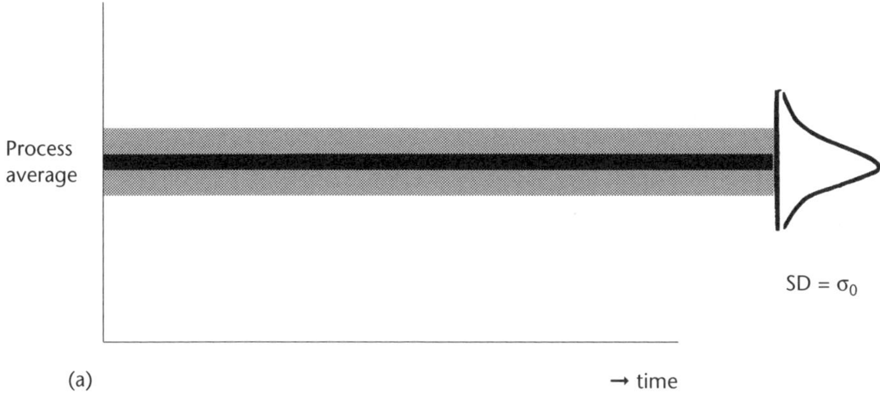

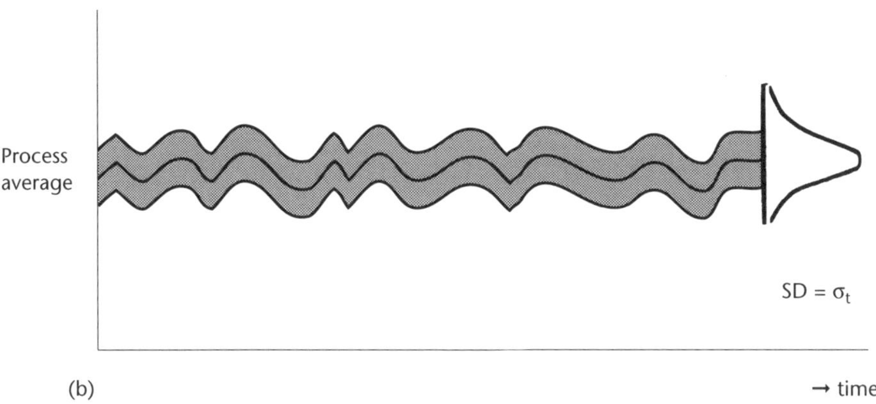

Figure 8.4 Random variation of the mean: (a) stable process average, (b) average subject to random variation

the assumption of constant mean, the expected value of this standard error is $\sigma_0/\sqrt{n}$ (where n is the subgroup sample size). The variance of the mean is obtained from the difference between the two variances:

$$\sigma_1^2 = \sigma_e^2 - \sigma_0^2/n$$

As an illustration, consider samples 8 to 13 in the example:

σ_0^2 is the average of the observed variances, that is
$\sigma_0^2 = 1/6\ (0.011^2 + 0.012^2 + 0.018^2 + 0.012^2 + 0.014^2 + 0.010^2)$
$= 0.000155$
($\sigma_0 = \sqrt{0.000172} = 0.0124$, which, as a check, is close to the value of 0.0129 obtained earlier from the entire data set.)

σ_e is the standard deviation of the $\bar{x}$ values, i.e. of 15.018, 15.004, 15.019, 15.012, 15.016 and 15.018, which gives $\sigma_e = 0.0057$.

The expected standard deviation under the assumption of constant mean is $0.0124/\sqrt{5}$ = 0.0055.

As the two values (σ_e and $\sigma_0/\sqrt{n}$) are almost the same (that is, the difference between them, representing σ_1, is effectively negligible), in this particular process the assumption of a stable mean is justified. From this, all the various indices are validated from this aspect, and there is no need to modify the assessment of process capability.

To illustrate a situation when this is not the case, and to show the effect on capability analysis, consider another set of process capability data shown in Table 8.4. The data consist of averages and ranges of samples of 5 drawn from a container filling process. The specification is 250 ± 2 ml.

The overall average is 250.07 ml. The average of the ranges, $\bar{R}$, is 1.281, giving an estimate of the standard deviation σ of $\bar{R}/d_5 = 1.281/2.326 = 0.55$ ml.

Using, initially, the simple approach assuming a stable mean, this gives capability indices:

$$C_P = 4/(6 \times 0.55) = 1.21$$
$$C_{Pk} = (252.00 - 250.07)/(3 \times 0.55) = 1.17$$

These indices show both that the process is highly marginal as regards capability (C_P falling short of the required value of 1.33) and could also benefit from more accurate centring.

To investigate the stability of the mean:

$\sigma_e = 0.396$ (by direct calculation from the $\bar{x}$ values)
$\sigma_0 = 0.55$ (i.e. σ as used above), giving $\sigma_0/\sqrt{5} = 0.246$

The value of σ_e is now much bigger than its 'expected' value, showing that there is instability in the mean. This could be due to an assignable cause, but a sample-by-sample plot of x shows no evidence of this, so the effect is a purely random one due to unassignable causes. The standard deviation of the sample average, σ_1, is evaluated by

Table 8.4 Process capability data for 26 samples

Sample no.	*Average* $\bar{x}$	*Range* R	*Sample no.*	*Average* $\bar{x}$	*Range* R
1	249.99	1.4	14	250.01	2.4
2	250.32	1.1	15	250.38	1.2
3	250.54	1.0	16	250.00	1.2
4	250.30	0.7	17	249.92	0.9
5	249.87	0.9	18	249.86	0.5
6	249.98	1.4	19	250.22	1.6
7	250.01	0.6	20	249.80	0.8
8	249.47	2.0	21	250.66	1.7
9	249.78	1.5	22	249.62	1.0
10	250.59	2.2	23	250.25	1.3
11	250.15	0.9	24	249.16	1.6
12	249.69	1.0	25	250.19	1.5
13	249.84	1.8	26	251.03	1.1

$\sigma_1^2 = \sigma_e^2 - \sigma_0^2/n$, that is $\sigma_1^2 = 0.396^2 - 0.55^2/5 = 0.0963$
$\sigma_1 = \sqrt{0.0963} = 0.310$

The overall process standard deviation σ_t will comprise both these within-sample and between-sample elements:

$\sigma_t^2 = \sigma_0^2 + \sigma_1^2 = 0.55^2 + 0.31^2 = 0.3986$
$\sigma_t = \sqrt{0.3996} = 0.631$

This total effect should be used in evaluating the capability. Revised values are:

$C_P = 4/(6 \times 0.631) = 1.056$
$C_{Pk} = (252.00 - 250.07)/(3 \times 0.631) = 1.02$

both of which show a situation somewhat worse than the previous analysis.

This example demonstrates that if there is random variation in the mean (and there very often is in real production processes), the conventional simple approach to process capability can give over-optimistic answers. Whenever a capability study appears to demonstrate marginal acceptability, an analysis similar to the example just described should be undertaken to ensure that the situation is not, in reality, one of unacceptability. These considerations will also have a bearing on limits for control charts for averages, as discussed in the next chapter.

Further Reading

See Chapter 18 for a combined reading list for Chapters 8 and 18.

CHAPTER **9**

Product Reliability

David Newton

Reliability is rightly perceived as one of the most important attributes possessed by any product or system. Accepting the importance of reliability, what can be done to achieve it? The first point to make is that reliability is not achieved by reliability engineers and managers, any more than quality is achieved by their quality equivalents. Reliability is achieved by getting the product design right, and ensuring subsequent manufacturing conformity to that design. Other chapters deal with manufacturing conformity. This chapter will concentrate on the design input to reliability.

Introduction

Definitions of reliability are legion, but all imply an extension of quality into the domain of time, or some other measure of product usage. Reliability is the ability to keep on doing what is required. This ability can be thought of in purely subjective terms, or it can be made apparently more objective and precise by being expressed as a probability under specified constraints (for example, the probability that a fire extinguisher will operate after storage for two years, or the probability that a motor car will survive the warranty period without failure). These probabilities can themselves be derived from other measures, such as failure rate.

The need for reliability is obvious, so it might be reasonable to ask why we so often fail to achieve it. The answer stems largely from the fact that reliability is unique among desirable properties of products and systems in that it cannot be immediately measured. The quality of the motor car you have just purchased can be assessed by inspection – it starts and goes, the paintwork shines, no bits are falling off, and so on. Other aspects, such as its performance, weight, and the like, can be measured with suitable instrumentation. There is, however, no such thing as a reliability meter.

Our expectations of reliability must come from trusting that the product designers and developers have done their job properly, and that the manufacturing processes conform fully to the design. Whether or nor our experience matches our expectations will only become obvious through use, when they will be replaced by knowledge. If our expectations are not met, it is too late: too late for us to change our minds about our unfortunate purchase (but not too late to resolve never to repeat the mistake, and probably tell all our friends as well), and too late for the manufacturer to do anything other than damage limitation about all the unreliable units that have been sold to other customers.

Value of prototype testing

There are two distinct approaches to assessing the reliability of a product or system:

1 at the design stage, before the 'hardware' exists
2 in the testing and subsequent use of the product.

The first of these is at the correct time in the design cycle because changes to the design can be made at minimal cost. The drawback is that the answers we get are only as good as our understanding of the design, which is bound (even from the designer's standpoint) to be imperfect.

The second gives us 'real' information, but is chronologically late in the development cycle, resulting in high costs for design modifications and/or service failures.

Some obvious strategies now begin to emerge for the achievement of reliability. It is obviously cost-effective to do as much as we can as early as we can, but we must also accept that incomplete understanding of the product implies risks that what we do might not be totally effective. The best information will come from product use, but will of necessity take time to acquire. An obvious corollary of this is the desirability of getting as much test information as we can as early as we can. This is an area in which industry is most often culpable – money spent on product testing will usually be recouped many times over in the avoidance of service failures.

It is unfortunate that industrial accounting procedures are frequently unable to tell the difference between a cost and an investment, with a resultant reluctance to invest in testing. One has only to look at the many instances where the reliability testing has been left to the customer to see the folly of this policy. It is perhaps noteworthy that the spectacular improvement in perceived reliability recently achieved by a large British motor manufacturer has been accompanied by a policy of producing large numbers of prototype vehicles purely for the purpose of reliability testing.

Relevance of reliability measurement

Comment is necessary on the issue of measuring reliability, as sometimes encountered in scathing references to the 'numbers game'.

The objective should always be total reliability. The only target we should have for a 'probability of working' is 1.0. The only acceptable target for failure rate is zero.

The various numbers that we estimate are simply measures of our failure to achieve these targets. Indeed, it might be more sensible to rename the quantitative approach to the subject 'unreliability'. Having said this, measures of imperfection need to be calculated. They are not of great value in themselves, but they do provide essential information as to what needs to be done to improve matters.

The great danger is that achieving a number can become obsessive, and become more important than making the product better. This is particularly the case in numerical predictions 'from the drawing board', as described in a later section of this chapter.

There is a possibly apocryphal story of a Japanese supplier of electronic components who, on encountering a purchase specification that stated a required reliability of 99.9 per cent, politely enquired if the customer required the unreliable items to be packed separately.

Reliability engineering in design and development

The final reliability of a product is built in at the design stage. While it is true that remedial improvement can sometimes be realized by eliminating 'quality of conformity' shortcomings and by design modifications, the concept of right first time is just as important in designing for reliability as it is in other aspects of quality – perhaps even more so.

Reliability cannot be considered as a bolt-on extra which is the responsibility of specialist reliability departments. It is an inherent property of the design, and nobody in a design team has the right to abrogate responsibility for reliability. The function of any reliability specialist is to act as a repository of the specialist skills sometimes necessary to assess and measure the effectiveness of the design. Some of these skills are outlined in this chapter.

The specialist techniques divide conveniently into 'before the hardware' and 'after the hardware' headings, as described earlier. This does not mean that the application of the two approaches should not overlap – on the contrary, the movement through research/feasibility/design/development/production is progressive, and only the emphasis on one or the other will change as work progresses.

The important thing is that reliability is considered right from the outset. The techniques described in the next three sections (FMEA, FTA and prediction) can be implemented at the earliest stage, and refined progressively as development takes its course.

Failure mode and effect analysis (FMEA)

FMEA is a component-by-component analysis of a system which sets out to identify the possible failure modes of the component, identify the resulting effects on the system, and assess whether these effects are critical.

'Critical' in this context includes such considerations as the severity of the potential failure, its likelihood of occurrence and its 'detectability' (the likelihood of its being foreseen through system degradation, inspection, maintenance and so on).

An important feature of FMEA is its value as a working document as a design evolves. It is essentially a tool for designers rather than for reliability specialists, and provides documented evidence that reliability has been kept in mind throughout the design process.

There are many suggested ways of laying out the details of an FMEA, but the general approach is that of a spreadsheet, as shown in Figure 9.1. This is in the form suggested by the Society of Motor Manufacturers and Traders (see SMMT, 1989), and is widely used in the motor industry. It is not suggested that this is the only format available (there are many others), but the procedures are essentially the same. As an example of alternative layouts, see, for example, Part 5 of BS 5760 or MIL-STD-1629.

Referring to Figure 9.1, the columns in the worksheet are completed as the design proceeds, with each failure mode of a component constituting a row of the worksheet. The columns are completed as follows:

Column	*Information required*
1 and 2	Identify the component.

SMMT

FAILURE MODE & EFFECTS ANALYSIS – DESIGN

FMEA NUMBER *F375*

SHEET *1* OF *12*

PART OR ASSEMBLY NAME *BOTTOM BRACKET (ENGINE MTG)* SUPPLIERS *PROFORM (RAW MAT'L)*

PART OR ASSEMBLY NUMBER *A 1234*

DRAWING ISSUE *A*

FMEA COMMITTEE *DESIGN, DEVELOPMENT, MANUFACTURING & QUALITY ENGINEERING*

FMEA APPROVED

NAME DATE SIGNATURE

AMENDMENTS	1	2	3	4	5	6	7	8	9	10
DATE	ORIGINAL									

1 ITEM	2 PART No NAME ISSUE	3 FUNCTION OR PROCESS	4 FAILURE MODE	5 EFFECT OF FAILURE	6 CAUSE OF FAILURE	7 CURRENT CONTROLS	CURRENT STATUS 8 OCC	9 SEV	10 DET	11 RPN	12 RECOMMENDED CORRECTIVE ACTION	13 ACTION BY	14 ACTION TAKEN	REVISED STATUS 15 OCC	16 SEV	17 DET	18 RPN
11	*A1234 BOTTOM BRACKET ISSUE A*	*TO PROVIDE ENGINE FRONT SUPPORT*	*BUCKLING FAILURE OF BRACKET VERTICAL WALLS*	*ENGINE DROP (COOLING FAN FOULS RADIATOR)*	*INCORRECTLY SPECIFIED MATERIAL THICKNESS*	*STRESS REPORT SR 100* *TEST TO TR 150*	*3*	*8*	*3*	*72*	*TESTS TO BE CARRIED OUT TO TR 150 TO VERIFY STRESS REPORT SR 100*	*TEST/ DEV'T*	*TESTS TO SPECIFIED LOAD PROVES ADEQUATE STATIC STRENGTH*	*2*	*8*	*2*	*32*
12	*"*	*"*	*"*	*"*	*SERVICE LOADS IN EXCESS OF DESIGN LOADS*	*NOT YET ESTABLISHED*	*4*	*8*	*9*	*288*	*VERIFICATION BY ROAD LOAD DATA/TEST BED REQUIRED & DRAWING CONTROLS ESTABLISHED*	*TEST/ DEV'T*	*ROAD LOAD/TEST DATA CONFIRM DESIGN LOADS ARE SATISFACTORY*	*2*	*8*	*3*	*48*
13	*"*	*"*	*CORROSION*	*GRADUAL LOSS OF STRENGTH LEADING TO STRUCTURAL FAILURE*	*INADEQUATE PROTECTIVE TREATMENT SPECIFIED*	*PROTECTIVE TREATMENT SALT SPRAY TESTS ARE SPECIFIED (TR 150)*	*2*	*8*	*2*	*32*	*INSTALLATION TO BE REVIEWED AFTER ROAD & LABORATORY TESTS*	*VEHICLE PROVING*	*LABORATORY & ROAD TESTS WERE CARRIED OUT & NO CORROSION WAS EVIDENT*	*2*	*8*	*2*	*32*
14	*"*	*"*	*FATIGUE FAILURE (STRESS CONCEN-TRATION)*	*ENGINE DROP (COOLING FAN FOULS RADIATOR)*	*SPECIFIED BEND RADIUS TOO SMALL*	*FATIGUE TESTS ARE SPECIFIED IN TR 150*	*3*	*8*	*3*	*72*	*VERIFY BY SPECIFIED RIG TEST*	*TEST/ DEV'T*		*2*	*8*	*2*	*32*

Figure 9.1 FMEA pro forma (Society of Motor Manufacturers and Traders)

3	Specify the component's function. If the component has multiple functions, a separate entry is needed for each function.
4	The failure mode being considered. If the component has multiple failure modes, a separate entry is needed for each mode.
5	The effect of this failure mode on the system.
6	The cause of this particular failure mode.
7	Narrative of the current controls in place to prevent this failure mode.
8	A numerical measure of the likelihood of this failure mode occurring. Any sensible scale can be used. The SMMT specify a 10-point scale from 1 = unlikely to 10 = certain. Other authorities require the use of a formally predicted 'failure rate' as described in a later section of this chapter.
9	A measure of the severity of the effect of this failure mode in one system. Again, the SMMT suggests a scale from 1 = 'no effect' to 10 = 'most severe' (in the motor vehicle context, meaning a safety-related failure).
10	A measure (again on a 1 to 10 scale) of the 'detectability' of the failure mode. SMMT define this as a measure of how likely a vehicle would be to reach the customer with this potential mode still present. An alternative might be to consider how likely it would be that its potential occurrence would be detected during routine operation, or in maintenance procedures.
11	This column contains the 'risk priority number' (RPN), which is the product of the numbers in the previous three columns. This provides a ranking index of each potential failure mode's importance, so prioritizing the action that needs to be taken to improve matters.
12 and 13	Identify any corrective action necessary to reduce or eliminate the consequences of the failure mode.
14 to 18	These columns act as a record of any subsequent action and revise the estimated RPN resulting from that action.

It must be emphasized that this is only one of many different pro formas for FMEA. It is, however, widely used as a standard method within the British motor industry. Other industries and other applications will require different adaptations of the principle. BS 5760 Part 5 provides several useful examples of FMEA layouts in different applications.

An interesting, and important, sidelight on Figure 9.1 is that the form can be used for both designs (as in the example) and processes. In high-volume manufacture, reliability of the manufacturing process is just as important as reliability of the product, and suppliers to the main manufacturers are expected to perform FMEAs on both.

Fault tree analysis (FTA)

If FMEA is viewed as a 'bottom-up' approach to design analysis from the reliability standpoint (starting at the component level), then fault tree analysis (FTA) can be viewed as a 'top-down' approach. Instead of investigating the system component by component, FTA starts by defining a particular failed state of the system, and then, through a logical decomposition of the system, evaluates the component failures which could cause that failed state. The standard conventions and procedures of FTA are largely due to work carried out at Bell Laboratories and at Boeing in the USA, and most of the foundations of the subject are reported in Barlow et al. (1975).

FTA is based on a graphical representation of the system in the form of a logic diagram. This involves two aspects – 'events' and 'gates' – with conventional symbols as shown in Figure 9.2.

EVENTS

These include the following:

1 **Fault events** (rectangles) are complex failure events whose values can be decomposed through logic gates (see below) into a combination of simpler events. A particularly important fault event is the 'top event', representing the failed system state being investigated.
2 **Basic events** (circles) are failure events that cannot be further decomposed.
3 **Undeveloped events** (diamonds) are complex events that could have, but have not, been further decomposed. This can happen either because we have chosen not to break them down further because the tree is not affected by the lower failure levels, or simply because we are at an interim stage in producing the tree, and further development will take place later (in which case the 'double diamond' symbol is sometimes used). In truth, all events are 'undeveloped', and we could continue decomposing events down to the molecular level. One of the skills acquired in using FTA is that of knowing when to stop.
4 **House events** – This name comes from the symbol. These are not failure events, but are simply events that occur routinely in system operation and switch parts of the tree on or off. Examples might be 're-heat on' for a gas turbine engine or 'it is raining' for a vehicle braking system.

There are several other types of events and accompanying symbols sometimes used in FTA, but those already described cover most circumstances.

GATES

The two most widely applicable gates in FTA are the OR gate and the AND gate, as shown in Figure 9.2.

For an OR gate, the output fault event will occur if any one (or more) of the input events occurs.

For an AND gate, the output fault event occurs only if all the input events occur.

Other types of gates are occasionally encountered, but these two will cover most circumstances.

TRANSFERS

In complex systems, it is often necessary to extend a tree over several pages. It also sometimes happens that sections of the tree repeat in other parts of the tree. The triangle symbol is used to denote the links between the various parts of the tree.

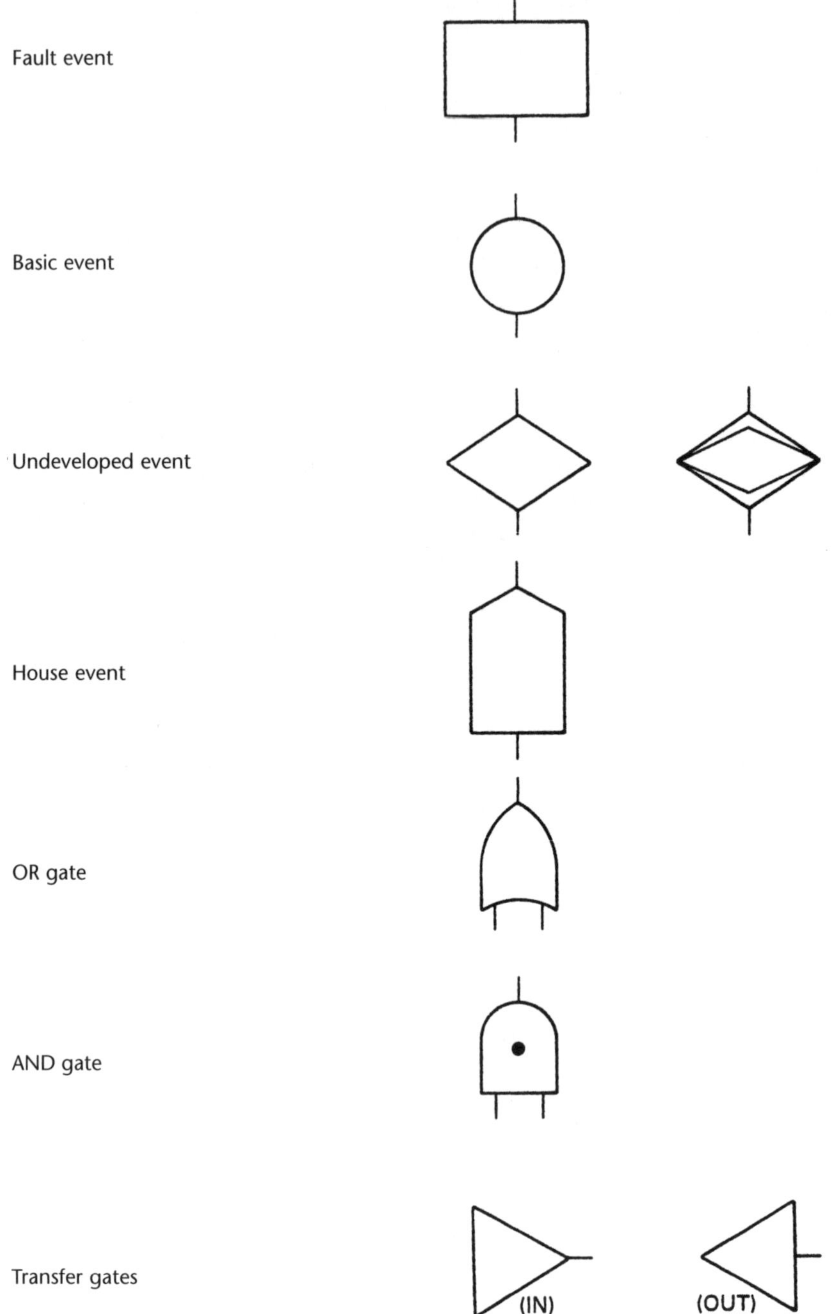

Figure 9.2 Fault tree symbols

EXAMPLES

An example of a realistic fault tree is given in Figure 9.3, which relates to the door control system for a public transport vehicle, and has as its top event 'door opens while vehicle is moving'. This example shows all the above symbols in use (and in reality carries on to many more pages through the various transfers).

To understand the principles of fault tree construction, it is necessary to use some much simpler examples.

Example 1

As a very simple example to illustrate the process of FTA, consider the simple circuit in Figure 9.4a. A d.c. motor is powered by a battery, and controlled by two switches in series. We are free to define any 'top event' of interest for this system. One possibility is that the motor fails to stop when required. Should the motor fail to stop when one switch is thrown, we would then throw the second switch. If the motor still fails to stop, the first reaction is that this can only be because both switches have failed to open. The fault tree is simply these two basic events linked through an AND gate, as in Figure 9.4b.

Further consideration might suggest other possibilities. For example, an alternative current path might be present. This will alter the picture to that in Figure 9.4c. Although the new event is shown 'undeveloped', there are all sorts of possibilities: an alternative path through another circuit perhaps, or someone leaving a spanner lying across the switch contacts. This illustrates one of the problems of FTA, in that it is limited only by the imagination.

An alternative top event for the same circuit would be that the motor does not start when the switches are closed. The simple explanations here are either a primary motor failure OR a failure of the power supply. The power supply failure needs further development: a possible suggestion is shown in Figure 9.4d.

Example 2

This example shows how a tree can change fundamentally for different top events.

A pressure reduction system in a gas distribution network consists of two regulators in series in the pipeline. A standard configuration is to have two of these pressure reduction systems in parallel, as shown in Figure 9.5a. Regulators have two possible failure modes: 'closed', where flow is blocked completely, and 'open', where gas passes freely through without any pressure reduction. The system's top events of interest are:

1 total loss of supply
2 overpressure downstream.

The two fault trees are shown in Figures 9.5b and 9.5c.

EVALUATION OF FAULT TREES: CUT SETS

A cut set is a set of events that makes the occurrence of the top event certain. The more events there are in a cut set, the less likely it is to occur, so particular interest centres on identifying cut sets with small numbers of events. In particular, we need to identify cut sets that cannot be further reduced and still remain cut sets. These are referred to as 'minimal cut sets' (MSC). For simple systems, MCS can be identified by inspection.

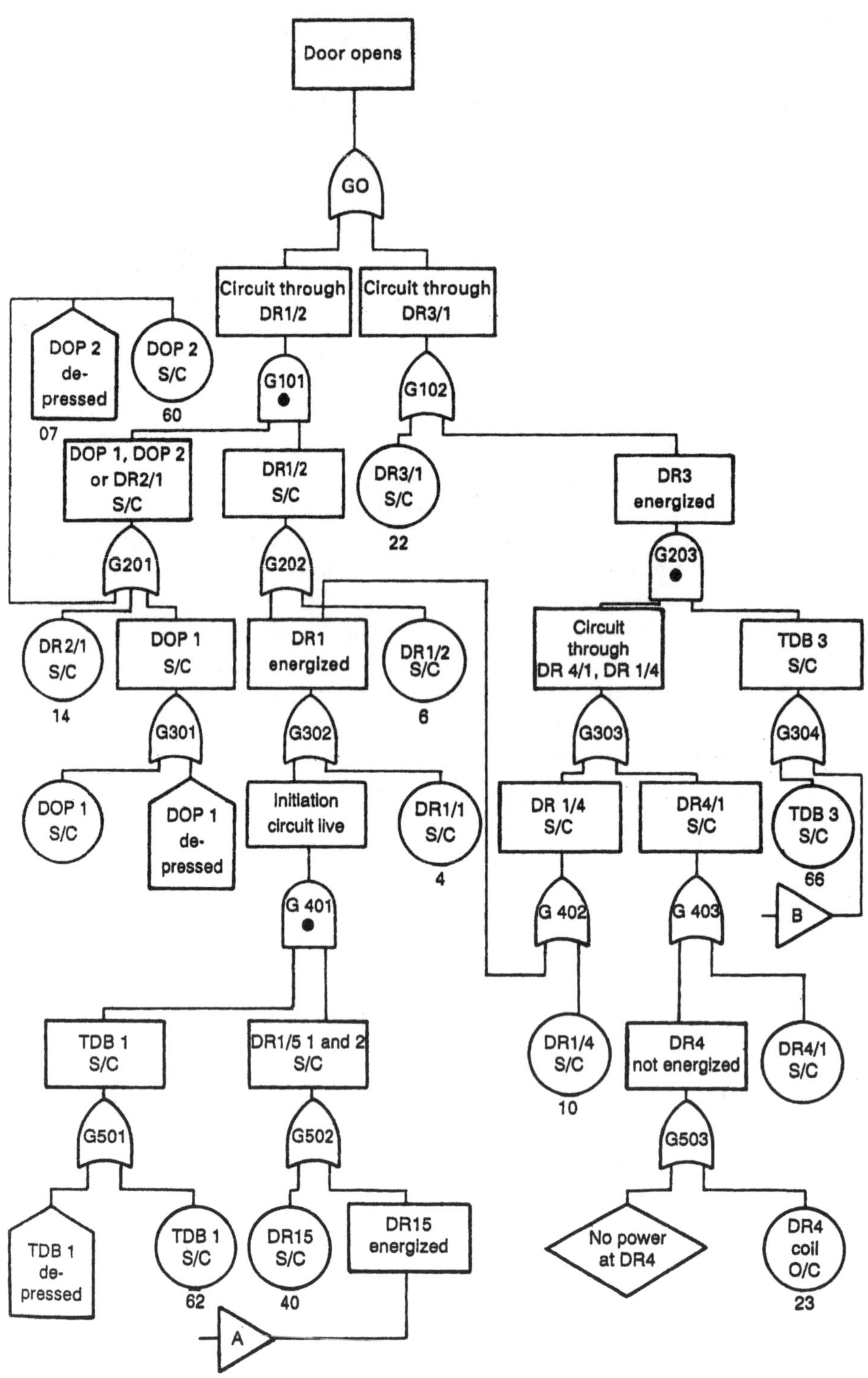

Figure 9.3 Fault tree for door control system

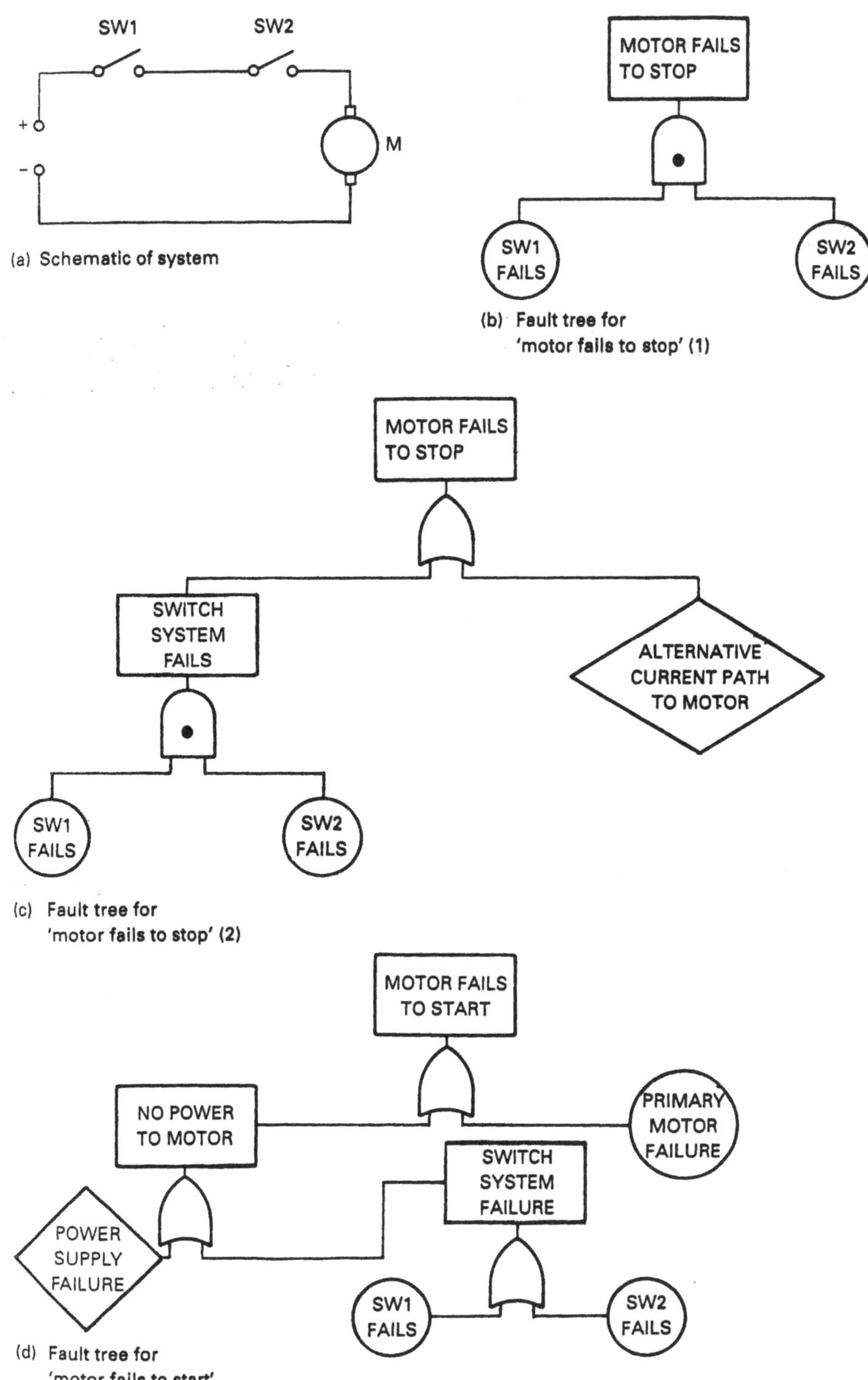

Figure 9.4 Fault trees for motor control system

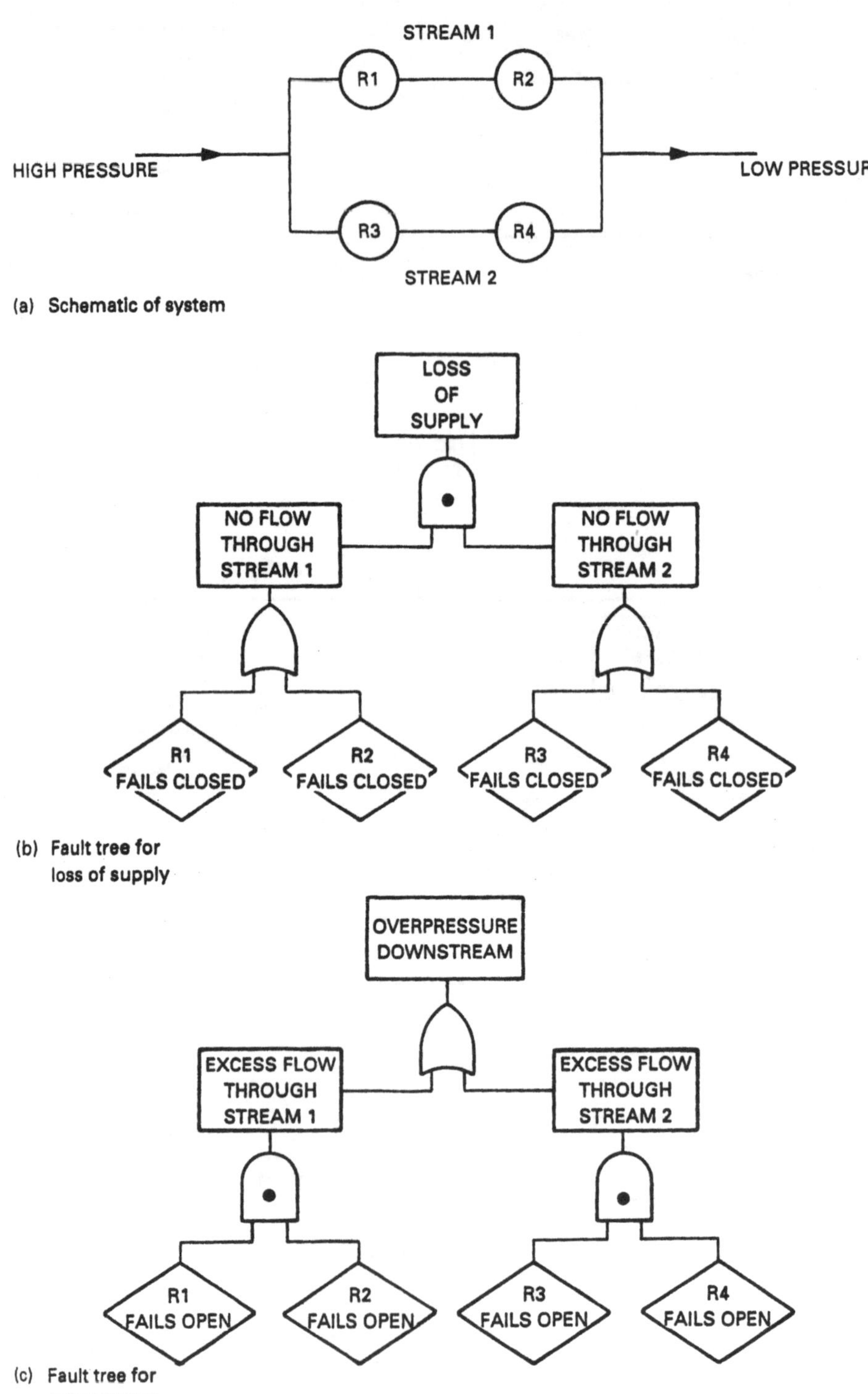

Figure 9.5 Fault trees for pressure reduction systems

Top event 1: Loss of supply

For the top event 'loss of supply', denoting the event 'regulator 1 fails closed' by R1C, and so on, the cut sets consist of:

1	R1C	R3C		
2	R1C	R4C		
3	R2C	R3C		
4	R2C	R4C		
5	R1C	R2C	R3C	
6	R1C	R2C	R4C	
7	R1C	R3C	R4C	
8	R2C	R3C	R4C	
9	R1C	R2C	R3C	R4C

of which numbers 1 to 4 constitute minimal cut sets.

Top event 2: Overpressure downstream

For the top event 'overpressure downstream', using a similar convention but with 'O' denoting 'fails open', the cut sets are:

1	R1O	R2O		
2	R3O	R4O		
3	R1O	R2O	R3O	
4	R1O	R2O	R4O	
5	R1O	R3O	R4O	
6	R1O	R3O	R4O	
7	R1O	R2O	R3O	R4O

In practice, most fault trees are much more complex than these simple examples and a disciplined procedure is required. A useful example of this is the MOCUS algorithm. This can be used 'manually', as explained in Barlow et al. (1975, pp. 19–23), but it also forms the basis for computer-based MCS identification – in fact, most FTA is computer-based throughout, and many packages are available.

Reference back to Figure 9.3 shows that there is a single-event cut set (event 22). Without any sophisticated analysis, it is obvious that this event (which is a relay 'hanging up') is critical to the system. Either the component must be super-reliable, or the system must be reconfigured to introduce an AND gate somewhere between this event and the top event. This problem is obvious by inspection. There are many less obvious but still significant problems. Computer analysis of this tree identified 17 two-event minimal cut sets, and over 5 000 MCS of higher order.

Another aspect to examine the tree for is any event appearing more than once, or 'common cause' failures. A simple example is a multiple-engined aircraft, where there is partial redundancy (AND gates) between the engines, but the event 'contaminated fuel supply' would appear in the sections of the tree for each engine, being a common cause of failure.

NUMERICAL EVALUATION IN FTA

If the probabilities of individual events are known, the probabilities at all the gates can be calculated, and hence the probability of the top event. This type of analysis is, of course, heavily dependent on the assumed probabilities and all the problems inherent in the assumptions (see the next section). It is, however, often the only way to proceed in evaluating events of high consequence and (hopefully) low probability. It featured heavily, for example, in the risk assessment of various proposed nuclear power stations.

Another quantitative aspect is that of 'importance' of events. If it is required to reduce the probability of the top event failure, it is not necessarily the least reliable component that should be improved. Instead, consider the most 'important' component as the one where a given proportional improvement in reliability has the greatest proportional effect on the top event probability. Procedures for identifying such a component are given in Barlow et al. (1975, pp. 77–100).

Summary: FMEA and FTA

FTA is a more 'surgical' approach than FMEA, in that it defines the system failure (top event) beforehand, rather than adopting the approach of looking at every component and seeing what horrors evolve. In an ideal (and totally unattainable) world, a perfectly executed FMEA covering all failure modes of all components and a series of perfectly executed fault trees for all top events would both amount to the same thing. They would also both consume an infinite amount of paper. More realistically, both need doing.

The FMEA is best viewed as a working document that evolves with the design, and is best carried out by the design team themselves. The FTA is more likely to be undertaken as a specialist activity at a later stage in the design as an assurance of critical aspects of system reliability.

FMEA and FTA are both necessarily imperfect tools, and largely limited by understanding of the system and foreseeing the sort of component failures that can occur. It is instructive (and sobering) to think of some fairly recent well-known and well-documented reliability disasters (such as the Clapham, Southall and Ladbroke Grove train accidents, Challenger spacecraft failure, Chernobyl nuclear reactor fire, Flixborough chemical plant explosion) and wonder whether what happened could reasonably have been foreseen in either FMEA or FTA.

Numerical reliability prediction

This type of prediction sets out to provide a numerical estimate for the mean time between failures (MTBF) of a system. The procedure is based on the use of databases of achieved reliability for particular types of component under specified operating conditions. The database information for particular components is quoted as a 'failure rate'. (It should, more properly, be called the 'hazard rate'.) The failure rate for the system is taken as the sum of the failure rates of all the constituent components. This summation procedure implies assumptions:

1 that the system is in series configuration (so that the failure of any one component causes system failure); in FTA terms, it consists entirely of OR gates.
2 that component failures are statistically random (that is, the probability of failure does not change with component age – they are 'constant hazard', as explained in the next section).

The procedure was developed originally for application to electronics. It was devised in the USA by the Rome Air Development Center (RADC) in response to a need to make considerable improvements in the reliability of electronic equipment that was being used by the US military in the late 1950s.

The procedures are documented in the US Department of Defense Handbook MIL-HDBK-217, which undergoes occasional reviews and reissues (it was at issue F-2 in 2002).

The effort in producing this document is enormous, as it needs to keep up to date with the rapid advances in electronic component technology. The general approach is consistent for all components, with the predicted component 'failure rate' being:

$$\lambda_p = \lambda_b \prod_{i=1}^{n} \pi_i$$

where:

λ_p is the component (part) 'failure rate'
λ_b is the base failure rate at the component's known operating temperature, obtained from a chart or graph in the standard
π_i are various factors that differ for each type of component, and allow for such things as vibration level, derating, application, level of technology, manufacturing quality, and so forth. These are multiplied together to give a composite correction factor.

The MIL handbook gives sufficient data on base failure rates and the various factors to yield a predicted 'failure rate' for most types of components currently in use.

There are other databases and procedures available as an alternative to MIL-HDBK-217F-2. For example, in the USA, AT&T Bell Laboratories publish their own equivalent, known as the 'Bellcore Reliability Prediction Procedure TR-332'. This uses a similar methodology to MIL-HDBK-217, but modifies the various factors and base failure rates to be more representative of non-military applications, and to correlate with AT&T's own field data. It also takes into account burn-in data and field and laboratory test data. In the UK, British Telecommunications plc maintain a database (HRD4) for electronic equipment. In the case of non-electronic systems, there are databases with particular emphases on specific areas of application, such as the SRS (Systems Reliability Service) Databank (with an emphasis on power generation and large-process plant) and the OREDA Databank directed towards offshore systems. In addition, many firms have their own in-house reliability databanks.

In all these procedures, there is a certain seductive element, in that by rigorously applying them it is always possible to obtain a figure for system failure rate – often to an impressive number of decimal places. It must be accepted, however, that such apparent precision is usually something of a delusion, and these predicted values often provide estimates that are eventually shown to be in error by orders of magnitude compared with the results obtained in service – in either direction. Within the many possible sources of discrepancy, there are three particular aspects that are worthy of consideration: historical averaging, generic families and independence.

HISTORICAL AVERAGING

With historical averaging, the database figures for a particular type of component are averaged over different manufacturers. Even for one manufacturer, they will be averaged over early production (where there may have been some quality problems) and later production (where these problems may have been sorted out).

GENERIC FAMILIES

RADC developed prediction methods in the field of electronics when electronic systems consisted of separate components individually mounted on circuit boards. In this application, components were of easily identifiable, distinct generic types whose reliability characteristics were similar, even when produced by different manufacturers. This approach of considering identifiable generic families has been continued in MIL-HDBK-217 through its successive issues, following the development of new technologies and, in particular, the increasing use of microelectronics.

It is conceivable that such groupings are meaningful in the case of electronic components where designs and production processes are similar for all suppliers (and are, in fact, often constrained by national and international specifications). The approach becomes more problematic in the case of mechanical and electromechanical equipment which is characterized by diversity of design and application, and comparatively small numbers of components in existence.

Whereas, for example, it makes sense to quote global reliability characteristics for plastic film capacitors of a given capacitance, voltage rating and type of construction, it makes much less sense to quote a figure for a gearbox. The gearbox reliability depends on so many things (size, function, application and, above all, the integrity of the design) that using a predicted failure rate is fairly meaningless. Such figures exist in databanks, but it is important to realize that they are simply the average of all such data reported to the bank, with no justification for supposing that they relate to the particular design and application of interest.

Before using such figures, it is always worth investigating the detailed sources of the data to see whether they are relevant, and the sample sizes used to produce the figure to see whether they are sufficient.

INDEPENDENCE

The use of component reliability data in prediction assumes that each component is an 'island', and that failures are caused only by the response of the component itself to the various stresses and environmental factors imposed upon it. No allowance is made for the interaction between functioning components, which is very often the primary source of failures – they are precipitated by a chain of events.

A possible solution to this problem would be to use the component data in a fault tree, but as already indicated, the preparation of a tree defining all events in even a modest system is a major undertaking.

SUMMARY OF NUMERICAL RELIABILITY PREDICTION

In summary, numerical prediction has a place in the development of reliable designs. It is a useful catalyst for a 'second look' at a design, particularly for the identification of over-stressed components, and it can provide valid data for the comparison of alternative designs. What is worrying is that its use is often over-emphasized to the extent that obtaining a number appears more important that getting the design right.

Argument over the merits or otherwise of the procedure has continued since the RADC notebook was first published, and the reader is referred to past issues of *Quality and Reliability Engineering International* and *IEEE Transactions in Reliability*, and in particular, the correspondence pages of these journals for a selection of views of both sides of the argument.

Reliability analysis of test and service data

The procedures so far introduced are based on a synthesis of the system – they are performed on the design on paper (or in software), rather than on hardware. They help to get the design right, but the real information on reliability only emerges when hardware is available for testing. Testing is, of course, a necessary adjunct to design.

Prototype testing falls into two broad aspects:

1 extreme stress testing ('type' testing)
2 endurance testing.

Extreme stress testing is directed at ensuring that the design is capable of meeting the extremes of stress and environment that it is likely to encounter (and is often proscribed by test specifications). It consists of such aspects as extremes of temperature, humidity, vibration, shock and so on, applied to electronic systems. The test programmes undertaken by motor manufacturers subject vehicles, at one extreme, to desert conditions to monitor effects of very high cabin temperatures, and at the other extreme, to testing starting reliability after prolonged exposure to very low temperature. Tests such as these are directed to major aspects of design, materials and so forth, and are characterized by there being no need to involve large samples because problems will be repeated on all system copies.

Reliability problems encountered in the routine use of systems do not necessarily involve high stresses and extreme environments. These problems occur relatively infrequently, because they result from aspects that have not been picked up by design or type testing. They are nonetheless crucial in establishing acceptable reliability. Laboratory testing has an important role to play in reliability, using such techniques as spectrographic stress analysis, or use of thermal imaging cameras to detect hot spots in electronic circuitry.

Sometimes the term 'durability' is used to describe reliability against major causes of deterioration, with 'reliability' used to describe the remaining issues arising from a multiplicity of causes at individually low levels.

Things become more difficult in the case of failures that are at a fairly low frequency and random in nature. The low-level failures might be individually of minor consequence, but spread across the plethora of components in the typical system, they are usually the major source of reliability problems because of their inherent diversity and unpredictability. The only sensible way of finding and eliminating such failures is by investing heavily in endurance testing. In contrast to type testing, this requires large samples and protracted test times at stress levels representative of routine in-service conditions (though modest stress increases can sometimes be used to accelerate the testing).

In considering the behaviour of equipment in operation, it is necessary to draw a distinction between components and systems. To clarify this distinction, it is convenient (if not completely rigorous) to define a component as an item that will only fail once. If such a component forms part of a repairable system, the system is restored to operation by replacing the failed component. In turn, replacement can be viewed as the restoration of the 'hole' in the system brought about by the failure. It is usually assumed that the replacement is 'as good as new', and is achieved either by physical replacement or by perfect repair of the failed component.

The validity of this 'good as new' assumption can be examined under the heading of repairable system analysis. The behaviour of individual components is examined under the heading of component reliability analysis. It is important for an understanding of the subject that these two aspects are considered separately.

Component reliability

The measure of component reliability is its age at failure. Failure needs some sort of prior definition – it might be something spectacular, or merely some parameter moving outside specified limits.

Age can also be any suitable measure of the component usage. The usual quantity is time (symbol t), but it should be whatever is relevant for the component. The choice is a matter of engineering judgement, but some examples are:

- elapsed time
- operating time (for non-continuous use)
- distance covered (for drive train components of motor vehicles, for example)
- cycles of operation (photocopier meter readings, for example)
- quantity of product (a chemical plant, for example).

The concept underlying component reliability is that of the 'lifetime distribution', as depicted in Figure 9.6. The function $f(t)$ is known as the probability density function. It is some mathematical function such that the area under the curve is 1.0. At any time we care to define, the area to the left of this time is known as the 'distribution function' (CDF), given the symbol $F(t)$. This measures the probability that the component will fail before time.

The area to the right is known as the 'reliability function' (or sometimes as the 'survival function'). This function $R(t)$ measures the probability of having survived to time t (the reliability). Note that $R(t) = 1 - F(t)$.

A related concept, central to the understanding of component reliability, is the 'hazard function', usually denoted as $h(t)$, although alternative notations of $z(t)$ or $r(t)$ are sometimes used. The hazard function defines the probability that a component which is working now will fail in a small interval of time beyond now. For example, it could measure the probability that the processor chip in the computer I am using to prepare this chapter will fail in the next minute (yes, it has happened before!). The units would be 'probability per minute', for which reason the function is sometimes referred to as the 'hazard rate'.

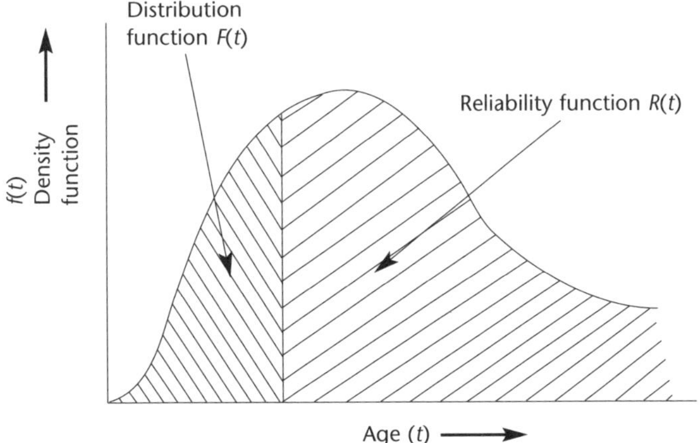

Figure 9.6 Lifetime distribution

The hazard rate is also sometimes referred to as the 'failure rate' or the 'instantaneous failure rate'. While there is nothing wrong in such terminology, it is the root of widespread confusion and misunderstanding in distinguishing between components and systems. To avoid this problem, a convention is beginning to emerge of using 'hazard function' in the context of components, and 'failure rate' for systems. This convention is adhered to throughout this chapter. The two concepts are fundamentally different.

Mathematically, it can be shown that the hazard function is simply the probability density function divided by the reliability function, which, referring to Figure 9.6, is the height of the distribution divided by the area to the right:

$$h(t) = f(t)/R(t)$$

Of particular interest is the way in which the function behaves. In particular, is it increasing, decreasing or staying more or less constant as component age increases?

Reducing hazard is exhibited by a component whose failure probability reduces as it ages. An example of this is provided by such things as ball and roller bearings, where initial slight misalignment on installation can cause high initial loadings that are then reduced as the component 'beds in'. Reducing hazard is characterized by comments to the effect that 'these items fail early or not at all'.

Note that reducing hazard is a characteristic of a given component. It should not be confused with reducing system failure rates arising through early failures of weak components, and associated issues of burn-in and stress screening. That is a separate issue, dealt with in a later section under the heading 'Reducing failure rate: Burn-in and reliability growth'.

Constant hazard arises in the case of components whose failure probability remains constant as the component ages. This implies that failures are due to random events where the applied load exceeds the strength of the component, and there is no deterioration through use. Constant hazard is widely assumed in the case of electronic components.

Increasing hazard describes the case where the component failure probability increases with its age. This will occur in any situation where the component deteriorates through use: for example, components subject to corrosion, wear, fatigue and so on.

It is generally unrewarding to try to predict the hazard pattern from a theoretical standpoint. Instead, it can be estimated statistically from observed failure data. Knowledge of the hazard behaviour is important in identifying failure mechanisms and their causes. It is also of fundamental importance on evolving preventive maintenance strategies. There is no point in replacing an unfailed component on a preventive basis unless it exhibits an increasing hazard function.

MODELS FOR LIFETIME DISTRIBUTIONS

Failure data analysis is facilitated by making some initial assumption about the form of the lifetime probability distribution and its attendant distribution and hazard functions. If, for example, we can assume a constant hazard function (usually denoted as λ, with the units 'failures per unit time', and with θ [= 1/λ] being the mean life), the lifetime distribution will be exponential:

Density function $f(t) = \lambda e^{-\lambda t}$
Distribution function $F(t) = 1 - e^{-\lambda t}$
Reliability function $R(t) = e^{-\lambda t}$
Hazard function $h(t) = \lambda$

(as in Figure 9.7)

If this model is assumed, data analysis consists simply of estimating the value of λ.

While this model is simple, in presupposing constant hazard it puts a severe constraint on the analysis, particularly as the most important aspect of data analysis in this context is to investigate the form of the hazard function. A particularly useful and flexible model that avoids this constraint is provided by an adaptation of the exponential distribution, known as the Weibull distribution. This introduces a second parameter, ß, known as the shape parameter. The usual form of expression (for the distribution function) is:

$$F(t) = 1 - e^{-(t/\eta)^{\beta}}$$

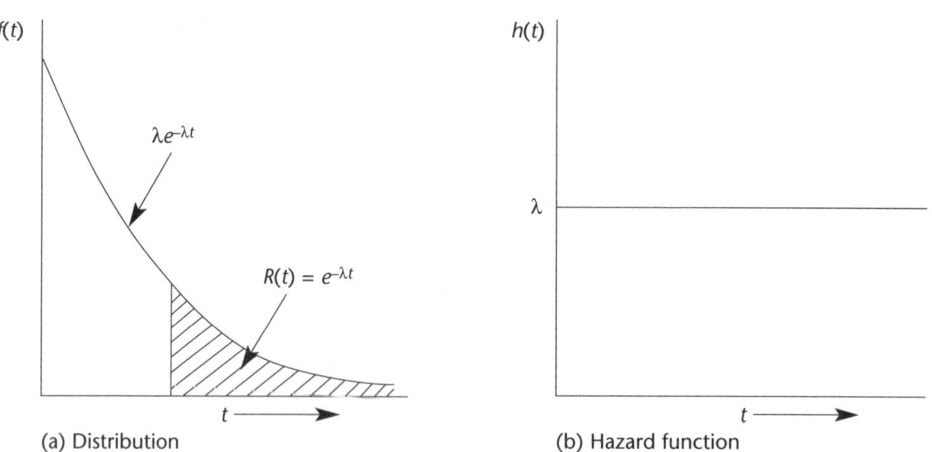

Figure 9.7 Exponential distribution

Putting $\eta = {}^{1}/_{\lambda}$, it can be seen that this distribution is the same as the exponential when ß = 1. The effect of changing ß is shown in Figure 9.8a for the distribution itself ($f(t)$), and in Figure 9.8b for the hazard function.

Values of ß greater than 1 indicate increasing hazard function: the greater the value, the more rapidly the component is wearing out. A value of 2.0 represents linearly increasing hazard. A value of about 3.5 approximates to a normal (symmetrical) lifetime distribution. Values much greater than this are rarely encountered in practice. Values less than 1 represent reducing hazard, with about 0.5 being the lowest value likely to be encountered.

η is known as the 'characteristic life'. It is an informal measure of the average life. It is only the true average (that is, expected life) when ß = 1. More precisely, it is the life at which 62.3 per cent ($100 \times (1 - e^{-1})$) of the components will be expected to have failed.

Further description of the Weibull distribution is given in Chapter 17.

WEIBULL ANALYSIS

Estimates of the two Weibull parameters (ß and η) will provide a comprehensive description of the component failure pattern. Weibull analysis is the process of producing these estimates. The input data will consist of an identified sample of components, some or all of which have failed.

Note that unfailed times must always be included in the analysis. A common mistake is to omit them, which results in a pessimistic estimate of reliability. While laboratory component testing can be 'to destruction', with all components failed, in the case of prototype testing of systems and their subsequent use in service, most components will be unfailed – or, at least, we hope so! This type of testing will generate a few 'times to failure' and a comparatively large number of non-failures, or 'censorings'.

Analysis in anything other than simple cases where all components have failed is not particularly straightforward. The usual methods are either to calculate maximum likelihood estimates, which involves iterative calculations necessitating the use of a computer, or to use a graphical method (probability plotting or hazard plotting).

A description of these techniques is beyond the scope of this chapter. Nelson (1982) is a comprehensive and authoritative text on component failure data analysis. A simple and useful outline of plotting methods is also given in Davidson (1988), both in Chapter 6 and in an accompanying video. The use of maximum likelihood methods is most easily approached through 'off the shelf' reliability software packages.

Repairable systems

We now move on from studying the lifetime behaviour of components to consider the systems in which such components are installed. Such systems are generally repairable, meaning that when a component fails, the system does not reach the end of its life. Instead, it is restored to an operating condition by repair or replacement of the failed component.

The reliability of a repairable system is most easily described by plotting a graph of total (cumulative) failures (denoted $N(T)$) against the cumulative elapsed system time T.

Consider initially just one component in a system. When failures occur, the failed component is replaced. Assume initially that replacement components are nominally identical to the ones that fail. In this case we should expect each component to last for the

β = 0.5, 1.0, 1.5, 2.0, 3.0 and 4.0

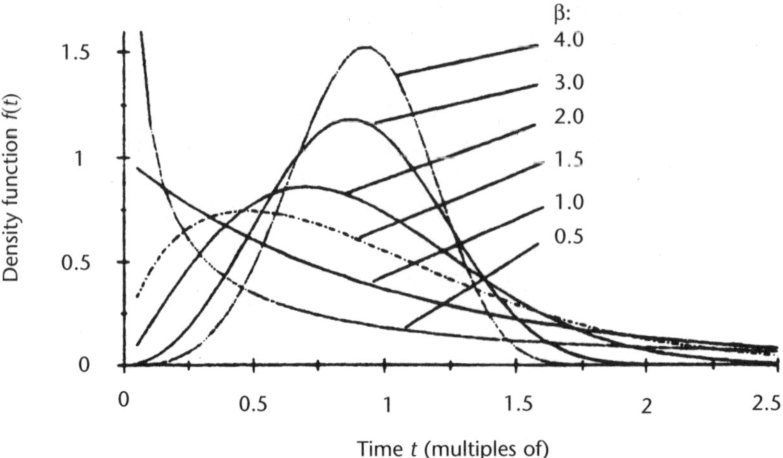

(a) Weibull density function

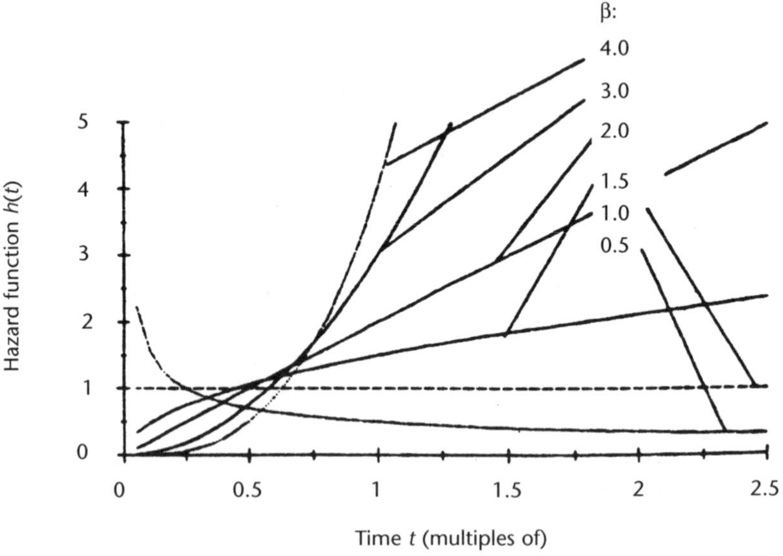

(b) Weibull hazard function

Figure 9.8 Weibull distributions

same time. In practice, of course, successive components do not last for the same time because their times to failure are distributed about their mean life: they constitute random samples from their lifetime distribution (as described in the previous section). This concept is sometimes described as the component lifetimes being 'independent and identically distributed' (IID). Because the average lifetime of successive components does not change, a plot of *N(T)* against *T* will therefore show a linear relationship, with individual points scattered about the line because of the distribution of the lifetimes (see Figure 9.9).

The slope of this line (failures per unit time) is the failure rate of the system due to this one component. The line is straight (and the failure rate constant) because of the assumption of IID components. This is irrespective of the form of the lifetime distribution: specifically, it is independent of the hazard function as indicated by the Weibull 'ß'. Constant failure rate *does not* imply constant hazard.

The argument can be extended by superimposing on this 'renewal process' all the other components in the system. There will now, of course, be many more points to plot, but the underlying argument remains the same: provided that replacement components are 'good as new' (that is, their lifetimes are IID), the system failure rate will remain constant irrespective of the hazard function behaviour of the components within the system. Later in this section, we shall consider the case of non-constant failure rates, but these arise through breakdown of the IID assumption rather than anything associated with component hazard functions.

There is a widely held view that the assumption of constant failure rate, and the consequent use of the various testing procedures and so on predicated on this assumption, also involves the assumption of constant hazard. As shown above, this is not the case. There is no need to restrict the use of such procedures (for example) to electronic systems where the constant hazard assumption might be valid.

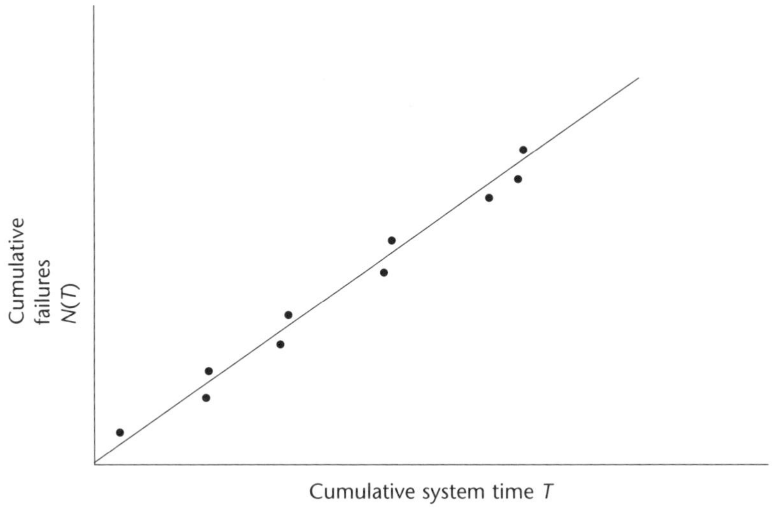

Figure 9.9 Repairable system example

RELIABILITY ANALYSIS UNDER CONSTANT FAILURE RATE

Under the constant failure rate assumption, there is only one parameter to estimate: the slope of the failure/time graph, that is to say, the system failure rate (usual symbol λ), or its reciprocal, the mean time between failures (MTBF; usual symbol θ). In producing these estimates, the assumption of constant failure rate implies that failures are statistically random, giving the resulting simplification that over any aggregated cumulative operating time T (over any number of identical systems), if the observed number of failures is x, the estimated failure rate is given by:

$$\lambda = x/T$$

and the estimated MTBF (θ) by

$$\theta = T/x$$

In any situation other than that of random failures as generated under the assumption of constant failure rate, this simple aggregation is no longer possible, as both λ and θ will then no longer be constants.

Note that the failure rate symbol is the same as that used in the previous section for hazard function, despite emphasis on the point that these two quantities are essentially different. This is a reflection of current usage, which is largely responsible for the confusion between the two concepts. This confusion is further confounded by the fact that when λ (in either guise) is constant, its mathematical relationships are the same in both applications. This chapter has adopted the approach of living with the existing imperfect situation, rather than embarking on a crusade for clearer terminology. This issue is pursued in depth (and with considerable vigour) in Ascher and Feingold (1984).

As an example under the assumption of constant failure rate, consider three identical systems:

System 1 had failures at ages 15, 231, 440 and 487 hours, and has now reached an age of 550 hours.
System 2 had failures at 110, 193 and 265 hours. It has now reached an age of 400 hours.
System 3 has had a single failure at 96 hours. It has now reached 150 hours.

The total system time T is:

$$(550 + 400 + 150) = 1100 \text{ hours.}$$

The total number of failures, $x = 8$

The estimated failure rate is therefore:

$$8/1100 = 0.00727 \text{ failures per hour}$$

The estimated MTBF is 1100/8, which is 137.5 hours.

Note that the calculation did not make use of the individual observed times of failure: it is not necessary to do so because of the constant failure rate assumption.

The assumption of constant failure rate can be seen as an attraction because of the simplicity of the resulting calculations. It is often worthwhile to test this assumption. A simple way is to plot the failure/time graph and check that it gives a straight line – or, at least, that there is no obvious curvature. In so doing, it is necessary to give some consideration to the origin of the T scale. In the example, it might be sensible to assume that the current lives of the system represent 'today's' situation, so that on an 'elapsed time' basis the situation was as shown in Figure 9.10.

The cumulative system ages at failure are, by vertical summation of the times over the three systems, 15, 312, 370, 536, 695, 770, 911 and 938 hours (at each failure time, the cumulative time is the aggregate of the times over all three systems at that instant). A failure/time plot of these values is shown in Figure 9.11.

From this it can be seen that there is no obvious curvature to the plot (although there is some expected random scatter about the straight line trend). The assumption of constant failure rate is therefore validated.

RELIABILITY DEMONSTRATION UNDER CONSTANT FAILURE RATE

There is frequently a wish to demonstrate that some minimal requirement for the reliability of a system has been achieved. This is sometimes formalized into a contractual requirement on the supplier. A common way of expressing this is to require a demonstration at a specified confidence level that a given MTBF has been achieved (or exceeded). Suppose, for example, that we require an MTBF of 500 hours to be demonstrated with 90 per cent confidence. How much testing is required?

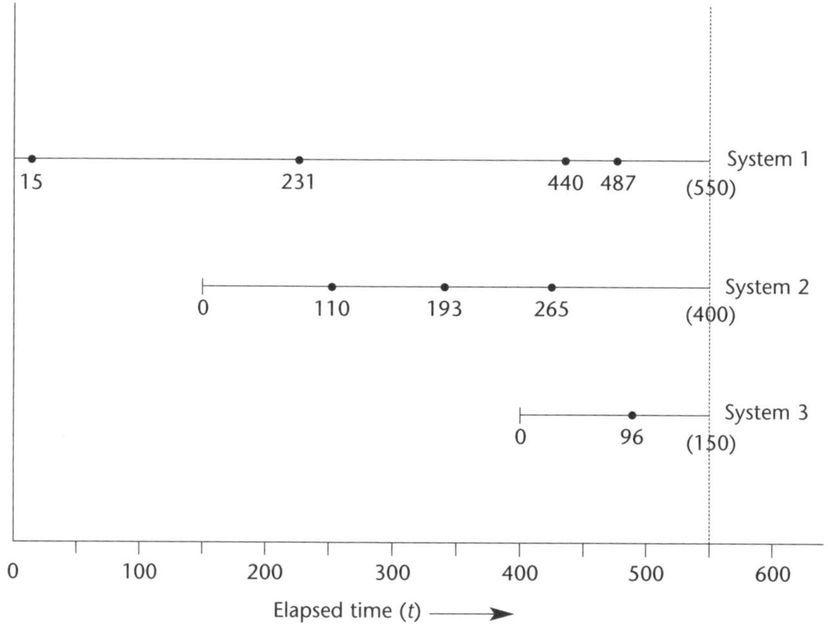

Figure 9.10 Data for failure/time plot

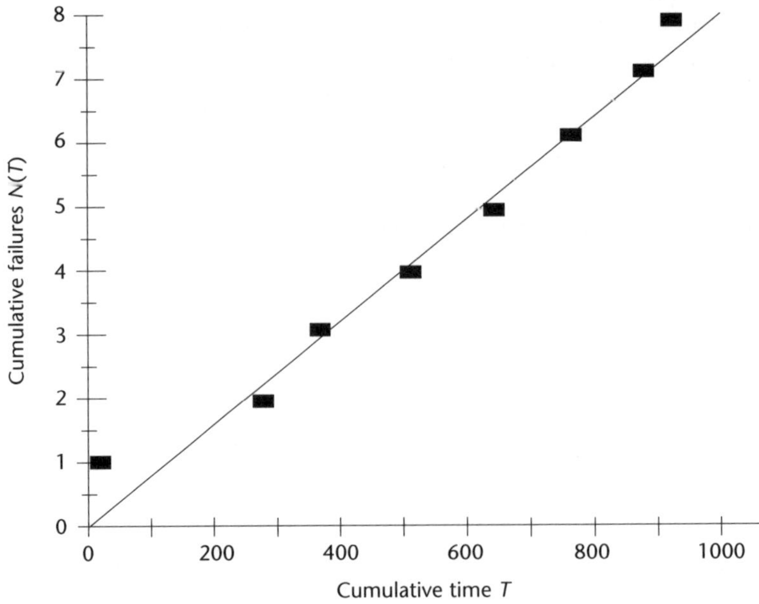

Figure 9.11 Failure/time plot for data in Figure 9.10

If no failures occur, the total test time required (T) is given by:

$$\theta \times \ln (100/(100 - C))$$

where:

θ is the required MTBF
C is the percentage confidence
ln is the natural logarithm (to the base *e*)

In the example, therefore, the total test time required (without failure) is:

$$500 \ln (100/(100 - 95))$$
$$= 500 \ln 20$$
$$= 500 \times 2.996 = 1498 \text{ hours}$$

The interpretation of 'confidence level' needs explanation. If, in this example, we succeed in accumulating 1498 hours without failure, we can make the statement 'the MTBF of this system is at least 500 hours'. The confidence level (95 per cent in this instance) is the probability that this statement is correct.

If we are prepared to accept a lower confidence level, the required test time is reduced. The reader may like to repeat the calculation to show that, for a confidence level of 75 per cent, the required test time is 693 hours. If failures occur during the demonstration, it is still possible that the requirement can be met, but further testing will be required. The relationship between test time and required MTBF becomes more complex when failures occur, but the requirements are summarized in Table 9.1. This table gives values of *K*, the multiple of the required MTBF which is to be accumulated for the given number of failures. Readers familiar with statistics can note that K is equal to 0.5 $\chi^2_{[\alpha,2(x+1)]}$, where $\alpha = (1 - c/100)$, and x is the number of failures.

Suppose that, in the previous example, we had a failure when 1230 hours of testing had been accumulated. To meet the same demonstration requirements we would now require a total of 4.74 x 500 = 2370 hours without any further failures, and so on.

Note that, under the constant failure rate assumption, it does not matter when, and over how many systems, the test time is accumulated so long as T is the product of units x time.

ACCEPTANCE TESTING UNDER CONSTANT FAILURE RATE

The demonstration procedure described above has the danger that for a system whose MTBF is lower than the requirement, testing or demonstration could continue for a very long time with the accumulated test time failing to 'catch up' with the target as it is further extended by the occurrence of more failures.

To avoid this situation, there is an alternative approach to testing and demonstration that also permits the system to be rejected if it is of inadequate reliability. To construct such a test, it is necessary to define two risks:

1 The risk of wrongly rejecting a system with a low failure rate λ_1. This risk is called the 'producer's risk' and is given the symbol α.
2 The risk of wrongly accepting a system with a high (unacceptable) failure rate λ_2. This risk is called the 'consumer's risk', and is given the symbol ß.

The ratio of λ_2/λ_1 is referred to as the 'discrimination ratio' of the test. The closer this ratio is to 1, the greater the amount of testing.

Note that for this type of test it is more convenient to work in terms of failure rate than MTBF.

Various testing procedures have been proposed, but a very different and simple procedure is that of the 'sequential probability ratio test' (SPRT) due to Wald, and incorporated into the widely used reliability testing specification MIL-STD-781C(14). The procedure is best explained with reference to the failure/time plot of $N(T)$ against T, as previously described. SPRT superimposes a template of decision lines on the plot, as shown in Figure 9.12. Test hours are accumulated and failures logged until the plot crosses one of

Table 9.1 Multiplication factors for MTBF demonstration (constant failure rate)

Confidence level (per cent)	*Number of failures* 0	1	2	3	4	5
50	0.70	1.68	2.67	3.67	4.67	5.67
75	1.39	2.69	3.92	5.06	6.27	7.42
80	1.61	2.99	4.28	5.52	6.72	7.91
90	2.30	3.89	5.32	6.68	8.00	9.27
95	3.00	4.74	6.30	7.75	9.15	10.60
99	4.60	6.64	8.41	10.04	11.60	13.11

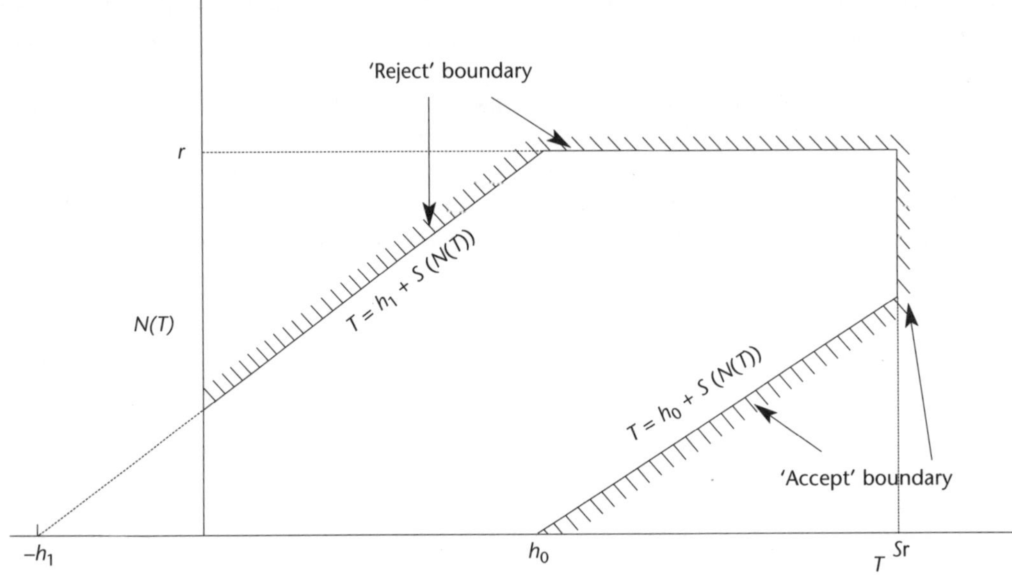

Figure 9.12 Sequential testing boundaries for failure/time plot

the decision lines. If the plot crosses the 'accept' line, the system is accepted as meeting the reliability requirement. If it crosses the 'reject' line, the system is rejected as unacceptable (meaning 'take it off test and do something to improve its reliability').

For the reject line, the slope is $1/S$ and the intercept on the $N(T)$ axis is h_1/S.

For the accept line, the slope is again $1/S$ and the intercept on the T axis is h_0.

The equation of the accept line is therefore:

$$T = h_0 + S(N(T))$$

and the equation of the reject line is:

$$T = -h_1 + S(N(T))$$

To avoid the risk of testing for a very long time, as might happen with a system whose true failure rate was somewhere between λ_1 and λ_2, the test envelope is truncated as shown, with the reject line truncated at a maximum of r failures and the accept line truncated at a maximum test time of Sxr.

The parameters for a required test plan are given by:

$$h_0 = \frac{\ln\left(\frac{1-\alpha}{\beta}\right)}{\lambda_2 - \lambda_1}$$

$$h_1 = \frac{\ln\left(\frac{1-\beta}{\alpha}\right)}{\lambda_2 - \lambda_1}$$

$$S = \frac{\ln\left(\frac{\lambda_2}{\lambda_1}\right)}{\lambda_2 - \lambda_1}$$

To determine *r*, it is necessary to use Chi-square tables, or sampling tables derived from them. A suitable table is Table 9.2 (where the tabulated values are $\chi^2_{ß} / \chi^2_{(1-\alpha)}$ with 2*r* degrees of freedom). In this table, identify the column referring to the α and ß values required, and find the highest row where the tabulated number is smaller than λ_2/λ_1. This identifies *r*.

As an example, we will define an SPRT that will give a 95 per cent chance of acceptance if the MTBF is 250 hours, and a 10 per cent chance of acceptance if the MTBF is 100 hours. This defines the test requirements as:

$\lambda_1 = 1/250 = 0.004$ failures per hour
$\lambda_2 = 1/100 = 0.01$ failures per hour
$\alpha = 0.05 \quad ß = 0.10$

so

$h_0 = ln\ 9.5/0.006 = 375.2$ hours
$h_1 = ln\ 18/0.006 = 481.7$ hours
$S = ln\ 2.5/0.006 = 152.7$ hours per failure.

Table 9.2 Limiting values of λ_2/λ_1 for producer's risk α, consumer's risk ß and rejection number *r* (to give truncation points for sequential testing)

r	α	*0.05*	*0.05*	*0.05*	*0.01*	*0.01*	*0.01*
	ß	*0.010*	*0.05*	*0.01*	*0.10*	*0.05*	*0.01*
1		44.89	58.40	89.78	229.1	298.1	458.2
2		10.94	13.35	18.68	26.18	31.93	44.69
3		6.509	7.699	10.28	12.21	14.44	19.28
4		4.890	5.675	7.352	8.115	9.418	12.20
5		4.057	4.646	5.890	6.249	7.156	9.072
6		3.549	4.023	5.017	5.195	5.889	7.343
7		3.206	3.604	4.435	4.520	5.052	6.253
8		2.957	3.303	4.019	4.050	4.524	5.506
9		2.768	3.074	3.707	3.705	4.115	4.962
10		2.618	2.895	3.462	3.440	3.803	4.548
11		2.497	2.750	3.265	3.229	3.555	4.222
12		2.397	2.630	3.104	3.058	3.354	3.959
13		2.312	2.528	2.968	2.915	3.188	3.742
14		2.240	2.442	2.852	2.795	3.047	3.559
15		2.177	2.367	2.752	2.692	2.927	3.403
16		2.122	2.302	2.665	2.603	2.823	3.269
17		2.073	2.244	2.588	2.524	2.732	3.151
18		2.029	2.192	2.520	2.455	2.652	3.048
19		1.990	2.145	2.458	2.393	2.580	2.956
20		1.954	2.103	2.403	2.337	2.516	2.874

To obtain r, find the column in Table 9.2 headed by our values of α and ß (which is the first column), and then the highest row for which the tabulated value is less than our discrimination ratio (λ_2/λ_1) of 0.01/0.005 = 2.5. This occurs on the eleventh row, where the tabulated value is 2.497 and r = 11. The failure truncation is accordingly at 11 failures, and the time truncation at Sr = 152.7 x 11 = 1680 hours. The resulting test plan template is shown in Figure 9.13.

NON-CONSTANT FAILURE RATE

The assumption of constant failure rate is a convenient one, in that it gives rise to simple analytical procedures, and is often a valid assumption to make. There are, however, common practical circumstances in which the assumption is invalid, and it is necessary to be aware of these in order to avoid misleading (and usually pessimistic) conclusions.

Departures from constant failure rate can be either in the form of increasing failure rate or decreasing failure rate. These are typified by cumulative failure plots as in Figure 9.14a and 9.14b respectively. Both are due to breakdown of the 'good as new replacement' assumption, invalidating the assumption of IID lifetimes. Increasing failure rate results from 'worse than new' replacements – for instance, due to imperfect repairs of failed items within the system. Reducing failure rates are encountered much more frequently, and are considered in more detail below.

REDUCING FAILURE RATE: BURN-IN AND RELIABILITY GROWTH

Reducing failure rate (as in Figure 9.14b) can be considered as having two distinct causes that both affect a system of given design.

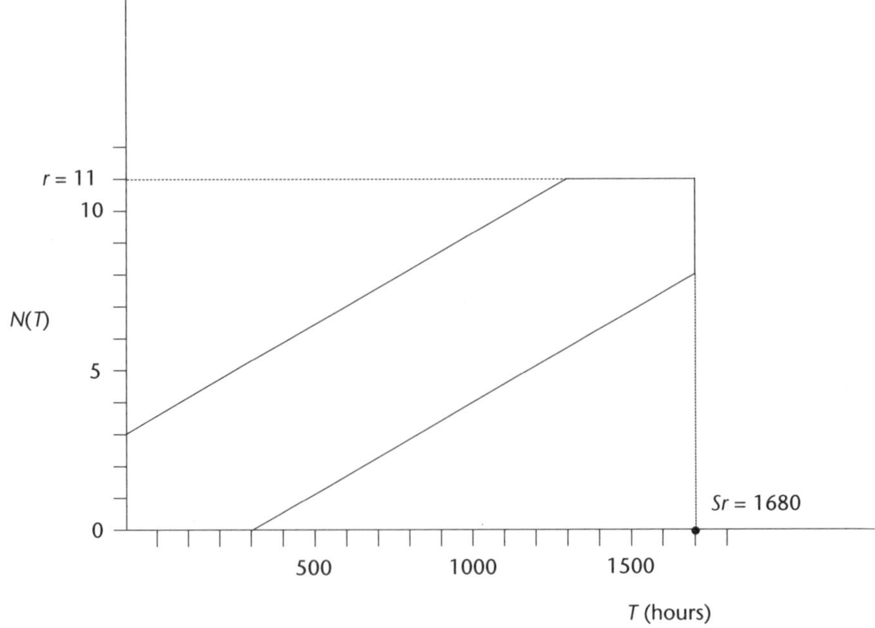

Figure 9.13 Sequential test example

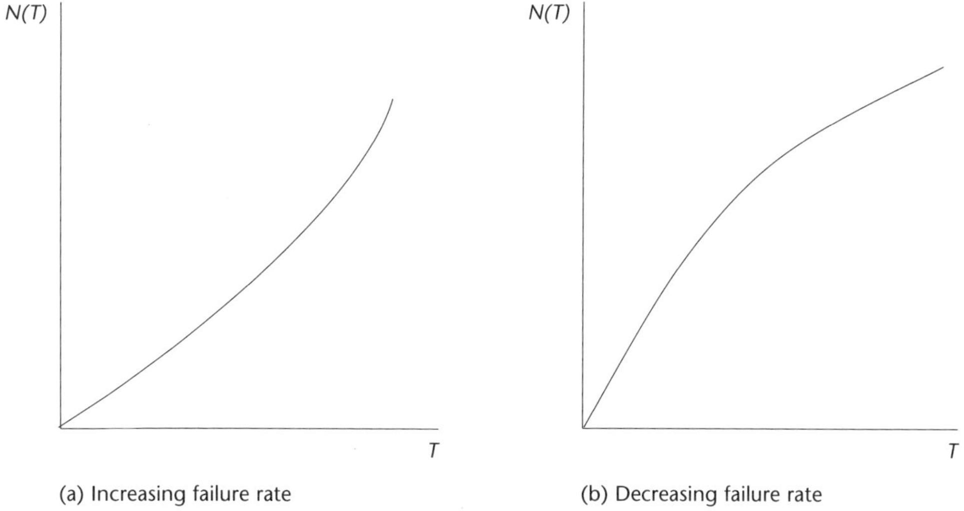

Figure 9.14 Failure/time plots for non-constant failure rates: (a) increasing failure rate, (b) decreasing failure rate

The first aspect is a short-term consideration affecting an individual 'copy' of a system. Consider, for example, a new motor car (or any other new repairable system). In its early life, a common experience is to encounter some initial failures due to shortcomings in manufacture – components that are defective in some way, or errors in assembly such as loose fasteners, misalignments, missed operations and so on. When such failures occur, they are put right by replacing the component or by correcting the assembly error. The 'replacement' (be it a component or an operation) is no longer 'good as new' – it is 'better than new', 'new' in this context having been unsatisfactory. This means that the IID assumption is not valid – the replacement 'good' items will have a lifetime distribution with a higher mean age to failure than that of the failed items. When all such failures have occurred and been corrected, the failure rate will have reduced to a level inherent in the design of the system (which is not necessarily zero).

In many applications (particularly with consumer goods), it is accepted by the manufacturer that such failures occur, and it is unjust to expect the purchaser to pay for any remedial work, so some sort of guarantee is offered (such as the warranty on new motor cars – recently typically for the first 1 year/12 000 miles, but now moving towards 3 years/36 000 miles). In other applications, a different approach is sometimes adopted in that the supplier is expected to 'burn in' the product by operating it, often under accelerated environmental conditions, for sufficient time to provoke all the early failures due to manufacturing shortcomings. This is widely practised, for example, in avionics, and is beginning to appear in consumer electronics, where some suppliers of personal computers use a pre-supply burn-in as a marketing strategy.

Another application of burn-in is that of component screening, often applied in the case of electronic components. Here, a batch of components is subjected to some form of environmental stress. This is usually passive, in that the components are not actually connected in a circuit. Components are inspected after this exposure, and failed ones removed. In the same way as before, components are assumed to fail because they are defective – typical good components are expected to survive the screening process. (The activity has no connection with any assumption of reducing hazard.)

In burn-in, it is obviously critical that the duration and stress are chosen so as to maximize the chance of provoking failure of 'weaklings', yet not reaching a level that causes failures that would not occur in normal operation. A substantial body of theory has developed in this area, for which a recommended reference is Jensen and Petersen (1982).

As well as the reducing failure rate observed in individual copies of a system, it is also to be hoped that the overall failure rates will be lower for later copies of systems than for earlier ones, as a natural consequence of design and development of the system. This is particularly the case in early stages of development – successive prototypes of a system should show rapidly reducing failure rates as design-related failures are encountered and subsequently eliminated through design modifications. It is also to be hoped that this will continue throughout the life of a design. This design-related aspect of 'reliability growth' will be superimposed upon the reducing failure rate for individual systems, the combined effect being shown in Figure 9.15.

Every failure has a cause, and all causes that are design-related should give rise to the consideration of modifications to eliminate them. It is a cause for concern that we sometimes fail to do this. There are several well-known British products in which design defects have been perpetuated, with the unfortunate results that must be expected in a competitive market. Complaining customers might be a nuisance, but they offer invaluable information that should not be lightly ignored.

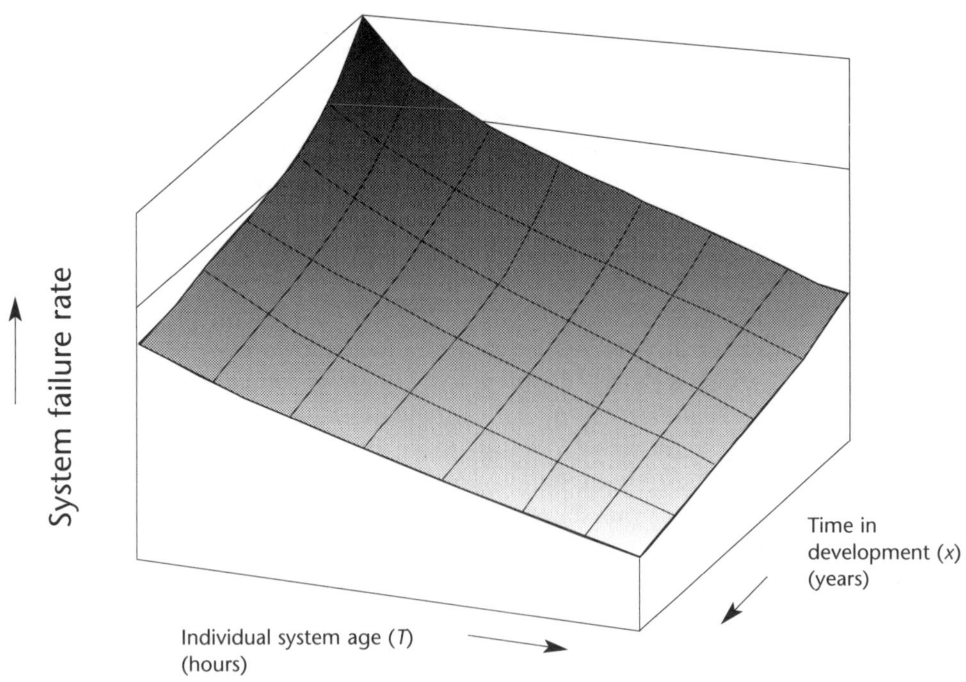

Figure 9.15 System failure rate patterns: Growth and burn-in

RELIABILITY GROWTH MODELLING

The usual occurrence of reliability growth has implications for reliability testing. In particular, if we performed an analysis of the type described in the example under the constant failure rate assumption in the presence of reliability growth, it would only show the current high level of early failures, and would not make any allowance for future improvement. In response to this, there have been various attempts to model reliability growth mathematically with the twin objectives of measuring the rate of growth and predicting future reliability.

The first, and still the most widely applied, reliability growth model is the Duane model which has more recently been adapted into an updated form known as the AMSAA model, which forms the basis of US specification MIL-STD-189 (14). It can be related to the constant failure rate case as follows:

	Constant failure rate	*AMSAA model*
Failure rate at cumulative time T	λ	$\lambda \beta T^{(\beta - 1)}$
Cumulative failures at time T ($N(T)$)	λT	λT^{β}

The growth parameter measures the rate at which the failure rate is reducing. It can be seen that $\beta = 1$ is the constant failure rate case. A value of around 0.4 would indicate an active and effective reliability improvement programme, and 0.8 would indicate the sort of 'creeping' improvement that would occur without too much effort. For those familiar with the original Duane method, $1 - \beta$ is the same as Duane's α, and λ is the same as Duane's K.

Example

This is the result of a 'test, analyse and fix' reliability growth demonstration on four systems. The four systems started their lives simultaneously, and the data give the system age at which failures occurred. We want to know whether growth is occurring, and see if there is any likelihood of this system eventually meeting a target MTBF of 100 hours.

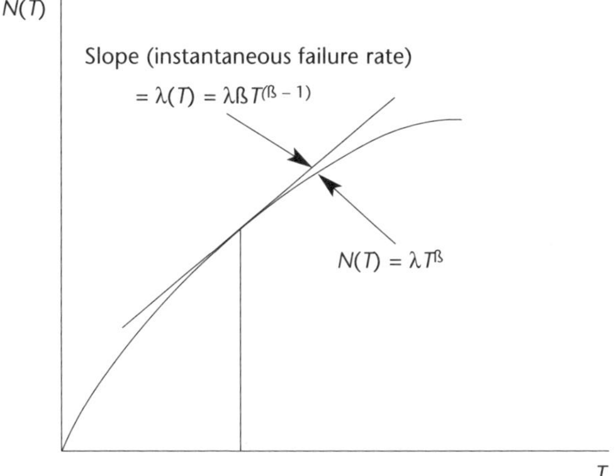

Figure 9.16 AMSAA reliability growth model

System	*Cumulative hours at which failures occurred*
1	4, 34, 38, 52, 76, 104, 202, 282, (300)
2	0.6, 20, 24, 30, 82, 174, (240)
3	6, 10, 22, 28, 46, 102, 132, 158, 226, (240)
4	1.8, 10, 12, 18, 34, 38, 106, 142, (200)

Figures in parentheses are current unfailed hours accumulated for each system.

As the systems started their lives simultaneously, we assume a common origin for their lives. (This is in contrast to the previous example in Figure 9.10, where it was more sensible to assume a common termination point.) On this assumption, the cumulative hours over all four systems at which failures occurred, assuming a common origin, are therefore 2.4, 7.2, 16, 24, 40, 40, 48, 72, 80, 88, 96, 112, 120, 136, 136, 152, 152, 184, 208, 304, 328, 408, 424, 456, 528, 578, 632, 696, 806, 878 and 962 hours, with a total time on test of 980 hours. The failure/time plot (Figure 9.17) shows a clearly reducing trend, so growth is present.

There are two ways in which to estimate β:

1 **Graphical** – Plot the cumulative failures against cumulative failure time as in Figure 9.18, but on log versus log graph paper. The slope of the line gives the estimate for β.
2 **Algebraic** –
Denote the cumulative time at the *i*th failure T_i
Denote the total cumulative hours T_0
Total number of failures = *n*.
Calculate *S*, the sum of the natural logarithms of all the failure times (T_i)

$$S = \ln 2.4 + \ln 7.2 + \ln 16 + \ln 24 \ldots + \ln 962$$
$$= 0.875 + 1.974 + 2.773 + 3.178 \ldots + 6.869$$
$$= 153.336$$

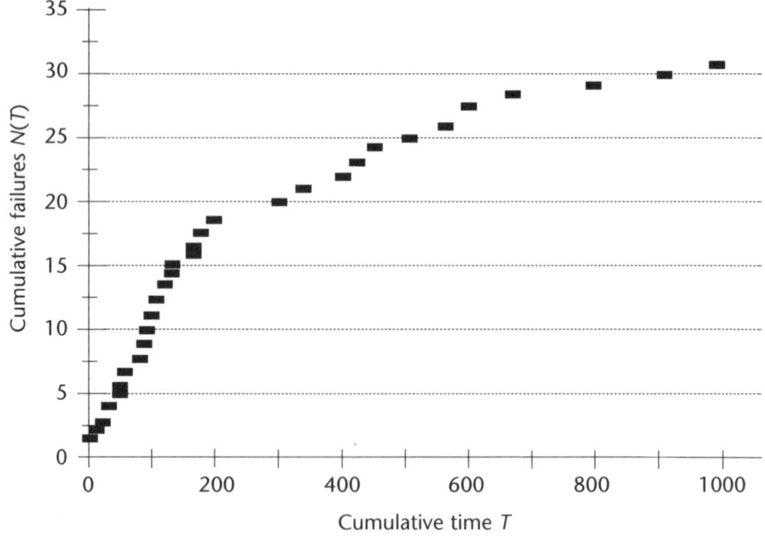

Figure 9.17 Failure/time plot showing reliability growth

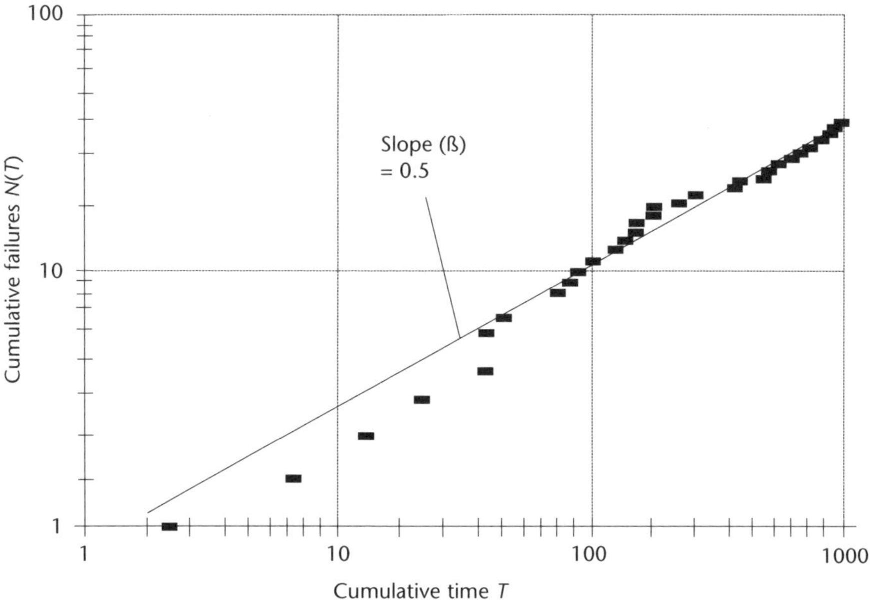

Figure 9.18 AMSAA plot using data from Figure 9.17, plotted on a log versus log graph

β is given by:

$$n/\ (n\ln T_0 - S)$$
$$= 31/\ (31\ \ln 980 - 153.336)$$
$$= 31/60.18 = 0.515$$

which indicates moderate growth.

However β is estimated, we can now estimate λ using

$$\lambda = n/T_0{}^{\beta}$$

thus $\lambda = 31/980^{0.515} = 0.893$

and the failure rate at any value of the cumulative hours T using:

$$\lambda\ (T) = ßT^{(ß-1)}$$

For example, at the current total time of 980 hours, the failure rate estimate is:

$0.893 \times 0.515 \times 980^{-0.485}$
$= 0.0163$ failures per hour
(MTBF = 1/0.0163 = 61.39 hours)

This result can be compared with that obtained by wrongly assuming constant failure rate, where:

$$\text{MTBF} = T_0/n = 980/31 = 31.6 \text{ hours.}$$

By omitting to allow for growth we have obtained an MTBF of only half the correct value.

Our target MTBF is 100 hours. We can use the same expression to estimate how much more 'testing, analysing and fixing' is required to improve the reliability to obtain this figure.

The required failure rate ($\lambda(T)$) is 1/100 = 0.01, and we require T.

$$0.01 = 0.893 \times 0.515 \times T^{-0.485}$$
$$T^{0.485} = 46.00$$
$$T = 2683 \text{ hours}$$

so we estimate that we will have to keep on running these systems, finding failures and eliminating their causes, at the same intensity of effort, until the total accumulated time is 2683 hours.

Further reading

BOOKS

Introductory books available in paperback

Bentley, J.P., *An Introduction to Reliability and Quality Engineering*, Longman, London, 1993.

Davidson, J. (ed.), *The Reliability of Mechanical Systems*, MEP (Institution of Mechanical Engineers), London, 1988. (A companion video to this text, *Weibull Reliability Analysis: Technique and Applications*, is also available from the IMechE.)

O'Connor, P.D.T., *Practical Reliability Engineering*, Student Edition, 3rd edn (Revised), J. Wiley, Chichester, 1995.

Smith, David J., *Reliability, Maintainability and Risk*, 4th edn, Butterworth-Heinemann, Oxford, 1993.

Publications dealing with specific aspects in detail

For FMEA:

BS 5760: Part 5 (see below)

Society of Motor Manufacturers and Traders, *SMMT Guidelines to Failure Mode and Effect Analysis*, SMMT, London, 1989 (available from SMMT, Forbes House, Halkin Street, London SW1X 7DS).

For fault trees:

Barlow, R., Fussell, J.B. and Singpurwalla, N.D., *Reliability and Fault Tree Analysis*, Society for Industrial and Applied Mathematics, Philadelphia, PA, 1975.

Martin, J., *Systems Performance: Human Factors and Systems Failures*, Open University Press, Milton Keynes, 1976 (this publication includes the IEEE [US] Standard 352-1975, *IEEE Guide for General Principles of Reliability Analysis of Nuclear Power Generating Station Protection Systems*).

For component reliability analysis:

Nelson, W., *Applied Life Data Analysis*, J. Wiley, Chichester, 1982.

For repairable systems reliability:

Ascher, H.E. and Feingold, H., *Repairable Systems Reliability: Modelling, Inference, Misconceptions and Their Causes*, Marcel Dekker, New York, 1984.

For burn-in:

Jensen, F. and Petersen, N.E., *Burn-in: An Engineering Approach to the Design and Analysis of Burn-in Procedures*, J. Wiley, Chichester, 1982.

STANDARDS

British

The principal British Standard on Reliability is BS 5760. This currently runs to 23 parts. Many of these are re-issues of earlier IEC reliability specifications. A visit to the BSI Web site (<http://www.bsi-global.com/index.xalter>) will provide a detailed list of what subjects are covered and what is under development. For initial reading, useful references are:

BS 5760-3: 1982, *Guide to Reliability Practices – Examples.*
BS 5760-5: 1991, *Guide to Failure Modes, Effects and Criticality Analysis (FMEA and FMECA).*

BS 5760 is continually being updated. For initial reading, Parts 3 and 5 are recommended. Part 5 is particularly useful in showing a variety of different FMEA layouts that have been used in real applications.

American

MIL-HDBK-217F-2, *Reliability Prediction of Electronic Equipment.*
MIL-STD-781C, *Reliability Design Qualification and Production Acceptance Tests: Exponential Distribution.*
MIL-HDBK-189, *Reliability Growth Management.*
MIL-SD-1629A, *Procedures for Performing a Failure Mode, Effects and Criticality Analysis.*

JOURNALS

Reliability is an active and developing subject, with areas of controversy. Textbooks rapidly become outdated, and continual reference to the journals is necessary to keep up to date. Many of the papers are highly academic and over-specialized, but there is usually a leavening of papers of more general interest. There is also much to be gained from the editorials and letters to the editor. In the UK, the main journal is:

Quality and Reliability Engineering International, published bimonthly by Wiley.
IEEE Transactions in Reliability (an American monthly journal) also carries a large number of papers covering a wide spread of applications, and has a reputation for particularly pointed editorials.

CHAPTER 10 Materials Handling

John Oxley

In any industrial context, handling, storage and delivery do not operate independently of each other or of their embracing function of logistics and supply chain management. This chapter therefore places these activities within the wider context of logistics and supply chain management, and develops their objectives from the overall objectives of logistics systems. The general thrust of these objectives is towards the control and reduction of overall system costs, while maintaining and improving standards of customer service. This chapter then suggests that these objectives will determine what a quality system for handling, storage and delivery activities should encompass, and what it should seek to define and monitor. The chapter concludes with comments on the implications of quality systems for these activities.

Introduction

LOGISTICS

Logistics and the management of supply chains encompass the planning, monitoring, and control of the movement of goods and materials into and through an enterprise, and the onward supply of finished products to the customers. Within a supplying company, logistics can encompass material procurement and storage, material flow and control through manufacturing and assembly operations, and the warehousing and distribution of finished product to the customer. It also includes intermediate work-in-progress handling and storage operations, and materials and inventory management. Consequently, the concept of integrating all these activities to optimize system performance is important, and this includes the use of integrated information systems to enable effective management and control.

Logistics is now widely recognized as a vital function within the context of industrial activity and management, and one which has a direct impact on at least two key business parameters: costs and customer service.

In any enterprise logistics activities consume considerable resources and require management time and effort. Some activities are labour-intensive, buildings and handling and storage equipment are required for the accommodation and handling of stocks, transport facilities are used to move goods along the supply chain from production to the customers, information and control systems are needed for effective management, and working capital is tied up as inventory. Consequently, there is a significant cost on the enterprise.

In addition to the cost implications, the quality of logistics performance has a direct and immediate impact on the levels of customer service achieved. If the component activities within the supply chain are not planned and managed effectively, the consequences can include late, incomplete or inaccurate order fulfilment, with resulting loss of credibility in the marketplace, and loss of business. Effective management and control is therefore vital.

It follows from the above that one of the overriding objectives of logistics management is to satisfy customer requirements in a cost-effective manner. Indeed, for many companies, continuing improvement in logistics performance is seen as the primary means of achieving competitive edge.

These considerations represent much of the driving philosophy behind logistics management, and have resulted in significant improvements in performance over recent years. The pressures for cost reduction continue, with the prerequisite condition that key performance parameters such as customer service must be at least maintained, and preferably improved. Any courses of action which help to improve performance and increase the confidence of customers in their suppliers, including such developments as supply chain partnerships, are seen as adding to marketplace competitiveness.

In this context, accepted and verified standards of quality as applied to the systems, control and management of logistics functions provide important motivation for monitoring and improving performance, and can also be seen as enhancing a company's image and competitiveness in relation to its customers. Taken a stage further, many businesses, and some public sector organizations, now require their suppliers or potential suppliers to obtain recognized standards of quality performance, such as ISO 9001 certification, and refuse to trade with them unless this requirement is met. There is also international pressure through the European Union for this standard.

Supplier companies are consequently recognizing the potential benefits or even the necessity of moving in this direction, and the penalties of not doing so. This trend will undoubtedly continue as European integration continues.

HANDLING, STORAGE AND DELIVERY OPERATIONS

The component functions which make up logistics and supply chain management include materials management and physical distribution. Key activities within physical distribution include the handling, storage and delivery of goods and materials, and it is these which form the subject of this chapter. It follows from the previous discussion that the detailed roles and objectives of handling, storage and delivery must ultimately be determined by the overall role and objectives of the logistics supply chain of which they are an integral part.

Within the overall function of logistics, the specific activities of handling, storage and delivery are major consumers of resources and time and they cost money. If not properly planned and managed, they will adversely affect the performance of the logistics function in terms of cost-effectiveness, resource utilization, and customer service. Hence there is a vital need for quality standards in the management and control of these activities if they are to function in the most effective way within the overall logistics function.

Over recent years, there have been a number of developments in the technology, planning, management and control of the activities of handling, storage and delivery of goods, and there have been continuing pressures to improve performance.

Technological developments in handling and storage have led to increasing levels of mechanization, progressing on to automation and robotic applications. These have had implications in terms of stock integrity and the maintenance of product quality, in reduced manual handling, in the accuracy and speed of materials handling, and in functions like the loading of vehicles prior to delivery of goods to customers.

Developments in computer-based information systems to manage and control physical distribution activities have resulted in dramatic improvements in operational, cost and customer service performance. They have enabled much faster and more accurate information handling, more immediate and up-to-date information, product traceability, and improved utilization of people and equipment. These developments have facilitated more effective operational planning of storage and handling operations, of load scheduling and routeing of vehicles for customer delivery, and have influenced the design of packaging to make the most effective use of handling and storage systems and the consolidating of goods into unit loads.

To an extent, these evolutionary developments have gone hand in hand, since it is the introduction of good management practices supported by effective information systems and appropriate technology which have enabled progress to be made in improving cost-effectiveness and the utilization of resources, and in achieving better customer service.

The thrust towards quality management systems imposes requirements for defined and recognized quality standards and quality accreditation for industrial and commercial enterprises. However, the standards required are no higher than those which should already be in place for the most effective management of an operation. The difference when achieving registration under ISO 9001 lies in the need to define, record and formalize the systems of good practice, and to be able to monitor and demonstrate that the required levels of quality performance are in place and are being achieved.

This is particularly important for companies in the business of logistics and supply chain management. The effectiveness of their operations has an immediate impact on the quality of service provided to their customers. Consequently, there is a need for effective, defined and validated management and information systems. There is also a caveat – which is that these systems must be compatible with, and derive from, the overall business plans and objectives if they are to avoid the pitfall of suboptimizing the subsystems.

OBJECTIVES OF HANDLING, STORAGE AND DELIVERY OPERATIONS

The objectives of handling, storage and delivery in the context of logistics can be summarized in the long-established and often quoted statement of requirements:

> to get the right goods, in the right quantities and condition, to the right place, at the right time in a cost-effective manner.

In other words, this means meeting customer service requirements. This statement encapsulates the essential customer service elements of timely, complete and accurately fulfilled orders. However, service increasingly includes additional concepts:

- effective communication between supplier and customer in terms of speed and accuracy of relevant information
- availability and transfer of relevant information between supplier and customer, including such things as material requirements, stock availability, and the status of orders in hand

- flexibility in the supplier's response to customer requirements
- traceability of customer orders and of goods
- monitoring of customer complaints and returns, and appropriate response.

In addition to primary objectives for meeting customer service requirements, however specified, other objectives for handling, storage and delivery operations are likely to include some or all of the following:

- stock management, including meeting conditions imposed by sell-by dates, stock rotation and 'first in first out', shelf line, and material quality standards
- product protection, and maintenance of product integrity
- condition monitoring, and ensuring that environmental requirements are met
- batch and lot tracking and traceability
- identification of product loss or damage
- monitoring and control of costs, which can include:
  - inventory, working capital
  - handling and storage, buildings, equipment, labour
  - transport (trunking), vehicles and drivers
  - transport (local distribution), vehicles and drivers
  - systems operation and maintenance.

These objectives of the handling, storage and delivery activities define the requirements of quality management, and identify those aspects of the management of these activities which should be defined, documented, monitored and recorded to ensure the required quality of performance.

What do handling, storage and delivery operations involve?

Before exploring aspects of quality for handling, storage and delivery activities, it is appropriate to give a more detailed description of what they comprise and how they operate. They can involve different levels of technology, from the manual movement and handling of goods to mechanized or automated handling and storage.

An example which brings all these activities together within a supply chain context is the operation of a finished-goods warehouse, as illustrated in Figure 10.1. This shows on the right of the diagram the flow of material through such a warehouse, involving various handling and storage activities, and culminating in packaging and labelling operations prior to vehicle loading and delivery of goods to customers.

Some of the principal flows of information are also shown on the right of the diagram, driven by the receipt of customer orders to be fulfilled, and replenished by purchase orders for goods from in-house or external suppliers. It is emphasized that a prerequisite condition for the successful operation of any storage and handling system is an effective information and management system.

Typical operations can include:

- unloading incoming goods from vehicles
- unpacking and restacking of goods

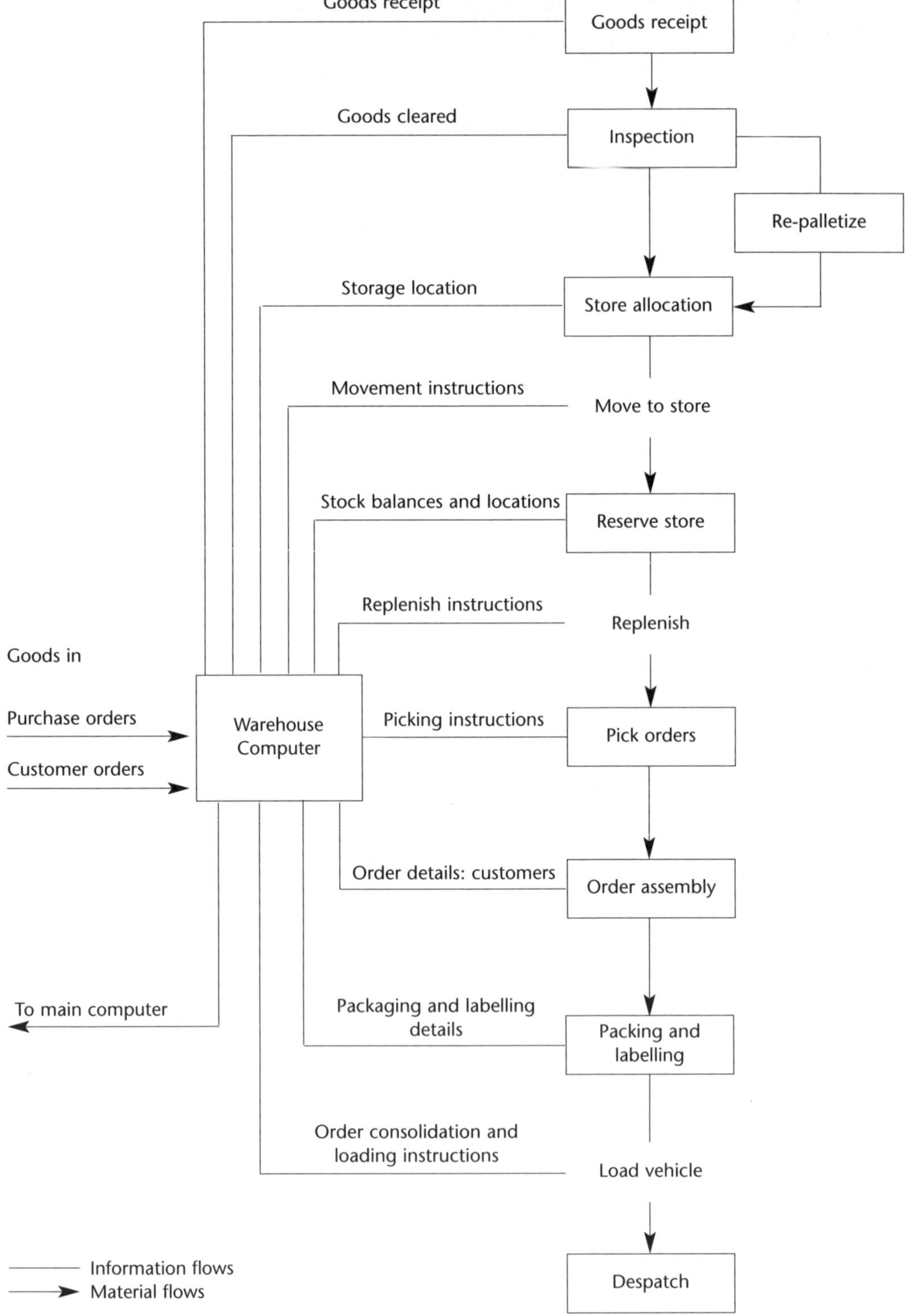

Figure 10.1 Material and information flows in warehouse systems

- inspection for correct quantity of correct goods, and for damage
- putting goods into reserve storage racking or other storage media
- break bulk or order picking operations selecting individual items from stock to make up customer order
- replenishment of break bulk stock from reserve stock
- collation of goods into orders
- packing into despatch packaging
- labelling
- load marshalling by vehicle load
- loading goods to vehicles
- delivery to customers' premises
- unloading and moving at customers' premises.

In the context of handling, storage and delivery, information and records are vital for monitoring and control, for ensuring performance to required standards, and for validating performance measures. This is clearly compatible with the requirements of any quality management system.

Examples of poor performance

There are some types of error and examples of substandard performance to which physical distribution activities are prone. They illustrate some of the more common situations which an effective quality management system can help to obviate.

Because of the physical and often labour-intensive nature of handling, storage and delivery activities, there is always the risk of damage to goods, and of accidents – when moving goods into or out of storage, or when loading and unloading vehicles. This can arise through the use of inappropriate handling and storage techniques, or when pressure is being exerted to carry out work to tight order or delivery time schedules, leading to short cuts or misuse of equipment. It can also occur if equipment is not properly maintained and fails or performs inadequately in service. Another consequence of equipment non-availability is delay to the movement of goods, and possibly to order completion.

Information systems are vital to effective system performance. Inadequate systems can cause significant failures. A common example is the incorrect location or recording of the location of goods when put away in a storage system. In such cases, when the goods are required (usually to enable a customer order to be completed), the system 'thinks' the goods are in a different location from their actual location. This often results in a late delivery or the despatch of an incomplete order.

Handling of goods for order selection depends on accurate order information presented to the operating staff in correct sequence. Inadequate information systems can lead to incomplete, inaccurate and delayed orders, and even to incorrect packaging and labelling.

A further example resulting from a poor information system is stock deterioration through exceeding shelf life, or failure to meet stock rotation or 'sell-by date' requirements.

A final example, also due to an inadequate information system, is the inability to advise customers quickly about the status of their orders, or to warn them in the event of delays.

All the above examples – and indeed others – can lead to poor performance, with implications for costs, utilization of people and resources, stock management, and customer service. The consequences can include loss of orders and loss of customers. There are examples of companies that have gone out of business through just such problems. More encouragingly, there are companies that have recovered from near failure by reforming and formalizing their distribution management and information systems with the direct aims of achieving their overall objectives and quality in their management and operating systems.

Quality monitoring

Following on from the objectives already discussed and the description of typical operations involved in handling, storage and delivery, the requirements for a quality system can be summarized as:

- ensuring that customer requirements are met in a cost-effective way
- managing people, inventory and resources efficiently in achieving customer service.

Expanding these concepts out to a detailed operational level, the following subsections specify the principal factors which will influence the ability of the system to meet the objectives, and which should therefore be recorded and monitored as part of any quality system. The list is not exhaustive, and every individual application must be examined in the light of its own particular requirements.

CUSTOMER SERVICE

Requisite information on service performance should be recorded so that service standards can be monitored and failures in performance identified and rectified. Typical records will include:

- numbers of complete orders despatched to time
- analysis of incomplete or inaccurate orders, with reasons
- analysis of delayed orders with reasons
- record of orders outstanding
- analysis of specific product shortages with reasons
- record and analysis of returned or damaged goods
- record and analysis of customer complaints.

MATERIALS RECEIPT, LOCATION, AND INVENTORY MANAGEMENT

The principal concern here is to ensure that required goods will be available (in stock) when they are needed to meet customer orders, at known locations in the system. The condition and integrity of stock must be maintained to specified standards. The records which will enable these factors to be monitored (and which should be as up to date and accurate as possible) include:

- product identification references and codes
- lot and batch identification codes
- quantities and condition of the goods received

- records of when stock items were received into the system, with sell-by dates, stock rotation or shelf-life requirements as appropriate
- stock balances, to minimize the probability of stockouts
- locations for all individual stock items, probably using location codes.

STOCK INTEGRITY AND CONDITION MONITORING

The condition and integrity of stock handled and stored is one of the responsibilities of management, and records to monitor these factors include:

- condition monitoring, including records of environmental conditions of storage where relevant, such as temperatures and humidity, standards of housekeeping and cleanliness
- loss levels, measured by the difference between recorded stock balances and physical stock checks.

STOCK ISSUES, ORDER ASSEMBLY, PACKING AND LABELLING

The main tasks to be achieved are to bring together the correct goods to make up specific order requirements, and to ensure that they are then packed and labelled correctly. The packaging and labelling requirements must be known, including such factors as order and shipping information, handling instructions, and hazard classifications and warnings, where appropriate. Typical records would include:

- numbers of orders assembled
- product lines and units issued
- details of stock shortages encountered
- the individual(s) responsible for each order.

ORDER DELIVERY

This aspect is concerned with the efficient use of delivery systems, with vehicle routeing and utilizations, and with ensuring satisfactory delivery of orders to customers. Parameters to monitor will include:

- vehicle utilizations
- vehicle maintenance and availability
- vehicle performance, fuel usage
- proof of order delivery
- security of vehicles and stock.

THE MANAGEMENT OF PEOPLE

Personnel performance can obviously have a great impact on quality. Records to monitor that staff are well managed and are performing effectively may include:

- measures of performance, such as units handled or orders fulfilled per unit time
- overtime records

- sickness and absence records
- staff turnover
- safety records and analysis of accidents and causes
- training carried out.

UTILIZATION OF EQUIPMENT AND OTHER RESOURCES

The management, use and condition of equipment is important in physical distribution, and in addition to ensuring that the appropriate type and capacity of equipment is being used for particular tasks, a quality system should monitor equipment performance in terms of:

- how effectively equipment is utilized
- service and maintenance tasks carried out, and any repairs required
- equipment availability and out-of-service time
- delays, damage or accidents involving equipment.

Quality systems

Quality management within an organization establishes guidelines for sound management practice. The philosophy underlying quality systems is to identify potential problems or poor or falling performance levels relating to the business enterprise, and to prevent them.

Key steps for establishing quality systems include:

- statement of policy and objectives
- defining the organization structure and areas of responsibility
- identifying key activities and operations within the organization, including how the organization relates and interacts with its customers
- defining and documenting specific operating methods and procedures and control mechanisms using accepted best practice
- setting out clear instructions on how they are to be carried out, and ensuring that these instructions are put into practice
- setting specific performance standards and corrective measures if performance falls below standard
- devising appropriate recording systems
- defining and implementing the necessary staff training.

These steps should be incorporated into an action plan, and prerequisites for establishing quality systems in any organization must include total commitment from senior management.

In the context of handling, storage and delivery activities, the systems and procedures which would be required for the monitoring and management of quality relate directly to the areas for monitoring described previously:

- customer service
- materials receipts, location and inventory management

- stock integrity and condition monitoring
- stock issues, order assembly, packing and labelling
- order delivery
- the management of people
- utilization of equipment and other resources.

There are various computer-based packages for use in the planning and management of handling and storage systems to optimize the utilization of people and equipment, and for vehicle route planning and loading for delivery. The functionality which these packages incorporate provides an invaluable information handling tool for quality management.

The ISO 9000 quality systems standard

European distribution operations are moving towards the international ISO 9001 quality systems standard. The main issues set out in this standard are described below.

The overall approach should be that all handling of goods and materials is properly planned and controlled, and systems put in place to ensure that the plans are monitored and effectively implemented. Suppliers of goods and materials must preserve the conformity of product during internal processing and delivery.

There should be defined controls, and probably documented systems for recording and checking all goods and materials coming into an enterprise, all materials in process, and all finished goods. This should apply along the whole supply chain, including delivery operations, and in some circumstances up to the time when the finished goods or materials are put into use.

HANDLING

Suppliers should implement handling methods and procedures, including the use of appropriate handling equipment, that prevent damage and deterioration to goods and materials, provide safe and secure handling, and prevent contamination. In circumstances where special handling is required for hazardous materials, appropriate special methods and procedures should be identified, documented and adopted. These requirements apply to handling in and through the supply chain, including the loading and unloading of vehicles.

Documented instructions and training requirements for safe and appropriate handling methods aimed at preventing injury to people and damage to goods and materials should be seriously considered.

Handling and storage operations have the potential to cause damage to goods and materials from shock, vibration, abrasion, corrosion, temperature and other potentially adverse conditions. The methods of handling and storage should therefore make use of suitable pallets, containers or other unit loads, and also appropriate handling equipment, such as conveyors, industrial trucks and vehicles.

STORAGE

Suppliers are required to provide secure and appropriate storage areas or stock rooms to prevent damage or deterioration to goods and materials prior to use or delivery. Appropriate methods and procedures for authorizing receipt and despatch into and out of such storage areas should be drawn up and used. Where appropriate, it will be necessary to implement procedures to ensure particular security requirements.

There should also be systems to detect any deterioration of stock, including monitoring the condition of stock at appropriate intervals. This monitoring should cover matters such as stock rotation, shelf life, and 'sell-by', 'use-by' or 'best-before' dates.

Storage methods and systems used should take account of any special conditions which may be required for particular stored goods and materials. Examples include limitations on stack heights to prevent crushing, special lighting for light-sensitive stock, segregation or special conditions for hazardous materials, separation of incompatible materials, and temperature-controlled storage.

PACKAGING

The packing operations, packaging materials used and the preservation and marking processes must be under the control of the suppliers of goods and materials, at least to the extent that they can ensure that the specified packaging requirements are being met.

All packaging details for goods and materials should be specified and documented. This will include cleaning requirements (where relevant), preservation and protection methods (such as packing and cushioning techniques and materials), crating, moisture elimination or control, or any other special measures needed.

An important feature of packaging is the identification of goods and materials, and the communication of such factors as special handling instructions, and hazard warnings and emergency actions. This involves marking the packaging. All such marking or labelling should be readily visible, legible and to specification. The methods of identification chosen should also be sufficiently durable to withstand the environmental conditions to be encountered in the supply chain from initial receipt to final destination. They must also be sufficient to identify a particular product in event of recall, or if special inspection becomes necessary.

DELIVERY

The responsibilities of a supplier include the preservation of the quality or integrity of goods and materials during delivery operations to final destination. This includes ensuring use of the appropriate packaging and protection. Procedures should be specified for items with a limited shelf life, or which require special protection in transit, to ensure their delivery in good condition. The procedures should also ensure that any items that have deteriorated are identified and withdrawn.

There might be occasions when it is appropriate to use specialist carriers who have particular expertise in the delivery of sensitive or hazardous goods.

USE OF CONTRACT WAREHOUSING

The considerations set out above for handling and storage will also apply to contract warehousing in the supply chain which is not under the direct control of suppliers. Procedures and work instructions for the contract operator should cover all handling, storage, packaging and delivery aspects.

The impact of quality systems on handling, packaging, storage and delivery operations

For any supplier of goods and materials, the management of handling, packaging, storage and delivery operations can influence its overall performance for good or for ill. Internal factors include cost-efficiency and the optimum use of resources. Externally, customer perception is one of the obvious important factors.

INTERNAL

Setting up quality systems involves a process of internal examination or audit, of clarifying objectives, of defining internal systems and good practice, and of setting standards and targets. This establishes a discipline of defined and understood working methods and procedures which embody the best standards and codes of practice. It should lead to higher levels of performance through monitoring and benchmarking, recognition of areas where further improvement can be achieved, and potential for improved staff motivation.

EXTERNAL

The adoption of formally drawn up and applied quality management systems, while demanded by some customers, can also present to other customers and potential customers an image of an effectively managed and committed organization with defined objectives and monitored performance targets. This helps to retain existing customers, and gives additional strength when negotiating for new customers. It therefore increases growth potential: in other words, it is a powerful marketing tool.

The role of information technology

A quality system requires the recording and availability of accurate and timely information, and the transfer of information between stages within a logistics supply chain. This is an obvious application for computer-based information handling. Many companies now use electronic data interchange within and between organizations. Using electronic data interchange, orders can be placed and invoiced, information on available stock and order status can be exchanged, and the movement and shipping of goods can be planned, monitored and reported.

The benefits of computer-based information technology in this sort of situation include:

- reduced clerical effort and paper flow
- reduction in data re-entry
- greater accuracy
- immediacy of information
- fast response time
- closer relationships with trading partners
- improved customer service
  - fewer stockouts
  - less mislaid stock

  - availability of order status information
- better utilization of people and equipment
- improved management planning and control.

Clearly, this has a direct impact on operational efficiency and costs, on the quality of business performance, and on reliability and customer service. In fact, without the facility in information-handling resulting from the use of computer technology, many of the performance improvements seen over recent years, including quality systems, would have been at a lower level, and much more difficult to achieve.

Conclusion

Systems for quality management are of vital importance in the handling, storage and delivery of goods and materials, if for no other reason than that these operations tend to be costly and have a direct impact on reputation and customer service. Quality systems require the identification and documentation of best practice for handling, storage, packaging and delivery operations, monitoring of performance, and taking corrective action where appropriate. They will involve maintenance of the appropriate documentation and records, and will help to identify the requirements for staff training.

Implemented quality management systems will have direct impact on levels of performance in:

- the quality of customer service
- effective and safe handling and storage
- protection of goods and materials against damage and deterioration
- the condition and integrity of stock
- goods receipts and issues
- stock levels
- use and availability of stores and handling equipment
- information and instructions, labelling and marking
- condition and protection of goods and materials during delivery
- vehicle conditions and utilization
- delivery times and consignment confirmations
- proof of delivery
- accuracy and quality of information and records.

Implementing quality systems requires commitment, determination and time, from the top to the bottom of the enterprise. The potential benefits are considerable, and pervade the whole of the enterprise. They add marketing strengths by convincing customers of an effectively managed enterprise. The operational disciplines of defined procedures and benchmarks lead to higher levels of staff motivation and performance.

Further reading

Bellinger, S., 'Quality is a waste of time and money!', *Focus*, Vol. 12, No. 4, 1993.

Betts, J.H., 'The quality challenge', *Focus*, Vol. 8, No. 1, 1989.
Boatman, J., 'Quality in retail distribution', *Focus*, Vol. 8, No. 2, 1989.
Hackett, R.A., 'Quality in commercial vehicle design and development', *Focus*, Vol. 8, No. 3, 1989.
Juran, J.M., *Quality Control Handbook*, 4th edn, McGraw-Hill, New York, 1988.
Rushton, A. and Oxley, J., *Handbook of Logistics and Distribution Management*, Kogan Page, London, 1991.
Short, M., 'Quality in warehousing', *Focus*, Vol. 8, No. 5, 1989.
Smith, C., 'EDI: technology for quality', *Focus*, Vol. 8, No. 4, 1989.
Stebbing, L. *Quality Management in the Service Industry*, Ellis Horwood, Chichester, 1990.

CHAPTER **11**

Servicing

Gordon Staples

All products undergo a further series of processing steps following their final inspection and test in the factory. These additional steps might include packing, storing, shipping, unpacking, installation, usage and servicing. The last of these – servicing – is the subject of this chapter.

Introduction

Servicing includes all the supplier activities associated with ensuring that a product continues to operate in its 'as supplied' condition after it has been put to use by the customer.

Servicing has not previously been an area subject to quality control in the same way as manufacturing. The automotive industry is perhaps the best-known industry in which servicing plays a big part, and has perhaps had more publicity (both good and bad) than most, but there are many other examples of products that require particular attention to servicing. Examples include domestic appliances (washing machines, for instance), central heating and air conditioning installations, and industrial electronic equipment such as telecommunication systems and computers.

The organization of these different servicing operations is quite varied. Most of the organizations that carry out automobile servicing, for example, are not owned by the manufacturers, but are dealers who enter into an agreement (usually with the marketing/distribution arm of the manufacturer) to sell and service that manufacturer's range of products. Such an agreement ties the dealer to working in a particular way. It mandates the manufacturer's assessment of the dealer or provides for on-site surveys, and it sometimes excludes trading in competitors' products, although the dealer may sell second-hand competitors' products and service any vehicle. The dealer, in turn, receives considerable support from the manufacturer. This will include training for all staff who are involved in working on the vehicles and/or all staff who deal directly with customers. It includes help in buying, installing and operating the latest technology in servicing and testing of products. As there is a huge and very profitable spare parts business usually associated with servicing, this may also be heavily supported by the manufacturer in terms of product knowledge for spare parts staff, troubleshooting knowledge and so forth.

Certain manufacturers (for example, the makers of many domestic electrical products such as electric irons and vacuum cleaners) might have only a very small service operation themselves. They would allow a network of dealers to service their products, given the provision of a basic amount of training and product knowledge by the manufacturer and the dealers' guarantee of facilities and resources.

Another example of a servicing arrangement is given by a manufacturer of steam plant control equipment (valves, desuperheaters, thermostats and so on). This company has its own service staff, who go to customers' sites to install, service and repair the equipment. No dealers or third-party organizations are involved, but the scale of the operation is, of course, very much smaller than that of a large automotive or domestic appliance manufacturer.

It will be useful, first of all, to consider an organization that provides a product which will need to be serviced regularly in order to minimize the risk of undue deterioration or failure.

Essential interfaces and support for the service organization

The service organization must obviously decide how often regular servicing is going to be required for each product.

Service intervals on newly developed products are generally somewhat arbitrary at first, but the intervals can be adjusted appropriately as experience is gained of the amount of wear or the types and frequency of failures. It is common, for example, to test domestic gas meters at intervals of several years. However, when data had been collected from a large number of meters which had been in continuous use for many years, it became possible to reduce servicing costs in many cases by allowing longer intervals between services.

Careful recording and collection of data have given rise to similar results in aircraft maintenance and servicing, which is perhaps the industry with the best safety record of all. The very rigorous safety requirements applying to commercial aircraft would imply a fair degree of redundancy in the amount of maintenance and servicing carried out, but this is not, in fact, the case.

The choice of interval for the servicing of any product therefore needs to be made on the basis of good data: not only of measured wear or performance deterioration and failures, but also on the parameters used by the designers, the conditions under which the equipment was designed to be used, legal or other mandatory requirements, safety, and so forth.

There is therefore a very strong need for the servicing personnel to be made aware of the basic design details of a product. The interface between design and servicing has to be well established and maintained.

Consider a company which has products in the field that continue to operate for many years. One particular product type has undergone several developments so that:

- product Mark 1, which was introduced 20 years ago, is still working on some sites
- Mark 2 was introduced 10 years ago, and Mark 3 products have been sold for the last 5 years
- both Mark 2 and Mark 3 include enhancements and are constructed differently from Mark 1, but all require servicing
- some components in Mark 1 fit Mark 2, but not Mark 3
- subassemblies in Mark 3 have replaced combinations of separate components used in Mark 1 and Mark 2, giving Mark 3 a better performance.

It can easily be seen that the product knowledge necessary, the documentation of replacement/equivalent parts, along with serial numbers and data on performance, become quite complex. (This subject is dealt with at greater length in Chapter 13.)

The servicing personnel need to have all such information available to them, they must be trained to be able to understand and deal with it, and the necessary replacement parts and materials have to be available when they are needed. If the servicing activity covers acceptance testing after repair or routine servicing, then, clearly, properly calibrated and maintained test equipment must also be available.

The servicing function requires effective interfaces with design, technical document control, parts provision (manufactured or bought out), calibration, and quality assurance (data collection and analysis).

Organization and resources

It might, or might not, be decided to regard the servicing function as a profit centre of the business. This question and the position of the servicing function within the organization are not discussed in detail here, and in any case these are matters that will depend very largely on the particular circumstances of the company and of the industry in which it operates.

Servicing is often associated with the sales and marketing functions because it is a highly exposed activity, providing a direct customer interface. Servicing is also frequently associated with the engineering function, because the servicing personnel are expected to be technically conversant with the product in all its versions and with its operation and operating environment.

SERVICE STAFF AS AMBASSADORS

Servicing personnel characteristically have to go to a customer's premises, represent their company to the customer, and repair/service/adjust the product causing minimum cost and inconvenience to the customer. They may also have to be diplomats, able to pacify an anxious, impatient or angry customer while working in a difficult technical environment.

FLEXIBILITY AND INVENTIVENESS

The skills demanded of servicing personnel are not limited to being able always to work to a standard procedure. In addition to being chosen for their technical ability, they will have to be innovative in their approach to the problems and environment encountered, capable of dealing personally with product operators or users, and also appear to give proper value for what the customer is paying.

The variety of equipment to be serviced may be so great that particular personnel, or even whole servicing departments in a very large company, might have to specialize in servicing a particular product or limited range of products from the total product spectrum of the company.

Some companies in the author's experience who manufacture and service photocopying equipment engage the services of small subcontractors for one very specific range of products in given geographical areas. Full product training is given to these subcontractors, all of whom are specifically approved, and full instructions (exploded diagrams, sequence of dismantling, trouble-shooting routines and so on) are clearly documented. Colour codes are used for different components to help identify them for ease of repair or replacement. In particular, specific subcontractors are used in countries where a foreign language is spoken. All parties benefit from these arrangements because overall costs are minimized, although initial costs are high for the manufacturer. The customer receives a speedier response from 'local' people and pays less for travel and time.

Of course, not all servicing takes place on the customer's premises. The example used at the start of this chapter – automotive servicing – is one which is usually undertaken in a workshop run by the servicing organization. In this situation, the people responsible for dealing with the customer are generally different from those carrying out the servicing. The workshop environment has all the necessary tools and equipment to hand, and supervision is present to monitor the activities of the servicing personnel or give expert advice when necessary. Interface with spare parts supply is easier, and any problem is passed from the servicing mechanic to the customer-contact people in reception.

Service reports and records

The following parts of this section concentrate mainly on aspects of the considerable amount of useful data that has to be gathered, recorded, digested and used during and after servicing operations.

SERVICING IN A SPECIALLY EQUIPPED WORKSHOP

One of the most contentious topics is the assessment made by a servicing department of a product brought or sent in for service or repair. Perhaps the customer has not maintained the product properly, or the information given to the customer upon purchase of the product was unclear. What faces the customer is extra expense and extended time without the use of the product, along with possible resulting disruption of other arrangements.

To give automotive manufacturers and dealers some credit, they have become much better at ensuring that only the expected servicing will take place, that it will take no longer than promised, and that it will be priced according to a standard rate or scale of charges. Most reputable dealers now go to considerable lengths to keep the customer advised about potential problems: perhaps the brake pads will need attention soon, tyres are nearing the minimum legal tread depth, and so on. Manufacturers have tried to educate customers about preventive action (such as regular servicing), and items like batteries and many engine components now need no servicing whatsoever during their usual life. There is competition among manufacturers, not only on warranty provisions, but on service intervals and on the costs to be borne by the customer. Legislative requirements have also assisted in ensuring more stringent and frequent tests for roadworthiness.

The report prepared by the service engineer stating the extent of servicing or repair needed must have a format and content that can easily be translated into time and money. These are the two factors that the customer particularly values and measures, and are, of course, also useful data to the dealer and the manufacturer.

The other aspects about which the customer is concerned are speed of response (the customer does not want to be kept waiting for a long time while the service people decide what to report) and the experience after the service. (Did they do exactly what they said they would do, and was it effective?)

SERVICE AT A CUSTOMER'S SITE

When an examination, service or repair is carried out at a customer's premises, the engineer should prepare a report on what was done or, if necessary, on what needs to be done at a future visit. If a service or repair has been concluded successfully, common practice requires that a customer's representative is asked to sign the engineer's report to indicate that, as far as they are aware, the work has been carried out to order and that the customer is basically satisfied.

Service reports are typically prepared on standard no-carbon-required (NCR) forms, which the engineer carries as a pad of duplicates or triplicates. The customer is usually given one copy to keep. Such forms often carry information about materials and parts used and the total time spent, to be used later as a basis for charging the customer. The customer's signature in such cases certifies that the customer agrees with the time and materials claimed.

The data collated on service reports are of value to the company for purposes other than cost accounting and administration. Wear measurements of certain components after a given life, or measures of efficiency, power usage or performance are all information that can lead to improved reliability for future versions and designs. Although the conditions of usage are difficult, if not impossible, for the manufacturer to prescribe (let alone control), such measurements are nevertheless of much greater value than those extrapolated from laboratory tests.

Another value of service reports, especially in larger organizations, is seen where an engineer develops a particular method, short cut or knack for dealing with a particular problem. A written description of such procedures in a service report can be of great benefit to colleagues servicing similar equipment. However, there must obviously be a routine mechanism:

1 to ensure that such all such ad hoc techniques are approved by the engineer's superiors
2 to circulate information about the newly approved methods to all the other engineers servicing similar equipment.

One company involved in the servicing of domestic and industrial heating and ventilating control equipment used suggestion schemes to great effect, rewarding the engineers when they came up with innovative solutions.

The engineering design function is undoubtedly the most important internal customer of servicing reports. It should be assumed that the engineers will design a new product in good faith, believing that they have contrived it so that it can be manufactured, tested and serviced as easily as possible. However, the design engineers cannot always know exactly where every product is going to be installed and used. For example, some products might require free space all round to allow withdrawal of long assemblies. A customer might reposition a product after its initial installation by the supplier, or crowd it with other equipment. The original process which the product was designed to perform might have changed (the product might still be operating within its design specification but at the higher, rather than the lower, limits set at the design stage).

Service labels

Some products need to carry service labels on which the engineer must certify that a service has actually been carried out. A familiar example is a car service book, which should be stamped by the servicing garage on each occasion. Other examples include apparatus concerned with safety, such as fire extinguishers, where the possibility of failure cannot be countenanced and regular servicing is usually mandatory.

Product modification during service

A service engineer's duties should include checking to ensure that all essential post-manufacture modifications have been carried out. Some products undergo continual improvement to enhance reliability or safety, and the products in such cases will usually carry modification labels on which modification numbers are stamped or written when they are incorporated.

Service reports should indicate where such modifications have been carried out in the field, and the information can then be recorded against the product entry in the customer's history file at headquarters.

Unscheduled servicing

The points made so far have dealt mainly with scheduled servicing (carrying out servicing at predefined intervals as planned preventive maintenance). However, the service department will also have to carry out unscheduled work to investigate and repair products whenever any unexpected failure occurs. The organization has to provide for being able to receive and register all calls for help from customers in such circumstances and respond with practical action within a short time.

Every unscheduled call for service should be treated as a customer order and given a service order serial number so that all subsequent actions and costs can be recorded and progressed against it. This procedure should be followed for every call, whether or not the service is to be provided free under a general maintenance and servicing contract. The order reference number should be told to the customer when the initial call is made (which will usually be by telephone, fax or e-mail). The use of such individual service order numbers is essential, and will enable any subsequent enquiries or complaints from the customer to be related to the relevant event and handled promptly.

The response to a customer's breakdown call might be to send a replacement part or assembly for the customer to install. In this case, the information supplied by the customer must be sufficiently accurate for the supplier to be able to confirm the fault diagnosis and identify the parts required without ambiguity. The equipment must therefore be identified by its type and serial numbers. The customer needs to have sufficient product knowledge, almost certainly supported by an effective user's manual, and may have to assume responsibility for any liability resulting from the repair.

The response to a customer's call might be to send an engineer. Here, again, the equipment must be identified by its type and serial numbers. The engineer will need to be provided with the exact site address, name of the person or department to contact on arrival, telephone number, times when access to the product is possible, kit of tools and test equipment, a carefully selected range of spare parts, and of course, a pad of blank service report forms.

Good data collection systems are essential in both the above situations, but the customer and product information has to be readily available within minutes for some industries (retrievable from the equipment serial number, if known, or from the data held on the customer's file). Retrievability is obviously far easier when detailed customer history files have been established and maintained. If the customer has a regular maintenance contract for the product, the contract number should give the path to all necessary information.

Very careful planning of spare part availability from stock is crucial to providing a speedy response. Means must be available for dispatching spare parts quickly from a central stock area to all geographical areas which contain users of the product.

Servicing as a quality product

The servicing function's output must be regarded as a company 'product', subject to quality management and control along with all other company products. It is worth emphasizing some of the characteristics of the service product which are vital to its quality.

RESPONSE TO SERVICE CALLS

Time is always of the essence in any service activity, and the reports and head office documentation should, together, record time taken to respond to the service call, time taken to carry out the service, and the amount of and reason for any excess time taken.

Systems in larger organizations for recording response times have means for automatically recording every call received, allocating a service order serial number, recording the time taken to respond, the interval between receiving the call and arrival at the customer's site, the time taken to restore the product to correct operation, and the time that has elapsed since the previous service call to the product. This last item, coupled with meter readings or other indication of the amount of product usage, are obviously useful data concerning the reliability of the product and/or the effectiveness of previous servicing and repair.

Such data must be of importance to the servicing function. It sets its own standards for service response, and provides the most accurate means possible for calculating the costs associated with the function. All of this information gives the means for monitoring and improving servicing standards.

Competition among manufacturers of communications equipment and computers, for example, is based to a large degree on the extent and speed of backup in the event of failure within the first years of operating the equipment.

BEHAVIOUR

The service engineer is perhaps the only representative of the company that the customer sees. The image portrayed by this engineer and the way in which he or she behaves is therefore a quality characteristic in the eyes of the customer. This behaviour includes courtesy to the customer and staff, and respect for them and their property. It includes obvious points like cleanliness of self, tools and working methods. It means communicating with the customer's representatives, keeping them advised, and, where necessary, educating, but it also means listening to their comments, suggestions, criticisms or complaints. The engineer needs to develop credibility and trust with the customer.

MANAGEMENT

People working away from headquarters in a servicing function can lose valuable identification with colleagues, and, if not given good support, can become disloyal to the company and damaging to it in the presence of customers. There must be good support systems for people who work remote from headquarters.

Training, updated regularly, is essential. This should not be product-based only, but also based on some of the feedback methods mentioned in the following section.

Means need to be provided to deal with employees' concerns about their status and security. Management style is important. Service engineers carry out much of their work away from headquarters, some regional engineers even working from home. Such remote workers need to feel that:

- They are useful.
- Their organization cares about whether or not they are doing a good job.
- They are appreciated.
- They are communicated with properly, not simply by means of circulars and memoranda.

FEEDBACK

Because of the remote nature of the work and of the difficulties of monitoring standards, means need to be provided for measuring the quality of service.

Most companies take some note of unsolicited complaints. These are obviously of concern to them. Other companies try to solicit complaints and feedback, although there are some dangers inherent in overdoing this. However, comment cards or customer surveys can be most useful.

The function of servicing must be audited regularly as part of the quality system, but more importantly, there should be a 'management presence' whenever any monitoring activity is carried out. Some service managers go out to a selected call with each engineer on a regular basis for this purpose.

Given an appropriate managerial climate, peer reviews can also provide useful feedback. Two engineers work together, and comment afterwards on one another's performance. Managers can also survey the engineers themselves, and ask for feedback (either anonymous or otherwise).

Metrics

In some industries, notably telecommunications, moves have been made to establish the regular collection of data on many aspects of suppliers' performance. These data are split into hardware, software and service, or combinations thereof. They are termed 'metrics'.

With regard to our topic here, servicing, some of the metrics being mandated are of interest.

Problem report fix response time is the overall responsiveness of the supplier to reported problems. The data are to be measured monthly as the percentage of the total number of overall fixes due to be closed during the month that were delivered on time.

Although this metric need not always be to do with servicing *per se*, it is of interest to those people who have to go out to the field and see to equipment which has been installed, is in operation, but has a reported problem.

This metric clearly bears a strong relationship to *mean time to repair* (MTTR). Not only would the customer and supplier be interested in knowing that the responsiveness had been improved over a period of time, but also that the time taken to become operational again had, on average, shortened.

Another metric is in the area of software. It is called *corrective patch quality*.

Following a fault found in installed software, a corrective patch may be used to put the situation right. Again, the measurement put on the supplier is the percentage of patches which are defective. The servicing function in the software supplier will want to be aware of such a metric.

The TL 9000 requirements include many such metrics. The idea is to require relevant metrics to be reported to a central databank and be published on the Web to enable suppliers to benchmark themselves against the industry means or averages. There are *normalization factors* and *counting rules* to ensure that the data are compared on exactly the same basis.

THE CUSTOMER

Customers always have a level of expectation before any service. Their perception of the service performance results from comparison between their prior expectation and their experience of the service actually provided.

The whole service process, as well as its result, is of key importance to the customer. This is particularly true where the service is unscheduled. A company that promises to provide a response to a customer must have staff available at all times when customers are most likely to call for help. If these times are outside conventional working hours, then that is the way the servicing function must be arranged.

Perhaps in future standards for quality systems there should be greater emphasis on the servicing function. It is not a straightforward process, and is worthy of considerable management attention.

All companies must have the objective of combining designed product reliability with planned preventive maintenance so that as many servicing calls as possible are scheduled, with product failures and their resulting unscheduled calls reduced to a minimum, if not prevented altogether. Achieving this state of affairs is the result of good design, excellent data collection, proper analysis of those data, and corrective action on the diagnoses. Servicing people need appropriate training to be fully equipped to provide a comprehensive service. Customers need to be kept well informed about the product and its correct operation and care.

Further reading

Juran, J. (ed.) *Quality Control Handbook*, 3rd edn, McGraw-Hill, New York, 1974.

TL 9000 Quality Management Systems Requirements Handbook (Book 1, Release 3.0), QUEST Forum, <http://questforum.asq.org>.

TL 9000 Quality Systems Metrics (Book 2, Release 3.0), QUEST Forum, <http://questforum.esq.org>.

CHAPTER

12 *Service Quality*

Denis Walker

Customers are the lifeblood of all organizations. Yet few organizations seem fully capable of matching their performance to the needs of their customers – in quality, efficiency or personal service. Managers must start to recognize that improving quality to their customers is not a matter of choice: the health, and ultimately the survival, of the organization depends on it.

The purpose of this chapter is to show what has to be done to create a total commitment to customers. It is aimed primarily at executives who recognize that achieving quality improvement coupled with total commitment to customer service requires a new style of management. It is a style which demands development of skilled and knowledgeable people at all levels through communication and training, and the use of their expertise to seek better ways of doing things. This style is based on agreeing clear standards and targets and the use of data and statistics to drive for continuous improvement. It combines the art of managing people with the science of reducing variability.

What is service?

Customers react differently to what appears to be the same service. The same customer can also react differently to the same service in different circumstances. The business executive flying out to make a difficult but important deal is not the same customer as the one returning home that night with a lucrative contract safely in his pocket. This represents the difficulty – and the challenge – for service providers and their organizations. Mood, culture and timing, as well as the customer's previous experience, all affect the way service is perceived.

This concept is one that many business people are uncomfortable with, since it demands flexibility in the use of resources, giving discretion to staff who deal with customers, and not relying on production-oriented routines. It means treating customers as individuals and setting up organizational systems which support, not hinder, this aim. Service reputation is all about what it is like doing business with you. Is it a pleasant, rewarding experience, or one your customers would rather not repeat? Is that little bit extra being done without asking, or is getting good service like going through an army assault course?

Service strategy

'Putting the customer first' is an admirable intention, but it will only be more than that if there is a proper service strategy for delivering it. The two main objectives of this strategy are to create a difference which is observable or measurable by the customers, and also to have real impact on the way things are done inside the company.

The service strategy must be a central part of the company's business strategy, which will also cover profit objectives, markets, technology and so on. It is central because it defines the company's internal culture as well as its desired external image. It needs to be put in writing and communicated widely, so that no one is in any doubt about what it is designed to achieve. It needs to be matched by an organization structure designed for customer response. The strategy must include:

1 **Customers' needs and expectations** – No company can survive if its customers' needs are either not fully defined or ignored when known.
2 **Competitors' activities** – Without knowledge of what your main competitors are doing, it is impossible to set out to gain advantage through the quality and innovation of your services. You need to know why customers are using your competitors' products and services rather than your own.
3 **Vision of the future** – Listening to customers and watching the competition are obviously important processes, but they may not be sufficient to sustain differentiation and customer satisfaction over the longer term. The companies that stand apart from the rest have visionary leaders who encourage experimentation and change and enable their people to create a vision of the future. This is not a projection of the future on the basis of present position, but a picture of where you would like to be and how to get there.

Areas 1 and 2 need regular audit and assessment, which itself should be part of your service strategy.

Now consider what customers receive, or at least expect to receive, for their money. It is usually a combination of material service and personal service – the tangible and the less tangible elements. If you are buying a toaster, the material aspect will be most important; if you are staying in a hotel, the personal aspects of service may be foremost. But in each case, you hope that both material and personal services will be excellent. This is an important consideration when developing a strategy for service: it has to ensure that the customer is consistently well served, both materially and personally.

MATERIAL SERVICE

Material service consists of a product plus the environment in which service takes place, and the service or delivery systems which get products to customers:

- **The product** must be reliable and do what it is specified to do (fitness for purpose).
- **The environment** must reflect the quality of the organization – shoddy premises invariably raise questions about other aspects of a company's standards and performance. Well-organized and well-presented premises create a favourable first impression.
- **The delivery systems** must work. These include distribution, scheduling, accountancy and computerized paperwork, job organization and so on. It does not matter how good a product is if it arrives late or damaged, if it is not to the customer's specification, of if the order and account paperwork do not match.

PERSONAL SERVICE

Personal service encompasses service style and the relationship between customers and the staff of an organization. How good a company is to deal with usually depends on the people it employs. Their knowledge and skills are crucial to the company's ability to fulfil the expectations expressed in the service strategy. Staff who have direct contact with customers have the greatest effect on the company's reputation. But those behind the scenes must not be ignored, because they service those who are dealing with the customers, as well as creating the product and many of the delivery systems:

- **Staff attitude** towards customers can strongly support or badly undermine a company's service strategy. If staff do not believe in, and demonstrate commitment to, the customer, then the service will not match the image being promoted. Therefore, it is important to know where they stand (using a carefully constructed attitude survey).
- **People systems** must be designed to motivate staff to support the service strategy. Selection criteria should reflect the need for customer focus, induction should introduce it at an early stage, 'technical' training should reinforce and not conflict, and performance appraisal should develop objectives relating to service performance. The way people are organized and the way they are managed must also be compatible with giving good service.

SERVICE HEALTH CHECK

Clearly, any organization determined to become more customer-oriented needs to examine its performance in each of the above areas. The activity of auditing 'organizational health' should become a natural part of the continuous improvement process. Try the following brief health check for your own organization:

- Do you know your customers and are you clear about their needs?
- Have you communicated these needs to your staff?
- Have clear service standards been set and communicated?
- Are you sure about how service can give you an edge over your competitors?
- Have you clearly defined the skills and knowledge required by your staff to deliver quality service?
- Have the skills of managing your service business been identified and programmes set up to give all managers these skills?
- Do you know how much poor quality is costing you and what the main causes of poor quality are?
- Do you have a customer complaints system?
- Do you have a corporate mission?
- Has this mission been communicated to your staff and set in the context of their work?
- Do systems exist which assure you of quality products or services?
- Do your selection procedures reflect a quality company?

SERVICE STRATEGY MODEL

The elements of the service strategy just defined can be presented in the form of a model to aid in auditing organizational health and devising service quality improvement programmes (see Figure 12.1).

Planning and running a service programme

The next stage is to develop a coherent framework of activities which will enable your service strategy to be implemented and create a real difference.

The coherent framework of activities is designed to produce awareness of the need to change, commitment to the process of change, and an environment in which change happens. This is a complex, long-term task. Ownership and commitment at all levels of the organization, starting with management, are crucial. Commitment programmes have to be designed and run, and levels of commitment monitored through regular audit and reviews of quality improvement plans and achievements. Although ownership concerns everybody, the improvement programme itself will need a 'kick-start' and continual coaxing. While the ultimate champion has to be the principal executive officer, a senior champion or co-ordinator may be required to present the total picture, co-ordinate design and implement activities.

The coherence of the activities is important: people must be able to understand how activities fit together and how they lead to achievement of the mission. The use of branding, traditionally an external marketing tool, helps to communicate the fact that a broad range of activities are all concerned with quality improvement.

Activities need to be designed to put the service strategy into practice – building understanding, emotional commitment and practical participation in improving service performance on a continuous basis. Improving performance requires standards of service to be defined and communicated and improvement targets set; staff need to be trained to deliver these standards and in problem-solving and innovation skills and techniques, and to be involved in carefully selected improvement projects. The process of improvement is continually fuelled by new survey data, by internal audits, by customer complaints, and by external audits through quality assurance (QA) programmes and supplier-partnership programmes led by customers. In other words, there should never be a time when improvement opportunities do not arise: there will always be unexpected variations, changes to requirements to satisfy. The improvement projects need to breach traditional organizational boundaries. As the service strategy model shows, most quality problems occur in the delivery and people systems areas, and these rarely have a single, clear owner. The bigger management processes cross many organizational boundaries yet still have to be improved – mechanisms for doing this have to be introduced as part of the service programme.

As the service improvement programme is to be long-term, ways have to be developed for reinforcing the messages and consolidating progress. Communication systems must be overhauled, every opportunity must be taken to repeat key messages, and successes have to be featured to keep service quality awareness to the fore.

All training programmes provide an opportunity to reinforce the principles of 'customer first' and the need to seek continuous improvement. Technical training should no longer be perceived as separate from customer relations training, whether on the job or in a classroom. Finally, service improvements need to be recognized, rewarding individuals and teams for achievement and providing encouragement to others.

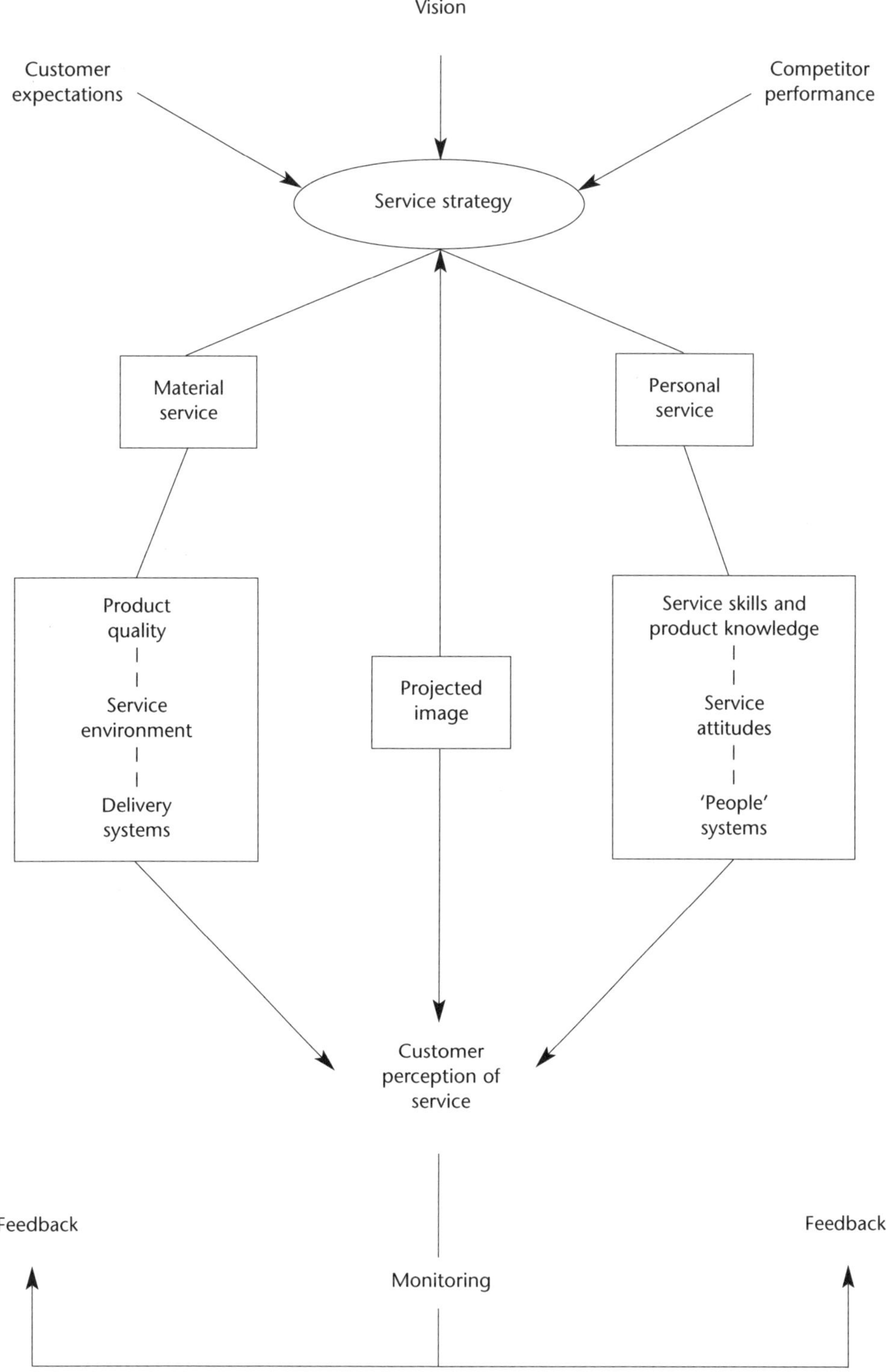

Figure 12.1 Service strategy model

We concentrate here on the role of the manager in implementing the service strategy and bringing about performance improvement. Deming and Juran have both stated that at least 80 per cent of quality problems are to do with systems weaknesses and bureaucracy, and can only be put right through management-initiated activity. Very few problems can be blamed on the workforce; it is usually the systems and processes they are asked to work with. Even apparent attitude problems often have their root cause in poor training – a largely management-led process. Management in a quality organization involves managing change for the better, rather than maintaining the status quo. Key result areas for managers should reflect this, as should management behaviour. Most employees take their behavioural cues from people only slightly higher up in the hierarchy of the company. Therefore, quality leadership must be widely spread. Managers have to be seen to be committed to customers, talking to them and acting on what they say, eradicating quality problems for good, and encouraging subordinates to do the same.

Managers need to produce and use their own local data on customer requirements and employee attitudes. They need to devise and communicate meaningful improvement plans and use these to drive personal review systems in a non-restrictive, participative manner. They should both seek and provide training for their subordinates in change management and in customer-oriented business management. They should set up improvement projects which cross traditional barriers between departments, rather than protecting parochialism. They should help their people to understand causes of variation and the control processes used to minimize them. 'Customer first' will only become a reality if managers want it and work for it.

Of course, the aim of all of these activities is to create a competitive edge which will enable the organization to prosper and grow. Image is part of the service strategy model. The way an organization promotes itself, deliberately or inadvertently, gives customers, or potential customers, certain expectations against which they will judge actual performance. Improved service can become a marketing tool, but timing is important. The organization must be sure that if it raises expectations, they will be fulfilled. Sustained improvement adds value to a basic product and has a market price. Customers will pay for reliably high quality.

The sternest test of a service strategy is its response to customer complaints, requiring clearly defined systems and procedures to handle complaints effectively.

In essence, the activities outlined above are designed to achieve:

- an awareness of customer service and quality principles
- commitment to implementing these principles throughout the organization
- regular review of data to show the difference achieved.

The importance of ownership

In order for service improvement to become a natural part of managing the business, and for its implementation and effects to be widely shared, the involvement (and therefore ownership) of managers must be deliberately cultivated by:

- involvement in research
- running workshops on the findings
- testing activities with them first

- encouraging local initiatives within the overall 'customer first' framework
- conferences to share learning and successes and to develop next steps.

Ignoring the issue of ownership and leadership will result in piecemeal activities for which managers will not get the support of their staff, and in managers actually undermining the service strategy.

Managing a service business

In any business, the onus is on managers to point the way and create the right environment for success. Employees look to their managers to set the style, to demonstrate what is important, and to decide the pace of work. Nearly all changes which are needed will have to be initiated by management – revolutions rarely happen 'bottom-up'. The following are some of the principal ways for managers in service organizations to manage their own performance and that of their departments in bringing about quality improvement.

VISION

All managers need to understand the corporate vision, mission or objectives, and to be able to explain them in a way which makes sense to their own people. They should consider working with their team to define departmental missions which are complementary to each other. They should be able to describe the department's main purpose and motivate people towards achieving that purpose.

KEY RESULTS

The work on vision should lead to clarification of the results and targets to be achieved in the coming months. These should be expressed as between five and seven key results, at least two of which would be mainly concerned with quality and customer service. Key results should be about change – improvement, innovation, implementation – not about maintaining the status quo. Targets, set in terms of quality, quantity, cost and/or timescale, should provide the milestones and review points.

It is difficult to measure some jobs in this way, but how else can their real worth to the organization be established? Objective systems designed purely to fill up the annual appraisal report, and not used to foster real performance improvement, are a waste of time. A 90-day review system is needed: two hours every three months with each direct report is managerial time well spent. A 90-day review period allows for changes in priority, correction of work which has gone off course, and reallocation of resources. The annual review and report then becomes more meaningful and less traumatic. If managers are not assessed for their contribution to customer service, then the organization is not really serious about putting the customer first.

Once a key result is implemented, it is much easier to reward managerial performance. The reward system should reflect and support the service strategy, rather than working against it by encouraging caution and mediocrity.

EXEMPLIFYING THE NEW VALUES

Managers will be observed carefully by their subordinates for signals of commitment to 'customer first'. Here are some of the ways in which managers can demonstrate their customer orientation:

- referring to customers and customer data frequently
- not accepting poor quality and 'it's near enough' attitudes
- making direct contact with customers on a regular basis
- breaking down barriers between departments, rather than protecting their own territory; demonstrating the importance of the internal customer concept
- praising people for good performance, particularly where it is overtly supporting the service emphasis
- being visible in their own department and in customer departments, and taking time to update people on performance successes
- implementing a 90-day review system for the department
- encouraging staff to be involved in performance improvement, problem-solving and innovation, and showing an interest in team and project activity
- keeping subjects such as quality, safety and customer high on their own and their department's agenda
- setting high personal standards in terms of presentation, courtesy, quality and rate of work.

Managers must be careful to avoid sins of omission: failing to take the trouble to acknowledge a particularly good piece of work can easily lead people to suspect lack of interest and commitment.

PERFORMANCE DATA

Managers who are serious about performance improvement measure it. 'What gets measured gets done' is a Tom Peters maxim which, put alongside a clear sense of priorities, is very powerful. Individuals and departments should set a handful of work standards which reflect the needs of customers (preferably developed jointly with those customers) by which performance can be measured regularly. The resulting data should be presented creatively and very visibly. Any department which cannot agree performance standards with its customers should consider whether it needs to exist at all. Some departments may even find it difficult to decide who their customers are! Using measurement in the key result areas can add meaning to the objectives and help chart progress towards them. Examples of performance standards are:

- answering telephones in the sales department within four rings
- accuracy of delivery to the warehouse by the production department
- monthly accounts delivered on time by the accounts department
- number of bug-free systems from management services department
- pay systems with no errors
- point of sale material available one week before product launch.

Each standard should reflect '100 per cent right first time' performance, and any which demand less must be seen as stepping stones towards that goal. This concept has to be interpreted for each department, but the sum of the parts must ultimately be perfect products and services every time. Accuracy of 98 per cent may sound great to managers who know how difficult it is to achieve, but the fact that 2 per cent of customers get wrong or damaged orders cannot be justified.

Data can be very boring, or they can provide you and your department with interest and excitement – a driving force for improvement. Displaying that data effectively is important. It should be done simply but attractively. Charts are better than columns of numbers. Use colour if possible. Provide special noticeboards, and keep the data up to date. Talk about them with staff when you are on walkabout. Encourage staff to seek training in simple measurement techniques to support their problem-solving. Establish statistical expertise within your department, and let people know what help is available. Use the data as a regular agenda item in meetings. Hold a regular performance meeting to review performance against service standards. Investigate shortfalls and praise improvements, and ensure that the right people see the data.

HOW TO AUDIT YOUR DEPARTMENT (OR COMPANY, DIVISION OR GROUP)

Announce your own material and personal audit to demonstrate commitment to the organization's service programme. Involve your people in identifying all the systems, procedures and rules which are unhelpful to the customers and which impede fast response and innovation. Scrap the worst offenders, and change the rest. Has the supervisor, for instance, become just the guardian of these inhibiting rules and procedures? Can the role be changed into an enabling one? How effective are your people? Do they understand what's expected of them? Are they capable of delivering it? Could they become so with the right training and other resources? If so, set this up.

Stand back from your department, and make sure you know:

- who your customers are
- what they expect of you
- how well you meet those expectations
- what needs to be done to improve
- what are the inhibitors and barriers to improvement.

Discuss these questions with your staff, and check your findings with your customers.

Create action plans for improvement using task forces, champions and work teams, and check these plans with your internal and external customers. With the latter group, you may feel you are taking a commercial risk, but as they already know your failings, you can only enhance your reputation by showing them that you are aiming to overcome them.

Eradicate the 'manager knows best' attitude; your years of experience may have become your own worst enemy. Establish what factors influence customers' success. Talk to them regularly, and use market research selectively and intelligently. Listen to your staff – the experts. Find out what they think is wrong and what needs to be done to put it right.

TRAINING

It is the manager's job to ensure that training programmes are put into place for their staff. But managers themselves need training to manage service businesses effectively. One area in which training programmes may be needed is the management of change – understanding current and future states, managing transitions.

Managers need to become comfortable with change, accepting it as part of normal life rather than constantly striving for stability which never comes. Managers need to debate in workshops, possibly with the help of external facilitators, the need for change, the process of change and their own roles in making it happen. Techniques can include vision exercises, domainal mapping, key result-generation, peer and subordinate data, action-planning and critical success factor analysis. Managers need to understand why people resist change, and to learn ways of overcoming the resistance of people who are territorial; who have a high need for structure; who dislike risk; who think in black and white; or who always see the negative aspects rather than the opportunities.

Other workshops may concentrate more specifically on customer service and the added value and differentiation it provides in the marketplace. Discussion of customer research and critical success factors leads to an understanding of the principles behind quality and service standards and monitoring mechanisms, and an understanding of the importance of managers providing a role model for the new corporate values.

An organization introducing key result systems to support its service strategy will need a workshop solely on the matter of managing performance, to cover:

- defining key results
- setting targets
- appraisal interviewing
- giving feedback
- counselling and coaching
- career management.

Discussions with colleagues in the workshop will help to clarify key result areas – those parts of your job that really count. Targets for change, improvement or innovation can be given deadlines, milestones, standards, success criteria or measurement methods, as appropriate.

INDIVIDUAL ATTRIBUTES

Quality organizations need quality managers. While this chapter provides a recipe of actions for managers to take, there are also some key attributes needed at a personal level:

- total commitment to quality and customer service
- capability for both strategic and tactical thinking
- ability to stand back and evaluate the unit's performance
- ability to demonstrate effective customer response by own example
- ability to build warm, friendly relationships based on trust
- ability to recognize good customer service and creative and innovative ideas
- visible concern for and care about people.

Pitfalls

'Customer first' is creating change in a real and lasting way. There will therefore be many areas of resistance to overcome; to you, these may appear to be based on illogical, irrational and emotional thinking. Just as with convincing customers to buy, people within the organization have to be motivated to 'buy in', so these perceptions cannot be ignored, however difficult they may be for you to accept or understand.

People facing change can experience a whole series of negative emotions – anger, denial, frustration and, at best, resignation. All of these have to be countered if you are seeking enthusiastic, fearless commitment to change. Resistance may have to do with having change imposed, rather than the change itself. Allowing people to become involved in defining the nature of the change required and the subsequent processes for its implementation will remove much of the resistance. People must be allowed to let go of their old way of doing things in a manner which maintains their self-esteem. If you wish them to be part of the new culture, bridges with their past have to be built. Although people often resist prescribed change, there will need to be some – new structures, specific techniques, carefully chosen projects, improvement targets and so on. Therefore time must be taken to help people understand reasons for change in order to accept these changes. 'Customer first' or total quality cannot be achieved by system improvements alone. People make system changes work, and, as such, their enthusiasm and commitment need to be won.

One obvious pitfall is not having a sufficiently coherent, well-thought-out framework of activities, with the result that improvement activities are seen to be sporadic and piecemeal.

Another pitfall is not recognizing the need to have a critical mass of believers and enthusiasts with organizational influence, either in the formal structure or the informal networks which are part of any organization. Critical mass is not an absolute figure, but the number required to give impetus and maintain momentum, and will be different according to the stage of the change programme. These enthusiasts can be used to start convincing the persuadable neutrals who constitute the bulk of most normal populations.

The biggest hurdle is often the middle management group, waiting for repeated signals of commitment from the top or contra signals and mixed messages which allow them to stay neutral. Blaming the attitudes of their workforce for quality problems, being threatened by the changing nature of their role, feeling increasingly isolated and fearful of the future are all characteristic behaviours, and they can quietly and insidiously undermine progress. This particular hurdle can only be overcome by persistent leadership from the senior team providing clear championing of 'customer first' and role-modelling quality behaviour, and by the training investment described earlier.

Other aspects which will soon undermine the programme if they are not anticipated are:

- Failure to start with improvement projects which are likely to be successful – teams soon get dispirited if they do not achieve success, and success in the early projects breeds confidence, and hence more success.
- Becoming stale after a few months as enthusiasm begins to drop – all improvement programmes will meet peaks and troughs of enthusiasm and progress. Be prepared with some new ideas, new champions and the odd surprise to keep people alert; keep the successes visible, use data constantly to renew energy levels.
- Managers not listening, either to customers or employees – 'manager knows best'

behaviour is always lurking, ready to resume control at the least opportunity. Listening to customers and staff means you are constantly challenging your thinking and testing your ideas. Listening is the biggest respect you can pay to people, while it also provides you with data. Its absence will be the biggest signal to the organization of your lack of commitment to improvement.

The potential benefits

Creating service as a key strategic value, listening to your customers and responding in a way that pleases them can have lasting benefits. The aim is to make 'customer first' behaviour a way of life by building a climate where continuous improvement in quality and innovation is natural and where the concept of the internal customer is a comfortable one for everybody in the organization.

None of this is achieved easily; it requires a long-term commitment and much effort in order for the difference to be noticed by your critical external and internal audiences. Yet the company's very survival may depend on making these changes. In addition to this perhaps rather threatening scenario, there are positive benefits if you can overcome the many hurdles and pitfalls associated with bringing about change.

The vision of what can be achieved is exciting – your organization *can* be a different place in which to work and a different company to do business with. There are many opportunities for stumbling and falling, but with care these can be overcome or avoided. The question is: 'Is it all going to be worth it?' While the question can be avoided by showing that there is no choice if you want to become or remain competitive, there are also many positive, certain benefits to provide an affirmative answer to the question. Hard benefits which make a contribution to the growth and prosperity of the company are as follows:

- Guaranteed service quality becomes a remarkable product in itself, with a price differential acceptable to customers.
- Quality improvement provides a cost-effective organization, since waste, rework and compensation become things of the past.
- A common purpose and alignment removes ineffective training and compartmentalization, and generates trust and enthusiasm.
- A better-educated, more numerate management and workforce are better prepared to face and handle change confidently and without fear, including market downturns; change becomes welcomed and sought after; cries for stability disappear.
- Management systems and processes are uprated, and the climate of continuous improvement ensures they are regularly reviewed for effectiveness, amended or removed.
- Customers see the company as:
  - responsive to their needs; good listeners
  - adding value through innovative products and services
  - sharing data in joint problem-solving, generally seeking a partnership approach
  - recognizing the importance of a third-party accreditation in creating customer confidence
  - understanding the customer's business and the factors critical to their success
  - caring about the way they deal with each customer.

- Competitors see the company as formidable.
- Shareholders regard the company as a safe, worthwhile investment.
- The communities within which the company exists see it as a caring partner, concerned for the social and economic environment.
- Future potential employees see the company as one they would be proud to work for.
- Energy and potential are released at all levels to create an altogether more powerful, innovative and responsive organization.
- Partnership programmes ensure only the best suppliers are kept and effort on new business generation is reduced as growth comes from customer loyalty and mutual development.

'Customer first' is a state of mind, producing an organization which is customer-led, quality- and safety-conscious, concerned for the development of its people, and, as a result, highly successful. The journey is worthwhile and enjoyable. The destination is worth aspiring to. The potential pay-off is immense.

Further reading

Deming, W.E., *Out of the Crisis*, MIT Press, Cambridge, MA, 2000.

Normann, R., *Service Management: Strategy and Leadership in Service Businesses*, John Wiley, Chichester, 2000.

Oakland, John, *Total Quality Management*, 2nd edn, Heinemann, Oxford, 1993.

Peters, Tom, *Thriving on Chaos*, Macmillan, London, 1988.

Walker, Denis, *Customer First: A Strategy for Quality Service*, Gower, Aldershot, 1990.

CHAPTER **13** *Documentation and Records, Part 1*

Documentation and Records, Part 1

Dennis Lock

Other chapters in this handbook describe various documented procedures or forms which are used specifically for quality management. This chapter will outline some of the principles that apply more generally to documentation in an organization which strives to provide quality goods and services. Paper forms are used here as illustrative examples, while recognizing that many working documents will in practice be generated from computer systems and stored on media other than paper.

Documents and quality

In any modern organization that provides goods or services, every sensible person should agree that proper documentation is essential to – indeed, an essential part of – quality management. Specific aspects of such documentation obviously include the drawings, specifications, work management forms and quality records that are familiar to anyone who has ever worked in an engineering or service environment. In more recent years, the quality system itself has become a subject which requires its own essential purpose-designed procedures, the most notable item being the *quality manual*. For an example of a quality manual based on ISO 9001: 2000, see Matt Seaver's book (Seaver, 2001).

It must be recognized that relevance to quality extends well beyond those documents which purport directly to define products, services and quality itself. Every system in an organization affects quality to some degree – if not directly, then at least indirectly. For example, the service provided to the customer must include correct delivery documents and invoicing. Systems used in human resource management can affect motivation and performance (and therefore quality), particularly if a system is badly documented and perceived to be inadequate, unfair or error-ridden. Other examples could be quoted *ad infinitum*, but this chapter will concentrate on documents that deal directly with products and work operations.

DEDICATED DOCUMENTATION

Once upon a time, many years before ISO 9000 had even been thought of, there was an engineering manager who could often be heard repeating to himself and anyone else within earshot: 'Dedicated documentation ... must have dedicated documentation.' The message was heard, and the word was spread. 'Dedicated documentation' became a guiding motto which lived on in the company long after its originator had departed. That engineering team's subsequent dedication to proper documentation helped to create a before, during and after sales service to its clients that was second to none.

Typical projects included designing and building complex processing plant installations far overseas, often in hostile climates. Yet even for 30-year-old installations, clients could always rely on the London-based engineers to deal promptly and expertly with operating problems, repairs, replacements and requests for modifications or plant extensions.

In addition to the obvious requirement for competent London staff, the quality of this service depended on:

1 having all records of each project safely on file (some dating back well before the Second World War) – these records included contract documents, process flowsheets, calculations, drawing and purchase schedules, drawings, specifications, site photographs, purchase orders for brought-out/built-in plant and equipment plus the vendors' own drawings, test certificates, and operating and maintenance instructions
2 protecting the files against loss by fire, flood, theft or damage from any other cause
3 having the files indexed and organized so that documents could easily and quickly be found
4 designing, documenting and implementing operating procedures for document management
5 ensuring that all staff, from clerks to senior managers, understood and followed the procedures.

In other words, the company practised dedicated documentation.

Document identification

In order to be able to identify any document in such a way that it cannot possibly be confused with any other document, or with incorrect versions of the same document, the identifying data should include:

1 the document type (for example, contract, specification, purchase order, drawing, inspection report)
2 a unique identification code (such as a serial number)
3 a title or description which explains concisely, but without ambiguity, the subject of the document. (Even if the document can be identified by its type and serial number alone, using the title as an additional identifier acts as a check against clerical or keyboard errors.)

If there is any possibility at all that a document could change in any way and be reissued with the same title and identification code, then it must also have:

4 a version code (revision number), or
5 the issue date of the current version.

The identifying data might also have to include:

6 The project, product, part, job or batch number to which the document applies.

DOCUMENT CODES

There are many reasons for allocating codes to items rather than simply describing them in words, not least of which is that codes can be designed to be concise and precise. They also have the advantage – essential in computer systems – of facilitating analysis, editing, retrieval and sorting for planning, reporting and control.

The functions of a code include the first or both of the following:

1 A code must act as a unique 'name' that identifies the item to which it refers.
2 The identifying code, either by itself or by the addition of subcodes, can be arranged so that it categorizes, qualifies or in some other way describes the item.

The best coding systems are those which manage to combine both these functions as simply as possible in numbers that can be used throughout a company's management information system.

In many cases, the identifier codes can be simple serial numbers, allocated from registers or pre-printed on standard forms (such as purchase orders). For other documents, particularly engineering drawings, part lists, bills of materials and other technical or work documents, there is much to be gained from devising a logical numbering system that conveys information about the characteristics of the documented item, as well as being related in some way to the company's management information system (MIS) and cost accounting codes.

A drawing for a manufactured part, for example, could be coded to indicate the assembly or sub-assembly on which the part is to be installed. It might also be used to classify the outline characteristics of the part (codes that identify shape or other physical characteristics are essential in group technology).

In an ideal arrangement, coding systems would be compatible throughout the organization's management information systems so that, for example, every project drawing could automatically be used as a cost code, or at least part of a cost code. An example which has been used successfully in a heavy engineering company (for special-purpose machine tools) is shown in Figure 13.1.

If codes are designed with the company's MIS in mind, they can include digits that denote responsible departments, engineering disciplines, and so on. However, it is possible to be too ambitious and try to make codes include to much information. It is not difficult to devise coding schemes that need 14, 15 or even more characters. The designer of such a system might feel quite proud, and computer systems are well able to accept and process such codes. But people are going to have to read and write these codes as part of their everyday work routine, perhaps in a noisy factory or on a building site. Even in ideal working conditions, simple codes save clerical time and result in fewer mistakes.

IDENTIFICATION OF COMPLEX DOCUMENTS

Many documents, such as proposals, design specifications and project contracts, comprise a principal document that is supplemented by a number of separate drawings and other related documents. It is obviously important to be able to identify the entire document

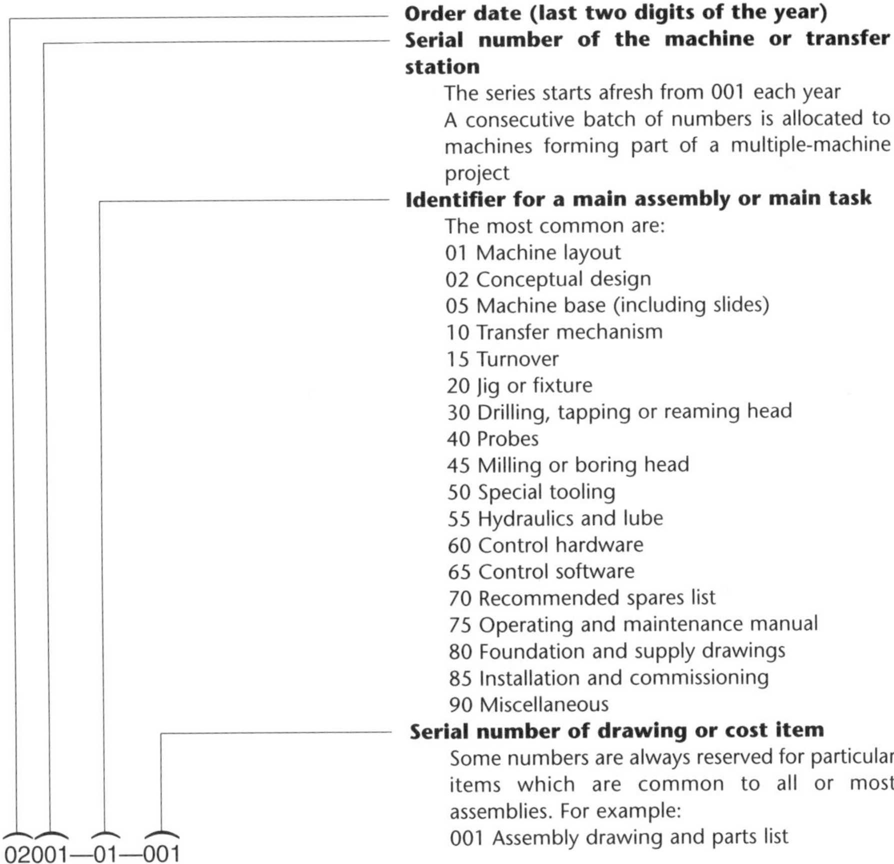
Order date (last two digits of the year)
Serial number of the machine or transfer station
The series starts afresh from 001 each year
A consecutive batch of numbers is allocated to machines forming part of a multiple-machine project
Identifier for a main assembly or main task
The most common are:
01 Machine layout
02 Conceptual design
05 Machine base (including slides)
10 Transfer mechanism
15 Turnover
20 Jig or fixture
30 Drilling, tapping or reaming head
40 Probes
45 Milling or boring head
50 Special tooling
55 Hydraulics and lube
60 Control hardware
65 Control software
70 Recommended spares list
75 Operating and maintenance manual
80 Foundation and supply drawings
85 Installation and commissioning
90 Miscellaneous
Serial number of drawing or cost item
Some numbers are always reserved for particular items which are common to all or most assemblies. For example:
001 Assembly drawing and parts list
02001—01—001

Figure 13.1 Example of a hierarchical coding system

completely, precisely, yet simply. Otherwise there might be doubt concerning the scope, content and correct version of the document.

The solution is to include a contents list with the main document which lists the serial and amendment numbers of all the constituent documents. When the main document or any attachment is amended, the contents list must also be updated and reissued with a raised amendment number. Every page of the contents list must itself carry the main document identifier code plus the latest amendment number. Then it is only necessary to refer to this code and amendment number to identify and define the complete document (including its various attachments).

Some of the attachments to a complex document might themselves also be complex or, at least, multiple-sheet documents. Those attachments will therefore also have to be identified precisely, either by giving them individual contents lists or by including every sheet separately on the main document's contents list.

A contents list for a complex document (a specification front sheet in this case) is shown in Figure 13.2. The sections below headed 'Amendments to multiple-sheet documents' and 'Version control' contain further comments that are relevant to complex documents. This is essentially the control that is used for a quality manual.

Specification	Specification No:	Rev:	Sheet: 1
Title:			

At the latest revision number as given above, this specification comprises all the sheets listed in the following table, with each sheet at the revision number stated. When this specification is revised, only revised or additional sheets will normally be issued, together with a replacement for this front sheet.

Sheet	Rev.	Sheet	Rev.	Sheet	Rev.	Sheet	Rev.	Sheet	Rev.	Sheet	Rev.	Sheet	Rev.	Sheet	Rev.	Sheet	Rev.	Sheet	Rev.

Attachments

The following attachments form part of this specification

Amendments

No.	Date	Reason

Authorization

Originator:	Checked by:	Chief engineer:

Figure 13.2 Front sheet of a complex document

The use of a front sheet such as this acts as a definitive contents list for any commercial or technical document that comprises several sheets plus other attached or related documents.

Documentation of changes

CHANGE RECORDS

All change requests, whether these are internal or external (such as contract variation orders from a project client or purchase order amendments from a customer), are part of project or product documentation. These are the documents which define the technical and/or contractual details of each change at origin. They therefore require the same degree of care in numbering, indexing, filing and safekeeping as other records.

There are several reasons why the ability to identify, locate and retrieve any of these documents from active files or archives is essential. Should any retrospective investigation or audit be required, these documents will help the investigators to determine the technical evolution and build state of the project or product. Contract changes carry a significant risk of subsequent dispute, and the reasons for safekeeping purchase order amendments and contract variations should be obvious.

Production permits and concessions can be regarded as a kind of change documentation, in the sense that they define a temporary or limited change from the relevant drawings or specifications. These documents must be subject to the same management care as all other change documents. They might be a vital source of information if backtracking is required after a product failure (see 'Traceability' later in this chapter).

AMENDMENTS AND REVISION NUMBERS

Although the issue date can be used to define the intended version of many general documents, most commercial or technical documents require a distinguishing amendment or revision number when they are reissued with changes. A familiar system is that used by software houses for the release of different program versions, which are identified as version 1.0, 1.1, 1.2, and so on until the program is reissued in a completely revised version in a new series version 2.0, 2.1 and so forth.

Many industrial companies use a coding method which distinguishes preliminary issues of documents from those which are fully authorized for construction or manufacture, as shown in Table 13.1.

HIGHLIGHTING CHANGED DATA OR INFORMATION

To assist document users, either when they receive changed documents or carry out retrospective investigations, it is necessary to highlight the area of each document which has been changed and, in some cases, to summarize the details of the change.

Table 13.1 Example of a coding method

Revision status	*Preliminary or draft issues*	*Fully authorized issues*
Original	A	0
First revision	B	1
Second revision	C	2
and so on		

On drawings, this is typically done by writing the revision number in an inverted triangle, both alongside the change and as a key in a revision summary panel.

For sales proposals, contracts, engineering standards and other documents comprising several pages of text, changed paragraphs are sometimes highlighted by ruling a vertical line in the margin. Provided that the number of amendments is likely to be low, several parallel lines can be ruled, the number of lines corresponding to the amendment number.

AMENDMENTS TO MULTIPLE-SHEET DOCUMENTS

When a multiple-sheet document, such as a long specification, commercial document or a schedule is first issued (say at amendment 0), all the individual sheets will also be labelled at amendment 0. Then the whole document can be referred to confidently, without ambiguity, as serial number so and so, at amendment 0.

When changes occur, some sheets may need to be changed, while others remain unaltered. It might also be necessary to insert additional sheets. Is it sufficient merely to reissue those sheets which have been amended or added, or should the complete document be reissued? If the whole document is not reissued, the amended version must contain sheets bearing a mixture of amendment numbers. This places reliance on all recipients of the original document to substitute, add or remove changed sheets correctly. Some, inevitably, will get it wrong. After several amendments, it is very likely that there will exist several different versions of what should be the same document.

The safest method is to reissue the whole document every time a change is made, but this can be wasteful (particularly for documents with many pages and a long distribution list). A more economical way is to issue only new or changed sheets, and to redefine the correct composition at each amendment by attaching a contents list at the front. This contents list should show the sheet and correct amendment number for every page. The contents list must always be reissued with every amendment, so that the amendment number of the contents list itself will be the same as the highest number amendment to be found among the sheets. Figure 13.2 shows a design used by one company for such a front sheet.

THE INTERCHANGEABILITY RULE

The effect on interchangeability is one of the important questions which much be answered whenever a change is considered to any product or component which is produced in repeating or continuous quantities. The golden rule is:

> If a change destroys interchangeability, it is not sufficient merely to reissue the changed drawing with a new revision number. The drawing must be issued as a new drawing, with a changed number, giving a changed part number to the new, non-interchangeable product.

VERSION CONTROL

Version control is a name which can conveniently be given to describe the process of being able to identify the correct version of documents that should be used to define commercial terms, scope of work or the build status to which a product should be manufactured, taking into account all authorized changes. This is obviously important in the event of contractual difficulties or disputes. In the case of manufactured equipment, the role of version control is to define exactly what the finished product contains. Documentation, at any time, should list all the relevant drawings and specifications, giving their serial numbers and their appropriate amendment or revision numbers.

The simplest case – the single product

In the case of a project to make and assemble a single item, version control can be a relatively simple procedure.

To produce a build schedule, it is only necessary to compile a list of all the drawings and specifications, giving the serial and correct amendment number for each document. The listing is quite straightforward, although – except for the very smallest project with very few documents – it is usually convenient to divide the list into a summary and sublists that correspond to the main project and its sub-projects or sub-assemblies in family tree fashion.

An essential requirement is that the schedule and its breakdown elements should be updated whenever a change is authorized, so that it always shows the correct build status of the product or project. The schedule must be given new amendment or revision numbers at each reissue. It follows that the actual build status of a completed project should be definable simply by quoting the number and final amendment number of the controlling schedule.

The controlling document for this process will be a bill of materials (for a manufactured product) or drawing and purchase schedules (for a petro-chemical or similar capital project). These schedules used always to be compiled by hand on pre-printed forms, which could be reproduced as photocopies or dyeline prints. Nowadays, they will invariably be issued as computer-generated schedules, possibly from files linked with progress and cost data in a relational database.

The complex case – the existence of more than one version

The complex version control case occurs with manufactured assemblies that are produced in batches or continuously. When changes are introduced from time to time for product improvement or for any other reason, it is important to:

1 specify the point in production at which the change is to be introduced (the 'point of embodiment') by giving the relevant batch number or product serial number on the authorized change request form
2 record the actual build status of every product; if a quantity of a product is scattered about the production area, stores, warehouses, wholesalers, retailers and in the hands of users, it is important for quality and safety reasons that the manufacturer can recall the exact modification status and parts content for every one of these items.

In order to satisfy the second of these requirements, each unit should be identifiable by some mark or number which distinguishes it from its fellows. This is usually achieved by supplementing the catalogue or part number with a serial number.

The most common method of recording this information is to compile a build schedule for each different version. This is tedious but unavoidable. A build schedule – often called a master record index (MRI) – is simply a list of all the drawings and specifications used in the manufacture of the product, giving the amendment numbers of all these documents as

Build schedule	No:	Rev:

Product:	Sheet 1 of:

Catalogue No:	For serial numbers from:	To:

Drawing number	Sheet	Revision	Drawing number	Sheet	Revision	Drawing number	Sheet	Revision

Modification numbers incorporated for this version							

Figure 13.3 Front sheet of a build schedule (or master record index)

A build schedule is used to define the content and modification status of products which are manufactured in different versions. Each issue is specific to a particular batch or range of serial numbers. Schedules can be written on pro formas such as this or, more conveniently and effectively, using a computer system.

they relate to a particular product serial number or (more usually) to a batch of serial numbers).

Build schedules are typically compiled as computer files and can be distributed in many ways, including microfiche. Figure 13.3 shows the essential elements of a build schedule in clerical form.

There is little point in maintaining build schedules of units with differing build standards if all the relevant drawing and specification amendment information is not archived, indexed and readily retrievable.

Note also that the comfortable premise that the latest issue of a drawing must be the correct issue is dangerous, and may not be valid. Batch manufacturing requirements or customized options can easily result in simultaneous or overlapping manufacture of different versions of a product in the same manufacturing plant.

The build schedule procedure should obviously be supported by labelling the actual products (by engraving, stamping or attaching durable tags). Each label should show the part number and the batch or serial number. Sometimes it is necessary to make provision on the labels to allow for modification numbers to be added as each modification is carried out (this is applicable particularly to products which may have to be modified in the field, after delivery to customers).

Suppliers' documents

A project contractor will need to keep a complete set of equipment suppliers' documentation safely in his own files.

Where bought-in equipment is installed in engineering projects or complex products, it may not be sufficient to rely on being able to obtain additional or replacement copies of documents such as operating and maintenance instructions, drawings, spares lists, test certificates, and so on from all the various suppliers in the future. Some of them might lose or destroy their records, be swallowed up in mergers or takeovers, or simply disappear from the commercial scene altogether.

Suppliers' documents are usually serially numbered and recorded in registers before filing. To ensure that these documents can easily be found again in the future, they must be kept in some recognizable and logical sequence. This indicates the need for a logical numbering system, which can usually be based on specification numbers, requisition numbers, purchase order numbers, or the project work breakdown code numbers.

It may be necessary to renumber some incoming documents (especially drawings from outside manufacturers) in order that they can be filed in a logical system from which they can later be found and retrieved. A cross-referenced index is essential so that, for example, a file can be found if only the equipment specification number of the supplier and approximate date of supply are known.

Traceability

There are several important aspects to traceability, all of which are dependent upon maintaining adequate build records or quality documentation.

BUILD STATUS

The ability to identify the build and modification status of products after manufacture and delivery is essential for servicing and repair, the supply of spares and replacements, and for post-delivery modifications. Performance in this respect depends on the existence of adequate build records, related to serially numbered products, as described above.

PRODUCT RECALL

There is an obvious safety connection with respect to traceability which becomes important when products in the field are found to be unreliable or unsafe. In order that they can be recalled or modified in the field, the supplier must be able either to trace all the customers for the affected items through sales records, or to quote the relevant product model and serial numbers in media advertisements.

Build status records are obviously vital in this respect. For some low-volume high-cost products, it should be possible to maintain sales records showing at least the first-time purchaser in every case.

QUALITY AUDIT TRAILS

In industries where operational safety is particularly important (which include, for example, the nuclear, aviation and defence industries), being able to trace the build status of the product is not sufficient. It is also necessary to provide audit trails for the source of supply for all the components used, right back to their raw material origin. It must be possible, through archived inspection release notes and other supplier documentation, to trace any component that has failed or developed a fault in service back to its purchase order and manufacturing batch number. This information can then be used:

1 to investigate possible causes of the failure
2 to trace the location of products in which components or materials from the same batch have been installed, so that these can be replaced to prevent further failures; an obvious example is when aircraft of a particular type are grounded until suspect components have been checked.

Records of production permits and concessions can be particularly relevant in these circumstances.

PRODUCT LIABILITY AND THE SUPPLY CHAIN

For purchasers who sell products on to others, being able to trace the supply chain from original manufacturer, through intermediaries, importers and so on can become vital in the case of product liability litigation. Product liability is dealt with in Chapter 3, but, from the traceability point of view, suppliers of faulty goods can be personally liable if they are unable to inform an injured person who the producer, importer or own-brander of the goods is within a reasonable time of being asked. This means that full records of the source of goods must be kept in order that such enquiries can be answered, and the liability placed where it belongs.

Document disposition

AUTHORIZATION FOR ISSUE

Rules should be established and documented which list those documents needing special authorization before issue. This applies particularly to documents issued for action, to give special permission, or to certify data.

Examples of 'action documents' are:

- works orders, which authorize work to start on a project or a manufactured batch
- purchase orders, and any other contract documents that commit expenditure
- requisitions for additional permanent or temporary staff
- drawings and specifications (typically requiring at least one signature to certify that they have been checked and another approving issue for action).

Examples of 'permission' documents are:

- production permits
- concessions.

Examples of 'certifying documents' are:

- inspection reports
- test reports.

The documented procedures should set out the minimum levels of authority needed in each case. For all documents where pro formas are used, it makes sense to print the relevant job title in or near the space allowed for the authorization signature.

DISTRIBUTION

The routes by which documents are distributed in a company include, but are not limited to:

1 display on notice boards or video screens in common areas
2 provision of reference copies at key points or in a library (often used for company, national and international engineering standards, for example)
3 provision of a copy for every member of staff, either distributed freely or formally addressed to each person (statement of the company's health and safety policy, for example)
4 distribution to a selected group of people (for a document such as a purchase order and its various copies)
5 placing in files or archives
6 general or selective distribution online through intranet.

This chapter is generally concerned with items 4 and 5. Procedures should be established to determine the standard distribution for each type of document, choosing the addressees on a 'need to know' basis. A document matrix is a useful tool for this purpose (Figure 13.4). In some companies, the standard distribution is very small (called the primary distribution), on the basis that those included will be responsible for, and be best placed to decide, any secondary distribution of copies to their subordinates or others.

Every document should carry a list of those to whom it has been distributed. Where standard forms are used, this list can be pre-printed. It is essential that the list should indicate which of the addressees (if any) is expected to take action. Otherwise, there is a risk that either no action will be taken, or that two or more people will attempt to duplicate the action required.

Standard distribution lists, especially when pre-printed on documents or described in procedures, should always be based on job titles or the names of departments, rather than the names of actual individuals. This is on the assumption that people move in, between and out of jobs more frequently than the organizational structure changes.

Each amendment should be issued to every person who received the original issue.

Recipient	Document: Customer orders	Works orders	Schedules	Assembly drawings	Detail drawings	Bought-out parts lists	Materials specifications	Purchase requisitions	Purchase orders	Delivery notes	Engineering changes	Production permits	Concessions	Inspection reports		and so on...
General manager																
Engineering director																
Project manager																
Project engineer																
Works director																
Production manager																
Production controller																
Quality manager																
Purchasing manager																
Stores manager																
Cost accounts																
Computing manager																
Customer/client																
Supplier																
and so on...																

Figure 13.4 Principle of a document distribution matrix

Filing and archiving

It is very easy to build up substantial, space-consuming files in a very short time. There are several ways of overcoming the filing space problem. These are:

1 Hire off-site space for the storage of non-active files, possibly in a secure repository managed by one of the specialist archive companies. This method has the drawback that the files can easily be forgotten, the only reminder of their existence being the regular receipt of invoices for space rental.
2 Label each file prominently with a review date, at which time the file must be considered for microfilming and/or destruction.
3 Invest in space-saving filing equipment.
4 For digitized documents, storage on CD-Rom can result in small storage space requirements, short search and retrieval times and good quality regeneration of hard copy. A documented backup procedure is essential.

INDEXING

Finding any document in a large file store, whether in electronic storage or as original 'hard copy', demands that all records are carefully indexed. It should be possible, for instance, to be able to search for an individual letter from a client either by reference to its subject, or by its date, or by both of these.

SAFE STORAGE

Records are usually at risk from fire, flood or loss through mistakes by staff, and it is always good sense to consider maintaining a security copy off site (on the basis that tragedy is unlikely to strike in two places simultaneously). However, if there should be a fire which consumes the original files, the backup copy will be of little practical use without an index of its contents. An up-to-date copy of the index for the main files must therefore form part of the security files.

Where records are kept electronically, a system of backups must be devised and followed scrupulously to safeguard against accidental erasure, loss or damage through any cause, or equipment failure. Copies must be made at specified, regular intervals using a suitable rotation strategy. The grandfather–father–son technique is a common method, where three complete copies of the the entire system are retained at all times.

RETENTION POLICY

Every company should have an agreed, documented policy for the retention of documents. The retention period chosen will depend on the type of document and the nature of the business, but the maximum expected life in service of any product must obviously be taken into account.

Further reading

Hyde, William F., *Improving Productivity by Classification, Coding and Database Standardization: The Key to Maximizing CAD/CAM and Group Technology*, Marcel Dekker, New York, 1981.

ISO 9001: 2000, *Quality Management Systems – Requirements*, British Standards Institution, London.

Lock, Dennis, *Project Management*, 5th edn, Gower, Aldershot, 1992 (for numbering systems, version control and build schedules).

Sargent, Philip, Chapters 27 and 28 in Lock, Dennis (ed.), *Handbook of Engineering Management*, 2nd edn, Butterworth-Heinemann, Oxford, 1993 (an account of information management and documentation ranging from manual methods to advanced computer technologies).

Turton, Alison (ed.), *Managing Business Archives*, Butterworth-Heinemann, Oxford, 1991.

CHAPTER

14 Documentation and Records, Part 2: ISO 9000 Documents

Matt Seaver

One essential feature of the ISO 9000 quality management system is that it is *documented*. The core elements of documentation that are required are a *quality policy* for the organization, a *quality manual* containing an overview of the system, objectives in relation to achievement of quality, procedures that are strictly necessary for proper operation, and *records* relating to quality that demonstrate that quality has been achieved.

Documents can be in different formats, not necessarily paper. More and more organizations are working with paperless quality systems. However, the same basic principles apply irrespective of the medium used.

Many people fail to see the benefit of having at least some procedures documented. Without written procedures, errors are often made because of confusion that could have been prevented by an appropriate document. Somebody fails to perform a task because it is not clear who is supposed to do it, or a task is performed incorrectly because the correct way has not been defined, or a change is introduced and not everybody implements it, or different people implement it in different ways.

However, contrary to what people used to think, it is not necessary to have 'a procedure for everything'. Many people used to believe that ISO 9000 demanded detailed procedures for all quality-related tasks. During the drafting of ISO 9001: 2000, the members of ISO Technical Committee 176 were determined that there should be less emphasis on documented procedures than previously. The result was that there are now only six instances where a documented procedure is required. They are:

1 internal audit
2 nonconforming product
3 corrective action
4 preventive action
5 document control
6 record control.

In all other cases, procedures are only required where the absence of a procedure would jeopardize the quality of the output or customer satisfaction. Whether a procedure is needed depends on the circumstances, such as the level of supervision, the experience and training of the people concerned, and the complexity of the task.

Documenting the system

When starting the task of documenting a quality system, one should begin from the premise that if the business is reasonably successful, then probably most things are being done right. So start by documenting existing procedures and methods, and then see what needs to be changed. Do not change the existing method unless there is clearly a problem with it, either because it is not effective, or because it does not comply with the standard.

It is most important not to make the mistake of writing the procedure you would *like* to operate. Sometimes when a manager writes down the current procedure, some weaknesses are evident. It can happen that the current procedure causes extreme embarrassment when it is examined in detail. The temptation then is to write down what you know is the correct procedure. An example from the food sector concerns the thawing of food. A frozen chicken, according to the theory, and all the best books and codes of practice, should be thawed in the refrigerator. If a chef were to put a frozen chicken in the fridge to thaw overnight and then cook it the following morning, it is probable that the customers would be quickly taken ill with salmonella poisoning, since the chicken would have been cooked while partly frozen. In that case, the temptation is to write down that chickens are thawed in the fridge, in the full knowledge that this does not – and in some circumstances, *must* not – happen.

That is a problem for later. At that point, it is necessary to analyse the situation honestly. What is important is that the actual practice can be justified.

The significance of writing down only what can be implemented is that the auditor regards the documented procedure as your definition of what is important for quality, and this is what will be used as one of the bases for the audit. For that reason, it is essential that you should only write down in your procedures what you are prepared to do. If you write it down, then you have to do it! Do not include aspirations posing as facts. The only place where you are allowed aspirations is in your objectives, and even then the aspiration should be achievable, with some effort.

There is no reason why documenting a procedure should result in inflexibility or stunt creativity. Proper wording of the procedure will allow you to maintain the level of control that you define as desirable or necessary, and at the same time allow the operator of the procedure to use whatever discretion is appropriate in the circumstances. Of course, this cannot be done in isolation from other aspects of the system, and would have an impact on such elements as responsibilities and authority, training and competence, risk assessment and record-keeping.

The quality manual

The quality manual is essentially an overview of the entire quality management system, and contains a brief description of the various elements of the system. It is usually structured strictly along the lines of the ISO 9001 standard. There is no explicit requirement that it should follow the ISO 9001 structure, but it is strongly recommended. A different structure will give rise to unnecessary difficulty during external audits, since the auditor will be using an audit checklist based on the ISO 9001 standard. The quality manual is a high-level document, and usually contains little operational detail. It is the sort of document that could be used as promotional material submitted with a tender for a contract.

It must contain an overview of the different processes of the organization, showing their interaction. This is most easily done by including a flowchart of the organization's principal process, showing how the various sub-processes interact.

The quality manual is the place where the policy and strategy for quality are described. It should contain an accurate and reasonably specific description of the quality management system. It does not, however, contain the detailed information on operating the quality management system. Under each clause heading of the standard, the manual should contain references to specific individual procedures. In some cases, the reference will be to another manual rather than to a list of individual procedures. By using references to procedures, the quality manual does not need to be amended every time one of the procedures referred to is changed.

Figure 14.1 shows the contents page of a typical quality manual that addresses the requirements of ISO 9001: 2000 for one particular company. The circulation list is included in the manual as a separate document. Typically, the circulation list for the quality manual includes all managers, since it usually defines individual responsibilities. While other manuals can be authorized (signed off) by managers at appropriate levels, the quality manual is normally authorized by the chief executive.

To facilitate changes to the manual, it has been sub-divided into separate sections. The sections are coded QM-01 to QM-35. This avoids the need to revise and reissue when a single change is made.

General operational documentation

Figure 14.2 shows the contents of a manual containing the operational procedures of a different company, in this case a service company with a management team of three. The manual has been titled the *operations manual*. This company has decided that all quality system procedures can be most usefully contained in one manual, including the procedures for maintaining the quality management system, such as internal audit. It has been divided into sections representing the main areas of activity. The different sections are circulated to the relevant people – that is, not every manager receives the entire manual, but only those sections that are relevant.

Note that the numbering system for individual documents does not bear any relation to the ISO 9001 standard headings. That is because this company found this a more convenient way of organizing the documents. There is no requirement to align the document numbering system with the clauses of the standard. Indeed, it is not easy to see how such alignment could be maintained in a practical manner. Detailed operational tasks are listed in Section 3. In a larger company, there might be so many such tasks that a separate manual would be justified – a 'production manual', perhaps.

Guidance on ISO 9000 procedures

There are certain issues that must be addressed when preparing ISO 9000 procedures.

ABC Ltd
Quality System Document

Reference **QM-00**	***Approved for use by*** **Mark Smith**	**Date of issue/revision** 25.7.2002	**Page 1 of 1**
Title :	**Contents**		

Document title	**Reference**	**Date of current version**
Circulation list	QM-01	15 Jan 2002
Scope of the quality management system	QM-02	20 Jan 2002
Company background	QM-03	15 Jan 2002
Quality management system	QM-04	20 Jan 2002
Quality documentation	QM-05	20 Jan 2002
Quality records	QM-06	20 Jan 2002
Management commitment	QM-07	15 Jan 2002
Customer focus	QM-08	15 Jan 2002
Quality policy	QM-09	25 Jan 2002
Quality objectives and quality planning	QM-10	20 Jan 2002
Management responsibility and authority	QM-11	20 Jan 2002
Management representative	QM-12	20 Jan 2002
Internal communication	QM-13	25 July 2002
Review of the management system	QM-14	20 Jan 2002
Resource management	QM-15	20 Jan 2002
Human resources	QM-16	25 Jan 2002
Infrastructure	QM-17	15 Jan 2002
Work environment	QM-18	15 Mar 2002
Production planning	QM-19	20 Jan 2002
Customer-related processes	QM-20	20 Jan 2002
Control of development work on products and processes	QM-21	20 Jan 2002
Purchasing	QM-22	25 Jan 2002
Product specifications	QM-23	15 Jan 2002
Procedures/work instructions	QM-24	15 Jan 2002
Servicing	QM-25	15 Jan 2002
Identification and traceability	QM-26	15 Jan 2002
Preservation of product	QM-27	15 Jan 2002
Measuring and monitoring devices	QM-28	15 Jan 2002
Measurement of conformity and improvement	QM-29	15 Jan 2002
Monitoring customer satisfaction	QM-30	15 Jan 2002
Internal audit of the quality system	QM-31	15 Jan 2002
In-process and final product testing	QM-32	15 Jan 2002
Control of nonconforming product	QM-33	15 May 2002
Analysis of data	QM-34	15 Jan 2002
Improvement	QM-35	15 Jan 2002

Figure 14.1 Typical quality manual contents page

ABC Ltd
Quality System Document

Reference PM-00	***Approved for use by* Mark Smith**	**Date of issue/revision** 25.7.2002	**Page 1 of 2**
Title :	**Contents**		

Document	**Code**	**Date**
Section 1 General management procedures		
Contents	PM-00	As above
Guidelines on planning and improvement	100	15 Jan 2002
Procedure for approval of changes to the process	101	15 Jan 2002
Control of documentation	102	10 Jan 2002
Control of quality records	103	10 Jan 2002
Procedure for management review	104	10 Jan 2002
Procedure for internal quality auditing	105	10 Jan 2002
Checklist for internal quality audits	106	25 July 2002
Guidance on dealing with customers	107	10 Jan 2002
Procedure for customer surveys	108	10 Jan 2002
Procedure for customer complaints	109	10 Jan 2002
Procedure for corrective action	110	10 Jan 2002
Procedure for risk assessment and preventive action	111	15 Jan 2002
Procedure for product recall	112	10 Jan 2002
Quality awareness	113	10 Jan 2002
Section 2 Purchasing		
Purchasing process flow-chart	200	10 Jan 2002
Procedure for selection and approval of suppliers	201	10 Jan 2002
Procedure for review of suppliers	202	10 Jan 2002
Procedure for purchasing and receipt of materials	203	10 Jan 2002
List of approved suppliers and materials	204	15 Jan 2002
Section 3 Service control procedures		
Process flow-chart	300	10 Jan 2002
Daily schedule for operators	301	15 Jan 2002
Procedure for handling customer orders/contracts	302	10 Jan 2002
Procedure for intake of product	303	25 Jan 2002
Procedure for storage/stock-rotation	304	10 Jan 2002
Procedure for release of product	305	10 Jan 2002
Maintenance and calibration of equipment	306	10 Jan 2002
Procedure for control of cold stores	307	10 Jan 2002
Control of storage temperature	308	10 Jan 2002
Procedure for identification and traceability	319	15 Jan 2002
Procedure for controlling nonconforming product	310	10 Jan 2002
Procedure for order preparation and dispatch	311	15 Jan 2002
Section 4 Inspection and testing		
Quality inspection plan	400	10 Jan 2002
Procedure for physical conditions inspection	401	15 Jan 2002
Section 5 Cleaning		
General cleaning rules	500	10 Jan 2002
Cleaning schedule	501	15 Jan 2002
Standard cleaning procedure	502	10 Jan 2002
Cleaning procedure – chills	503	10 Jan 2002
Cleaning of dry storage areas	504	10 Jan 2002

ABC Ltd
Quality System Document

Reference PM-00	*Approved for use by* Mark Smith	Date of issue/revision 25.7.2002	Page 2 of 2
Title :	**Contents**		

Controlled copies

Controlled copies of the various sections of this manual are circulated as follows:

Section 1: General Manager; Stores Controller; Office Manager
Section 2: General Manager; Office Manager
Section 3: General Manager; Stores Controller
Section 4: General Manager; Quality Inspector
Section 5: General Manager; Stores Controller
Section 6: General Manager; Stores Controller
Section 7: General Manager; Office Manager

Figure 14.2 Contents of a manual of operational and quality management procedures from a small service company

DOCUMENT IDENTITY

Every document must have a unique identification, which is usually a code number. This number may or may not bear any relation to the numbering of ISO 9001 clauses, and is usually chosen on the basis of the sub-sections of the organization itself. Thus, all purchasing documents might have a prefix 'P', and service-related documents a prefix 'S', for example. In addition, it must show some distinguishing mark that indicates its revision status. This is to enable the user to determine whether it is the current version of the document. In fact, there is nothing that can be put on a document that, independently, shows its revision status. This can only be done by reference to another document, normally a master list of the current revisions of all documents. See Chapter 13 for a more detailed treatment of this aspect.

NUMBER OF PAGES

Each page should be marked with the page number, and the document should display the total number of pages it contains. This is to prevent a document being used from which pages are missing – perhaps an attachment. Each page must show the document revision identification.

RELEASE FOR USE

It should be clear that the document has been released for use, and is not merely a draft. That usually means displaying the name and/or signature of somebody who has been given the authority to release, or approve, the document in question. Note that this person may not have written, drafted or even issued the document, but is the person who has authorized it – that is, has taken responsibility for the content of the document. It is most effective if the person authorizing the individual procedures is the manager responsible for the process described in the manual – the *owner* of the process – often a departmental manager. This has the benefit of ensuring that the manager takes full responsibility for the consequences.

OBJECTIVE

It is very useful to state what the objective of the procedure is. What, precisely, is the procedure trying to achieve? What problems will be prevented by its implementation?

SCOPE

To what, precisely, does the procedure apply? Does it apply universally, or only in certain circumstances, or only to certain products or processes, or certain sections or departments?

METHOD

The prescribed method for performing the task in question constitutes the major part of the procedure. A documented procedure is required where the absence of a procedure could put quality in jeopardy. That fact will also determine the level of detail that is appropriate; it should not contain unnecessary detail. Excessive detail can cause problems later, since whatever is stated in the procedure must be implemented. After all, procedures are provided on the basis that what they contain is important for quality, and since these details have been included in the procedure they are obviously considered important for quality. An auditor is therefore quite entitled to raise a non-compliance where procedures are not implemented fully.

The description of the method should answer the questions:

- What is to be done?
- How is it done?
- When and where it is to be done?
- How will one know that it has been done properly (for example, by testing, inspecting or measuring)?
- What is to be done if there are problems (for example, failure)?

RECORDS

It should be specified what record, if any, is to be kept.

RESPONSIBILITIES

It should be stated clearly who is to carry out the task described. This is particularly important if several people are involved, or if it is not obvious who is to do it.

KEEP IT SHORT AND SIMPLE

Procedures should not be long or complex. They should be worded in the same way as simple verbal instructions:

1 Check that the widget adjuster is working properly.
2 Carefully remove the outer cover. Do not allow X to touch Y.
3 Adjust the widget according to the relevant specification.
4 Replace the outer cover, ensuring that there are no leaks.
5 Complete Form Z.

Note that if the operator has been trained, there is no need to go into detail in step 3. If the work is also closely supervised, then detail is doubly unnecessary. The training records will show whether the omission of these details in the procedure is justified.

For a more complex task, it may be better to break it down into a number of short procedures to facilitate document control (see Chapter 13).

Since the purpose of a procedure is to clarify and prevent confusion, it is important that it should state *exactly* what is intended, and not allow misinterpretation. Imprecise words should be avoided. Statements such as 'The operator measures the temperature *regularly*' and '*Most* records need to be retained' are open to different interpretations, and are not precise enough to ensure that everybody does the task the same way. Avoid the passive voice as far as possible. A statement like 'The problem is reported to the manager' leaves the possibility open that nobody will actually take it upon themselves to inform the manager. Better to state: 'When this happens *the operator must inform* the manager.'

OPERATING CONDITIONS

It is not usually necessary to describe in detail how a machine or instrument should be operated, since this information is usually available in the supplier's manual, and the person will have been trained in its use. But it may be important to specify the operating conditions for your particular circumstances, since these will be unique to your operation.

Where a process is controlled by maintaining some variable at a target level, the procedure should specify the acceptable limits, rather than simply the target. Thus, it is more instructive to the operator to state that the temperature of the process is to be maintained between 148°C and 152°C than to state that it should be maintained at 150°C.

TESTING AND INSPECTIONS

The procedure must include any quality checks to be carried out and any samples that must be taken. The inspection method should be described. Alternatively, the inspection can be described in a separate procedure, and a cross-reference made to it.

DUPLICATION

It is not usually a good idea to duplicate information in different procedures. When information is duplicated there is a risk that the information may be changed in one place and not in the other, resulting in one of them containing inaccurate information. It is better to use cross-references.

REVIEW OF DOCUMENTS

If the quality management system is going to be dynamic it will be necessary to review the documentation to ensure that it is kept up to date. ISO 9001: 2000 contains a requirement to 'review and update as necessary and re-approve documents'. This requirement should be included in the defined responsibilities of the appropriate managers. In practical terms, a simple approach to document review is to request the users of the document to confirm that the written method does reflect the actual situation. To make a record of this review simply make an uncontrolled copy of the contents page of the manual and get the reviewer to initial the margin opposite the document reviewed.

Further reading

Seaver, M., *Implementing ISO 9000: 2000*, Gower, Aldershot, 2001.

CHAPTER

15 *Controlling Changes*

Dennis Lock

The concept of a project that proceeds from initial concept to fulfilment without any change is a Utopian dream. There are many possible reasons for changes at any stage in the lifecycle of a product or project. However, even where the need for a particular change is seen as compelling, formal procedures must be in place to ensure that all the implications are considered and, if appropriate, to authorize the change and then see that it is properly implemented.

This chapter describes control procedures for design changes that have been proven in many companies. Related procedures for dealing with difficulties in complying with drawings and specifications are also described. Further aspects of change documentation and methods for recording the as-built state of products are described in Chapter 13. There is more on the subject of deviating from manufacturing instructions in Chapter 27.

The material covered in this chapter is especially relevant to engineering operations, but the principles and many of the practices are applicable to most operations, whether production or service.

The impact of changes

A significant change, perhaps ordered by a client or customer, can obviously have a big impact on a project, ranging from altered scope or basic objectives to complete cancellation. However, the impact of every proposed change, whatever its apparent scale, must be assessed before it can be authorized. That impact will depend on many factors, including the point in the project or production cycle at which the change is to be introduced. Things which a change can affect, directly or indirectly, adversely or advantageously, include (but are not limited to):

- performance and quality
- contractual obligations
- subcontracts
- purchasing
- costs and profitability
- plans and schedules
- work-in-progress (with possible scrap or waste)
- manufacturability
- reliability
- repairability

- interchangeability
- jigs, fixtures and tooling
- machining settings and control software
- inspection and test equipment
- health and safety
- product liability
- environmental pollution or damage
- documentation of all kinds, both internal and as issued to suppliers, customers and others
- motivation of personnel
- customer service.

The change committee

A change can affect commercial, technical or other factors well beyond the awareness or competence of its originator. For that reason, it is prudent (and common practice) to identify those managers or other suitably qualified individuals whose consideration and approval should be sought whenever a change is requested. These individuals, when brought together, make up a body which is typically known as a change committee.

The individuals on the full change committee should comprise relevant departmental managers or their delegates. These must include people who are able to answer for the likely safety, reliability, performance, cost and timescale consequences of changes, the effects on work-in-progress and the practical feasibility or otherwise of introducing the change into manufacture or construction.

The composition of a change committee at any particular sitting will depend to some extent on the nature of the change and the stage of progress that has been reached in the work. Usually, the committee has an essential core, which can be supplemented by co-opted specialists if necessary.

The functions that should be represented on the committee are discussed below.

THE DESIGN AUTHORITY

Responsibility for the technical design of a product or project must be vested unambiguously in one place, which can be recognized both inside and outside the company as the design authority. The design authority might be the chief engineer for an engineering project, the project manager, the quality manager or a consultant. The design authority is responsible for seeing that the design aspects of any proposed change are considered carefully, particularly for their effect on performance, safety, reliability and interchangeability.

THE INSPECTING AUTHORITY

The inspecting authority will often be a senior quality controller, chief inspector or the quality manager. The person responsible should report to a high level of management, preferably independently of the direct line management organization of manufacturing. This reporting structure, in theory at least, should help to ensure that the inspecting authority is able to function without undue pressure or bias if ever matters of quality or safety appear to be at odds with commercial or production commitments. The role of the inspecting authority must not be compromised.

For some government contracts, and for other work where safety is a special factor (such as in aviation), the inspecting authority might be an external inspectorate. It is common for such an external inspectorate to delegate its authority, under supervision, to the company's own quality assurance management.

THE COMMERCIAL AUTHORITY

Changes typically threaten budgets and delivery programmes. Those requested by the customer for a project or for a special product will probably provide the basis for negotiating contact changes (especially concerning price and delivery date extensions). A contracts manager or similarly qualified person should be available to consider such questions, with the background support of cost estimators and planners.

THE MANUFACTURING AUTHORITY

The manufacturing authority (typically represented by a senior production manager) will need to consider the consequences of each change on inventory and manufacturing.

CHANGE COMMITTEE MEETINGS

Sensible administration is needed to ensure that no change request is unduly delayed for consideration, while avoiding the creation of a large number of time-wasting and possibly hastily summoned meetings. On engineering projects in large organizations, formal change committee meetings are typically held at regular intervals, their frequency depending on the number of changes being experienced and the urgency of the work. In other cases it might be more sensible to conduct change committee business during other meetings at which the relevant members are expected to attend regularly. It must, however, always be possible to arrange for ad hoc meetings or other short-notice arrangements to deal with particularly urgent changes.

Decision criteria

Questions which might have to be considered before a change can be authorized are likely to include several from the list given below (some of the questions in this list obviously relate only to projects, and others are specific to products manufactured continuously or in batches):

- Is the change actually possible to make?
- What are the estimated costs (or savings) of the change:
  - once-only costs?
  - costs or savings per unit of production?
- For projects or custom-built items, will the customer pay for the change? If so, what should be the price?
- If the change is not customer-requested, is it really necessary? Why?

- What will be the effect on progress? Is there enough time in the work programme to allow the change?
- How will safety, reliability and performance be affected?
- At what stage in production should the change be introduced (the point of embodiment)? The manufacturing authority's recommendation would usually carry weight in this decision unless the change is intended to remove a safety hazard (requiring immediate and possibly retrospective action).
- Are any items to be changed retrospectively? Are these:
  - in progress?
  - in stock?
  - already delivered to the customer?
- Will scrap or redundant stocks be created?
- What internally used drawings, specifications and other documents will have to be modified?
- What externally issued or published documents will have to be modified?

Where the change is to be applied to an item that is being manufactured in batches, interchangeability must also be considered:

- Will the items which accommodate the change be interchangeable with those manufactured in earlier batches?

When the committee has considered all these questions, it has the option to:

- Authorize the change as requested.
- Give restricted approval only, authorizing the change with specified limitations.
- Refer the request back to the originator (or elsewhere), asking for clarification, or for an alternative solution.
- Reject the change, giving reasons.

Design freeze

The further into design and (especially) production a design project has progressed, the more potentially expensive or disruptive any change will be. It is easily possible for a keen originator to believe that a proposed change will bring benefits to the product, to the customers and to the company when, in fact, the disruption caused would far outweigh the foreseen benefits. Indeed, one change committee known to this author applied the following rule to all late changes unless they were customer-funded:

> If it's essential, we do it.
> If it's desirable, we don't.

In most design projects a point is reached where any change would be particularly damaging. This can lead to the imposition of a design freeze, after which no change request will be considered unless there are exceptionally strong reasons – such as malfunction, safety or a request from a paying client or customer.

If a design project is for a new product development, a design freeze might be imposed on early production, allowing changes to be made at later, specified and more convenient points of embodiment. This kind of arrangement is clearly required to allow for continuous product improvement. For this reason, product batches released to the outside world over a period of time can differ from each other in varying degrees. For many reasons, it is obviously necessary to keep track of these differences (for example, to recall unsafe products). Documentation for recording these variations is described in Chapter 13.

Change requests

Change requests can arise internally for many reasons. An engineer, designer or quality controller might discover a design error, recognize the need to comply with some standard or regulation, or simply have a good idea somewhat late. Change requests can also result from other internal sources or procedures, for example when a documented query points to the need to change a specification. The marketing department could request some change to a product in an attempt to improve sales. Changes can also arise from a variety of participative quality improvement techniques.

In theory, at least, any person should be allowed to ask for a change, because requests can have no practical effect until they have been considered and authorized by the change committee. If a company is concerned about possible time-wasting through requests that are frivolous or obviously unsuitable, it can rule that every application must be countersigned by a supervisor or departmental manager before it can be considered. This author has never found such a restriction to be necessary in practice.

Change requests may have to be originated following an instruction from a customer or client. These circumstances apply particularly to engineering projects and custom-built products. Changes are generated by such documents as project variation orders (also known as contract variations) and purchase order amendments. Some aspects of these documents are described in Chapter 13. These changes may have nuisance value because they are usually compulsory and can disrupt or cancel work in progress. They do, however, give the manufacturer or project contractor the chance of recouping at least the costs of the change, and possibly more.

CHANGE REQUEST FORMS

Change originators should always put their request in writing using a standard engineering change request form, the purpose of which is to describe, document and seek formal permission for a permanent design change. Change requests of the type shown in Figure 15.1 are used widely, although they may be known by different titles.

CO-ORDINATION AND PROGRESSING

Many change committees include a change co-ordinator, often considered essential in engineering situations. This is a person who can be given responsibility for following every change request through, to ensure that it is put before the change committee, that the actions authorized do in fact take place, and that the relevant documents are revised and reissued. This co-ordinator might be a project co-ordinating engineer, a technical clerk, or

Change Request Form

Process involved		
Products affected		
Reference documentation attached Important: See Document Control Procedure		
Details of proposed change		
Reason for change (e.g. current problems, benefits)		
Change has potential impact on:		
Signed:		**Date:**

Change assessed for impact on	**Impact (Y/N)**	**Change Committee Instructions**
Product quality		
Product safety		
Other processes		
Cost		
Environment		
Occupational health and safety		
System documentation		
Other:		

The above change is approved subject to any instructions noted above.

Signed: ______________________ Date: _______________
pp Change Committee

Figure 15.1 Change request form

some other suitable member of the engineering department. He or she will maintain some form of register to:

- allocate a serial number to each change request
- record the committee decision
- progress the change through all stages
- act as a permanent record and index of changes.

In a typical arrangement, the co-ordinator will be responsible for submitting change requests to the change committee. The co-ordinator will distribute copies of authorized change forms for action. If rejected, the originator must be informed. Follow-up activity includes ensuring that changed drawings or specifications are issued. Original request forms should be kept on file to become part of the particular project or product's technical documentation.

EMERGENCY CHANGES

There are occasions when a change has to be carried out with urgency, so that the process must be modified before revised drawings or specifications can be issued. If time allows, a change request can be processed quickly, possibly by taking it to the change committee members in turn. If authorized, the change note itself then becomes an attachment to the issued drawings or specifications, to be used for all manufacturing, inspection and testing purposes. The original documents must, of course, be revised: normal distribution of the change request action copies, coupled with follow-up monitoring from the co-ordinator, should ensure that this happens.

There are other times when changes have to be made even before they can be considered by the committee. Such changes can arise, for example, when a vital production operation is held up awaiting correction of a specification or drawing error. The engineering query procedure described later in this chapter can sometimes be used to unblock such problems. Again, the use of a formal procedure should ensure that the mistake is corrected on the original file drawing.

Another method which is often used to clear manufacturing problems which arise from design errors or unclear drawings is for the engineer or appropriate technical expert responsible to visit the work station, sort out the problem on the spot, and mark up the offending print of the drawing or specification. The engineer's signature would be required against the correction to authorize the change and allow the 'nonconforming' job to proceed through subsequent inspection or test stages.

Many people, however, do not look kindly upon the use of marked-up documents. They are right to object. There is always a risk that changes made on the spot will not find their way into the official documents system, and there is the added danger that all the implications of the alteration have not been properly considered. Short of banning the practice altogether, marked-up documents should only be allowed under strictly controlled conditions, within some formal procedural framework. An emergency change procedure which can include the use of marked-up documents will now be outlined.

The change originator writes out a change request and has it registered and serially numbered by the change co-ordinator. After seeking the immediate approval of the relevant responsible manager (or deputy), the originator attaches a signed copy of the change request form to the manufacturing documents, where it becomes part of the manufacturing instructions, allowing production to resume or continue. The co-ordinator will see that the change is put before the next change committee meeting, after which action copies of the authorized change can be distributed in the usual way (triggering revision of the original documents in the official files).

Once an emergency change instruction has been issued to a production area, the change request form must remain attached to the manufacturing documents through all subsequent stages of manufacture and inspection. In the event of the working prints having to be marked up (which might be unavoidable if there is insufficient space on the change request form), an identically marked-up print must be provided simultaneously for the engineering or quality department, as appropriate, from which the original documents can be altered when the change is properly authorized. It is better to produce the second marked-up copy by photocopying the first, to eliminate any risk of clerical error.

Production permits and related procedures

The flow of manufacturing information is hardly ever a one-way affair from the technical department to the manufacturing organization. More typically, questions begin to arise when the production personnel attempt to achieve the results demanded in newly issued drawings or specifications. There are several ways in which questions or difficulties can manifest themselves within a production department. Sometimes these can lead to hardware that does not conform strictly to the designer's intentions, or to the need for drawings or specifications to be changed to make manufacturing easier or possible.

Several recognized procedures exist for dealing with such questions in a formal manner, so that quality is not put at risk and proper records are kept. Each procedure has its own purpose-designed form, but there is no reason why the administrative procedure should differ from that already described for change requests. Where the organization allows, the same co-ordinator can often deal with the registration and progressing of all these documents.

The most usually encountered procedures are described below. These are not mutually exclusive, and two or more of them might be operated together in the same organization.

ENGINEERING QUERY NOTES

There might be a particular feature of a drawing which is difficult to understand, or a specified operation that is proving difficult or impossible to perform in practice. Perhaps, for example, a specified material cannot be machined to the required surface finish, or it might be found that the adhesive named on a drawing will not produce a satisfactory bond. The obvious course for the perplexed manufacturing staff is to refer the problem back to the engineering department. In many companies, this might be done simply by picking up a telephone or visiting the engineers. Other companies operate formal engineering query procedures.

In one company known to this author, a formal written procedure was insisted upon because the engineering manager disliked having workmen in dirty (or even clean) overalls within his office boundaries, leaving tarry footprints from the wood-blocked shop floor. However, there are often more valid reasons for a formal procedure. This is especially the case in industries where reliability and safety are critical, and where every manufacturing difficulty that could be attributable to engineering design must be properly assessed, be seen to receive suitable expert attention, and be adequately documented (triggering engineering change action if appropriate).

The answer to an engineering query will often consist of a more detailed or alternative description of the existing instructions. It might be, however, that the documents are inadequate or actually wrong, in which case they must be revised. In cases where a drawing change is required, production can usually be allowed to proceed without waiting for revised drawings to be issued, by considering the annotated engineering query note as part of the officially issued manufacturing documentation. The existence of the completed query form alongside the relevant drawings allows the work to be passed through subsequent inspection or test stages. The query note has, in effect, become a kind of production permit.

Figure 15.2 illustrates an engineering query form which can double as a production permit.

PRODUCTION PERMITS

A procedure closely related to formalized engineering queries is seen when manufacturing departments find that they need to apply for permission to depart from the issued instructions. Here, there may be no implied criticism or questioning of the manufacturing documents or design quality; the manufacturing department is simply stating that it cannot, on this occasion, for reasons beyond its reasonable control, carry out the instructions as issued. The permit request will propose and seek authorization to proceed with some alternative solution.

Procedures for production permits vary greatly from one company to another. They can range from the very informal 'Is it all right if we do it this way instead, George?' to a strictly controlled procedure. Rigid procedures can be expected in the defence, aerospace and nuclear industries, and in any other case where safety and reliability rank high as objectives.

The use of alternative materials, different adhesives, modified assembly and acceptance of wider tolerances are all possible reasons for requesting production permits. Any of these might represent a risk to performance, reliability, safety or interchangeability. As a general rule, therefore, production permits require the formal approval of the design authority. For some industries, the approval of the inspecting authority may also be required. The general administrative procedure can be similar to that already described for engineering query notes. An example of a production permit is shown in Figure 15.3.

Because a production permit implies a departure from the designer's intentions, consequential revision of manufacturing documents will usually not be relevant. The validity of a permit should normally be restricted to one unit, or to a limited number of units which are identified by their batch or serial numbers. The manufacturing department would be expected to take steps to obtain the correct materials or take whatever other action is needed to comply with existing drawings and specifications for future manufacturing.

Records of all production permits must be kept. The permit serial numbers should be indexed (preferably using a computer database) in such a way that they can be related to the relevant manufactured items. This is essential to be able to track back over any particular unit's history should it become necessary to investigate causes of failure in use.

Engineering Query Note	EQN number:
Drawing/part no: Issue/rev:	Project or job number:
QUERY: to engineering department: Is the work held up?	
Queried by: Department: Date:	
ANSWER:	
Answered by: Telephone ext: Date:	
PRODUCTION PERMIT (if appropriate): The above instructions to deviate from drawings will not affect reliability, safety or interchangeability. Drawings will be changed*/Drawings will not be changed and this permit applies only to this batch or job *Delete as appropriate Signed (Senior or chief engineer):	

Figure 15.2 Engineering query note

This form allows queries to be converted into production permits, where the answer instructs production staff to deviate from the relevant drawing or specification.

Production Permit Request	PPR number:
	Project or job number:

Name of part of assembly:
Drawings or specification number: Rev:
Batch or serial numbers affected:

Is the work held up?	
Yes	No
Tick as appropriate	

DETAILS OF REQUEST:
Permission is requested to deviate from the drawing/specification listed above as follows:

REASON FOR REQUEST:

Requested by: Department: Date:

ASSESSMENT	DECISION: Refused/Granted
Quality:	Comments:
Health and safety:	
Interchangeability:	
Other:	Design authority: Date:
For Technical Department: Date:	Inspecting authority: Date:

Figure 15.3 Production permit

A form such as this can also be used to request a concession for a manufacturing or functional nonconformity.

CONCESSIONS

Concessions are very similar to production permits, and some people make no distinction between the two terms. The requirement for a concession can arise if a product fails marginally an inspection stage, or does not quite satisfy the specified performance in all respects during testing. If rectification is not possible, there might be reluctance to scrap the product owing to the very slight degree of nonconformity.

Where the product embodies a relatively high investment of time and materials, or where its completion is eagerly awaited for an urgent programme, then the production management or the project manager might wish to try to obtain the inspection release of the product. One way of going about this would be to raise a request for a production permit, as described in the preceding section. But this would be a needless proliferation of paper; it is simpler and more efficient to use the foot of the nonconformity report as a concession request (see Figure 15.4).

The criteria for authorizing concessions are the same as those described above for production permits. The design authority must give approval, and that of the inspecting authority might also be required.

As with production permits, concessions imply a failure to satisfy the designer's intentions, so that associated revision of manufacturing drawings or specifications is usually neither necessary nor desirable. Each concession must be identifiable (by its serial number) with the particular unit or production batch to which it relates. Suitably indexed files must be kept (preferably using a computer), in order to be able to track back over all concessions in any particular unit's history should it become necessary to investigate causes of failure in use.

<table>
<tr><td colspan="2" rowspan="2">Report of Nonconformity</td><td>Report number:</td></tr>
<tr><td>Report date:</td></tr>
<tr><td colspan="2">JOB INSPECTED OR TESTED:
Name of part of assembly:
Part or drawing or number: Rev:
Specification number: Rev:</td><td>Job, batch or serial number(s) affected:</td></tr>
<tr><td colspan="3">DETAILS OF NONCONFORMITY:

Reported by: Department: Date:</td></tr>
<tr><td colspan="3">REQUEST FOR CONCESSION (if applicable):
The nonconformity detailed in this report will not affect quality, safety or interchangeability.
Further comments:

Requested by: Supported by: (Design authority)</td></tr>
<tr><td colspan="3">DISPOSAL INSTRUCTIONS:</td></tr>
<tr><td>Scrap and remake</td><td>Rectify and reinspect/retest</td><td>Concession granted</td></tr>
<tr><td></td><td></td><td></td></tr>
<tr><td colspan="3">Authorized by: Date:</td></tr>
</table>

Figure 15.4 Nonconformity report form with provision for conversion into a manufacturing concession

CHAPTER **16**

Standards, Standardization, Conformity and Compatibility

Charles Corrie

Standards affect all of us, in many different facets of our lives, even though many of us are not necessarily cognizant of this fact. While formal standards originated historically from the engineering and manufacturing industries, today they are developed and applied in diverse fields such as public administration and services.

What are standards?

Standards are documented agreements containing technical specifications or other precise criteria to be used consistently as rules, guidelines or definitions of characteristics to ensure that materials, products, processes and services are fit for their purpose.

The key to determining the content of a standard is its scope. This will have been agreed collectively by the interested parties involved in the development of an individual standard. What they want may be an agreed terminology or classification, or methods of measurement or testing, or they may want verifiable criteria for a standard product or some practical recommendations or guidance for its use.

The resulting 'documented agreements' may take a whole variety of formats, from a printed A4-sized document, a pocket-sized booklet, a loose-bound folder, or increasingly, a fully electronic format.

Why are standards created?

Industry-wide standardization exists within a particular industrial sector when the large majority of products or services conform to the same standards. It results from consensus agreements reached between all economic players in that industrial sector – suppliers, users, and often governments. They agree on specifications and criteria to be applied consistently in the choice and classification of materials, the manufacture of products, and the provision of services. The aim is to facilitate trade, exchange and technology transfer through:

- enhanced product quality and reliability at a reasonable price
- improved health, safety and environmental protection, and reduction of waste
- greater compatibility and interoperability of goods and services
- simplification for improved usability
- reduction in the number of models, and thus reduction in costs
- increased distribution efficiency, and ease of maintenance.

For international standardization the existence of non-harmonized standards for similar technologies in different countries or regions can contribute to so-called 'technical barriers to trade'. Export-minded industries have long sensed the need to agree on world standards to help rationalize the international trading process.

International standardization is well established for many technologies in such diverse fields as information processing and communications, textiles, packaging, distribution of goods, energy production and utilization, shipbuilding, banking and financial services. It will continue to grow in importance for all sectors of industrial activity for the foreseeable future.

The main reasons for this are:

- **World-wide progress in trade liberalization** – Today's free-market economies increasingly encourage diverse sources of supply and provide opportunities for expanding markets. On the technology side, fair competition needs to be based on identifiable, clearly defined common references that are recognized from one country to the next, and from one region to the other. An industry-wide standard, internationally recognized, developed by consensus among trading partners, serves as the language of trade.

- **Interpenetration of sectors** – No industry in today's world can truly claim to be completely independent of components, products, rules of application and so on, that have been developed in other sectors. Bolts are used in aviation and for agricultural machinery; welding plays a role in mechanical and nuclear engineering, and electronic data processing has penetrated all industries. Environmentally friendly products and processes, and recyclable or biodegradable packaging, are pervasive concerns.

- **World-wide communications systems** – The computer industry offers a good example of technology that needs quickly and progressively to be standardized at a global level. Full compatibility among open systems fosters healthy competition among producers, and offers real options to users, since it is a powerful catalyst for innovation, improved productivity and cost-cutting.

- **Global standards for emerging technologies** – Standardization programmes are now being developed in completely new fields, such as the environment, life sciences, urbanization and construction. In the very early stages of new technology development, applications can be imagined but functional prototypes do not exist. Here, the need for standardization lies in defining terminology and accumulating databases of quantitative information. An example of the impact of standards in a new technology is the MP3 format for digital audio systems, where manufacturers agreed the format of the new media prior to producing and releasing consumer versions of their machines for playing music.

- **Developing countries** – Development agencies are increasingly recognizing that a standardization infrastructure is a basic requirement for the success of economic policies aimed at achieving sustainable development. Creating such an infrastructure in developing countries is essential for improving productivity, market competitiveness and export capability, according to the International Organization for Standardization.

Users have more confidence in products and services that conform to recognized standards. Assurance of conformity can be provided by manufacturers' declarations, or by audits carried out by independent bodies.

Standardization at national and international level

NATIONAL

Around the world, national standards bodies vary considerably in their constitution, ownership, areas of responsibility, participation, revenue-generation and funding models.

Some are directly constituted and controlled through their national governments, some are owned on the basis of a collective association (where subscribing members are considered to be the owners of the organization), and others are fully independent private organizations. Those closer to government tend to be more heavily financed through direct funding mechanisms, whereas those closer to the private sector tend to be dependent on other revenue-generating mechanisms (for example, through the sale of standards).

Within a single country, there may be more than one recognized national standards body, each with a differing area of responsibility. For example, there may be one body responsible for standardization on electrotechnical issues, with a separate body for all other standards.

Independent of their ownership and funding, there is a wide variety of mechanisms for the participation in the actual work of developing standards. Some national standards bodies use systems of representational participation (for example, only trade associations, professional associations or the government may send delegates to meetings), others use individual subscription schemes, and some are by invitation only.

INTERNATIONAL

There are two levels of international standards bodies: those that are fully international, and those that represent a geographic region.

At the fully international level are the International Organization for Standardization (ISO), the International Electrotechnical Commission (IEC) and the International Telecommunications Union (ITU).

Regionally, there are groupings of standards bodies that cover national standards bodies in distinct geographical areas:

Europe – CEN, CENELEC, ETSI (see below)
Asia/Pacific – ASEAN Consultative Committee for Standards and Quality (ACCSQ) and the Pacific Area Standards Congress (PASC)
Africa – African Standards Regional Organisation (ARSO)

North/South America – Pan American Standards Commission (COPANT)
Arab States – Arab Industrial Development and Mining Organization (AIDMO)
Euro-Asia – Asian Council for Standardization, Metrology and Certification (EASC).

For ISO, the IEC and the relevant regional groups, each country is invited to nominate a standards body to act as its representative in their proceedings. About 145 countries are members of ISO, and 61 are members of the IEC.

Both ISO and the IEC use formal rules of procedure. These have been developed jointly by the two organizations, and are entitled the ISO/IEC Directives. They detail the responsibilities of their central secretariats, the committee secretariats, and those of the participating national standards bodies and liaison organizations.

Generally, ISO and the IEC use a system of technical committees, sub-committees and working groups to develop their international standards, to which the national standards bodies may send delegates. The national standards bodies are not required to participate in all of them, and may be selective as to which committees they send delegations. There are approximately 730 technical committees and sub-committees in ISO, and about 180 in the IEC.

At the technical committee and sub-committee levels, the delegations work to a national briefing, and represent their own national standards body's views. At the working group level, individual experts are nominated by a national standards body or liaison organization, but they are then expected to work from their avowed expertise, not from a national briefing.

The development of standards proceeds on the basis of the achievement of consensus among the participating bodies, with final ratification by ballot. ISO adheres to a policy of 'one member one vote' in its ballots.

ISO, IEC and the ITU are not empowered to compel anyone to use their standards. The standards that are adopted therefore remain voluntary unless national laws intervene. The participating national standards bodies are encouraged to adopt international standards as national standards, but there is no obligation that they do so.

OUTPUT FROM INTERNATIONAL STANDARDIZATION

ISO produces a variety of products, with differing levels of consensus requirements and differing development processes. The IEC offers a similar range of products.

Foremost among these is the International Standard (IS). Publication of an International Standard requires that the highest degree of consensus has been sought under ISO's and IEC's development processes. Usually, this involves the following stages before publication of the International Standard is permitted:

- balloting of a New Work Item Proposal (NWIP)
- preparation of Working Drafts (WDs)
- balloting of a Committee Draft (CD)
- balloting of an Enquiry Draft, also known as a Draft International Standard (DIS)
- balloting of a Final Draft International Standard (FDIS).

A Technical Specification (TS) may be developed when the subject in question is still under development or where for any other reason there is the future but not immediate possibility of an agreement to publish an International Standard. In such circumstances, a technical committee or sub-committee may decide that the publication of a Technical Specification is appropriate. The reasons for publishing the Technical Specification, and an explanation of its relationship to the expected future International Standard, is required to be given in its Foreword. In addition, when the required support cannot be obtained for a final draft International Standard to pass the approval stage, or in case of lack of consensus, the technical committee or sub-committee may decide that the document should be published in the form of a Technical Specification.

A Publicly Available Specification (PAS) in an intermediate specification published prior to the development of a full International Standard. IEC also publishes the PAS as a 'dual-logo' document in collaboration with an external organization. The PAS does not fulfil the requirements for a standard.

A Technical Report may be developed when a technical committee or sub-committee has collected data of a different kind to those normally published as an International Standard. These may be, for example, data obtained from a survey carried out among the national bodies, data on work in other international organizations, or data on the 'state of the art' in relation to standards of national bodies on a particular subject.

An International Workshop Agreement (IWA) may be developed following the acceptance of a proposal from a variety of sources, including ISO member bodies, liaison organizations and corporate bodies. They are developed outside of the usual committee process by a 'workshop'-style meeting. The date and venue for the workshop are widely advertised to ensure that as many interested parties as possible can attend. Workshops decide on the content of their own deliverables. Competing IWAs on the same subject are permitted, and the technical content of an IWA may compete with the technical content of an existing ISO or IEC standard, or the proposed content of an ISO or IEC standard under development. After three years, an IWA is required to be reviewed to determine whether it should be confirmed, developed into an International Standard, or be withdrawn.

A Technology Trends Assessment (TTA) is developed by pre-standardization research organizations with which ISO has a co-operation agreement, or is one that may be developed in a pre-standardization workshop.

REVIEW OF STANDARDS

In order to ensure the continuing currency and relevance of a specific standard, ISO, the IEC, the regional standards body groupings and most national standards bodies require that individual standards be reviewed at least every five years. The result of a review may be to confirm a standard without alteration, to decide to revise or amend it, or to decide that it is now obsolescent and to withdraw it.

INTERNATIONAL LIAISON ORGANIZATIONS

ISO and the IEC allow for the participation of other international bodies (for example, the International Accreditation Forum) in their committee proceedings through the creation of formal liaison arrangements. (ISO currently recognizes about 500 such organizations.) Such liaison organizations are not permitted to participate in the voting on standards (or other documents) under development, but are invited to provide technical comment on drafts.

There are several categories of liaison member, with varying degrees of participation in committee proceedings being permitted for the differing categories. The benefit of such liaisons is that they bring the specific expertise and focus from a particular sector to bear on the development of standards. Sometimes, the collaboration with a particular liaison organization results in a standard (or other type of publication) being jointly published by both organizations. Such documents carry the logos of both organizations on their covers.

EUROPEAN STANDARDS BODIES

The European grouping of regional standards bodies includes:

- European Committee for Standardization (CEN)
- European Committee for Electrotechnical Standardization (CENELEC)
- European Telecommunications Standards Institute (ETSI).

These directly mirror the work of ISO, IEC and the ITU respectively, at the full international level. Formal agreements on co-operation exist between ISO and CEN and between the IEC and CENELEC. These seek to avoid the duplication of work between the paired institutes in common areas of interest, and allow for parallel voting on draft standards between the paired institutes.

Countries which are members of the European Union (EU) or the European Free Trade Area (EFTA) are entitled to be members of CEN, CENELEC and ETSI.

The development of standards proceeds on the basis of the achievement of consensus among the participating bodies, with final ratification by ballot. As with ISO and the IEC, most standards development is through the use of technical committees, sub-committees and working groups. However, a key difference to ISO and the IEC is the use of a system of weighted voting in CEN and CENELEC, with the larger countries being assigned higher-weighted votes.

CEN and CENELEC are not empowered to compel anyone to use their standards. The standards that are adopted therefore remain voluntary unless national or European law intervenes.

EUROPEAN STANDARDIZATION DOCUMENTS

The main types of CEN and CENELEC publication are European Standards (designated EN), Harmonization Documents (HD) and European Prestandards (designated ENV). ENs and HDs constitute CEN and CENELEC standards, while ENVs are prospective standards for provisional application.

An EN carries the obligation on CEN or CENELEC members to implement it at national level by giving it the status of a national standard and by withdrawing any conflicting national standards. The technical content of an EN is therefore presented in identical form in each country, and is of equal validity. The only possible exception to this is in EFTA countries whose members have not supported its adoption.

An HD carries the same obligation to withdraw any conflicting national standards, but public announcement of its number and title is otherwise sufficient. HDs are established if transposition into national standards is unnecessary, as in the case when a CEN or CENELEC member has already adopted the ISO or IEC standard being endorsed in Europe, or is impracticable, or, particularly, if agreement is subject to the acceptance of national technical deviations.

SECTOR ARRANGEMENTS

CEN and CENELEC have the facility to administer, or to associate formally with, such other organizations as may exist on a sufficiently authoritative and participative basis for the purpose of preparing standards in particular sectors:

- The European Coal and Steel Community used to maintain a separate, official committee structure for drawing up iron and steel standards, then issued as 'Euronorms'. Nowadays, it sponsors the European Committee for Iron and Steel Standardization (ECISS) administered by CEN.
- The European Aerospace Manufacturers' Association (AECMA) is recognized by CEN as an Associated Body competent to conduct all preparatory standards work in the aerospace field prior to formal CEN voting.
- CEN also has a protocol with the European Cooperation for Space Standardization (ECSS) for the development of European Standards.
- CEN also provides the secretariat to the European Board for EDIFACT Standardization, which supports the United Nations Rules for Electronic Data Interchange for Administration, Commerce and Transport (UN/EDIFACT) process in Europe.

EUROPEAN UNION

Most European standards are prepared at the behest of industry. However, the European Commission can also request CEN, CENELEC and ETSI to prepare standards in the context of the implementation of European Community legislation. This is known as 'mandated' standardization work.

REMOVING TRADE BARRIERS WITHIN THE EUROPEAN UNION – THE OLD APPROACH

An ambitious European Community programme intended to eliminate technical barriers to trade was launched in 1969. Directives issued under Article 100 of the Treaty of Rome established free circulation objectives for Member States, linked to detailed annexes setting out technical requirements. Keeping these annexes up to date proved an unexpectedly heavy burden, the flow of new directives dried up, and the Commission reviewed its policy ten years later.

THE LOW VOLTAGE DIRECTIVE

As an exception to what was then normal practice, the 1973 Low Voltage Directive was drafted in such a way that national standards harmonized through CENELEC would provide the detailed criteria for assessing the safety of a wide range of products against a list of the minimal essential requirements to be taken into account. Much of the work of CENELEC has since been directed towards providing the necessary standards, mostly in the form of HDs, as far as possible by endorsement of pre-existing IEC standards.

MUTUAL RECOGNITION

The *Cassis de Dijon* judgment in 1979 established the principle that any product lawfully produced or marketed in one Member State must be admitted to the market of any other Member State by virtue of Article 30 of the Treaty of Rome ('general prohibition of quantitative restrictions on imports between Member States and all measures having equivalent effect'), unless Article 36 can be invoked ('justification of restrictions on grounds of public morality, public policy, protection of health and life etc.'). Following this principle, it was recognized that directives should promulgate only the essential requirements needed as a harmonized basis for national regulations, relying on the subsequent provision of voluntary safety standards that would not fall foul of safeguard clauses or the general application of Article 36. The principle of mutual recognition was stated in the Commission's 1985 White Paper on completion of the internal market, which first listed the programme of Community measures to be adopted no later than 1992:

> In cases where harmonization of regulations and standards is not considered essential from either a health/safety or an industrial point of view, immediate and full recognition of differing quality standards, food composition rules etc. must be the rule. In particular, sales bans cannot be based on the sole argument that an imported product has been manufactured according to specifications which differ from those used in the importing country. There is no obligation on the buyer to prove the equivalence of a product produced according to the rules of the exporting state. Similarly, he must not be required to submit such a product to additional technical tests nor to certification procedures in the importing state. Any purchaser, be he wholesaler, retailer or the final consumer, should have the right to choose his supplier in any part of the Community without restriction. The Commission will use all the powers available under the Treaty, particularly Articles 30–36, to reinforce this principle of 'mutual recognition'.

THE NEW APPROACH

Directives under the new approach are based on Article 100A introduced by the Single European Act. They are no longer dependent on unanimity in the Council of Ministers, but are subject to the requirement that the Commission, in its proposals concerning health, safety, environmental protection and consumer protection, will take as a base a high level of protection.

Under these directives:

- legislative harmonization is limited to the adoption of essential requirements only
- preparation of supporting technical specifications is entrusted to standardization organizations
- such technical specifications maintain their status as voluntary standards
- national authorities are obliged to recognize products conforming to harmonized standards as presumed to conform to the essential requirements.

PROCUREMENT DIRECTIVES

Article 6 of the Treaty establishing the European Community (formerly Article 7 of the

Treaty of Rome) prohibits discrimination on grounds of nationality within the scope of application of the Treaty. Liberalization of public procurement is seen as an important element in establishing the Single Market – an area in which the free movement of goods, persons, services and capital is assured. Under the amended Public Supplies and Public Works Directives, and the new Public Services and Utilities Directives, those responsible for inviting tenders for contracts above certain values are required to define their technical specifications by reference to national standards implementing European standards, where these exist, subject to permission derogation. On this basis, no authority likely to be bound by the outcome can afford to ignore European standardization developments.

In the absence of suitable European specifications, the Utilities Directive envisages that contract specifications should, as far as possible, be defined by reference to other standards having currency within the Community. The Supplies and Works Directives indicate more explicitly that in this case it is appropriate to make reference in order of preference to:

1 national standards implementing international standards accepted by the country of the contracting authority
2 other national standards (and national technical approvals) of the country of the contracting authority
3 any other standard.

However, contracting entities bound by the directives are advised to qualify with the words 'or equivalent' any specification requirement referring to a purely national standard, in order to be able to verify compliance with their technical conditions without running the risk of unlawfully restricting the initial opportunity to tender.

LEGAL STATUS OF STANDARDS

Few standards are directly enforceable in law, and either compliance with or conformity to a standard is generally a voluntary action. Use of standards may be enforced by law only through their incorporation in contracts, in trade descriptions or in legislation. Such actions are outside the control of the standards bodies. However, codes of practice, guidance notes and practice notes are increasingly being used to complement statute law. They underpin the law and provide further guidance on standards, implications and procedures. Failure to comply with an approved code of practice may be cited in criminal proceedings against a company or an individual. Other codes merely indicate practices which would support a company's claim to have exercised 'due diligence', or in the case of 'occupational exposure levels', determine acceptable standards for healthy working with substances.

There has been increasing legislation in the areas of trade descriptions, health and safety, food safety, consumer protection, environmental protection and product liability (often supported by European Union directives). As standards are based on scientific and technical knowledge, they can clearly play a vital role in defining expected performance or safety levels. Furthermore, the operation of standards-based quality management systems and procedures designed to identify and control components, materials and methods to ensure a safe and reliable product enable suppliers to give their customers, and the public at large, greater confidence in the expected performance of their goods and services.

ADOPTION, AVAILABILITY AND DESIGNATION

Standards are made publicly available through the national standards bodies that collaborate in the global and regional standards organizations. Only where there has been express difficulty in procuring a standard will one of the regional or international bodies intervene to provide copies of their standards. Users should always direct their enquiries to their own national standards body in the first instance. However, searchable catalogues of standards are available through the Websites of the international organizations, as well as through those of many of the regional and national standards bodies.

The adoption of ISO or IEC standards by a national standards body is voluntary, whereas for members of CEN or CENELEC the adoption of the relevant standards is mandatory. Of the approximately 12 000 ISO standards, the UK has adopted approximately 7000. Of the 6000 CEN standards, the UK has implemented about 5000. For comparison, the full portfolio of British Standards numbers about 20 000.

The methods used for the designation of adopted standards are in transition from one system to another. Formerly, when CEN adopted an ISO standard, it added 20 000 to the number of the ISO standard, but did not indicate ISO within the designation (for example ISO 9001: 1987 became EN 29001: 1987). This is now changing to a clearer designation system, which allows for traceability to the originating organization and the original document. Under the new system, CEN merely needs to add EN in front of the ISO designation (for example, ISO 9001: 2000 became EN ISO 9001: 2000). The national standards bodies are also following this revised system, and adding their national prefix to either the EN or ISO designation as appropriate. For example, while ISO 9001: 1987 had the designation BS 5750: Part 1, ISO 9001: 2000 is known as BS EN ISO 9001: 2000.

CONFORMITY

Conformity assessment is defined in EN 45020: 1998 as: 'any activity concerned with determining directly or indirectly that relevant requirements are fulfilled'. This very general definition conceals a complexity and wide-ranging applicability to the activities of industry, which uses conformity assessment to examine a product, process or service to determine whether it fulfils a defined expectation. The defined expectation may be a standard, or it may be a contractual requirement, stated or implicit.

Four levels of conformity assessment activity can be recognized. The first level is the determination of the characteristics of a product, process or service. There are three main ways in which this can be done. Testing is a technical process which uses a specified procedure to measure one or more characteristics of a product. (The closely related activity of calibration provides traceability of physical measurements to the national measurement system.) Physical inspection can be carried out on either newly manufactured products, or as an in-service check on the continued operation of plant and equipment. The third activity is the assessment of a quality management system.

At the second level, conformity of the results of the determination of characteristics to an appropriate standard is evaluated. This may be done by:

- the supplier or manufacturer
- the purchaser
- an organization independent of, but contracted to, either manufacturer or purchaser

- an independent agency for the purpose of enforcement or regulation.

Action by the manufacturer leads to the supplier's declaration of conformity. Action by the purchaser leads to the acceptance of a piece of equipment, batch of products or service, all of which were the subject of a contract. Many major purchasers, such as the utilities, have for many years carried out their own 'second-party' assessment of suppliers.

There has been a general move towards greater reliance upon independent certification. An independent organization may be contracted by either supplier or purchaser to certify either a quality management system or products in the form of a piece of equipment, batch or consignment.

Use of the term 'certification' in a generic sense has tended to obscure the distinction between product testing and conformity certification on the one hand, and systems capability assessment and registration of firms on the other. The generic term 'registration' is now preferred as an indication of third-party endorsement of a firm's capability following systems assessment to ISO 9001, or to ISO 14001. These standards list the key requirements of a quality or environmental management system respectively, and registration gives independent assurance that a compliant system is in place, so that the need for customers to carry out their own assessments is reduced or eliminated. This confers operating and market advantages on the supplier, and provides confidence to regulators and purchasers. This latter point has developed to the stage where it may be a contractual requirement in many cases.

Product certification is a procedure under which a distinctive mark may be applied to a product certified as having been manufactured to conform to a specific product standard. In addition to product testing and inspection, it may require compliance by the manufacturer with a quality management system standard (for example, ISO 9001). It will also usually involve regular surveillance.

Completion of assessment procedures leads to the assurance of conformity of a certified product or a registered manufacturer's quality system. This assurance is strengthened if the third-party body has been through the procedure of accreditation, in which an authoritative body gives formal recognition that a body or person is competent to carry out specific tasks. Accreditation demonstrates the competence of a conformity assessment body to certify that a product can conform to a product standard, or that a system can conform to a system standard (for example ISO 9001). For conformity assessment activities, the EN 45000 series of system standards provides relevant accreditation criteria. (The EN 45000 series of standards will shortly be replaced by new documents in the EN ISO 17000 series.)

Internationally, the various accreditation bodies work towards the harmonization of their procedures and practices. In addition, they seek mutual recognition of their services across national boundaries. This is facilitated by organizations such as the International Accreditation Forum (IAF) and the International Laboratory Accreditation Cooperation (ILAC).

In the UK, accreditation of testing and calibration was until recently the responsibility of NAMAS (National Measurement Accreditation Service), whereas accreditation of certification was the responsibility of NACCB (National Accreditation Council for Certification Bodies). These two organizations merged in 1995 to form a unified national accreditation service, the United Kingdom Accreditation Service (UKAS). Accreditation of inspection bodies and quality/environmental verifiers in the UK is covered by UKAS.

The aim of all these conformity assessment procedures is to achieve acceptance of a product on the market. They may have a part to play in the enforcement of regulations or in reducing technical barriers to trade.

THE EUROPEAN DIMENSION

Technical barriers to trade stem from two sources. They are caused by differences between national regulatory regimes, which require manufacturers to make their products to different specifications for different markets. They also arise from the actions of individual purchasers and customers, who may lack confidence in the quality and consistency of the goods and services they buy and use, and therefore require products to be checked and re-checked for each part of the market on which they are to be sold. A solution to these problems was sought in the Global Approach to certification and testing adopted by the European Council of Ministers in December 1989. A key feature of the Global Approach was the establishment of the European Organization for Testing and Certification (EOTC) as the focal point for the rationalization of voluntary conformity assessment activities in Europe. EOTC provides encouragement and a mechanism for the providers of conformity assessment services to enter mutual recognition arrangements product by product. In this way, it provides assurance that mutual recognition is technically sound, and so reduces the need for repeat testing or certification. It ensures that mutual recognition arrangements are market-responsive, and not anti-competitive in structure.

CONFORMITY MARKING

The European Union's Low Voltage Directive originally provided for nominated bodies' certification marks and test results to be accepted by the relevant national authorities. The New Approach Directives, instead, provide for a single, distinctive marking (the letters 'CE') to be displayed on products marketed as conforming with the applicable essential requirements. CE marking is now also required by the Low Voltage Directive as amended. Any product that comes under a European directive and is to be placed on the market in the EU must, by law, bear CE marking. CE marking is the manufacturer's claim that the product meets the essential requirements of all relevant EU Directives.

CE marking requirements vary from directive to directive, and even within directives. Third-party testing, systems assessment and technical file assessments can be mandatory, but sometimes the manufacturer's unverified claim is all that is demanded.

While CE marking is beginning to have an impact on both manufacturers and consumers (toys are CE-marked), there is still significant demand for the use of national product conformity marks, such as BSI's Kitemark in the UK.

COMPATIBILITY

In 1987, ISO published the first editions of the ISO 9000 quality management system standards. This was followed in 1996 by the publication of the ISO 14000 series of environmental management system standards.

Many users of the two series of standards realized that they contained common elements, but that these were expressed differently in each series of standards. Fearing that this could lead to cost implications for the implementation of both series, requests were made to ISO to ensure that the standards would be 'compatible' (that the use of one series would not preclude the use of the other, and that where possible, similar requirements would be harmonized).

During the development of the year 2000 edition of ISO 9001 a great deal of effort was devoted to improving its compatibility with ISO 14001. In addition, work is ongoing to improve the compatibility of ISO 14001 against ISO 9001: 2000.

While the ISO 9000 and ISO 14000 series of standards are probably the most widely known of ISO's management system standards, others have also been developed, such as ISO/IEC 17799 on information security management.

Furthermore, there have been many discussions within ISO about the possibility of producing standards in a diversity of management systems fields, such as occupational health and safety, risk management, the protection of personal data, sustainability and complaints management, to mention but a few.

While ISO continues to deliberate, other external organizations have not been so hesitant. For example, the International Labour Organisation has published its own *Guidelines on Occupational Safety and Health Management Systems*, and the OHSAS Project Group has published OHSAS 18001, *Occupational Health and Safety Management Systems – Specification.*

There have also been other management systems initiatives outside of the control of ISO, such as the European Eco-Management Audit Scheme (EMAS) for environmental management systems.

With each new publication, the concerns of users about the cost implications have also grown. In an attempt to allay such fears, ISO has published ISO Guide 72, *Guidelines for the justification and development of management system standards*. Guide 72 lays down stringent evaluation criteria for determining real market need for future management system standards, as well providing an outline structure for such standards to follow.

It is hoped that this Guide 72 will be used by those developing management systems standards outside the control of ISO, and that it will provide a much-needed platform for all future initiatives. Already, evidence is gathering that the desired result is beginning to happen. Many of those that are developing standards (or other documents) for use by specific industrial sectors against the ISO 9001: 2000 standard have taken note of its guidance.

Useful references

<http://www.iso.org> – the Website for ISO
ISO Journal: *ISO Management Systems*
<http://www.iec.org> – the Website for the IEC
<http://www.wssn.net/WSSN/> – the World Standards Services Network (for details of regional standards body groups)
<http://www.cenorm.be> – the Website for CEN
<http://www.cenelec.org> – the Website for CENELEC
<http://www.eotc.be> – the Website for the EOTC
<http://www.bsi-global.com> – the Website of the British Standards Institution
<http://www.iaf.nu> – the Website for the IAF
<http://www.ilac.org> – the Website for ILAC
<http://www.ukas.com> – a Website for UKAS
<http://www.ukas.org> – another Website for UKAS
<http://www.newapproach.org> – for advice on the EU's 'New Approach' Directives
<http://europa.eu.int/comm/enterprise/newapproach/legislation.htm> – also for advice on the EU's Directives

<http://www.ilo.org> – the Website for the International Labour Organisation
<http://europa.eu.int/comm/environment/emas> – the Website for EMAS

PART 3 *Check*

CHAPTER 17

An Introduction to Statistics

David Newton

Statistics is concerned with the analysis and interpretation of data in situations of uncertainty and variability. Such variability is inescapable in most industrial situations, so statistical thinking should permeate all analyses of industrial data. This is particularly the case in the control of manufacturing processes. The following three chapters are concerned with statistical methods in quality assurance. This chapter gives an introduction to statistical analysis. Chapter 18 shows how the ideas contained in this chapter are applied to the assessment of process variability and its comparison with what is required of the process – referred to as *process capability analysis*. Chapters 18 and 19 then build on these principles to establish methods for continuing control of production processes.

Data

Numerical data in statistical analysis can take two forms:

1 continuous data
2 discrete data.

Continuous data are observations of continuous variables. A continuous variable is a measurement that has no restriction on the values that can be observed apart from the physical constraints of the process that is generating them. For example, the dimensions of any machined component have ranges of values within which manufacture is possible, but within such a range there is no constraint on the values that can be achieved. The only limit to the number of decimal places to which a dimension is quoted is the resolution of the measuring equipment.

In contrast, discrete data can consist only of non-negative integers. These comprise counts of the number of times something happened (known as frequency) rather than measurements. In the quality assurance context, the count is usually of the number of items in a sample that are in some way defective. When such counts are being used in a quality control procedure, the procedure is described as 'by attributes' (as in 'control charting by attributes' and 'acceptance sampling by attributes'), the attribute in question being the defectiveness (or otherwise) of the item.

Examples of data are shown in Tables 17.1 and 17.2. Table 17.1 shows an example of a continuous variable, and Table 17.2 a discrete variable. As they stand, these tables give little

Table 17.1 Breaking loads for 20 test specimens of aluminium wire

Breaking load (kg)				
5.41	4.81	5.02	5.56	5.31
4.73	5.19	5.00	4.95	5.07
5.74	5.10	5.25	5.44	4.88
5.32	5.16	4.78	5.38	5.22

Table 17.2 Number of breakdowns in a machining centre observed in 59 successive weeks of operation

Week no.	*No. of breakdowns*	*Week no.*	*No. of breakdowns*	*Week no.*	*No. of breakdowns*
1	2	21	3	41	7
2	4	22	1	42	1
3	2	23	2	43	2
4	0	24	3	44	1
5	1	25	5	45	2
6	2	26	1	46	0
7	0	27	2	47	1
8	3	28	1	48	0
9	3	29	0	49	3
10	0	30	2	50	0
11	1	31	0	51	3
12	2	32	4	52	1
13	0	33	2	53	0
14	1	34	1	54	2
15	1	35	5	55	1
16	0	36	2	56	4
17	0	37	2	57	4
18	1	38	1	58	1
19	2	39	1	59	0
20	1	40	3		

information about the patterns of variability, and methods must be found for describing the data in a more helpful form. There are two ways of doing this – using pictures, and using numbers.

DESCRIBING DATA USING PICTURES

Slightly different approaches are needed for continuous and discrete data.

Continuous data

The data are represented pictorially using a 'histogram'. This is obtained by dividing the observed extent of the variable into a number of convenient 'class intervals' of equal width, and counting the number of data items (the frequency) that occurs in each interval. From the data in Table 17.1, we get:

Class interval	*Frequency*
4.6 a.u. 4.8	2
4.8 a.u. 5.0	3
5.0 a.u. 5.2	7
5.2 a.u. 5.4	5
5.4 a.u. 5.6	2
5.6 a.u. 5.8	1

The abbreviation 'a.u.' stands for 'and under', simply to resolve arbitrarily the issue of which class interval includes values (such as 5.20) that occur exactly on a boundary. These values can then be displayed as a histogram, as shown in Figure 17.1, where each frequency is represented by the scale height of a block drawn across its associated class interval. Figure 17.1 shows the way in which most of the data are in the interval 5.0 to 5.2, with the frequencies reducing symmetrically on either side. The choice of class interval is fairly arbitrary – either too wide or too narrow an interval width will reduce the information to be obtained from the picture. Trial and error is the usual way to the best choice, though there is a rule known as 'Sturges' Rule', which helps in choosing a sensible number of class intervals:

$$k = 1 + 3.3\log(n)$$

where the number of class intervals used should be a convenient number close to k for a sample size of n data items. For the data in Table 17.1, Sturges' rule gives

$$k = 3.3\log(20) = 5.29$$

showing that the choice of six intervals was reasonable.

There are variations on the histogram that are sometimes useful. A common modification is to rescale the vertical axis by dividing the frequencies by n, the sample size, to give relative frequencies. In the example in Figure 17.1, this would replace 1, 2, 3, 4, 5, 6

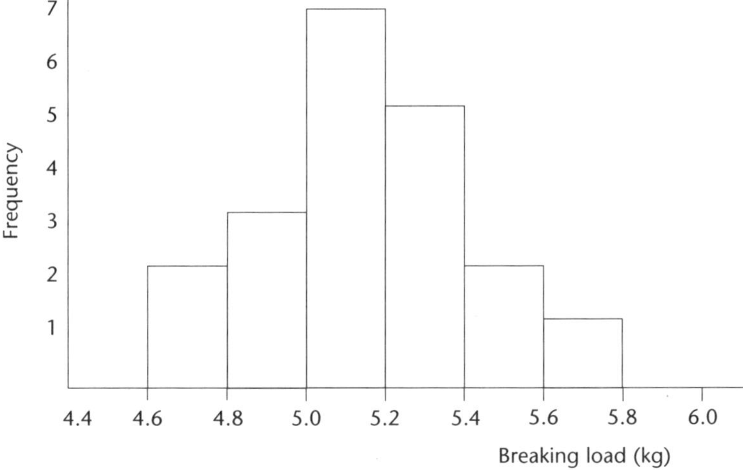

Figure 17.1 Histogram for the data shown in Table 17.1

and 7 by 0.05, 0.10, 0.15, 0.20, 0.25, 0.30 and 0.35, respectively. This permits comparison of two samples, or (as described later) comparison of a sample with a theoretical model without the comparison being confused by differences in sample size. Another variation is to use a cumulative frequency diagram (sometimes called an 'Ogive') in which the cumulative frequency less than the top of each class interval is plotted, as in the histogram which is shown, together with its data table, in Figure 17.2.

Discrete data

As discrete data can only take integer values, it is not necessary to use class intervals. A frequency diagram is usually similar to that in Figure 17.3, which is based on the data from Table 17.2 (as summarized in the table included with Figure 17.3).

DESCRIBING DATA WITH NUMBERS

While pictures are a very succinct way of summarizing and presenting data, they do have the drawback that they cannot be stored and manipulated algebraically. To do this we need numbers, but numbers which summarize the data rather than the data points themselves. Such numbers are known as *summary measures*, different measures being used to quantify different aspects of the data. The most useful summary measures are *measures of location* and *measures of dispersion*.

Class interval	Frequency	Cumulative frequency	Cumulative relative frequency
4.6 a.u. 4.8	2	2	0.10
4.8 a.u. 5.0	3	5	0.25
5.0 a.u. 5.2	7	12	0.60
5.2 a.u. 5.4	5	17	0.85
5.4 a.u. 5.6	2	19	0.95
5.6 a.u. 5.8	1	20	1.00

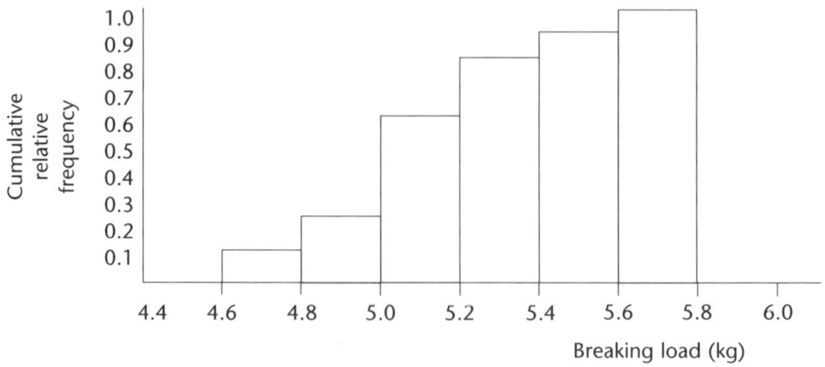

Figure 17.2 Cumulative frequency table and histogram derived from the data in Table 17.1

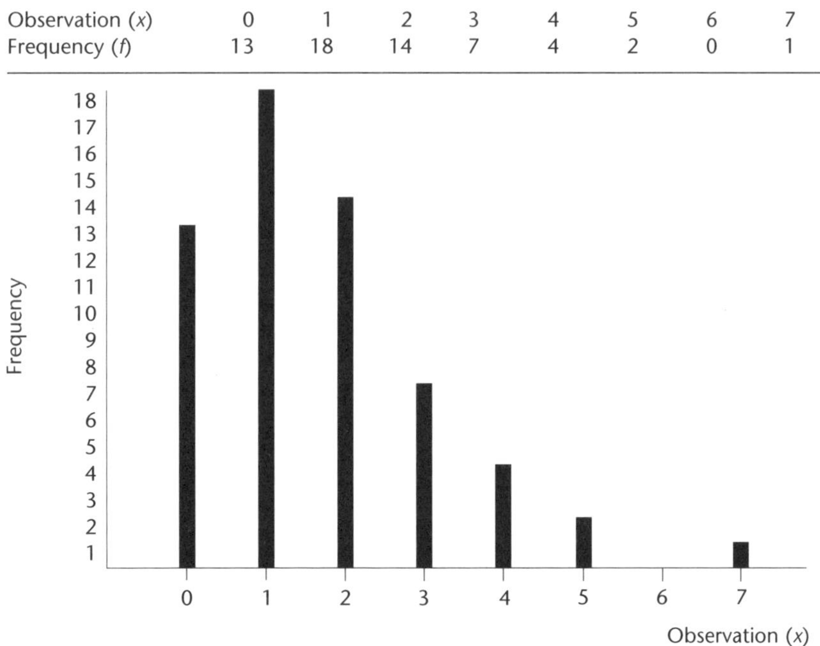

Observation (x)	0	1	2	3	4	5	6	7
Frequency (f)	13	18	14	7	4	2	0	1

Figure 17.3 Bar chart (histogram) for discrete data
Note: The table is a summary of data from Table 17.2.

MEASURES OF LOCATION

Measures of location describe where the 'middle' of the data is located. There are three measurements generally in use: the mode, the median and the arithmetic mean.

Mode

The mode is usually defined as the most frequently occurring value in a sample. This makes sense in the case of discrete data. By inspection of the table accompanying Figure 17.3, it can be seen that the mode for this data is one breakdown, which occurs with a frequency of 18, the highest value in the sample. For the continuous variable in Table 17.1, however, we cannot define a mode because all the 20 values are different, each having a frequency of 1. What we have to do instead is use the mid-point of the class interval with the highest frequency, giving a value of 5.1. Although the mode is useful for discrete data, and can be obtained simply by inspection, it is less satisfactory for continuous data. It has further drawbacks. It is not necessarily unique (there can be ties for the highest frequency), and it can be misleading for data which are markedly non-symmetrical (referred to as 'skewed').

Median

The median is the central observation when the data are arranged in ascending order. For example, writing the data of Table 17.1 in ascending order gives:

4.73, 4.78, 4.81, 4.78, 4.95, 5.00, 5.02, 5.07, 5.10, 5.14, 5.16, 5.19, 5.22, 5.25, 5.31, 5.32, 5.38, 5.44, 5.56, 5.74

As there are 20 values, there is no central value (true for any sample of an even number of items), so we have to adopt the convention of using the mid-point of the 10th and 11th values, 5.14 and 5.16, respectively, giving a median of 5.15.

For the discrete data in Table 17.2, the ordered data set is:

0000000000000111111111111111111222222222222223333333444455 7

As there are 59 items, the median is the 30th ordered item, which is 1.

The median, like the mode, is obtained simply by inspection of the data without any calculations. Although it will always give a unique value, it is still misleading for skewed data. It finds application in control charting, where its simplicity as a measure of location for a small, odd-numbered sample size is attractive.

Mean

The most widely used measure of central tendency is the arithmetic mean (usually referred to simply as the mean) – the sum of all the observations in the sample divided by the number of observations.

For the continuous data in Table 17.1, the mean is:

(5.12 + 4.81 + 5.02 + ... 5.38 + 5.22) ÷ 20
= 103.05 ÷ 20
= 5.152

For a general notation for the mean of a sample, the observations in each sample are denoted by a subscripted letter. For example, the data in Table 17.1 can be denoted by x_1, x_2, x_3, etc., up to x_{20}. Which particular value of x is given a particular subscript value is unimportant, so long as all 20 are uniquely identified.

The mean, in the general case of a sample of n observations, is given by:

$$\frac{1}{n} \quad (x_1 + x_2 + x_3 + x_4 + \ldots x_{(n-1)} + x_n)$$

for which the conventional notation is:

$$x = \frac{1}{n} \sum_{i=1}^{n} x_i$$

The symbol Σ (Greek upper-case sigma) stands for 'summation' – all the values following are added together. The terms 'i = 1' and 'n', respectively, above and below the Σ indicate the starting and finishing points for the summation – it starts at x_1 and finishes at x_n. When the range of summation is obvious, these limits are often omitted.

When the same numerical value occurs several times in a set of data, as in the discrete data in Table 17.2, rather than give each reappearance of the same number a different subscript, it is usual to re-express the formula for the mean as:

$$\bar{x} = \frac{1}{n} \sum_{i=1}^{k} f_i x_i$$

where the subscript i now represents each of the k different numerical values in the sample, and f_i the frequency with which that value occurs. For example, from the data in Figure 17.3, $\Sigma f_i x_i$ is calculated as:

$$(13 \times 0) + (18 \times 1) + (14 \times 2) + (7 \times 3) + (4 \times 4) + (2 \times 5) + (0 \times 6) + (1 \times 7) = 100$$

and the total number of observations (the sample size, n) is:

$$13 + 18 + 14 + 7 + 4 + 2 + 0 + 1 = 59$$

so the mean $\bar{x}$ is 100/59 = 1.695.

For continuous data which are presented in class intervals without access to the original data, the same procedure can be used, with x_i being the mid-point of the ith class interval, and f_i the observed frequency in that interval. This method should *not* be used when the original ungrouped data are available – this would introduce unnecessary errors due to the assumption that all the observations in an interval are at the mid-point. If their actual location in the interval is known, this information should be used.

MEASURES OF DISPERSION

Measures of dispersion measure the spread of the data about the mean. Consider the sample of 20 observations shown in Table 17.3. These are seen to have an initial similarity to those in Table 17.1. Calculation confirms that they have exactly the same sample mean of 5.153. Further inspection, however, shows that there is a very important difference in that the data are clustered much more closely round the mean. This can be confirmed by drawing a histogram of the data. The purpose of a measure of dispersion is to provide a single number for each sample that quantifies the 'spread'.

Range

An obvious measure to use is that of the range within the sample – the difference between the largest and the smallest value. In Table 17.1, the range is 5.74 – 4.73 = 1.01, whereas in Table 17.3 the value is 5.27 – 5.03 = 0.24. The range does have its uses. As shown above, it provides a usable measure with minimal calculation. It does, however, have severe drawbacks. The most important one is sheer inefficiency – whatever the size of the sample, it only makes use of two observations. The value obtained will also tend to increase as the sample size increases, because extreme observations become more likely. For these reasons, it should be used with care and only in tightly defined situations. As will be seen in Chapter 18, it is widely used in control charting, where sample sizes are usually small and it is important to obtain a rapid measure with the minimum of calculation.

Table 17.3 20 observations of a continuous variable

5.14	5.03	5.12	5.21	5.18
5.12	5.19	5.08	5.12	5.09
5.22	5.17	5.15	5.19	5.05
5.27	5.10	5.13	5.21	5.20

Variance and standard deviation

For a single observation, the quantity $(x_i - \bar{x})$ measures its deviation from the mean. At first sight, adding together all such values might form the basis for a measure of spread including all the observations, but this summation would always come to exactly zero, as the positive and negative values would cancel each other out. This problem can be circumvented by using the absolute values (that is, ignoring the signs). To eliminate the effect of sample size, the summation is divided by the sample size to give a measure known as the *mean absolute deviation* (MAD):

$$\text{MAD} = \frac{1}{n} \sum_{i=1}^{n} |x_i - \bar{x}|$$

While this measure does work (and finds some applications in work study), problems are presented by the discontinuity of this measure. Instead, we make the measure always positive by squaring it. The average is then the *mean square deviation* (MSD):

$$\text{MSD} = \frac{1}{n} \sum_{i=1}^{n} (x_1 - \bar{x})^2$$

For reasons that will be explained later (under the heading 'Populations and estimation'), one further modification is necessary. Instead of using the sample size as a divisor, we use $(n - 1)$ (known as the 'degrees of freedom'). This results in a measure known as the sample variance, denoted s^2:

$$s^2 = \frac{1}{n-1} \sum_{i=1}^{n} (x_1 - \bar{x})^2$$

The sample variance is the definitive measure of dispersion. The fact that it is dimensioned in the square of the original unit of measurement of the data can cause confusion, for which reason it is usual to refer to its square root, known as the standard deviation (s):

$$s = \sqrt{\frac{1}{n-1} \left(\sum_{i=1}^{n} (x_i - \bar{x})^2 \right)}$$

By squaring out the term in brackets, an alternative form of the expression for variance emerges that is slightly easier for calculation, and does not involve explicit use of the calculated sample average:

$$s^2 = \frac{1}{n-1} \left[\Sigma(x_i)^2 - \frac{(\Sigma x_i)^2}{n} \right]$$

As an example, consider again the data in Table 17.1.

$$\begin{aligned} \Sigma(x_i)^2 \text{ is } & (5.14)^2 + (4.81)^2 + (5.02)^2 + \ldots + (5.38)^2 + (5.22)^2 \\ & = 26.4196 + 23.1361 + 25.2004 + \ldots + 28.9444 + 27.2484 \\ & = 532.2795 \end{aligned}$$

Σx_i was previously calculated as 103.05, and n is 20, so the variance is given by:

$$s^2 = \frac{1}{19} \left[532.2795 - \frac{(103.05)^2}{20} \right]$$

$$= \frac{1}{19}\ [532.2795 - 530.9651]$$

$$= \frac{1.3144}{19} = 0.0692$$

and the standard deviation, $s = \sqrt{0.0692} = 0.263$.

For the data in Table 17.3:

$$\Sigma(x_i)^2 \text{ is } (5.14)^2 + (5.03)^2 + (5.12)^2 + \ldots + (5.21)^2 + (5.20)^2$$
$$= 531.0387$$

Σx_i is again 103.05 and $n = 20$, so the variance is:

$$= \frac{1}{19}\ (531.0387 - 530.9651)$$

$$= \frac{0.0736}{19} = 0.00387$$

and the standard deviation, $s = \sqrt{0.00387} = 0.0622$.

In both the above variance calculations, the quantity in brackets is a very small difference between two large numbers. Any small error in calculation of either of the numbers gives a possibly very large error in the final result. For this reason, it is important to maintain accuracy in calculation. Rounding during the calculation must be avoided, and all significant figures must be carried. It is, of course, acceptable to round the final result.

Variance calculations with grouped data

As for the mean, when observations x_i occur with frequency f_i, it is easier to use a modified expression for variance, namely:

$$s^2 = \frac{1}{n-1}\left[\ \Sigma(f_i x_i^2) - \frac{(\Sigma f_i x_i)^2}{n}\right]$$

Applying this to the data in Table 17.2, we have already obtained the result that $\Sigma f_i\, x_i = 100$. $\Sigma(f_i\, x_i^2)$ is calculated as:

$$(13 \times 0^2) + (18 \times 1^2) + (14 \times 2^2) + (7 \times 3^2) + (4 \times 4^2) + (2 \times 5^2) + (0 \times 6^2) + (1 \times 7^2)$$
$$= 0 + 18 + 56 + 63 + 64 + 50 + 0 + 49 = 300$$

that is:

$$s^2 = \frac{1}{58}\left[300 - \frac{100^2}{59}\right] = 2.25$$

and standard deviation $s = \sqrt{2.25} = 1.5$.

POPULATIONS AND ESTIMATION

Information contained in samples is rarely of much interest in its own right. Its value lies in estimating the corresponding measures in the 'population' from which the sample was drawn. This terminology comes from the use of statistics in demography – if we wanted to know, for example, the average height of the adult male UK population, practical constraints would prevent us measuring the 20 million or so subjects in this category, so we would obtain an estimate by measuring a small sample. The same principle would apply to the variance of the height, or to any other summary statistic for any other measurement. In many industrial situations, the population cannot even be viewed as having a finite number of members. If we are sampling items from some manufacturing process, and measuring a particular property or dimension, the mean and variance obtained from the sample are estimates of the mean and variance of the process at that time. The population is conceptually all the components that could be produced from the process when it is operating under the conditions applying when the sample was taken.

It is obviously important that the sample results provide 'good' estimates of the corresponding population values (known as population 'parameters'). There are several criteria of 'goodness', but one of the more important ones is that of lack of bias. Repeated sample estimates from a single population will themselves be subject to variation, but are 'unbiased' if the average of an infinite number of such estimates is exactly equal to the corresponding population parameter. As population parameters are generally unknown, there is no way of testing any particular estimated value for bias – we have instead to rely on theoretical justification beyond the scope of this book. This will confirm that:

Sample mean ($\bar{x}$) is an unbiased estimator for population mean (μ).
Sample variance (s^2) is an unbiased estimator for population variance (σ^2).

Note, in the case of variance, that the mean square deviation,

$$\text{MSD} = \frac{1}{n} \sum_{i=1}^{n} (x_i - \bar{x})^2$$

gives a biased estimator of population variance – it underestimates by a factor $(n - 1/n)$. To unbias the estimate, it is multiplied by $(n/n - 1)$, giving the result for s^2. (It should be noted that there are a few texts which quote the value with n in the denominator for s^2, and therefore require multiplication by $(n/n - 1)$ to give an unbiased estimate of σ^2.)

Use of calculators

Most calculators on the market described as either 'statistical' or 'scientific' have built-in functions for the calculation of sample means and standard deviations, and their use can in most circumstances bypass the stages of calculation described above. There are, however, two points of caution. The first is that very few machines include a facility for dealing with grouped data, so it is necessary either to enter each observation individually, or use the method shown above. The second is that of a lack of consistency in what emerges when the 'standard deviation' button is pressed. Some use n as the denominator, others use $n - 1$. It doesn't matter so long as it is known which, an issue that can be resolved by checking a sample calculation. One popular make of calculator gives the choice of either – denoted σ_n or σ_{n-1}, respectively. (Strictly, the keys should be labelled s rather than σ, as even electronic calculators cannot produce population parameters from sample data.)

Other summary measures

The measures of location (mean, median, mode) and dispersion (variance, standard deviation, sample range) described above are usually sufficient to describe the data. Occasionally, other measures can be invoked to give further information on the shape of the distribution of data. For consistency in terminology, define:

$$m_1 = x$$

$$m_2 = \frac{1}{n-1} \sum_{i=1}^{n} (x_i - \bar{x})^2 \ (= s^2)$$

$$m_3 = \frac{1}{n-1} \sum_{i=1}^{n} (x_i - \bar{x})^3$$

$$m_4 = \frac{1}{n-1} \sum_{i=1}^{n} (x_i - \bar{x})^4$$

From these statistics (where m_1, m_2, m_3, m_4 are, respectively, the first, second, third and fourth moments of the sample data) two further summary measures can be produced:

coefficient of skewness = m_3^2/m_2^3
coefficient of kurtosis = $(m_4/m_2^2) - 3$

The *coefficient of skewness* measures the symmetry of the data, and the *coefficient of kurtosis* measures whether the shape of the distribution is flat (platykurtic) or peaked (leptokurtic). Such information can sometimes be of use during process capability analysis, as described in the next chapter. The behaviour of these coefficients is illustrated in Figures 17.4 and 17.5.

Probability

Probability theory is a very large area of study. This section is restricted to a very brief outline of some of the aspects necessary for the remainder of this chapter and the following three chapters.

Consider some event A. The probability must be somewhere between 0 and 1 inclusive:

$P(\mathrm{A}) = 0$ means that A cannot occur (it is impossible).
$P(\mathrm{A}) = 1$ means that A must occur (it is certain).

More generally, if we consider the total extent of possible outcomes to a 'trial' (which is simply an opportunity for an event to occur), $P(\mathrm{A})$ is the proportion of these outcomes that consist of event A as the number of trials tends to infinity. This probability can be quantified in various ways:

1 **Experimentally** – If n trials were undertaken, and event A occurred in x of them, then the *estimate* of $P(\mathrm{A})$ is x/n.
2 ***A priori*** – There are some situations where the answer is obvious from prior knowledge of the physical process generating the events. For example, it can be said before the event that the probability of an unbiased tossed coin coming up 'heads' is 1/2; the

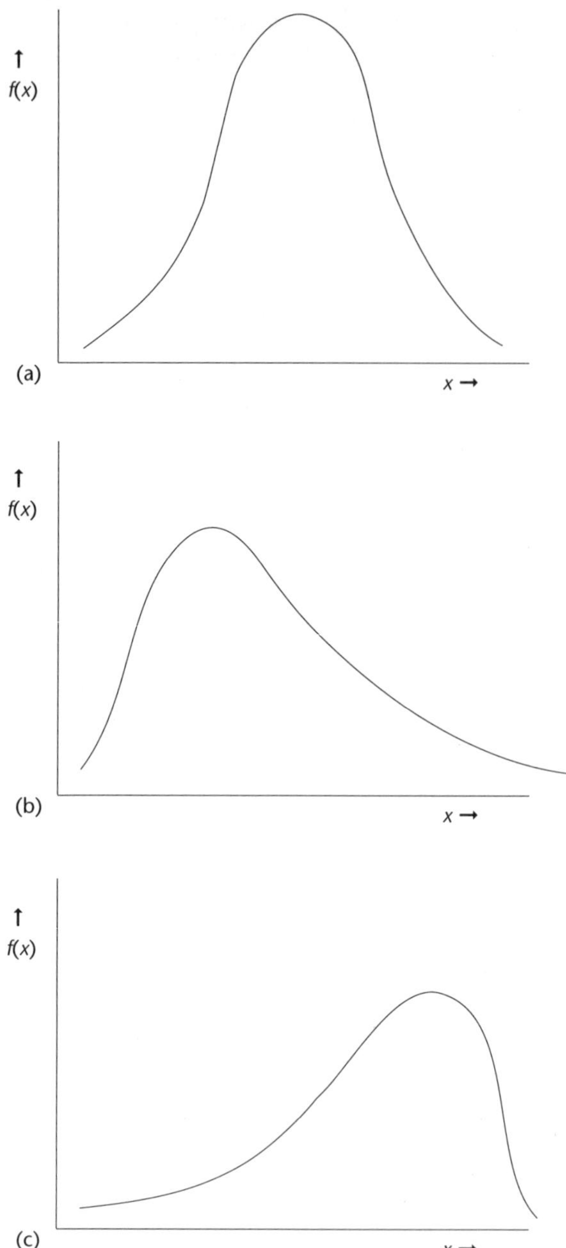

Figure 17.4 Skewness: (a) symmetrical (coefficient = 0), (b) positively skewed (coefficient > 0, (c) negatively skewed (coefficient < 0)

probability of a randomly selected playing card being the ace of spades is 1/52, and so on, without any need to undertake experiments. (There are many situations where it is easy to be tempted into *a priori* judgements which cannot be justified. This often happens in industry. It is also prevalent in gambling, where the profitability of that particular industry depends almost exclusively on the customer's insistence on making incorrect *a priori* assessments.)

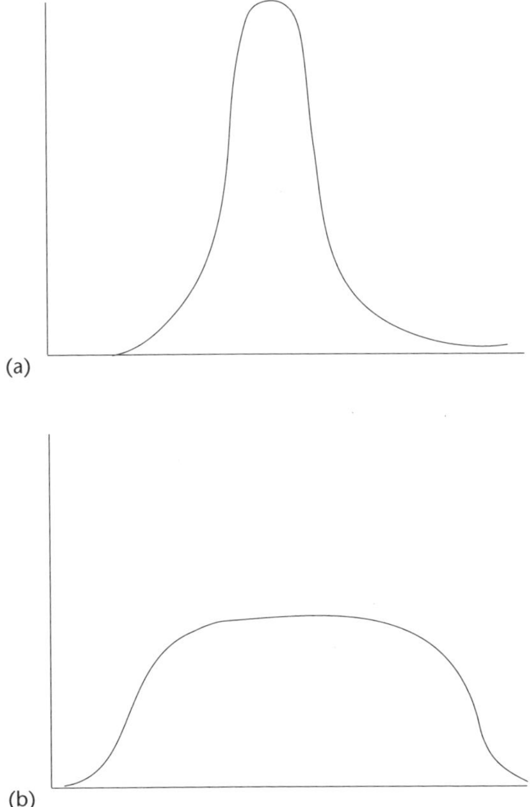

Figure 17.5 Kurtosis: (a) leptokurtic (coefficient > 0), (b) platykurtic (coefficient < 0)

3 **By modelling** – In situations where experimentation is impractical and there is no immediately obvious *a priori* value, some theoretical model of the situation can often be developed in the guise of a 'probability distribution', as described later.

COMPOUND PROBABILITIES

The event A has so far been considered as a *simple event* which is not readily decomposed into further events. A *compound event* is an event consisting of two or more simple events. For simplicity, this discussion will be limited to compound events that consist of two simple events only – denoted A and B.

Multiplication rule

For the two simple events A and B, the probability of both A *and* B occurring is denoted $P(AB)$ (or $P(A \cap B)$, where the $\cap$ implies the 'intersection' of the two events:

$$P(AB) = P(A) \times P(B \mid A)$$

$P(B \mid A)$ is the probability of event B given that event A has already occurred. For example, consider an almost-finished packet of mixed peanuts and raisins, which now contains 7 peanuts and 5 raisins. If A is obtaining a peanut when one item is selected at random from the bag (assuming that we can neither see nor feel what is being selected), and B is obtaining a raisin, then obviously $P(A)$ is 7/12 and $P(B \mid A)$ is 5/11, giving $P(AB) = 35/132 = 0.265$.

Note that if the peanut and the raisin had been considered in the reverse order, the same result would have been obtained: $P(A) \times P(B \mid A) = P(B) \times P(A \mid B)$ (known as Bayes' formula). In many situations, $P(A \mid B) = P(A)$ and $P(B \mid A) = P(B)$, in which case A and B are said to be *independent*. This means that the occurrence of A has no influence on the probability of B, and vice versa. This would be the case in the above example if, after obtaining our first sample peanut or raisin, instead of eating it, it was returned to the bag before the second sample was taken. In this case:

$$P(AB) = P(A) \times P(B) = 7/12 \times 5/12 = 35/144 = 0.243$$

Such independence is usually assumed in quality control applications – the value of a sample observation from a manufacturing process is usually assumed to have no influence on the value of a subsequent sample.

Addition rule

For two simple events A and B, the probability of A *or* B occurring is denoted $P(A + B)$ (or $P(A \cup B)$, where the $\cup$ implies the 'union' of the two events):

$$P(A + B) = P(A) + P(B) - P(AB)$$

$P(AB)$ is the probability of both A and B, as described above.

For example, further complicate the bag of peanuts and raisins by adding 15 cashew nuts, so there are now 27 items in the bag. The probability that our selection is either a peanut or a raisin is obtained from:

Probability of a peanut, $P(A) = 7/27$
Probability of a raisin, $P(B) = 5/27$
Probability of our selection being simultaneously a peanut and a raisin, $P(AB) = 0$ (obviously, by definition);
so $P(A + B) = 7/27 + 5/27 - 0 = 12/27$

The fact that $P(AB)$ is zero defines the two events as being *mutually exclusive*. If this is so (as in the above example), then we have the simple result:

$$P(A + B) = P(A) + P(B)$$

This also is usually assumed to be the case in the later exploration of techniques in quality control, but it is wise to always be alive to the possibility of both the assumptions of independence and mutual exclusivity not being valid.

PROBABILITY DISTRIBUTIONS

Probability distributions are theoretical models of the behaviour of random variables. Descriptions of the behaviour of variables usually consist of a combination of an assumed probability distribution and estimates of the parameters of the distribution from sample data. As with the analysis of sample data, it is convenient to treat separately the applications to discrete and to continuous data.

CONTINUOUS PROBABILITY DISTRIBUTIONS

Consider a continuous random variable, X, with probability distribution as shown in Figure 17.6. The shape is determined by the function $f(X)$. This function is always such that the total area under the curve is unity:

$$\int_{-\infty}^{\infty} f(X)\, dX = 1$$

and is known as the *probability density function* (PDF). The area under the curve between any two defined values of X represents the probability of the variable being between these values. More specifically:

$$\int_{-\infty}^{\infty} f(X)\, dX = F(x) \text{ (the cumulative density function [CDF])}$$

and

$$\int_{-\infty}^{\infty} (X)\, dX = R(x) \text{ (the survival, or reliability, function)}$$

where, of course, $F(x) + R(x) = 1$ for all values of x.

The mean of a continuous probability distribution, μ, is given by:

$$\mu = \int_{-\infty}^{\infty} Xf(X)dX$$

and the variance by:

$$\sigma = \int_{-\infty}^{\infty} X^2 f(X)dX$$

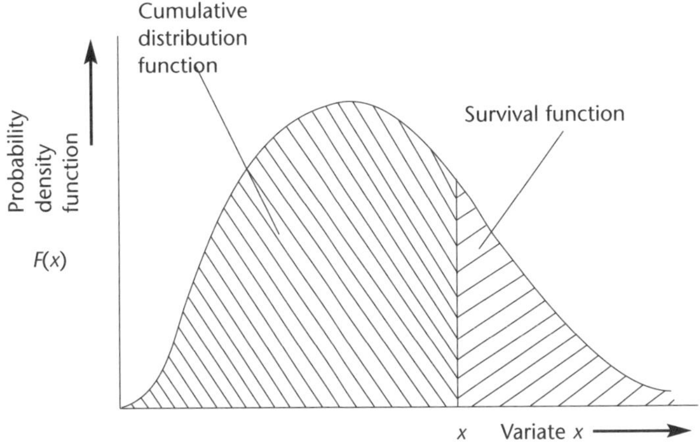

Figure 17.6 Continuous probability distribution

SPECIFIC MODELS FOR CONTINUOUS PROBABILITY DISTRIBUTIONS

There is an endless list of possibilities for the function $f(X)$, giving an equally endless list of possible shapes for probability distributions. The only constraint is that the total enclosed area is unity. There are, however, relatively few that find practical application, usually through a combination of realistic underlying assumptions, mathematical simplicity and observed correspondence to the actual behaviour of real variables. Of the many possible models, just four of the more widely used ones will be introduced: the normal, log-normal, exponential and Weibull. The normal distribution will be explained in detail, followed by brief descriptions of the others.

NORMAL DISTRIBUTION

The normal distribution is arguably the most useful and widely used model in statistical analysis. It is certainly the one on which most of the standard techniques of statistical testing depend. Its origin is usually attributed to the French mathematician Demoivre in 1733, though others such as Gauss and Laplace also lay claim. Its mathematical form is:

$$f(X) = \frac{1}{\sigma\sqrt{2\pi}} e^{\frac{-(x-\mu)^2}{2\sigma^2}}$$

where μ is the mean and σ^2 is the variance, and its shape is the well-known symmetrical bell-shaped curve as shown in Figure 17.7. The derivation assumes that X is diverted from its target by a large number of small factors whose effects are additive and whose average value is zero (the negative and positive ones cancel each other out). This has an immediate similarity to manufacturing processes where such factors can be imagined as affecting, for

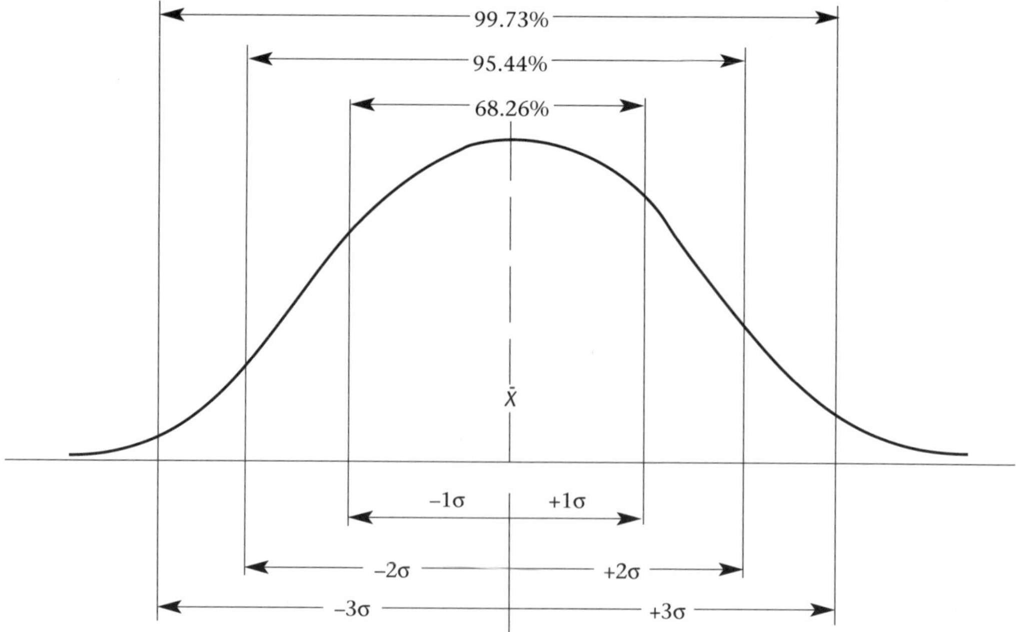

Figure 17.7 Normal distribution

example, a machined dimension. It is important to recognize that no physical dimension of property will ever be exactly normally distributed, as this would imply finite probabilities for all values between $\pm\infty$. What can be done is to accept it as an adequate model for many such dimensions and properties, where its use is helpful and does not give rise to unacceptable inaccuracies, as is often the case in statistical process control as described in the next two chapters. Another consequence of its widespread use is a school of thought that there is, by definition, something wrong with a manufacturing process that does not give rise to normally distributed properties. This is, of course, nonsense – there is nothing automatically wrong in a situation simply because a particular bit of theory does not fit. In such cases it is usually the theory that is wrong, and we need to find a more suitable distribution.

Calculating normal probabilities

To avoid the need to evaluate areas under normal curves by integration, it is usual to use tables of such values. As there are infinite possible values of both μ and σ, it is clearly impossible to tabulate all possible normal distributions. Instead, tables are provided for only one pair of values, namely $\mu = 0$ and $\sigma = 1$. This is known as the *standardized normal distribution*, which has the form:

$$f(u) = \frac{1}{\sqrt{2\pi}}\ e^{(-\frac{\mu^2}{2})}$$

and is shown in Figure 17.8.

The variate is known as *standardized normal deviate*, with the conventional symbol u. To convert an x from any normal distribution into a u, so that tables of the standardized normal distribution may be used, the conversion is:

$$u = \frac{(x - \mu)}{\sigma}$$

(that is, u is the distance of x above the mean expressed as a number of standard deviations).

A table of the normal distribution is given in Table 17.4. Its use is best illustrated by example. Suppose a dimension of a component is specified as 5.00 ± 0.10 mm. If it is known that this dimension is normally distributed with a mean of 5.02 mm and standard deviation

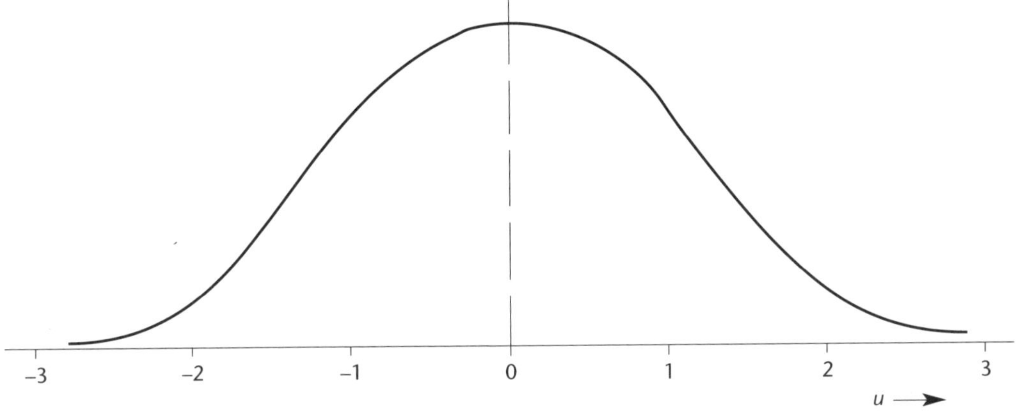

Figure 17.8 Standardized normal distribution

Table 17.4 Normal distribution table

The function tabulated is 1 – f(u), where f(u) is the cumulative distribution function of a standardized normal variable u.

$$\text{Thus } 1 - \phi(u) = \frac{1}{\sqrt{2\pi}} \int_{\mu}^{\infty} e^{-u2/2}\, du$$

is the probability that a standardized normal variable selected at random will be greater than a value of

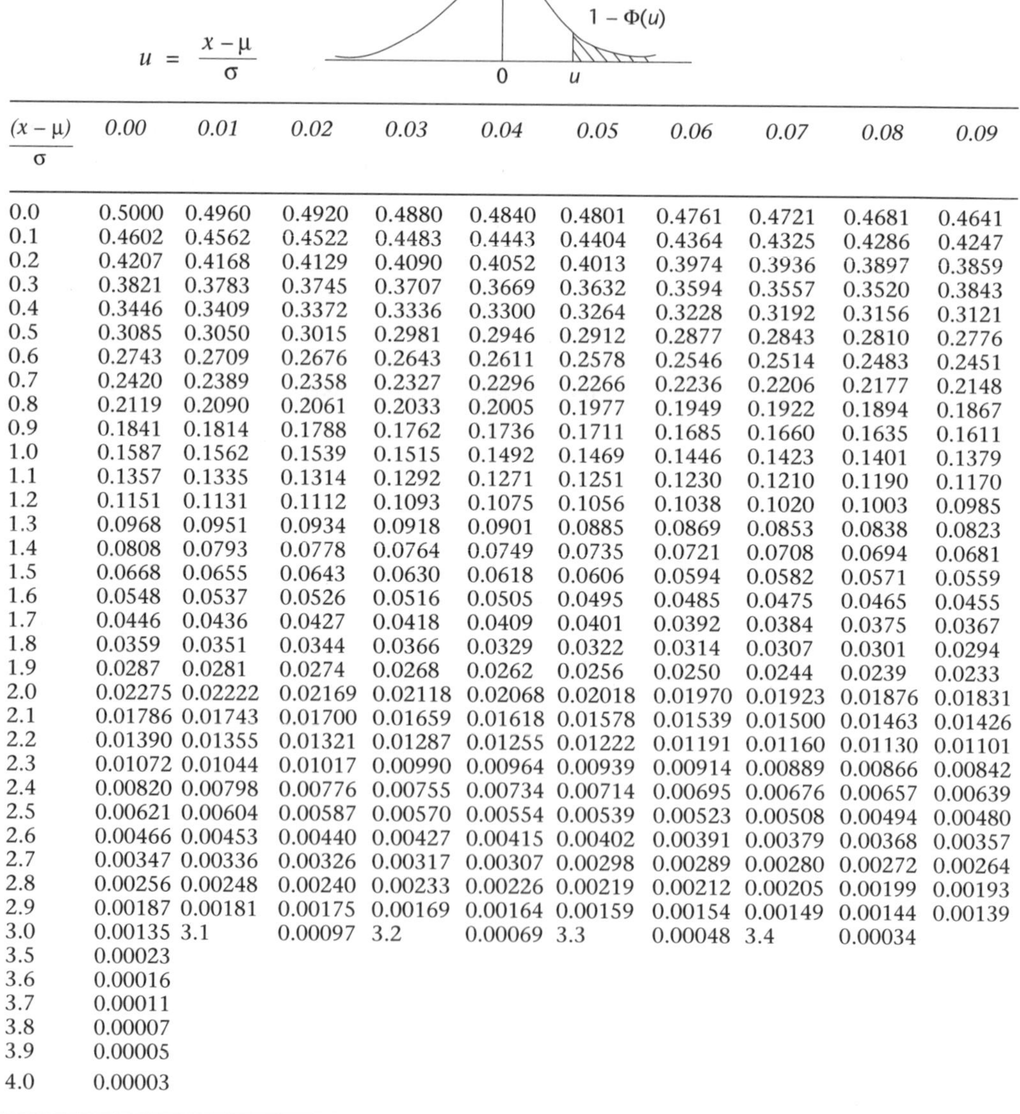

$$u = \frac{x - \mu}{\sigma}$$

$\frac{(x-\mu)}{\sigma}$	*0.00*	*0.01*	*0.02*	*0.03*	*0.04*	*0.05*	*0.06*	*0.07*	*0.08*	*0.09*
0.0	0.5000	0.4960	0.4920	0.4880	0.4840	0.4801	0.4761	0.4721	0.4681	0.4641
0.1	0.4602	0.4562	0.4522	0.4483	0.4443	0.4404	0.4364	0.4325	0.4286	0.4247
0.2	0.4207	0.4168	0.4129	0.4090	0.4052	0.4013	0.3974	0.3936	0.3897	0.3859
0.3	0.3821	0.3783	0.3745	0.3707	0.3669	0.3632	0.3594	0.3557	0.3520	0.3843
0.4	0.3446	0.3409	0.3372	0.3336	0.3300	0.3264	0.3228	0.3192	0.3156	0.3121
0.5	0.3085	0.3050	0.3015	0.2981	0.2946	0.2912	0.2877	0.2843	0.2810	0.2776
0.6	0.2743	0.2709	0.2676	0.2643	0.2611	0.2578	0.2546	0.2514	0.2483	0.2451
0.7	0.2420	0.2389	0.2358	0.2327	0.2296	0.2266	0.2236	0.2206	0.2177	0.2148
0.8	0.2119	0.2090	0.2061	0.2033	0.2005	0.1977	0.1949	0.1922	0.1894	0.1867
0.9	0.1841	0.1814	0.1788	0.1762	0.1736	0.1711	0.1685	0.1660	0.1635	0.1611
1.0	0.1587	0.1562	0.1539	0.1515	0.1492	0.1469	0.1446	0.1423	0.1401	0.1379
1.1	0.1357	0.1335	0.1314	0.1292	0.1271	0.1251	0.1230	0.1210	0.1190	0.1170
1.2	0.1151	0.1131	0.1112	0.1093	0.1075	0.1056	0.1038	0.1020	0.1003	0.0985
1.3	0.0968	0.0951	0.0934	0.0918	0.0901	0.0885	0.0869	0.0853	0.0838	0.0823
1.4	0.0808	0.0793	0.0778	0.0764	0.0749	0.0735	0.0721	0.0708	0.0694	0.0681
1.5	0.0668	0.0655	0.0643	0.0630	0.0618	0.0606	0.0594	0.0582	0.0571	0.0559
1.6	0.0548	0.0537	0.0526	0.0516	0.0505	0.0495	0.0485	0.0475	0.0465	0.0455
1.7	0.0446	0.0436	0.0427	0.0418	0.0409	0.0401	0.0392	0.0384	0.0375	0.0367
1.8	0.0359	0.0351	0.0344	0.0366	0.0329	0.0322	0.0314	0.0307	0.0301	0.0294
1.9	0.0287	0.0281	0.0274	0.0268	0.0262	0.0256	0.0250	0.0244	0.0239	0.0233
2.0	0.02275	0.02222	0.02169	0.02118	0.02068	0.02018	0.01970	0.01923	0.01876	0.01831
2.1	0.01786	0.01743	0.01700	0.01659	0.01618	0.01578	0.01539	0.01500	0.01463	0.01426
2.2	0.01390	0.01355	0.01321	0.01287	0.01255	0.01222	0.01191	0.01160	0.01130	0.01101
2.3	0.01072	0.01044	0.01017	0.00990	0.00964	0.00939	0.00914	0.00889	0.00866	0.00842
2.4	0.00820	0.00798	0.00776	0.00755	0.00734	0.00714	0.00695	0.00676	0.00657	0.00639
2.5	0.00621	0.00604	0.00587	0.00570	0.00554	0.00539	0.00523	0.00508	0.00494	0.00480
2.6	0.00466	0.00453	0.00440	0.00427	0.00415	0.00402	0.00391	0.00379	0.00368	0.00357
2.7	0.00347	0.00336	0.00326	0.00317	0.00307	0.00298	0.00289	0.00280	0.00272	0.00264
2.8	0.00256	0.00248	0.00240	0.00233	0.00226	0.00219	0.00212	0.00205	0.00199	0.00193
2.9	0.00187	0.00181	0.00175	0.00169	0.00164	0.00159	0.00154	0.00149	0.00144	0.00139
3.0	0.00135	3.1	0.00097	3.2	0.00069	3.3	0.00048	3.4	0.00034	
3.5	0.00023									
3.6	0.00016									
3.7	0.00011									
3.8	0.00007									
3.9	0.00005									
4.0	0.00003									

Source: Murdoch, J. and Barnes, J.A., *Statistical Table for Science, Engineering, Management and Business Studies*, Macmillan, London, 1986.

of 0.05 mm, what proportion of the components will have that dimension outside the specified limits? The situation is shown in Figure 17.9. The shaded areas represent the probabilities of dimensions being outside the two limits.

For the lower limit, $x = 4.90$ and

$$u = \frac{(x - \mu)}{\sigma} = \frac{(4.90 - 5.02)}{0.05} = -2.4$$

The minus sign simply tells us that we are dealing with the lower tail of the distribution. Reference to Table 17.4 gives a tail area of 0.0082, which is the probability of obtaining a component below the bottom limit. Similarly, for the upper limit at $x = 5.10$,

$$u = \frac{(x - \mu)}{\sigma} = \frac{(5.10 - 5.02)}{0.05} = 1.6$$

for which the tail probability is 0.0548.

The total proportion outside these limits is the sum of these two areas: 0.0082 + 0.0548 = 0.063.

Sampling from the normal distribution

If a large number of sample observations was taken from a normal distribution of mean μ and standard deviation σ, a histogram of the observed values could be drawn. As the number of observations becomes very large, so the width of the class intervals can be reduced, as shown in Figure 17.10.

Taking this idea to its conclusion, as the number of observations tends to infinity, so the class interval width tends to zero and the histogram's envelope becomes a smooth curve. If the histogram is of relative frequencies, this curve is the probability distribution. At the same time, the calculated estimates of mean and variance, $\bar{x}$ and s^2, from this infinite sample would become equal to μ and σ^2. (This, of course, assumes that the 'unbiased' form for s^2 is being used, with $(n - 1)$ in the denominator.)

This fact – that sample observations from an infinite sample assume the probability distribution of the sampled variable – while being fundamental, may not seem of much interest. The interest lies in the extension of this idea to samples that do not consist of individual observations, but instead consist of n observations (n = sample size). In such

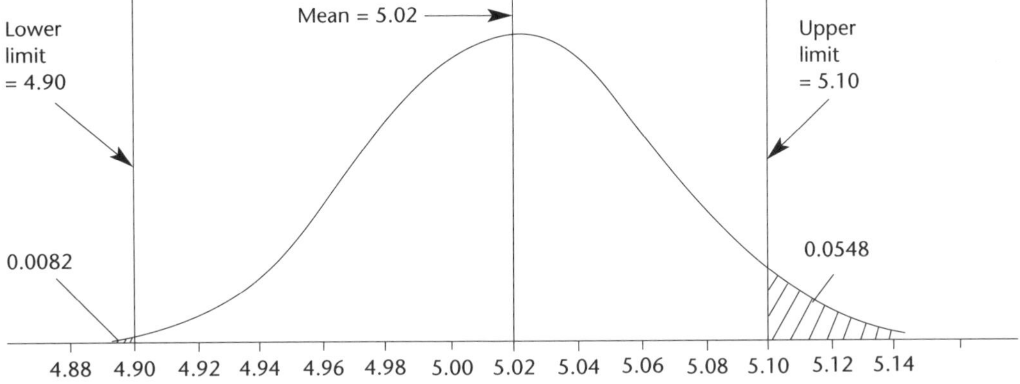

Figure 17.9 Normal distribution example

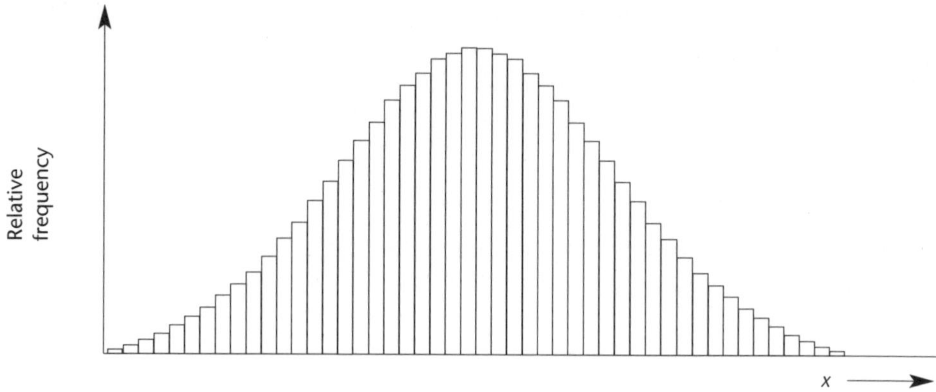

Figure 17.10 Frequency distribution: Histogram for a very large sample

cases, we can examine the behaviour of statistics (such as the sample means) calculated from the samples. The probability distributions of such statistics are known as sampling distributions.

Sampling distribution of sample means

Consider the situation where a sample of n independent observations is drawn from a normal distribution. The sample mean, $\bar{x}$, will be an unbiased estimator of the true mean μ, but will not be equal to μ. We could continue to take an infinite number of such samples. Each sample would have its own individual x. The probability distribution of these $\bar{x}$ values (that is, the sampling distribution of x) will have a mean equal to the population mean μ (as did the distribution of individual observations), but will have a smaller variance than σ^2, the variance of the distribution from which the samples are being drawn. This is, of course, to be expected, as each sample mean must be closer to μ than the outer extreme single observation in the sample.

Specifically, the variance of the distribution of the averages of samples of size n drawn from a normal distribution of mean μ and variance σ^2 will be a normal distribution with the same mean, μ, but with variance σ^2/n (that is, with standard deviation $\sigma/\sqrt{n}$), as shown in Figure 17.11. The standard deviation of sample averages ($\sigma/\sqrt{n}$) is known as the *standard error.*

As an example, consider a packaged product where it is a requirement that the average nett weight of a randomly selected sample of 50 packages must not be less than 250 g. If the standard deviation of the filling processes is 2.0 g, where should the mean contents be set to ensure that there is a probability of 0.95 that the requirement is met when such a sample is taken? The situation is shown diagrammatically in Figure 17.12.

The standardized normal deviate is now

$$u_{0.05} = \frac{(\bar{x} - \mu)}{\sigma/\sqrt{n}}$$

$$=1.645 \text{ (from Table 17.4)}$$

$$\text{giving } \mu = 1.645 \times (2.0/\sqrt{50}) + 250$$

$$= 250.47 \text{ g}$$

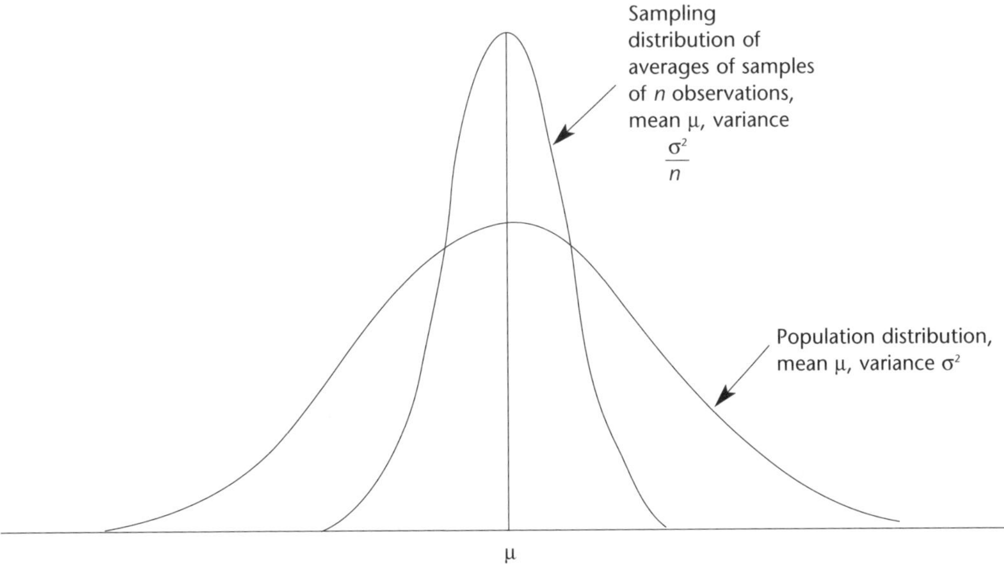

Figure 17.11 Sampling distribution of sample averages

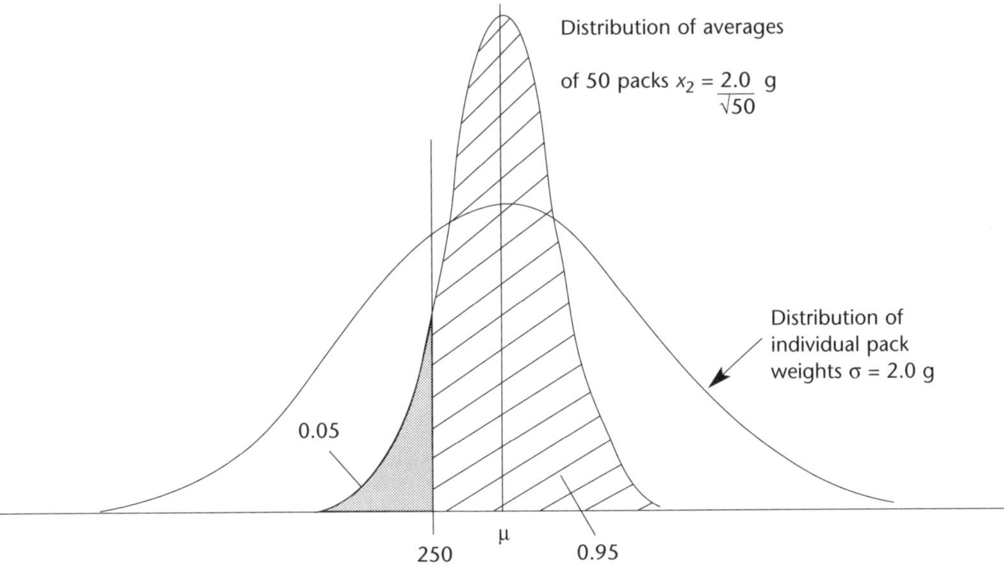

Figure 17.12 Sampling distribution of averages of 50 packs

Note that for *individual* packages, the standard deviation is 2.0, and the proportion below the declared weight will be obtained using:

$$u = \frac{(x - \mu)}{\sigma} = \frac{(250 - 250.47)}{2.0} = -0.235$$

from which reference to Table 17.4 tells us that the corresponding value of α is 0.4071 (averaging the results of u values of 0.23 and 0.24). This tells us that even though the risk of an average of 50 packages will be under this value – an interesting comment on the effect of the current practice of declaring contents by average rather than the previous use of minimum contents declaration.

The Central Limit Theorem

This provides the major justification for the widespread use of the normal distribution in statistical analysis in general, and in SPC in particular. It states simply that irrespective of the form of the distribution from which samples are drawn, the distribution of the sample averages will tend to a normal distribution as the number of observations in the samples (the sample size) tends to infinity.

The beauty of this theorem is that the sample size does not have to tend very far towards infinity. In most practical situations, the distribution of averages of samples of size $n = 5$ will approximate closely enough to the normal distribution to validate its use, as long as the distribution from which the samples are drawn is not too heavily skewed.

In the case of heavily skewed distributions, taking the means of the logarithms of the individual values will usually suffice.

THE LOG-NORMAL DISTRIBUTION

This distribution occurs when the variable X is such that log (X) follows a normal distribution. This distribution is positively skewed, as shown in Figure 17.13. This distribution is often used to model variables that have a target value of zero, but where in practice there will always be small positive values – such things as impurities in chemicals, and distortion measurements such as squareness, eccentricity, parallelism, and so on.

Analysis of log-normal variates is undertaken by transforming them into normal variates. For example, consider the ovality measurement of a turned cylinder which is log-normally distributed with a mean of 20 μm and a variance of 16 μm^2. What proportion will have ovality greater than the specification maximum of 35 μm?

The logarithm of the ovality will be normally distributed with mean log (20) (= 1.3), and

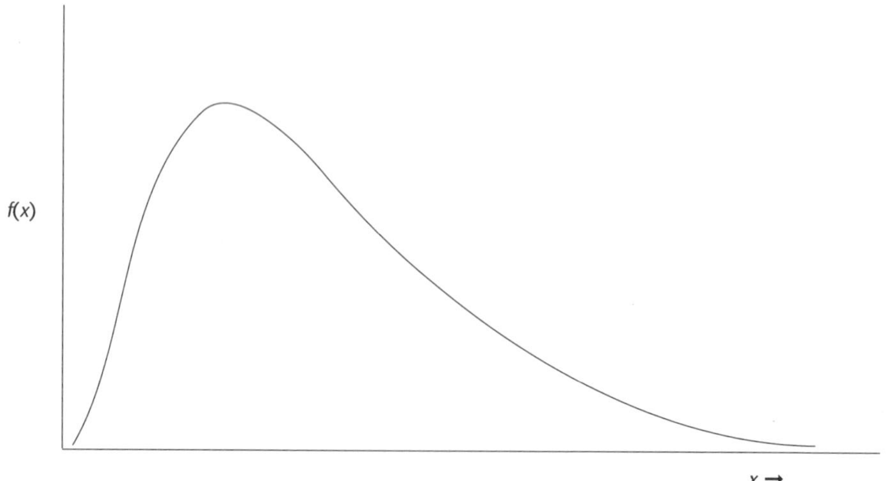

Figure 17.13 Log-normal distribution

standard deviation log ($\sqrt{16}$) (= 0.6). We want to know the proportion of this distribution greater than log (35) (= 1.54). In the unusual normal distribution terminology:

$$u_\alpha = \frac{(x - \mu)}{\sigma} = \frac{(1.54 - 1.30)}{0.6} = -0.40$$

Table 17.4 gives the corresponding α value as 0.345: about 35 per cent of the cylinders would be expected to have eccentricities above the specification limit.

THE EXPONENTIAL DISTRIBUTION

This distribution is used to describe the extent of sample space between successive occurrences of events that occur in a completely random manner, but at a constant underlying rate. Such events are said to be generated by a *homogeneous Poisson process* (HPP). In manufacturing, common examples are such things as blemishes in painted surfaces, insulation defects in coated conductors, assembly defects and so on. The exponential distribution would describe, respectively, the distribution of the area painted between the occurrence of each blemish, the length of conductor between each defect, and the number of assemblies (or assembly operations) between each defect. Another popular application in quality assurance is in the field of reliability and life testing, where the distribution is used to describe the times between successive failures of randomly failing equipment.

The distribution itself is extremely simple. It has only one parameter, λ, which is the rate (events per unit of sample space) at which events occur. The density function is an exponential curve.

$$f(x) = \lambda e^{-\lambda x}$$

as shown in Figure 17.14. The term e is the exponential constant, 2.7183. The mean is at $1/\lambda$, and this is also equal to the standard deviation. By inspection, the mode is always at zero. To evaluate probabilities under the exponential distribution, tables are unnecessary as the area under the curve between zero and x (the distribution function, $F(x)$) is simply $1 - e^{\lambda x}$. Consider an item of equipment that fails on average at a rate of one failure per 427 hours of operation. What is the probability that it will last for 500 hours without failure?

The rate of failures, λ, is 1/427 = 0.00234 failures per hour. The probability of there being a failure in the interval 0–500 hours is $e^{-(500 \times 0.00234)} = e^{-1.17} = 0.31$. The probability of there *not* being a failure is therefore:

$$1 - 0.31 = 0.69$$

Note that for any probability calculated under the exponential distribution, the value of the sample space at which $x = 0$ is completely arbitrary. The time represented by $x = 0$ in the above example, for instance, need not necessarily be the time of the previous failure. The underlying basic principle is that events are totally random, and therefore uninfluenced by the point in the sample at which they occur.

The sample estimate of λ is obtained from the mean of sample data. For example, if a randomly chosen 200 metre length of wire contained three insulation defects, the estimate of λ is simply 3/200 = 0.015 defects per metre. To test the assumption of the exponential distribution, a simple way is to calculate the estimate of the standard deviation of the x

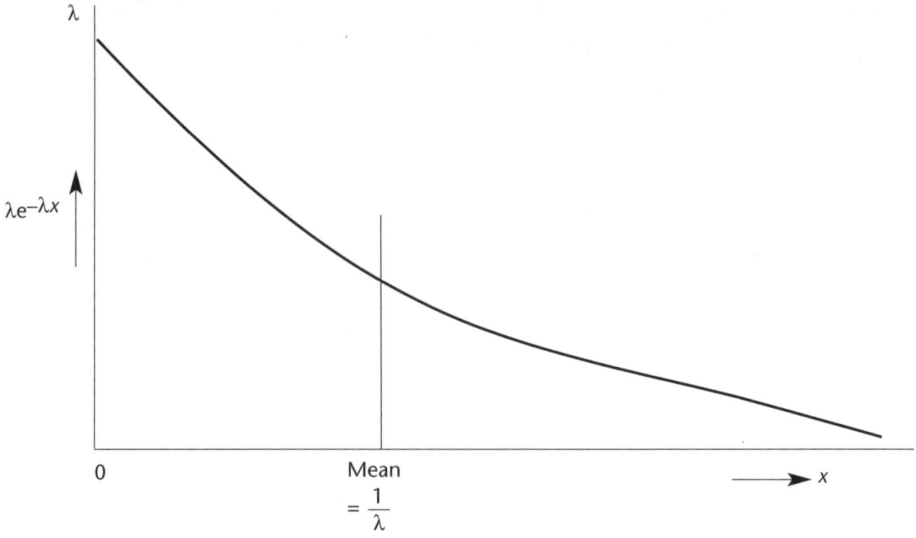

Figure 17.14 Exponential distribution

values. If this is close to $1/\lambda$, the assumption is likely to be valid. In any estimation involving sequenced data, it is important that the sample is randomly selected. In particular, any sample that is terminated by an event (such as a sample that is terminated by a defect in the wire, or at the time of an equipment failure) is *not* random, and will overestimate the rate.

THE WEIBULL DISTRIBUTION

This is is a simple extension of the exponential distribution, whose distribution function is given by:

$$F(x) = 1 - e^{-(\lambda x)^{ß}}$$

or, more usually, by using the symbol η for $1/\lambda$

$$F(x) = 1 - e^{\left(-\frac{x}{\eta}\right)^{ß}}$$

η is known as the *characteristic life* – it is a measure of location, but is only equal to the mean when $ß = 1$. More generally, it is the value of the variate at which the area under the distribution (the distribution function) is equal to $1 - e^{-1} = 0.632$.

ß is known as the *shape parameter* – as can be seen from Figure 17.15, changing its value changes the shape of the distribution. If $ß = 1$, it is an exponential distribution (as is apparent from the above formulae). For $ß = 3.44$, it forms a close approximation to the normal distribution. For values in between these two, it approximates to a log-normal. It can therefore be seen that it has potential as a very flexible distribution that is none the less mathematically fairly simple, with only two parameters. In practice, it is widely used in failure data analysis, but only rarely elsewhere. This is largely due to difficulties in estimating ß and η from sample data. Algebraic methods need iterative solution of equations (usually using computer algorithms). The distribution does, however, lend itself to graphical parameter estimation using probability plotting, as described below.

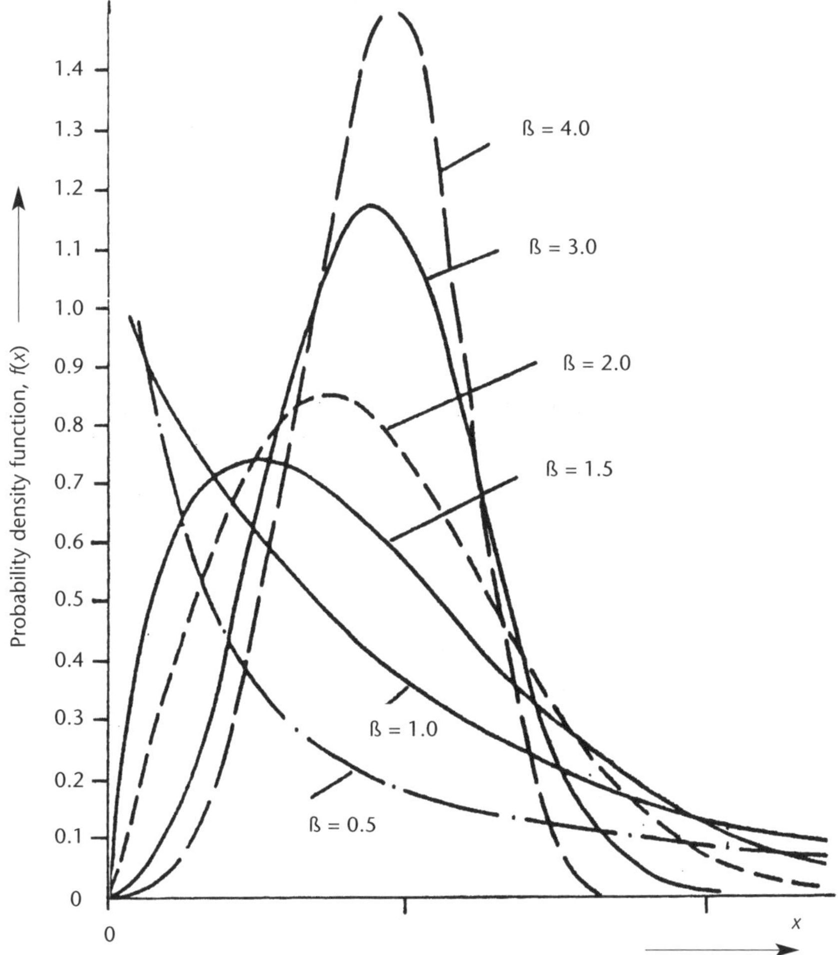

Figure 17.15 The Weibull probability density function, *f*(*x*), for different values of the shape parameter ß

Probability plotting

Probability plotting is a simple graphical technique that is used for assessing the fit of sample data to continuous probability distributions. It also provides informal estimates of the parameters of the distributions.

The procedure consists simply of drawing a curve representing the distribution function as estimated from the data. This is compared with the distribution function of the assumed model. To obviate the difficulty of comparing curves, special graph paper is available with transformed probability scales that give a straight line plot for data conforming exactly with the distribution for each particular type of paper.

As an example, consider the data that were introduced in Table 17.1. To produce the distribution function, it is first of all necessary to write the data down in ascending order of magnitude. In Table 17.5, the data in Table 17.1 are rearranged in this way, with $x_{(i)}$ being the *i*th ordered observation ($x_{(1)}$ is the first, $x_{(2)}$ is the second, and so on).

The sample estimate of the distribution function at any randomly chosen value of x (that is, the proportion of the population less than that of x) is given by i/n. Care must be taken, however, in treating sample data as the $x_{(i)}$ values are not random samples – they are fixed at the observed data points. A modified, and less biased, estimate of the distribution function is obtained by a modified statistic. Many have been proposed – a suitable one in most circumstances is 'mean rank', $i/(n + 1)$. In the example, as the sample size, n, is 20, the mean ranks are the order number, i, divided by 21. A further consideration is the fact that most commercially produced probability plotting graph paper expresses the distribution function estimate as a percentage rather than a proportion, so it is necessary additionally to multiply the estimate by 100 if this is the case. The distribution functions in the final column of Table 17.5 have been calculated on this basis.

NORMAL PROBABILITY PLOTS

Plotting paper is available for most of the more widely used distribution models. For illustration, the above data are plotted on one of the commercially available normal probability plotting papers (Chartwell ref. 5571) in Figure 17.16. From the plot the following comments can be made:

1 The fact that it gives a reasonable straight line confirms that the normal distribution is a reasonable fit to the data. A near-perfect fit should never be expected. Remember that all the sample points are subject to sampling variation. Too good a fit should, in fact, raise suspicions that the data are not truly random, but may have been 'adjusted' to fit

Table 17.5 Calculation of distribution function values from the data in Table 17.1

i	$X_{(i)}$	$(i/21) \times 100$
1	4.73	4.76
2	4.78	9.52
3	4.81	14.28
4	4.88	19.04
5	4.95	23.80
6	5.00	28.57
7	5.02	33.33
8	5.07	38.09
9	5.10	42.86
10	5.14	47.62
11	5.16	52.38
12	5.19	57.14
13	5.22	61.90
14	5.25	66.67
15	5.31	71.43
16	5.32	76.19
17	5.38	80.95
18	5.44	85.71
19	5.56	90.48
20	5.74	95.24

the required answer. Note that, in fitting the line to the data points, the fit should emphasize the points towards the centre. Because of the highly non-linear probability scale, apparent outliers at the end of the line (as in Figure 17.16) are not as much in error as they initially appear.

2 The mean and the median for a symmetrical distribution (such as the normal) are coincident. The mean can therefore be estimated by reading the value of x corresponding to 50 per cent probability. This is shown in Figure 17.16, giving a value of 5.145.

3 The slope of the plot estimates the standard deviation – the steeper the plot, the greater the value. To obtain a value from the non-linear scales, the usual method is to identify the 5 and 95 per cent points from the plot. From our knowledge of the normal distribution, these points are 3.29 standard deviations apart, so the distance between the 5 and 95 per cent points, divided by 3.29, estimates the standard deviation. Specifically, in this example:

The 5 per cent point is at $x = 4.69$
The 95 per cent point is at $x = 5.60$

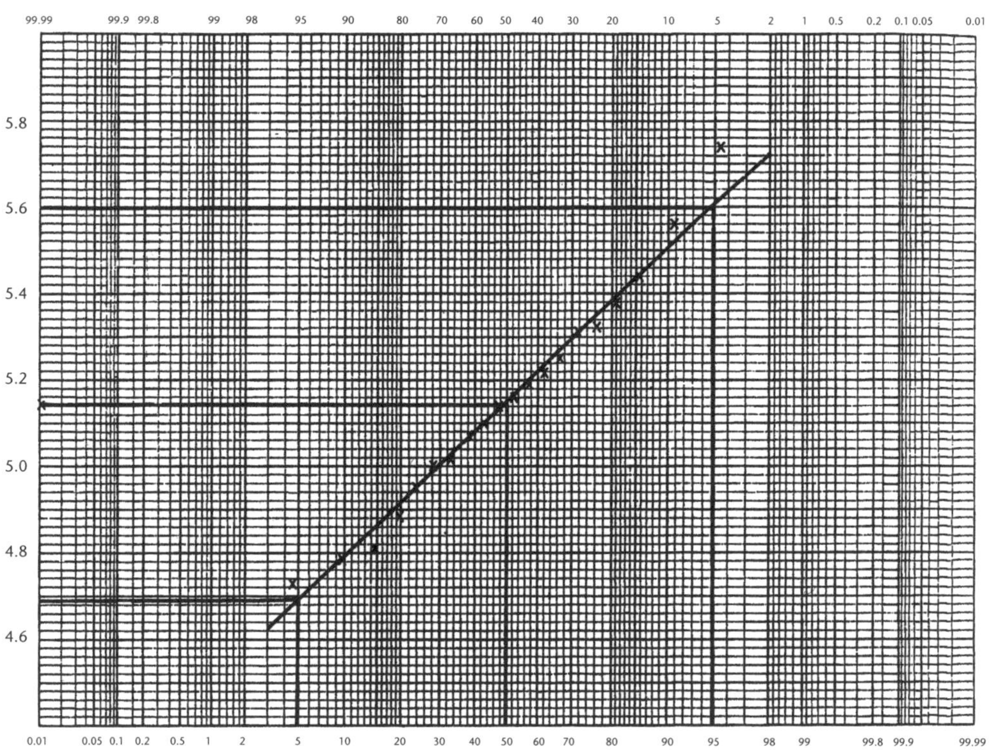

Figure 17.16 Normal probability data plot
Note: Data from Table 17.1.

so the estimate of the standard deviation is:

$$\frac{(5.60 - 4.69)}{3.29} = 0.277$$

It can be seen that the results agree reasonably closely with those obtained previously by calculation ($\bar{x}$ = 5.153 and s = 0.263).

PROBABILITY PLOTTING WITH GROUPED DATA

When data are grouped into class intervals, the approach to probability plotting has to be slightly modified. The variate values are plotted at the *top* of each class interval against the cumulative proportion at that point. The procedure is illustrated in Table 17.6, again using the data from Table 17.1.

Note that when using class intervals, the cumulative percentages are plotted direct, without using $i/(n + 1)$. This is because the points are now plotted at predetermined variate values rather than predetermined cumulative percentages. It does give the drawback, however, that the last point cannot be plotted. The reader can verify that the plot gives similar results to those in Figure 17.16, but there is less certainty about the fit of the line as there are now only 5 points instead of the previous 20. This repeats the point made in discussion of mean and various estimates in general that analysis using grouped data should *not* be used if the individual 'raw' data are available. The plotting procedure for grouped data should only be used in the cases of discrete data, or of continuous data that are available only already categorized into groups.

PROBABILITY PLOTTING FOR NON-NORMAL DISTRIBUTIONS

For log-normal data, either the logarithms of the data can be plotted on normal probability paper or, alternatively, plotting paper is available with a logarithmic variate scale. Probability plotting is a particularly well-used method of parameter estimation for the Weibull and exponential distributions (the exponential being simply a special case of the Weibull with the shape parameter ß equal to one). These distributions are mainly used in modelling the distribution of lives to failure, both in engineering reliability and human mortality studies. Special plotting paper is again available (for example, Chartwell ref. 6572).

Table 17.6 Probability plotting with the data from Table 17.1 grouped into class intervals

Top of interval	*Cumulative relative frequency (per cent)*
4.8	10
5.0	25
5.2	60
5.4	85
5.6	95
5.8	100

A comprehensive description of its use is given in Davidson (1988). A general overview of probability plotting for a wide range of distributions is given by King (1971).

DISCRETE PROBABILITY DISTRIBUTIONS

For a discrete random variable X, the probability that X takes a particular discrete value x is denoted $P(x)$. This is called the *probability function*, which can be represented graphically as shown in Figure 17.17. Note the similarity to the discrete frequency distribution in Figure 17.3.

There are two separate discrete probability distribution models that find widespread use in quality assurance: the binomial distribution and the Poisson distribution.

THE BINOMIAL DISTRIBUTION

The binomial distribution (literally 'two names') is concerned with trials that have two possible outcomes, usually referred to as 'success' and 'failure'. This terminology, while perfectly sensible for general application, becomes the source of some confusion in quality assurance applications where a 'success' is usually the occurrence of a defective item. For the purposes of this chapter's aim of describing applied statistics in a quality assurance context, this confusion will be avoided by making the two classifications 'defective' and 'good'. (There are further dangers in the use of the word 'defective' that are discussed in Chapter 18.)

Suppose a process generates a small, random proportion of defective items, p. If we were to take a random sample of n items from the process, consider the possibility of getting x defective items followed by $(n - x)$ good items:

DDDDDD.......................DDDDGGGGGGGGGGGGGG.........GGGGGGG
| ◄— x defectives —► | ◄———— $(n - x)$ good ————► |
(each with probability p) (each with probability $1 - p$)

The product rule of probabilities tells us that the probability of obtaining x consecutive defective items, each with probability p, is

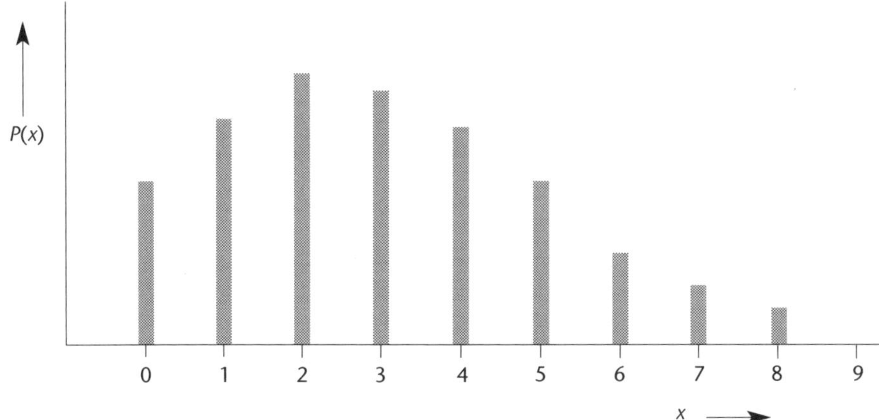

Figure 17.17 Discrete probability distribution

$$p \times p \times p \times p \times p \ldots \times p \text{ (x times)} = p^x$$

and similarly, the probability of obtaining $(n - x)$ good times, each with probability $(1 - p)$, is:

$$(1 - p) \times (1 - p) \times (1 - p) \times (1 - p) \ldots \times (1 - p) \text{ ($(n - x)$ times)}$$
$$= (1 - p)^{(n - x)}$$

The probability of both these occurring is, again using the product rule,

$$p^x (1 - p)^{(n - x)}$$

The particular sequence we have considered (x defective, followed by $(n - x)$ good) is, however, only one of a large number of possible combinations. It can be shown that the number of combinations of x defective and $(n - x)$ good (denoted $_nC_x$) is:

$$\frac{n!}{x!\,(n - x)!}$$

where the '!' denotes 'factorial', the factorial of a number being that number successively multiplied by the previous number minus one until the multiplier reduces to one (for example, 5! = (5 x 4 x 3 x 2 x 1)= 120).

As there is not usually any interest in the precise order in which defectives occur in a sample, but only with the total number, these results can be combined (now using the addition rule) to give the general result that the probability of x defectives in a sample of n that is drawn from a population that is proportion p defective is given by $P(x)$, where:

$$P(x) = \frac{n!}{x!\,(n - x)!}\, p^x (1 - p)^{(n - x)}$$

This is the *binomial probability formula*. The mean (that is, expected) number of defectives is np, and the variance of the number of defectives is $np\,(1 - p)$.

As an example, consider the case of a sample of 20 items drawn from a population that is 8 per cent (0.08) defective. The probability of zero defectives is:

$$P(0) = \frac{20!}{(0!\ 20!)}\ 0.08^0\ 0.92^{20} = 0.92^{20} = 0.1887$$

(Note that 0! = 1.) Similarly:

$$P(1) = \frac{20!}{(1!\ 19!)}\ 0.08^1\ 0.92^{19} = 0.3282$$

$$P(2) = \frac{20!}{(2!\ 18!)}\ 0.08^2\ 0.92^{18} = 0.2711$$

$$P(2) = \frac{20!}{(3!\ 17!)}\ 0.08^3\ 0.92^{17} = 0.1414$$

and so on up to $P(20)$. (Note that if all the terms are evaluated, their sum will be exactly 1.)

These probabilities form a binomial probability distribution. The complete picture of this particular distribution is shown in Figure 17.18. This distribution has mean = np = 20 x 0.08 = 1.6 and variance = $np(1 - p)$ = 20 x 0.08 x 0.92 = 1.472 (standard deviation = 1.213).

A particular distribution is identified by its two parameters, n and p. A selection of distributions for other values of n and p is shown in Figure 17.19.

From Figure 17.19, an overall appreciation of the different shapes of the distribution can be obtained. Note in particular the exact symmetry of the distribution when $p = 0.5$, and the closeness to symmetry when (n x p) (which is the mean, that is the expected number of defectives) becomes large. This is of particular relevance in the consideration of attributes control charts in Chapter 19.

A note on calculation of binomial probabilities

In most practical applications, rather than wanting to know the probability of exactly x defectives, it is usual to want to know the probability of 'c or fewer' or 'r or more' (c and r simply being conventional symbols for the integer in question).

To calculate the probability of c or fewer, simply add all the binomial probabilities from zero up to c. For example, in the case already explored of $n = 20$ and $p = 0.08$, the probability of two or fewer defectives is:

$$P(0) + P(1) + P(2) = 0.1887 + 0.3282 + 0.2711 = 0.7880$$

The evaluation of successive binomial probabilities can be simplified by using the recursion relationship:

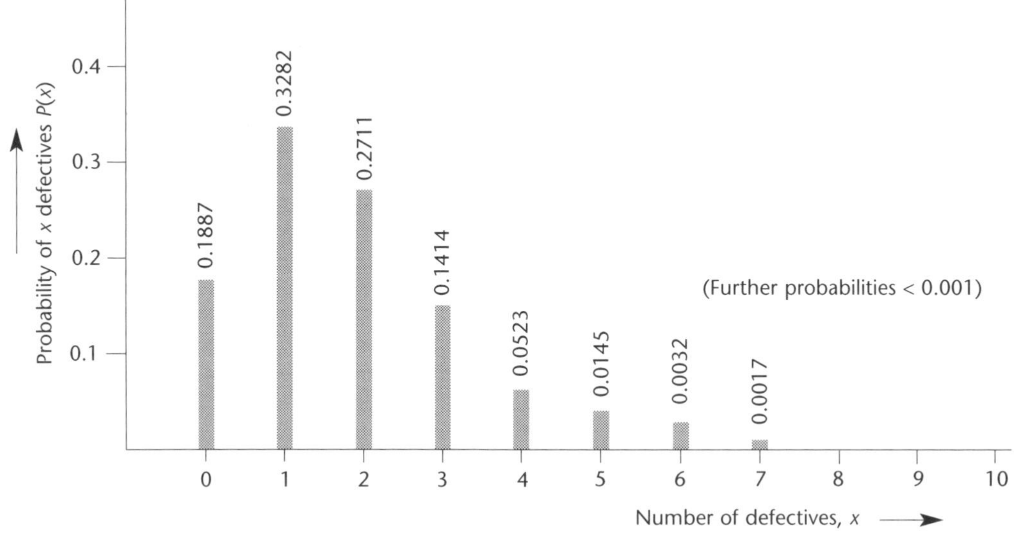

Figure 17.18 Binomial distribution with $n = 20$, $p = 0.08$

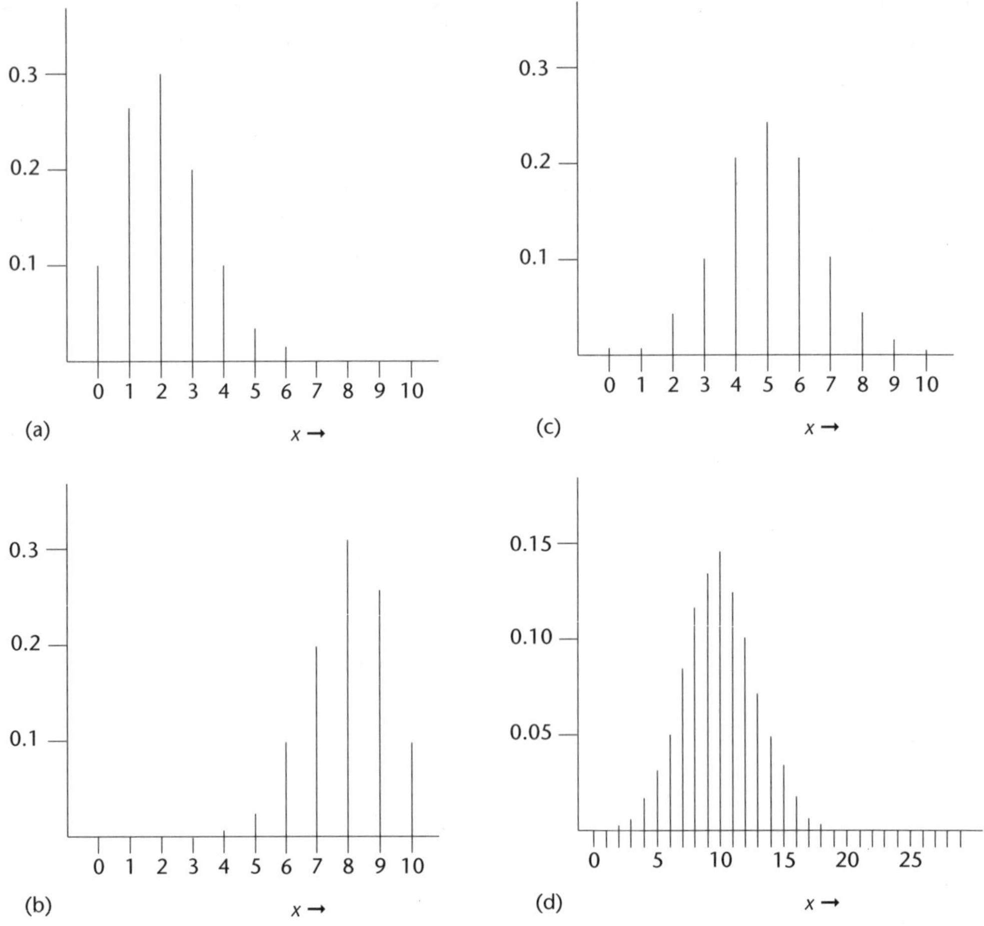

Figure 17.19 Binomial distributions: (a) $n = 10$, $p = 0.2$; (b) $n = 10$, $p = 0.8$; (c) $n = 10$, $p = 0.5$; (d) $n = 50$, $p = 0.2$

$$P(x) = P(x-1) \times \frac{(n-x+1)}{x} \times \frac{p}{(1-p)}$$

Reverting again to the example of $n = 20$ and $p = 0.08$, it is simple to calculate $P(0) = 0.92^{20} = 0.1887$. From this:

$$P(1) = 0.3282 \times \frac{20}{1} \times \frac{0.08}{0.92} = 0.3283$$

$$P(2) = 0.3282 \times \frac{19}{2} \times \frac{0.08}{0.92} = 0.2711$$

and so on, as far as is required.

An even simpler alternative, of course, is to obtain the values from a set of tables. The difficulty with the binomial is that it is not possible to standardize the variates, so a table containing even a restricted set of values of n and p is going to be a massive document. A very restricted set of tabulations for the probability of r or more defectives is given in Murdoch and Barnes (1986, Table 2), but this is only for n values of 2, 5, 10, 20 and 100. If tables are to be used, it is more usual to use the Poisson distribution (see below) as an approximation.

POISSON DISTRIBUTION

The Poisson distribution is used to describe homogeneous Poisson processes (HPPs) as already introduced under the heading 'Exponential distribution'. Whereas the exponential is a continuous distribution describing the amount of sample space between events, the Poisson is a discrete distribution describing the number of events in a given sample space. The equation for the distribution (the Poisson probability function) is:

$$P(x) = \frac{e^{-m}\, m^x}{m!}$$

where $P(x)$ is the probability of x events occurring in an HPP when m events are expected. The term m is the only parameter of the Poisson distribution, and is equal to both the mean and the variance of the distribution. Referring to the section dealing with the exponential distribution, m is equal to λx, where λ is the rate per unit sample space at which events occur and x is the extent of the sample space.

For example, if a painting process produces blemishes at an average rate of one per 3.7 m^2, the expected number of blemishes on a panel of area 2.5 m^2 is 3.7/2.5 = 1.48. Using this for m:

Probability of 0 blemishes on a panel, $P(0) = e^{-1.48} = 0.228$

Probability of 1 blemish, $P(1) = \frac{e^{-1.48}\ 1.48^1}{1} = 0.337$

Similarly:

$$P(2) = \frac{e^{-1.48}\ 1.48^2}{2!} = 0.249$$

$$P(3) = \frac{e^{-1.48}\ 1.48^3}{3!} = 0.123$$

and so on. There is a very simple recursion formula for Poisson probabilities:

$$P(x) = P\,(x-1) \times \frac{m}{x}$$

so, in the above example, from $P(0) = 0.228$ it follows that:

$$P(1) = 0.288 \times \frac{1.48}{1} = 0.337$$

$$P(2) = 0.337 \times \frac{1.48}{2} = 0.249$$

and so on.

THE POISSON AS AN APPROXIMATION TO THE BINOMIAL

The only situation modelled exactly by the Poisson is that of the HPP. While this does have applications in quality assurance (as, for example, in the use of *c* charts, which will be described in Chapter 18), it is more usually applied as an approximation to the binomial. This opens the field of application to other types of attributes control chart, and also to acceptance sampling by attributes (as, for example, in British Standard BS 6001 and its international equivalent, ISO 2859).

The approximation is applied by putting the Poisson mean (m) equal to the binomial mean (np). Referring to the example used to illustrate the binomial distribution with $n = 20$ and $p = 0.08$, the mean $np = 20 \times 0.08 = 1.6$. Using 1.6 as the Poisson 'm', this gives:

$P(0) = e^{-1.6} = 0.202$
$P(1) = 0.202 \times 1.6 = 0.323$
$P(2) = 0.323 \times 1.6/2 = 0.258$
$P(3) = 0.258 \times 1.6/3 = 0.138$

and so on.

Comparison with the binomial figures shows that while there is some disparity, the agreement is probably close enough for practical purposes. Provided that np is suitably small (usually taken as being less than 0.1), this approximation can be made use of as it greatly simplifies the calculations. It also facilitates the use of tabulated probabilities (for example, in Table 2 of Murdoch and Barnes, 1986), as there is now only one parameter to enter in the tables, and it will deal with any value of sample size.

The smaller the value of p, the better the approximation, with the limiting value of 0.1 merely being an arbitrary value. In quality assurance applications, it is to be hoped that real proportions defective never get this high, so the use of the Poisson in such applications is generally justified. A distinction should always be made, however, between the exact application (in an HPP) and the approximation to the binomial.

THE NORMAL DISTRIBUTION AS AN APPROXIMATION TO BINOMIAL AND POISSON DISTRIBUTIONS

Inspection of Figure 17.19 shows that for large values of the binomial mean, the distribution becomes fairly symmetrical, with a shape similar to that of the normal distribution. The Poisson behaves in a similar way. This opens the possibility of using the normal as an approximation to the binomial and the Poisson with large means. This can sometimes simplify calculations of cumulative probabilities, but it is a procedure that must be used with care as it uses a continuous approximation to a discrete situation. It is best illustrated by example.

Suppose it is required to calculate the probability of there being between 15 and 25 (inclusive) defective items in a sample of 75 with a proportion defective 0.3. Calculation using the binomial is perfectly possible, but would necessitate the calculation of 20 separate terms, with some rather large numbers involved (the doubting reader is invited to try it!). The Poisson is no use as an approximation, as p is far too large.

The use of the normal as an approximation involves equating the normal and (in this case) binomial means and variances. For this binomial:

The mean is $np = 75 \times 0.3 = 22.5$
The variance is $np\,(1 - p) = 75 \times 0.3 \times 0.7 = 15.75$
The standard deviation is $\sqrt{15.75} = 3.97$

The approximating normal therefore has $\mu = 22.5$ and $\sigma = 3.97$. The distributions are as shown in Figure 17.20.

The required part of the binomial is shown superimposed on the approximating normal. Note that the 'cut-off' points for the required tails are at 14.5 and 25.5. The problem as to whether to add or subtract this 0.5 continuity correction is a frequent source of difficulty. Rather than try to provide a necessarily complex set of rules, the simple solution is always to draw a sketch of the situation (as in Figure 17.20) when the solution becomes obvious. For the lower tail,

$$u_\alpha = \frac{14.5 - 22.5}{3.97} = -2.015$$

for which the tail area (which is the probability of *less than* 15 defectives) is 0.022, and, for the upper tail,

$$u_\alpha = \frac{25.5 - 22.5}{3.97} = -2.755$$

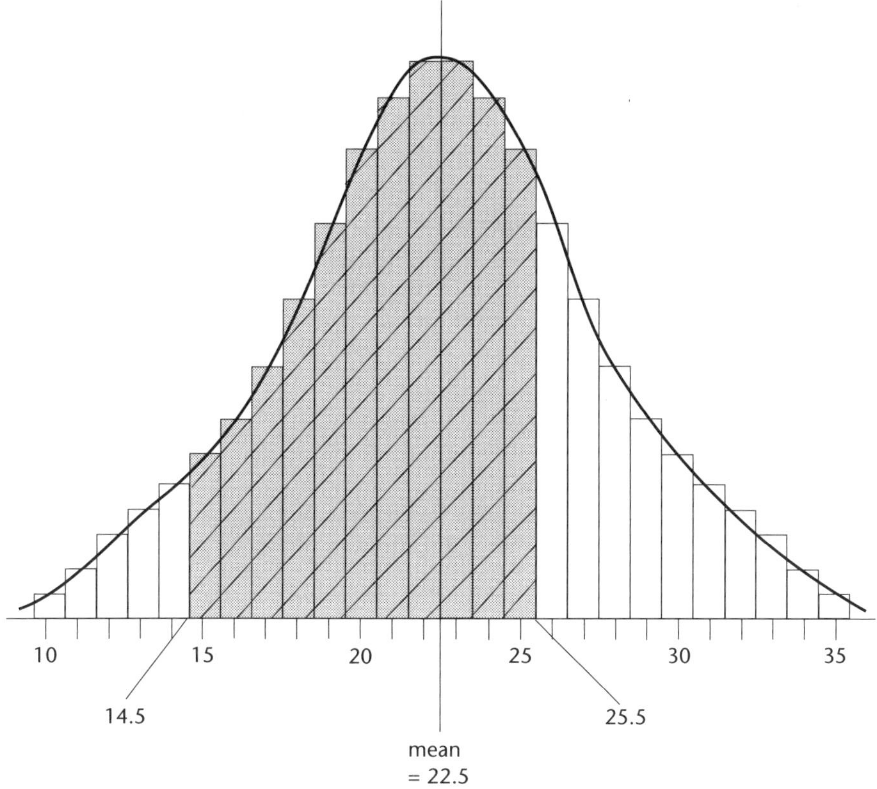

Figure 17.20 Example: Normal approximation to the binomial
Note: the required area is shaded

for which the tail area (the probability of more than 25 defectives) is 0.225. The probability of obtaining between 15 and 25 (inclusive) is therefore 1 – (0.022 + 0.225) = 0.753.

In dealing with attributes control charts (in Chapter 18), it will be seen that this approximation is often used implicitly even where the criteria for it being an adequate approximation are far from being met. The justification for this is that it is more important to have simple procedures than accurate probabilities – an issue that is discussed more fully in that chapter.

Further reading

This chapter has been limited to fundamental ideas with particular relevance to quality assurance. The subject of statistics goes far beyond this introduction. There are many hundreds of books on applied statistics, very few of which are unworthy of recommendation, so suggestions for further reading are to some extent personal preferences. On this basis, Chatfield (1983) is a very readable text, which has a particular leaning towards industrial applications and quality assurance. Miller and Freund (1977) is a rather more comprehensive text along the same lines. A classic, and very readable, text is Moroney (1951). Another useful little book is *The Pocket Statistician*, compiled by members of the Quality Improvement Group of the Royal Statistical Society. This links the basic concepts of statistics with specific quality topics such as *process capability* and *process control* (covered in the subsequent chapters in this handbook) and quality improvement through experimentation (which is beyond the scope of this text). Beyond these, the best text is the one that the reader finds most 'user-friendly'.

It is not possible to proceed very far with formal statistical analysis without being able to evaluate probabilities from the various sampling distributions (binomial, Poisson, normal, etc.). This is usually effected through the use of statistical tables (an alternative being to use one of the computer packages which are available). Murdoch and Barnes (1986) is, in common with most 'compact' tables, mainly a compilation of standard tables that have mostly been published elsewhere, but they are particularly clearly presented, and contain in one volume many of the more usual tables and several that are of specific application to quality control.

References

Chatfield, C., *Statistics for Technology*, 3rd edn, Science Paperbacks, Chapman & Hall, London, 1983.

Coleman, S., Greenfield, T., Jones, R., Morris, C. and Puzey, I., *The Pocket Statistician*, Arnold, London, 1996.

Davidson, J. (ed.), *The Reliability of Mechanical Systems*, Mechanical Engineering Publications, London, 1988.

King, J., *Probability Charts for Decision Making*, Industrial Press, New York, 1971.

Miller, I. and Freund, J.E., *Probability and Statistics for Engineers*, Prentice-Hall, New York, 1977.

Moroney, M.J., *Facts from Figures*, Penguin Books, Harmondsworth, 1951.

Murdoch, J. and Barnes, J.A., *Statistical Tables for Science, Engineering, Management and Business Studies*, Macmillan, London, 1986.

CHAPTER

18 Control Charts, Part 1: Shewhart Charts

David Newton

Chapter 8 described how the variation inherent in a process is measured and how it is compared with specified limits in order to quantify process capability In so doing, the idea was introduced of a time-based chart on which were plotted sample averages of the process characteristic in question. Control charting is simply an extension of this procedure into the routine production operation of the manufacturing process. The purpose of the chart now becomes that of detecting change from the inherent, 'in-control', situation defined in the process capability analysis. Objective decision criteria are introduced for decisions as to whether or not such a change has occurred. The need for control of the variation of the process as well as its mean level is explained. The definitive control chart for measured variables is the '$\bar{x}$, *R*' chart, which combines these two requirements with data from the same sample being plotted on both charts simultaneously. Similar approaches can be applied to attributes control, where the process characteristic is a count of nonconforming items or of defects. Control charts such as these, both for variables and for attributes, are sometimes referred to as Shewhart Charts (Shewhart, 1931).

To interfere or to ignore?

When a process is 'in control', it is behaving in a completely random (that is, unpredictable) manner influenced only by its 'common causes' of chance variation. The objective of any control chart is to signal any departure from this situation due to 'special' (sometimes called 'assignable') causes, whether they affect the mean level or the variability of the process. The objectives are accordingly twofold:

1 to take action when a change occurs
2 to refrain from action in the absence of a change.

It is easy to lose sight of the importance of the second aspect. Human nature is to 'fiddle' with a process when any apparent change occurs. It is easily demonstrated that if the variation is purely random, any such fiddling is bound to make the process deteriorate. Table 18.1 shows 10 consecutive samples from a stable 'in-control' process. Column 1 shows the averages from samples of 5 observations. Column 2 shows the value of these sample averages if the process mean is corrected to counteract the deviation from the target of 250. Column 3 shows this observed deviation, and column 4 shows the process means after applying the correction.

Table 18.1 Data for 10 samples taken from a stable 'in-control' process

Uncorrected sample average (1)	*Corrected sample average (2)*	*Deviation from 250 (3)*	*Process mean after correction (4)*
251.23		+1.23	248.77
250.94	249.71	–0.29	249.06
248.26	247.32	–2.68	251.74
250.99	252.73	+2.73	249.01
249.81	248.82	–1.18	250.19
251.87	252.06	+2.06	248.13
249.98	248.11	–1.89	250.02
249.35	249.37	–0.63	250.65
248.85	249.50	–0.50	251.15
250.10	251.25	+1.25	249.50

The increased variation of column 2 compared with column 1 is immediately apparent, the standard deviations of the averages being 1.753 and 1.139 respectively. The increase can also be seen in Figure 18.1, where the two sets of data are charted. Even if the process had not been 'corrected' on every sample, or if the corrections had been less than the total error, the variation would still have increased.

While it is, of course, important to take some form of action if a process really changes due to a special cause, any attempt to correct or adjust a process where no special causes are present will *always* make matters worse than if the process were left alone.

The control chart for sample averages

The use of control charts for sample averages is an extension of the process capability analysis into the production process. It relates to measurements of a single process characteristic. Samples are taken from the process at regular intervals. Each sample is of n items. The value of n, the sample size, is usually between 1 and 8.5, and is a popular value – it is sufficiently large to take advantage of the Central Limit Theorem in any assumption of normality, and any further increase in size is subject to diminishing returns in that the information contained in the sample increases only in proportion to the square root of the sample size.

The choice of the time interval between successive samplings from the process is largely an economic one, based on the maximum time it would be considered tolerable for the process to remain in an undetected 'out-of-control' state. The intervals between samplings should be approximately equal. It is, however, worthwhile bearing in mind the risks of being too predictable, particularly in the case of processes influenced by operators who might be inclined to make a special effort when a sampling is due.

Figure 18.2 shows a simple averages control chart for averages of samples of size five. The target value is 50.00 and process capability analysis has produced an estimate of 0.73 for σ. There is no obvious pattern to the plots except that there appears to be a downward movement of the averages towards the end, and, in particular, the most recent value, 48.87,

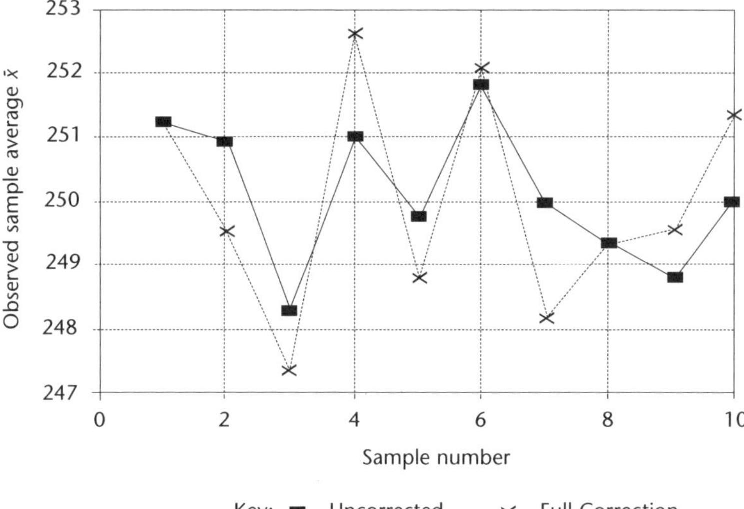

Figure 18.1 The effect of correcting the mean

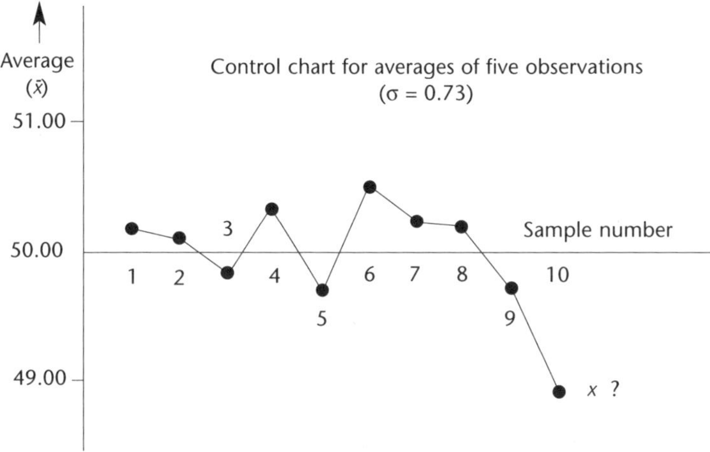

Figure 18.2 Averages control chart. Has the process average changed?

seems particularly low. Bearing in mind what has been said about the dangers of trying to correct an in-control process, however, we need to be fairly certain that this apparent move downwards is a real change in the process before they move to reset it.

This can be assessed by reference to the probability distribution of the averages under the 'in-control' assumption. This will have a mean equal to the target value of 50.00. From what was learned in Chapter 17, the standard deviation of averages of samples of size n (the standard error) will be the inherent standard deviation σ divided by the square root of the sample size (i.e. $\sigma/\sqrt{5}$). We also learned that, as a result of the central limit theorem, these averages will be approximately normally distributed, so we can use normal distribution tables to assess probabilities.

In this example, the standard error is $0.73/\sqrt{5} = 0.326$, so the last plotted point is $(50.00 - 48.87)/0.326 = 3.47$ standard errors away from the target value. Reference to tables of the normal distribution (see, for example, Table 17.4) shows that the probability of obtaining an average this far away from the target under the assumed distribution is very small (approximately 0.00025, or one chance in 4000), so we are justified in assuming that our observed value comes from some other distribution. The obvious conclusion is that it came from one with a mean of less than 50.00, so it now makes sense to readjust the process upwards, taking several additional samples until it is demonstrated that the mean is back on, or near to, the target value.

CONTROL LINES

Rather than assess the probabilities of each point as it is plotted, it is more usual to set decision criteria in advance by drawing control lines on the chart equispaced either side of the mean, at a distance such that a plotted point on or outside the lines makes it fairly certain that a change has occurred. The conventional position for these lines is three standard errors either side of the target: $T \pm 3\sigma/\sqrt{n}$. (Note that it is acceptable, or even preferable to use $T \pm 3\sigma_e$ if a value of σ_e has been obtained direct from the process capability study, as was discussed in Chapter 17.)

The probability of getting a point on or outside a line (assuming normality) is approximately 1 in 1000 (0.00135, to be more exact), so if we interpret such a point as meaning a change in the process, there is approximately a 0.999 probability that we are correct in doing so.

Other positions for control lines are of course possible – the use of 3 as the multiplier has evolved as a value that works satisfactorily in most circumstances. British Standards use a value of 3.09, for which the number of standard errors away from the mean corresponds to a normal distribution probability of exactly one-thousandth. The difference this makes in practice can be ignored. Values of less than 3 are quite common in circumstances where it is critical to detect changes in mean level. If such values are adopted, there is a concomitant increase in the risk of a spurious action decision where no change has in fact occurred. The value of this risk (known, in general, as the 'Type I' or 'α' risk) can be read from normal distribution tables. For example, if we use ±2.5 instead of ±3, the Type I risk increases from 0.00135 to 0.0062.

It is very easy to become obsessive about the normal distributions and exact probabilities. Remember that the normal distribution does not represent some great truth, nor does close conformance to it imply a better process than one that is not normally distributed. Its only value is its attractive mathematical properties – in particular, the Central Limit Theorem (see page 248). For this reason, arguments about whether to use British Standard control limits (based on 3.09 standard errors) or American/International ones (based on 3 standard errors) are futile. It is worth remembering that in describing the procedure to which he gave his name, Shewhart (1931) used a factor of 3, not because of any relation to the normal distribution, but simply because it seemed to work better than any other value.

REFINEMENTS TO DECISION CRITERIA

Warning lines

Sometimes, an additional pair of lines is positioned inside the control lines, with the rule that two consecutive points outside the same line constitute an action decision. This increases the sensitivity of the chart. Conventionally, these are positioned at ±2 standard errors either side of the target, which is approximately at the 1 in 40 probability point. (British Standards use ±1.96 to give an exact $^1/_{40}$ probability under the assumption of normality.) If warning lines are in use, once one point is obtained outside a line it is a signal also that the next sample should be taken sooner than usual, so that the suspicion of change can be confirmed or allayed as soon as possible.

A control chart with both control and warning lines is shown in Figure 18.3.

Runs of observations

If a chart shows either a run of several plotted averages the same side of the target (as in Figure 18.4a), or a run of several averages where each one is consistently greater than or less than its predecessor (as in Figure 18.4b), this can again be taken as a criterion for action. Conventionally, a run of 8 such observations is needed – the chance of either of these happening purely by chance is no greater than $0.5^8 = 0.004$.

Other criteria

Plotting a control chart reveals aspects of the process that might not necessarily be encompassed by any of these decision criteria. For this reason, the plot should always be studied for evidence of any patterns which could indicate problems that might be anticipated for a particular process. This must, however, be done with great care, bearing in mind what has been said about the dangers of interfering with a stable process.

Control of variation: The ranges chart

In processes controlled by a measured variable, there are possible out-of-control situations other than a movement in the average away from the target. Specifically, it is essential to detect any increase in variation above the inherent value demonstrated by the process capability analysis. Such an increase can often happen without any change in the process average. To detect such increases, it is necessary to plot some statistic that measures the variation of the process as reflected by the sample. The statistic most widely used is the

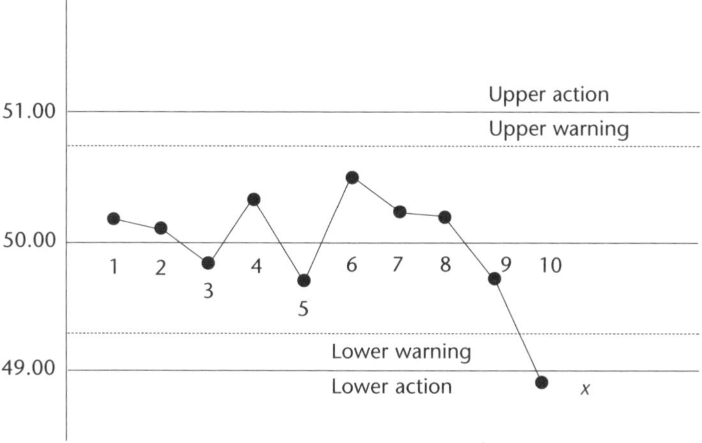

Figure 18.3 Averages chart with action and warning lines
Note: the data are the same as in Figure 18.2.

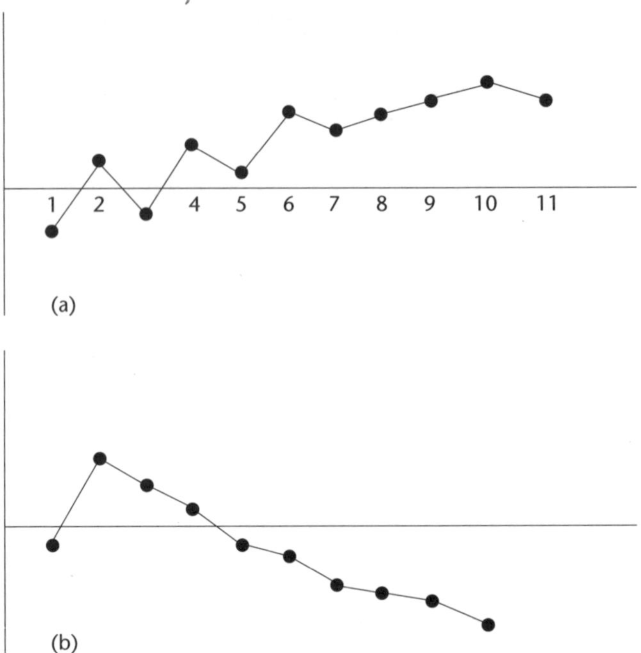

Figure 18.4 Examples of runs of consecutive points: (a) run of points above target (samples 3–11), (b) run of consistently reducing points

sample range (*R*), which is simply the difference between the largest and smallest observations in the sample. (The sample will be the same one that was used to provide $\bar{x}$, the sample average.)

CONTROL LINES FOR RANGES CHARTS

The probability distribution for sample ranges is not normal, even for normally distributed measurements, unless the sample size is much bigger than those in conventional use in control charting. Further, the distribution is asymmetrical, which precludes the use of simple '±' rules as for the averages chart. Factors for these lines have been calculated, and are available in many sources. The values in Table 18.2 have been reproduced from British Standard BS 5700: 1984, and are used as follows:

For an inherent process standard deviation σ:
The action line is at σ multiplied by $D_{0.001}$
The warning line, if used, is at σ multiplied by $D_{0.025}$

The option is also given for calculating these limits from process variation expressed as an expected average range, μ_R (which was estimated by the observed range, $\bar{R}$). In this case:

The action line is at μ_R multiplied by $D'_{0.001}$
the warning line, if used, is at μ_R multiplied by $D'_{0.025}$

An 'American' factor for sample range, D_4, is also given. This is an empirical factor due

Table 18.2 Table of control line factors for charts for sample range

Sample size (n)	*Factors for standard deviation, σ*		*Factors for average range, μ_R*			*Conversion factor d_n*
	Control $D_{0.001}$	*Warning* $D_{0.025}$	*Control* $D'_{0.001}$	*Warning* $D'_{0.025}$	*Control (US)* D_4	($\sigma = \mu_R \div d_n$)
2	4.65	3.17	4.12	2.81	3.27	1.128
3	5.05	3.68	2.98	2.17	2.57	1.693
4	5.30	3.98	2.57	1.93	2.28	2.059
5	5.45	4.20	2.34	1.81	2.11	2.326
6	5.60	4.36	2.21	1.72	2.00	2.534
7	5.70	4.49	2.11	1.66	1.92	2.704
8	5.80	4.61	2.04	1.62	1.86	2.847

Note: Taken from BS 5700 by permission of the British Standards Institution.

originally to Shewhart, which is commonly used in the United States. It gives risk values between those of BS type control and warning lines. It is based on μ + (3 x the standard deviation of μ_R).

In the example previously used for calculating the averages chart limits, with $\sigma = 0.326$,

For sample size 5, $D_{0.001} = 5.45$
$D_{0.025} = 4.20$

giving an action line at 0.326 x 5.45 = 1.777 and a warning line, if required, at 0.326 x 4.20 = 1.369.

THE STANDARD DEVIATIONS CHART

Control charting was developed in the days before electronic calculators. It was essential that calculations in the use of such charts were kept to a minimum to permit easy application on the shop floor. For this reason, range was used as the measure of variation instead of the theoretically much sounder use of standard deviation. Range has the related drawbacks of inefficiency (in that it only uses two pieces of information from the *n* available in the sample) and a dependency upon the assumption of normality in the derivation of the control lines. The use of standard deviation is nowadays much more acceptable as the complexities of its calculation can be avoided by the use of a calculator – the result is just as easy to obtain as the range. Despite this, the traditional use of range predominates, largely as a result of its use in various national and company standards. Table 18.3 gives control chart factors for standard deviation – in the same simple empirical '±3σ' theme that applies to American limits, it is simply σ + (3 x the standard deviation of σ). The control limit is at B_4 x σ.

Table 18.3 Table of control limit factors for charts for standard deviation

Sample size	2	3	4	5	6	7	8
B_4	3.27	2.57	2.27	2.09	1.97	1.88	1.81

LOWER LIMITS FOR CHARTS FOR RANGES AND STANDARD DEVIATIONS

It is unlikely that any manufacturing process will, without outside intervention, become more precise through a reduction in its variability. For this reason, there is no usual need for lower limits for range or standard deviation charts, although it is straightforward enough to derive factors for such limits. They are, for example, given in BS 2564 for D and D^1 factors, the suffixes for control and warning limits being 0.999 and 0.975 respectively (referring, as with the upper line, to the probabilities of obtaining a point above the line when 'in control'). The 'American' equivalent factor for the lower control line is given in Grant and Leavenworth (1972) as D_3. The corresponding factor for standard deviation charts is given in the same reference as B_3.

There is one reason for the application of lower limits that is perhaps worth consideration. This is the possible apparent reduction of variability due to errors in measuring equipment – an example once encountered was a cylindrical grinding process whose remarkable consistency was found to be due not to the process at all, but the fact that the pointer on the air gauge dial was firmly stuck to the glass.

OUTLIERS AND THE RANGE CHART

The designed intention of the range chart is to detect any change (usually an increase) in the variation inherent in the process. It also serves a very important additional function of signalling any individual sample observations that are a long way from the target value. Such values would often not have sufficient effect on the average to give an 'action' signal on the $\bar{x}$ chart (due to the centralizing effect of the others in the sample), but a single 'rogue' value would be more likely to give an upper 'action' signal on a ranges (or standard deviations) chart. Such values can occur due to a single faulty component in the sample, or simply due to an error in recording the data. This function of the range chart alone is sufficient justification for such a chart always to be used in conjunction with an averages chart, as described below.

The average and range ($\bar{X}$, R) chart

The definitive control chart for measured variables is one which controls mean level and variability simultaneously. The most widely used version of this is the chart for average and range. In such a chart, the average and the range are both calculated from the same sample.

An example of production data from which such a chart might be constructed is given in Table 18.4. The process is the press-forming of a spring clip, where the process is monitored by the free length dimension which has specification limits of 20.00 mm ± 1.5 mm. An earlier process capability study showed that when in control, the process gave a mean very close to the nominal, and a standard deviation of 0.50 mm. This standard deviation converts into an expected range for samples of five of 0.50 x d_5, that is 0.50 x 2.326 = 1.16.

THE $\bar{X}$, R CHART IN ACTION

Figure 18.5 shows the data in Table 18.4 plotted on a typical charting form as used in

Table 18.4 Example data for $\bar{X}$, R chart

Sample number	*Measured values*					*Average* $\bar{X}$	*Range* R
	1	*2*	*3*	*4*	*5*		
1	19.3	19.4	20.7	20.0	20.6	20.00	1.4
2	20.3	19.8	19.7	20.8	20.3	20.18	1.1
3	19.5	21.4	20.5	19.7	20.5	20.32	1.9
4	20.3	19.9	19.9	20.6	20.2	20.18	0.7
5	20.3	19.6	19.9	20.4	19.5	19.94	0.9
6	20.0	20.6	19.3	20.7	19.5	20.02	1.4
7	20.3	19.7	20.0	20.2	19.7	19.98	0.6
8	20.1	19.5	18.5	20.5	19.3	19.58	2.0
9	19.8	19.2	19.1	20.6	20.6	19.86	1.5
10	20.9	19.5	19.8	21.7	20.6	20.50	2.2
11	19.7	20.1	20.1	19.9	20.6	20.08	0.9
12	20.0	19.2	20.2	19.7	19.2	19.66	1.0
13	19.0	20.8	19.8	19.3	20.7	19.92	1.8
14	21.2	19.7	20.0	20.0	18.8	19.94	2.4
15	20.3	21.0	20.3	20.4	19.8	20.36	1.2
16	20.3	19.9	19.6	19.6	20.5	19.98	0.9
17	19.6	20.0	20.1	19.9	19.9	19.90	0.5
18	19.8	20.2	21.1	21.2	19.6	20.38	1.6
19	19.5	19.7	19.8	19.4	20.2	19.72	0.8
20	20.7	21.4	20.3	20.6	19.7	20.54	1.7
21	19.4	19.4	19.6	20.1	19.1	19.52	1.0
22	20.3	19.6	20.3	20.2	20.9	20.26	1.3
23	19.2	18.9	20.0	18.4	19.3	19.16	1.6
24	20.5	19.6	20.3	20.0	20.8	20.24	1.2
25	21.0	19.6	19.8	20.2	19.5	20.02	1.5

industry. This particular example is reproduced by kind permission of the Ford Motor Company.

Choice of sample size

The sample must be sufficiently large to give adequate precision to estimates of mean and range, and also for the Central Limit Theorem to make reasonable the assumption of normality implicit in the averages chart limits. Conversely, we need a sample small enough to provide an instant 'snapshot' of the process. Experience has shown that the best compromise is reached with sample sizes in the range 4 to 8, with 5 being a particularly popular value. There are times when the nature of the process constrains the choice – for example, a sample size of 6 would be sensible for a six-spindle automatic lathe. (Although more rigorous control would be provided by plotting a separate chart for each spindle, to do so would probably result in too much effort devoted to plotting charts and insufficient to running the machine. A compromise has to be achieved between effectiveness of the control procedure and the effort necessary to achieve it.) In contrast, there are processes where the sample size has to be one: for example, where the measurement cannot be referred to discrete sample items, but may be a single reading of a meter, or a sample drawn from a bulk

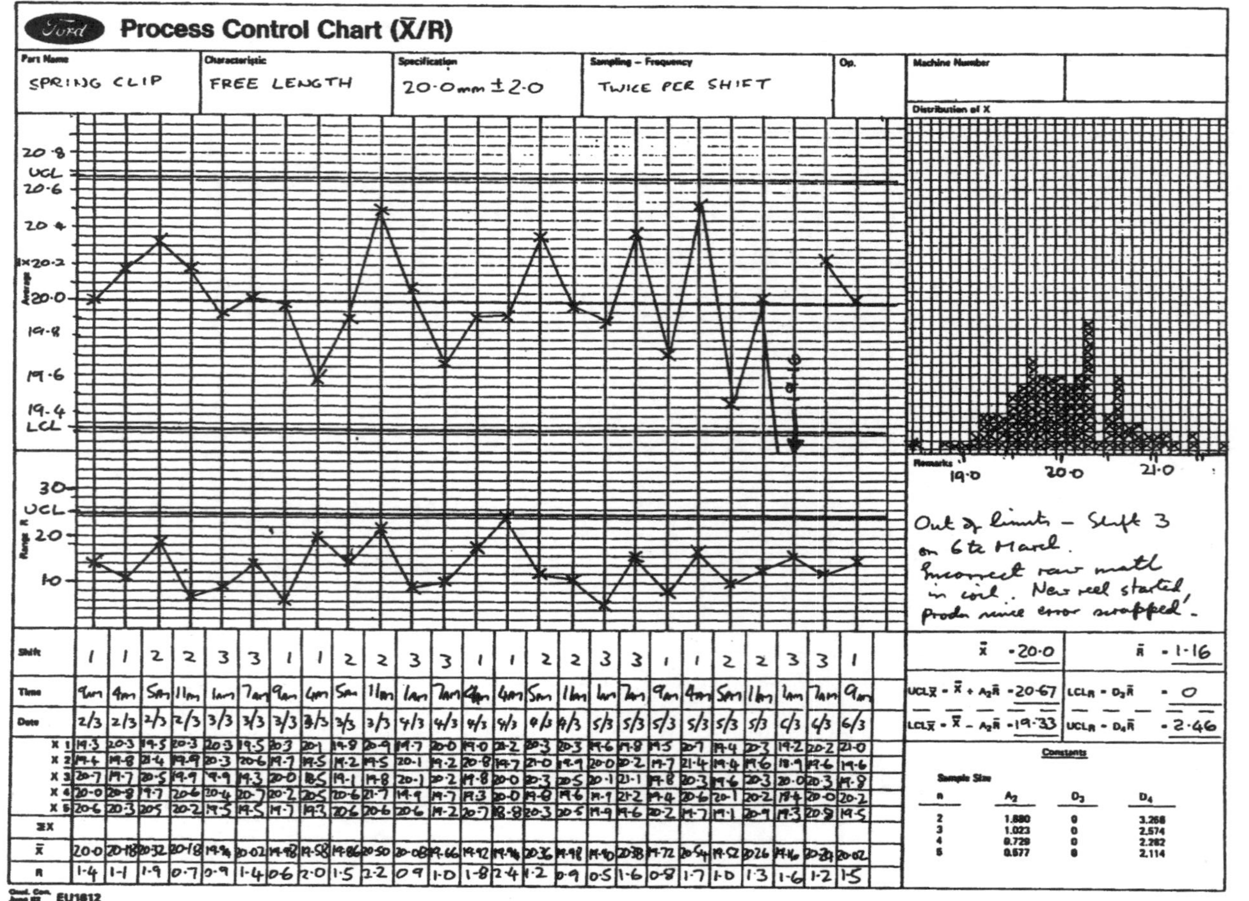

Figure 18.5 A typical charting form as used in industry, containing data from Table 18.4
Note: The form is reproduced by permission of the Ford Motor Company. The data used are for illustration only and have no connection with Ford.

tank of liquid. In such cases the averages chart becomes one for individual observations, which is statistically very inefficient, and a ranges chart cannot be plotted. In these circumstances, the use of cumulative sum methods as described in BS 5703 is an attractive alternative.

Choice of interval between samples

This choice is largely based on the economics of the process. The interval should not exceed that within which the maximum tolerable amount of unacceptable produce would be produced, on the pessimistic assumption that the process went out of control immediately after the previous sampling. Implicit in this approach is the requirement that all product between one sampling and the next is suspect until the state of the process is defined by that next sample. Should that sample show the process to be out of control, this intervening product must be identified and recoverable for any inspection, rectification or scrapping that subsequent investigation deems necessary.

Plotting the data

Reference to Figure 18.5 shows that this chart requires all the observations in the sample to be individually recorded. This is a valuable discipline in that it helps to ensure that all the samples are taken and measured correctly, and allows a check to see if any out-of-control points are a result of mistakes in calculations. Another noteworthy aspect is the recording on the chart of *everything* that occurs that might have some bearing on the behaviour of the process. The majority of such comments may eventually turn out to be of no relevance, but the occasional one may be of vital importance in the investigation of a serious problem. If they are always noted, there is no need to rely on uncertain memories in unravelling the history of a process.

It can also be seen that provision is made for building up a histogram of the data as they arise. This can be of assistance in revealing any problems reflected in any obvious non-normality in the data, and in informally relating the process to specification limits.

Comments on Figure 18.5

The only out-of-control point on the chart was at sample 23, when the sample average was so far below the control line that it was off the chart. The appropriate investigation action and the subsequent correction of the process were noted on the chart.

Although the ranges chart gave no action decisions, one point came extremely close to the control line, which merits a reassessment of the process variation. The average of the observed sample ranges was calculated, the result being 1.32 mm, that is the standard deviation is estimated to be 1.32/2.326 = 0.57 mm. This is rather larger than the process capability figure of 0.50, and has reduced the effective C_P value from 1.33 (which was barely adequate) to 1.17 (which is unacceptable), so some action is necessary to improve the process precision even though the chart did not give an action decision on any individual point.

The histogram does not show anything particularly useful in this instance, except for the strange absence of values of 20.4, and the contrasting high frequency of 20.3. Together, these may merit an examination of the measuring process.

The chart used action lines only. These were calculated using the constants given in the bottom right of Figure 18.5. The averages chart limits are effectively straightforward $\pm 3\sigma/\sqrt{n}$ values. The range chart limit is the D_4 value as in Table 18.2.

WHO DOES THE PLOTTING?

The obvious person to plot the chart is whoever is responsible for the operation of the process. This ensures that what is plotted has the best chance of being accurate, and that all production conditions are recorded. Even more important, it ensures that the operator has the information to control the process immediately available. For operator control to be effective, very careful training is necessary in the principles of control charting. To invest in this is a far preferable alternative to having the charts run by a small coterie of 'experts' with the operator taking the role of bemused spectator.

WHAT ABOUT SPECIFICATION LIMITS?

There has been no mention of specification limits in the description of control charting. This is deliberate – the chart is concerned only with the consistency of the process. The process capability study established the relation between the inherent capability of the process and the specified limits. Having done so, the function of the control chart is to detect any changes from this pattern and requires correction action whatever the notional precision of the process. The climate should be one where at worst this consistency should be the goal, but an even better objective in a long-running process is to aim to improve the process by making 'assignable' some of the hitherto 'unassignable' causes of variation, and progressively eliminating them. This idea of 'never-ending process improvement' is in sharp contrast to the more relaxed view that the arbitrary presence of a wide tolerance is something that is to be exploited.

RETROSPECTIVE PROCESS CAPABILITY

The objective of the chart is to assess the current behaviour of the process using the information from the process capability analysis as a basis for comparison. This will, *inter alia*, tell us when the variation has increased. For any long-term process, the aim should be to improve the process through a reduction in variation. This can usually only be achieved by a relentless elimination of causes of variation that we originally judged to be 'unassignable'. Such improvements will generally be individually fairly small, such that they would not be detected by, for example, a lower limit on a ranges chart. They will, however, be revealed by revaluating process capability over several recent samplings from the process over which the control chart shows it to be stable and 'in control'. A survey over a number of such samples over a stable process gives more information than individual samples on their own, and such a periodic retrospective analysis should be an integral feature of control charting.

The process capability is usually recalculated after approximately 20 to 30 samples (that is, typically after the completion of each sheet as in Figure 18.5). The average of the sample ranges is multiplied by the appropriate value of d_n (see Table 18.2) to give an estimate of the current value of the inherent standard deviation, σ. If this is substantially lower than the previous value (conventionally, reduced by 10 per cent or more), the reduced value should be used for recalculating the limits for both the $\bar{x}$ and R charts. Figure 18.5 also provides a grid on which the individual observations can be entered as a histogram as the results are obtained. This gives a developing picture of the overall variation, and highlights any departure from the distribution pattern (normal, log-normal, and so on) that was revealed in the original capability analysis. If the new value is higher, the previous value should still be used, and efforts made to identify and eliminate the assignable cause of the deterioration of the process.

Control charts for attributes

Charts in this category can be applied to two distinct situations:

1 Discrete items that can be classified as acceptable or as nonconforming. These can arise as either what can be termed genuine attributes (where the item is placed into one or the other category without any measurement being involved), or through limit gauging on a measured variable. Control charts for this application can be either:
   - control charts for number nonconforming (*np* charts) or
   - control charts for proportion nonconforming (*p* charts).

2 Processes that generate nonconformities where the sample is not defined by a number of discrete items, but by a sample 'space' within which the nonconformities occur. Examples might be assembly nonconformities in a television set, or blemishes in a painted panel. The situation is characterized by it being impossible to define the number of nonconformities that did not occur – it is impossible to state the number of blemishes that were not present on the painted panel. Control charts for this application can be either:
   - control charts for nonconformities (*c* charts)
   - control charts for nonconformities per unit (*u* charts).

TERMINOLOGY

The use of the terms 'nonconforming' and 'nonconformities' may seen rather laboured in contrast with simpler terminology such as 'defective' and 'defects'. The problem with the use of this latter terminology is that the ever-increasing emphasis on product liability gives rise to a risk that such terminology could imply safety shortcomings. While such an implication is very rarely valid, it has become accepted practice to use the more cumbersome terminology to avoid any possible problems.

CONTROL CHARTS FOR NONCONFORMING UNITS (DEFECTIVES)

Such charts are based on the premise that there is a small proportion (*p*) of nonconforming items being produced when the process is 'in control'. The chart's purpose is to signal any change in this proportion. It needs to be established at the outset that the procedures of attributes charting imply that a small finite value of *p* is therefore acceptable, so they are not applicable to situations where the 'in-control' *p* is truly zero. It is perhaps too easy to use this as an excuse for not using attributes control, as there are many circumstances where non-zero proportions nonconforming arise in intermediate stages of manufacture. An example occurs in the manufacture of electronics. Individual circuit boards are manufactured in large quantities, and 100 per cent functional inspection at the board stage would be time-consuming and expensive. When the final assemblies are produced, they are all subjected to a rigorous testing programme that is certain to detect any malfunction due to a faulty board. Provided that the level of faulty boards is kept low, the cost of removing and replacing them at final test can often be tolerated. In such a case, the attributes chart would be used to control the proportion of nonconforming boards to a suitably low level. The only difference between an *np* chart and a *p* chart is that the former assumes a sample of fixed size, and the latter allows the sample size to vary to a limited extent.

CONTROL CHARTS FOR NUMBER NONCONFORMING ('*np*' CHARTS)

Samples of size n are taken at intervals from the process. The nonconforming items in the sample are identified and counted, and this number is plotted on the control chart, as shown in Figure 18.6. (The charting form used is again reproduced by kind permission of the Ford Motor Company.) It will be seen that the same basic form can be used for all four types of chart: it can be used for p, c and u charts, in addition to *np* charting.

The number of nonconforming units in the sample will be described by a binomial distribution of parameters n (the sample size) and p (the proportion nonconforming), as described in Chapter 17. It would therefore be reasonable to expect that the control lines would be based on this distribution. For reasons of simplicity, this is not the case, and simplifying approximations are used. There is, however, a complication in that there are two widely used, but quite different, methods of obtaining control limits. Both will be described, but before doing so, it is necessary to consider the choice of sample size.

Choice of sample size

The amount of information in a sample for an attributes chart is a function of the number of nonconforming items in the sample. The sample size should therefore be selected to give an expected number of nonconforming units (which is the product $n \times p$) that is reasonably large. The British Standard on Attributes Charting, BS 5701, recommends that this number should be between 1 and 4. It can be seen that this will yield sample sizes that are considerably larger than those used in variables charting. For example, if a process has an 'in-control' proportion nonconforming of 0.025 (2.5 per cent), a sample of 40 would be needed to give an expected number nonconforming of 1, a sample of 80 would give an expected value of 2, and so on.

Control limits ('American' method)

The 'American' method uses the 'mean $\pm 3\sigma$' heuristic familiar from variables charting. The fact that the normal distribution is nowhere near to applying to binomial situations with small expected values is simply viewed as irrelevant. No claim is made that the limits are related to any particular probability values.

The mean of the binomial distribution is np and its standard deviation is $\sqrt{[np(1-p)]}$. Accordingly, the control limits are set at

$$np \pm 3\sqrt{[np(1-p)]}$$

For small values of np, this will yield negative values for the lower limit. In such circumstances, the lower limit is taken as zero, and it is not possible to signal an improvement in the process (a reduction in p).

As an example, consider the case of $p = 0.035$ with a sample size of 50. The expected number nonconforming is $np = 0.035 \times 50 = 1.75$. The control limits are therefore

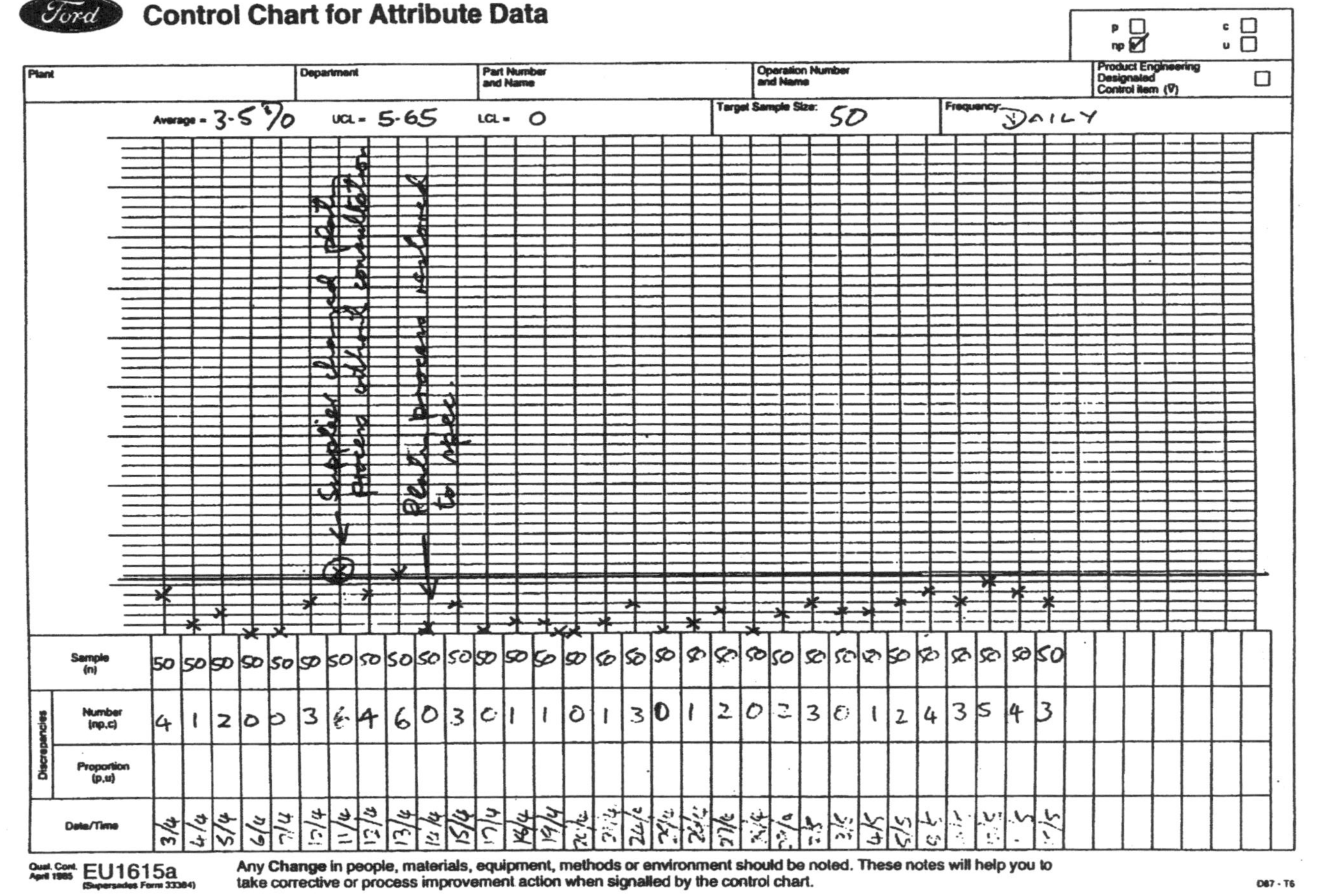

Ford Control Chart for Attribute Data

Plant | Department | Part Number and Name | Operation Number and Name | p ☐ np ☑ c ☐ u ☐ | Product Engineering Designated Control Item (∇) ☐

Average = 3.5% UCL = 5.65 LCL = 0 Target Sample Size: 50 Frequency: DAILY

Date/Time	Sample (n)	Number (np,c)	Proportion (p,u)
3/4	50	4	
4/4	50	1	
5/4	50	2	
6/4	50	0	
7/4	50	0	
10/4	50	3	
11/4	50	[illegible]	
12/4	50	4	
13/4	50	6	
14/4	50	0	
15/4	50	3	
17/4	50	0	
18/4	50	1	
19/4	50	1	
20/4?	50	0	
21/4?	50	1	
22/4?	50	3	
[illegible]	50	0	
[illegible]	50	1	
27/4?	50	2	
[illegible]	50	0	
[illegible]	50	[illegible]	
[illegible]	50	3	
[illegible]	50	0	
4/5	50	1	
5/5	50	2	
[illegible]	50	4	
[illegible]	50	3	
[illegible]	50	5	
[illegible]	50	4	
[illegible]	50	3	

Discrepancies

Qual. Cont. April 1985 EU1615a (Supersedes Form 33384) Any Change in people, materials, equipment, methods or environment should be noted. These notes will help you to take corrective or process improvement action when signalled by the control chart. D87-T6

Figure 18.6 Attributes chart (*np* chart for numbers nonconforming)

Note: Chart reproduced by permission of the Ford Motor Company. The data are for example and have no connection with Ford.

$$1.75 \pm 3\sqrt{(1.75 \times 0.965)}$$
that is, 1.75 ± 3.90

that is, at 5.65 and zero (as the lower limit is negative). If these limits are superimposed on Figure 18.6, it can be seen that an action decision was in fact given at sample number 7.

Control limits (British Standard BS 5701)

These are based on the Poisson distribution used as an approximation to the binomial – an approximation which is valid provided p is less than about 0.1, which should apply in any organization that is still in business! The control lines are at approximately the 1/200 probability point. They are chosen from the value of m, putting $m = np$, the expected number of units nonconforming in the sample, and are given in Table 18.5, which is an extract from BS 5701. The lines are not drawn at integer values, but at 0.3 below, so that points cannot occur on the line. A further, optional refinement in BS 5701 is the provision of warning lines. These are always exactly one below the control line, and are associated with a 'critical gap'. Action is taken if the gap between any two points outside the warning line is less than this critical gap.

In using Table 18.5, should the value of m not coincide with one in the table, the next higher value should be used. The limits under Group 1 are 'non-preferred' and should only be used where it is essential that very small sample sizes are used such that the expected number nonconforming per sample does not reach the recommended values. Group 2 limits are recommended for general use.

Repeating the previous example with $m = np = 1.75$, Table 18.5 gives the control line at 6.7, the warning line at 5.7 and a critical gap of 4 (using tabulated $m = 2.04$). This would fail to give the action decision at sample number 7, but would give one at sample number 9 as this second warning line is within the critical gap.

NUMBER NONCONFORMING CHARTS FOR MEASURED VARIABLES

A control chart for number nonconforming can be used to control a measured variable by

Table 18.5 Table of control limits for attribute charts

m	*Control line*	*Warning line*	*Critical gap*	
0.10	1.7	0.7	1	
0.33	2.7	1.7	2	**Group 1**
0.67	3.7	2.7	2	
1.08	4.7	3.7	3	
1.53	5.7	4.7	3	
2.04	6.7	5.7	4	**Group 2**
2.57	7.7	6.7	4	
3.13	8.7	7.7	4	
3.72	9.7	8.7	4	

Note: Extract from Table 1, BS 5701, by permission of the British Standards Institution.

considering any measurement outside specification limits as making the item nonconforming. In general, this is much less efficient than using a chart for variables, and will require much larger sample sizes. It does have a compensating advantage in that limit gauging is usually quicker and cheaper than measurement.

A further problem is contained in the fact that a process of adequate precision will not, when in control, produce any nonconforming ideas, so there is no value of p on which to base the chart. This problem can be circumvented by the use of *compressed limits*. These are gauging limits that are set inside the specification limits so that a significant proportion of the output will be outside the limits and deemed 'nonconforming' for the purposes of charting (but still acceptable with respect to the 'true' limits). BS 5701 recommends that the compressed limits are chosen so as to produce about 10 to 15 per cent outside the limits when 'in control', adjusting the sample size to give an expected 1 to 4 per sample outside limits. Use of such limits is explained in detail in Newton (1986).

'PRE CONTROL'

'PRE control' is a method of using attributes control (using limit gauges) for measurable dimensions. It has achieved some popularity as an extremely simple control procedure, and was promulgated specifically as a method suitable for operator control. It is described in detail in Juran (1974). Its only advantage over other methods is its simplicity – its sensitivity to process changes is is inferior to other methods. It has also the fundamental drawback of being based on specification limits rather than process performance. None the less, it has had some successful applications in industry, where it has been the first step in introducing SPC prior to the introduction of more efficient methods.

PRE control acts as integrated process capability and process control loop. The basis is the division of the specification limits into four bands of equal width as shown in Figure 18.7.

The central two bands are referred to as the 'green' region and the outer two bands as the 'yellow' region. Anything outside the specification limits constitutes the 'red' region. The intention is that limit gauges are appropriately coloured. It is sometimes the case that measuring equipment is used, but the measurement scales are replaced by appropriately coloured bands.

The procedure is as follows.

Set-up

The process is operated and adjusted, with every resulting component being gauged. When five consecutive items are in the green region, the process is judged satisfactory, and sampling control is introduced.

Sampling

Every twenty-fifth item produced is sampled. If the result is in the green region, production continues. If it is in the yellow region, another sample is taken immediately. If this second sample is in the same yellow band as the first, the process is investigated and adjusted (with the suspicion being that the process average has moved in the direction of the yellow band in question, although it would also be possible for the explanation to be an increase in variability). If the second sample is in the opposite yellow band, the obvious conclusion is that the variation has increased, and appropriate corrective action is necessary. Should the second sample be in the green region, no action is taken, and sampling continues. Should a sample appear in the red region, corrective action is of course required immediately.

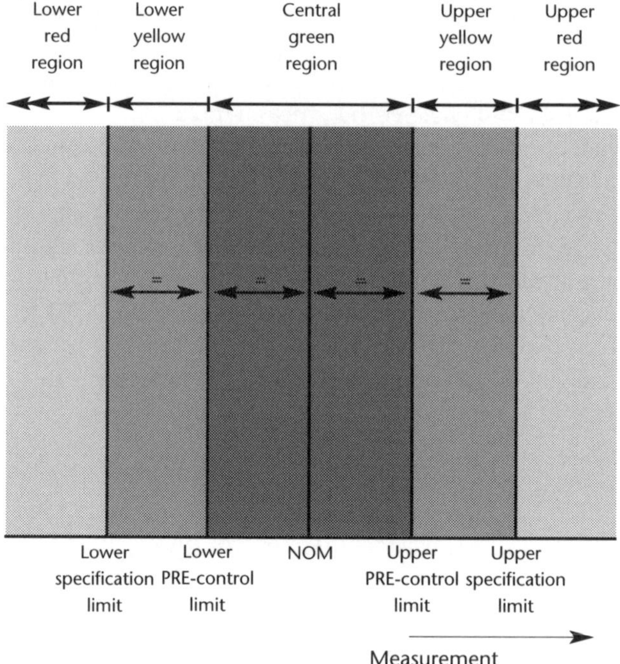

Figure 18.7 PRE control

Whenever corrective action has been necessary, the process reverts to the 'set-up' procedure.

CONTROL CHARTS FOR PROPORTION NON-CONFORMING (*p* CHARTS)

These charts are similar to charts for number nonconforming, except that they allow for variations in sample size. (For fixed sample sizes, they are effectively the same as number nonconforming.) The plotted value is x/n, where x is the observed number nonconforming in a sample of n items.

As the standard deviation of x/n is $\sqrt{[np(1 - p)/n]} = \sqrt{[p(1 - p)/n]}$ the control limits are $p \pm 3\sqrt{[p(1 - p)/n]}$.

It is seen that the control limits will therefore have to be adjusted for different sample sizes, which would at first sight negate the point of having such a chart. Conventionally, however, this is not deemed necessary unless the sample size varies more than 25 per cent from the value for which the limits were calculated. Unless circumstances dictate variations in sample size, it is recommended that number nonconforming charts are used in preference to this type of chart.

CONTROL CHARTS FOR NONCONFORMITIES

These charts are used for the second situation outlined on page 275, that of nonconformities arising in a sample that is described by a 'sample space' (such as a length, an area, elapsed time, etc.). The in-control situation is defined by c, the expected number of nonconformities per sample. Charts for this situation can be c charts, for nonconformities per sample or, less frequently used, u charts for nonconformities per unit.

CHARTS FOR NUMBER NONCONFORMITIES PER SAMPLE (*c* CHARTS)

The plotted value is simply the number of nonconformities per sample. Control limits are based on the Poisson distribution (in this case, without any approximation involved). The control limits can be either 'American'

$$c \pm 3\sqrt{c}$$

or based on BS 5701, where c is equated to m in Table 18.5.

As an example, consider a painting process which, when in control, generates minor appearance blemishes at the mean rate of one per 3.5 m². A sample area of 5 m² is inspected every production shift to control against any deterioration of the process. The value of c is therefore $5\sqrt{3.5} = 1.43$ blemishes per sample. Using the 'American' limits, the control lines would be at:

$1.43 \pm 3\sqrt{1.43}$, that is 1.43 ± 3.59
that is an upper limit only, at 5.02.

Using Table 18.5, the upper limit would be at 5.7. In both cases, the answer is effectively the same: we would need to observe 6 blemishes in the sample to give an action decision.

The c charts can also be used for controlling the level of nonconformities in discrete complex assemblies such as televisions, car engines, and so on. The sample consists of a fixed number of such assemblies ('units'), which can be anything from one upwards. The plotted value is the total number of nonconformities across these units. For a target value of c, the control limits are calculated in the same way as described above.

CONTROL CHARTS FOR NONCONFORMITIES PER UNIT (*u* CHARTS)

In using a c chart in the way described in the previous paragraph, it could be that the number of units sampled varied from one sampling to the next. This might occur, for example, if the time and resources available to perform the inspection were not constant. In such a case, the chart limits would have to be recalculated for each sample, making the chart confusing and difficult to read. A way out of this difficulty is to divide the observed number of nonconformities, c, by the number of units sampled, n. Then c/n is denoted by u.

A control chart plotting nonconformities per unit would have limits of

$$u \pm 3\sqrt{(u/n)}$$

where u is the 'in-control' value of nonconformities per unit.

The limits are affected by the number of units sampled, but conventionally, it is not considered necessary to recalculate them unless this varies by more than 25 per cent.

Software for statistical process control (SPC)

The industrial practice of control charting often, and increasingly, makes use of computers. This can be at various levels of sophistication. At one extreme there is the online gathering and recording of data from measurement transducers networked to a powerful central computer. At the other extreme there is the use of simple applications software on a standalone microcomputer, with keyboard entry of the data. Systems on the market fall into two broad categories:

1 Integrated measurement and analysis systems, usually developed and marketed by suppliers of metrology equipment.
2 Applications software for microcomputers, which can usually accept direct input from measuring equipment via a suitable interface.

The use of computers in control charting is effective in eliminating some of the more tedious aspects of calculating suitable statistics and plotting them on graphs. They also facilitate storage of data, which is becoming ever more important in demonstrating that effective quality procedures have been used in manufacture. It is important, however, that the system used does not let its impressive technology obscure the simplicity and immediacy of charting. If control charting is being introduced into an organization, it is usual to do so initially on a manual basis, so that learning to use the method is not complicated by simultaneously having to learn to use the software.

Journals provide a useful source of information on applications and on new developments. In the UK, *Quality World*, *Quality Today* and *Quality and Reliability International* often contain articles on SPC. The equivalent American journal is *Quality Progress*. For the statistically brave, such journals as the *Journal of Quality Technology* and *Technometrics* nearly always contain papers on SPC methods and applications.

The extent of software available is considerable, and ever-expanding. The maximum of 'try before you buy' applies here as for all other software. A good source of guidance is the annual software review in *Quality Progress*.

Further reading

The references given below relate to Chapters 8 and 18. Montgomery (1991) is a comprehensive and readable text covering all aspects of SPC and the use of statistical methods in quality improvement. Grant and Leavenworth (1972) is a similarly comprehensive text with a solid reputation, but is perhaps now becoming a little dated. In addition, both books contain considerable material on sampling inspection, an aspect of SPC not covered in these chapters. They both, naturally, base their procedures and examples on the American way of doing things. Oakland and Followell (1990) is a British text that has comprehensive coverage, is more up to date and describes both UK and American conventions. For a briefer description, the Open University text by Newton (1986) is available. The British Standards on the subject are also worthy of consideration. BS 2564 (for variables) and BS 5701 (for attributes) are 'how to do it' standards with minimal explanatory text. BS 5700 is, in contrast, a guide to the methods involved and their statistical origins. Also, the original British Standard on the subject, BS 600, is another 'classic' that is still available and well worth consulting. A revised and updated version of BS 600 was published in 2000.

BOOKS

Grant, E.L. and Leavenworth, R.S., *Statistical Quality Control*, 4th edn (international student edition, paperback), McGraw-Hill, Kogakusha, Tokyo, 1972.

Juran, J. (ed.), *Quality Control Handbook*, McGraw-Hill, New York, 1974.

Kotz, S. and Lovelace, C.R., 1998, *Process Capability Indices in Theory and Practice*, Arnold, London.

Montgomery, D.C., *Introduction to Statistical Quality Control*, 2nd edn, Wiley, New York, 1991.

Newton, D.W., *Statistical Quality Control of Production*, Open University Press, Milton Keynes, 1986.

Oakland, John S. and Followell, Roy F., *Statistical Process Control*, 2nd edn, Butterworth-Heinemann, Oxford, 1990.

Shewhart, W.A., *Economic Control of Manufactured Product*, Van Nostrand, New York, 1931.

JOURNALS

Journal of Quality Technology (published quarterly)

Quality and Reliability Engineering International (published quarterly by J. Wiley, Chichester, UK)

Quality Progress (published monthly)

Quality Today (published monthly by Whitehall Press Ltd, Maidstone)

Quality World (published monthly by the Institute of Quality Assurance, London)

Technometrics (published quarterly)

BRITISH STANDARDS

BS 600: 1935, *Application of Statistical Methods to Industrial Standardisation and Quality Control.*

BS 600: 2000, *A Guide to the Application of Statistical Methods to Quality and Standardization.*

BS 2564: 1955, *Control Chart Technique when Manufacturing to a Specification.*

BS 5700: 1984, *Introductory Guide to Control Charting and Cusums.*

BS 5701: 1980, *Guide to Number-defective Charts for Quality Control.*

Note: Extracts from British Standards used in this chapter are reproduced with the permission of BSI.

CHAPTER **19**

Control Charts, Part 2: Cusum Charts

David Newton

This chapter describes a type of control chart which has the same objectives as the conventional (or Shewhart) charts described so far, but uses a completely different method of plotting. A conventional chart shows the current state of the process by the vertical position of a plotted point. A cumulative sum (cusum) chart uses instead the slope of the plot to show the current level. The procedure is applicable to any of the variables and attributes situations described in Chapter 18.

Basic cusum procedure

For the charted quantity, the reference value (T) is first defined. This will usually be the nominal, or target, value for that quantity. If the ith measurement of the quantity is denoted x_i, the target value is first subtracted, giving $(x_i–T)$. The cusum is then calculated by adding this value to the sum of all the previous values:

$$\text{Cusum} = \Sigma_i(x_i–T)$$

As an example, consider the following 10 observations from a process which has a target value of 10:

11, 8, 5, 20, 12, 10, 11, 9, 15, 13

The cusums are calculated as shown in Table 19.1.

The cusum is simply the cumulative deviation from a target value. While the concept is sometimes viewed as a rather sophisticated one in SPC, it is encountered in everyday life without any problems of understanding. For example, Bissell (1984) instances the fact that scoring in golf is by cusum – rather than count the total number of strokes, it is easier to consider the cumulative score above or below par. This is, in fact, a rather sophisticated cusum where the reference value (par) changes from one sample (hole) to the next.

Table 19.1 The cusums of 10 process observations

Observation number (i)	x_i	$(x_i - T)$	*Cusum* $\Sigma(x_i - T)$
1	11	1	1
2	8	–2	–1
3	5	–5	–6
4	20	10	4
5	12	2	6
6	10	0	6
7	11	1	7
8	9	–1	6
9	15	5	11
10	13	3	14

Cusum charts for variables

Just as in conventional Shewhart charting, charts can be produced for sample average, for sample ranges and for single observations.

CUSUM CHARTS FOR SAMPLE AVERAGES

Table 19.2 shows a sequence of 30 averages of samples of size 4 from a process with target value 150.0. The table also shows the cusum values. These are plotted in Figure 19.1, which demonstrates the essential features of a cusum chart.

The most important aspect to understand is that the average of the process measurement is shown by the *slope* of the plot. Referring to Figure 19.1, it can be seen that the plot has three distinct sections:

- From sample 1 to 8, the slope is slightly upwards, showing that the average is slightly above the reference value of 50.
- From sample 9 to sample 19, the slope is strongly downwards, showing an average below 50.
- From sample 20 onwards, the slope is steeply upwards, showing a mean well above 50.

These observations can be quantified by measuring the slope. Over any sequence of consecutive points, the average between the $(j + 1)$ and $(j + r)$th points is given by:

$$\frac{[S_{(j+r)} - S_j]}{r} + T$$

where S is the cusum at a point indexed by the subscript. For example, the mean between sample 2 and sample 8 is:

$$\frac{S_7 - S_1}{6} + 150 = \frac{(-2.7) - (-10.0)}{6} + 150 = 151.21$$

Table 19.2 Cusum tabulation for sample averages

Sample no. (i)	*Average* $\bar{x}_i$	*Corrected average* $(\bar{x}_i - 150)$	*Cusum* $\Sigma_i(x_i - 150)$
1	140.0	−10.0	−10.0
2	156.7	6.7	−3.3
3	146.7	−3.3	−6.6
4	146.6	−3.4	−10.6
5	156.7	6.7	−3.3
6	153.3	3.3	0.0
7	147.3	−2.7	−2.7
8	140.0	−10.0	−12.7
9	146.3	−3.7	−16.4
10	149.2	−0.8	−17.2
11	152.3	2.3	−14.9
12	140.0	−10.0	−24.9
13	148.9	−1.1	−26.0
14	155.6	5.6	−20.4
15	145.6	−4.4	−24.8
16	148.8	−1.2	−26.0
17	138.9	−11.1	−37.1
18	142.1	−7.9	−45.0
19	145.5	−4.5	−49.5
20	155.3	5.3	−44.2
21	155.2	5.2	−39.0
22	155.0	5.0	−34.0
23	158.9	8.9	−25.1
24	146.1	−3.9	−29.0
25	148.7	−1.3	−30.3
26	151.5	1.5	−28.8
27	152.4	2.4	−26.4
28	161.5	11.5	−14.9
29	155.6	5.6	−9.3
30	150.8	0.8	−8.5

Similarly, between points 8 and 19 the mean is:

$$\frac{S_{19} - S_7}{12} + 150 = \frac{(-49.5) - (-2.7)}{12} + 150 = 146.10$$

and between points 20 and 30 is:

$$\frac{S_{30} - S_{19}}{11} + 150 = \frac{(-8.5) - (-49.5)}{11} + 150 = 153.72$$

The clarity of the indications of the different mean values, and the points at which changes occurred, is one of the main attractions of cusum plotting. This clarity is such that it is often

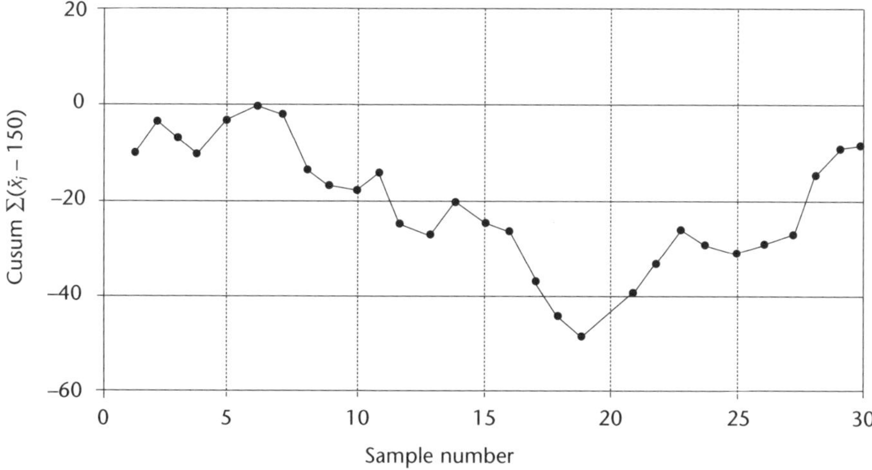

Figure 19.1 Cumulative sum chart using data in Table 19.2

deemed unnecessary to use any control limits for this type of chart – the location and magnitude of any changes are obvious from the plot. This should be contrasted with the conventional 'Shewhart' chart of the same data where these aspects are much less obvious – see Figure 19.2.

CHOICE OF SCALE

The impression of mean level and the magnitude of any changes as shown in a cusum chart will be influenced by the choice of scale, as illustrated in Figure 19.3.

Compression of the vertical scale, as in Figure 19.3a, suppresses the effect of short-term 'ripples' on the chart, but gives the impression of small changes in mean value. Conversely, for the same data, expansion of the scale as in Figure 19.3b exaggerates the changes in mean. Both charts are of the same data as in Figure 19.1.

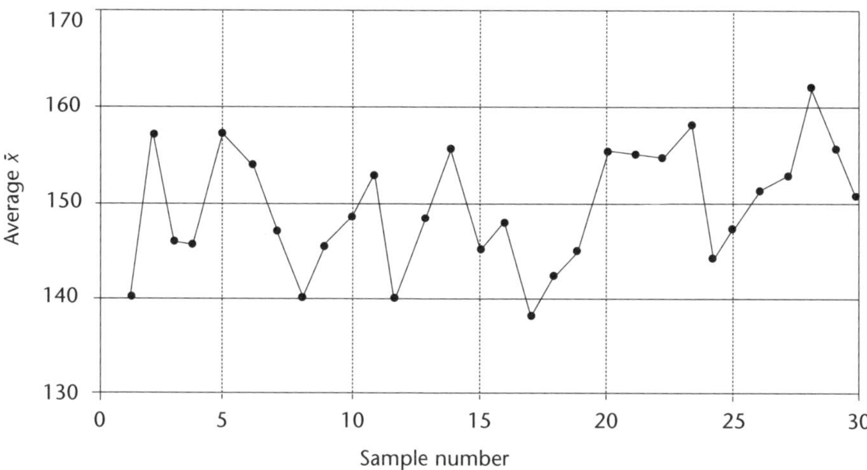

Figure 19.2 A Shewart chart using the same data as Figure 19.1

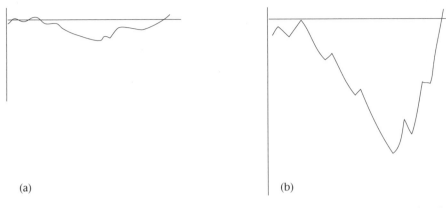

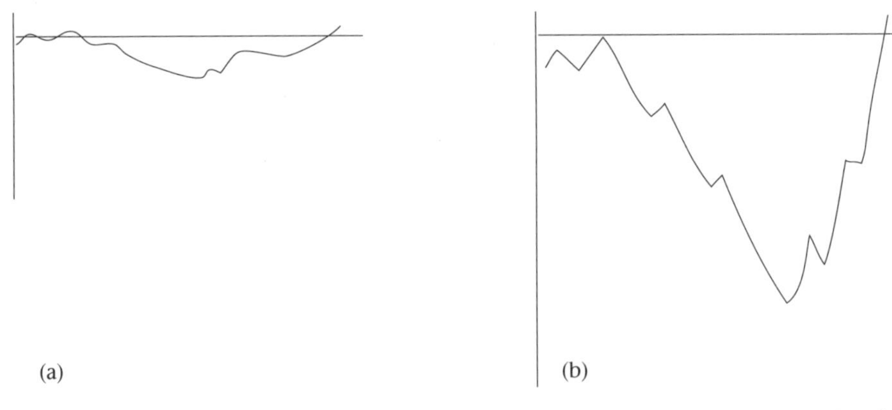

Figure 19.3 Effect of scale ratio on cusum plots for similar data: (a) compressed vertical scale (a large), (b) expanded vertical scale (a small)

The choice of scale is an arbitrary one which is related only to the visual impact and interpretation of the chart. The recommendation in British Standard BS 5703 is that the scale ratio a is equal to 2 standard deviations of the plotted variable, rounded to the nearest convenient scale. The term a is defined as the distance on the vertical scale equal to the horizontal distance between successive plots (the 'horizontal plotting interval'). For example, if the x_i values had a standard deviation of 4.3 units, and the horizontal scale was 1 cm per horizontal plotting interval, the recommended vertical scale would be 1 cm = 8.6 units. This would be rounded to the nearest convenient usable scale of 1 cm = 10 units. As another example, consider the data in Table 19.2, and assume that the standard deviation σ of the process was 4.22 units. The cusum plot is of averages of samples of 4, so that the expected standard deviation of these averages (the expected standard error) is σ divided by the square root of the sample size, i.e. $4.22/\sqrt{4} = 2.11$. The value of a is therefore 2.11 x 2 = 4.22 – which, for simplicity of scaling, has been rounded up to 5 in Figure 19.1 (exemplifying the fact that the a values are merely a guide that can be adapted to suit particular circumstances).

DECISION CRITERIA FOR CUSUM CHARTS FOR AVERAGES

Although the cusum chart gives a much clearer indication of changes than a conventional control chart, there is still a need for objective decision criteria analogous to control lines. Control lines cannot be used in the conventional way, as it is the slope of the chart that needs to be monitored rather than the vertical position of plotted points. Various decision criteria have been suggested as the subject of cusums has developed. These have culminated in a standardized procedure in BS 5703 known as the 'decision mask'. The mask is in the form of a template that is superimposed on the chart as each point is plotted. Various masks are available in the standard, but they all have the general shape shown in Figure 19.4.

The most widely used mask is known as the '5–10–10' mask, where H in Figure 19.4 is set at 5 standard deviations of the plotted variable, and the slope of the sides of the mask is set at 0.5 standard deviations per plotting interval. Thus, at a position 10 plotting intervals to the left of the 'vertex' of the mask, the sides of the mask are [5 + (0.5 x 10)] = 10 standard deviations either side of the central line. In use, the vertex of the mask is placed on the last plotted point, with the central line horizontal. If any of the previous plot intersects the sides of the mask, this gives an 'action' decision. Otherwise, no change is deemed to have

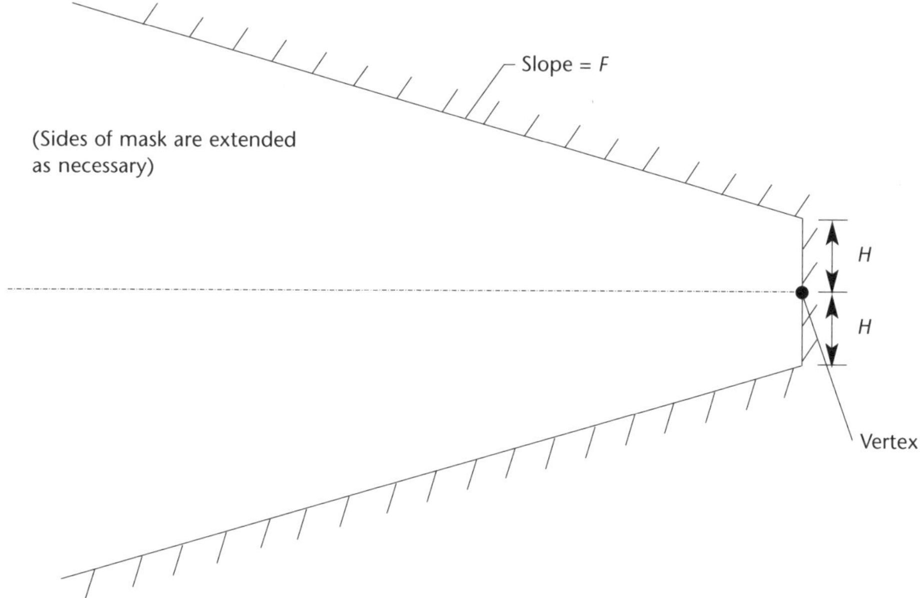

Figure 19.4 General form of decision mask

occurred, and the process mean is assumed to be still 'under control'. This is illustrated in Figure 19.5. The mask can take any convenient form – they are usually either cut from card, or engraved on Perspex or similar material.

The '5–10–10' mask is widely used because it behaves in a similar way to a conventional chart with action and warning lines when the process is 'in control'. It is, however, much more sensitive to small changes in process mean than conventional charts. It is also possible to 'tune' the mask to make it more or less sensitive to changes of particular magnitudes by altering the slope and intercept of the mask away from the '5–10–10' convention. This is explained in detail in Part 3 of BS 5703.

CUSUM CHARTS FOR RANGE

It is no less important to control average and range simultaneously when using cusums as when using conventional charts. The sample range could, of course, still be monitored with a conventional chart whilst using a cusum chart for the averages, but is is more usual to use cusums for both. The cusum range procedure is based on μ^R, the expected average range whose value is estimated as described in Chapter 8.

The cusum is now of $\Sigma(R_i - \mu_R)$, where R_i are observed sample ranges. The mask used for such a chart is usually only 'single sided', as shown in Figure 19.6. It consists of the lower half only of the masks as it is only necessary to detect increases in process variation, as reflected in an upward movement in the chart.

The intercept of the mask, H, is given by $h \times \mu_R$ and the slope, F, by $f \times \mu_R$ where h and f are constants whose value depends on sample size and desired risk behaviour of the chart. For a 'middle-of-the-road' scheme whose behaviour when the process variation is 'in control' is again similar to a conventional ranges chart with action and warning lines, values of h and f are shown in Table 19.3, which is an extract from Table 10 of BS 5703 Part 3. The a values are the recommended scale ratios.

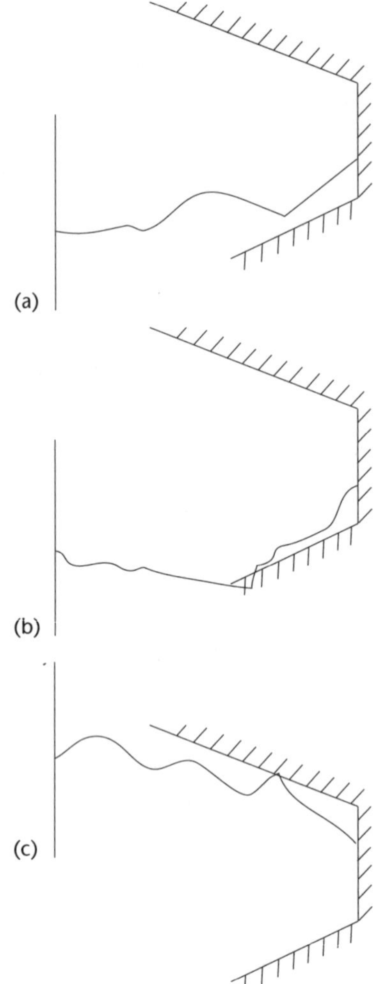

Figure 19.5 Use of decision mask: (a) no decision, (b) upward change, (c) downward change

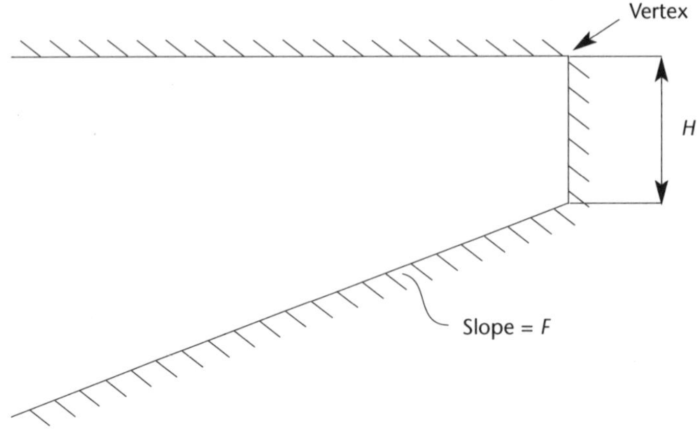

Figure 19.6 Half mask for cusum ranges chart

Table 19.3 Mask parameters for cusum range charts

Sample size *n*	*h*	*f*	*a*
2	2.50	0.85	1.50
3	1.75	0.55	1.00
4	1.25	0.50	0.85
5	1.00	0.45	0.75
6	0.85	0.45	0.65

Note: Taken from Table 10 of BS 5703, Part 3, by permission of the British Standards Institution.

As an example of a cusum range chart, consider the process whose average values are shown in Figure 19.1. The process standard deviation was 4.22, so μ_R is estimated by $\sigma \times d_4$. The value of d_4 is obtained from Table 18.2, and equals 2.059, so the expected sample range is 4.22 x 2.059 = 8.69. A tabulation of observed sample ranges for the first 12 samples is given in Table 19.4. These data are plotted in Figure 19.7. The plotting scale ratio is obtained from Table 19.3 as $a \times \mu_R = 0.85 \times 8.69 = 7.39$, which is rounded up to 10.

The mask parameters are:

$H = 8.69 \times 1.25 = 10.86$, and $F = 8.69 \times 0.5 = 0.35$.

The reader may wish to produce this mask, and confirm that it gives an action decision at sample number 11. It is also of interest to note that the conventional action and warning lines would be 22.33 and 16.77, respectively (calculated using the constants in Table 18.4), which would not have given any 'action' decision.

Table 19.4 Cusum range chart data

Sample number *i*	*Range* R_i	*Range* – μ_R $(R_i - 8.69)$	*Cusum* $\Sigma(R_i - 8.69)$
1	7.06	–1.63	–1.63
2	5.37	–3.32	–4.95
3	12.15	3.46	–1.49
4	9.10	0.41	–1.08
5	8.24	–0.45	–1.53
6	11.67	2.98	1.45
7	9.56	0.87	2.32
8	11.04	2.35	4.67
9	15.82	7.13	11.80
10	13.16	4.47	16.27
11	19.94	11.25	27.52
12	15.27	6.58	34.10

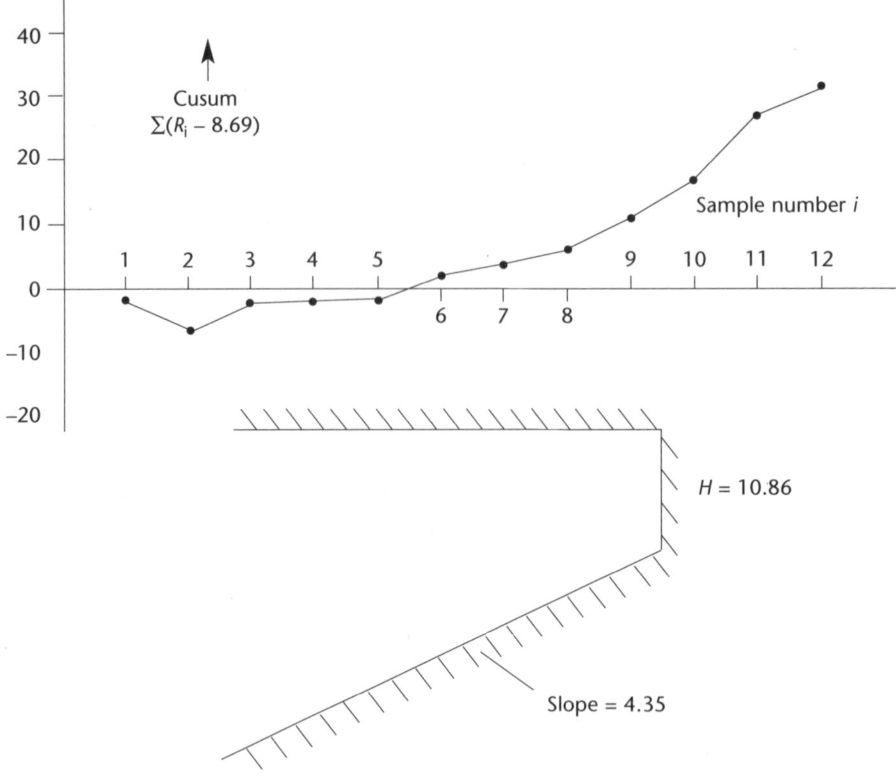

Figure 19.7 A cusum range chart using data in Table 19.4

CUSUMS FOR SINGLE OBSERVATIONS

When the observations (x_i) are individual observations rather than sample averages, the procedure for the averages chart is the same, except that these sample observations are used directly in calculating the cusum. It is, of course, not possible to produce a ranges chart for single observations. One way of circumventing this difficulty is to plot a ranges cusum chart for ranges of samples of 2, each sample range being the difference between the current sample and the previous one. Although this is theoretically unsound (as the ranges would also be affected by any change in mean), it is better than doing nothing to control variation, and seems to work adequately in practice.

CUSUM CHARTS FOR ATTRIBUTES

Cusum charts can be applied to any of the attribute charting situations described in Chapter 18. The reference value for the cusum is always *m*, the expected number of nonconforming items (defectives) or nonconformities (defects) per sample. The sample size criteria are also the same as for conventional charting in that the sample should produce an expected 1 to 4 nonconforming items (or nonconformities) per sample when the process is stable and 'in control'. However, the increased sensitivity of the cusum method permits smaller samples to be used if necessary, and mask parameters are tabulated for values of *m* as low as 0.1 per sample.

As an example, consider the '*np*' chart in Table 18.5. The target proportion nonconforming is 0.035 and the sample size is 50, giving an expected number of nonconforming items per sample of 50 x 0.035 = 1.75. This is the value used for m in Table 19.5, where the data of Figure 18.6 are re-expressed as cusums. These data are plotted on a cusum chart in Figure 19.8. The recommended scale ratio for an attributes plot is simply $2\sqrt{m}$ – in this case, it is $2\sqrt{1.75} = 2.65$. The actual value used in Figure 19.8 is 2.5. Note the way that the cusum is restarted at sample 10, after the identified problem has been dealt with. This is a useful convention, highlighting the fact that there is a discontinuity in the process.

Comparison with Figure 18.6 emphasizes the clarity with which the cusum reveals

Table 19.5 Data of Figure 18.6 expressed as cusums

Sample no.	*Nonconforming items (x)*	*(x) – 1.75*	*Cusum* $\Sigma(x - 1.75)$
1	4	2.25	2.25
2	1	–0.75	1.50
3	2	0.25	1.75
4	0	–1.75	0.00
5	0	–1.75	–1.75
6	3	1.25	–0.50
7	6	4.75	5.25
8	4	2.25	7.50
9	6	4.75	12.25
*10	4	2.25	*2.25
11	3	1.25	3.50
12	0	–1.75	1.75
13	1	–0.75	1.00
14	1	–0.75	0.25
15	0	–1.75	–1.50
16	1	–0.75	–2.25
17	3	1.25	–1.00
18	0	–1.75	–2.75
19	1	–0.75	–3.50
20	2	0.75	–2.75
21	0	–1.75	–4.50
22	2	0.25	–4.25
23	3	1.25	–3.00
24	0	–1.75	–4.75
25	1	–0.75	–5.50
26	2	0.25	–5.25
27	4	2.25	3.00
28	4	2.25	–0.75
29	5	3.35	2.50
30	4	2.25	4.75
31	3	1.25	6.00

Note: *Cusum restarted after corrective action.

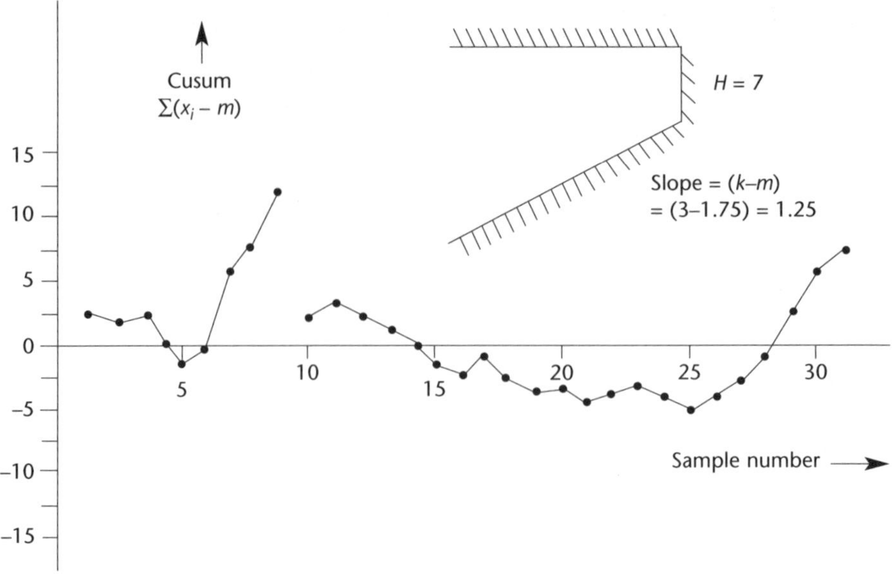

Figure 19.8 Cusum range chart for number nonconforming using data from Figure 18.6

changes. The large increase in the number of nonconforming items around samples 7 to 9 is obvious from both charts. There is an improvement between samples 10 and 25, and a deterioration from sample 26 onwards, which are much more clearly shown on the cusum.

MASK PARAMETERS FOR ATTRIBUTE CUSUMS

As in the case of variables, there is a wide choice of mask parameters available to suit differing circumstances. The values tabulated in Table 19.6 are taken from BS 5703 Part 4, and are chosen to give similar properties to conventional charts for an 'in control' process.

The intercept of the mask is H, and the slope is $(K - m)$. In this example, the parameters are chosen for $m = 2$, being the nearest value to the 'true' m of 1.75. (If the use of BS 5703 mask procedures is intended, it is preferable to choose a sample size that gives an m value coinciding with one in Table 19.6.) The mask is shown in Figure 19.8. Superimposition of the mask on the plot will demonstrate that the change at sample 7, which was detected by the conventional chart, is also detected. The mask also gives an 'action' decision at sample 30 showing an increase in the level of nonconforming items. Although this increase is visible on Table 18.5, it does not give an action decision using either of the variants of conventional control lines.

Summary and recommendations for further reading

Cusums have two significant advantages over conventional (Shewhart) charts:

1 They give a much clearer pictorial representation of the behaviour of the process.
2 Objective decision criteria (such as the BS mask) are much more sensitive to small changes than control lines on conventional charts.

Table 19.6 Table of mask parameters for cusums for attributes

m	0.1	0.2	0.4	0.5	0.8	1.0	2.0	4.0	5.0	8.0	10.0
H	1.5	3.5	2.5	3.0	5.0	5.0	7.0	8.0	9.0	9.0	11.0
K	0.75	0.5	1.5	1.5	1.5	2.0	3.0	6.0	7.0	11.0	13.0

To offset these advantages, it is sometimes argued that they are more complicated to use. Whilst this may be marginally true, the real source of objection is more likely to be rooted in conservatism, compared with the fifty-year tradition of more conventional methods.

There is only one reference work on cusums to be recommended, namely the four parts of British Standard BS 5703. This has distilled, simplified and developed the work of various earlier authors, and is comprehensive in its coverage of all aspects of cusums. It also includes computer program listings for the charting and decision procedures to permit the user to automate the cusum. The development of the standard is largely due to Prof. A.F. Bissell, who has also written an outline guide to the subject, reference below.

References

Bissell, A.F., *Cusum Techniques for Quality Control*, Institute of Statisticians, London, 1984.

BS 5703: 1980, 1981, 1982, *Guide to Data Analysis and Quality Control using Cusums*, Parts 1–4, British Standards Institution, London.

CHAPTER 20 Inspection

R. Plummer

Inspection has always been a part of the quality management process. Unfortunately, it has been used by many managements as a prop of quality management systems rather than a tool, in the belief that quality can be somehow 'inspected in' to the product.

When management finds that nonconforming product is reaching the customer, their traditional reaction is to increase the level of inspection. Not surprisingly, the increased level of inspection detects an increased volume of nonconforming product. Management now believe that they have a bigger problem than they thought they had, so pressure is put on for ever more inspection. The increased volume of nonconforming product thus detected results in an increased level of rework. Sooner or later, the processes which are producing the nonconforming product start to creak with the level of rework, and they produce even higher levels of nonconforming product. This result is not the aim of inspection.

Quality management seeks, among other things, to remove to the greatest possible extent the need for inspection, and therefore inspection itself. Inspection is essentially wasteful. Inspection by sampling the product or service gives no more than an indication of the number of defectives or defects in a batch, lot or process. It is well known that 100 per cent inspection fails to find as much as 15 to 20 per cent of the defects or defectives in the inspected lot, even when the same lot has been 100 per cent inspected three times. It is for these reasons that quality management seeks to eliminate the causes of imperfection, and thus the imperfections themselves. In trying to achieve this, there has for some years been a move towards self-inspection of the product or service, to exercise quality control at the point of operation.

The fact remains that inspection does need to be carried out, for a number of reasons. This chapter deals with those reasons, and with how to run efficient inspection activities. Yet once the inspection itself is over, management is still not finished. Even if the product fails inspection, it may still be fit for purpose. Even if it fails inspection and is not fit for purpose, it may be possible to repair or rework the product. If it is possible, then there is one final question to be asked: 'Do we tell the customer?'

Inspection therefore consists of what Juran has for years called 'the three questions':

1 Does the product meet the specification?
2 Is it fit for purpose?
3 Do we tell the customer?

Does the product meet the specification?

DEFINITION OF INSPECTION

In general terms, inspection means determining the quality of some characteristic of a product or service in comparison with an agreed standard.

The form which inspection takes can be divided into two broad categories – inspection with measuring equipment and inspection without it. Both of these broad categories are used to determine information about products or services.

REASONS FOR INSPECTION

The reasons for inspection fall into some clear categories, which are typified by the following:

- **Can we make it OK?** – Here, inspection of the product or service is conducted to see if it is even possible to make it to specification. This form of inspection will take place during pilot runs or during process capability analysis.
- **Are we making it OK?** – When processes are running, it is necessary to make periodic checks that the process continues to be capable and that it is producing an output within specification. The frequency of this type of inspection will depend on a number of things, including the length of time over which the process is known to remain stable, the number and type of changes in the inputs to the process, and the time between these changes. These inspection observations are usefully recorded on Shewhart charts, containing control lines which warn when the process is probably producing out of control, and advise when action is necessary to stop the process producing out of control.
- **Have we made it OK?** – Sample inspection is used to distinguish good batches or lots from bad. It can be used at any time in the process such as:
  - acceptance sampling by a production inspector
  - goods inwards inspection
  - interdepartmental inspection (remember that in total quality management, the incidents of failure tend to be interdepartmental)
  - final inspection prior to despatch of the goods or service to the customer.
- **Which bits did we make wrong?** – In this case, inspection is used to sort the bad from the good. One hundred per cent inspection may be used when a bad batch has been detected and the defectives are being sought for replacement – remembering always how ineffective this usually is.
- **Product audit** – Inspection may be carried out by in-house inspectors or customers' auditors, so that a view can be formed of the quality of the product.

PLANNING INSPECTION

For inspection to be as efficient and as effective as possible, it is necessary to plan inspection activities as an integral part of the process to which they relate. Such inspection plans are often referred to from *quality plans*.

An extremely powerful tool in the analysis of processes is flow charting. The resulting flow chart can be analysed, and the number of occurrences of each type of activity, including inspection, counted. Once the process has been fully charted and reduced to optimum, the inspection activities should be planned rigorously.

Where the process in question is unique, such as with project management of large capital projects, the flow chart is, in practice, the *project management plan*. Every project management plan should have incorporated in it, or coexisting with it, a quality plan, of which an inspection plan should be a part. Identifiable milestones, at natural breaks in the project, should have inspection activities integrated into them.

In designing and charting processes, one should keep sight of the potential for self-inspection. One principle of self-inspection is that where the process itself subjects the product to more stress than the customers' express or implied requirements will ever do, that aspect of the product does not need to be inspected later.

In other cases, the process itself may be self-inspecting. For example, disc brake pads and callipers are mechanically keyed so that if the fitter attempts to insert the wrong pads they simply will not go in. In other words, the process cannot proceed beyond this point unless and until the correct pads have been used.

Care should be taken to ensure that the inspection activities avoid, where possible, the potential for human error. Potential human error can be reduced in several ways. One example is where inspection requires human senses to be used as the tools of the inspection. Periodic audits of the inspected product may be necessary to allow a view to be formed of the inspectors' ability. Clearly, this potential for human error can be reduced by replacing the use of human senses with the use of sensing equipment. Advances in data processing capability contribute greatly on this front. However, where the human senses must be used and there is unavoidably an element of subjectivity about the inspection criteria, the process of inspection must be controlled to the greatest practical extent. Consider the professional water taster. In order to retain an undefiled palate, the water taster has to stick to a regime in life which does not permit the consumption of alcohol, tea, coffee, spiced food, tobacco, and so on.

In a second example, sometimes there is potential for a process to be conducted in such a way that a product could be assembled or service conducted in more ways than the correct one. In this case careful design should be brought to bear to ensure that only the correct assembly or execution can be made, as in the case of car brake disc pads. Unfortunately, the reverse of this can also be true. Proper quality-assured design should ensure that problems are not designed into a product or service which later demand inspection to filter them out.

Having planned the system of inspection as an integral part of the process, a set of specifications must be provided to the inspectors which state the acceptance criteria in clear and precise terms. The inspection specification must say what it means, and mean what it says, in language that is both comprehensible and meaningful to the inspectors. Remember that the inspectors may not have the knowledge or ability to understand the implications of the specification, and therefore need to have an unequivocal statement of what they must do. Useful tools to assist sensory inspection are photographs and samples. These are especially useful if the photographs or samples show both acceptable and unacceptable product. The factory of one client of the author assembled certain visual signalling equipment. It was a straightforward, low-tech assembly, but one that required precise axial alignment of the coloured lenses in their mountings. On the wall at the end of the large assembly bench was a bank of photographs of all aspects of assembly. Horizontally, through the middle of the array of photographs ran a wide dividing line. Above the line were examples of good assembly, below the line, bad assembly. The assembler had the criteria for workmanship and inspection criteria constantly in view.

One pitfall to avoid is making the inspection specification more stringent than the customer specification in the belief that doing so will result in fewer defects reaching the customer. In fact, such excessive stringency increases the cost of inspection, and adds other quality-related costs such as additional disposal and rework facilities. It also imposes unwarranted stress on the inspectors, which arises when, after their best efforts to filter out 'defectives', the inspectors see them passed to the customer as meeting the customer's specification.

The typical reaction in British industry – increasing the level of inspection when increased numbers of defectives are found – causes further problems. Firstly, the increase in inspection runs counter to the principles of quality management, which seeks to eliminate causes, not just their effects. Secondly, a wasteful by-product of these inspection purges is that they tend to remain in place long after the reasons for them have disappeared. As with the rest of the quality management system, inspection activities must be reviewed to ensure that they continue to be effective and to ensure their preparedness for forthcoming change.

Planned inspection should include inspection of all the activities within a company. For example, is packaging being performed correctly? Is the handling of product during loading and transportation compliant with specification?

To encourage co-operation from people whose work is to be inspected, or who will inspect their own work, it is useful to carry these people along the path of inspection with you. To this end, it is beneficial to involve the operators and inspectors in the planning process. No one knows more about any three square metres of floor space than the person who has to work in them, so get them on board! This is generally best done at the flow charting stage, and at a stroke it is possible to refute the allegation that management is using a 'police force'.

The extent to which inspection should be performed with measuring equipment should be carefully considered in planning the inspection system. In general terms, the more clearly defined and repetitive the inspection operation, the better suited it is to instrument or machine inspection. The more complex, imprecise or subjective the inspection decision, the better suited it is to human inspection. Where possible, design of the process should remove attributes or variables that need to be inspected for, or should downgrade the complexity of the inspection decisions to be taken so that inspection effort is reduced and, where possible, consigned to machines.

Having specified in a comprehensive, meaningful and unambiguous way what the inspectors must do, the entire inspection activity must be enshrined in an inspection manual or a set of operating procedures as part of the quality management documentation, which will be subject to review. Review enables planners to avoid too many special or custom-made inspection activities. Where a set of good inspection techniques exists, they should be built upon rather than proliferated.

Finally, the results of inspections must be recorded, and the records periodically analysed. This is pivotal to quality management. If you don't know what has been going wrong, then you don't know what to put right. Then, perversely, if the capability of the process is such that its output is almost never outside specification, the discovery of an out-of-control point will produce both wonderment and an opportunity to improve further.

The knowledge accumulated from collected inspection data assists in revising existing inspection plans and in evolving new ones, in lengthening or shortening inspection frequencies or in increasing or reducing inspection sample sizes. Inspection planners should take pains to devise inspection records that are simple to use, unambiguous and comprehensible. A fine example of an inspection record is the Shewhart chart, which was devised and has been used since before the days of the pocket calculator. The ability of the operator to use an inspection record of some sophistication should not be underestimated. Ask your workforce how much they would win on a four-horse accumulator with doubles and trebles, and you will soon see the extent of their ability to grasp concepts!

HOW MUCH TO INSPECT

The amount of inspection of a product or service depends on many factors, including:

- how much is known about the process
- the extent to which a sample of a lot or batch is representative of the lot or batch as a whole
- what will be the effect on the finished product or service of defects in its component parts.

If a process is known to run stably and in control, or if the product is known to be of quality simply because of its means of manufacture – through self-inspection – then inspection may not be required. If the process is known to run stably and in control over a certain length of time, then the frequency of inspection should be correspondingly low. If the homogeneity of the product is such that one can be very confident that a small sample is highly representative of the product at large, then the number of samples and consequent inspection effort can be small. If a new process is being run and no knowledge of its performance exists, then much more frequent inspection with larger samples is called for until sufficient data have been acquired about the process that the inspection effort can be reduced. If a process is producing a product or service which critically affects a finished product into which it is to be incorporated, of if the process capability is too poor to meet the customers' requirements, then the most stringent inspection may have to be applied in the short term. Purists will argue that it is the purpose of total quality management to eliminate the causes which demand inspection, and so it is. However, the use of uninterruptible power supplies as a backup power supply to computer or telecommunications equipment is seen by some as the last resort, and their reputations or even careers may depend upon the quality of the backup. Under these circumstances, it is difficult to persuade them that final, pre-handover inspection in the most stringent form might be unnecessary. Invoices which have not been checked, even by the invoice writer, will find themselves being reworked when an overcharged company returns them. If an invoice undercharges a customer, it may hang on the wall for a few weeks before the short payment is made! Either way, a quality-related cost is incurred. One hundred per cent inspection, even if it is only self-inspection, may be called for here.

SERIOUSNESS CLASSIFICATION

One method to reduce inspection effort is the use of seriousness classifications, whereby product defects are classified by the extent to which they affect fitness for purpose.

The extent of this effect can be determined from a failure mode effect and criticality analysis (FMECA). The results of an FMECA will show, for example, that if the upper tolerance limit of a process is exceeded, then it would be critical to fitness for use, and would result in catastrophic failure. Exceeding the lower tolerance limit would, on the other hand, be of minor importance. By understanding the importance of this contrast, it is possible to reduce the level of inspection and the complexity and number of sampling plans, to say nothing of reduced rework, scrap and other quality-related costs associated with the disposal of what was once thought unfit product.

Three seriousness classifications are generally used to make this distinction – critical, major and minor. In broad terms, these classifications are defined as follows:

- **Critical defects** are those certain to cause failure in either the product itself or the assembly (or process) of which the product is a part, and the customer will have a product unfit for use at some unspecified future time within the normal useful life.
- **Major defects** are those where there is a high probability of failure, and which will require major effort on the customer's part to maintain continued fitness for purpose.
- **Minor defects** are often divided into two sub-categories. In the first sub-category, defects are unlikely to cause failure but will probably cause noticeable substandard performance, and will require effort on the part of the customer to maintain continued fitness for purpose. Defects in the second sub-category do not affect operation or fitness for purpose, but are noticeable to the customer.

Once these classifications of defect have been made, the effect of the classification on process tolerances can be assessed. It should be clear by now that with the second type of minor defect, process tolerances may be slackened or even ignored, provided that the defects cause no interactive effect with any other part of the system with or into which they will be integrated. Subject to this condition, inspection can be dispensed with. In the case of the first type of minor defect, process tolerances may be eased by carefully monitored amounts, as long as no interactive effects occur, and inspection continued to the new tolerances. For major and critical defects, there is no difference to either process tolerances or inspection. Thus a significant reduction in inspection effort can be achieved by this method.

INSPECTION STAMPS

As each stage of the process is concluded, and inspected at a planned and integrated inspection milestone, a record of the inspection or test status must be updated to comply with quality system standards. One of the most commonly used methods of recording is to stamp the product (be it hardware or software). Room on the product for stamping should be designed in at the inspection planning stage. Self-inspection operates here, in that successive operations in the process are not permitted to continue until a positive vet has found a satisfactory stamp mark from the previous operation. In the absence of such a mark, a defect or incident report should be issued, stating that the inspection status of the product is unknown.

In the move towards self-inspection, teams of workers have been given their own inspection stamps. The purpose is to bring quality control to the point of operation, to remove the feeling of a 'police force' presence, to instil in the team of workers an increased sense of pride in their workmanship, involvement in the decisionmaking process, responsibility for the quality of the finished product, and more involvement in the improvement of capability to meet the customer's requirements. The inspection stamp is entrusted to the team leader, who may delegate authority for its use. Periodic inspection of the work of each team is required by an inspection supervisor or auditor to ensure that a sample of the work is indeed within specification. The interval between these inspections will vary in accordance with the degree of conformance found in the samples. If an unacceptably high level of nonconforming work is found, then the inspection stamp may be removed from the team leader, and inspection may revert to the more traditional methods until an acceptable level of conformance has been regained.

ERRORS IN INSPECTION

The true capability of a process is often masked by variabilities introduced by different process operators, because of the way that each operator prefers to operate the process. Similarly, it is possible for different inspectors to introduce variability into the inspected product which exceeds the intrinsic capability of the process. The variability may be due to different inspectors being too lenient or too stringent, or lacking sufficient discrimination between good and bad. Precise and meaningful inspection specifications, coupled with sufficient training, are required here, along with an appropriate level of inspection supervision or auditing.

Reference was made earlier to the fact that 100 per cent inspection of the same lot, even as many as three times, can fail to find up to 15 per cent of defects and defectives. Experiments requiring participants to count the number of occurrences of a given letter in a piece of prose invariably give results whose spread is about 20 per cent of the true number of occurrences. Experience gives no clear indication that the percentage of missed occurrences reduces as the length of time available for inspection increases. Time for inspection is not unlimited, of course, and there is in any case a natural human tendency to inject some pace into inspection. Consequently, potential improvement in percentage defects found with increased inspection time tends to be lost as a consequence of trying to be quick. It is worth observing that participants in these experiments who are counting the occurrences of a given letter in prose of a language not their own tend to produce results much closer to the true number of occurrences. This fact may be a useful pointer to discovering the reasons why inspectors make errors of such wide diversity.

Some methods for reducing inspector errors have been mentioned already, but are worth summarizing. They include error-proof methods of assembly, use of instruments or inspecting equipment, the use of paradigms to obviate judgement, and the use of control loop theory to improve human sensory capability. This interesting method relies upon the fact that the inspection control loop – consisting of the eye, the brain, the shaking hand and a measuring tool held by it – can reduce the shake of the hand by interposing a magnifying glass between the measured object and the eye. This effectively increases the feedback path gain of the control loop. The remarkable result that can be achieved is a factor of reduction in hand shake equal to the power of the magnifying glass, up to certain limits. This agrees with experience, and has an applicability beyond simple optical aids.

The stressful pitfall of over-specifying the acceptance criteria is a well-known device that managers use in the belief that it will reduce the number of defects. Managers have also knowingly used batch inspection to try to pass off nonconforming product, or have been sufficiently uninterested in the process operators' views on quality-related matters that the stressed operators have become uninterested in quality. Poor management attitudes can induce in the workforce a bad approach to quality. This can result in inspection errors ceasing to be inadvertent or technique-based, and becoming conscious and witting. Examples of this are where defectives are held back waiting for an unusually good batch to be produced, with which the defectives can then be mixed and still meet the sample plan pass level. There are occasions when 'management by terror' causes the workforce conveniently to neglect to declare defectives, which are later 'lost'. Nobody is going to volunteer to face a firing squad. Misunderstanding of management requirements can lead to inspection returns being falsified to appear to meet requirements, only to have the books 'balanced' at a later date when quality levels are better. Finally, inspectors naturally tend to round off results when reading instruments. A quality-related cost arises if the inspection specification is diluted by rounding errors. The key is to use instruments of an appropriate resolution.

COST OF INSPECTION

The cost of inspection takes the form of prevention, appraisal and failure cost:

- **Prevention costs** include inspection activities performed during the pilot stage of a new process. Here, inspection is being conducted to assist evolution of the process, so that the process will have minimum quality costs when it is in full operation.
- **Appraisal costs** include the cost of inspection incurred during normal operational running of a process. In this case, the inspection is conducted to appraise the process to determine whether or not it is continuing to produce within the control limits.
- **Failure cost** – The recurrent theme of this chapter has been to use quality management to reduce the need for inspection solely as a means of detecting nonconforming product. Where inspection is used purely in this category, then it is classed as a cost of failure. It is into this category that inspection activities fall when there has been an increase of inspection activity due to increased levels of product failure. It is up to the quality management system to remove the causes of failure, and therefore the need for this category of inspection.

The cost of all metrology facilities and equipment, plus all the time of inspectors and laboratory staff, must be included. However, correct apportionment of these costs to the appropriate category of quality-related cost soon reveals how much inspection effort is being wasted in inspecting solely to separate the good from the bad. Quality improvement projects should then be instituted to remove the need for the inspection costs classed as failure costs.

Is it fit for purpose?

'Fitness for purpose' is one of the widely accepted definitions of quality. Often, a finished product may not meet the specification and yet still be fit for purpose.

Consider scratches on the surface of a photographic lens. By defracting the light, the scratches will degrade the resolving power of the lens, reduce the contrast of the resulting negatives, and render the lens unsightly to the customer. This makes the lens unfit for its original purpose. In this case, the lens is both outside specification and unfit for purpose. Consider identical scratches on the silvered reflector inside an ordinary, domestic, ceiling-mounted luminaire. The scratches neither impair the purpose of the luminaire nor are ever likely to be seen by the customer. The luminaire does not meet specification, but is still fit for purpose.

As another example, consider the crankshaft on a 20 tonne press, where the amount of slop between the crank journals and the bearings is so extensive that the press is no longer precise. Upon dismantlement of the journal bearings, it is discovered that the journal surface itself is so pitted and worn that simply replacing the worn-out bearings will not solve the problem. The journals could be ground to a smaller diameter and reassembled with oversized bearings. The assembled crankshaft no longer meets the original specification, but is quite definitely fit for purpose. It may not, therefore, be necessary to clean up, remetal and regrind the journals to the original specification.

Questions such as these must be addressed and criteria need to be prepared for management to work to, otherwise subjective decisions on fitness for purpose will probably introduce costly rejection of fit product, and increase quality costs such as disposal and rework.

Do we tell the customer?

The implications of this question must also be considered by management. The issues to be considered include:

- How many customers would need to be notified?
- How easy would it be to explain the technicalities of the condition, compared to the clear lack of implication for fitness for purpose?
- What other implications are there for the customer?
- What does the contract say?

The first two questions are self-explanatory and are germane to the case of the scratched luminaire.

The third question has implications for the holding of spares for the owners of the crankshaft, if they carry replacement bearings with a view to preventing a recurrence of the sorry state of their journals.

In the fourth question, a wisely thought-out contract will state those types of apparent defect which must be brought to the attention of the customer. Industry knowledge will guide the customer in this, and it becomes the subject of proper contract review to ensure that such considerations for reporting are included.

This is particularly true in the case of rework and repair.

In the case of the crankshaft journals, with correct diameter and surface hardness, the remetalled and ground surface may be acceptable to the customer, owing to the relatively slow speed at which the crankshaft rotates. But if it was a shaft designed to rotate at high speed that had been remetalled, there is potential for the metalling to come off at high speed, and such a solution might be totally unacceptable. As the customer, I would ensure by careful use of contract review that the proposed use of such repair was contractually notifiable.

Further reading

The reader is referred to the work of John Oakland and Joseph Juran.

CHAPTER **21**

Functional Testing

Geoffrey Leaver

The requirements of any product or service vary widely depending on whether one is the supplier or the user. Users require *fitness for purpose* (Will the product or service 'perform'?). Suppliers, on the other hand, can only work to a 'specification', and in their terms quality must be defined as *conformity to specification*.

An inspector or tester provided with the product, specification, measuring equipment and skill can adequately assess conformity to specification, but may not be in a position to judge fitness for purpose. It is thus not uncommon for products to be supplied that 'comply with specification' even though they may not meet the customer's requirements (indeed, the question of fitness for purpose may not even be raised unless the product fails to comply with specification).

The role of testing

Before examining the methods and techniques, we will first consider the philosophy behind inspection, measurement and testing, and the reasons for carrying them out. It is important to appreciate the following:

- Separate testing, including goods inwards and final product testing, does not add value to the product or service. It only adds cost. Time spent in eliminating test or inspection operations *without loss of confidence* will be financially rewarding.
- Separate test operations carried out by the organization's 'independent' testers or inspectors take responsibility away from the person who carried out the operation being inspected. The *producer* of a product or the *supplier* of a service is ultimately the controller of quality. Operators should be totally responsible for their own operations. They should monitor work received from the previous work stage (that is, from their supplier) and should have the ability and facility to check their own work before it passes to the next stage (customer). Each operator then becomes a tester or inspector.
- The later in the work cycle or the further down the production line that testing is carried out, the more expensive it will be to correct any faults found. Where testing is necessary, the earlier in the process the better: control at each stage promotes finished product or service that is 'right first time'.
- Minimizing overall cost requires the elimination of causes of faults – *prevention*, not *detection*. It is necessary to concentrate on reducing variation within the process to give

confidence that the process is capable of producing a product or service that meets requirements every time, all the time.

If it is to be of value, testing should be considered for the following purposes.

1 *To help establish customer confidence* – Customers need to know that products, components or services supplied to them will be fit for purpose. For commercial or industrial customers, this means that products, components or services supplied can be slotted into their process without having to check, inspect or test. Testing carried out as a supplier is designed to enable customers to buy with confidence – good business practice.

2 *To establish the design* – Design of the product and design of the process should develop side by side. Testing during the development stages should be conducted to obtain sufficient information for subsequent production to proceed under established, controlled conditions, minimizing the need for costly inspection and testing.

3 *In-line process control* – Where testing can be built in as part of the process, it can be used to provide a warning that problems are going to arise before they actually do. This, combined with an automatic correction, can lead to prevention of defects, instead of allowing them to happen and subsequently having to sort them out.

In Utopia, all designs would be fully proven, all processes would be under complete control at every stage, every customer would have complete confidence in their supplier, and separate testing would be unnecessary. In the real, less than ideal world, however, these conditions do not exist and a degree of testing is necessary.

Functional requirements (those which relate to use) must be distinguished from non-functional requirements (those which allow the functional requirements to be met). *Functional requirements* are aimed at such aspects as ensuring performance, meeting health and safety requirements, ensuring agreed lifetimes, and so on. *Non-functional requirements* provide the means to the end (they enable manufacture or supply).

Functional testing is therefore carried out to verify that a product will perform under its operating conditions for a given length of time. Such testing may be conducted on the finished product or system (which is the major interest for the user) and at intermediate stages, such as at component or sub-assembly level (which may be of significant economic value to the producer).

The requirements can be divided into three main areas:

1 *Performance* – These requirements, specific to the product, are defined qualities or quantities such as the expected light output from an electric luminaire, the output capacity and stability of a generator, and so on.

2 *Environmental conditions* – These requirements cover such things as the temperature range, humidity, vibration, presence of corrosive or other harmful substances to which the product is likely to be exposed during its stored or operating life.

3 *Time requirements* – These are the expected lifetime requirements for the product, usually relating to operating life, but also, in many cases, to storage or shelf-life. Thus an electric light bulb may have a quoted life of 1200 hours under typical conditions, an automobile

engine could have a target life of 100 000 hours before major overhaul, and an exhaust silencing system could have an expected life of three years.

Each of these factors will vary between individual units of the same product and steps are necessary to determine the requirements, estimate the variation (determining the distribution) and finally testing to verify that the product can meet the requirements.

In many cases it is unrealistic, time-consuming and extremely costly to 'test to destruction' over the lifetime of a product, and accelerated testing is commonly used by applying excessive stresses or exaggerated environmental conditions to deliberately accelerate the effects.

Before testing, the actual requirements must be defined, and what is to be expected of the product or service (the design requirements) as compared with how well the product or service actually achieves the design requirements (this degree of achievement being the conformity or production requirements).

Design testing is directed towards the approval of a design. The tests are conducted to determine whether an item is capable of meeting the requirements of the product specification.

Production testing (or conformity testing) is directed towards the approval of production. It is intended to determine whether the units, as produced, actually do meet the requirements of the product specification.

Fitness for purpose

For modern products, attainment of fitness for purpose involves striking a balance between many competing factors. Costs and other information must be obtained as necessary in such areas as:

1 minimum functional requirements
2 maximum environmental expectations
3 cost limitations
4 safety requirements
5 reliability requirements.

MINIMUM FUNCTIONAL REQUIREMENTS

What performance does the customer have a reasonable right to expect under specified conditions of use? This information can be obtained by market research (prior to design), field trials (during design finalizing stage) or feedback from customers (after supply).

The minimum functional requirements should be set out clearly in the functional specification, which describes in detail the characteristics of the product with regard to its intended capability. This specification should, as far as possible, be written in quantitative terms giving the limits of acceptability.

MAXIMUM ENVIRONMENTAL EXPECTATIONS

Environmental factors have to be considered from two viewpoints:

1 discovering or predicting what the environmental conditions will be
2 testing to ensure that the product can cope with these conditions (which might include temperature, speed, acceleration, pressure, humidity, vibration, altitude and many other factors).

COST LIMITATIONS

The product design will have certain restrictions imposed by the final price (and overall cost) of the product or service supplied, and it is necessary to clearly define the intended market. What sector of the market are we aiming for:

- the leather-bound or paperback book buyer?
- the 'designer label' or the 'mass market'?
- the long lifetime or the 'disposable'?

SAFETY REQUIREMENTS

Safety is defined as 'freedom from *unacceptable* risks of personal harm'. It must be realized that there is no known way of attaining absolute safety, and there will always be a degree of risk while any hazard is present.

A *hazard* is a set of conditions in the operation of a product or system with the potential for initiating an accident sequence. Hazards can be classified in a number of ways, including:

- **catastrophic** – causing death, severe injury to personnel, or total loss of product
- **critical** – will cause personal injury or major product damage unless immediate corrective action is taken
- **controlled or marginal** – can be overcome without injury to personnel or major product damage
- **negligible** – will not result in personal injury or product damage.

A *risk* is the combined effect of the probability of occurrence of an undesirable event and the magnitude of the event. It can be defined in terms of the probability of occurrence of a hazard or the effect of this occurrence.

Although absolute safety cannot be attained, it must be realized that legally, a manufacturer or supplier must show that all possible steps to minimize the risk of hazards have been taken.

RELIABILITY REQUIREMENTS

Reliability is the ability of an item to perform a required function under stated conditions for a stated minimum period of time.

Purchasers need to be told not only how a product should be used and maintained and what the expected initial performance will be. There is also a requirement to assess how long the product will continue to function, and what will be its chance of failure.

Reliability sets an objective or a requirement of a product from its inception to the end of its working life. In those products where reliability is of prime importance, quantitative requirements should be included in the functional specification.

FAILURE

Failure is defined as 'the termination of the ability of an item to perform a required function'. In practice, some kinds of failure are more important than others. It is necessary to distinguish between these – they can be classified by cause, as follows:

- **misuse failure** – attributable to the application of stresses beyond the stated capabilities of the item
- **inherent weakness failure** – the item fails when it is subjected to stresses within the stated capabilities of the item
- **wear-out failure** – failures which have increasing probability of occurrence with time.

TESTING FOR RELIABILITY

Reliability tests are conducted to verify that a product will work under operating conditions for a given length of time. Results are assessed on failure accumulated during the testing. The emphasis is usually placed on:

- the component and individual parts level
- the complete system or assembly level.

Tests focus on three elements:

1. **The performance requirements** – These are specific to the product, and tests must be conducted to verify that the product can withstand the expected stress for the required time period.
2. **Environmental conditions** – Testing may well be needed to determine the conditions, before conducting tests to verify that the product can operate and withstand these conditions for the required period.
3. **Time requirements**.

One common form of reliability testing, allowing reduced costs, is *accelerated testing*. The products are made to perform at abnormally high stress or environmental levels in order to make them fail earlier. Great care is needed in correlating accelerated test results with those expected under normal service conditions.

For any reliability testing to be valid, it must provide statistically significant results. Special problems can arise in such cases as:

- a requirement for extremely high reliability (a low failure rate, or a high mean time between failures)
- a requirement for an extremely long life
- high cost or shortage of test samples.

There are two basic types of error in evaluating significance: rejecting an acceptable item, or accepting a rejectable item. Both of these risks are present in any sample testing.

The sample size taken depends on the chosen sampling risks, the size of the smallest time difference which is going to have to be detected, and the amount of variation in the characteristic being measured.

In general, the higher the sample size (or the greater the number of tests) relative to the standard to be attained, the greater the validity of the testing. For example, if there is an objective of a maximum of one defective component per million produced, a sample of only 100 would have a low validity. On the other hand, if the target is that a minimum of 90 per cent of trains shall arrive on time, then a sample of 100 could yield a significant result.

Although increasing the sample size or number of tests improves the precision of estimates obtained, this improvement does not usually vary linearly according to the number of tests. Doubling the number of tests, for example, does not double the precision. Also, the degree of precision obtained is not dependent simply on the size of the sample chosen in relation to the total batch size. The size of the total batch itself affects the result. This is illustrated in the following example, taken from ISO Standard 2859, inspection level 2. Table 21.1 shows the sample size needed to obtain the same level of testing for three different total batch sizes.

TWO SAFEGUARDING APPROACHES TO IMPROVE RELIABILITY

There are two main safeguards that can be incorporated to improve reliability:

1 **Derating** – A margin of safety is built into the design so that components and systems are operated well below their specified limits. For example, the use of a capacitor rated at 3000 volts in an application where the actual level is only 200 volts.
2 **Redundancy** – This is the case where the designer provides more than one means for accomplishing a given task in such a way that, should one method fail, the system will still operate. An example is the multi-engined aircraft: if one engine fails, the aircraft should still be able to land safely.

DEFECTS

Defects, or defectives, relate to items that do not comply with the specified requirements, where the non-compliance is the responsibility of the manufacturer or supplier. Defects can be classified according to their degree of seriousness as:

1 **Critical** – Such a defect which is likely to result in hazardous or unsafe conditions for individuals using, maintaining or depending on the product. A critical defect is also one which will cause the failure of a major product. As an example, the failure of a car steering mechanism would be classed as a critical defect.

Table 21.1 Samples size needed for the same level of testing for different total batch sizes

Batch size	*Sample size*	*Sample size as % of batch size*
40	8	20.0
800	80	10.0
400 000	800	0.2

2 **Major** – Such a defect, although not critical, will result in failure or will significantly reduce the performance of the product. Thus a defect causing a car engine to fail would be classed as major.

3 **Minor** – Such a defect will not appreciably affect the use of the product. Staying with the automobile industry for our example, a slight paint blemish on a car could be classed as a minor defect.

Defects can also be classified in terms of cost. It must be remembered here that costs of consequential damage can go well beyond the costs of parts and labour for repairing the defect itself. For example, if a lorry carrying components breaks down on a delivery run to a customer, the user's costs might include (in addition to the repair costs) the value of the lorry while it is out of action, the driver's pay, and the customer's lost factory production time caused by late delivery of the components.

Other examples include the breakdown of a deep freeze cabinet (in which the contents may have to be scrapped), and the costs of making alternative arrangements when a car breaks down.

Normal legal responsibility concerning defects is twofold:

1 General disclaimers in cases of injury to human beings are usually not valid.
2 Disclaimers on consequential monetary loss not involving safety are usually upheld.

Measurement

Product conformity is determined by measurements made by test equipment, and it is necessary to have sufficient knowledge of the equipment to be sure that the results are valid (that is, sufficiently accurate and precise for the required purpose).

Any error in measurement has a direct bearing on the ability to judge conformity, and a clear understanding of the meaning of the measurements requires an understanding of the nature of the measurement error.

ACCURACY

If a number of measurements are made on a product, the mean of these measurements is calculated, and this mean is compared with the true value; the extent to which this measured mean agrees with the value is a measure of the accuracy of the equipment used.

The difference between the measured mean and the true value is the error, which can be either positive or negative, and is the extent to which the equipment is out of calibration. The equipment can still be considered accurate if the error is less than the tolerance or maximum allowable for that grade of instrument.

PRECISION

Irrespective of the accuracy of calibration, an instrument will not give identical results on repeat readings even when making a series of measurements on a single unit. Instead, there will be a scatter of readings, and the dispersion, or spread, of these readings is a measure of the precision (irrespective of the relationship with the true value).

In measurements, it is necessary to have both adequate accuracy *and* precision, but it should be appreciated that recalibration will normally improve the *accuracy* of an instrument, but will not change the *precision*.

There are many sources of measurement error which can be attributed to the operator (differences in skill levels, experience or technique of different operators), the test equipment (variations due to drift caused by changes in environmental conditions, backlash, wear, and so on) or the test procedure (where several different procedures are available).

The overall measurement error is, of course, the result of all the contributing errors. The *observed* error can be expressed in the form:

$$S_o^2 = S_a^2 + S_b^2 + S_c^2 \ldots$$

where S_o is the observed error and S_a, S_b, S_c and so on are the individual contributing errors. In a measurement system, the observed variation (S_o) will comprise the *product* variation (S_p) and the *system* variation (S_s). The relationship is of the form:

$$S_o^2 = S_p^2 + S_s^2$$

which can be expressed as:

$$S_p^2 = S_o^2 - S_s^2$$

It is apparent that if the variation due to the system is less than 10 per cent of the observed variation, then the effect on the product will be less than 1 per cent. That is the basis of the commonly accepted practice of specifying that the measuring instrument should be capable of distinguishing to an accuracy of 10 per cent of the required product tolerance.

CALIBRATION

In publishing results, it is necessary to make clear the extent of possible errors, and it is essential to be able to demonstrate that the equipment used is capable of providing precise measurement before any assurance of conformity can be given. This requirement means that the measuring equipment used must be capable of an accuracy higher than that specified for the product.

Any measuring equipment has at some time been adjusted or graduated to the required accuracy within known limits (usually as one of the final steps during its manufacture). Unfortunately, this by itself is insufficient, as all measuring and test equipment is subject to change caused by wear, damage and so on, and it is necessary to check at a predetermined frequency.

Ideally, an instrument should be checked immediately before and after each occasion of use. The pre-check will prevent a faulty instrument from being used and thus producing incorrect results, while the post-check will detect whether any changes have occurred during the period of use. This, however, is a policy of perfection, being both time-consuming and expensive. Stable equipment can, in the absence of damage, normally be relied upon for periods measured in months, and checking equipment at regular intervals provides a good assurance that measurements taken are satisfactory.

With any test equipment, it is therefore necessary to establish a calibration procedure that will detect any deterioration beyond tolerable levels of accuracy. This demands a calibration schedule to determine when each piece of equipment must be reassessed to ensure that it is still maintaining its required accuracy. There are generally three possible methods of determining calibration schedules:

1 **Time** – calibration on the basis of fixed calendar times or intervals, such as one week, three months, annually, and so on

2 **Usage** – calibration based on the amount of actual usage which the instrument has received, such as the number of units of product measured; recalibration times can be determined by recording clerically the number of times the equipment has been used, or by automatic counting or in-built computer programming
3 **Hours** – calibration according to the number of hours for which the measuring equipment has been operated; for electrical equipment, for example, this may simply be a matter of metering the actual time for which the equipment has been drawing current.

In any calibration system, it is important to measure and record the results before any recalibrating adjustments are made. This is the only way in which drift can be measured, and used as a basis for adjusting calibration periods sensibly.

Testing

Testing may be one of two basic types:

1 **condition termination tests**, where the testing is continued until failure or some predetermined change of state occurs
2 **fixed-time sequence testing**, which is based on specified acceptable values of the characteristics being assessed.

Testing to expose design weaknesses should be planned to generate failures. Weaknesses are only demonstrated by failure, so a test that generates no failures has provided no information on which to base improvements. Tests should therefore be as severe as is compatible with the planned operation of the products.

Once the design has been established, the actual performance parameters are specified and fixed-time or sequence testing is used to monitor the continuing product conformity. The aims of a test programme generally are to:

- ensure that the item meets the specified performance or operational requirements
- minimize manufacturing faults and defective parts
- highlight systematic errors so that design deficiencies can be overcome
- provide information which can be fed back to design as part of an improvement plan.

While the performance requirements under normal or anticipated conditions of operation may be readily specified and tested for an item as produced, in certain cases this may be of limited value, since subsequent operations including packaging, transportation, installation/commissioning and usage may all have an effect on subsequent field performance. In such cases, it is necessary to specify clearly and test for these conditions, which may include:

- **Packaging** – protection of the product during handling, transport and storage; this may require special attention, such as verifying the effectiveness of rustproofing of steel, or the shielding of sensitive electronic components
- **Transportation** – tests to check that damage will not occur due to temperature, humidity, vibration, shock, sabotage and so on
- **Storage** – testing to ensure that shelf-life is determined and specified, and that the product is clearly dated
- **Installation, commissioning and handover** – special facilities and tests may have to be specified to support commissioning and to demonstrate the product to the customer before handover
- **Usage** – problems can arise when the user fails to observe the operating instructions, or overstresses or fails to maintain the product; tests may be necessary to determine the consequences of foreseeable misuse.

Ideally, testing should compare actual service performance with users' service needs, and the most significant aspect is the need for the manufacturer to find out the actual usage which takes place. There are numerous sources of such information, such as direct observation, complaint analysis, positive feedback and so on, and it is essential to ensure that all such data are used and incorporated into the functional specification, and hence into the functional test programme.

It is not always possible or economical to test complete systems; it may be necessary to test components and sub-assemblies, and hence predict the behaviour of complete systems.

In a similar way, testing under normal or anticipated operating conditions can be unrealistically time-consuming or expensive, and accelerated testing may be carried out, whose primary purpose is to provide failures and/or performance data more quickly than if the item were tested under normal conditions. To be valid, an accelerated test should not alter the modes of failure, and the relation between the accelerated data must be understood. In accelerated testing, the stresses applied are more severe than those encountered in normal use in order to speed up the ageing process, and may be applied either as constant stress or step stress. Care must be taken when predicting performance under normal conditions from results obtained under exaggerated conditions, since different factors may come into play.

Automation of testing

Automated inspection and testing is designed to reduce costs, improve efficiency, reduce time, overcome staff shortages, increase accuracy and eliminate human monotony.

Commonly, automation involves substantial investment in capital equipment, and there are drawbacks with automated testing which need to be overcome. However, its use is rapidly increasing, for very good reasons, and just as computer-aided design (CAD) and computer-aided manufacture (CAM) are widely used, computer-aided testing (CAT) and computer-aided inspection (CAI) are becoming more and more widely adopted.

When examining the possibility of using automatic test equipment, it is necessary to consider many aspects, including an awareness that any automated process requires:

- criteria which can be expressed exactly (numbers)
- decisions which can be made in advance (What happens if ...?)
- repetitive activities
- decisions must be right or wrong, good or bad, and so on
- a high degree of order.

In addition, it is necessary to consider the cost of automated testing and the economic justification for its introduction, comparing the anticipated benefits in time saving or improved information with the capital cost of the equipment together with the cost of obtaining, maintaining and protecting the software.

Once all these factors have been resolved, automatic test equipment offers many advantages in terms of speed and the number of parameters which can be evaluated. The major factor limiting speed of test may be the time taken to position the item in the test equipment.

Automatic test methods can generate a tremendous amount of data of varying degrees of usefulness, and it is essential to identify the information which is really needed for evaluation. Only data which are required should be processed, whereas there is a danger of processing all data for no other reason than that they are available.

Both attribute and variables data require processing. Attribute data are used to identify major defect types, determine yields, classify into different grades, and so on. Variables data may be processed for analysis and presented in various statistical forms (such as distributions, central tendency, and so on).

Two needs must be satisfied when testing is automated: the inspection itself, and the calibration of the test equipment. Automatic testing may be used on high-volume production lines to provide go/no-go answers. When multiple properties are measured or the product must be sequenced through a variety of environmental conditions or monitored over time, computer systems can continually follow the product under test, and it is therefore possible to combine data collection and exception reporting with automatic testing.

Test procedures

Test procedures are usually tailor-made for a specific product type. They normally include some or all of the following:

- **Scope** – the product to be tested must be identified by name or by a specific reference number
- **Field of application** – the intended usage of the procedure itself and of the item which is its subject; sufficient information should also be given of any secondary or partly applicable uses
- **References** – other relevant standards, procedures or other documents
- **Definitions** – all specialized terms used must be defined, following the relevant international standards

- **Responsibilities** – the responsibility for conducting the testing and for determining the subsequent course of action must be defined
- **Purpose and context of use** – this part describes the role that the item is intended to perform; environmental conditions and other factors associated with the performance of the item in service must be listed
- **Equipment** – equipment to be used for the testing should be listed, together with acceptable alternatives, where applicable
- **Performance requirements** – each performance requirement should be defined in terms of a function which is to be fulfilled, together with the physical, chemical or mechanical property on which assessment or verification can be assessed; wherever possible, terms and expressions capable of quantification should be used in accordance with any applicable international standard; requirements should be listed so that those which always apply are distinguished from those which apply only under certain circumstances
- **Method of assessment or verification** – for each performance requirement, this part will describe fully (or cross-refer to) the means by which the achieved performance of the product will be assured or verified, and in addition, the means for predicting the performance over time; cross-reference should be made to international standards wherever possible
- **Performance values** – for each performance requirement, the upper and lower acceptable performance values or grades against which the product will be required to perform must be stated; the relationship between the values or grades to the purpose and context of use should be indicated
- **Frequency of testing** – this part defines the frequency of testing, which may be based on time or quantity
- **Follow-up action** – the procedure for action to be taken in the case of either acceptance or rejection should be defined.

Test procedures within a company may conveniently be drawn together into a test and inspection procedures manual. This typically contains:

- authorization, by the responsible person or department
- list of contents, with amendments
- statement of responsibilities and authorities
- general policy on the classification of defects
- sampling plans
- copies of test reporting forms
- procedure for identification and labelling of the product and its test status
- nonconformity procedure
- individual product test procedures (either included in the manual or referenced from it).

Test specifications are derived from design documents, and they cannot be fully defined until the following questions have been resolved:

1 What constitutes acceptable performance? The need is to define the purpose of the product or service and to specify the conditions which must prevail for this purpose to be considered as having been met. When the purpose is defined in detail, it becomes clearer which failures will impair the performance and which will not.

2 What are the loads or stresses to which the item will be subjected during its life? Many failures result from misunderstandings between the designer and the user. For example, a component may be designed for continuous operation at 150°C with intermittent exposure to temperatures of 180°C. But what does this term 'intermittent exposure' mean in this case? What happens if, on occasions, the temperature rises to 200°C?

3 What are the reliability targets? These should be specified in quantifiable terms (for example, a failure rate not exceeding 1 per cent per annum, or a specified mean time between failures).

In some cases the customer may specify these requirements, but in many other cases, the manufacturer or supplier must taken the initiative in establishing specifications.

TEST STRATEGY

One quality problem with assembled products has been inadequate expertise among field service engineers. In addition to improvements in product designs to achieve greater reliability, there has been a vast increase in the use of modular construction, in which sub-assemblies or modules are designed to allow easy removal and replacement. Thus a failure in a television set or a computer can usually be dealt with by the speedy replacement of one or more modules on site, and where possible, repairing the defective modules later at a factory or service workshop.

This use of modular construction also has benefits for the manufacturer, since sub-assemblies can be tested and accepted on the basis of defined criteria before they are built into the total assembly or system.

During the design stages of a new or modified product, the system, subsystems and units must be defined precisely in terms of their functional requirements and the conditions which constitute acceptable or unacceptable performance. At this stage, the interfaces between the various components must also be clearly defined.

The critical parts must be identified. These can be defined as those which:

- have a high population in the product
- have a single (or unreliable) source of supply
- have to function within unusually tight limits
- would have serious consequences in the case of failure
- are unproven owing to lack of data.

For each critical part, a list must be made of all the factors which are relevant to its performance or its reliability, such as the actual functions, ratings, internal environment and stresses, expected external environments and stresses, and the actual duty (operation time) cycle.

Once the requirements for each component and/or assembly have been defined and specifications and procedures have been written, testing can be conducted on a bottom-upward basis. This approach will ensure that the satisfactory operation (or nonconformity) of each module is discovered at the earliest possible stage. Integration of accepted modules into the main assembly should then be followed by a final functional test to ensure that the complete product or system meets the test specification – and hence the design requirements.

CHAPTER

22 Inspection and Measuring Equipment

Trevor C. Ashton

Introduction

There are several obvious principles concerning the maintenance of inspection tools and equipment in the contribution to quality. These combine:

- maintaining traceability of all measuring equipment in the organization and keeping it in good working condition
- using equipment of proven accuracy for confirming the calibration of production measuring and inspection tools
- choosing correct tools for the degree of accuracy required.

Consistent quality in manufacture is only assured by reliable measurement. These measurements are performed:

- on bought-in components and material at the goods receipt stage (possibly in conjunction with supporting documentation from the supplier)
- throughout the manufacturing process, either in the control of the processing machinery or the components being produced
- during and after final assembly, to confirm that the product is operating satisfactorily before shipping to the customer.

Measuring and test equipment is not confined to production areas. It is found also in design laboratories and in associated workshops and offices. Standard procedures must be applied throughout the organization.

To achieve true total quality, the same attention to correct use and performance must include not only measuring instruments used in inspection and testing, but also the tools used within the manufacturing process. These considerations obviously apply to machine tools and process equipment (temperature gauges and recorders on ovens, for example). However, monitoring and correct maintenance of simple hand tools, such as soldering irons and crimping tools, are also important.

Many quality and inspection problems can be avoided by proper attention to tolerancing and standardization of design and production processes.

There are considerable benefits from incorporating test and inspection facilities into the manufacturing process (possibly assisted by the use of custom-built automatic measuring or testing equipment). This outmodes the principle of having two sets of measuring equipment: one for the operator and one for the inspector. The only recognized difference now is that between working equipment and the higher-accuracy equipment used in the calibrating room to maintain it.

Quality assurance and standards

Reference to relevant standards specifications for measuring tools and equipment is vital to the test methods adopted. Some relevant standards are listed in the further reading section at the end of this chapter.

For quality assurance techniques, ISO 10012-1 can be referred to when the product or process quality depends heavily on the ability to measure accurately. This standard contains the quality assurance requirements for measuring equipment, and is more detailed than those found in ISO 9001.

The ISO 9000 series standards provide sound advice in recommending that documented procedures be produced and maintained to control, calibrate and maintain inspection, measuring and test equipment, including test software, used to demonstrate conformity of product to the specified requirements of a customer. This standard states the procedures needed and what they should include. It emphasizes the need to control special processes which may be particular to a service or industry: for example, describing paint spraying in the automobile industry and printed circuit production in an electronics company.

General control principles

To comply with most second- and third-party quality systems, suppliers must demonstrate their control of all inspection, measuring and test equipment, whether this is a bought-in proprietary instrument or a custom-designed unit built in-house and including not only hardware but also any associated software.

Documented procedures should provide for the monitoring and maintenance of the measurement process, including equipment procedures, statistical method (if applicable) and operator skills. Procedures and in-house company standards should be based on the ISO 9000 series of standards. Good work instructions should explain the extent of their control, avoid confusion, and provide a means of delegating authority and responsibility.

Measuring equipment should be regularly audited internally to review its method of use, recalibration requirements and the recalibration facilities actually available. It is the manufacturer or service provider's duty to establish the extent and frequency of all calibration checks and to maintain records as evidence of control.

Where appropriate, advice should be given to make sure that any degree of measurement uncertainty is known, matching the accuracy requirement with the appropriate measurement capability.

Some products require regular maintenance or after-sales service. Measuring and test equipment used in field installation must be brought under a similar control umbrella. Special-purpose tools or equipment for handling and servicing during or after installation should have their design and function validated, and instruction manuals should be comprehensive.

There are often instances where technical data on the adequacy of inspection and measuring equipment are a customer-specified requirement. In any such case, the relevant data must be available to the customer or his agent.

CONTROL CHECKLIST

The following should be considered in drawing up a quality control regime:

- Determine the accuracy needed for the measurements, and then choose appropriate inspection, measurement and test equipment, including range, accuracy, precision and robustness, under specified environmental conditions.
- Specify the equipment selected, either in the relevant process or servicing specification or on a production planning layout.
- Identify all equipment in the organization. Each piece of equipment should be given a unique identifying number or code that will appear in all associated inventory, maintenance/recalibration and disposal records.
- Specify initial calibration requirements before first use, in order to validate the measuring accuracy (bias and precision).
- Establish procedures for testing the software and procedures controlling automatic test equipment.
- Specify procedures for recalibrating and adjusting equipment against certified equipment at prescribed intervals.
- Ensure that the calibration status of equipment used to check and recalibrate measuring equipment is traceable to nationally recognized measurement standards. (Nationally certified bodies accredited by UKAS can provide this service – see Chapter 23). Where no such standards exist, for example with home-built test equipment, the basis used for calibration must be documented.
- Control the process of equipment calibration. For every relevant piece of equipment, this involves recording details of type, unique reference, location, frequency of checks, checking method, acceptance criteria and corrective action.
- Implement a loan procedure so that the location of each item is always known, and so that it can be recalled periodically for adjustment, repair and recalibration.
- Label all tools and equipment with their calibration status.
- Maintain calibration records for each identified tool, instrument and piece of equipment, to provide documentary evidence covering the frequency of calibration required and its actual calibration status.
- Provide suitable facilities for handling, preserving and storing equipment to ensure that accuracy and fitness for use are maintained.
- Safeguard equipment against unauthorized tempering with adjustments. This might be necessary for health and safety reasons, in addition to safeguarding calibration validity.

- Reassess the validity of a product and its documentation if ever it has been inspected or tested with equipment subsequently found to be out of calibration.
- Ensure that all equipment used during off-site installation and commissioning, servicing, field repairs and other after-sales activities remote from the factory is included in the control system and procedures.

Selection of checking equipment

Measuring equipment in an organization is either:

1 used for verifying the production process (equipment such as workshop micrometers, vernier gauges, digital comparators and electrical indicating instruments for measuring inputs, outputs or physical parameters)
2 laboratory equipment used for checking and maintaining the accuracy and calibration of the first group (for example, slip gauges and surface blocks).

The second group will have an accuracy at least one order better than the first, and is normally used in a separate and secure environment. It must be certified by a UKAS-approved laboratory, which will use equipment traceable to national reference standards. The calibration checks on working tools should be conducted in this controlled environment so that the accuracy of the calibrating equipment is maintained.

Checking and calibrating

Maintaining tools and measuring equipment in a good state of repair and reliable accuracy entails constant vigilance and regular calibration against reference standards of known accuracy, traceable to national standards.

Normally, hand tools and portable measuring instruments would be returned to a central recalibration point, but items such as ovens, pressure gauges and flow meters on processing equipment, not coming under the normal definition of inspection measuring equipment, should also be identified in the control system, labelled, and subjected to similar regular recalibrations.

IN-HOUSE CALIBRATION SERVICES

A company calibration service section or metrology laboratory must be aware of all relevant legal requirements and national standards. It must ensure that:

- Its own equipment is within calibration limits.
- The correct environment exists for calibration.
- The tests are carried out according to the relevant instructions or procedures.
- Records are maintained of items calibrated (see Figure 22.1).
- Individual equipment records (described earlier in this chapter) are updated at each new calibration.

Tool and gauge system record						
Tool number	*Description*	*Date in use* (d/ww/yy)	*Calibration* Interval (weeks)	*Date calibrated* (d/ww/yy)	*Location*	*Repair frequency*
AP 601 001	Flow solder service	1/25/93	026	1/39/01	416 D Kirk	0000
AI 601 001	Flow solder analysis	5/33/00	012	1/50/01	489 A Wilkinson	0000
AI 602 001	Roller tin analysis	5/33/00	012	1/50/01	489 A Wilkinson	0000
AI 091 733 01	Screw plug gauge M4 LH	4/33/95	039	5/40/01	414 S Lawrence	0000
AI 244 002	Gap gauge 2,3 - 2,25	5/46/98	104	1/23/00	414 S Lawrence	0000

Figure 22.1 Tool and gauge record

- External certifications (such as those obtained from UKAS) are maintained and recorded.
- Documented procedures are up to date.

The department operating the calibration service should be responsible for identifying and recording all the equipment in the organization (as described earlier) and for confirming that it is in acceptable condition. They should introduce control procedures via written instructions (see Figure 22.1, for example).

The process of checking and maintaining the accuracy of equipment generally falls into one of three categories:

1 electrical
2 mechanical
3 in-house automatic test equipment (ATE) for measuring electrical and/or mechanical properties; this category includes the software required for all computer-assisted hardware.

Further subdivisions of test equipment categories provide a guide to the appropriate calibration checks. Examples are:

- test equipment used where the actual measured results are of significance for verification to the customer (this equipment would be fully calibrated against national standards)
- test equipment used for output of measured quantities, such as power supplies and signal generators
- meters for indication only, and needing no accuracy
- equipment that it is not practicable to measure, such as VDUs, lamps or switches.

Checking and calibrating should be conducted against published standards wherever possible. For example, methods of test and calibration will be found in BS 6468, BS 870, BS 1734 or BS 959 for various types of micrometers. There are many other British Standard specifications for other types of measuring equipment; however other standards, such as the German DIN, International or other European standards, may be referred to if a British Standards specification has not been produced. Suppliers' literature and regulations are also potential sources for the specification of metrological characteristics.

Calibration environment

It is usual to isolate the checking and calibration services from the workshop, to improve environmental control, ensure the security and stability of its measuring equipment and electrical supplies, and keep the error attributable to calibration as small as possible. In most areas of measurement, this should be no more than one-third, and preferably one-tenth, of the permissible error of the confirmed equipment when in use.

The temperature should be maintained at 20°C or 23°C ± 1°C or 2°C, with a relative humidity of 40–60 per cent, depending on the accuracy class of the instruments (see the appropriate British Standards for reference conditions). Environmental control is particularly important for electrical instrument calibration. A controlled ambient temperature of 20°C is very common in Britain, but there is a trend for international standards to be referenced to 23°C, which provides a better working environment and is in line with the standards more easily maintainable in other climates.

It is usual to carry out calibration under reference conditions. However, where operating conditions differ significantly from these reference conditions, calibration can be carried out under appropriate values; otherwise, allowance is made for the difference.

CALIBRATION FREQUENCY

The interval between calibrations should be agreed between the user and the inspection authority. It must be reviewed regularly to take account of changing circumstances. The user indicates the rate or degree of use, and the inspector correlates this with the intrinsic reliability of the item.

The frequency of checking and/or recalibration must be decided with reference to the intrinsic stability of the equipment being checked, the accuracy specified for the measuring equipment and the degree of use. ISO 10012 Part 1 is recommended for its guidelines, which are based on OIML International Document No. 10.

The UKAS register lists organizations offering services for checking inspection, measurement, testing or calibration, to avoid costly additional investment, but the requirements to keep records mentioned above are still appropriate. It is possible for companies providing a calibration service and obtaining UKAS accreditation for their own purposes to offer their services elsewhere to workshops not having their own facilities.

Some instruments need periodic rechecking only in the restricted sense of checking to ensure that they are functioning. A very useful check that a measuring instrument continues to measure correctly, particularly on a specific manufacturing operation, is obtained by using a checking measurement standard applied to the instrument by the user. This will demonstrate whether the instrument is still functioning correctly at the values and conditions of the check. The checking standard must be simple and robust in order to be reliable, and must in no way be regarded as a substitute for regular calibration.

CALIBRATION OF SPECIAL-PURPOSE EQUIPMENT

There are instances where calibration turnaround time or some other specialized requirement demands special-purpose equipment in the laboratory. A process might take one or two hours using conventional methods, but is possible within only a few minutes with purpose-designed equipment.

Such special equipment, even though it is maintained and guaranteed to be accurate within the essential limits, might not be obtainable with the necessary UKAS accreditation because of its source of manufacture. It cannot, therefore, subsequently be used to provide UKAS certification because of the loss of first-generation traceability to national standards. In-house-designed and -manufactured inspection equipment is in the same category.

Equipment without UKAS certification may be used for calibrating production tools, but it should not be used for calibrating measurement references such as slip gauges or surface tables unless some other assurance is available. In some cases, foreign or international standards are used as references. 'Proprietary' certification rather than UKAS certification may be offered on the basis of alternative assurances, although this might not be as readily accepted by third-party auditors.

The design and production as well as the use of in-house automatic test equipment should be controlled within the company's quality system, taking account of any in-built measuring gauges or instrumentation. Occasionally, specialized equipment is checked by specialist functions such as the chemical laboratory or photographic department. Any or all of these may be approved in-house facilities or subcontracted services selected from the UKAS approved list.

The extent and regularity of checks on things such as electrical supplies, substances in use and equipment should be specified by the supervisor. Equipment subjected to checks such as earthing must be identified with a label stating the date of the check and the void date. In the case of electrical equipment, this is a requirement of the Electrical Safety at Work Regulations 1989. The user of the equipment should be advised not to use equipment beyond its void date. In the case of particularly hazardous equipment, a 'permit to work' may be needed, forbidding access to such hazards without prior instruction and permission.

Control discipline

While it is the responsibility of management to establish control procedures within a quality system, the user must taken responsibility for ensuring that the equipment in use is in a satisfactory condition and within the calibration period. Users must be educated to report any suspected deficiencies.

Any equipment that has passed its due recalibration date (which must be marked on the equipment) or which does not carry an official registration label or identification mark must be declared unfit for use. Anyone found knowingly using such 'illegal' equipment should be liable to disciplinary procedures.

Records

The procedure for recording all existing equipment, addition of new equipment and the disposal of surplus or worn-out tools must be regularized.

All tools and equipment must be identified uniquely. The calibration of each must also be clear and traceable. Often, the means of identifying the calibration status of an instrument is to affix a calibration label showing the 'calibration void' date. Access to adjustable devices can be sealed with a tamper-proof label that must be torn before further adjustment can be made (see Figure 22.2).

In situations where the label could easily be destroyed or damaged, the tool may have

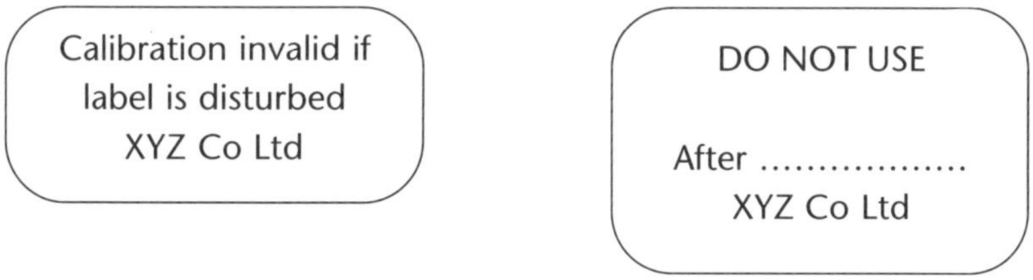

Calibration invalid if
label is disturbed
XYZ Co Ltd

DO NOT USE

After ....
XYZ Co Ltd

Figure 22.2 Calibration label

to be engraved. Alternatively, the calibration status may be shown by means of appropriate documentation, such as calibration records or instrument log sheets. The important point here is that the user has direct and immediate access to the calibration status, and that the risk of using an instrument that is beyond its 'calibration void' date is minimized.

Equipment used for making critical measurements must come under the scope of the calibration scheme. In this context, a critical measurement is one that is used to determine whether an item meets the 'fitness for use' requirements. Many measurements are made which do not fall into the category, either because they relate to characteristics that do not affect the ability of the item to function perfectly, or there is a further test later which fully identifies any defects. In both situations, the non-calibration of such instruments can be justified, even if not recommended. Calibration can be an expensive business, and as always, it boils down to a balance between cost and benefit. No equipment used for critical measurement or tests in the organization must be allowed to slip through the net. The thoroughness demanded in the identification, traceability, and record keeping indicates a preference for a centralized control system in any organization. There are computer systems and proprietary software available that have been designed for this purpose.

A system for controlling the calibration of inspection tools and equipment should provide a master file detailing:

- a short description of the item
- a reference code or serial number
- the name of the holder
- the permanent location (and temporary location, if the item is available for loan)
- date first used
- calibration department responsible for checking
- frequency of calibration
- date received for calibration
- time needed to calibrate
- date last calibrated
- calibration period
- previous history
- return from checking date
- status (in use, lost or missing, bonded, for repair, temporarily out of the factory, and so forth).

An active system is essential, because updating must be regular. Obviously, it should record all design laboratory and production equipment. It should also include spares and personal measuring equipment (such as micrometers purchased by individuals for their own use). An organization might or might not authorize the use of personal equipment, but if it does, the equipment must be controlled under the same system as company-owned tools.

The records system should be structured on a comprehensive coding system that embraces all equipment in use. It should include arrangements for issuing regular reminders to users that equipment is approaching 'calibration void' date. The system should, on demand, provide data on items overdue, recalibration date, calibrated items held at particular locations, and the condition or useful life expectancy. The procedure should provide for scheduling the calibration internally or externally, and should act as a recording system for the loan of items away from their usual locations.

Queries from a computerized control system might either be selective and immediate from the computer screen for questions relating to a particular item, or programmed to output on paper or cards for weekly recalibration notices (see Figure 22.3).

Computer networking enables further development of the control system by allowing the responsibility for maintaining equipment to be allocated locally to charge-hands or foremen. They can assess the centralized computer database directly in order to check the status of tools in use within their areas, so counteracting some of the inertia of a centrally operated system.

Archives and records can be in the form of manuscript, microfilm or any electronic or magnetic medium. Those concerned with principal measurement standards might have to be retained indefinitely, but there are no specified rules for the minimum period of retention other than the purchaser's requirements and regulatory factors covering manufacturers' liabilities. All reasonable steps must be taken to ensure that records cannot be destroyed inadvertently, for example to avoid loss through operator error or computer system failure whenever computer files are being updated or backed up.

Storage

Inspection and test equipment should be kept in special racks which provide stable and secure storage, and prevent accidental damage. The storekeeper must ensure that all items in store are within calibration date. He or she must record any items taken out on loan, not only for security purposes, but also to ensure that they are traceable for recalibration.

Any damage sustained in storage or use must be reported. The damaged item should be checked and, if necessary, rectified and recalibrated or, if necessary, replaced.

Special environmental conditions are not usually necessary for working tools and equipment. Users of the equipment should be reminded, perhaps by a prominent notice at the stores counter, that measuring and inspection tools have to be treated with respect at all times, which includes guarding against accidental damage during temporary storage when not in actual use and overnight.

Items of equipment that become surplus to requirements or rendered obsolete should (if worthy of retention) be placed in a secure bonded store under the control of a person who will ensure that the store is kept locked. All items in this store should be clearly labelled as 'bonded' and showing the date of bonding. Items should only be released under authorized conditions, ensuring in particular that those items to be disposed of are not reintroduced into the production system.

Reminder Card

YD500B TOOLS AND GAUGES RECALIBRATION SCHEDULE RUN DATE: 6 07 01

DEPT 414
NAME: R. STOREY

PREVIOUS REFERENCE DATE REQ D WW YY
1 18 01

TOOL NUMBER DESCRIPTION CAL COMPLETE
AI 678 330 01 TORQUE DRIVER HAND
DATE TO CAL DEPT:

OVERDUE CARD

YD500B TOOLS AND GAUGES RECALIBRATION SCHEDULE RUN DATE: 05 08 01

DEPT 414
NAME: R. STOREY

PREVIOUS REFERENCE DATE REQ D WW YY
7 26 00

TOOL NUMBER DESCRIPTION CAL COMPLETE
AA 827 126 01 PYROMETER
DATE TO CAL DEPT: REASON FOR OVERDUE:

OVERDUE

INSTRUCTIONS

1 GIVE THIS REMINDER CARD AND THE EQUIPMENT TO THE CALIBRATING DEPARTMENT.

2 FOR ITEMS WHOSE NUMBERS START WITH 6, CHECK THE EQUIPMENT YOURSELF, SIGN THE CARD, AND RETURN IT TO THE INSPECTION OFFICE.

3 THROW AWAY ALL 'OVERDUE' CARDS EXCEPT THOSE DELIVERED THIS WEEK.

4 WRITE THE REASON FOR THE OVERDUE ON THE CARD, AND RETURN IT TO THE INSPECTION OFFICE.

IT IS THE USER'S RESPONSIBILITY TO ENSURE THAT TEST OR MEASURING EQUIPMENT IS IN CALIBRATION.

Figure 22.3 Computer-produced reminder and overdue cards, showing also the reverse side

Education and training

The results from all measuring and testing, including customer satisfaction surveys and questionnaires, need to be examined to ensure that they are valid and reliable. An important factor in lending confidence to these results is the competence of the relevant staff, at all levels. This demands training in the proper use of equipment and in the application of control procedures for the calibration and maintenance of all measuring and testing equipment.

Training operators to perform specific tasks is essential to attaining quality and maintaining their quality awareness. The way in which tasks and operations affect quality can be identified, and the individuals' training needs can be set against these requirements as being required for satisfactory performance.

General quality education programmes can heighten quality awareness, but it is also necessary to plan and organize appropriate specific training on the use of metrological or test equipment. The extent of the training and levels of achievement must be recorded in an easily retrievable form so that records can be updated and gaps in training identified. After-sales service should also be considered, and training arrangements made for commissioning and repair workers.

Use of automatic test equipment (ATE)

Any proposal to develop or purchase automatic test equipment is best considered early in the product design phase, so that the design and test specifications are considered jointly, and appropriate test points, input and output facilities can be built into the product. This approach will allow the test equipment to be comprehensive, compact and self-contained with all the necessary testing performed as part of the production process.

Much of the new technology can be usefully employed to facilitate foolproof testing. For instance, visual display units (VDUs) can be used to display test prompts and calibration results and to prohibit further progress if satisfactory results are not obtained. The computer can store the results, and where relevant, reformat them to suit the customer's specification.

Such equipment provides a good example of the need for various calibration control systems to verify the electrical reference sources, the computer hardware and the computer software. In-house test equipment must itself meet all the conditions already listed in this chapter covering calibration and control.

If a company is designing its own test equipment, then the design procedures must also be consistent with the quality system procedures for product design in terms of control of design, purchasing, production, test and documentation.

Customized test equipment purchased from an outside supplier must be specified as if it were conventional measuring equipment, demanding conformity with national standards, traceability of references and certified calibration. The control and calibration should be consistent with all other measuring equipment in the organization.

The software for computer-controlled equipment should itself be recorded. In particular, records should be kept of the supplier's name and address, the title of the software, the version and date of issue, and any identification serial number. It may also be relevant to register with the owner of the software for information on upgrades.

Companies regularly using or creating software should seek TickIT accreditation incorporated into an ISO 9001 assessment.

Further reading

AQAP 7 (NATO), *Guide for the Evaluation of a Contractor's Measurement and Calibration System.*

ISO 9000: 2000, *Quality Management Systems – Fundamentals and Vocabulary.*

ISO 9001: 2000, *Quality Systems – Requirements.*

ISO 9001: 2000, *Quality Management Systems – Requirements.*

ISO 10012-1: *Quality Assurance Requirements for Measuring Equipment Part 1: Metrological Qualification System for Measuring Equipment* (same as BS 5781).

ISO/IEC Guide 43: 1997, *Proficiency Testing by Interlaboratory Comparison.*

OIML International Document No. 10, *Guidelines for the Determination of Recalibration Intervals of Measuring Equipment used in Testing Laboratories.*

OIML International Document No. 16, *Principles of Assurance of Metrological Control.*

CHAPTER

23 Metrology

Joyce Brick

This chapter is concerned with the role of measurement in assuring quality, and with the national measurement system available in the UK for achieving and verifying quality. The considerable extent of the UK measurement industry will be indicated, both in terms of its scale and in terms of the range of facilities provided. It will also be shown that, just as measurement plays a vital part in assuring quality, so equally the principles of quality assurance can themselves be applied to the conduct of the measurement process. Emphasis will be placed on the fact that measurement technology cannot be static, but must develop apace with (indeed, ahead of) the changing needs of industry. And it will be shown that, increasingly, the development of measurement technology must be a co-operative enterprise, both nationally between government and industry, and internationally between laboratories and authorities in different countries.

Some definitions

A variety of definitions of the term 'measurement' can be found in national and international vocabularies, and in technical glossaries throughout the world. While the various definitions differ in detail, they all convey the basic idea that measurement is the process of assigning a value to a given physical quantity, such as the length of a rod, the temperature of a furnace, and the electrical resistance of a heating element.

Like measurement, the term 'quality' is also the subject of a variety of definitions. Again, fortunately, most definitions convey the same general idea: in this case the notion that quality is the capability of a product (or a service) to meet or exceed someone's legitimate expectation. The expectation may be that of a consumer, or of a manufacturer, or it may be that of a retailer who passes a product from manufacturer to consumer. Equally, it may be the expectation of a regulatory body that is concerned, say, with the electrical safety of a class of domestic or industrial products.

An expectation can be a mainly qualitative one (for example, a connoisseur's expectation of a wine's body and bouquet), or it may be a quantitative expectation (such as that of an excise inspector concerned with the alcohol content of that same wine). Where an expectation is quantitative, it can be formalized in a written technical specification such as a British Standard (BS) specification, an International Standard specification (ISO), or more locally as a manufacturer's or a purchaser's own in-house specification. This chapter is concerned with the application of measurement to achieving quality, in the sense of a specified quantitative expectation.

The role of measurement in achieving quality

The most obvious and familiar way in which measurement is involved in product quality is through the testing of products against a relevant specification, after completion of manufacture. The tests may be carried out on every product or on selected samples of the product; they may be conducted by the manufacturer or a purchasing body, or by a representative of consumer or legislative interests. Further, similar tests may be performed during a product's life on the shelf or in service, to monitor its continuing compliance with its specification.

While testing of the completed product may be the most obvious intervention of measurement into product quality, the role of measurement can begin much earlier in a product's life. In many cases, tests are carried out during manufacture, on the partially assembled product or on key components, to ensure that the manufacturing process is going as planned, and to enable any necessary process adjustments to be made. On-line analysis or measurement is common to check for compliance with specification – the penalty for postponing deficiency detection until after a production run has been completed can be catastrophic.

Measurement will often also play a part in other less direct ways during production. An example is provided by the close monitoring and control of environmental conditions that are necessary in the manufacture of certain sophisticated electronic products or components.

For many or most types of products, the measurement process will have made a significant impact even before manufacture commences. One example arises in the testing of models or prototypes, in order to predict performance of planned products, or to demonstrate their compliance with legal requirements such as those arising from environmental or weights and measures legislation.

More generally, the development and installation of manufacturing equipment will have entailed detailed prior measurement activities or considerations; this is necessary in order to ensure that the equipment concerned operates within the tolerances necessary to yield an end-product that meets the intended design or performance characteristics. It is not practicable to establish a manufacturing facility of any appreciable technical sophistication without planning one's measurement requirements well in advance and taking account of the technical (and economic) constraints arising from measurement considerations.

So far, the emphasis has been on the application of measurement to achieving product quality, leading to industrial competitiveness, consumer protection and related benefits. However, measurement has a vital part to play in enhancing quality in the more global sense of quality of life. In the medical field, measurement contributes, for example, to diagnosis and treatment through tissue analysis, radiography and tomography, and automatic monitoring of patients in intensive care. Also, our everyday environment is made safer and more pleasant through the monitoring of land, air and water (seas, rivers and reservoirs) for unacceptable levels of pollutants. Measurement is important in safeguarding us from dangerous levels of radiation in and around the workplace, or at home. Crime is detected, solved, and ultimately discouraged or prevented, by measurement carried out in the course of forensic investigation.

Measurement is used to combat counterfeiting and fraud. In the form of blood alcohol analysis and vehicle speed monitoring, it helps to make our roads safer. In the field of national security, advanced measurement is indispensable in the detection and guidance systems intended to safeguard the integrity of our frontiers.

Some of the principal direct users of measurement services are listed in Table 23.1. The full number of those using and depending on measurement, in its various forms, is legion. Most aspects of daily life are touched by measurement in one way or another. Materials for the clothing we wear are tested for shrink-resistance, colour-fastness and durability. Petrol is accurately metered when we purchase it from our local filling station. The food we eat, the beverages we drink, even the air we breathe, are subjected to testing. We live from day to day in a 'sea of measurement' of which most individuals are, for the most part, not aware.

The role of government

For those who rely on the results of measurement in the achievement of quality, it is vital not simply to have access to an adequate range of testing and other services, but also that the measurements are performed competently and with appropriate accuracy. The UK government recognizes the need for organizations and individuals throughout the UK to be able to place confidence in the results of measurement, and accepts it as a government responsibility to promote the conditions for reliable measurement at all levels.

Government policy on measurement is implemented through the Department of Trade and Industry (DTI), and most notably through the Department's National Physical Laboratory (NPL), which is the UK's national measurement standards laboratory. (NPL is currently operated on behalf of the DTI by NPL Management Ltd, a wholly owned subsidiary of Serco Group plc.) The National Engineering Laboratory and the Laboratory of the Government Chemist have the responsibility for flow and chemical metrology.

The original requirements were for the basic units of mass, length, time, temperature and electricity. Over the years, industry has needed standards in new fields, for example colour, ulatrasonics, fibre-optics and microelectronics, and the programme of work at NPL has developed in response to these requirements. Today, many standards are related to atomic phenomena which are the same wherever measured. For example, the metre is no longer realized by a platinum–iridium bar, but by very precise laser systems which are capable of accuracies of a few parts in 100 000 million. The only base unit which is now defined by an artefact is the standard of mass – the kilogram – and NPL is working towards a new definition of the kilogram which could be reproduced by any suitably equipped laboratory. NPL's work is of vital strategic importance to the country's present and future measurement needs. NPL serves the future by developing the new and more accurate and more economic measurement standards and measurement methods that will be demanded by new and evolving technologies.

Table 23.1 Some organizations requiring measurement

- Government departments – regulations, defence, forensic, and so on
- Procurement bodies – compliance with specifications
- Manufacturers – quality control, compliance and specifications
- Health services – analytical services, safety of equipment, therapy services
- Consumers – safety tests, compliance with specifications
- Certification bodies – correctness of test data for certification of products
- Contracting bodies – compliance with specifications

NPL's core skills are:

- acoustic metrology
- dimensional metrology
- electromagnetic metrology
- environmental measurement
- fundamental metrology
- ionizing radiation metrology
- materials measurement and technology
- mechanical metrology (including mass and density, force, pressure)
- optical metrology
- software engineering
- thermal metrology
- time metrology.

NPL's services include:

- consultancy
- contract research
- collaborative projects
- technology and knowledge transfer
- test and calibration
- transfer standards and reference materials
- training.

There are two principal ways in which the government strategically influences current metrology in the UK. The first is through the work of NPL measurement centres, which maintain the UK national standards of measurement and disseminate these by calibration to industry, commerce, health, defence and other fields, thereby providing the basis for national *measurement traceability*. NPL issues approximately 5000 calibration certificates to its customers annually. The second way is through the activities of the United Kingdom Accreditation Service (UKAS), which assesses and accredits laboratories, thereby providing the basis for national *measurement assurance*. The activities of UKAS are described later in this chapter.

Measurement traceability and measurement assurance

It may be helpful at this stage to digress briefly in order to explain the distinction between the notions of measurement traceability and measurement assurance mentioned earlier.

If asked what is the principal factor influencing the accuracy of a measurement, most metrologists are likely to answer, quite correctly, that the accuracy of the measuring equipment is the most significant determining factor. The way to establish the accuracy of an item of measuring equipment is to test that equipment, in the appropriate way, using a more accurate measuring instrument; or, phrased in specialist metrological terminology, to calibrate the equipment against a measurement standard. (Calibration is, quite simply, the testing of metrological characteristics of measuring equipment.)

The accuracy of the measurement standard concerned may in turn be established, in a similar way, by calibration of the standard against a higher, more accurate standard, and so on, through an unbroken chain of calibrations, stretching back to the national measurement standards held at NPL. This ability to relate the properties of an item of measuring equipment through an unbroken chain of calibrations, back to a national measurement standard, is known as *measurement traceability*. A simple example of a traceability chain, for length measurement, is shown in Figure 23.1.

The national measurement standards held at NPL form the anchor for traceability chains serving different levels and sectors throughout the UK (see Figure 23.2).

Standard	Calibration chain	Uncertainty
	Definition of the unit of length	
NPL primary standard	Iodine-stabilized helium–neon laser	<3 in 10^{11}
NPL working standards	Stabilized lasers	<1 in 10^{8}
Accredited calibration laboratory standards	Reference-grade gauge blocks	1 in 10^{6}
Industrial metrology standards	Laboratory-standard gauge blocks	1 in 10^{5}
Shop floor	Micrometers, transducers, and so on	1 in 10^{4}

Figure 23.1 Traceability chain for length measurements

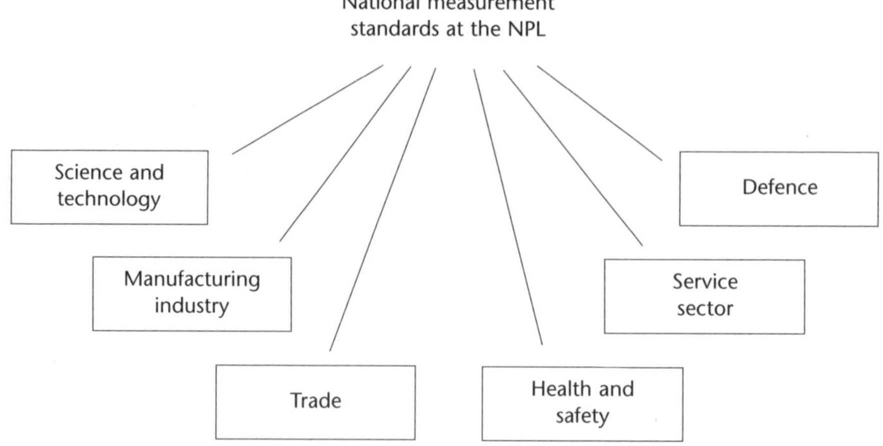

Figure 23.2 How National Physical Laboratory measurements serve the UK

Traceability of measurement is essential if accuracy of measurement is to be assigned meaningfully, and if measurements made on different instruments or at different times and locations are to be combined validly or compared successfully with like devices.

While traceability of measurement is essential to the accuracy of measurements, a number of other important considerations can significantly influence the credibility of a measurement result. For example, it is possible for a laboratory to possess accurate equipment, properly calibrated, but for the laboratory's measurements to be carried out with the equipment (or the object to be measured) at the wrong temperature, or the item to be measured may be incorrectly prepared (inadequate surface finish, for example), or may be confused with another similar item, say through inadequate labelling. An incorrect or out-of-date measurement procedure may be used. Measurement staff may be insufficiently skilled, supervised or briefed in their tasks. Staff may be subject to organizational or operational pressures that impair their judgement. Even where a measurement has been carried out satisfactorily, its usefulness may be undermined due to the result being reported or recorded in an ambiguous or misleading way. A list of major factors influencing the credibility of a laboratory's measurements is given in Table 23.2.

Only when authenticated measurement traceability exists and when a laboratory has proper control over all other aspects influencing credibility can there be proper measurement assurance, giving overall confidence in a laboratory's capability to produce correct measurement results. It is the purpose of UKAS to provide measurement assurance within the UK, by assessing laboratories and awarding accreditation (that is, formal recognition of competence) to those demonstrating measurement traceability and proper control over all relevant aspects of laboratory responsibility and activity.

In order to help locate laboratory accreditation more clearly within the overall context

Table 23.2 Factors affecting credibility

- Nature of equipment
- Measurement traceability
- Calibration schedule
- Maintenance
- Protection of equipment
- Environmental control
- Staff expertise
- Allocation of responsibilities
- Supervision
- Sample preparation
- Sample protection
- Sample identification
- Measurement method
- Measurement records
- Reporting results
- Organizational pressures
- Control of subcontracted work
- Documentation
- Quality audit
- Management review

of quality assurance in general, let us return briefly to consider the manufacturing process. Manufacture can be considered to be the application of a sequence of operations or processes to basic raw materials. To ensure acceptable quality in the finished product, it is necessary to achieve a corresponding level of quality in each of the processes constituting the manufacturing processes. (Looked at in this way, the notion of quality assurance for processes could be considered as more fundamental than that of product quality assurance.) Measurement is just one of the processes, albeit a very important one, involved in manufacture, and the laboratory accreditation activities of UKAS consist largely in the application of accepted quality assurance principles to the measurement process.

The operation of UKAS

Laboratories that wish to be accredited by UKAS, and that believe they can meet the necessary requirements, submit a formal application to UKAS. Applicant laboratories are visited in due course by skilled UKAS assessors, and are assessed against an international standard covering the responsibilities and activities mentioned above. This international standard is ISO/IEC 17025, *General Requirements for the Competence of Testing and Calibration Laboratories*. Laboratories meeting the criteria are awarded accreditation; they are listed, together with the tests or calibrations for which they hold accreditation, in the UKAS *Directory of Accredited Laboratories*; accredited laboratories are permitted to display the UKAS mark on relevant test reports or calibration certificates, and on their company notepaper.

Maintenance of accreditation by UKAS is conditional upon laboratories continuing to comply with the criteria in ISO/IEC 17025; UKAS assessors visit laboratories annually following accreditation, to ensure that these criteria continue to be met.

UKAS is a private non-profit-distributing company which is recognized by the UK's DTI as the national body responsible for providing national accreditation of laboratories, certification and inspection bodies. Accreditation is voluntary, and Table 23.3 lists some of the principal advantages that UKAS accreditation may be considered to confer on laboratories.

These are all benefits that relate directly to an accredited laboratory's increased confidence in the accuracy and validity of its calibration or test results. That laboratories and their customers perceive these to be real practical benefits is shown by the large number of laboratories that hold UKAS accreditation for various types of testing and calibration.

UKAS-accredited laboratories include independent testing and calibration laboratories,

Table 23.3 Benefits of accreditation

- Confidence in test results
- Confidence in management system
- Confidence in quality system
- Improvement in testing capability
- Provides assurance of the traceability of measurements
- Reduction in multiple assessments
- Wide acceptance of UKAS certificates in UK
- International acceptance of UKAS certificates

as well as laboratories that form part of larger organizations including government departments, public corporations, research and educational establishments, and manufacturing companies.

The fields of calibration and testing served as UKAS-accredited laboratories are shown in Table 23.4.

Accredited measurements range from classical electrical and dimensional calibration, with an accuracy of 1 part in 10^6, to testing thermal insulation and strength of concrete, with rather less exacting accuracy demands of a few per cent. The scheme covers fields as widely diverse as electrical safety testing, chemical analysis and computer software validation.

UKAS enjoys a considerable measure of support throughout all sections of industry and government, being recognized by manufacturing, certification and regulatory bodies, and by major procurement organizations in both public and private sectors. Like the list of accredited laboratories, the list of support organizations continues to increase over time, as the advantages of using accredited laboratories are recognized, and as the technical scope for the scheme grows.

Securing the acceptance of UKAS-accredited test reports and calibration certificates abroad, as well as at home, is regarded as very important in breaking down technical barriers to trade. UKAS-accredited calibration certificates and test reports are, in fact, widely accepted

Table 23.4 UKAS fields of calibration and testing

Calibration	*Testing*
Electrical measurements: d.c. and l.f.	Acoustic
Electrical measurements: r.f. and microwave	Ballistic
Dimensional measurements	Biological
Fluids: flow, pressure, viscosity and density measurements	Chemical analysis
	Corrosion
Optical measurements	Dimensional testing
Temperature measurements	Electrical product
Radiological measurements	Electromagnetic compatibility
Chemical analysis and reference materials	Environmental
Hardness measurements	Fire
Acoustical measurements	Forensic
Humidity measurements	Geological
Force measurements	Health and hygiene
Accelerometry measurements	Information technology
Magnetic flux measurements	Ionizing radiation
Fibre-optic measurements	Mechanical
Mass measurements	Metallurgical
	Microbiological
	Non-destructive testing
	Performance testing
	Physical
	Safety
	Sampling
	Sensory

in many overseas countries on account of the excellent reputation enjoyed by the scheme. Some 700 000 calibration certificates are issued by UKAS-accredited calibration laboratories annually.

UKAS participates in the activities of the European Co-operation for Accreditation (EA) and the International Laboratory Accreditation Co-operation (ILAC).

The European Co-operation for Accreditation covers accreditation in all fields of conformity assessment activities. The EA plays a key part in eliminating technical barriers to trade by working to ensure that reports or certificates issued by accredited laboratories are recognized in all other member states. This is done through the signing of a Multilateral Agreement (see below).

At the global level, the equivalent organization is the International Laboratory Accreditation Co-operation. Its objective is to ensure that international standards are applied consistently, so that nationally accredited certificates are accepted throughout the world – thereby facilitating the passage of goods and services in international trade.

Agreements with accreditation bodies in other countries

It is UKAS policy to negotiate agreements with other national accreditation bodies through the international and regional accreditation networks. These agreements recognize the equivalence of the accreditation granted in the countries concerned, and are referred to as Multilateral Agreements (MLAs). Each signatory to the EA MLA promises to:

- accept the other accreditation schemes operated by other signatories as equivalent to their own scheme(s)
- recognize these on an equal basis with its own the certificates and/or reports from the organizations accredited by the signatories under their schemes.

The MLAs have been reached as a result of a formal, detailed evaluation of each of the accreditation body's policies and procedures and the criteria used, and by observation of assessment and surveillance visits. These evaluations are performed by a team of experts in the relevant area of accreditation.

Mutual recognition agreements between countries that are not members of the EA and the EA MLA also operate on a bilateral basis where there is no framework for multilateral agreement. Each country is required to sign a contract of co-operation with EA, and is evaluated in the same manner as EA signatories. The list of countries participating in MLAs may be found via the UKAS Web site.

Future measurement needs

Measurement does not remain static, nor can national metrology institutes afford to do so. As the apex of the UK national measurement system, NPL must foresee the future measurement needs of UK industry, and must respond by evolving more advanced measurement standards and by developing or promoting the new and more economical measurement techniques that will be required to keep UK industry competitive. It is not sufficient to await the development of an industrial need before initiating research on a measurement problem: to do so would be a recipe for industrial obsolescence. As part of a research programme, NPL metrologists are continually investigating the possibility of new methods in the various disciplines of physical measurement. NPL also co-operates internationally with other national measurement institutes (NMIs).

International co-operation

The scale and sophistication of today's technology have made increased international co-operation a necessity for large industrial projects. The measurement industry is not immune to similar pressures. Even in well-established measurement fields, the wisdom of pooling resources is evident.

In 1987, the European Collaboration in Measurement Standards (EUROMET) was established by a Memorandum of Understanding between the NMIs in western Europe to promote the co-ordination of metrological activities and services with the purpose of achieving higher efficiency. The current members are Austria, Belgium, Commission of the European Communities, Czech Republic, Denmark, Finland, France, Germany, Greece, Hungary, Iceland, Ireland, Italy, Luxembourg, the Netherlands, Norway, Poland, Portugal, Slovak Republic, Slovenia, Spain, Sweden, Switzerland, Turkey and the United Kingdom.

The aims of EUROMET are to:

- encourage co-operation in the development of national standards and measuring methods
- make optimum use of resources and services
- improve measurement facilities and make them accessible to all members.

To achieve these aims, EUROMET works in ten subject fields through four types of collaboration.

The fields are:

- mass and related quantities
- electricity and magnetism
- length
- time and frequency
- thermometry
- ionizing radiation
- photometry and radiometry
- flow
- acoustics, ultrasound and vibration
- amount of substance.

The types of collaboration are:

- co-operation in research
- comparison of measurement standards
- traceability
- consultation on facilities.

EUROMET focuses its efforts on:

- ensuring that the co-ordinated European measurement infrastructure meets all Europe's industrial needs
- supporting and serving its member in their endeavours to serve their customers better
- participating in inter-laboratory comparisons for the world-wide recognition of its measurement standards
- strengthening the collaboration with other regional metrology organizations and the BIPM (see below).

EUROMET and UK industry

EUROMET aims to improve the overall provision of measurement standards in Europe with the purpose of achieving higher efficiency. In many areas, those using NPL calibration services will be unaffected by this initiative in their day-to-day dealing with the NPL. However, for industry, NPL's EUROMET participation will mean that:

- Measurement standards to support emerging technologies will be available more quickly and be widely acceptable in European markets.
- Improvements to existing measurement standards should be more speedily implemented.
- It will be possible to designate primary standards for the UK for quantities where previously no national standards have existed.
- In some areas, other European countries will now be looking to the UK for primary standards and for calibrations at the highest level of accuracy.
- In other areas, the UK will be devolving the responsibility for maintaining a primary standard to another European laboratory which will also provide calibrations at the highest level of accuracy.

EUROMET is just one of a growing number of regional metrology organizations (RMOs), all of which play an important role on the world scene, and particularly the implementation of the recently signed Mutual Recognition Arrangement (MRA).

Global metrology and the MRA

Global metrology is based on an international diplomatic treaty, the Metre Convention, signed in 1875. The treaty established the International Bureau of Weights and Measures (BIPM), the International Committee for Weights and Measures (CIPM) and the General Conference on Weights and Measures (CGPM). The CGPM, which meets every four years, is an assembly of the 48 member states of the Metre Convention. It discusses and agrees on the arrangements to ensure the propagation and improvement of the International System of Units (SI). The CIPM meets annually and makes detailed proposals to the CGPM. The CIPM is, in effect, the world's top metrology body, and is the ultimate authority and technical reference. NPL sits on the CIPM and on all 10 of the Consultative Committees (CCs) which cover the various fields of measurement. The CCs provide detailed recommendations to the CIPM.

The CIPM also oversees the work of the BIPM. The BIPM is an international laboratory situated in France which, together with the major NMIs in the world, carries out work leading to world-wide agreement on units of measurement and the practical provision of accurate measurement standards.

For many years, the credibility and confidence in measurements world-wide have been based on the results of international comparisons of the major NMIs' primary measurement standards and on a detailed knowledge of their skills. The MRA was developed to establish a more formal basis for this confidence. It was necessary as there has been a significant growth in the number of NMIs in the world offering an increasingly wide range of measurement services. The objectives of the MRA are:

- to establish the degree of equivalence of national measurement standards maintained by NMIs
- to provide for the mutual recognition of calibration and measurement certificates issued by NMIs
- thereby to provide governments and other parties with a secure technical foundation for wider agreements related to international trade, commerce and regulatory affairs.

The process by which this is achieved is through:

- international comparisons of measurements, known as Key Comparisons
- supplementary international comparisons of measurement
- quality systems and demonstration of competence by NMIs.

The major outcome will be a statement of the measurement capabilities of each NMI in a database maintained by the BIPM which will be publicly available on the World Wide Web. The BIPM Web address is: <http://www.bipm.fr>.

It will take a few years to include in the database entries for all of the measurement capabilities of the 48 NMIs in the member states of the Metre Convention. NMIs throughout the world are busy carrying out Key Comparisons and familiarizing themselves with the quality systems in other NMIs. In both of these tasks, the RMOs have an important role. In Key Comparisons, for example, a model has been developed whereby the comparisons take place in two stages. In the first stage, two or three NMIs from each RMO will participate in a so-called CIPM Key Comparison. The participating NMIs must have the highest technical competence and experience, and they are normally member laboratories of the appropriate CC. In the second stage, there is a further set of comparisons within each RMO. Those NMIs which participated in the CIPM Key Comparison must participate, and any other NMI in the RMO may nominate itself to participate. In this way, it is possible for all participating NMIs to determine the degree of equivalence of their measurement standards with all of the other NMIs in the world.

Contact points

For information on UKAS accreditation, a list of UKAS-accredited laboratories and a copy of *How to get UKAS Laboratory Accreditation*, contact UKAS: <http://www.ukas.com>.

Detailed scopes of accreditation for UKAS-accredited calibration laboratories may be found at <http://www.ukas.org>.

Technical information may be obtained via e-mail: <technicalenquiries@ukas.com>.

For free and independent advice on techniques, practices and standards for physical measurement, contact the NPL, e-mail: <enquiry@npl.co.uk>.

For advice on flow measurement, contact the National Engineering Laboratory (NEL).

For advice on analytical measurement and reference materials, contact the VAM, e-mail: <vam@lgc.co.uk>.

For advice on legal metrology and mass, length and volume calibration, contact the National Weights and Measures Laboratory (NWML), e-mail: <info@nwml.dti.gov.uk>.

CHAPTER **24**

Quality Audits and Reviews

Gordon Staples

An audit is the means by which management of a company determines whether the people in the organization are carrying out their duties in the way that management intends them to. A review is the means by which management determines whether the organization is being effective in meeting corporate goals (increased customer satisfaction, growing market share, rising profit) and whether the audits carried out are doing their part in monitoring the organization's effectiveness in moving towards those goals.

Reasons for audits

Any business which is going to undertake quality audits needs to make the requirement for audits a clear mandate from the top. It would be expected that the belief in and the authority for audits would be enshrined in the quality policy of the business. In this case, management want audits to be carried out so that they can control operations.

Of course there are other reasons for carrying out audits. All quality standards contain a requirement – explicit in some, implicit in others – that companies conduct audits. However, if carried out for this reason alone, audits are unlikely to be particularly searching or useful. Unfortunately, there are still many companies in which audits are carried out to show that procedures are still slavishly followed, regardless of whether these procedures are contributing to the health of the business. The company may even proudly proclaim that it conducts audits, and the auditors within it may be extremely busy working the prescribed programme of audits and maintaining lots of file space full of audit reports.

To consider the best way to set up an audit system, therefore, it is as well to be clear about why the audit system is wanted and what the company will have, or potentially have, when series of audits have been completed. In order to determine that, it is necessary to consider what the systems are there for, and whether there is a way to think about the systems which allows the needs of the business to be addressed and the audit to be related directly to those needs.

NEEDS OF A BUSINESS

While profit undoubtedly figures very highly when considering what businesses need, it can be appreciated fairly quickly that sustained profit – and particularly increases in profit – can only come from an established base of satisfied customers.

So the organization's main goal is to create and increase this base of happy customers. But there is another step which must be taken. Is the 'customer' always the 'user' of the product? The answer often is a negative one; therefore any business in the marketplace has to determine exactly how its product is going to be used and what expectations the user has of that product. Anything a business can do in order to make its products actually *fitter for use* than those of the competitors will give that business a market edge, provided it can bring those quality characteristics within the perception of the marketplace.

The needs of a business must thus be very closely aligned with the needs of the user/customer.

Having established its needs, the business must decide how it is going to achieve them through its functional divisions and departments. Their duty is to work within that stated policy and provide their own policy, and hence their output, to the requirements developed in line with the policy. Departments within an organization are required to work to timescale, budgets, output targets, capital allocations, and so on. Each department then has to work to conform with the requirements so that the customer/user is supplied with a service which is progressively thought of as excellent. The word 'service' is used deliberately, since every perception which a customer or user has of a product, including the way it was supplied, is going to influence the opinion held about it. *All* businesses are in the service business.

Now, within the business, each of these functional departments is working away to meet the requirements laid down for it, but few departments work in total isolation from the rest of the company. Each is dependent on others for information. In processing areas, one department is dependent on another for the timely receipt of the product in a state *fit for their use*. The same is true for those departments which merely exchange information. These days, it is possible to move and distribute large amounts of data around a company, and it can be painful to identify and extract the little piece of useful information which the package contains.

Therefore, it becomes clear that each department (and ultimately each person in an organization) is at one time or another playing one of three roles. These roles may be considered in any order.

The first role is that of *customer/user*. Other departments supply information or product (often both), so that the user can process it and pass it on to the next user. The departments supplying the input are suppliers. Any customer is entitled to get what is fit for their use, provided, of course, they have told the supplier precisely and unambiguously exactly what is wanted, when it's wanted, and so on.

In passing the product on to the next user, the department concerned is acting in a second role – as a *supplier*. In order to be a good supplier, it should find out what its customer's needs are, and define in conjunction with this customer how quality will be determined. In the ideal situation which is being expounded here, it requires no great intellect to realize that the internal customers and suppliers in a company need to work very closely together in order to cut down the barriers which can exist and which prevent the even flow of fit-for-use product information. Only by working in that way will a satisfactory compromise – which may be necessary – be worked out. Anything which restricts the efficient flow is waste and should be removed. It is termed the 'cost of nonconformity'.

There is also the third role, perhaps the most important – that of *processor*, of fulfilling the function the department or person is employed to carry out. The function can be conducted correctly provided the input for it is correct and fit for conversion to the output. Of course, the process of conversion must be fit for purpose too. Any process is subject to variation. In order to keep a process under control, it is necessary to recognize the variables which are going to prevent the output being achieved. These variables are unwanted inputs.

Now this picture is complete. Every department – no, every *individual* – is at one time or another a supplier, a customer and a processor. If every one of those supplier–customer links is improved one iota, shouldn't the organization be more effective, measured in terms of cost and time? Might it not satisfy the external customer more quickly, more often, and engender that confidence which customers like so much – perhaps with an edge over the competition?

That's what quality is about. That's where audits and reviews should be aimed. If audits and reviews do not instigate more benefit than they cost, then their effectiveness must be questioned.

The base for setting up a programme for audits is therefore established. It is a strategic position. The implementation consists of planning, of doing, of reporting, of follow-up, and of getting corrective action taken and providing feedback.

Types of audits

Before launching into an audit programme, it is necessary to distinguish between the different types of audits. For example, a customer may audit a supplier against the contract requirements to examine how closely this supplier is working to the agreed contract conditions. This audit may include requirements invested in a quality standard system, such as ISO 9000.

A company may audit a potential supplier against requirements proposed to operate were a contract to be placed. These requirements can be prescribed in suppliers' internal documents, and may include the requirements invested in a quality systems standard.

Audits can obviously take place before, during or after contracts, and are known as external audits, commonly called 'second-party' audits.

A company may carry out audits internally to determine for management purposes how closely the various departments are working to the procedures prescribed for each department. The results of these audits are provided to management for use in determining effectiveness of the company's systems in meeting objectives within current policy.

Such audits are internal audits, and are commonly called 'first-party'. Some organizations subcontract the audit to an outside organization, where an external party comes into the company and audits it against the company's own procedures perhaps because the organization planning the audit is limited in experience and/or resources.

Provided the audit is carried out within the expressed policy and requirements of the company and is not designed by the auditor to lead to more work, perhaps consultancy, then the audit may still be considered as a proper internal audit within the 'intent' of the quality systems of the company.

As far as the subcontracted auditor is concerned, of course, an audit carried out in such a way is an external audit.

There is of course, a third type of audit within the scope of this discussion. The huge number of second party audits which were taking place in the 1960s and 1970s in the industrial world were carried out to differing standards under limited qualification systems for audit practices and auditors. This created a great deal of confusion and was very wasteful of both customers' (auditors) human resources and of suppliers' (the auditees).

In the late 1970s in the UK, it was proposed that all the major second party customers (government-controlled entities in the main) which were carrying out these audits, often on the same suppliers, should get together and agree to share assessment results from each others' audits. If assessments were agreed, then it might reduce the need for different customers to audit the same suppliers. This led to the formation of third party certification bodies. Since 1978 (the first third party audit), the number of third party certification bodies (also known as registration bodies or registrars in the USA) has increased to many hundreds throughout the world.

These companies assess organizations against the relevant quality systems standard, such as ISO 9001. A certificate is provided if the audit's results show compliance. Regular surveillance of the quality system takes place, and regular reassessment is carried out every two or three years. A fee is charged for this service, and the certificate can be withdrawn if continued compliance is not established.

This third-party method is considered to provide customers of the registered companies with confidence about the quality of their services. There is very little objective information available to show whether customers are receiving better services as a result of third-party quality systems certification.

This chapter is concerned with audits, whether first-, second- or third-party. The principles of audit, as far as this author is concerned, apply equally whether the audit is first-, second- or third-party, whether the audit covers environmental systems or quality systems, health and safety, financial, and so on. The focus of this chapter will be quality systems audit.

Internal audits

Many organizations write down their business mission, then their quality policy, then their business objectives in the long and short term, then more detailed procedures for the troops to achieve those objectives. The first three may be thought of as strategy, the last as tactics. Such a hierarchy of documents is often pictured as a triangle (as shown in Figure 24.1).

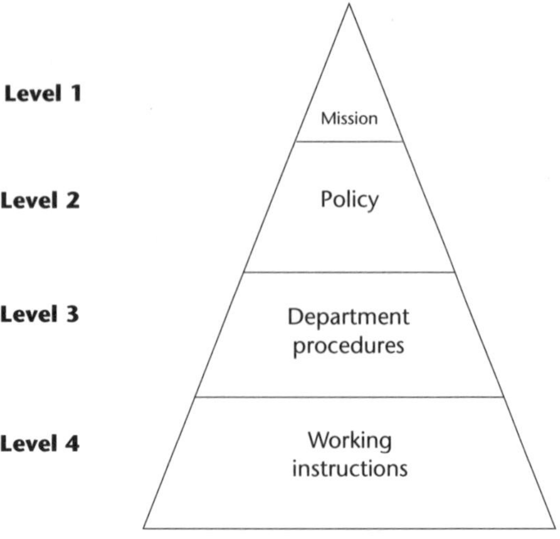

Figure 24.1 Document hierarchy

If the management of an organization sees the need for internal audits in order to check that each step in the hierarchy is operating properly, then it is clear that the need for internal audits should be enshrined in the quality policy (along with the need for relevant corrective actions). Having established this belief from the top of the company, the question must then be asked: 'Who is going to do the audit?'

Definitions of audit nearly always stress the element of independence. Some companies have therefore provided a separate department in the organization to carry out audits. This department exists to audit everyone else. Typically, the quality department gets the job. Some companies which originally organized their audits in this way have been suspicious that the department is not really being as effective as it should be in this respect. Certainly, the correct forms are being filled in at the appropriate times against programmes and schedules of audits, but the same order and types of deficiencies continue to arise. The fault may, of course, lie with the procedures which are being audited. The audit may be doing no more than ensuring that the status quo is being maintained. In these circumstances, it may not be inappropriate to translate 'the status quo' as 'the mess we are in'.

Those companies which originally set up their own independent departments began to ask:

> Why do we have to have these people? They add to our costs without adding value to our product or service and we are only duplicating activities that management throughout the company should be doing in any case.

So these companies began to train their managers, supervisors and specialists in the art of audit. Thus at the very senior level managers were required to ensure that departments got together and established their customer–supplier links. Questions took the form: 'What are the features and characteristics by which one department can measure the performance of another?' Having established the answers, a means of measurement had to be provided for both parties, in quantifiable units (the units may have differed in each case, but to ensure full understanding, they had to be 'translated' into the same units of measurement). Then, within each department, a similar arrangement was set up among sections and people.

It follows from this development that the three basic questions of auditing can be asked at each stage:

1 Is there a way of doing things?
2 Has it been put into practice?
3 Is it effective?

Thus procedures must be documented to the extent necessary to establish the best way of doing things. Then there is the need to show that this is being done, using records. Finally, there must be a measure of whether the effort was worthwhile, via a satisfied 'customer' (who will also keep a record).

An auditing schedule can be established, not very different from traditional schedules in format, but perhaps with an emphasis placed on what the company is in business for. Schedules are illustrated in Figures 24.2 and 24.3.

The operating forces (managers, supervisors and specialists) would decide what the relationships are, what measurements are necessary, how forward communications and feedback will be determined, the timescales for action, and when problems are likely to arise.

Customer department		Supplier's departments →			
Research and development		Marketing	Finance	Administration	Purchasing
Stages ↓	Relationship established				
	Products defined				
	Quality criteria agreed				
	Performance measured				
	Review of system				

Figure 24.2 Internal audit schedule: Suggested content for examining customer–supplier links

Senior management must be determined that these activities be extended throughout the organization. They would therefore initiate reports, perhaps collated and summarized by the quality department. This department has not totally disappeared, but it now provides a service in training for auditing, assistance in problem solving and enables managers to collect relevant data. Thus the quality assurance department has become quality assistance, which is a more useful role. The extent of assurance necessary is left in the hands of the experts, the people employed to do the job, with less need for the 'QA paper chase'.

Based on the triple role model explained earlier, it would first of all be necessary for series of individuals from each pair of interacting departments to have met and for them to have determined the major products and services passed between them – in what specific ways are they customers (users) and suppliers of service, what gives difficulty to the other party, and what improvement opportunities are available. There would need to be measurements made in units agreed by both parties, and a means of recording performance. The two parties in each case will need to review these on a regular basis as the 'products' change.

The basis for the relationship and its functioning would need to be formally defined and agreed, much as a standard procedure might be. In this condition, it can easily be audited.

The audits early in the development of this process would be searching for the existence of a growing number of formal relationships between departments, and subsequent development of waste removal and efficiency improvements.

There are some different possibilities for who carries out the audits. A concept of 'internal second party' might operate, whereby each user audits their suppliers. A concept of internal third party might operate whereby one party audits sets of other users/suppliers. One could maintain an independent department doing the audits – itself audited by the chief executive or nominee. There is no ideal answer to this. It would seem that a combination of these options is likely to prove most effective.

The natural development of this process must lead to whatever the objectives of the organization are. Areas of improvement may be a reduction in staff turnover, in absenteeism

Function/ department	*Month of audit*	*Report issued*	*Corrective actions agreed*	*First follow-up*	*Second follow-up*	*Close-out*
Administration	1	√	√			
Date:						
Mechanical	2	√	√			
Date:						
Electrical	3					
Date:						
Textile	4					
Date:						
Physical	5					
Date:						
Chemistry	6					
Date:						
Metallurgy	9					
Date:						
↓						

Figure 24.3 Internal audit schedule: Traditional style, department by department

and lateness, a cost reduction, an increase in business, a reduction in external complaints/returns/warranty, and so on.

There is something blocking the development process somewhere if some of these things do not happen. The management review of operations is naturally interested in reviewing the effectiveness of the user–supplier process, driven by the ultimate user. Like any management tool requiring careful and prolonged attention, it may be sacrificed on the altar of short-term gains.

There has been considerable discussion about the ability of external bodies, particularly those which are not customers, to determine, by audit, 'effectiveness' of an auditee's quality management system. It is generally accepted that third parties cannot. First-party, and more forward-looking training organizations and their customers have been developing ways of going well beyond compliance (which is the third party's province, anyway – why duplicate the effort?) and driving real improvement in the company towards effectiveness.

One approach is for a company to work to its own set of criteria. Quality systems standards, almost by definition, and definitely in practice, are the lowest minimum standards. Compliance is the basic level. The intent of these standards is clearly more, but those who state that are considered almost as heretics by the establishment, which always works to the minimum standard.

Deming, Juran and Crosby, to name but three, are examples of those who have provided in their writings the kinds of criteria that the most successful companies strive to meet. Some of these criteria are being included in quality systems standards, as they have been in the various quality models such as EFQM (European Foundation for Quality Management) established in the 1980s, and MBNQA (Malcolm Baldrige National Quality Award – USA) established some time earlier.

Some of the limitations on applying such criteria are the knowledge and experience of the auditors. Unless the auditors are trained and have experience in some of these (advanced) practices, they will be unable to audit them satisfactorily.

Other limitations are associated with the traditional view of 'quality' – that it had more to do with just making things than with all the support functions as well. If that traditional role also considers the auditor as a firefighter rather than as a fire prevention officer, the system will make no progress, and the audits within it will reflect that.

Some companies decide that they will give their internal auditors terms of reference and a role (with associated training for them and the organization as a whole) which enables them to facilitate quality improvement thinking by auditees and auditors alike. It is known that the major quality problems in any organization are cross-functional, and as such are not solvable by internal or external audits, which consider only compliance to a standard like ISO 9001. Audits should be carried out at all levels in an organization, and across departmental and functional boundaries. If audits consider only the traditional procedures developed as part of ISO 9001 compliance, the opportunities for real improvement will remain hidden. The triple role model, described earlier, is one approach that can aid this. However, the major issues in companies can only be identified and prioritized by persons with the highest authority in the company. Analysis may be carried out by others, but the responsibility for making sure that the issues are identified and that action is taken can only come from the top. The ultimate responsibility for quality cannot be delegated by the CEO (Juran).

The internal auditor therefore takes on a much more important role than the external auditor, who is too limited by lack of knowledge, by the rules, and lack of time to have any hope of being anything more than an evaluator of compliance.

External audits

Both second- and third-party audits come within our definition of external audits; therefore the two can be seen to be very similar. However, it should be made clear that a third-party auditor has to abide by the rules to which certification bodies have to work (in the UK, those set by UKAS – United Kingdom Accreditation Service – and IAF – International Accreditation Forum).

These rules forbid the auditor from providing anything other than objective evidence of compliance or noncompliance. Auditors may not provide consultancy or advice about implementation of quality systems.

Second-party auditors may not have that limitation placed on them. It may indeed be the customer's policy that the auditor provides help, advice and therefore a strengthening of the relationship between customer (auditor) and supplier (auditee).

That being said, there need be little difference between second- and third-party audits. A second party, of necessity, may have technical and capability assessment needs which are specifically avoided by third-party auditors.

The mechanics of audit are defined in ISO 19011: 2002, *Guidelines for Quality and Environmental Management Systems Auditing*, which includes:

- A clear explanation of the principles of management systems auditing
- Guidance on the management of audit programmes
- Guidance on the conduct of internal or external audits
- Advice on the competence and evaluation of auditors.

This document defines the practices now accepted as part of audit protocol and is a good basis for audits, whether first-, second- or third-party.

PREPARATION FOR AN EXTERNAL AUDIT

Second-party

The whole auditing activity must be planned in a formal and systematic manner, and it is necessary to formulate a forward programme of vendor audits. This programme should be documented so that it can be shown to and discussed with interested parties inside and outside the company (for example, user departments and/or visiting auditors). There are a number of factors to be considered along with those already mentioned earlier in this chapter:

- the requirements of current and pending contracts; it may be desirable to carry out audits early during a major contract to assure effective QA during the design/development and early procurement phases
- the time which has elapsed since a particular vendor was last audited
- the number and nature of the findings of previous audits
- the resources available for auditing.

The programme must be reasonably flexible, to allow for contingencies. For example, it may be desirable to arrange an immediate audit on a vendor whose products are failing to meet standards. The purchasing department may wish to open a new source of supply for some product, and it may be decided that an evaluation of the vendor is needed prior to contract award.

The first step taken in the audit preparation is the selection of the audit team leader, who will be responsible for planning, performance and reporting of the audit.

The team leader therefore needs to be fully briefed about the objectives of the audit. What decisions can be made, and what actions can be taken when the audit has been carried out? Audits may be carried out to assess a vendor's ability to supply a given product, to manage a given project, to complete a given project within a timescale, and so on. Unless the team leader knows this, the audit will be unsuccessful.

Similarly, the team leader must be advised of the scope. Are all products, all parts of the vendor to be audited, or just some?

Once objectives and scope are clear, then some decisions can be made about the person-days necessary to complete the audit. These decisions must be made at this early stage.

The company to be audited should be given ample warning of the intention to carry out an audit and the proposed date(s). Who does this is immaterial. It often falls to the procurement function, but it is reasonable, and not untypical, for the audit team leader to make this initial contact.

In order to plan properly, the auditors need a considerable amount of information about the company – its activities, organization, policies and procedures. The usual source of such information is the quality manual. Different companies have very different ideas about what a quality manual is and what should be in it. The manual may include all documented procedures, or it may be only the part dealing with policy.

Companies are often unwilling to release a copy of procedures which may be confidential and useful to competitors. They may, however, allow the auditor to see procedures while on the company's premises.

Companies may have no quality manual which they can pass over to the auditor. What is important to the auditor is that he or she gains sufficient information before the audit about the way the company controls its operations. Depending on cost and the resources available, there are many ways open.

The auditor can make detailed preparation if the company has a document or set of documents which describe the company operations in sufficient detail for him or her to understand the management controls used in the various areas of interest. The company may call this a quality manual, but it may have been written for the company's own benefit, not for external auditors. The auditor may have some work to do in order to find the information he or she wants. This is not a criticism of the manual, unless a requirement within the scope of the audit is violated.

Where difficulty in procuring the information is experienced or there appears to be no such information available, the auditor has two choices.

First, he or she can visit the company on a preliminary basis, and discuss with management the information required. This has an added benefit, as the relevant personnel meet one another, thereby removing some of the formality present at the start of any new relationship. This is, however, impossible where great distances are involved, and therefore great time or costs would be incurred by a preliminary visit.

The second choice, therefore, is to make preparations without the more detailed information requested.

There may be other choices, according to the auditor's own company policies. These may require the vendor to prepare such a document. In its absence, the audit is either put on hold or is cancelled, along with the business between the two companies.

Assuming that documented information has been supplied by the vendor, the auditor must prepare his or her own checklist or *aide-mémoire* for carrying out the audit.

The initial information-gathering being complete, a decision is now necessary about how many auditors, for how long, will be needed to achieve the objectives of the audit within the required scope. Many audits are undertaken by one person alone, and internal audits are often done this way quite satisfactorily. External audits may also be conducted this way, especially if the audited company is small and the auditor is comfortable with the technology involved.

However, if it were considered that eight person-days were required as audit effort, it might be preferable to have four people for two days or two for four days, rather than one person for eight days. Audits can be disruptive, and the less time spent conducting them the better.

Audits carried out by one person can be productive, but audits carried out by two auditors working together as a team can be more than twice as successful. An audit team where the members corroborate notes and statements where necessary, and provide each other with support and help, is a joy to behold. The second person in any audit team is often able to view the situation more objectively than the leader when the situation becomes 'heated' or where the line of questioning is yielding little of value. The second person may also act as timekeeper, to help to keep the audit on schedule.

The second team member may be someone who has technical knowledge or direct experience of working in the industry being audited. Some major auditing organizations in the UK, for example, make up audit teams of experienced systems team leaders and assessor(s) from mechanical, electrical, chemical, and other disciplines as necessary. This is considered to keep the auditors in a more pragmatic frame of mind regarding the industry being audited, and the organization's objectives from the audit.

Third-party

The overall process for planning a third-party audit is similar to that above, but there are a number of particular differences.

The decision to have its quality systems registered by a third party through audit rests with the organization. This decision may have been arrived at for a number of reasons:

- Its customers are requiring quality system registration as a prerequisite for doing business.
- It sees registration as a marketing advantage.
- It decides that having independent auditors register the company will help to improve its quality system, and therefore its service to its customers.

Once a decision has been made, a choice of certification body must be made. Application to the certification body then follows, agreement of the contract between the two parties, establishment of the scope of the quality systems to be registered, and agreed date(s) for the audit.

A team leader is nominated by the certification body, plus other auditors if necessary, according to the size and type of organization.

The third-party audit process is defined very clearly in terms of the following:

- Intent
- Implementation
- Effectiveness.

The 'Intent' stage is the assessment of the company's documented quality manual. This document must be supplied to the auditor prior to the site visit, and assessed for completeness against the standard – for example, ISO 9001. This is termed 'Adequacy', 'Desk', 'Book' or 'Intent' audit, and is designed to ensure, before the audit on site, that the company has addressed all the applicable parts of the quality standard.

In general, on a third-party audit, auditors work alone. Third parties compete on a commercial basis, and cannot afford the luxury of two or more auditors auditing at the same time.

PROGRAMME FOR THE AUDIT

Once the auditors have decided how much time is needed at the auditee company, it is necessary to lay down a programme for the visit. It is reasonable to do this, since the auditors cannot see everything in the company during the audit; they take a 'snapshot' of activities in selected parts of the company in order to arrive at a conclusion about the organization's degree of compliance with a set of criteria. They will therefore take a sample of departments throughout the company, and allocate some time to each.

The programme needs to be agreed with the auditee before the audit. The auditee may be able to make suggestions about the route proposed in order to save time (or the auditors' legs) during the audit.

There is another more important reason for agreeing the programme with the auditee before the audit. Few companies are willing to allow auditors (or any other visitors for that matter) to wander around their facilities unaccompanied. It is discourteous to the auditors, and may in fact be hazardous to them. The auditee will be requested to supply a guide who is responsible for taking the auditors from point A to point B, and so on. The auditee will also need to have someone of requisite authority – a management representative – available in each department, to explain to the auditors how the department works and to answer the auditors' questions. The guide and the management representative may be the same person for parts of the audit.

Figure 24.4 is a typical programme for an audit covering three days with two auditors. The example is a manufacturing company with some design activities. In preparing this programme, the auditors will also have decided their strategy for the audit. There are various options.

Some auditors favour starting at the point in a company where enquiries and orders are received, then following the process through various departments, finishing with the despatch area, taking in specialized areas along the way. This may be termed 'top-down' or 'downstream audit'. The auditors follow a specific order through the system, examining other examples, documents and stages as they go. They follow the process route and take examples of other orders at each stage, and thus gain their 'snapshots'. This has certain advantages, particularly if making comparisons among a number of vendors with the same kind of service. However, it can be superficial unless the auditors use other techniques as well.

Another approach is to go in entirely the other direction. Take a completed product or its records, and go back 'upstream' and check the systems that got it there. This can be very searching, but if only one order or product is being examined, it may 'bias' the audit conclusion.

The answer, of course, is that there is no 'right' way. The audit has an objective, and the combination of techniques must be geared to achieving that objective.

CHECKLISTS

The auditor must remember that the quality system is made up of many parts. There is that part which is written down in manuals and procedures, the people who are expected to follow those procedures, plus the machinery, equipment and materials used in the process. The auditor must always ask whether there is a system, whether this is put into practice, and whether it is effective by taking into account the people, the procedures, the machines, the equipment and the materials, otherwise the audit may not be considering properly all the factors that it should.

Having established the overall audit programme, the auditors need to establish the detailed samples within each chosen area. This will entail the preparation of checklists or

Audit Programme

Company: XXXX Limited

Dates: ....

Auditors: **Team leader:**

Auditor:

Day 1

09.30–10.00	Opening meeting
10.00–10.30	Quality manual
10.30–12.30	Contracts Department
13.30–15.30	Design Department
15.30–17.00	Purchasing Department

Day 2

09.00–09.30	Review meeting
09.30–11.30	Storage: Stockyard Covered stores
11.30–12.30	Instrument shop
13.30–15.00	Test house
15.00–17.00	Fabrication shop

Day 3

09.00–09.30	Review meeting
09.30–11.30	Assembly shop
11.30–12.30	Drawing office and standards
13.30–14.30	Quality office
14.30–15.15	Paint shop
15.15–16.00	Preparation, closing meeting
16.00–17.00 (proposed)	Closing meeting

Figure 24.4 Typical external audit programme

aides-mémoire. The word 'checklist' has an unfortunate connotation and smacks of ticks and crosses or 'yes' and 'no' answers. These checklists are not meant to be like that at all. They will define the sample. This sample cannot be statistically valid (though some auditors would like to make it so), but it should be as representative as the auditor can make it.

The style and format of a checklist are at the auditor's discretion. An inexperienced auditor may frame full questions on a checklist, while a more experienced auditor may use keywords instead. A good guide to the preparation of checklists is to think in terms of 'what to look at' and 'what to look for'. Thus it may be decided to look at documents, records, products, equipment. Respectively, these may be examined for approval, completeness, status and condition. This is a very simple example. It may be decided to look at the internal audit system, and to look for statement of its authority, comprehensive coverage of the system, training of auditors, timely action on findings, procedures and understanding of them by auditors, and so on. The objectives of the audit must therefore be clear in the auditor's mind when these checklists are being prepared.

To return to the preparation of a representative sample, it is reasonable that, if the audit is to examine a given department, it should include a look at what the department spends most of its time doing. Thus a drawing office may be mainly preparing drawings and parts lists, a merchandiser in a retail organization may be mainly assessing products and placing orders, and a laboratory may be mainly making up standard formulations. If the purpose of the audit is to establish the degree of compliance with established criteria, then the representative sample should reflect the major activities of each relevant department.

All departments have 'their job'. There are also special or different activities they may undertake. Thus drawing offices may also carry out troubleshooting, provide technical advice, prepare sales literature and take technical customer enquiries. Merchandisers may influence outlet pricing, methods of display and safety policy. Laboratories may conduct special studies and experiments and provide specialist advice, and so on.

Yet another aspect must be considered by the auditor. What happens when a department's systems fail? How does the department attempt to put things right and prevent the error from occurring again? Perhaps audits in some organizations should look at this aspect and no other!

There is therefore considerable choice open to the would-be auditor. The selection of subjects is up to him or her. The leader of an audit team may insist that certain samples are taken, but another team of auditors may make a different choice. Neither is necessarily wrong. It would be impossible to define the sample (though some believe they can).

Few auditors are given total freedom in their choice. The auditor has a purpose and is initiated by management, so there are management priorities and concerns which have to be addressed. This collection of requirements can often be quite large. Auditors look at it and consider that the time allowed for the audit must therefore be used very carefully. One of the essential features of planning the audit before the audit itself is to ensure that no time during the audit will be wasted. It must be spent auditing, not planning what is next.

Some auditors believe that they can carry out a good audit by arriving at the auditee with a blank piece of paper and then 'following their nose'! No one has been shown to have completed an effective audit in this way, and all such auditors have done the profession a great disservice. Such audits are generally biased, and provide good material for the individual auditor's particular 'hobby horse'. It is likely that such an audit will reach a conclusion based on very scant information, or which is unrelated to the audit objective.

The audit team leader, with the team members (or subteams), therefore draws up a total sample for the audit.

There is a school of thought which says that checklists should be sent to the auditee before the audit. This may have the advantage of saving time during the audit, as certain information can be made available in advance. However, other schools of thought would be opposed to this. It depends on what the checklist contains. In principle, it should not matter that the checklists are sent out if they are understood by the auditee and if this contributes to the achievement of audit objectives.

This point is related to another. Some auditors prefer not to advise the auditee that an audit is going to be carried out. In this way, it is argued, the 'tidyings up' are not carried out and the audit will find a more typical condition. However, at least once in a while the place does get tidied up so the audit instigates some improvement. The sort of management system error that can be easily tidied up is generally not major, and therefore does not deserve any lengthy attention from the auditor.

Once the programme has been agreed with the auditee and checklists have been prepared by the audit team, the planning stage ends and the the audit stage starts.

OPENING MEETING

Good audit practice would recommend that the team leader telephones his or her contact at the auditee organization the day before the audit is to start and checks that all arrangements are in hand. It is disconcerting to find that nobody is expecting the audit team when they arrive after a long and expensive journey.

The same good practice would recommend that the team arrives promptly – neither early nor late. Either is embarrassing for both parties, and is unprofessional.

The opening meeting or pre-audit conference is typically held in a conference room at the auditee's premises. The audit team leader should come prepared with an 'agenda', and ensure that certain points are covered quickly and efficiently. It should be remembered that this meeting may be the first time the two parties – auditee and auditor – have met. The way it is carried out can set the style or 'tone' of the audit. The meeting is the occasion to set the rules for conduct of the audit. Matters to be addressed include: introduction of personnel; purpose and scope of the audit; reviewing the audit programme, and administration arrangements.

Introduction of personnel

The audit team leader should introduce him or herself and the team, explaining how the people are organized (whether there is more than one team, for example). It may be the case that the auditee representatives are not particularly senior. While the audit team leader may have expected to find some senior management representative available, there is no need for concern if all the preparation has been completed beforehand. The auditors cannot insist on meeting someone senior.

If a large number of people appear at the opening meeting, it is easier for the audit team leader to pass around a sheet of paper and ask for names and titles to be recorded. Some say that the number of people at an opening meeting is inversely proportional to the number of deficiencies the auditors will find.

Restatement of purpose and scope

Just in case there is any doubt in the auditees' minds about why the audit is being carried out and the extent to which the company is going to be examined, the audit team leader needs to restate these. As the nominated leader of the team, he or she may also tell the auditee about the auditing organization and the way it is organized to carry out such audits. The restatement of purpose and scope may also include a statement about the authority for conducting it.

The programme will have been discussed and agreed. Confirmation that auditee 'management representatives' are aware and available is necessary, as is an assurance from the audit team leader that he or she will keep to the programme.

Administration arrangements

Introductions are necessary for those auditee's staff nominated to act as guides for the audit team or teams. Part of the audit preparation will have included setting aside a room or suitable space for the auditors to use during the audit. Lunch arrangements need to be confirmed. Typically, these take the form of a working lunch or something fairly simple. Audit legend contains all the usual stories of huge three- or four-hour banquets laid on for the auditors, usually at some distance from the company. These are no longer practical, and should be avoided.

If it is a large site, it may be necessary to arrange for transport. If there are areas of the company where restrictions may be placed on the auditors, these should be discussed and agreed. These can be various:

1 **Clean or hazardous areas** – If it is necessary for the auditors to visit these areas, the team leader should ask that any essential protective clothing is made available in advance, to avoid wasting time.

2 **Sensitive union–staff relationships** – Where there have been redundancies or rumours of them, or where there have been bitter exchanges between staff, management and unions, personnel in companies can be rather concerned to see strangers walking around on an official basis and taking notes. Once these people realize who the audit team is and what they are doing, there is little difficulty. It is amazing to find how many companies do not tell all their staff that some visitors from or representing their customer are going to be in the company for a time.

3 **No-go areas – secrecy** – Where the Official Secrets Act operates in companies, there are obvious restrictions. Appropriate clearances must be raised and received prior to the audit. However, purely from a commercial point of view, it may be that the company has an area where it is carrying out work that it knows would be of value to its competitors, so it may place a restriction on auditors' access. Unless it is specifically a part of the audit scope to examine such areas, the auditors must accept this limitation.

4 **Audit is a representative sample** – The audit team leader should make it clear that the programme is a sample of the company's operations, and that what will be examined within that is also a sample, and therefore subject to the limitations of sampling. Both acceptable and nonconforming aspects will be seen and missed.

5 **Confidentiality** – The fact that the audit is taking place is confidential between the auditee and the auditors' company. Similarly, everything the auditors see and discuss during the audit is confidential between the parties. Auditors with professional auditing qualifications are bound by their own code of ethics, but it is the duty of all auditors to be discreet and professional about the information they may become privy to. The team leader should therefore make a statement about confidentiality.

6 **Response to auditee's questions** – Other questions of a general nature might arise. Such questions may be concerned with the method of reporting to be used by the auditors. This should be explained, especially if there are documents which will have to be signed during the audit. When all these matters have been cleared, the team leader should bring the meeting to a close by thanking the management, and by confirming the date and time of the closing meeting.

THE AUDIT INVESTIGATION

At any given time during the audit, there may be many people involved. This is not conducive to easy control by the team leader. Those involved could include:

- the team leader
- the leader's colleague or second person
- the nominated guide
- the management representative from the area being audited
- other staff
- observers accompanying the audit party (possibly trainee auditors)
- interpreter, where there are foreign language difficulties.

It is in the auditor's interest to limit the size of the group. But with patience, and by keeping in mind the audit objectives, the team leader can carry out the audit even with a large following.

In keeping control of the audit, the audit leader is looking for three things:

1. **Compliance with the standard** – Examination of documents before the audit will have led the leader and the team to consider the extent to which the apparently prescribed system conforms with the appropriate standard (ISO 9001, for example). The prescribed system defined by the company therefore becomes the ruling document for the audit.
2. **Implementation of the prescribed system** – Examination of what people are doing will reveal the extent to which they are operating as laid down in their own documents.
3. **Effectiveness** – Each procedure, both written and in practice, is there for a reason. Each procedure must produce some result, and there must be a means of showing what has been achieved.

Information will come to the auditors in many ways. For this information to be of use, it must be objective evidence. Objective evidence is fact that is established in a manner that would be acceptable in, for example, a court of law. It therefore includes what is seen by the auditors and what is said to them.

It is essential to have a 'management representative' at each department visited by the auditor, to act as the department's 'expert witness'. Statements made by this person are 'admissible evidence', provided they relate to the areas within his or her responsibility. Anything that this expert says about matters outside the range of his responsibility is hearsay evidence, and not admissible. The auditor therefore needs to be able to differentiate between evidence which is admissible and inadmissible, and keep the audit on course while also considering things he or she may hear from subsequent investigation later in the audit.

The investigation involves talking to people about the working of the quality system and verifying its operation by examination of documents, materials, equipment, and so on. The auditor must develop skills in both these types of activity.

The biggest problem facing the audit team leader is the management of the audit in terms of keeping to programme, looking at and examining enough evidence in each area, and slowly building up an informed judgement about the degree of compliance seen. Any auditor will therefore be well advised to have his or her own way of working within any area, and then adapt the various techniques as each situation demands.

On entering an area and being introduced to the management representative by the guide, the auditor should run over the audit plan for that area with the guide and management representative, and take their advice as to the most logical sequence to follow. The amount of time the auditor has to spend talking to the management in each area about their system will vary according to how much information was originally made available to the auditor. Where there was very little, more time may need to be spent on the audit to determine some of the basic controls.

The items on the checklist can then be worked through in a systematic manner. If the auditors find no evidence of noncompliance, they can and should proceed quickly. Having covered the 'sample', they should move on. Auditors should never continue the investigation 'until we find something wrong'.

As the investigation proceeds, the auditors need to make notes of what they see and hear. Only the most experienced auditors make sufficient notes of all the relevant things seen and heard, and that is yet another reason why audits carried out by different people can yield such different results.

Perhaps the biggest challenge for the auditor is the fact that finding out information depends on his or her communication skills with people. Within a very short time of meeting someone, the auditor needs to have developed a degree of rapport yet remain sufficiently objective to gain the facts essential to the investigation. If these facts are indicative of a lack of management control in the area, it does not take much imagination to realize that if not done correctly, the implied criticism can produce a very unfavourable reaction from the auditee.

The auditor's main method of gaining information is by asking questions in a series of interviews. Although it is not always fully appreciated, the best interviewers are those who say least and have an ability to listen and hear what is said. By applying the right sort of technique, the auditor generates the kind of environment in which good communication can take place.

In all circumstances, the auditor needs to be polite, have respect for everyone he or she questions, and needs to show an interest in the person being questioned. Being polite covers many activities, and some auditors will never achieve it, for it means not openly disagreeing or arguing, but it also means not contradicting people; it means allowing them to have their say; it means giving the auditee the benefit of the doubt. Showing respect demands that the auditor is not obsequious in his or her approach to senior people nor superior to more junior people, but maintains the discussions around the point and strives for facts.

Showing interest in the people being addressed means maintaining a degree of eye contact, showing by small verbal acknowledgements ('I see', 'Ah, yes', and so on) that the communication is being received. Facial expression is important, as are head movements (as long as these are normal).

Questioning techniques

An apt quotation is that by Rudyard Kipling, which though in danger of being overquoted, is nevertheless the basis of all successful questioning:

> I keep six honest serving men/(they taught me all I knew);/their names are What and Why and When/and How and Where and Who.

Elsewhere, particularly in quality circle teaching, they are called 'five Ws and an H'. Although a clumsy description, the idea is the same. Questions beginning with these words will elicit more than 'yes' and 'no' answers, and are therefore called *open-ended questions*. It takes longer to answer such a question than it does to ask it, so the auditor gains some thinking time. The auditor can control the tone of discussion to advantage with the use of these questions.

There are, of course, different types of open-ended questions. For example, there are questions which provide a topic before the question is asked: 'Talking of calibration control, how do you ... ?' Topics needing expansion demand questions that create a high level of empathy between the auditor and auditee, showing obvious interest by the auditor: 'How important is it for you to have this document ... ?' and 'Why do you feel ... ?' or 'What other areas are you thinking of ... ?'

Questions which ask for the auditee's opinion are often neglected, but apart from the danger of straying from fact, *opinion questions* can be useful for gaining someone's attention or for gaining new approaches to problem-solving. It can also encourage auditees who consider they are the 'local expert' to say more, or encourage junior people to talk.

Investigation questions are most useful when the auditor is not sure whether the auditee has fully understood what has been said, but does not want to make this obvious: 'To what extent to do you feel documented methods would fit into the way you work at the moment ... ?' and 'How do you actually approach this test ... ?' The auditee can feel at ease, and the point gets clarified.

Non-verbal questions may seem to be a contradiction in terms, but raising your eyebrows while maintaining eye contact can, with proper timing, encourage the auditee to give yet more information.

Repetitive questions are used to gain time and to establish confirmation of a situation. They keep the conversation going. For example, if the auditee says 'I don't think procedures are necessary', and you ask 'You don't think procedures are necessary?', the auditee is obliged to some degree to continue. This question should be used like the *dumb question*. No question should be considered too stupid for the auditor to ask if fact is going to be the result. However, repetitive or dumb questions should be used sparingly. If over-used, repetitive questions indicate that the auditor is unable to communicate. Dumb questions imply something abut the auditor's competence.

Hypothetical questions should also be used with care. It is reasonable to ask people what they would do if an instruction is not received, for example, or if things went wrong, but there is usually enough material in actual current practice rather than overdoing hypotheses. It can be a good way to find out what people's priorities are, and can also give an insight into the sort of contingency planning which has gone into the department's operations.

Closed questions are ones which can be answered 'yes' or 'no'. They are assumptive, and can be powerful. They also save time. However, they should only be used when the 'yes' or 'no' answer can be quite definitely given because of what has gone on before. To ask such questions without having had an opportunity to explain is equivalent to the auditee sitting in the witness-box being grilled by an opposing advocate.

Leading questions are common in bad audits, but very sparse in good ones. The auditor should not lead the auditee to an answer before attempts have been made to reach a conclusion by all other methods.

A number of organizations find that an understanding of the foregoing is particularly useful before undergoing external audit by a second or third party. While making no recommendation here of such a practice, it is true to say that if an auditee answers precisely and only the question the auditor asks, the auditee has to work very hard. Some auditors have been heard to complain at such a tactic. Who is at fault?

After each and every contact the auditor has with people, he or she should thank them for their time, give recognition for good management control if that has been apparent, and get on with the rest of the audit.

Recording nonconformities

Much could be written about definitions in quality assurance, and nowhere is this truer than when discussing deficiencies, discrepancies, non-compliances, nonconformities, findings, and so on. These words are used almost interchangeably to describe a condition which is found during an audit and is adverse to quality (that is, it violates a specified requirement). The word used in ISO 19011 for a condition which does not conform with specified requirements is 'nonconformity', so that is the word which will be used here.

Specified requirements are the following, in order of precedence:

1 legal requirements
2 contract requirements within the audit scope (including quality standard)
3 quality assurance manual and procedures.

The auditor examines all the evidence with these requirements in mind. As the audit proceeds, situations will arise which appear to conflict with one or all of these.

These situations are not meant to be kept secret by the auditor. As soon as concern arises that what is said or seen is in conflict with requirements, he or she should voice these thoughts to the management representative. In this way, both their understandings of the situation can be improved. By establishing what the exact situation is and determining what the facts are around the issue, the auditor may have a nonconformity and the management may have an opportunity to improve. Some time must be allowed to determine all the facts and decide the extent of the problem. If an isolated case, the auditor might note it, but not as a nonconformity. If more serious, then it is necessary to dig deeper and ensure that all the information is obtained.

A golden rule for auditors is to write the relevant information down as soon as possible, along with all the necessary references – document numbers, product identity, place (department), and so on.

Some organizations are required to have a signature from the management representative that he or she understands the written statement. This can be done, but there are certain disadvantages:

- **The time taken** – It can take quite a long time to write these statements out in a form that the management representative can understand clearly and put his or her signature to.
- **Subsequent information** – It is often the case that other information arises on another part of the audit which can alter or even remove the nonconformity. The auditor may be better advised to take this broad view.
- **'Parking ticket'** – The auditor must be careful not to 'play the numbers game' or

initiate this within the auditee company. Issuing these documents at the time in each department can be effective, but can also degrade the audit, with the receipt of documents perceived in a similar way to motorists 'getting tickets'.

To ensure that there are no unpleasant surprises for the company at the conclusion of the audit, the auditor must ensure that the management in a given area is clear about any nonconformities which are going to be reported in that area at the time, and before he or she leaves it. Providing a record can at least accomplish that.

The wording of a nonconformity document is crucial. It needs to contain an exact observation of the facts, state where, what and who (but avoiding names of people, and certainly those of very junior staff). The statement needs to make it clear why there is a nonconformity with specified requirements.

The reasons for using specified requirements are twofold. First, these provide both parties with a set of agreed criteria. Second, the nonconformities stated can depersonalize the findings, because it is a management system that is being criticized. The auditor must avoid 'pointing the finger', although it might often be clear where the responsibility lies.

There are four criteria to be used in assessing nonconformity statements:

1 **Is the statement factual?** – If it contains words like 'think', 'opinion', 'dislike', 'feel', 'seems', and so on, then there may be a shortage of fact.

2 **Is the statement complete?** – If it doesn't contain enough information, so that anyone with the need to could go back and find it again after the audit, then it is incomplete.

3 **Is the statement helpful?** – In stating the exact nonconformity, the requirement which it violates and the evidence, the statement should point to what has to be done to put it right.

4 **Is the statement brief?** – This is the last point, and is the least important, but writing out very long statements and presenting these at the conclusion of the audit is time-consuming. The auditor needs to practise conciseness, though not at the expense of objectivity and completeness.

It is also a good idea to use the company's or the industry's terminology. It will be more easily understood, and shows the auditee that the auditor has made sufficient effort to 'talk in our language'.

Here are some examples of nonconformity statements:

- 'Contract 5730/6 requires prior client approval of all changes to Quality Plan 5730/QA/016. Procedures HP29 issue 3 to 4, HP38 issue 1 to 2 and HP86 issue 3 and 4 have been changed without this approval. (Nonconformity is a violation of a contract requirement.)'
- 'Engineering Instruction 10/009 states that panels will be painted within 1 hour of shot blasting. Panel 968/a in Paint Bay 3 on [date] was blasted at 11.15 and painted at 15.45 hours – 4.5 hours between blasting and painting. (Nonconformity is a violation of an internal procedure requirement.)'

- 'There is no procedure to ensue that copies of modified drawings are removed from the Shop Central Drawing Store. Outdated copies of drawing numbers 10835/B, 10952/D, 102/A, 1409/C were found in the 'Current Drawing' file in the Store. Drawing Office Master Register and relevant drawings show that 10835 is now issue 'D', 10953 issue 'E', 102 issue 'D' and 1409 issue 'F'. The changes had been in effect for two months. Drawing Office Manager stated that the Technical Clerk should periodically check the Store drawings. (Deficiency is a violation of a quality management standard – Document Control.)'

These statements are not all brief, but they are factual, complete, and, as far as possible, are helpful.

A golden rule for auditors when writing nonconformity statements is to ensure the following are included:

1 **The source of the requirement** – This may be a QA manual, a procedure, or something stated by someone in authority who states the requirement. The reference in the manual or the procedure should identify it unambiguously; in the case of the statement, the person's position needs to be recorded.

2 **The requirement** – Whatever the requirement is must be recorded. Where it is a quote from the standard, it may be shortened. The standard is not always helpful. A person's oral statement must be quoted verbatim.

3 **The source of the evidence** – Wherever the evidence came from, for example a record (with identifier), the statement (person's position) and so on need to be clear.

4 **The evidence** – The evidence needs to be clearly different from the requirement, making it clear that there is a nonconformity.

In presenting nonconformities, auditors may be asked for suggestions about how to correct them.

As a second-party auditor, the policy of the customer is what defines what the auditor may do. The responsibility within a company for the way it runs its business is that of all the company's management at all levels. The auditor's job is not to run that company, but to collect factual information so that an informed decision can be reached about the compliance of the management systems with the specified requirements. A auditor is therefore not in a position to make suggestions and should avoid it, particularly as an external auditor. It is not his or her duty to make suggestions, and it may even be held against the auditor, particularly if the company spent money on the suggestion and it did not work! The policy for all third-party auditors is quite clear: they are prohibited from offering consultancy or advice in this respect.

As an internal auditor, the situation is different. If invited to participate in decisionmaking which is going to assist in improvements, the auditor should throw the checklist away, roll up his or her sleeves and help.

So external auditors must be careful about any constructive comments they might reasonably be expected to make. The nonconformity statement should say it all, but there are some aspects not yet addressed. There can be many nonconformity statements raised during an audit over two or three days, varying from complete lack of a necessary management system to isolated occurrences due to minor lapses.

There needs to be some means of differentiating between those which are considered serious and those which are not. The auditor is not always able to make this decision, but needs to be able to answer two questions about each nonconformity:

1 What could go wrong if this nonconformity remains uncorrected?
2 What is the likelihood of such a thing going wrong?

A comparative exercise can then be carried out which will allow the findings to be put in some kind of perspective.

Certain organizations use numerical values or class findings such as 'major' or 'minor'. These systems provide some guidance. What is important is that the auditor realizes when something is important or serious, and also when something is not.

The auditor has some freedom about the method used for assembling all the information. If there is a common theme in the findings – for example, they are all a failing of the same management system and the same department – then they can possibly be put together. However, this is not recommended if they are all serious and require extensive corrective action. It is then better to have them separated, so that they can be discretely identified and corrected.

As the audit proceeds, the audit team leader should make a practice of bringing the overall management representatives up to date at lunchtimes and at the end of each day with the process, any nonconformities raised, any minor difficulties or alterations to the programme, and so forth. Keeping the company well advised is professional and conventional, and has become an expectation of auditees.

During the course of the audit, the audit team needs to review its progress and make any changes necessary. While the extensive planning undertaken was designed to prevent wholesale alteration of the programme, the audit team leader is entitled to change it with proper consultation. This can arise through the finding of nonconformities. As an audit progresses, a number of 'leads' appear which an auditor can follow or ignore. Sometimes, the correct course of action is to follow these leads, sometimes it is not, and this may not be apparent until some considerable time has elapsed. Making the right decision comes from considerable experience. The auditor who sticks absolutely rigidly to the checklist can be as bad as the one who does no preparation at all.

Once management realizes that the auditor is not just looking for failure, they will assist in most helpful ways and become as interested as the auditor in examining the management systems. In fact, one school of thought says that the management representative should be a full member of the audit team.

Distractions during the audit

Audits present a vast amount of information to the auditors – some of it useful, some of it not. Some of the distractions which occur may not be accidental. Such things include film shows about the company, new technology areas, unusual or brand new equipment, and detours to see all these things. Unless the audit is going to benefit, the team leader must be firm and politely resist such distractions.

Other time-wasters include the situation where the auditor asks for a piece of information and the auditee disappears for a lengthy time to fetch it. It is better if the auditor accompanies the auditee, as it will take far less time, or they can send someone else while the audit continues.

Auditee reactions

It is necessary for the auditor to develop considerable skills in questioning, note-taking, time management, 'thinking on his or her feet' and doing all this while maintaining the momentum and pace of the audit. This can only be done with practice and a significant amount of patience and diplomacy. Not everyone auditors meet is pleased to see them.

Here is a list of some of the possible reactions:

1 **Authority** – Auditees who are very senior or who have previously not been audited feel threatened and sometimes react by suggesting they are above the audit. While this is usually a result of ignorance, the auditor must avoid openly stating this, and must be very patient and explain, perhaps many times during an audit, what he or she is there to do.

2 **Antagonism** – This usually arises from ignorance or lack of knowledge, and tests the auditor's patience, politeness, objectivity, impartiality and so on, to their utmost.

3 **Information volunteered** – Sometimes people give auditors information they do not request. The auditor must listen very carefully, and if the information is relevant, a determination of the facts must follow, then or later.

4 **Internal conflicts** – Audits stress people, and auditees may get into arguments and differences of opinion while the audit is in progress. These can be highly entertaining, and may even tell the auditor something about the management style of the company, but the auditor must politely insist that the audit continues and that they discuss it another time.

5 **Deception** – The auditor may find that the auditee has deliberately lied or prepared false documentary information. This is most serious, and the auditor must avoid making accusations. It is crucial that facts establish this beyond any doubt.

Quality system effectiveness

The aim of the audit investigation is to assess the effectiveness of the auditee's quality system. The auditee management should be interested too, regardless of the auditor. The auditor may look at many management systems during an audit, but there are some of a general nature that give a broad measure of the company's approach to quality:

- **Failures – internal** – What is the extent of avoidable mistakes, problems and nonconformity? Is there a report of scrap, rework, modification? What are they doing about these?
- **Failures – external** – Are complaints, warranty recalls and replacements measured, and the causes determined and corrected?
- **Frequency/trends** – Are the problems increasing, or decreasing?
- **Internal audits** – Do management at all levels take an interest in these, and take responsive corrective action?
- **Management attitude** – Do they take part in the system's management and improvement? Are they aware of the kinds of problems which exist at the lower levels of the organization?

No single finding is going to answer all these questions, but it is evident from bitter experience in the West that nothing worthwhile gets done and stays done unless senior management in a company want it. Management get the systems and people they deserve.

As the investigative part of the audit concludes, the audit team should be gathering the information so that an adequate summary can be prepared. While pieces of this are put together overnight, the team should meet to plan the closing meeting and present the findings in a balanced and objective way.

AUDIT TEAM PREPARATION FOR CLOSING MEETING

At some point about an hour before the closing meeting, the audit team leader should gather the audit team together to prepare the presentation to be made to the auditee management at the closing meeting.

Auditors sometimes feel they should 'try to get some more auditing in quickly'. The law of diminishing returns operates, unfortunately, and rushing the audit will yield little of extra value.

The audit team leader is responsible for control of this meeting. The priority must be to ensure that team members complete their nonconformity statements. Those 'findings' which have not been discussed and agreed with management are discarded. The leader needs to be able to understand the findings, and may suggest alterations. He or she will also decide with the team members who will present all the findings.

An agenda should be prepared for the closing meeting. An example is given in Figure 24.5.

The other major duty of the team leader at this time is to prepare a summary report. A key purpose of this report is to make clear to the audited company the informed judgement of the auditors. This report must be presented before the auditors leave.

The audit team leader can do worse than answer the three original questions in the summary:

1 Is there a system?
2 Has it been put into practice?
3 Is it doing what it's meant to be doing?

Item	*Duty*
1 Introduction and thanks	Team leader
2 Restatement of objectives	Team leader
3 Restatement of audit scope	Team leader
4 Report introduction	Team leader
5 Report limitations	Team leader
6 Principal findings	
Items 1 to 8	Team leader
Items 9 to 12	Second auditor
7 Summary	Team leader
8 Clarifications	Team leader, assisted by second auditor as necessary

Figure 24.5 An agenda for a closing meeting

In any audit, the auditors have an obligation to make it clear what is going to be said in the written report – and if they know, what the 'result' of the audit is.

In a second-party audit, the auditee wishes to know how the relationship between it and the (potential) customer is likely to change as a result of the audit.

In a third-party audit, the auditee needs to know whether the company will be recommended for registration or not.

Although third-party bodies have different systems for classifying nonconformities, all operate a system which prevents a recommendation for registration if one or more major nonconformities are found in the audit.

The nonconformities raised will give certain pointers to the kind of weaknesses that exist in the management systems examined in the audit. Conversely, lack of nonconformities may indicate a stronger system in a given area. The findings are, of course, tempered by the limitations of any audit – subject as it is to sampling errors.

Lastly, in this meeting the team leader should delegate to a colleague the duty of collecting the names and positions of everyone who attends the closing meeting.

THE CLOSING MEETING

Promptly, at the pre-agreed time, the audit team should assemble at the chosen venue for the closing meeting (also called 'wash-up', 'post-audit conference', 'exit meeting', and so on). Typically, they are welcomed by a member of the company management, who looks forward to hearing the findings and conclusions of the audit.

The audit team leader is now in the chair, and is responsible for conducting the meeting. This point is an added strain on the team leader, having led the audit, perhaps over a number of days, met many people, been in some stressful situations, possibly having had to reschedule some audit activities, and generally keeping the audit running on time. Auditors therefore need stamina if, at the end of all this, they are to be able to make a good final presentation.

Good planning will again assist the team leader, and the agenda items can be taken in turn. Most companies do not mind being given copies of the agenda, but it is then necessary to know in advance who will be attending, or at least the numbers.

The agenda may take the form shown in Figure 24.5, upon which the following item descriptions are based:

1 The team leader should start by thanking the company for their courtesy, for giving access to the team, and for the facilities and help provided. The guides and company representatives for the audited areas should be thanked. The remainder of the agenda can then be followed.

2 It is good practice to remind the company what the objectives of the audit were. The audit may have covered many areas, and it can clear up any possible misunderstandings if the original objectives are restated.

3 For similar reasons, the scope should be restated. The specified scope may necessarily have limited the audit to certain areas/products/plants.

4 The system of reporting should be stated. Some companies give auditees full reports, others less, but certainly the auditee should be given copies of the deficiencies found and a statement of conclusion.

5 Any audit cannot examine everything. Therefore, the report will carry a statement, which the team leader should make at this time, such as: 'The audit was a representative sample of activities only. The possibility therefore exists that there are similar deficiencies in areas not audited.'

6 It is strongly recommended here that the findings are read out one after another. This may seem strange to some, but the findings are statements of fact. When people (and auditors) try to present the deficiencies orally, the presentation often becomes unnecessarily wordy, and other odd words creep in. These should be avoided. Auditee management may want to intercede during this presentation to discuss deficiencies. The team leader should politely request that they hear all the findings first, then they will be given an opportunity to clarify anything afterwards.

Many inexperienced auditors are almost apologetic about the deficiencies. Reading out the words as they are written will help to alleviate this problem. They can be read in a clear, firm voice.

Opinions differ in the profession, but it is recommended here that if copies of deficiencies have not already been given out, they are given out now.

7 The overall summary of the audit findings is then presented. At this stage it is a rough draft. The 'sense' of it should not change, though the content may, and the prose and spelling and so on will be changed for the final report. A typical second-party summary might be as follows:

> This audit evaluated the quality management systems of the noted company for the possible supply of ... products.
>
> The company has only recently adopted ISO 9001 as a policy, and has undergone no previous audits by external parties.
>
> The quality system seen in this audit is not yet fully documented, and is still undergoing some development. Aspects of inspection status and product nonconformity control are not yet fully covered.
>
> A total of 12 deficiencies was found, 8 of which were concerned with nonconformity to operating procedures mainly in areas of goods inwards and final test. One major finding in design was the lack of follow-up action on design review.
>
> Corrective action from internal audits and management reviews was well documented, and verification of improvements noted as a prominent feature.
>
> It is recommended that the company provides a corrective action plan and a further audit to be carried out when action is completed. The CEO affirmed her company's determination to take appropriate action.
>
> Supplier status to remain at B2.

A typical third-party summary report might be as follows:

> This audit evaluated the quality management systems against ISO 9001 and the scope agreed.
>
> The company has a fully documented quality system via its QA manual and procedures.
>
> The audit discovered 12 nonconformities, one of which was major and concerned the lack of follow-up on design review.

> The other nonconformities were concerned mainly with lack of implementation of procedures in goods inward and test areas, particularly with regard to inspection and test status, and control of nonconforming product.
>
> It was noted that internal audits and management review are well documented, with evidence of noted quality improvement.
>
> The company is not recommended for registration. It is proposed that a partial re-audit be programmed once corrective action has been taken on the 12 nonconformities noted. The company's Managing Director affirmed the company's commitment to the programme.

Second-party auditors rarely, if ever, actually make the decision of whether to purchase, so it is often difficult if not impossible to tell the company whether they can supply or not at this stage. The team leader can usually state that a response from the company within, say, two to three weeks from receipt of the report about proposed corrective action will be likely to impress the customer. Similarly, third-party auditors do not make the decision to register. They make recommendations to a board, which makes the decisions.

The team leader should not expect the company to suggest corrective action at the closing meeting. Proper, effective corrective action needs careful thought and analysis of the deficiency to get at the cause. Decisions like that cannot properly be made at the closing meeting.

Of course, closing meetings do not go always to plan. What can go awry?

It is reasonable to expect that somebody fairly senior from the company will represent them at the closing meeting. The team leader cannot insist on who attends, but if the representative is not senior enough, the leader should ask whether there is somebody also available and attempt to persuade him or her to attend.

However, if nobody senior is forthcoming, then the closing meeting should be held with those who attend. If that person is presented as being the representative of the company, then anything said in that capacity is admissible as reflecting company policy. Naturally, the audit report reflects this.

Sometimes a deficiency is raised and evidence is then produced that it is no longer a deficiency. If the auditor was originally wrong and is sure of this, he or she should gracefully withdraw it. If the deficiency has been corrected since it was found, the deficiency stays in the report, but if the auditor is satisfied, it can be closed out there and then.

Often, the senior representative was not present during any of the audit, so he or she is dependent upon the Findings Statements. There should be no discussion of facts, since these have been discussed and agreed with the various management representatives during the audit – the people responsible for operating the quality system.

If the audit team has done a thorough job, then the closing meeting becomes what it is meant to be – a formality in which to present the collective factual findings of the audit to the company management. Once that is done, the audit team leader should restate the team's thanks, appreciate that the company management's time is valuable, and depart.

If the audit team departs from the company and both parties still fully respect one another, regardless of the findings, the team has been successful.

Audit reports and records

EXTERNAL AUDIT REPORTS

Someone back at base is interested in the findings of the audit, so a full and proper report must be prepared. The team leader needs to know who is interested.

The content outlined in the previous sections is probably the minimum which is produced. However, the recipients of the report do not usually want a lengthy treatise, so the summary prepared during the audit but polished up a little, plus the findings, are all that is necessary.

One aspect of the report which must be available, perhaps as a record, is the defined sample. Therefore, the auditor's checklists should be part of audit records.

There are many formats for reports. Common headings might include:

- Audit number
- Date
- Team:
  - Leader
  - Members
- Contacts:
  - Opening meeting
  - Closing meeting
- Purpose of audit
- Scope
- Ruling standard
- Reference documents
- Summary (in 'polished' form)
- Nonconformities (exactly as worded for audit)
- Prepared by
- Approved by.

Depending upon company policy, there may be space on the report for recommendations. The list above does not include these for the reasons stated – they are likely to be of only limited value.

After preparation and approval, the report should be submitted within the timescale agreed, together with an expected date for response and corrective actions proposed.

INTERNAL AUDIT REPORTS

Internal audit reports are initiated to activate corrective action. There is less need generally for summaries, though a short one is often prepared for senior management. Usually, all that needs to be prepared is a corrective action request (CAR), which contains spaces for the nonconformity, for the auditee to propose corrective action, for the auditor to agree it, and also space to provide evidence that the auditor has followed up and closed out the corrective action.

The report format might include:

- Audit number
- Date
- Auditor
- Auditee manager
- Department/Section/Function
- Nonconformities
- Proposed corrective action
- Follow-up dates and close outs
- Prepared by
- Approved by.

AUDIT RECORDS

The reports (and summaries) provide evidence of the audit. Checklists are retained to show the audit sample, and also to use for future audits. It is not necessary to look at exactly the same things on successive audits. Examining old checklists can provide for a different approach.

The last items which should be discussed are the auditors' notes. All auditors make many notes, often rather untidily, but these are evidence. As such, they should be retained. Retention times are difficult to specify, but a decision must be made. There are already precedents set in different countries of the world where the auditor has been ordered to attend a legal gathering and to produce the notes made at the time.

Many auditors now write all their notes in easily retained form (such as in a large diary) for this reason. This diary should not be taken into different companies, but should be kept at the home office.

Follow-up activities

EXTERNAL AUDITS

The audit is not complete until the nonconformities have been followed up and closed out. The only exception to this is where the audit was part of a vendor selection process. If it is decided that there will be no business, then there is little point in carrying out follow-up.

Even so, it is remarkable how many major organizations go to the trouble of carrying out audits and do not have an active follow-up system.

As a result of issuing the report, the auditor expects from the auditee a response with a commitment of corrective action to be taken by a given time. The time is agreed between the two parties, and for major nonconformities, may be weeks or months.

The action proposed is best evaluated by the team leader and/or team member who raised the nonconformity; to evaluate it correctly, the auditor needs to be able to understand the likely root cause. In fact, this is very difficult unless the auditor has many more facts. In all but the most trivial of nonconformities, finding the root cause may need considerable data analysis. However, if it is felt that the proposals would, in fact, remove the nonconformity, then the proposals can be endorsed.

Verification of the corrective action is then necessary. Again, in trivial matters some of this evidence can be provided by correspondence, copies of documents, and so on. In other cases, a further visit by the team leader, team member or suitably trained local representative can carry out verification.

A basic difference exists between typical second-party and third-party audits in this follow-up process. In second-party audits, if deemed necessary by the customer, follow-up is conducted to close out all nonconformities. Clearly, if corrective action has not been taken effectively in the time agreed, this could have serious consequences for the supplier. If action has not been effective, then there must be some form of 'escalation'.

In third-party audits, once major nonconformities are closed out, a company may be registered. Thereafter, a surveillance programme operates in which the auditor returns to the organization two or three times per year and audits parts of the system. Any nonconformities from previous audits (and of a minor nature only) are checked and closed out. Any new nonconformities are followed up at the next surveillance visit. Some bodies automatically reassess fully every two or three years; others use a continual surveillance technique, but covering the whole quality system over a defined period.

Escalation in third-party registration takes the form of de-registration – removal of the organization's certificate of quality systems registration. The ultimate escalation in the external case is removal of business.

INTERNAL AUDIT FINDINGS

The actions outlined in the foregoing are applicable to the external audit (which they basically describe) and, in principle, to the internal audit. However, internal audits to examine a department's compliance with its own procedures do not generally require the formality of a detailed programme for an audit, or the setting up of opening and closing meetings. But courtesy obviously demands that the responsible manager is advised of the audit and its results at the time. He or she should be encouraged also to take part in it.

Escalation resulting from nonconformities in internal audits is often viewed as a difficult subject. It need not be if the escalation system provides for the nonconformities to be brought to the attention of successively higher levels of management until the situation is corrected. The quality policy statement of the company should make this clear. It must not be the auditor who requires this escalation but the management system owned by the chief executive and the board.

If the principles outlined in earlier sections of this chapter have been followed so that each department, section and person is viewed as supplier, processor and customer, the abrasive situations historically associated with the auditor–auditee relationship will not exist. Any nonconformities in the system are opportunities for improvement. If corrected, they will make the company better able to supply the customer.

Conclusion

The stage is set. Now the review of the company's operations can look at departmental improvements, interdepartmental improvements, increases in understanding of the corporate goals, and measured achievements in reducing the avoidable costs in the business.

Clearly, the audit systems outlined have a great part to play. It is a serious business, but it needs imagination, honesty and single-mindedness from the top to the 'bottom' of the company. If this chapter assists in developing true control of quality, then let the audits commence.

Further reading

Mills, D., *Quality Auditing: A Tool for Excellence*, Chapman & Hall, London, 1993.

CHAPTER **25** *Quality- and Safety-related Costs*

*David J. Smith**

Every industrial company needs to be aware of the cost of quality, and this awareness must permeate the whole organization. A company may survive if individual projects or products fail to meet requirements, but if the most senior management fail to appreciate that costs must be identified and measured in relation to quality as part of company-wide policy, then the company will cease to trade competitively, and may eventually cease to trade at all.

To survive and compete, companies must provide products and services that not only satisfy requirements, but often exceed them in terms of quality, cost, product variety and time of production. Consumer protection and product liability legislation are reinforcing the social and individual pressure to meet these criteria.

In order to satisfy these conditions and provide 'value for money', companies need to identify, measure and control all quality costs related to production by establishing a quality cost system. This system will very often have to collect costs across the whole lifecycle of the product or service to include user and operational failure costs. Only this approach will give the total cost of quality in design, manufacture and installation.

When the total cost of the lack of quality is identified by management, it is soon appreciated that the cost of improving quality is small in comparison. This understanding leads to the allocation of more resources and better-trained personnel, and the general need for value and value-added engineering and production.

Quality costs should be recorded and presented on a periodic basis (for example, monthly), and the quality cost system itself should be monitored and reviewed regularly to gauge its effectiveness.

Categories of quality-related costs

The need to identify the costs of quality is far from new, although the practice is still not widespread. Furthermore, budgeting for the various types of quality-related costs is rare, and planning activities to identify, measure and control these costs is even rarer.

Quality costs are generally grouped under three headings:

1 **Prevention** – expenditure aimed at preventing failures
2 **Appraisal** – the costs of revealing failures

3 **Failure** – the penalty costs of failure such as repair, modification warranty, and so on.

Table 25.1 shows an example breakdown of operating costs for a three-month period in an organization which manufactures and assembles electronic equipment.

The total quality cost if £171 200 and sales for the three-month period are £2 000 000. The ratio of quality costs to sales is the usual way of expressing the relationship. The ratio is then converted into a percentage, to give the cost of quality as a percentage of sales.

In this case, the result is 8.57 per cent. It is well known, however, that the reported costs of quality are very frequently much lower than the actual costs. It is not uncommon for the cost of quality to be as high as 25 per cent of sales.

Referring to the headings in Table 25.1, the activities described below summarize the quality costs.

Table 25.1 Operating quality cost subtypes

1 January – 31 March 1995 (Sales £2 000 000)		
Prevention costs	*£000*	*% of Sales*
Design reviews	0.5	
Quality and reliability training	2.0	
Vendor quality planning	2.1	
Audits	2.4	
Installation prevention activities	3.8	
Production qualification	3.5	
Quality engineering	3.8	
	18.1	0.91
Appraisal costs		
Test and inspection	45.3	
Maintenance and calibration	2.0	
Test equipment depreciation	10.1	
Quality engineering	3.6	
Installation testing	5.0	
	66.0	3.3
Failure costs		
Design changes	18.0	
Vendor rejects	1.5	
Rework	20.0	
Scrap and material renovation	6.3	
Warranty	10.3	
Commissioning failures	5.0	
Fault-finding in test	26.0	
	87.1	4.36
Total quality cost	171.2	8.57

PREVENTION COSTS

Design reviews

Reviews of the design can be conducted at various stages in the design cycle, and prior to the release of drawings to production.

Design review is not concerned with progress, but with whether the design (at the particular stage in the design cycle) meets the technical requirements of the specification. It is a formal technical activity that needs to be defined in advance and carried out against specific specifications and drawings.

Quality and reliability training

The quality department needs to be staffed by people with an understanding not only of quality control, but also of quality assurance and quality management. The quality department may include personnel with competence in a specific discipline (reliability engineers, for example).

Vendor quality planning

All vendors must be able to satisfy product or service requirements; where they do not, the manufacturing company will produce inadequate products, and both it and its vendors will suffer. A vendor's ability to meet requirements will be evaluated by assessments, surveillance reports, meetings with clients or the vendors, questionnaires, product and company appraisals and audits.

Audits

Audits can be internal to the manufacturing company, carried out by its own quality personnel or independent auditors. Audits can also be external, examining the company's vendors, and these audits can be performed by the manufacturing company's quality personnel or independent auditors.

Installation prevention activities

These can include a wide range of activities which must be fulfilled if contract conditions are to be satisfied – for example, availability of proper tooling, equipment and instrumentation, manuals, drawings, other documents and data. All these activities need to be reviewed, planned and often audited.

Product qualification

This involves testing the design against its engineering specifications, to ensure conformance to the specifications, under different operational modes and stress conditions. Only when tested satisfactorily against its engineering specifications should the product's drawings be released to manufacturing.

Quality engineering

This includes preparation of quality manuals, guidelines and quality plans relating to a product or service.

APPRAISAL COSTS

Test and inspection

These are the traditional quality control costs of inspection and test covered by the hierarchy of inspection and test procedures. Only actual appraisal should be included here. Re-inspection and re-test, after rework, is not an appraisal cost, but a failure cost. The quality cost procedure needs to extract these items separately as training time, waiting time, and so on.

Maintenance and calibration

These are the costs of labour, subcontract and items needed to ensure the correct calibration upkeep, usability, availability and repair of all test and inspection equipment.

Test equipment depreciation

Test and measuring equipment is expensive, and will depreciate over accounting periods. It will also 'age' as technology advances. Include the depreciation here.

Quality engineering

Quality engineers carry out a very variable role, and it is likely that, hour by hour, their activities cover prevention, appraisal and failure activities. One approach is to assess a breakdown and then split the cost into the three categories on that basis. Alternatively, it might be assumed that the majority of their effort is concerned with line quality engineering (for example inspection and test documentation), and therefore allocated to appraisal. This can be addressed when setting up the quality cost recording system.

Installation testing

Installation and commissioning also involves appraisal (test) costs, which need to be collected.

FAILURE COSTS

Design changes

Failures found in manufacturing (or indeed later) will often result in design changes. Modifications are re-design, and invoke most of the activities in the design cycle. It is therefore necessary, in setting up quality cost recording, to be able to distinguish between time booked to design and time used for re-design.

Vendor rejects

Purchased items which are found to be defective must be reworked, worked around or written off. Costs need to be collected.

Rework

With each rework, production costs are incurred. Design changes might result from workaround. With all reworks, testing will be needed. Reworks will often result in idle time on other parts of the shop floor, which must be costed. Re-inspection and re-test must be distinguished from appraisal.

Scrap and material renovation

This cost is the difference between the cost of purchased items which are found to be defective and any reclaim from the vendor.

Warranty

Any products recalled under warranty must be investigated. Losses associated with a poor product or service and a falling reputation are difficult to quantify in the short term. Depending on the nature and complexity of the problem, many of the headings of preventive costs might have to be addressed. All labour and part costs must be accurately recorded.

Commissioning failures

These costs can be particularly high where delays result in deadlines not being satisfied and revenue being lost. Specialist labour is often needed during installation; there will also be rework, spares and testing costs.

Fault-finding in test

Production personnel will usually 'bunch' test products, and if easily remedied faults are found, will correct them. However, where less easily modifiable defects are found, whether by production personnel or test personnel, they need to be included under this heading. The cost of investigating these faults must be carefully recorded.

Introducing a quality cost system

In order to introduce a quality cost system, it is necessary to:

1 **Convince top management** – Initially, a quality cost report similar to Table 25.1 should be prepared. The accounting system may not allow for the automatic collection and grouping of the items, but this can be carried out on a one-off basis. The object of the exercise is to demonstrate the magnitude of quality costs, and to show that prevention costs are small by comparison with the total.

2 **Collect and analyse quality costs** – The data should be drawn from the existing accounting system, and no major change should be made. In the case of change notes and scrapped items, the effort required to analyse every one may be prohibitive. In this case, the total may be estimated from a representative sample. It should be remembered when analysing change notes that some may involve a cost saving as well as an expenditure. It is the algebraic total which is required.
   - Step one is to calculate those costs which are directly attributable to the quality function.
   - Step two is to identify costs that are not directly the responsibility of the quality function (for example, stores, purchasing) but which should be included as part of the total costs of the company.
   - Step three is to identify internal failure costs for which budgets were allocated, such as planned overproduction runs where failures were anticipated.
   - Step four is to identify internal failure costs for the unplanned failures, for example reworks, scrap.

- Step five is to identify the cost of failures after the change of ownership, such as warranty claims.

Sources of quality cost data will be varied in most companies, from payroll/time sheet analysis to material review boards. For the data to be collected consistently, tabulated data sheets are needed, addressing each of the quality cost types identified.

3 **Quality cost improvements** – The third stage is to set budget values for each of the quality cost headings. Cost-improvement targets are then set to bring the larger items down to an acceptable level. This entails making plans to eliminate the major causes of failure. Those remedies which are likely to realize the greatest reduction in failure cost for the smallest outlay should be chosen first.

Things to remember about quality costs

They are not a target for individuals, but for the company.

They do not provide a comparison between departments, because quality costs are rarely incurred where they are caused.

They are not an absolute financial measure, but provide a standard against which to make comparisons. Consistency in their presentation is the prime consideration.

Lifecycle costs

So far, this chapter has addressed the costs of the producer. However, there are costs which arise outside the production organization once the ownership of the product or service has been transferred to the user. The user has costs associated with acquiring, operating and maintaining the product or service. These are the total lifecycle costs. The user's costs can be described as follows:

- **Acquisition costs** – the capital expenditure in acquiring the product (or service) and adapting the user's facilities to the new product
- **Ownership costs** – the day-to-day costs of keeping the product operational; these will include modifications and enhancements, as well as preventive and corrective maintenance; special test/diagnostic instruments may have to be purchased; idle time costs and all revenue losses must be recorded
- **Operational costs** – the day-to-day costs of spares, consumables and energy; there could also be costs in training operators and providing suitable personnel backup
- **Administration costs** – the need to keep records, logs and other product documentation; this could entail the storage of electronic and paper media under controlled conditions, for long periods, especially where safety is involved.

It is necessary to find the optimum set of parameters which minimize the total lifecycle costs. Figures 25.1 and 25.2 show the relationships graphically. Each curve represents cost against availability (a function of reliability and maintainability).

Figure 25.1 shows the general relationship between availability and quality costs. The manufacturer's achievement costs increase with product availability. Its failure costs decrease as product availability improves. The total cost curve suggests a trade-off point for availability at some minimum total cost.

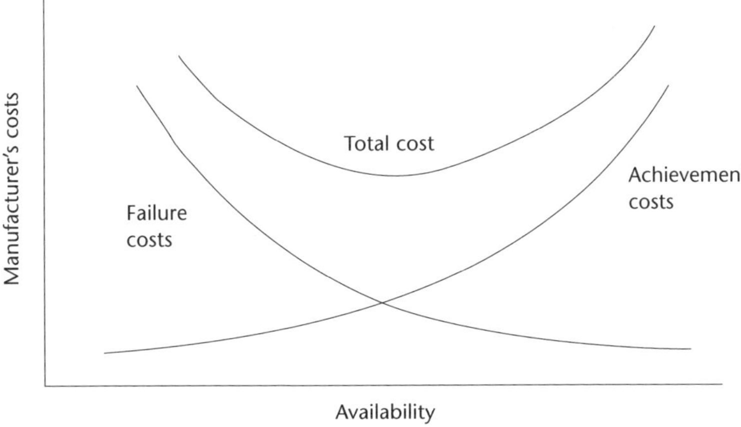

Figure 25.1 Availability and cost in manufacturing

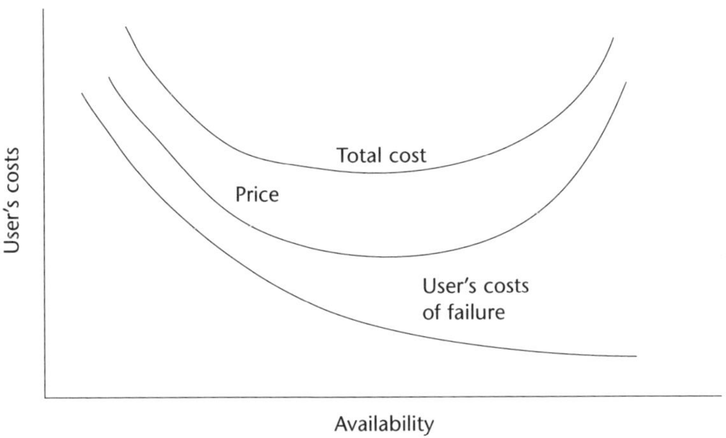

Figure 25.2 Availability and cost for the user

In Figure 25.2, the total quality cost curve has been repeated from the point of view of the user. The ultimate price of the product to the user will be related to this total quality cost. The user's quality costs must include any losses and expenses which have to be borne owing to the product's failure. The result is an optimized price curve, which shows the trade-off relationship between availability and cost.

Clearly, these diagrams are conceptual, and it would hardly be practical to calculate absolute values for the curves. However, they illustrate a concept whereby one would seek to assess any proposal as to whether it offered benefits in excess of penalty costs. In other words, would implementation of the proposal move one closer to the optimum cost point?

Consider applying this principle to the following example, where:

- A duplicated process control system has a spurious shutdown failure rate of 1 per annum.
  Triplication reduces this failure rate to 0.8 per annum.
- The mean down time, in the event of a spurious failure, is 24 hours.

- The total cost of design and procurement for the additional unit is £60 000.
- The cost of spares, preventive maintenance, weight and power arising from the additional unit is £1000 per annum.
- The continuous process throughput, governed by the control system, is £5 million per annum.

The potential saving is (1 – 0.8) x 1/365 x £5 million per annum = £2740 per annum, which is equivalent to a capital investment of, say, £30 000.

The cost is £60 000 plus £1000 per annum, which is equivalent to a capital investment of, say, £70 000.

There may be many factors influencing the decision, such as safety, weight, space available, and so on. From the reliability cost point of view, however, the expenditure is not justified.

ESCALATING LIFECYCLE COSTS

Lifecycle costs escalate where there is a lack of management commitment to quality; this attitude flows down through the organization, to the shop floor. All products (and services) go through lifecycle phases such as: initial conception, feasibility, system requirements definition, engineering system design and detailed design, manufacturing/production, component and integration testing, system and client acceptance testing, operations and maintenance, and withdrawal from operations or service.

As we move through these lifecycle phases, the cost of correcting defects and failures increases dramatically. In an electronics manufacturing company, with machining, assembly, wiring and functional test activities, the following relative costs may be incurred for defects found at various lifecycle phases:

- a component at incoming inspection and before it is used in engineering – 1 cost unit
- the same component used in detailed engineering design pre-production prototypes – 10 cost units
- this component in the integrated product undergoing system testing – 100 cost units
- component failure when the product is in operational use in the field – 1000 cost units.

Thus, when the defect is revealed in the field, failure costs can be punitive.

Companies using the most up-to-date technology (for example, computer-aided design, engineering and manufacturing, computer-integrated manufacturing, flexible manufacturing systems) still find the cost of the lack of quality crippling. It is not uncommon in the high-technology industries that for every 1000 cost units spent on product development, 700 cost units are then spent on maintaining the product in the field.

Even these product quality costs can be overshadowed. If senior management fail to think through the consequences of new policies and developments – a product brought late to the marketplace or a contract broken – there is not just a product failure, but a company failure.

The lessons of the cost of lack of quality do not seem to have been learned. UK industry turnover for 1990 was £150 billion. As quality costs were estimated at between 4 and 15 per cent, the average was taken as 8 per cent. Related to the total turnover, this amounted to £12 billion. Since failure costs account for about half or the total quality cost, it was therefore costing industry some £6 billion in failures and defects. If a 12.5 per cent reduction in failures could have been achieved, an extra £750 million would have been released into the economy over this period.

Several research studies have been funded by the UK government into the economics of quality control practices and the implementation of statistical process control (Followell and Oakland, 1985). The findings were not encouraging. The main conclusions were that there was a lack of understanding of how the practices and processes could lessen quality costs; there was little management commitment, and inadequate attention to training.

In one study (Plunkett et al., 1985), it was claimed that very many managements had little idea of what quality-related costs their organizations were incurring. This study put quality-related costs at between 5 to 25 per cent of an organization's sales turnover. It also found that very few companies used statistical techniques to monitor and control costs.

Software now has an impact on the operational and administrative functions of many companies. Software quality-related costs are huge. A 1988 Price Waterhouse study for the Department of Trade and Industry reported that:

> Poor software quality results in substantial costs to both suppliers and users. These 'failure costs' include costs of correcting errors before and after delivery of the software, overruns and unnecessarily high maintenance costs.
>
> At a conservative estimate, UK users and suppliers currently suffer failure costs of over £500 million a year. This figure includes domestically produced, marketed software only; if we were to include imported software and software produced in-house, failure costs would be much higher. There are in addition indirect costs, which are clearly substantial but which we were unable to quantify. These costs represent the potential benefits to be achieved from improving software quality. (Price Waterhouse, 1988)

The figure given is just for domestically produced marketed software. If we could quantify over the other areas mentioned plus any costs incurred due to hardware/electronics, the high-technology industries alone probably have quality-related costs of well over £1 billion a year.

The Price Waterhouse study and a further study by Logica (Logica, 1988) for the Department of Trade and Industry gave rise to the TickIT software programme, which is making a global impact (TickIT, 1997). The distribution of software costs and benefits is only fully appreciated where the developer (supplier) and purchaser (user) have common quality objectives through implementing the TickIT interpretation of software.

The lifecycle costs and benefits associated with the TickIT approach are illustrated in Figure 25.3. It is clear that the developer's (supplier's) net costs are increased by the application of quality measures, when compared with development costs without a quality system. However, if there is a TickIT-like joint developer/purchaser quality policy or system in place, the incremental benefits and reduced failure costs are larger, to the benefit of the purchaser (user). Maintenance costs are reduced dramatically, and the overall lifecycle costs (described earlier) are monitored and controlled more effectively.

One study (CSC-Index, 1992) identified that approximately 18 per cent of staff expenditure on computer systems development and acquisition is lost through incorrect specification of requirements and poor-quality software. This study reinforced the Price Waterhouse report findings of 1988: as computer systems become more complex,

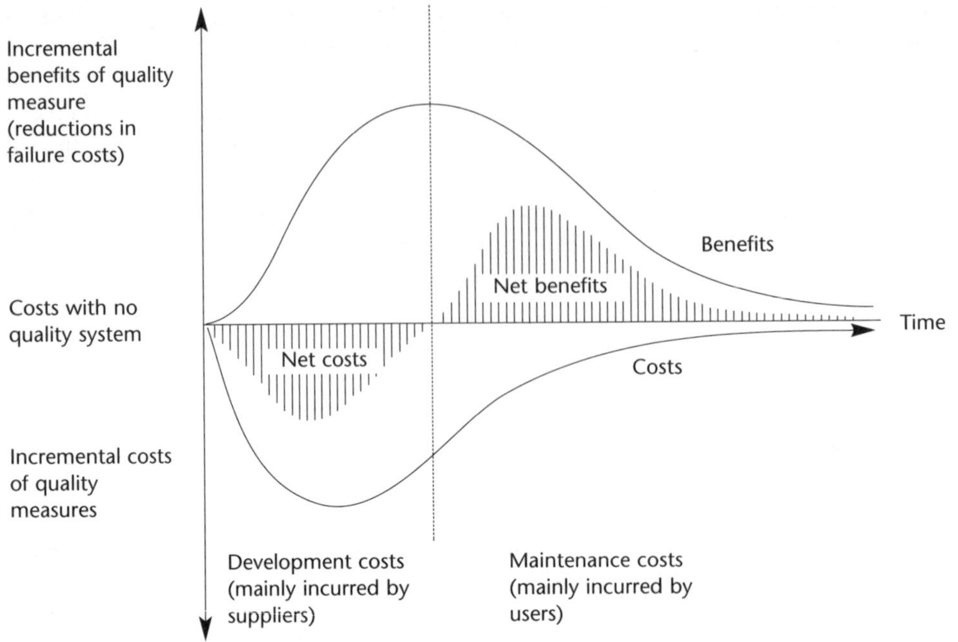

Figure 25.3 Quality system lifecycle costs and benefits

management must learn how to monitor and control cost by a quality management programme that follows the best practice guidelines of TickIT.

Safety and the cost of risk reduction

Once the probability (frequency) of a hazardous event has been assessed, the cost of measures which can be taken to reduce that risk must be considered.

Before the cost of potential safety improvements can be addressed, the question arises of setting a quantified level for the risk of fatality. The meaning of such words as 'tolerable', 'broadly acceptable' and 'unacceptable' becomes important. There is, of course, no such thing as zero risk, and it becomes necessary to think about what levels are 'tolerable' or even 'broadly acceptable'.

In this context, 'broadly acceptable' is generally taken to mean that we accept a particular probability of fatality as reasonable, having regard to the circumstances, and would not seek to expend much effort in reducing it further.

'Tolerable', on the other hand, implies that while we are prepared to live with the particular risk level, we would continue to review its causes and the precautions we might take with a view to reducing it further. Cost now comes into the picture, in that any potential reduction in risk can be compared with the cost needed to achieve it.

'Unacceptable' means that we would not tolerate that level of risk, and would not participate in the activity in question nor permit others to operate a process that exhibited it. Cost in that event is irrelevant, since alternative measures must be taken in any case.

The principle of ALARP (As Low As Reasonably Practicable) describes the way in which risk is treated legally and by the UK Health and Safety Executive. The concept is that all reasonable measures will be taken in respect of risks which lie in the 'tolerable' zone to reduce them further until the cost of further risk reduction is grossly disproportionate to the benefit.

It is at this point that the concept of 'cost per life saved' arises. Industries and organizations are reluctant to state specific levels of 'cost per life saved' which they would regard as becoming grossly disproportionate to a reduction in risk. Nevertheless, a value must be chosen by the operator for each assessment. The value selected must take account of any uncertainty inherent in the assessment, and may have to take account of any company-specific issues, such as the number of similar installations. The greater the potential number of lives lost and the greater the aversion to the scenario, then the larger the choice of 'cost per life saved' criteria. Values which have been quoted include:

- about £1 000 000 where there is a recognized scenario, a voluntary aspect to the exposure, a sense of having personal control, and small numbers of casualties arise per incident – an example would be passenger road transport
- about £2 000 000–£5 000 000 where the risk is not under personal control, and is therefore an involuntary risk – an example would be transport of dangerous goods
- about £5 000 000–£15 000 000 where there are large numbers of fatalities and there is uncertainty as to the frequency – an example would be multiple rail passenger fatalities.

The cost of a safety improvement can now be compared with the 'cost per life saved' target, as shown in the following hypothetical example.

A potential improvement to a motor car braking system is costed at £40. Currently, the number of fatalities per annum in the UK is in the order of 30 000. It is predicted that 500 lives per annum might be saved by the design. Given that 2 million cars are manufactured each year, then the cost per life saved is calculated as:

$$\frac{\pounds 40 \times 2 \text{ million}}{500} = \pounds 160\,000$$

Judged against the above criteria, the modification would be deemed essential under the ALARP principle.

References and further reading

BS 6143, *Guide to the Economics of Quality: Part 1, Process Cost Model*, British Standards Institution, 1992.

BS 6143, *Guide to the Economics of Quality: Part 2, Prevention, appraisal and failure model*, British Standards Institution, 1990.

CSC-Index, *Key Issues Affecting Quality in Information Systems*, a report for the Department of Trade and Industry, HMSO, London, 1992.

Department of Prices and Consumer Protection, *A National Strategy for Quality*, HMSO, London, 1978.

Followell, R.F. and Oakland, J.S., 'Research into Methods of Implementing Statistical Process Control', *Quality Assurance*, Vol. 1, No. 2, 1985.

International Standards Organisation (ISO): Relevant standards are listed above under their BS (British Standards) equivalents.

Logica, *Quality Management Standards for Software*, a review for and published by the Department of Trade and Industry, London, 1988.

Ministry of Defence Procurement Executive, *The Planning and Cost Management of Major Development Contracts*, DEFCON Guide No. 1, Ministry of Defence, London, 1975.

Plunkett, J.J., Dale, B.G. and Tyrell, R.W., *Quality Costs*, Department of Trade and Industry, London, 1985.

Price Waterhouse, *Software Quality Standards: The Costs and Benefits*, a review for and published by the Department of Trade and Industry, London, 1988.

Smith, David J., *Reliability, Maintainability and Risk*, 5th edn, Butterworth-Heinemann, Oxford, 1997.

The Consumer Protection Act 1987, HMSO, London.

TickIT, *Making a Better Job of Software: Guide to Software Quality Management System Construction and Certification*, Issue 3, Department of Trade and Industry/TickIT Office, London, 1997.

CHAPTER

26 Benchmarking

Sylvia Codling

Benchmarking is the process of continually measuring and improving products and services against the best that can be identified world-wide, with the objective of achieving market superiority and significant competitive edge. Unlike traditional competitive analyses which focus on outputs, benchmarking is applied to key processes within a business. It relies on determining the critical success factors across the organization. Processes governing those factors are analysed. The best performances against the key parameters are established, and these are then used to target improvements. Only a thorough understanding of the in-house processes makes it possible to recognize and integrate the differences, improvements and innovations which are found in the best-practice organizations.

In 1960, the *Harvard Business Review* published Theodore Levitt's landmark paper, 'Marketing Myopia'. In this, Levitt delivered his research findings, which showed that significant innovations in any sector frequently come from outside the industry. In ever more sophisticated and demanding markets, the need to develop an external perspective has never been more acute. Yet many firms have continued myopically to look internally or within their industry for clues to achieving or maintaining competitive edge.

Benchmarking – a rational, structured technique for continuously improving key business processes and practices through comparative measurement against best practice regardless of industry or location – is potentially the most powerful tool in the strategy armoury. Its flexibility and applicability across the whole range of business processes have led to its becoming a way of life in some of the world's leading organizations. Where competitive analyses helped countries understand and improve their relative industry position, benchmarking carries this forward and enables companies to learn from the best, regardless of sector of location, thus achieving superiority in the key areas which are imperative to their continued success. As Dean Rusk (1963) said:

> The pace of events is moving so fast that unless we can find some way to keep our sights on tomorrow we cannot expect to be in touch with today.

Applying benchmarking

As a strategic tool, benchmarking is most effective when applied to processes which, when improved, would make a significant contribution to the business's overall competitive position. The decision regarding what to benchmark at this level should incorporate examination of the following, and if resources and returns are to be optimized, the process or processes selected for benchmarking should ideally influence, or be influenced by, one or more of these:

- **Core competencies** – defined here as the strategic business capabilities which provide marketplace advantage (such as fast-track product development, giving rapid time from the start of design to full production)
- **Key business processes** – those processes which influence the external customer's perception of the business; examples include the quality of product development, effective distribution, and customer service
- **Critical success factors** – the quantitative measures of effectiveness, economy and efficiency of the business; examples of these are mean time between failures (MTBF), inventory turn ratio and production cycle time.

Having examined these factors, attention should be given to the level or category of process to be selected. When visualizing processes, it helps to imagine a Spanish onion. Like the onion, processes consist of a number of layers, each of which only becomes visible for analysis when the previous one has been 'peeled away'.

Processes within most organizations fall within three broad categories. The first, often called 'strategic' or 'level one', encompasses the central business processes. These generally reflect the values, mission and objectives of the business and, as such, affect its direction. Safety, health and environment, corporate planning, finance mechanisms and innovation, for instance, would come into this category.

The second category incorporates the main operational processes within the organization. These will largely be influenced by factors such as business type and sector, size and location. They may also reflect the culture and style of the organization and are essential to survival. Included in this category are logistics and human resource management, for example. Each of these processes can themselves be 'peeled away' to reveal numerous subprocesses (supply management, inventory management, distribution and so on in logistics), which in turn will have their own subprocesses, such as just-in-time delivery or Kanban systems.

Finally, every organization has a mass of support processes which make up the third category. Site maintenance, cleaning, catering and laundering fall into this group, as do documentation and employee induction processes, for instance.

Managers often face a dilemma when introducing the organization to benchmarking. The greater the competitive pressures, the more tempting it is to launch straight into benchmarking a central or strategic process. However, many have found to their cost that this is not necessarily the best place for 'cutting teeth'. As with every new technique or skill, it is necessary to master the basic principles in order to develop the facility of interpretation which enables it to be readily applied in a multitude of situations. This can most effectively be developed in a relatively low-profile environment where the priority can be given to learning and gaining experience rather than delivering substantial cost improvements. Thus it is that many of the most effective benchmarking programmes start with seemingly non-core activities (order processing, for instance) and gradually develop into more strategic areas.

Having decided the process which is to form the subject of a benchmarking exercise, attention then turns to locating the 'benchmark' – the standard against which your own process can be measured or judged. Since the objective is to improve your process, the 'benchmark' must obviously be 'better'. While this is simple in concept, managers have found it less easy to identify in reality. Essentially, it means defining what is meant by 'better' in the context of your own organization. For example, the 'better' (or benchmark) recruitment process may be the one which costs the least in overhead terms, or which delivers the highest calibre of first degree graduate entrants, or the lower rate-per-hour secretarial recruits. While there is great demand for instant assessment of and access to benchmark processes, each 'seeking' organization must first decide its own criteria and definition in the context of the process in question as well as the broader context of its operating environment.

The validating criterion should ultimately be that the selected benchmark process is measurably or demonstrably better. It may not be the best in the world, but it should certainly be the best that can be identified within the parameters outlined, and which, if emulated or adapted in your own organization, will bring significant improvement.

Locating benchmarking partners

Unlike competitive analyses which stress the anonymity of contributors during collection of relevant data, benchmarking is most successful when carried out as a partnership between two or more teams of people. The teams may comprise people from the same or different organizations. The starting point for the search will be influenced by:

1 the position of the benchmarking team on the learning continuum, from absolute beginners to highly experienced practitioners

2 the nature, scope and level of the process selected for benchmarking; it might be necessary, for instance, to go further afield to find a partner at the strategic rather than the operational level, particularly if your business is in a very narrow industry sector (nuclear power generation or steel manufacture, for example).

Although benchmarking has acquired many adjectival prefixes (such as 'generic', 'competitive', 'supplier', 'customer') during its development, there are essentially three locations to consider when looking for partners:

1 **Internal** – within the same organization or group, whether at the same site or elsewhere
2 **External** – a different organization or group, probably in the same general industry sector
3 **Best practice** – with deliberate disregard for industry sector or location in the search for best practice.

Each of these options has distinct advantages and disadvantages, the chief of which are detailed in Figure 26.1.

Emphasis on the short term, coupled with a demand for instant results, has led to an upsurge in the (mis)interpretation of benchmarking as merely making a visit. Proponents of this approach subsequently claim that the technique fails to deliver the expected benefit! Such visits have been variously dubbed 'Industrial Tourism', 'Wow Visits' and 'Feel-Good Trips'. Often ill conceived and lacking sufficient focus, the results of these may vary slightly in the detail, but are generally characterized by their irrelevance, lack of applicability or

Internal	External	Best practice
Functions, departments, projects, businesses in the same company or group at the same or another location.	Other companies in a similar sector.	Any organization, regardless of sector or location.
Advantages • Similar language, culture, mechanisms and systems. • Ease of access to data. • Existing communications. • Low profile, low threat. • Relatively quick returns possible. • Good test bed.	*Advantages* • Similar structure and constraints. • Relative ease of access to data. • Relatively low threat. • Helps to overcome complacency and arrogance.	*Advantages* • Less sensitive to ethical and political reservations. • Possibility of breakthrough. • Broadens corporate perspective. • Stimulates challenge.
Disadvantages • Might inhibit external focus and foster complacency. • Possibly results in returns that are merely adequate.	*Disadvantages* • Legal, ethical and political considerations. • Sector paradigms might restrain creativity.	*Disadvantages* • Relatively difficult to access data. • Change ramifications are greater. • Higher profile.

Figure 26.1 Locating benchmarking partners

managers' inability to comprehend what they see. Such visits may promote complacency, thus impeding change or improvement. This was certainly the situation which prevailed at Rover Body & Pressings, part of the Rover Group, in the early days of its partnership with Honda Cars. One performance aspect noted in particular was that Honda changeover times were more than ten times quicker. At the time, this was dismissed on the basis that such speed could not be applied to Rover's own seemingly older machines. Following the introduction of benchmarking, however, a team was established to focus specifically on press line performance and changeover times. After two months of improvement actions, the team visited Honda plants in Japan where members were surprised to see that in many cases the Japanese equipment was no better than their own. The difference was found to result largely from attention to detail: not *what* machinery was being used but *how* it was used enabled Honda to achieve such high performance levels.

Properly planned, therefore, and executed within the context of a benchmarking exercise, a visit can be crucial in gaining understanding of how the partner's process delivers superior results.

The 12-step benchmarking model

There are many different models of the benchmarking process, but they are all variations on one theme. The version about to be described here is a synthesis of these various models. It incorporates all the steps which have been found to characterize successful benchmarking programmes in leading organizations.

It is not suggested that this model must be adhered to rigidly. Indeed, it is likely to be more effective when translated to suit the particular organization, culture and language. However (rather like the Ten Commandments), once learned, its component steps should provide the guiding principles or framework within which benchmarking is conducted.

Some elements of the model, such as corrective improvement plans or flow charting, might already be present within the standard management mechanisms. It is one of the great strengths of benchmarking that it harnesses many existing practices plus only a few new ones within a rational, coherent format. Practitioners are usually required to learn only the sequence, framework and direction, rather than having to adopt a totally new set of tools.

The model comprises 12 steps arranged in four stages. The first three stages are *planning*, *analysis* and *action*. The fourth stage is a final, all-embracing *review*, but constant monitoring and feedback take place throughout the process, which is illustrated in Figure 26.2.

PLANNING STAGE

Step 1: Selecting the subject area

In this context, the subject area means the broad area of the business which contains the process to be benchmarked (for example, logistics, finance or manufacturing). The chief criterion is that improvement will make a significant improvement to the overall business results.

By way of example, here are key strategic questions and answers seen from the perspective of a videotape manufacturer:

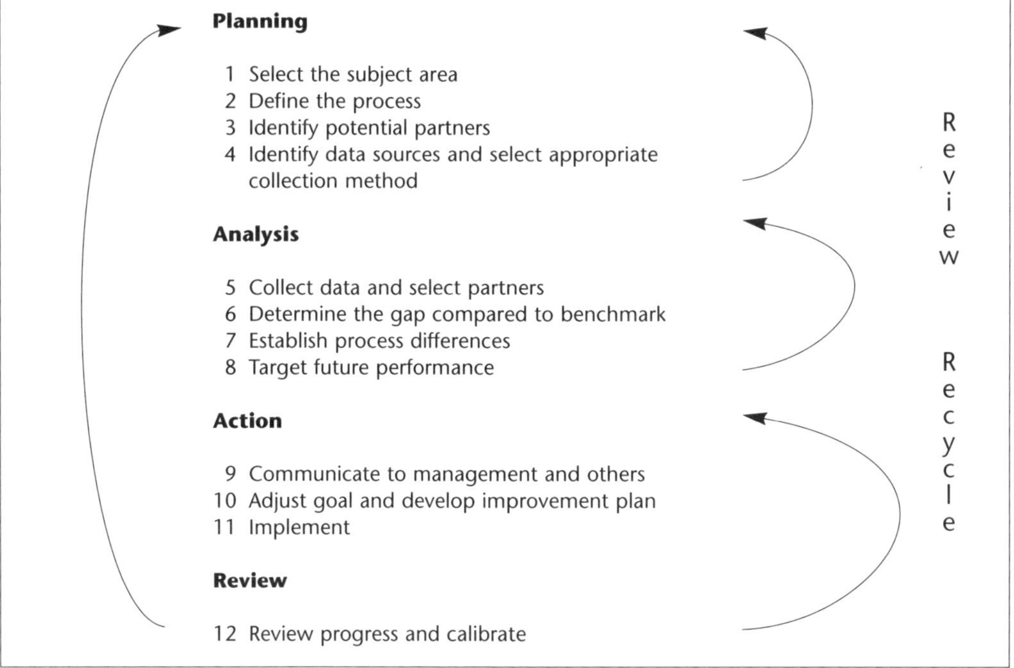

Figure 26.2 The benchmarking process model
© 1993 Oak Business Developers

Q. What business are we in?
A. Home entertainment.

Q. What must we do to remain in business?
A. Obtain rights to films.
Produce video copies efficiently.
Have effective marketing.
Achieve fast distribution.

Q. What must we do to be successful?
A. Be the best supplier of popular videos.

Q. What would make the most significant improvement to our customer/supplier/employee relations?
A. Faster delivery on demand to customers.

Q. Which area, if improved, would make the most significant contribution to our bottom line?
A. Increased market share as a result of more effective distribution.

Additional factors, such as supply-chain considerations, might influence the choice of subject area – particularly if costs associated with suppliers account for 50 per cent or more of the total cost of goods. In such cases, improved management of this area could have greater impact on profitability and competitive edge than internal factors such as speeding up new product launches or improving sales planning.

Step 2: Defining the process

When embarking on benchmarking, most companies find that some of the biggest surprises and earliest gains come from analysing the business processes. Frequently, the way things are done has developed as a result of habit and circumstance, with few people having time or reason to question or alter long-standing patterns. Process analysis plays a fundamental role in successful benchmarking; in the absence of rigorous analysis, it is impossible for managers to identify, appreciate and interpret best practice effectively in later stages of benchmarking. The key elements of process analysis are as follows:

1 **Working definition of the process** – Everyone understands a specific process from the perspective of how it relates to their work, their input to it, or output from it. This is subjective and personal. Unequivocal definition of each word which describes the process is required, so that there can be no doubt at any time precisely what is being studied. Definitions such as 'order scheduling', 'customer service' or 'reducing cycle time' are ineffective. Does 'order' mean export or home orders, for example? The process by which each is dealt with could be quite different. Does 'service' mean face-to-face, over the telephone or after-sales? Again, the process by which service is delivered might be quite different in each instance.

2 **Identifying process boundaries** – Boundaries are often the root of problems or dysfunctions. The more interfaces or junction points there are in a process, the greater

the potential for delay and failure. It is therefore essential that boundaries be described precisely and clearly. The following questions will help:

- What is the output of the process? (For example, is it an order fulfilled, a complaint handled, a delivery made?)
- Who is the customer? (That is, who is the recipient of the output?)
- What are the customer's expectations? (How, what, when, where, why?)
- Is this what the process delivers? (Not quite? Can it be improved? If not, is it the right process?)
- Who owns the process? (Who is the named person responsible for improvement and with control over resources?)

3 **Clarifying process steps** – This stage involves documenting, in sequence, what happens on the ground – not what is defined in the quality manual! Since few processes are the concern of single individuals, this activity should include the view of anyone with an input to, or output from, the process. An effective way of dealing with the variety of views is to write the individual process steps on notes that can be collected together on a board or table (Post-it notes are suitable). When consensus on the steps is reached, these can be transferred to a standard form. Each step should be accompanied by a measurement note (such as weight, frequency or quantity) or a description of whether it involves transport, storage or delay (for instance).

4 **Flowcharting and mapping** – These are the final steps in the analysis. They provide an overall view of the process in pictorial form. Charting details the passage of materials or documents through a process. Mapping enables the relationships, interfaces and potential failure points to be seen. The flowchart and map are essential reference documents for later comparison with benchmark processes. Much time, effort and potential confusion is spared at a later stage if the chart and map are completed painstakingly at this point.

Step 3: Identifying potential partners

This is the third and creative step of identifying which organization has a comparable process which is perceived to be better. Two questions which help at this stage are: 'Who or what is better at this process than us?' and 'To whom is this process key for survival?' It is also necessary to be clear about the definition of 'better' or 'best' as outlined earlier. In much the same way as Ferrari or Rolls-Royce cars have unique features which add up to a perception of 'best' in the eyes of buyers, so processes have unique features which make them particularly suitable, or efficient. Language, culture (organization and national), politics, locations, ethics and environmental factors also have a bearing on the selection of potential partners.

Step 4: Identifying data sources and selecting the appropriate collection method

This is the final step in the planning stage. Virtually all the data required for successful benchmarking already exist. The skill lies in obtaining the greatest amount of useful information from the smallest amount of data. It is useful to consider the following questions:

- What is the objective?

- What do we need to look for and why?
- How accurate must the data be?
- How much information do we need?
- How much time and resource can we allocate to this?

Sources of data range from corporate publications to special media reports and surveys; from personal networks to professional networks, trade associations and industry analysts; from corporate libraries to global databases. Table 26.1 provides a quick, though by no means comprehensive, reference guide for sources of information. Methods of collecting data will be influenced by the time, resources and skills available. Using business school information services may seem expensive, but could prove far more efficient than detailing a highly paid manager or an inexperienced graduate to search for the information required.

When the planning stage has been completed (see Figure 26.2) benchmarking moves into the analysis stage, which contains a further four steps.

THE ANALYSIS STAGE

Step 5: Data collection

Effective data collection and analysis will reduce the list of potential partners identified in Step 3 to just one or two names. These should be co-operative practitioners of a measurably more efficient process than your own. Furthermore, analysis of the data provides information on the performance metrics which indicate that a gap exists, and may also clarify what the process differences are. However, it is usually at this point that a visit is needed to validate metrics and provide vital evidence on how and why a process delivers improved performance. It should be regarded as the conclusive port of call for information, and planned accordingly. Correctly conducted, the visit will lead not only to understanding of the methodology, but also the combination of skills, attitudes, values, pride and culture which motivate people to produce superior results.

Every aspect of benchmarking – particularly outside your own organization – requires a sensitivity to the public relations, marketing, political, ethical and diplomatic ramifications of the exercise. This is nowhere more marked than in the area surrounding the conduct of visits, and has resulted in the drawing up of a code of conduct 'to contribute to efficient,

Table 26.1 Sources of information

Internal	*External*
Company libraries and databases	National and business school libraries
Corporate publications, including annual reports	International databases/Internet
Internal surveys and market research	Media broadcasts and reports
Personal networks	Trade shows, associations and journals
Planning and financial documents	Professional networks and institutions
	Industry analysts and consultants
	Suppliers and customers
	The Global Benchmarking Network

effective and ethical benchmarking' which is reproduced later in this chapter. This code was compiled initially for the benefit of practitioners in the United States, where it is now used extensively. The code has been adopted by, and is being promoted among, European companies by the UK-based Benchmarking Centre Ltd, an international membership organization dedicated to promoting the introduction and practice of benchmarking to achieve superior performance in Europe. Adherence to the code of conduct is already becoming a prerequisite to partnership arrangements, since it provides an effective way of gauging whether or not a company has embraced the spirit as well as the practice of benchmarking. It is particularly relevant in view of the degree of openness and collaboration required between partners.

Each visit should be preceded by briefing the host on the information and answers you are seeking, the people you would like to speak with, and the time the visit will take. Immediately following the visit, a report should be written. It is surprising how differently people assess the nature and quality of what they have seen. Reaching a consensus as soon as possible after the visit maximizes this learning. The report should incorporate what has been observed or learned under the four key areas of differences in process, management, structure and culture.

Steps 6, 7 and 8: Determining the gap, establishing process differences and targeting future performance

These three steps complete the analysis stage. Gap analyses include:

- descriptive and numeric data on the process
- calculation of the current and future estimated size of the difference
- explanation of the most likely causes
- assessment of the scope and nature of changes needed to close the gap and exceed the benchmark performance
- priority of these to produce optimum improvement
- evaluation of suitability and practicability of implementation
- assessment of the time frame and costs
- conclusion and recommendations
- a graphic illustration of the performance gap.

Gaps are 'positive' when the internal practices produce a better performance than comparative ones, and 'negative' when worse. In the early stages, gaps will tend to be negative. If analysis should prove a positive gap (especially in early benchmarking exercises), it is preferable to go back to Step 3 in the process and identify other potential sources of best practice, rather than assume directly that there is no need to improve your own!

The clearest and most comprehensive way to highlight differences in performance is by direct visual comparison of the process maps, accompanied by a documentary synopsis of the changes.

The improvement targets, together with the dates when they are to be implemented and completed, should then be set, bearing in mind that they must deliver results which substantially exceed those currently delivered by the benchmark process if they are to result in superior performance. The rate of improvement over the target period will have to be far greater than the partner's, whose own level of improvement will continue to rise.

THE ACTION STAGE

The action stage incorporates four more steps (see Figure 26.2) which, if pursued with thoroughness, will ensure that the performance gap swings to positive through effective implementation.

Step 9: Communicate to management and others

Communications play a key role in the change process, and if managed sensitively, can dissipate natural resistance. Change usually results from dissatisfaction with the present, combined with an understanding of what and how to change, and a clear picture of the desired future. Since it provides information across all three parameters, benchmarking can be a powerful motivational element in a broader change programme. Central questions should address 'Who is most affected by what has been discovered?' and 'How will this affect them?' Strong cases of resistance can often be dissolved by including the person or persons in a visit to the benchmark company.

Step 10: Corrective improvement plans

Plans should describe the solution or change suggested by the foregoing work, plus a plan to implement this, and a method for monitoring and reviewing the impact on outputs, results and critical success factors. Bearing in mind that most changes will occur over a period of time, the metrics and monitoring mechanisms should be clear and unequivocal. Goals should be sufficiently flexible to allow for the continual minor adjustments provoked by external factors, such as fluctuations in the political climate or feedback from customers, and internal factors such as leadership or budgetary changes. They will remain realistic only if synchronized to such feedback.

Step 11: Implementation

Implementation depends for its success on diligence and attention to detail combined with constant monitoring and measurement of results to determine whether the process is improving. Regular review of contingency plans and deadlines, along with concise and precise documentation of progress, are essential to maintain momentum and provide impetus. Frequent communication of progress and success stories will help maintain commitment not only from those actively involved in carrying out the improvement, but also those who must be relied on to provide essential background support (such as sanctioning expenditure) over the longer term.

Step 12: The review stage

An iterative and extremely important element of the improvement cycle, this is also the last of the 12 steps in the methodology (see Figure 26.2). Progress throughout the exercise should be monitored to ensure objectives are met or targets modified. In the final step, the level of improvement is reviewed, along with its impact on process performance and consequent effect on competitiveness. Assuming superiority has been achieved, decisions will be made about custodianship of the process (simply moving on to the next thing leaves the field wide open for regression) and frequency of continuing review to maintain the edge.

A broader review should conclude the benchmarking process. This completes the cycle, and provides the ultimate feedback loop which ensures that benefit to the organization as a whole is optimized. It should supply evidence and information on which to base decisions about future courses of action, such as which other processes should be benchmarked, and facilitate consideration of how benchmarking skills, or the technique itself, might be enhanced. It is at this point that companies, having become familiar with the 12-step methodology, can most sensibly 'customize' the approach to suit their particular circumstances.

The iterative process of constant monitoring, review and recycling, and the learning that accompanies it, ultimately lead to integration of benchmarking into organization and management practice. Reviews at this mature stage will incorporate efficient co-ordination of benchmarking resource and effort to maintain competitive superiority.

Managing benchmarking in the organization

Benchmarking alone is not enough to guarantee superior or world-class performance, but the evidence of its exponents suggests that it is a prerequisite to achieving that status. Once it is gained, companies rarely maintain competitive edge by accident. Furthermore, the better an organization is perceived to be, the more is expected of it. Throughout benchmarking, management must ensure optimum effectiveness of the process itself and its contribution, through other management mechanisms (the planning and budgetary cycles, for example), to the development of the business. Balancing the interests of the company with customer needs while maintaining the 'best-practice' philosophy can be a difficult juggling act. Ultimately, benchmarking is continuous learning, becoming more powerful the more it is practised. It is a philosophy of continuous improvement encapsulated in *Dantotsu*, the Japanese for continually 'striving to be best'. This philosophy permeates the Japanese work ethic, and is demonstrated by their attention to detail.

To deliver sustainable continuous improvement, benchmarking activity should constantly challenge the status quo. This requires 'proactive' management of the practitioners, and recognition of the depth of integration of the technique with other standard mechanisms in the organization. It demands top-level commitment to ensure that the improvement philosophy is mirrored in the strategies pursued by the various components of the firm. Research (Sweeney, 1992) has shown that the processes of a company frequently have little congruency with strategy. Top-level commitment will help co-ordinate an overview of total business strategy and sub-strategies (for manufacturing or marketing, for instance), thus helping in the selection of processes chosen for benchmarking which will steer the organization in the desired strategic direction.

With the integration of benchmarking will come the need to redirect resources or make trade-offs that ensure that the right things are done at the optimum time and in the best interests of the firm. It is the role of senior management to ensure that benchmarking is absorbed into the strategic planning processes of the company. Leading exponents of the technique, Motorola executives try to start every new product and capital programme with a search for 'best of breed' in the world at large. The demand for consistency with strategy becomes more critical as external activity develops, since this impacts on the image and reputation of the company. The final stages of integration are characterized by the need to sustain motivation and energy for the technique while also maintaining the humility to recognize that improvement is still possible and desirable.

Inevitably, the company with recognizably 'best' processes will receive numerous demands from others wishing to benchmark against it. Senior management must be clear on their policy for handling these requests. Where relevant, they will need to develop the organizational flexibility to provide positive assistance with the least possible interruption or disruption to the business.

Modern strategy incorporates co-operation and collaboration among best-practice organizations to the advantage of all participants without compromising competitiveness. The search for world-class benchmarks is never likely to end, and it is this realization which underpins the success that benchmarking is enjoying throughout the industrial and commercial environment.

Benchmarking codes of conduct

The Benchmarking Centre Ltd advocates the following code of conduct originally produced by the Council of Benchmarking in the Strategic Planning Institute. A European code of conduct has also been produced which takes cognizance of the European Community. While the wording differs slightly, the spirit of these codes is identical. All organizations and individuals involved in benchmarking are encouraged to adhere to the most appropriate one for their particular needs. Both codes are available from the Benchmarking Centre Ltd and the Global Benchmarking Network.

THE CODE

To contribute to efficient, effective and ethical benchmarking, individuals agree, for themselves and their organization, to abide by the following principles for benchmarking with other organizations:

1 **Principle of legality** – Avoid discussions or actions that might lead to or imply an interest in restraint of trade, market or customer allocation schemes, price fixing, dealing arrangements, bid rigging, bribery or misappropriation. Do not discuss costs with competitors if costs are an element of pricing.

2 **Principle of exchange** – Be willing to provide the same level of information that you request in any benchmarking exchange.

3 **Principle of confidentiality** – Treat benchmarking interchange as something confidential to the individuals and organizations involved. Information obtained must not be communicated outside the partnering organizations without prior consent of participating benchmarking partners. An organization's participation in a study should not be communicated externally without their permission.

4 **Principle of use** – Use information obtained through benchmarking partnering only for the purpose of improvement of operations with the partnering companies themselves. External use or communication of a benchmarking partner's name with their data or observed practices requires permission of that partner. Do not, as a consultant or client, extend one company's benchmarking study findings to another without the first company's permission.

5 **Principle of first-party contact** – Initiate contacts, whenever possible, through a benchmarking contact designated by the partner company. Obtain mutual agreement

with the contact on any delegation of communication or responsibility to other parties.

6 **Principle of third-party contact** – Obtain an individual's permission before providing their name in response to a contact request.

7 **Principle of preparation** – Demonstrate commitment to the efficiency and effectiveness of the benchmarking process with adequate preparation at each process step, particularly at initial partnering contact.

Etiquette and ethics

In actions between benchmarking partners the emphasis is on openness and trust. The following guidelines apply to both partners in a benchmarking encounter:

- In benchmarking with competitors, establish specific ground-rules up front, such as: 'We don't want to talk about those things that will give either of us a competitive advantage. Rather, we want to see where we can mutually improve or gain benefit.'
- Do not ask competitors for sensitive data or cause the benchmarking partner to feel that sensitive data must be provided to keep the process going.
- Use an ethical third party to assemble and blind competitive data, with inputs from legal counsel, for direct competitor comparisons.
- Consult with legal counsel if any information gathering procedure is in doubt, for example before contacting a direct competitor.
- Any information obtained from a benchmarking partner should be treated as internal privileged information.
- Do not:
  - disparage a competitor's business or operations to a third party
  - attempt to limit competition or gain business through the benchmarking relationship.

Benchmarking exchange protocol

As the benchmarking process proceeds to the exchange of information, benchmarkers are expected to:

- Know and abide by the benchmarking code of conduct.
- Have basic knowledge of benchmarking and follow a benchmarking process.
- Determine beforehand what to benchmark, identify key performance variables, recognize superior performing companies and complete rigorous self-assessment.
- Develop a questionnaire and interview guide, and share these in advance if requested.
- Have the authority to share information.
- Work through a specified host, and mutually agree on scheduling and meeting arrangements.
- Follow these guidelines in face-to-face site visits:
  - Provide meeting agenda in advance.
  - Be professional, honest, courteous and prompt.
  - Introduce all attendees, and explain why they are present.

- Adhere to the agenda.
- Maintain focus on benchmarking issues.
- Use language that is universal, not your own jargon.
- Do not share proprietary information without prior approval for the proper authority of both parties.
- Share information about your process, if asked, and consider sharing study results.
- Offer to set up a reciprocal visit.
- Conclude meetings and visits on schedule.
- Thank the benchmarking partner for the time and for the sharing.

Benchmarking and quality awards

Quality awards, introduced to raise standards of excellence within and across national boundaries, often provide a powerful incentive for organizations to strive for continuous improvement.

In the United States, the Malcolm Baldrige National Quality Award carries considerable prestige. It requires that companies provide performance comparisons, backed by benchmarking evidence, in their application details. Consequently, the award has been directly responsible for promoting the use of benchmarking among American organizations since its introduction in the mid-1980s.

In Europe, the European Quality Award was first presented in 1992. Subsequently, many countries in Europe have developed their own National Quality Awards based on the European model. These implicitly incorporate the need for benchmarking in the self-appraisal and application criteria. They will therefore exert considerable influence on European organizations to adopt the technique in their efforts to achieve excellence and gain recognition for superior processes, practices and products. The European Best Practice Benchmarking Award, first presented in 1995, was initiated by the Benchmarking Centre Ltd to encourage businesses and academics across Europe to document their best benchmarking case studies and research. Presented annually, the award facilitates the sharing and transfer of knowledge on the realities of benchmarking projects, and the gains to be had from them.

Useful organizations

Benchmarking Centre: <http:www.benchmarking.co.uk>.
British Quality Foundation: <http:www.quality-foundation.co.uk>.
Global Benchmarking Network: <http:www.globalbenchmarking.org>.

References and further reading

Camp, Robert C., *Benchmarking: The Search for Industry Best Practices that Lead to Superior Performance*, Quality Press, American Society of Quality Control, Milwaukee, WI, 1989.

Codling, Sylvia, *Best Practice Benchmarking: The Management Guide to Successful Implementation*, Industrial Newsletters, Toddington, 1992.

Hart, C.W.L. and Bogan, C.E., *The Baldrige: What It is, How It's Won, How to Use It to Improve Quality in Your Company*, McGraw-Hill, New York, 1992.

Levitt, T., 'Marketing myopia', *Harvard Business Review*, Vol. 38, No. 4, July/August 1960, pp. 45–56.

Rusk, D., *Time Magazine*, 6 December 1963.

Sweeney, M.J., *Benchmarking for Strategic Manufacturing Management*, Working Paper No. SWP 43/92, Cranfield School of Management, 1992.

Walleck, S.A., O'Halloran, J.D. and Leader, C.A., 'Benchmarking world-class performance', *The McKinsey Quarterly*, 1, 1992, 3–23.

PART 4 *Act*

CHAPTER

27 Managing Nonconformity

Ray Spencer

Even with well-defined specifications and capable processes, there are occasions when products or services fail to conform to requirements in some way. In such cases, a decision is required. The way a business manages such decisions can say more about its approach to quality than any quality policy statement ever could. It provides the acid test for commitment and integrity. This chapter examines the distinction between nonconforming and defective, the pitfalls and the opportunities presented by nonconformity, the process for managing nonconformity, and how to use it as a springboard for improving the quality of products, processes and systems.

Definitions

Before discussing the management of nonconformity, it is helpful to understand the difference between nonconforming and defective:

- Nonconforming – A unit or service is nonconforming when at least one quality characteristic results in a specified requirement not being met.
- Defective – A unit or service is defective when at least one quality characteristic results in its failing to satisfy an intended purpose.

In simpler terms, nonconforming means 'specification not met', and defective means 'intended purpose not achieved'. This is a subtle but important distinction.

The pitfalls and the opportunities

In the absence of a well-defined approach for managing nonconformity, a number of hazards will emerge, sooner or later. When nonconformity does occur, it can jeopardize schedules or outputs and demand urgent attention. Views on the seriousness or level of risk posed by the nonconformity can vary depending on the goals and objectives of individuals involved. The first question frequently asked is: 'Can it still be used?' This is a perfectly reasonable question, but dangerous if answered by the wrong person with the wrong motive.

In most organizations, the arbitrator on nonconformity is the quality manager. If the quality manager takes an intransigent view and rejects nonconformity without fully considering cause and effect, there is little prospect of co-operation for improvement, and a high probability of damaging internal conflict. On the other hand, if the quality manager is unduly influenced by peer or senior pressure, personal credibility will be the first casualty, quickly followed by the company's reputation as dissatisfaction, returns and claims increase. Any process must therefore take full account of all facts, risks and opportunities. A business that consistently applies such a process can expect the following benefits:

- a common understanding of requirements
- methodology that identifies causes and preventive measures
- knowledge that can be applied in future developments
- performance gains from problem resolution
- increased profitability from cost reduction.

The quality manager can expect these additional benefits:

- trust, by involving others
- credibility, from using objective decisionmaking
- peace of mind, by employing a sound process.

Decision criteria

SPECIFICATIONS AND STANDARDS

When considering any item potentially nonconforming or defective, it is necessary to make reference to existing specifications or standards used to define acceptability. Specifications relate to individual products, processes or services, defining such things as performance, reliability, capability, function, materials and appearance. Standards relate to a range of products, processes, services and systems, rather than individual items. They can be generated by departments, businesses, trade associations, professional institutions, buying groups, government institutions, defence agencies and national or international standards organizations.

Ideally, specifications or standards adequately define the boundaries of acceptability. In practice, they often fail to cover all eventualities completely, adding spice to the investigation process.

SUBJECTIVITY AND OBJECTIVITY

Subjectivity implies a dependence on personal taste or views. Where no definition of acceptability exists, subjectivity thrives. Production functions interpret things differently to quality functions, suppliers disclaim liability for rejections, and even within the quality function, individuals can reach different conclusions based on personal views or experience. Even when the design authority or the customer is consulted on acceptability, unless standards are established, limits or acceptability are clearly defined and the conditions for acceptance or rejection are known, the same problem will probably occur time and time again.

To make objective decisions, all parameters and characteristics must in some form be measurable or comparable. Using a suitable measurement instrument to determine length, weight, speed or electrical current is normally quite straightforward, but problems occur when appropriate measuring instruments do not exist, or would be difficult to conceive, such as with paint finish and solder joints. In these situations, it is necessary to produce standards that demonstrate limits of acceptability. Examples are charts, samples, diagrams and photographs. The process of establishing such standards is often preceded by long and heated discussions, and it may take several attempts to get it right, but this is a small price to pay for avoiding the continuing chaos created by uncertainty.

PRECEDENT

Using a previous case as an example to be followed has limitations. Something that is acceptable in one set of conditions can be totally unacceptable in another. A minor deviation in the output of a device may work perfectly well in one application, but could have major reliability or safety implications when used in others. Bypassing analysis and formal approval in granting concessions based on precedent is hazardous at best, and sets a poor example that others will all too easily follow.

ATTITUDE

Attitudes towards nonconformity can vary greatly according to circumstance, particularly when any of the following conditions exist:

- lack of information
- conflicting priorities
- inadequate traceability.

When there is insufficient information available to determine the cause or effect of nonconformity, it is prudent to err on the side of caution and place a hold on the product pending the outcome of further investigation. For straightforward issues, this is normally acceptable; but for complex issues, the time involved can be long and the skills for solving the problems may be lacking. Faced with these dilemmas, it is easy to assume that lack of information indicates lack of evidence of risk, and to trust that everything will turn out all right.

Conflicting priorities can add weight to this view when individuals have other reasons to play down the risks posed by nonconformity. Project managers faced with missed schedules, production managers faced with lost output, designers faced with late model introductions, materials managers faced with increased inventories, sales managers faced with lost orders and general managers needing better results could all have alternative motives for supporting a view that nonconformity may not be a problem. Such views can make life difficult for the quality manager, particularly when these individuals are not accountable for the consequences.

There are also those inclined to turn a blind eye if there is little chance that a nonconformity will be detected, or cannot be traced to them personally.

The reasons such disappointing attitudes develop are generally due to poor leadership, internal rivalry and individual rather than common goals. No one wins in the long run, and ultimately the customer suffers. The attitude only changes when the business leader is truly customer-focused and everyone works to satisfy the needs of their own internal and external customers.

Process for dealing with nonconformity

The level of detail involved in dealing with nonconformity can vary considerably. In a large company producing complex components in the aerospace industry, representatives from many functions follow rigidly defined procedures to review nonconforming items. In a small distribution company employing just a handful of staff, the proprietor alone may deal with nonconforming items. Whatever the size or complexity of the business, though, the process for dealing with nonconformities will involve the following activities, in some form:

1 discovery
2 identification
3 segregation
4 analysis
5 approval
6 action
7 disposal
8 closeout
9 tracking.

An illustration of the stages involved in managing nonconforming material is shown in Figure 27.1.

DISCOVERY

Whether discovered at incoming inspection, in process, during inspection or from customer returns, nonconformity requires investigation to decide what needs to be done with affected units and what action must be taken to prevent recurrence. To enable tracking of the process, a document or computer file is used to record occurrence, conditions, liability, disposal and other action taken. The record is often called a nonconforming material record or report (NMR). An example is shown in Figure 27.2.

The information entered at the discovery stage is typically:

- material or part number, issue and description
- specified and actual results
- quantity or ratio of nonconforming items
- batch or order number
- originator's name and the date raised.

The NMR is normally initiated by the quality function, and then used to record inputs, approval and agreed action. Dependent upon the approach adopted and the urgency of the situation, the NMR may be distributed manually, electronically, or held pending a meeting of individuals involved in the decisionmaking process. Such a meeting is termed a Material Review Board (MRB) in more formal procedures.

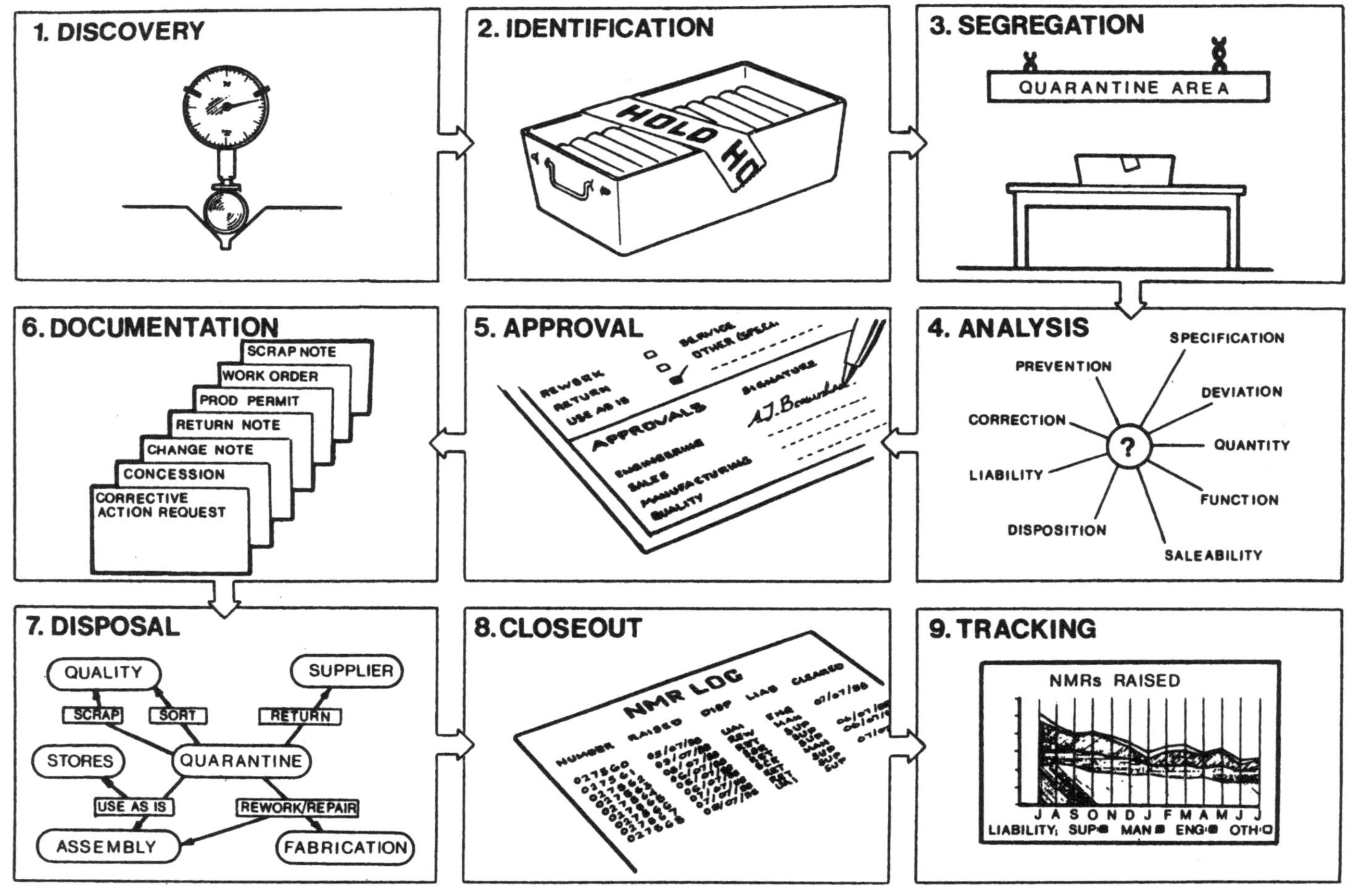

Figure 27.1 The stages of nonconformity management

RAGLETTS plc	**NONCONFORMING MATERIAL REPORT**			NMR: 01625
Part Number:	Issue:	Description:	Vendor/Operation/Customer:	Ord/~~Op/Acc~~ No:
6P90642	B	Support Shaft	ZT Jones Ltd	P/0 39468

Used on:	Lot Size:	Accept:	Reject:	Originator (Print):	Signature:	Date:
30S92431	500	27	5	KJ ROBBINS	KJ Robbins	10 Aug 2002

Specification:

Zone D-5 16.00dia. +/– 0.05 mm

DISPOSITION

DISPOSITION		LIABILITY		RELATED DOCUMENTS Name	Number
Use as is	❑	Supplier	☒	Return Note	07008
Sort	❑	Design	❑		
Rework	❑	Manufacture	❑		
Repair	❑	Other (Specify)	❑		
Return to supplier	☒				
Scrap	❑				

Deviation

Below bottom limit – to 15.87 mm

APPROVALS

	Name (print)	Signature	Date
Quality	BJ BROWN	BJ Brown	12 Aug 02
Manufacturing	N/A		
Design	LB ELLIOT	LB Elliot	12/08/02
Sales	N/A		

Comments

Undersize shaft diameter is unacceptable.

LBE Design Dept 12/08/02

DISTRIBUTION

Quality	☒
Manufacturing	❑
Design	❑
Sales	❑
Other (identify)	❑

Figure 27.2 A typical nonconforming material report

IDENTIFICATION

Following discovery of nonconforming material, it is important that all such material is marked 'Nonconforming material – DO NOT USE.' The wording and methods can vary, but red labels or red letters are commonly used to deter the use of such materials, and are available in the following forms:

- tote box label inserts
- adhesive tape
- tie-on labels
- sign plates.

Alternatively, nonconforming materials are stored in defined areas, pending segregation or analysis.

SEGREGATION

Once material has been clearly identified as nonconforming, it must then be segregated from all other material to prevent unintended use of installation until a decision on disposition is made. This area is commonly referred to as a 'Quarantine area', with restricted access for placement and disposal of material only.

ANALYSIS

The first stage of analysis is to determine whether an item is truly nonconforming, defective, or both. This involves examining drawings, specifications, standards, job instructions or purchase orders to establish whether requirements are met and whether requirements are adequately defined to make this judgement.

The second stage is to determine the extent of nonconformity, in two respects:

1 the deviation from specification or the failure to meet intended purpose
2 the quantity or rate of nonconforming items.

The third stage determines what effect the nonconformity or defect will have on the function or saleability of the product. Where the specification or function is in question, the design authority is consulted. The design authority will be internal in many organizations, but for suppliers this can involve asking the customer for clarification or making a request for concession.

The fourth stage identifies liability and responsibility for corrective and preventive actions. Although the assignment of liability is normally straightforward, it is sometimes less obvious, and liability can be altered following identification of the root cause during subsequent corrective action investigations.

The final stage is to decide what to do with the nonconforming units. The key factors in deciding disposition are acceptability, urgency and feasibility. The main options, in various combinations, are:

- sort
- use as is, on concession

- re-grade and use in a different application
- rework or repair, including re-inspection upon completion
- return to the supplier
- scrap.

APPROVAL

Approval involves completing the NMR to indicate liability, disposition and other action required, which affected parties sign to indicate approval. This can involve a meeting of nominated representatives, it can involve bringing the NMR to those concerned, or, increasingly, it means using an electronically integrated system to inform, respond, approve and distribute the NMR. In a small company, it may involve just one individual completing a document to record occurrence, liability and disposition. Where required by contract, the use of nonconforming or repaired product is reported to the customer for concession.

The quality function normally has overall responsibility for control of the process. Where many nominated representatives are involved, an elevation process to address major issues may be required, with limits of authority to the level of chief executive if necessary.

ACTION

An outline of various action documents that can be used depending on the disposition agreed is shown in Figure 27.3, and a brief outline of the purpose of each document is given below.

- **Concession** – a written authorization prior to use or release of a quantity of items that do not conform to specified requirements; see Chapter 15 for more information
- **Work order** – an order for repair or rework or any other form of action in addition to standard work content
- **Scrap note** – authorization to dispose of material that cannot be reworked, repaired or used for any other purpose
- **Return note** – notification to a supplier of the reason for returning material; this document sometimes incorporates a corrective action request document
- **Corrective action request** – a request to the individual or function deemed liable for nonconformity to define the root cause, corrective action and measures to prevent recurrence; an example is shown in Figure 27.4
- **Tool order** – an order for new or modified tooling
- **Operation instruction** – a written instruction detailing materials, methods and tooling required to perform an operation
- **Engineering change note** – an authorization for a permanent change to a specification or drawing; this is covered in detail in Chapter 15
- **Production permit** – a written authorization prior to production or provision of a service to deviate from specified requirements for a defined quantity of units or for a defined period of time; see Chapter 15 for more information.

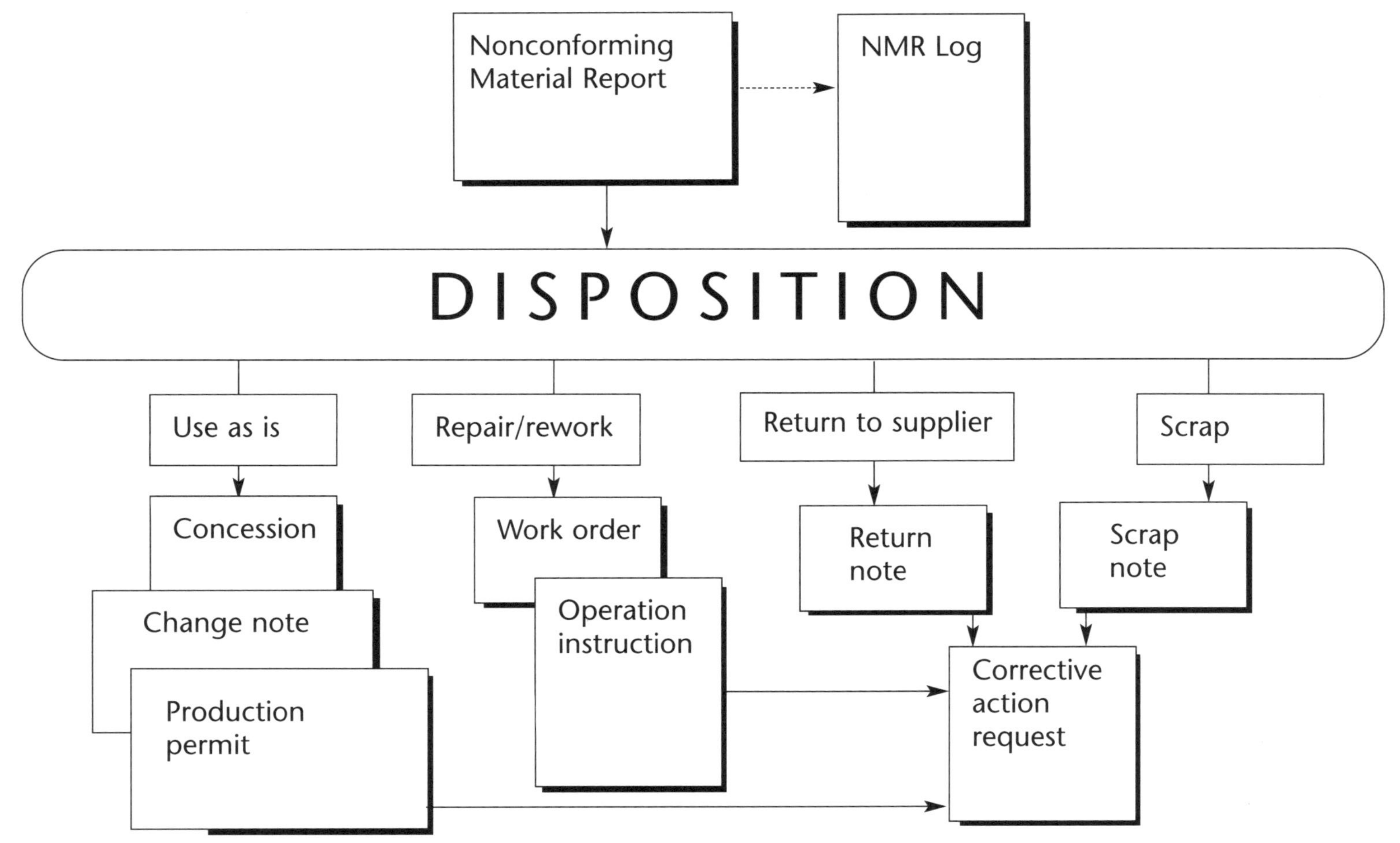

Figure 27.3 Documents used, depending on disposition

RAGLETTS plc

CORRECTIVE ACTION REQUEST

Complete and return sections 2 and 3 to Raglettsplc@ragletts.co.uk

CAR No: 00172

SECTION 1 – PROBLEM STATEMENT

Part number: ☐ Issue: ☐ Description: ☐

Purchase / W.O. No: ☐ Supplied by: ☐

Requirement: ☐ Nonconformity: ☐

Qty Inspected: ☐ Qty Rejected: ☐ PPM: ☐ % ☐

Originator: ☐ Department: ☐ Date: ☐ Tel: ☐

Issued to: ☐ Issue Date: ☐

SECTION 2 – ROOT CAUSE ANALYSIS

Analysis conducted:

☐

Root cause:

☐

Prepared by: ☐ Date: ☐

SECTION 3 – ACTION

	Completion Dates	
	Plan	Actual
Remedial Action:		
Corrective Action:		
Preventive Action:		

Prepared by: ☐ Title: ☐ Date: ☐ Tel: ☐

Figure 27.4 A corrective action request form

DISPOSAL

Based on the disposition agreed, the material is released from quarantine as defined for disposal on the NMR, with notification to the accounts function.

CLOSEOUT

The controlling function, normally quality, confirms that materials have been treated or disposed of as approved on the NMR, that units reworked or repaired have been re-inspected, and that follow-up actions for correction or prevention have been implemented.

TRACKING

NMRs are used to determine the effectiveness of actions to correct and prevent the occurrence of nonconformities. NMR data are also used to identify trends in liability sources and major types of nonconformity. The subject is covered further in this chapter under 'Trend analysis'.

Controls

An important step leading to the reduction of nonconformity is to ensure that all occurrences are exposed as soon as they occur, whatever their source.

SOURCES OF NONCONFORMITY

Sources of nonconformity include design, manufacturing planning, suppliers, material supply, fabrication, assembly, test/inspection, warehousing and distribution. This offers a wide range of possibilities, but the discovery of nonconformities normally occurs in one of four areas:

1 incoming inspection
2 in process
3 final test and inspection
4 customer returns.

Incoming inspection

Increasingly, suppliers are required to demonstrate the capability of their processes and to guarantee the quality of materials supplied, obviating the need for incoming inspection. As a result, incoming inspection tends to be limited to items that have a history of problems, or those where insufficient evidence of capability exists to discontinue inspection. For all inspection conducted, by the supplier or at incoming inspection, it is important that all parts in each sample lot are inspected. Ceasing inspection when sufficient nonconformities have been found to reject a lot risks failing to identify other nonconformities that may be present in the lot, and it can also distort process average data.

When supplier liability has been confirmed and disposal decided, the supplier is requested to identify clearly the root cause and action being taken to prevent recurrence. To trigger and track this activity, many companies issue a Corrective Action Request (CAR) form to suppliers. A CAR does provide a useful method of confirming that a supplier is addressing nonconformity, but the best indicators of successful supplier corrective action are adequate process capability and defect-free supply.

In process

Nonconformity discovered in process is frequently manifested in the form of defects or failures that hamper production output. If they are not resolved rapidly, there is always a risk that the production function may resort to measures that allow production to continue until a formal solution is found. However, local solutions do not always take full account of later production needs, intended function or the long-term reliability of the finished product. When an issue cannot be resolved immediately, it is necessary to quarantine finished or partly finished production pending resolution.

Nonconformity that directly affects output will rightly receive high-priority attention, but infrequent or isolated cases of nonconformity can easily be overlooked. Although they cause only minor irritations in production, they can sometimes point to issues that can later become major field problems. By providing operators with collection areas for random parts or items that have failed or are unusable, supervisors or inspectors are able to collect them at suitable intervals for investigation, as for any other nonconforming item.

Final test and inspection

Being the final stage before shipment, these results are often crucial for customers and producers. When deadlines are threatened, this area can experience strong internal and external pressure to reduce testing or relax standards. Such pressures should be steadfastly refused without a formal concession being granted.

Customer returns

In some businesses, customer returns are handled by a service function, and in others by the quality function. Whichever is used, any nonconforming units should undergo the same process applied to those discovered internally. In addition, there is a need to give careful consideration to customer responses and settlements, particularly when contributory negligence, false claims, inadequate specifications or potentially serious reliability or safety issues are involved. Whatever the outcome, any response to the customer requires the full knowledge and approval of all affected functions within the business.

APPROVAL RULES AND RESPONSIBILITY

To ensure a common understanding of the process and responsibilities, an outline procedure is required, as a minimum. An example is shown in Figure 27.5.

Implementation

Any company requiring certification to ISO 9001 or QS 9000 needs no additional justification for implementing a process for controlling nonconforming product. Where no formal quality system exists, or where the process for managing nonconforming product is clearly inadequate, justification for implementation of a new or improved process may be

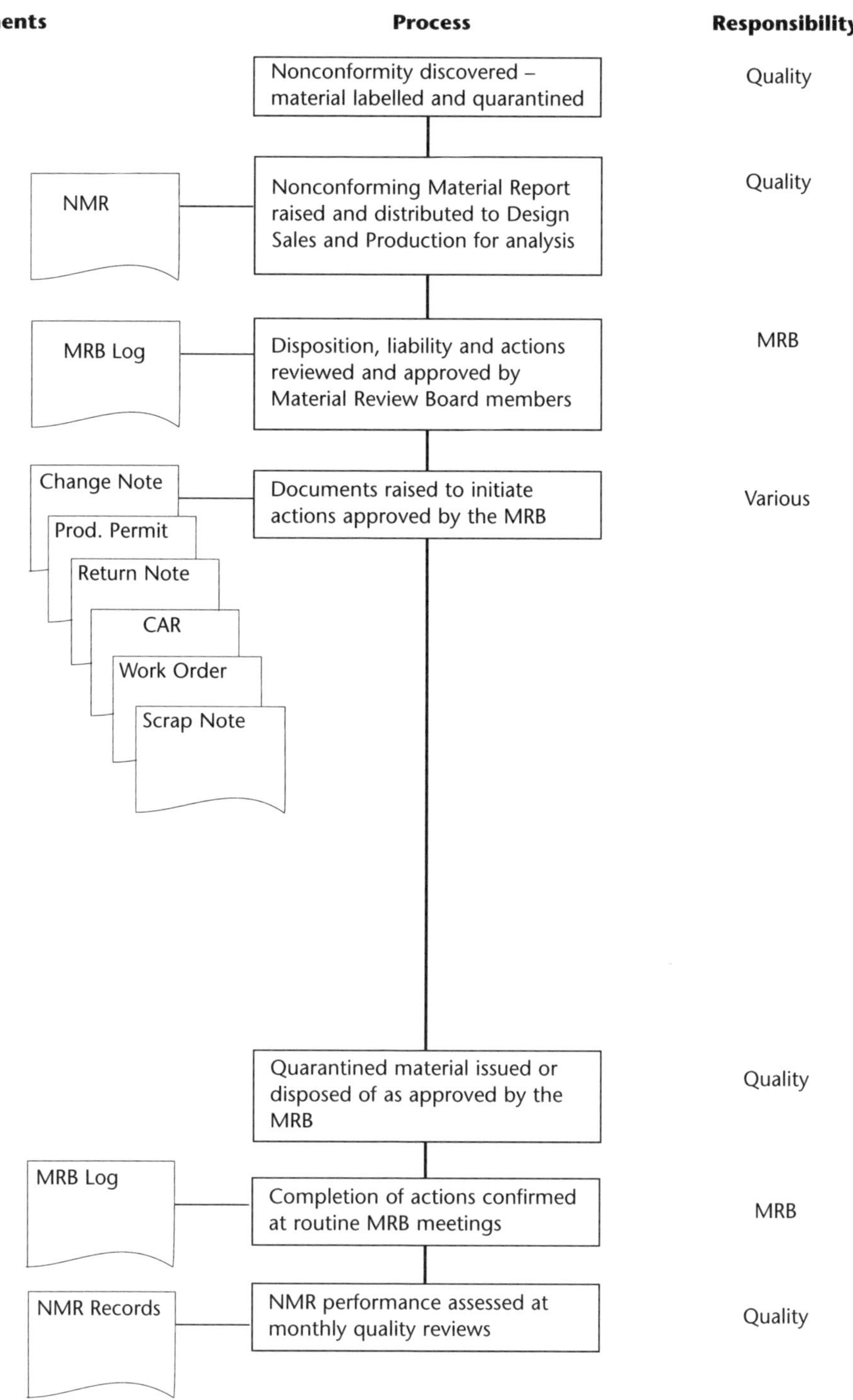

Figure 27.5 Example of an outline nonconformity management procedure

required. Making a conservative estimate of nonconforming materials costs is a good place to start. A modest cost-reduction target is likely to be more than sufficient to offset any implementation costs. Nonconforming costs include:

- failure, in the form of scrap, rework and repair
- appraisal, involving sorting and purging
- returns, including refunds and claims settled
- recovery of lost production
- sales and goodwill lost.

Costs for implementing the process include:

- Implementation – documentation, hardware and software
- Maintenance costs – incremental staffing, meetings, and so on.

Preparing and cost-justifying the case for implementation makes the selling and budget approval process much easier. Once approval is gained, addressing and overcoming operational issues before implementation is vital in preventing a negative reaction. This includes describing the process clearly to all potential users and addressing any concerns positively. A trial run in a selected area is a good way of ironing out any flaws and gaining acceptance before full implementation. As with all systems, when fully operational it should be reviewed for effectiveness, and improved if necessary. This is a routine activity for companies already certified to ISO 9001 as part of the management review process.

Improvements

The management of nonconformities is basically a reactive process, but it does serve to trigger actions that prevent further occurrences when used in conjunction with an effective corrective and preventive process that helps to improve products and processes in the future.

CORRECTIVE ACTIONS

Corrective actions cover remedial (immediate) interim and long-term actions. Remedial actions are measures enabling the recovery of nonconforming materials, where rework and repair are possible. Short-term or interim corrective actions are measures taken to reduce the risk of recurrence pending a longer-term solution. They include increased inspection, visual aids, samples and operating instructions. Interim measures are often reversible changes. They may reduce the risk of occurrence, but there is no guarantee that the problem will not happen again. Long-term corrective actions are intended to be permanent changes, and are frequently subject to resource, lead time or funding constraints. They address causes rather than symptoms, and include modifications to systems, design, processes, capability and tooling. Note that the term ‘preventive actions’ relates to potential nonconformities: problems that have not yet actually happened.

TREND ANALYSIS

A by-product of managing nonconformity is the ability to monitor improvement trends from analysis of NMRs raised. Useful indicators include:

- overall nonconformity rate
- customer nonconformity rate
- purchased material nonconformity rate.

These indicators provide a good source of data for selecting improvement projects, and a means for measuring their effectiveness.

Overall nonconformity rate

By tracking the total number of NMRs raised on a weekly, monthly or quarterly basis, the overall nonconformity rate of a business can be seen at a glance. Further analysis – by liability and type, for instance – can reveal areas most in need of attention.

Customer nonconformity rate

Tracking customer NMRs does not provide a reliable measure of customer satisfaction, since too many never complain, but it does indicate whether corrective and preventive measures have been effective.

Purchased material nonconformity rate

This provides a measure of purchased material quality, and focuses attention on areas that need to be addressed with individual suppliers and internal departments. It also provides one of the major components of a supplier performance rating system.

COST REDUCTIONS

A well-managed system for dealing with nonconformity can result in substantial cost reduction, as long as the corrective action process is effective. Reductions in the number of design changes, process deficiencies, operator errors, supplier returns, rework and remakes, stemming from the avoidance of problems identified previously, are just a few of the many tangible benefits that result.

DESIGN AND PROCESS CAPABILITIES

A nonconforming material process will expose and address design weaknesses, manufacturability issues and process capability limitations not identified in design reviews and design verification. Used positively, it leads to improvements in future products from changes made to design rules, standing orders and process guidelines.

Conclusion

The management of nonconforming material is perhaps the least positive area of quality management. In spite of measures taken in design, planning, manufacturing and throughout the business, this process is all about facing up to the fact that specifications or standards have not been met or may not be adequate. Managed badly, nonconformity will be a constant source of internal dispute and external dissatisfaction. Managed well, the rational analysis of nonconformity prevents more costly incidents, and points the way to improvements.

To err is human. To learn from errors made and to prevent them happening again is both sensible and profitable.

Further reading

Feigenbaum, Arnold V., *Total Quality Control*, 3rd edn, McGraw-Hill, New York, 1991.

Juran, J.M., *Quality Control Handbook*, 4th edn, McGraw-Hill, New York, 1988.

Juran, J.M. and Gryna, Frank M., Jr, *Quality Planning and Analysis*, 2nd edn, McGraw-Hill, New York, 1982.

CHAPTER 28 *Improvement*

John Edge and Matt Seaver

Managing the process for improvement

Improvement is the key to survival and prosperity for any organization. We must assume that our competitors are not standing still, so if we want even to keep up with them, we must improve our performance. Much has been written about improvement, and everybody is committed to it. But how to go about it?

To translate the aspiration into a working methodology is not too difficult, in theory. All that is needed is to adopt an intelligent and structured approach, and give it the appropriate commitment. What is difficult is to achieve the sort of results that are headlined in the quality press. But everybody can achieve some improvement, however small. This chapter attempts to give some guidance on the practicalities of implementing quality improvement initiatives. It cannot be considered a comprehensive treatment of the issue. Many readers will identify pet techniques or concepts that are not covered – or not, in their view, adequately. That is probably fair. What I have attempted is to provide the average manager with a flavour of what some of the many techniques involve and can achieve. More information and detailed descriptions of how to implement them can be found elsewhere. In the meantime, what follows will be sufficient to enable many readers to try out some of the techniques.

This chapter will look at some of the ideas of people such as Ishikawa, Deming, Juran, Crosby and other leaders in the field of quality over the years.

Benchmarking

Benchmarking is a very effective improvement technique that permits an organization to compare its performance with other highly effective organizations, and to identify the best practices that lead to the best performance in those organizations. Benchmarking has been defined as a 'continuous, systematic process for comparing performances of organisations, functions or processes against the "best in the world", aiming to not only match those performance levels, but to exceed them' (European Community DG III, 1996). The basis of benchmarking is the identification of one or more other organizations which are known to be the 'best in the class' in terms of performance. It is not necessary for the model company to be in the same sector.

An organization needs to have reached a certain level of maturity in terms of quality management if it is to reap the full benefits of benchmarking. There is little value in attempting benchmarking is there is not a sound base already in place consisting of the fundamentals, such as effective investigation of nonconformity, detailed knowledge of current levels of rejected product or service failure, an effective staff training system, and critical processes and tasks documented, where appropriate. It is not necessary to incur the costs of benchmarking in order to discover that these basics are part of the secret of success of the best in the class!

The selection of the right benchmarking partner is critical to the success of the project. But it should be remembered that no organization is best at everything, so it is likely that more than one partner will need to be selected, each a model for a different process or aspect of the business. It should also be remembered that in a large organization, the best benchmarking partner may be another section within that organization.

It is not possible to give a comprehensive treatment of this topic in this chapter, but the process of benchmarking can be summarized in the following steps:

PLAN

1. Set up the project team.
2. Define and document the current process of the organization.
3. Identify the scope and objectives of the project.
4. Define a set of performance 'metrics'.
5. Define the criteria for benchmarking partners.
6. Identify potential benchmarking partners.
7. Survey potential partners for suitability.

DO

8. Develop methodologies for obtaining the data.
9. Arrange and manage the visit to the partner's site.

CHECK

10. Analyse the information obtained during benchmarking visits and other interaction with the partner.
11. Determine current performance gaps.
12. Develop an improvement plan to eliminate the gaps.

ACT

13. Implement the improvement plan.

PLAN

14. Review the project, and measure its effectiveness.
15. Plan for continuous improvement.

And so the cycle of improvement goes on continuously.

Banking is covered in detail in Chapter 26.

Balanced scorecard

The balanced scorecard is a concept introduced by David Norton and Robert Kaplan in the early 1990s as a new approach to strategic management to assist an organization in translating its strategic objectives into a set of performance indicators. The balanced scorecard is both a management system and a measurement system. Kaplan and Norton describe the innovation of the balanced scorecard as follows:

> The balanced scorecard retains traditional financial measures. But financial measures tell the story of past events, an adequate story for industrial age companies for which investments in long-term capabilities and customer relationships were not critical for success. These financial measures are inadequate, however, for guiding and evaluating the journey that information age companies must make to create future value through investment in customers, suppliers, employees, processes, technology, and innovation.

The balanced scorecard addresses the organization from four perspectives. The organization is required to develop metrics for measurement of performance with respect to each of these perspectives:

- The Learning and Growth Perspective
- The Business Process Perspective
- The Customer Perspective
- The Financial Perspective.

Under each of the four perspectives, the organization identifies targets, each with its own set of metrics for measuring performance, with the overall view of achieving the strategic objectives of the organization.

Kaizen

Kaizen is the Japanese term for 'improvement'. It is very much a hands-on process. The members of the kaizen team do not simply plan the improvement, but get involved in cleaning machinery, moving it about, and making changes to processes. A refinement of the kaizen approach is to conduct a 'kaizen blitz'. As the name implies, this is a short, sharp campaign to achieve an immediate result. Kaizen is particularly suited to generating improvement in an engineering operation. Kaizen is based on a number of principles, loosely stated as follows:

- Maintain a positive attitude.
- Look for solutions rather than accept excuses.
- Everybody can contribute, and everybody's contribution can be valuable.
- Take action. Just do it!
- Do it now. Don't wait for perfection. Whatever you do now will achieve something.

One of the most attractive aspects of the kaizen approach is that it can be low-cost. It is very important not to make the mistake of thinking that throwing money at a problem is the best way to solve it. Sometimes it is, but usually a low-cost solution will achieve a significant improvement. However, the low-cost solution often involves attitude change on the part of staff at all levels, and this can be much more difficult to achieve than the approval to spend money on an investment solution to the problem.

ISHIKAWA'S SIX FEATURES OF QUALITY WORK

To explain the Japanese quality miracle, Ishikawa gave six features of quality work (Ishikawa, 1978, 1985):

1 a company-wide quality control programme
2 top management subject to quality audits
3 industrial education and training
4 quality circle (QC) activities
5 nationwide quality control promotion activities
6 application of statistical techniques.

A company-wide quality control programme

Every department and all levels and types of personnel within the company are engaged in systematic work, guided by written quality policies. These quality policies are endorsed by upper management, and their successful implementation is driven by management.

The consequence of this approach is that all personnel are committed to producing a quality product or providing a quality service, since management is itself consciously seeking to achieve this objective by known and agreed means.

In Europe and the USA, quality control often relates to the day-to-day activities of personnel implementing quality, with quality assurance being the management function of auditing and reviewing those activities. In Japan, quality control embraces both these notions, and is more akin to total quality management.

Top management subject to quality audits

A quality executive team visits each company department to identify, isolate and help remove any obstacles to the production of quality products or services. Normally, audits are done by the quality experts, but periodically a quality executive team is required to calibrate the department management and its products or services. Conversations are directed at the users of the product or service, company quality experts, departments production and manufacturing management, and shop-floor workers.

Industrial education and training

Education and training in quality must be given to everybody in all departments at each level, since company-wide quality requires participation by everyone involved.

The initial training has to take place within the quality department, so that the quality personnel 'train ourselves before we are fit to train others'. Only then do quality personnel start to train personnel in other departments.

These training programmes are intensive, and are attended by all managers and workers. This is a necessary step, but not sufficient to make personnel quality managers or quality workers. Training has to be complemented by continuing education, which brings awareness and discipline; from these the quality consciousness evolves.

The training is given by the quality personnel involved in the day-to-day activities of the department. They are aware of its problems and their evaluation. Personnel from the department bring uniformity to the educational process, and provide a common pool of experience, from which all can draw.

Quality circle activities

A quality circle is: 'A small group which meets voluntarily to perform quality control within a workshop to which they belong' (JUSE, 1980). The QC had traditionally been applied to the manufacturing process, but was expanded to include management and engineering quality. The QC provides a forum to discuss the department's problems; its full benefits are only seen in a company-wide quality approach.

Nationwide quality control promotion activities

November is Quality Month in Japan; the Deming Prize is awarded that month. The Deming Prize is used to advertise a company's products, since it ensures such a high degree of customer confidence that the customer can be sure of a quality product. This type of quality awareness reinforces quality ideas across the whole of society.

Application of statistical techniques

Statistical techniques for quality control include: Pareto analysis, cause-and-effect analysis, process analysis, histograms and various Shewhart-type control charts.

These statistical techniques enabled the Japanese to quantify quality and give it a high degree of 'scientific' objectivity. Deming was largely responsible for their introduction, and his guidance laid the foundation for the quality revolution.

JURAN'S THREE TARGET QUALITY AREAS

Another thinker who realized the link between management and quality was Juran (1981a, 1981b). He has highlighted three target quality areas to challenge assumptions and to change thinking:

1 upper management leadership of each company's approach to product quality
2 massive quality-oriented training programmes
3 structured annual improvements in quality.

Upper management leadership of each company's approach to product quality

An example of Japanese upper management commitment to quality was made by Sandholm to the International Quality Control Conference held in Tokyo in 1978. Almost half of the Japanese participants at the conference were from upper management – presidents, general managers, division heads and directors.

At conferences held in Europe or the USA, almost all participants are from the quality profession – quality assurance engineers, reliability engineers, quality managers and so on. There are few upper managers (Sandholm, 1983).

Deming (1975) also observed that in Japan top people in the companies take hold of the problems of production and quality. All the reports quoted by Deming showing successful implementations of quality principles were written by those with the rank of company president, managing director or chairman of the board. As Deming has stressed:

> All the top management came, not only to listen, but to work. They had already seen evidence from their own engineers that what you've got is this chain reaction. As you improve the quality, costs go down. You can lower the price. You capture the market with quality and price. Americans do not understand it. Americans think that as you improve quality, you increase your cost. (Gottlieb, 1975)

The need for upper management leadership, emphasizes Juran, stems from the need to create major changes, two of which include annual improvements in quality and a massive quality-oriented training programme, discussed below. The recommended step for Western upper management is to perform a comprehensive company-wide quality audit to understand what needs to be done.

An organizational weakness in the West is the large-company central quality department with the numerous functions of quality planning, engineering, co-ordination, auditing, inspection and testing. In Japan, most of these quality-oriented functions are carried out by line personnel who have the necessary training.

The Japanese do have quality departments, but they are small in terms of personnel, and they perform a limited array of functions: broad planning, consulting services and audits. Upper management quality audits calibrate the effectiveness of the organization, and only upper management has the authority to institute the necessary changes.

The commitment of all upper manufacturing management is necessary to instigate the needed quality changes, then to delegate the responsibility for implementation to the manufacturing departments. This helps foster close links and collaboration.

Massive quality-oriented training programmes

Selective training in quality in the West has been largely confined to members of the specialized quality departments, which constitute only about 5 per cent of the managerial and specialist personnel of companies. In contrast, the Japanese have trained close to 100 per cent of their managers and specialists in quality and made it a quantifiable science.

This massive quality-oriented training programme carries the education and training philosophy of Ishikawa to its logical conclusion. Juran points out that common quality training must include an understanding of:

- the universal sequence of events for improving quality and reducing quality-related costs (creation of beneficial change)
- the universal feedback loop for control (prevention of adverse change)
- the fundamentals of data collection and analysis.

Structured annual improvements in quality

In the early 1950s, the Japanese faced a grim reality: they had an inability to sell products. Since their major limitation was quality, not price, they directed their revolution at improving quality. They learned how to improve quality, became proficient at it, and are now reaping the rewards. Their managers are equally at home in meeting current targets and planning improvements for the future.

The story of the Japanese electronics industry with transistor radios, for example, illustrates the dedication to annual improvements in quality that exists in Japan.

With regard to programmable automation, computer-based manufacturing systems require a radically new approach by management. Too many systems will never meet their requirements, to either internal or external customers.

Manufacturing management must plan for and make a total commitment, like Japan's, to quality improvement from within. The programmable systems require a structured strategy and implementation if they are to be successful. Structured annual improvement programmes by companies should provide the overall framework for this. To accomplish these annual quality improvements, Juran (1981b) advises that a team:

1 study the symptoms of the defects and failures
2 develop a theory on the causes of these symptoms
3 test the theory until the cause(s) is (are) known
4 stimulate remedial action by the appropriate department(s).

Well-established manufacturing quality techniques have been able to identify and categorize defects in products, although this is less easy when dealing with programmable systems. As techniques for defect identification mature, the steps required for annual quality improvements can be applied to computer-based manufacturing.

Defects can be separated into those which are worker-controllable and those which are management-controllable. The latter category includes defects that cannot possibly be avoided by workers. Whether a certain defect should be regarded as a worker-controllable defect or a management-controllable defect depends on the extent to which the following conditions are met:

1 The workers know what to do.
2 The workers know the result of their own work.
3 The workers have the means of controlling the result.

If all three conditions are met and the work is still defective, the worker is responsible. However, if one or more of the conditions have not been met, this is a management-controllable defect (Juran, 1966).

On the responsibility for defects, Deming (1975b) has made the following point:

> To call to the attention of a worker a careless act, in a climate of general carelessness, is a waste of time and can only generate hard feelings, because the condition of general carelessness belongs to everybody and is the fault of management, not of any one worker, nor of all workers.

Many managers assume they have solved all the problems once they have brought worker-controllable defects under control. In fact, they are, as Deming also reminds us, just ready to tackle the most important problems of variation, namely the management-controllable causes (Deming, 1967).

During programmable manufacturing processes, many worker-controllable defects can be controlled by the workers. However, there is a wide class of defects in such systems that arise because the worker does not know what to do. This condition occurs because of the inevitable intertwining of hardware, software, specification and implementation.

Limitations of available implementation technology may force a specification change. The hardware hosting the computer software may require software workarounds because of technological limitations. Implementation choices may suggest enhancements to the original specification: that is, as more is accomplished, more is learned, making it reasonable to take a different approach than was originally specified.

To learn more and take a better approach, problems need to be identified and isolated. There has to be analysis and synthesis with every problem, yet everything has to work as an integrated system, and be understood in that framework.

That the workers know the result of their own work in programmable automation and software is very immediate and sometimes humbling for the worker who has made a 'silly mistake'. The worker receives the results, whether correct or incorrect, immediately from the computer exactly as commanded. On the other hand, there are the subtle defects that are not found for years. This is a worker-controllable defect, but one where the workers do not know the result of their work. Quality programmable automation must continually search to resolve this type of defect.

In programmable automation, the worker has the means of influencing the result. Assuming a reasonable task assignment, the worker is directly involved in the production of the resulting product and is often the first to see that result. Consider, for example, a situation in which the worker loses that influence because the FMS is unavailable. It is usually not worker-controllable that the FMS is or is not available.

To summarize this discussion of the annual quality improvements suggested by Juran, it is clear that, in the automated environment, the workers must first know the conditions before setting up the programme for improvement. In this area, knowing where one stands from a quality viewpoint is essential.

SANDHOLM'S FOUR-POINT ATTACK

To achieve high-technology management quality, a four-point attack is needed, as advocated by Sandholm at Westinghouse Defence Center in May 1983. The points are:

1 quality policy
2 quality objectives
3 quality system
4 quality organization (Sandholm, 1983b).

The quality policy

This is a statement that expresses the need for corporate-wide quality, supported by a statement of commitment to quality by the corporation. It provides the direction for all employees to implement the quality policy. As with all policies, it emanates from the highest executive in the corporation.

High-technology companies like IBM and Digital Equipment Corporation (DEC) take management commitment very seriously. DEC held their Second European Quality Symposium in 1986. Falotti, the European President of DEC, said:

> We as managers are responsible for too many compromises. We compromise every day and we think it is not important but people see that management is compromising and, therefore, it is all right to compromise. Extend this chain along and the result is a poor quality company. (Falotti, 1986)

Quality objectives

These are statements of measurable improvements, usually achievable on an annual basis. The implication is that a quality baseline is established so that the quality improvements may be measured. The presumption is that each professional manager and worker knows the quality of the items being manufactured.

In practice, it depends on maturity, degree of professionalism and many intangibles about people. With that awareness in mind, quality objectives should be set with the manufacturing managers to improve in a quantifiable way the quality of the manufacturing process and items produced: for example, records of the number of errors, their circumstances and severity during the enhancement of a programmable system.

The quality system

The means used to achieve the quality objectives was, traditionally, the heavy tome of standards and procedures for quality personnel to follow step by step – not very effective, but usually necessary to meet contractual and specifications requirements. To have really all-pervasive quality awareness throughout the organization would be more effective, with every manager and worker striving to achieve the company-wide quality objectives.

For developments using programmable automation, a quality system should include standards and procedures, methods, tools and techniques decided by, and committed to by, senior management. Examples of these include, but are not limited to: programmable quality assurance (PQA) procedures, design methods and aids, programmable and coding standards, testing strategies, and diagnostic guides. All these documents need to be produced and integrated within the framework of the management requirements for the product and the company. The PQA procedures and guidelines need to be particularized for each programmable product; this is usually accomplished by means of a PQA project plan for each product.

The quality assurance organization

A small and efficient quality assurance organization, in keeping with the previous statements, can act as a monitoring mechanism to focus the total organizational effort towards quality improvement.

CROSBY'S MANAGEMENT MATURITY GRID

Crosby, in his book *Quality is Free* (1979), sought to measure the management attitude to quality by the five categories shown in Table 28.1, the quality management maturity grid.

Stage 1: Measurement category of uncertainty

This clearly highlights that managements who lack an understanding of quality, and have the wrong attitude to it, will never have the quality organization to handle problems, cost quality, improve it, and have a quality posture or policy.

In this stage of management uncertainty, there are a number of deeply rooted beliefs that everyone holds:

- Quality means goodness; it cannot be defined.
- Because it cannot be defined, quality cannot be measured.
- The trouble with quality is that European and American workers don't give a damn.

Table 28.1 Quality management maturity grid

Measurement categories	*Stage 1: Uncertainty*	*Stage 2: Awakening*	*Stage 3: Enlightenment*	*Stage 4: Wisdom*	*Stage 5: Certainty*
Management understanding and attitude	No comprehension of quality as a management tool. Tend to blame quality departments for 'quality problems'.	Recognizing that quality management may be of value, but not willing to provide money or time to make it happen.	While going through quality improvement programme, learn more about quality management; becoming supportive and helpful.	Participating. Understand absolutes of quality management. Recognize their personal role in continuing emphasis.	Consider quality management an essential part of company system.
Quality organization status	Quality is hidden in manufacturing or engineering departments. Inspection probably not part of organization. Emphasis on appraisal or sorting.	A stronger quality leader is appointed, but main emphasis is still on appraisal and moving the product. Still part of manufacturing or other.	Quality department reports to top management, all appraisal is incorporated, and manager has role in management of company.	Quality manager is an officer of company; effective status-reporting and preventive action. Involved with consumer affairs and special assignments.	Quality manager on board of directors. Prevention is main concern. Quality is a thought leader.
Problem-handling	Problems are fought as they occur; no resolution; inadequate definitions; lots of yelling and accusations.	Teams are set up to attack major problems. Long-range solutions are not solicited.	Corrective action communication established. Problems are openly faced and resolved in an orderly way.	Problems are identified early in their development. All functions are open to suggestion and improvement.	Except in the most unusual cases, problems are prevented.
Cost of quality as percentage of sales	Reported: unknown Actual: 20%	Reported: 3% Actual: 18%	Reported 8% Actual: 12%	Reported: 6.5% Actual: 8%	Reported: 2.5% Actual: 2.5%
Quality improvement actions	No organized activities. No understanding of such activities.	Trying obvious 'motivational' short-range efforts.	Implementation of the 14-step programme with thorough understanding and establishment of it.	Continuing the 14-step programme and starting 'Make Certain' programme.	Quality improvement is a normal and continued activity.
Summation of company quality posture	'We don't know why we have problems with quality.'	'Is it absolutely necessary to always have problems with quality?'	'Through management commitment and quality improvement, we are identifying and resolving our problems.'	'Defect prevention is a routine part of our operation.'	'We know why we do not have problems with quality.'

Source: Crosby: *Quality is Free*, 1979.

- Quality is fine, but we can't afford it.

With this management understanding and attitude, these beliefs are self-evident truths. Management education is needed to dispel these erroneous notions.

When education is completed, there is usually lip-service to quality: people will say 'yes' from their minds while they feel 'no' in the pits of their stomachs; they will pay lip-service to quality without really realizing it. They will say they want quality, but will continue to judge performance solely by schedule and budget.

There seems to be an implied assumption that the three goals of quality, cost and schedule are conflicting, and therefore mutually exclusive. This is not true. Significant improvements in both cost and schedule can be achieved as a result of focusing on quality (Craig, 1983). A fundamental premise of Deming's teachings is that the only way to increase productivity and reduce costs is to increase quality (Deming, 1982).

Any company's policy must be to supply exactly what the customer wants. It sounds too elementary to be important. This is Crosby's first absolute: conformity to requirements (Crosby, 1984). Too often, managements emphasize making a shipment or delivering a service, whether it is right or only close to being right.

Costs will be incurred from the massive educational, organizational and procedural effort that will be required. Each manager and worker will have to learn what it really takes to achieve quality in manufacturing and associated services. In order to improve quality effectively, the quality personnel will have to get involved with the management of the company to ensure that relearning takes place for all managers and workers, in all aspects of engineering and manufacturing.

Stage 2: Measurement category awakening

Quality personnel are sought out in times of crisis. Difficulties with customers and internal engineering, manufacturing and service departments will lead to quality personnel being asked to act as a buffer, and even begin asked to carry out investigations into the reasons for the difficulties.

The value of audits begins to be appreciated. Checklists start to be generated and used, against which all products and services can be gauged for their conformity to specification and the customer's requirements and conditions. For the first time in the company, management can begin to sense the real quality perspective.

Stage 3: Measurement category enlightenment

This stage is reached when it is understood that quality contributes in a meaningful way, for the benefit of both management and workers.

Quality goals and objectives must be established first as a matter of corporate policy, and then enforced through management involvement, company organization, procedural policy and universal commitment. In essence, the quality role becomes a management role, in which quality principles and objectives are upheld at the start of each new contract by management and workers. Engineering, manufacturing and service practices must be driven by these quality objectives.

With the organizational changes, the need for planning to a common purpose becomes clear – the old inter-departmental fights and accusations become things of the past. Each department has its own job to do and gets on with it, within the framework of the overall planned company environment, which is increasingly driven by upper management.

Quality requirements begin to be considered before manufacturing and even research and development. That quality must be built in – not added (which it can't be) – becomes widely appreciated.

Quality planning and quality plans are considered. Audits are complemented by reviews at various points in the engineering, manufacturing and service processes. Control points begin to be used against which quality can be compared, data collected, and measurements and accurate predictions made. The scene is being set for a company-wide participative quality programme.

Stage 4: Measurement category wisdom

This stage is reached when everyone knows that a real, conscious effort has to be made by everyone to build in quality. Quality is a stated management objective, which is known to the total workforce. Quality matters appear as the first item on agendas; quality requirements are firmly established before the first engineering, manufacturing and service activity has taken place; all subcontractors will come within the quality objectives.

Very significant gains are seen as a result of the quality improvement. Productivity increases, the order book grows. Satisfied customers tell potential customers about the quality of the product or service.

Quality is also good marketing. For example, American industry, particularly the car industry, has undergone an inquisition on the subject of poor quality. A study by the Ford Motor Company revealed that customers who are happy with a product are going to tell, on average, 8 other people that they are really happy. The interesting thing is, a customer who is not happy is going to tell 22 (see Falotti, 1986)!

Stage 5: Measurement category certainty

This stage arrives when quality becomes the 'ideas centre' of the company. Quality is everyone's total commitment.

DEMING'S INFLUENCE

W.E. Deming introduced the Japanese to statistical techniques in 1948. Together with Juran, he transformed the Japanese perspective on quality. Deming, in particular, introduced them to data analysis and simple analytical and statistical techniques. He also introduced the Plan–Do–Check–Analyse approach. This is shown in Figure 28.1, and is known to the Japanese as the Deming Circle. This approach urged that everyone learned a common method of describing and attacking problems. This commonality is an absolute requirement if personnel from different parts of the same company are to work together on company-wide quality improvement. Thus when the executive audit team or the company executive visits any of the company's operations, there is a well-established framework, the Deming Circle, within which all parties can discuss problems and suggest improvements.

This is in stark contrast to management by exception, described by Tribus, where when things go wrong, the management have to try to work out where it went wrong, why it went wrong, and what they have to do to correct it (Tribus, 1984). By subjecting each department, activity and process to this common framework, attention is focused on the problem area.

By the late 1960s, the data analysis and statistical techniques Deming introduced were upsetting the economy of the world. They demonstrated what could be achieved by the serious study and adoption of statistical techniques and the implementation of statistical

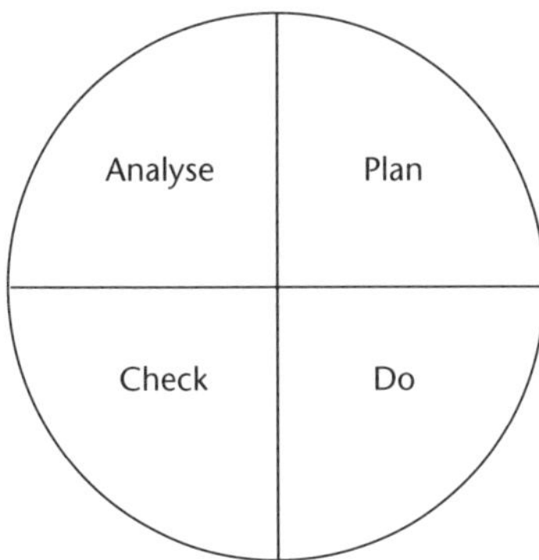

Figure 28.1 The Deming Circle

logic in industry. It must, however, be at *all* levels of the company, from the chief executive downwards, and it must be company-wide and within the framework of known policies and objectives.

Although statistical methods have wide applications, Deming (1967) argues that there is only one statistical theory. There are no separate and distinct theories for process control, acceptance sampling, reliability, estimation, experimental design, material testing and engineering – there is only one statistical theory. That statistical theory, incorporating the statistical control of quality, is directed at the economic satisfaction of demand; it includes all aspects of the lifecycle of the product (or service), from initial conception to operations and disposal, when all the data collected become part of a corporate database (Deming, 1975).

As Deming (1980) also points out, by doing 100 per cent testing, using automatic testing equipment, you cannot put quality into a process or product. Quality is either there to satisfy the economic demand of customers, or it is not.

When applied comprehensively throughout a company, data analysis and statistical techniques can make a dramatic impact. A structured company-wide approach is needed, incorporating all aspects of the company's functioning. It is pointless to delegate responsibility for the introduction of the techniques to the quality department. There must be company-wide organization, planning, communications and training.

To succeed, this structured approach must be driven by all levels of management; the whole company must be committed. This means that management must understand the subject, must be able to explain it to all workers, and must know how to introduce the techniques into the company.

Its introduction starts with an emphasis on what the customer wants, then how it is to be specified, then the company's ability to produce and control the product or service and its continuing quality.

To Deming, the most important part of the production line is the customer:

> It will not suffice to have customers that are merely satisfied. An unhappy customer will switch. Unfortunately a satisfied customer may also switch, on the theory that he could not lose much, and might gain. Profit in business comes from repeat customers, customers that boast about your products and service, and that bring friends with them. (Deming, 1986)

Deming also writes about the need to stay ahead of the customer. Customers do not know what they will need one, three, five years from now. If you, as the product manufacturer or service provider, wait until then to find out, you will hardly be ready to serve them. Only if the quality approach is company-wide can sales and marketing report meaningfully what customers want (or think they want). Only then can research and development have prototyped potential products and services to satisfy stated or implied needs. Only then can management have planned appropriately for the introduction of programmable automation, new tooling, new suppliers, retraining and evolving a new company culture of teamwork, open communications and never-ending company and worker improvement, to bring the best out of everyone.

There is a systems approach underlying all of Deming's thinking. This was noticed as early as July 1950. Thus there was a:

> chain reaction ... [which] ... was on the blackboard of every meeting with top management in Japan from July 1950 onward. (Deming, 1986)

This chain reaction is summed up in Figure 28.2.

A central thesis of Deming is that productivity improvement must begin with attention to quality (Deming, 1982, 1986). The reasoning, supported by the empirical data from Japan's economic growth, is as follows:

1 As a starting point, you need stability (lack of variation) of products and personnel.
2 Stability gives management and workers increasing control over the manufacturing and service environment.
3 With control, you can start to keep consistently collected records, for comparison and contrast, using various statistical techniques.
4 With such records, you can begin to isolate and measure areas of malfunction.
5 Measurement enables you to identify 'leverage points' so that improvements can be applied to these malfunctioning areas.
6 Leverage point improvement then increases quality.
7 Only with increased quality can you get an improvement in productivity.
8 Only with increased productivity can you improve your price competitiveness in the commercial world.

What European and American companies have to do is well known. The information, techniques, methods and policies are available in the public domain, from many sources and countries, mostly Japan and the USA. They have to learn not only from their own mistakes, but from others in related situations. Deming has developed 14 points for the transformation of industrial quality. These are listed in Table 28.2.

The Deming philosophy can be summarized as an equilateral triangle, Figure 28.3. It is also known as the Joiner Triangle (Joiner, 1988). This representation shows quality as the apex, achieved by the coalescence of two forces: total teamwork and the 'scientific approach'. The scientific approach requires understanding of the nature of variation, particularly its division into controlled and uncontrolled variation due to management-controllable common and worker-controllable special causes.

It is only by management and workers correctly diagnosing the most important sources of variation, and then reducing or even eliminating them, that quality (reliability,

Improve quality
Fewer mistakes
Fewer snags
Less scrap and rework
Fewer delays, better use of materials and machine time
Reduced inventory and work in progress
Reduction in overall costs
Improved productivity
Better quality at lower selling price captures bigger market share
Stay in business!
More and more jobs created

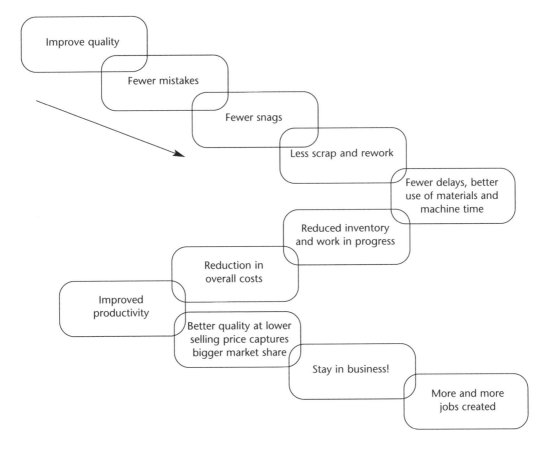

Figure 28.2 The chain reaction

consistency, predictability, dependability) can be improved. The scientific approach calls for decisionmaking and policymaking on the basis of solid information, both numerical and non-numerical, and not by 'gut feel', opinion or mere short-term considerations.

It includes the use of data collection and analysis and statistical techniques – but also knowledge and understanding of their limitations and awareness of the crucial importance of phenomena which cannot be quantified. These phenomena are Deming's seven 'deadly diseases' of Western management (Deming, 1986). They are listed in Table 28.3.

Deming frequently quotes Dr Lloyd Nelson, Director of Statistical Methods for the Nashua Corporation:

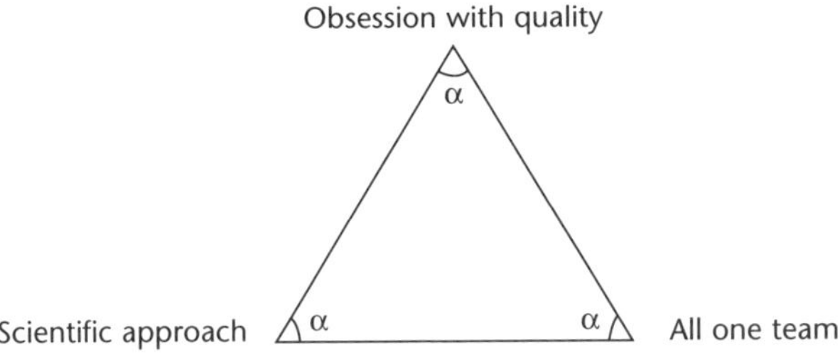

Figure 28.3 The Deming philosophy

Table 28.2 Deming's 14 points for the transformation of industrial quality

1 Create constancy of purpose towards improvement of product and service, with the aim of becoming competitive, staying in business, and providing jobs.

2 Adopt the new philosophy. We are in a new economic age. Western managers must awaken to the challenge, must learn their responsibilities, and take on leadership for change.

3 Cease dependence on inspection to achieve quality. Eliminate the need for inspection on a mass basis by building quality into the product in the first place.

4 End the practice of awarding business on the basis of price tag. Instead, minimize total cost. Move towards a single supplier for any one item, based on a long-term relationship of loyalty and trust.

5 Improve constantly and forever the system of production and service, to improve quality and productivity, and thus constantly decrease costs.

6 Institute training on the job.

7 Institute leadership. The aim of leadership should be to help people and machines and gadgets to do a better job. Leadership of management is in need of overhaul, as well as leadership of production workers.

8 Drive out fear, so that everyone may work effectively for the company.

9 Break down barriers between departments. People in research, design, sales and production must work as a team, to foresee problems in production and in use that may be encountered with the product or service.

10 Eliminate slogans, exhortations and targets for the workforce asking for zero defects and new levels of productivity. Such exhortations only create adversarial relationships, as the bulk of the causes of low quality and low productivity belong to the system, and thus lie beyond the power of the workforce.

11 (a) Eliminate work standards (quotas) on the factory floor. Substitute leadership. (b) Eliminate management by objective. Eliminate management by numbers, numerical goals. Substitute leadership.

12 (a) Remove barriers that rob the hourly worker of his or her right to pride of workmanship. The responsibility of supervisors must be changed from sheer numbers to quality. (b) Remove barriers that rob people in management and in engineering of their right to pride of workmanship. This means, among other things, abolishment of the annual merit rating and of management by objective.

13 Institute a vigorous programme of education and self-improvement.

14 Put everybody in the company to work to accomplish the transformation. The transformation is everybody's job.

> The most important figures needed for management of any organization are unknown and unknowable.

Those who find this statement surprising have not begun to understand Deming's teachings. All our calculations, business policies and decisions have to begin with assumptions and incomplete data. Some assumptions, however, are more soundly based than others, since there are variation records and data to support our decision. They are statistically under control. This encourages constancy of purpose and long-term planning.

Figures which are usually unknown are the cost of quality, reworks, warranty claims and concessions. Figures which are unknowable concern people:

Table 28.3 Deming's seven deadly diseases of Western management

1	Lack of constancy of purpose to plan product and service that will have a market and keep the company in business, and provide jobs.
2	Emphasis on short-term profits: short-term thinking (just the opposite from constancy of purpose to stay in business), fed by fear of unfriendly takeover, and by push from bankers and owners for dividends.
3	Personal review system, or evaluation of performance, merit rating, annual review, or annual appraisal, by whatever name, for people in management, the effects of which are devastating. Management by objective, on a go, no-go basis, without a method for accomplishment of the objective, is the same thing by another name. Even management by fear would be better.
4	Mobility of management: job hopping.
5	Use of visible figures only for management, with little or no consideration of figures that are unknown or unknowable.
6	Excessive medical costs.
7	Excessive costs of liability, fuelled by lawyers that work on contingency fees.

- being able to take a pride in their work
- being motivated and loyal
- doing the job well
- keeping the customer delighted.

These 'unknowable figures' depend on the company culture being people-driven.

The Taylor command and control management style renders genuine teamwork almost impossible, as does management by results, annual performance appraisals, and the use of arbitrary numerical goals and targets – all of which foster competition and conflict between company personnel, and sometimes between whole departments, as opposed to their working together for the true benefit of the company.

Several well-intentioned quality improvement notions can constitute similarly serious obstacles if they are not all-embracing within the company as a system: examples are cost of quality and Crosby's zero defects (Crosby, 1984). Concepts which are essentially beneficial can do more harm than good if used in an unsuitable environment: these include quality circles and just-in-time (JIT) systems.

JIT depends on zero defects; the production line must be continuous, and not stop–start. However, that can only happen when the total management approach is that of an integrated system, with known policies and procedures, operating within statistical control limits.

True comprehension of Deming's message comes when he talks of the need for the total transformation of Western style managements – and he means it!

Conclusion

To conclude this chapter, here is a final quotation – a stark warning from Deming's book *Out of the Crisis* (1986). This is a short section entitled simply 'Survival of the Fittest':

> Who will survive? Companies that adopt constancy of purpose for quality, productivity, and service, and go about it with intelligence and perseverance, have a

chance to survive. They must, of course, offer products and services that have a market. Charles Darwin's law of survival of the fittest, and that the unfit do not survive, holds in free enterprise as well as in natural selection. It is a cruel law, unrelenting.

Actually, the problem will solve itself. The only survivors will be companies with constancy of purpose for quality, productivity, and service.

This chapter has outlined what quality has come to mean in the early twenty-first century, and the thinking of the experts behind it. New company-wide quality policies, procedures and techniques to integrate management, workers, suppliers and customers have come to the fore, and are still undergoing rapid evolution.

Further reading

BS 5750: Part 8, 1991, ISO 9004–2, *Guide to Quality Management and Quality Systems Elements for Services*, British Standards Institution, Milton Keynes.

BS 7850: Part 1, 1992, *Total Quality Management: Guide to Management Principles*, and Part 2: 1992, *Guide to Quality Improvement Methods*, British Standards Institution, Milton Keynes.

Craig, W., 'Management Commitment to Quality: Hewlett-Packard Company', *Quality Progress*, 1983, Vol. XVI, No. 8, August, pp. 22–4.

Crosby, P.B., *Quality is Free*, Mentor, New American Library, New York, 1979.

Crosby, P.B., *Quality Without Tears*, McGraw-Hill, New York, 1984.

Day, R., *Design and the Economy*, The Design Council, London, 1991.

Deming, W.E., 'What Happened in Japan', *Industrial Quality Control*, 1967, Vol. 24, No. 2, August, p. 91.

Deming, W.E., 'My View of Quality Control in Japan', *Reports of Statistical Application Research*, 1975a, Vol. 4, No. 8.

Deming, W.E., 'On Some Statistical Aids Towards Economic Production', *Interfaces*, 1975b, Vol. 5, No. 4, August, p. 8.

Deming, W.E., 'It Does Work', *Quality*, 1980, Vol. 19, No. 8, August, 31, (Q26–Q31).

Deming, W.E., *Quality, Productivity and Comprehensive Position*, MIT Press, Cambridge, MA, 1982.

Deming, W.E., *Out of the Crisis*, MIT Press, Cambridge, MA, 1986.

Falotti, P.C., Opening Address on Quality, *Second European Quality Symposium*, Digital Equipment Corporation (DEC), February 1986.

Gottlieb, D., 'The Outlook Interview: W. Edwards Deming, US Guru to Japanese Industry, talks to Daniel Gottlieb', *The Washington Post*, 15 January 1975.

Hiromoto, T., 'Another Hidden Edge – Japanese Management Accounting', *Harvard Business Review*, 1988, Vol. 66, No. 4, July–August, pp. 22–6.

Ishikawa, K., 'Quality Control in Japan,' *13th International Association of Quality*, 1978, Kyoto, Japan.

Ishikawa, K., *What is Total Quality Control? The Japanese Way*, Prentice-Hall, Englewood Cliffs, NJ, 1985.

Japanese Union of Scientists and Engineers (JUSE), 'General Principles of the QC Circles', *QC Circle Koryo*, Tokyo, 1980.

Joiner Associates Inc., *The Team Handbook: How to Use Teams to Improve Quality*, Joiner Associates, Madison, WI, 1988.

Juran, J.M., 'Quality Problems, Remedies and Nostrums', *Industrial Quality Control*, 1966, Vol. 22, No. 12, pp. 647–53.

Juran, J.M., 'Product Quality – A Prescription for the West: Part 1, Training and Improvement Programs', *Management Review*, 1981a, July.

Juran, J.M., 'Product Quality – A Prescription for the West: Part 2, Upper Management Leadership and Employee Relations', *Management Review*, 1981b, July.

Kaplan, R., 'Yesterday's Accounting Undermines Production', *Harvard Business Review*, 1984, Vol. 62, No. 4, July–August, pp. 95–101.

Kaplan, Robert S. and Norton, David P., *The Balanced Scorecard: Translating Strategy into Action*, Harvard Business School Press, Harvard, MA, 1996.

Keegan, Richard, *Benchmarking Facts: A European Perspective*, Oak Tree Press, Dublin, 1998.

Laria, Anthony C., Moody, Patricia E. and Wall, Robert W., *The Kaizen Blitz*, John Wiley and Sons, New York, 1999.

Little, Arthur D. Ltd, *Corporate Competitiveness: Achieving Best Practice Through Managing Interfaces*, Arthur D. Little, London, 1990.

Open University (OU) and University of Manchester Institute of Science and Technology (UMIST), *The Benefits and Costs of Investment in Design*, Open University Press, Milton Keynes, 1990.

PA Consulting Group, *Manufacturing into the late 1990s* (A report prepared for the DTI), HMSO, London, 1990.

Sandholm, L., 'Japanese Quality Circles – A Remedy for the West's Quality Problems?' *Quality Progress*, 1983, February, pp. 20–3.

Sandholm, L., 'Quality Overview', *Quality Department Lecture Series*, Westinghouse Defense and Electronics Center, 1983b, May.

Schonberger, R.J., *World Class Manufacturing: The Lessons of Simplicity Applied*, The Free Press, Macmillan, New York, 1986.

TickIT, *Making a Better Job of Software: Guide to Software Quality Management System Construction and Certification*, Issue 5, Department of Trade and Industry/TickIT Office, London, 1992.

Tribus, M., 'Prize-winning Japanese Firms' Quality Management Programs Pass Inspection', *Management Review*, 1984, February.

CHAPTER **29**

ISO 9001 Certification

Matt Seaver

This chapter deals with the process of ISO 9001 certification, and some of the practical aspects of navigating through the journey to certification. There is a move towards use of the term 'registration' for the certification of management capability, to prevent confusion with product certification – see Chapter 16.

Introduction

There are two principal reasons why an organization would embark on the process of achieving certification to ISO 9001: pressure from customers, and a desire to improve performance. In recent years, more and more companies have been coming under pressure from customers to demonstrate their ability to supply a quality product or service. The usual way to do this is to have independent assessment of the operation, which in most cases means ISO 9001 certification. In some cases, the customer will make ISO 9001 certification a requirement for placing an order or contract. However, a growing number of companies now realize that ISO 9000 is an effective method of generating improvement in performance, and even where certification is not strictly necessary, assessment by an independent external certification auditor puts pressure on the company to keep up the effort.

ISO 9001 and ISO 9004

Before looking at the details of ISO 9001 certification, it is necessary to look at some of the other related quality management standards. What we call 'ISO 9000' is actually a family of standards, the most important ones being ISO 9001 and ISO 9004. The standards in the ISO 10000 range also deal with closely related quality management system topics, such as auditing.

ISO 9001 is entitled *Quality Management Systems – Requirements*. ISO 9004 is entitled *Quality Management Systems – Guidelines for Performance Improvements*. The ISO 9000 standard itself is actually entitled *Quality Management Systems – Fundamentals and Vocabulary*, and gives an introduction to the whole 'ISO 9000' scene. As well as giving definitions of terms that have different usage to the normal dictionary definitions, it contains some useful, though not very detailed, discussion on selected topics related to quality management systems.

ISO 9002 and ISO 9003 no longer exist, having been incorporated into ISO 9001: 2000.

As well as referring to a specific standard, the term 'ISO 9000' is often used as shorthand for the entire family of related ISO 9000 standards. Thus we may speak of an 'ISO 9000 quality management system', meaning that the system is based on the principles outlined in ISO 9000, was designed using the guidance in ISO 9004, and complies with the requirements of ISO 9001.

When the standards were first published in 1987, it was intended the ISO 9004 should be the first port of call on the journey towards excellence. The quality management system was to be based on it, rather than on ISO 9001 or ISO 9002. With the demand for ISO 9001 and ISO 9002 certification, however, organizations started to take the fast-track approach, and designed their systems on the much narrower requirements of ISO 9001 or ISO 9002. This resulted in many companies being disappointed in the level of benefits that they derived from ISO 9000, and frustrated at the huge effort they had to put into maintaining the certification, whose primary use was external to the company.

ISO 9004 should be the starting point when setting up a quality management system, since it addresses the entire range of initiatives that should be considered. While ISO 9001 is primarily concerned with ensuring customer satisfaction – that is, product or service quality – ISO 9004 strives to create an organization that is successful in all aspects of its operation, including financial success. ISO 9001 describes the minimum requirements for a quality management system if it is to be effective in ensuring customer satisfaction, whereas ISO 9004 gives broad guidance on all aspects of the quality management system.

Nowadays, however, it is recognized that people start with ISO 9001, so we now tend to look upon ISO 9004 as the guidance for progression towards excellence after the basics have been put in place.

It is very important to understand that ISO 9004 does not give guidance on how to comply with ISO 9001 requirements. To quote from ISO 9004 itself:

> ISO 9004 is recommended as a guide for organizations whose top management wishes to move beyond the requirements of ISO 9001 in pursuit of continual improvement of performance.

To use a motoring analogy, ISO 9001 represents the statutory checklist for roadworthiness (minimum requirements for road safety), whereas ISO 9004 represents the car maintenance manual (best practice for prolonging the life of the car and achieving efficiency).

The standards were first revised in 1994. The revision did not significantly change either the structure or the requirements. The revision in 2000 was a total restructuring, and addressed the main criticisms of the previous two versions: for example, the perceived emphasis on documented procedures, and the lack of emphasis on achieving results. It incorporates a number of additional requirements, and stresses the need to take the process approach to quality in all aspects of the organization's business. It also addresses another criticism: that the earlier versions were aimed primarily at large manufacturing companies, and were difficult to interpret for service companies and small manufacturing companies.

Benefits of certification

The benefits that a company derives from ISO 9001 certification depend largely on the company's motivation for seeking certification. If the prime reason for certification is to enable the company to compete for orders, where certification is a requirement for supply, then the benefits will largely have been achieved once the certificate is hanging on the wall. In that case, the company will probably have put minimal effort into setting up the quality system. Very often, such companies have a negative view of ISO 9001, since, essentially, it has been forced upon them.

However, where the company adopts ISO 9001 for reasons of quality improvement, the principal obvious benefits are internal. The overall objective of ISO 9001 is to facilitate the supply of a product or service which meets the customer's needs. This is achieved by organizing the entire operation as an integrated process, through effective planning, controlling, monitoring and correcting.

This almost invariably results in fewer mistakes, less waste, less management time spent firefighting, and more time to stand back and identify further improvements. The degree to which any individual company achieves these benefits depends on many things, not least of which are the knowledge of what the potential benefits are, and the commitment of all personnel, particularly senior management, to achieving them. It does not depend, to any significant degree, on the complexity or size of the operation, or the nature of the business, whether manufacturing or service supply, though, clearly, these factors will have a severe impact on the effort needed to set up the system.

The certification process

The process of achieving certification follows a broadly similar path in all companies:

1. Know what is involved.
2. Produce a quality policy.
3. Select somebody to co-ordinate the project.
4. Demonstrate commitment.
5. Document what you currently do.
6. Determine the scope of the system.
7. Integrate your activities.
8. Try it out.
9. Audit it internally.
10. Review the performance of the system.
11. Have a pre-assessment audit carried out.
12. Select a certification body.
13. Go through the audit!

KNOW WHAT IS INVOLVED

Many companies embark on the process without fully realizing the commitment that is necessary and the difficulties they will encounter. The first thing to do is to purchase a copy of the two standards, ISO 9001 and ISO 9004.

Speak to a number of people who have experience with ISO 9001. The more information you gather, the more informed you will be. You will certainly find people who say that ISO 9000 is 'all bureaucracy, paperwork and so on'. You should listen carefully to them, and find out exactly what difficulties they encountered. Try to figure out the root cause of their difficulties, and identify what you can do to avoid these problems. You must also speak to people who have had good experiences with ISO 9000. From them, you must try to find what factors made it work for them. Only when you have heard both sides can you have a broad vision of the benefits and pitfalls. You should consider taking expert advice from a consultant. However, be careful when choosing your consultant. Select one who comes well recommended by somebody whose opinion you value. Unfortunately, some of the problems experienced by companies have been caused by consultants who don't have a good grasp of ISO 9000. If a consultant does not have an in-depth knowledge of the ISO 9000 requirements and how they are to be interpreted, he or she will recommend 'overkill' so that the client will not be found to have omitted anything during the audit and blame the consultant for the omission – 'Better do it anyway, just to be sure.' This approach will cost you dearly before too long. Choose a consultant who has personal experience of the pressures of the *real world*, and who will think hard before imposing unnecessary additional workload on you.

PRODUCE A QUALITY POLICY

Once you know what is involved, you are in a position to formulate a policy that will actually mean something. Your policy must address the central position of the customer, and all quality activities must be geared towards satisfying customer expectations. Indeed, you should aim to exceed expectations – 'delight your customer'. Your policy should commit your organization to real improvement in performance, both in the quality of the product or service and the performance of the organization. You should address the whole question of developing your personnel – providing a suitable work environment and the resources to help your people develop their personal skills to the benefit of both them and the organization.

SELECT SOMEBODY TO CO-ORDINATE THE PROJECT

The usual advice is to set up a quality committee. This is certainly recommended, for several reasons, where the company size makes it a practical option. Firstly, there is a lot of work involved – writing procedures, trying out different controls, organizing people to make changes to the way they operate, and so on. It is impossible for one person to do all this except in the smallest companies, but a group can share the work, making the whole project easier to complete. Secondly, and more importantly, involving a group will ensure commitment throughout the company. If someone is involved in setting up a system, they will be more likely to work it, and will not be able to opt out on the basis that it has been imposed or is impractical.

In smaller companies, instead of a group you may have one person, a project co-ordinator, who will drive the project. In this case, also, it is critical that he or she receives support from everybody in the company. Equally, the co-ordinator must keep everybody else informed of progress. Regular briefing sessions for other staff should be held to ensure that the entire team is behind the project, even if they are not yet involved in the details of setting it up.

DEMONSTRATE COMMITMENT

It is critical that the senior manager is seen to be committed to the success of the project. There will be times when there is a clash between the interests of the ISO 9001 project and operational necessities. At times like this, the senior manager must, at least sometimes, give the quality project precedence, to demonstrate its importance. Senior management must be very conscious of the messages that their actions give to all employees. Apart from giving support in terms of resources, senior managers must be willing to participate frequently in routine project activities, particularly attending meetings, briefings and training sessions, whenever practicable.

DOCUMENT WHAT YOU CURRENTLY DO

ISO 9001 asks you to regard your business as a process, rather than looking at it piecemeal. You have your customer at both ends of the chain, firstly telling you (by placing an order or giving you the contract) what you need to do to give satisfaction, and finally receiving your product or service and expressing an opinion on how well you have met his or her expectations. In between is your process, which may be a service delivery activity, such as a solicitor's practice or a restaurant, or a manufacturing operation.

If you are running a successful business, you are probably doing most things approximately right. This should be your starting point. Start with what you have, and then see what needs to be changed. In the past we were often led to believe that ISO 9001 required us to 'document everything'. In fact, this was never the intention of the authors of the standard. Documented procedures are only required where the absence of such procedures could adversely affect quality. Furthermore, the amount of detail in the procedure should depend on the complexity of the work, the methods used, and the skills and training needed by personnel. In other words, you only have to have a written procedure *where it is necessary*. This topic has been covered in detail in Chapter 14.

The documentation you produce will be organized into one or more manuals. In a small office-based service company, it may be sufficient to have a *quality manual* describing the overall system in general terms (consisting of perhaps thirty pages, some carrying only half a page of text), and a *procedures manual* containing procedures for individual key tasks. In a major manufacturing operation, on the other hand, there might be twelve or more manuals, some with several hundred pages.

When writing procedures, use the in-house experts, namely the people who actually perform the tasks. Don't make the mistake of getting the co-ordinator to write out the procedure which you would like to operate. Take your existing method, and use that as the starting point. At this point, do not change it unless there is clearly a problem with it, either because it is not effective, or because it does not comply with the standard. Leave *improvements* till later.

DETERMINE THE SCOPE OF THE SYSTEM

The system you set up will depend entirely on your particular circumstances – the number of employees, whether family-owned or part of a large multi-national enterprise, whether public or private, the culture within the organization, the physical size of the premises, and so on.

In the past, many people failed to understand that if a particular requirement did not apply to an organization, then there was no need to include it in the system. The 2000 revision of the standard allows you to define the scope of your system. You may exclude certain elements if they do not apply to your operation. There is, however, a strict proviso on this: you may not exclude any requirement if this affects your ability to supply a quality service or product. You cannot exclude something simply because it is too much trouble! Having examined your existing system, you must then ensure that its scope complies fully with the conditions defined in ISO 9001. Where there are gaps, you must fill them.

No two systems are identical, and only you can decide on the best one for you. There is no single correct way of addressing any individual requirement. The best one for you is the one which works most effectively and comfortably for you. If it does the job, then it is correct for you.

You have to put in the effort when setting up the system. There is no easy way, no instant solution. You may be tempted to purchase a ready-made system where you fill in the blanks, or to copy somebody else's system. While these may seem to be cost-effective options, you will pay many times over later on. Some companies have actually had such systems installed by consultants. In the course of an audit, I once came across a record sheet that contained a results column which was always left blank. As I couldn't understand the heading on the column, I queried what it meant, and received the reply: 'We were told that this column didn't apply to us, and not to bother filling it in.' The consultant hadn't even bothered to delete the redundant column from the form he had drafted for the previous client! And amazingly, the client didn't see anything strange in that. A system that has not been designed specifically for your needs and circumstances can *never* work for you!

INTEGRATE YOUR ACTIVITIES

There is a definite trend nowadays towards integration of management systems. The three principal areas involved here are:

- quality
- environment
- occupational health and safety (OHS).

With the exception of the last, these are largely discretional. The quality management system was the first to be adopted widely by companies, first in its national form, BS 5750 in the UK, and later as the ISO 9000 series. The second to arrive was the environmental management system, with its separate ISO standards, the ISO 14000 series. In parallel with this, the Europe Union has the Eco-Management and Audit Scheme (EMAS). More recently has come the OHS management system, though, in fact, some of the more progressive companies have been working on this for many years. In the UK, this first appeared as BS 8800, and more recently as a certifiable specification: OHSAS 18001.

Looking at these three management systems more closely, it can be seen that they are essentially three different manifestations of a single requirement. This requirement can be stated simply as the need to control and improve a particular aspect of the organization's operation: customer satisfaction (quality), impact on the environment, or the welfare of the organization's employees and others who come into contact with it.

Looking at it still more closely, we see that each of the three addresses the following core issues:

- definition of the requirements to be met
- definition of what constitutes nonconformity
- control of critical information
- documenting the methods of keeping control
- training of personnel
- monitoring of activities and results
- control of inputs to the operation
- control of outputs from the operation
- dealing with nonconformity
- implementation of corrective action
- identification and implementation of appropriate preventive action
- auditing of the system
- review of the system
- improvement.

Consequently, it makes sense to have a single basic system with common methods of dealing with the generic problems that arise. This can be achieved in several ways. One extreme is to have a single totally integrated system, in which every (written) procedure addresses quality, environmental concerns, and health and safety. At the other end you could have a single approach to managing the business, with separate documented systems. In this case, the individual systems, though separate, are totally compatible, and ideally have a recognizably related structure. The important thing is to have a single company-wide approach to managing the different aspects, understood by all employees. The issue of integration is covered in depth in Chapter 33. See also Seaver and O'Mahony (2000).

TRY IT OUT

Your management system must become a dynamic entity – one which works effectively to help you achieve your objectives, both your overall company objectives and those at every level in the organization. You must therefore get used to the idea of making changes to suit changing circumstances. You must facilitate this by making it easy to introduce necessary changes, but without losing control. This is a very fine balance. Make it too difficult to introduce changes to the system and you will find that the changes are made anyway, but unofficially, and without control. On the other hand, if it is too easy, changes will be made without adequate consultation and deliberation.

Your system should deliver benefits. If, after serious and informed deliberation, you decide that a particular initiative is not beneficial, then it is sensible to drop it altogether, or amend the way in which you implement it. Remember that whatever you do should deliver benefits. Keep working on it until you find a practical way that suits your circumstances.

AUDIT IT INTERNALLY

The typical setup period for a reasonably complex ISO 9000 system is about twelve months, though much depends on the resources that are deployed in the development stage. When the system (or even a substantial part of it) has been running for a period of about three months, you should consider carrying out an audit. This is a prerequisite for certification, anyway, but doing it at this point can help to identify any remaining gaps. Review the audit findings, and try to find the most practical way of resolving the problems.

REVIEW THE PERFORMANCE OF THE SYSTEM

It is also a requirement of ISO 9001 that you review your system. This makes sense considering the resources you have invested in setting it up – management time, finance, training, lost production, and so on. So you need to know whether it is delivering the benefits promised or expected. If the review identifies deficiencies in the system, you must take the necessary action to correct the problems.

HAVE A PRE-ASSESSMENT AUDIT CARRIED OUT

When you believe that you are complying completely or substantially with the requirements of ISO 9001, you may consider it useful to engage an external auditor to carry out a pre-assessment *consultancy* audit. One significant difference between this audit and the certification audit is that you should be as open as possible with the auditor, and facilitate his or her efforts to find all significant nonconformities. In this case, the auditor is working for you, and you should make the best use you can of the audit. Make sure that all personnel understand the significance of each nonconformity found, and exactly why it contravenes the standard. After a pre-assessment audit, you may be able to get some suggested corrective action from the auditor. It is then for you to decide how best to correct the nonconformity. It should be part of your arrangement with the auditor that he or she will review your corrective action afterwards, and confirm whether it solves the problem.

SELECT A CERTIFICATION BODY

ISO 9001 certification is controlled in each country by a government-sponsored body. In the UK, this is the United Kingdom Accreditation Service (UKAS). This body is responsible for ensuring the accreditation of certification bodies working in the ISO 9001 and other fields. An accredited certification body must comply with certain specified requirements in exactly the same way that an individual company has to comply with ISO 9001 requirements in order to achieve certification. Accreditation by UKAS is intended to be your assurance that the certification body you choose will act responsibly and fairly. It should also ensure that the certification body has the competence to carry out audits in your sector.

However, in order to achieve UKAS accreditation, the certification body must first show a track record. That means finding a number of client companies who are satisfied to use a non-accredited certification body in its start-up phase. Everybody has to start somewhere! Before selecting your certification body, you must decide how significant accreditation is for you – and your customers!

Whether you select an accredited body or a non-accredited body, you should make sure that it will give you the quality of service you require. You should interview the prospective certifiers and establish that you can work with them. What companies have they audited previously? What do they regard as a major nonconformity? What level of detail do they expect in your written procedures? What hobby-horses do they have? How often will they carry out surveillance audits? What are their changes? Remember that you will probably be dealing with these people for a number of years, so it pays to select an organization with which you can develop a long-term relationship.

GO THROUGH THE AUDIT!

The certification audit is invariably a stressful time for everybody involved on the company side. There are few things you can do to make it easier for yourself:

- Realize that the certifier actually *wants* you to pass. When you have passed, you are a client, and a source of income!
- Be familiar with the standard, and understand the underlying concepts and principles. The auditor is working strictly to the requirements set out in the ISO 9001 standard. If you are taken by surprise by a question from the auditor, it may be that you have not read the standard in detail. If you have covered everything, you should have no problems.
- Be well prepared. Make sure everybody knows what the audit will entail. Have all your records and manuals to hand.
- Answer questions fully, but don't volunteer unnecessary or irrelevant information. You may say too much and lead the auditor down a path that you will regret. (This is where the certification audit differs from the pre-assessment consultancy audit.)
- If you commit to presenting some document later in the audit, the auditor may not ask for it a second time. Do not then think that you have 'got away with it'. If you do not present the document, this may appear in the final audit report as a non-compliance.
- Don't try to defend the indefensible. If you have been caught, you must show the auditor that you realize the significance of the nonconformity. If you try to argue that it is not a problem, you may be simply showing the auditor that you do not understand the standard. The auditor may then wonder whether other serious problems have not been uncovered in the audit. And one could argue that such a fundamental misunderstanding of the standard on the part of a key person in itself constitutes a major nonconformity.

The actual audit process is covered in more detail in Chapter 24.

Maintain the system

Once the initial certification audit is over, there is a great temptation to relax in a euphoria of self-congratulation. If this lasts too long, you may find that the implementation of the system has slipped – records not being completed, training or induction not being carried out in all cases, documents being changed without going through the correct procedure, and so on. If this happens, it will take an effort to bring it back under control. But, more importantly, the message will have gone out that ISO 9001 is not so important after all, and you will have established the classic cycle of Audit–Relax–Panic–Audit so familiar in many companies.

You have now passed the initial audit, so next you simply have to continue to implement the defined controls until you identify some areas for improvements. If you have set up a system which is practical and beneficial, you should be able to maintain it without too much pain. If you find that the pain is not worth the benefit, you probably have the wrong system for your circumstances, and must set about correcting the situation.

Remember, the system should be working for you – not the other way round!

Summary

Your ISO 9000 quality management system is something that should be working *for* you, to deliver real benefits in terms of quality of product or service and customer satisfaction. That is the principal objective. As a secondary objective, you may wish to have independent certification, so that you can demonstrate to customers your ability to produce a quality product or deliver a quality service.

The task of setting up a system which will achieve certification is long and involved, usually taking about a year. Over that period you must develop a full understanding of the ISO 9001 requirements, and implement appropriate controls, looking at your operation in terms of an overall process. Part of this phase is to audit and review the performance of the system.

When your system is operating satisfactorily, you will select a certification body with which you can develop a long-term relationship.

When you have achieved certification, you must then be very careful to maintain the discipline of following all your procedures all the time.

Further reading

Seaver, M. *Implementing ISO 9000: 2000*, Gower, Aldershot, 2001.

Seaver, M. and O'Mahony, L., *ISA 2000: The System for Occupational Health and Safety Management*, Gower, Aldershot, 2000.

CHAPTER **30**

Cultural and Organizational Aspects

Pat Donnellan

Cultural perspectives

Organizational culture is widely accepted to have an influence on an organization's success or failure. Employees and those who have direct contact with an organization, such as suppliers and customers, frequently mention its culture. What does it mean? People refer to the way 'things get done', the way change is embraced, or not, as the case may be, the ease with which new employees fit into the daily routine, core values and ideologies associated with working in the organization, or whether employees like the idea of belonging to the company family.

Whatever definitions one chooses to apply, serious thought must be given to the implementation of new management systems for quality, safety or environment. Within these systems, people will have their own core values and beliefs, and issues such as personal safety and the local environment often arouse emotional responses, whereas customer satisfaction and product quality are seen as more distant issues and must be presented in terms that strike closer to home, such as job security and the continued survival of the enterprise. The idea of perpetuity of the enterprise has been associated with the Japanese approach to quality. Furthermore, a criticism of Western enterprises has been the focus on short-term gain and stock market performance based on annual returns for stakeholders. Another factor working against the long-term view has been the short tenure of senior management. This promotes short-term gain, and fails to focus on the more strategic nature of quality, safety and environmental issues. Of course, throughout the life of the organization, the rate of change of the workforce is often slower than at management level. If there is a high turnover of staff, it is usually indicative of working conditions such as poor remuneration, lack of opportunity for personal development, or stress levels associated with the work environment. Maslow's hierarchy of human needs (see Figure 30.1) has a major bearing on workers' state of mind at any given time in the organization's existence. This might be referred to as the organizational climate, as opposed to organizational culture. These terms are often used interchangeably.

ORGANIZATIONAL CLIMATE VERSUS ORGANIZATIONAL CULTURE

Let's take a step back and look at some of the ideas presented about safety culture and safety climate as applied to organizations. These ideas can also be applied to developments in quality management. Glendon and Stanton (2000) cover the functionalist and

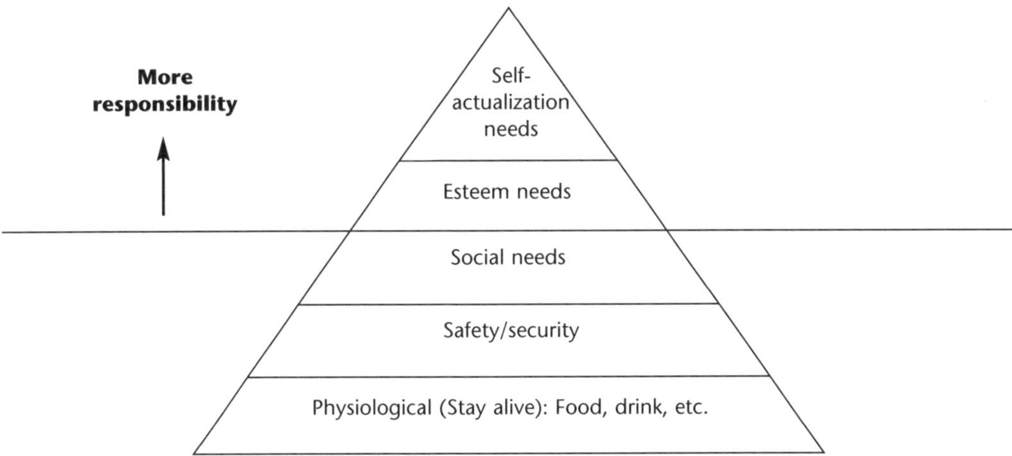

Figure 30.1 Maslow's hierarchy of human needs

interpretative perspectives on organizational culture. The functionalist approach assumes that culture exists as an ideal to which organizations should aspire, and that it can therefore be manipulated to serve the interests of the corporation. The basic model is one of prediction and control. The interpretative approach assumes that 'organizational culture is an emergent complex phenomenon of social groupings, serving as the main medium for all members of an organization to interpret their collective identity, beliefs, and behaviours'.

Alternatively, the interpretative approach reflects the pattern of assumptions developed by a group as it learns to adapt to its environment. New members are indoctrinated by the cognitions and behaviours in response to problems. Top management uses a similar idea when implementing new strategies, such as management systems, whereby the desired positive behaviour is rewarded by interest and enthusiasm, and alternative behaviour is received in a cool manner. Likewise, although all ideas are encouraged, unpopular ideas are put through several tests and trials until they die. This management behaviour soon gets the message across that some ideas and behaviours are not acceptable, without having to come out and say so. This behaviour indicates that managerial attempts to drive rapid organizational change are unlikely to succeed. The functionalist approach is 'top-down' and is used by top management for strategic objectives. The interpretative approach is 'bottom-up' and allows for the existence of subcultures across departments, groups etc.

Within the context of safety, Cooper (2000), in discussing a definition of safety culture as 'a product emerging from values, attitudes, competencies, patterns of behaviour, etc.', suggests that it reflects both the functionalist view in terms of purpose and the interpretative view, in that 'safety culture is also an emergent property created by social groupings in the workplace'. Similar definitions apply to quality and environmental issues in the workplace. This requires that the management system incorporate 'practices' that take account of culture. Some specific practices should emerge from further discussion of the ideas of Glendon and Stanton (2000) on safety culture.

Other dimensions of culture presented include depth, breadth, progression, strength, pervasiveness and direction (referenced by Glendon and Stanton from Eldridge and Crombie and Gorman). Culture *depth* is the way in which culture is reflected in policies, programmes, procedures, practices, values, strategies and behaviours. *Breadth* is the lateral co-ordination of the different organizational components. *Progression* is a time dimension. Gorman's idea of *strength* is the extent to which people embrace the core level meanings. *Pervasiveness* is the extent to which beliefs and values are shared, and *direction* the extent to which culture embodies behaviour that is consistent with company strategy.

The most recent publications on culture have dealt with safety, and build on experiences from the developments in quality over the last twenty years. Three meanings attached to safety culture were reviewed by the Institution for Occupational Safety and Health (IOSH). The first includes aspects of culture that affect safety. The second refers to the shared attitudes, values, beliefs, and practices concerning safety and the necessity for effective controls. The third, from the Health and Safety Commission (HSC) UK (1993), relates to 'the product of individual and group values, attitudes, competencies and patterns of behaviour that determine the commitment to, and the style and proficiency or, an organization's safety programs'. The Chernobyl disaster, and subsequently the Kings Cross and Piper Alpha disasters, cited breakdown in safety culture as a major contributor.

A methodology for changing safety culture (from Cooper, 2000) incorporates risk assessment, audits, training, climate surveys and behaviour change. Most of these basic elements appear in quality, safety and environmental management systems. The risk assessment element is manifested in the quality world as the consequence of poor-quality performance, using tools such as failure mode effect analysis and fault tree analysis.

Consideration of organizational climate may offer more opportunity for the implementation of a new management system for quality, safety or environment. Organizational climate relates to perceived quality of the organization's internal environment – it is an index of organizational health. Glendon and Stanton (2000) used the definition by James and Jones (1993), who referred to climate as 'psychologically meaningful cognitive representation of the situation'. Although climate is more superficial than culture, it is necessary to be aware of the current climate before embarking on a new initiative. Koys and Cotiis in Glendon and Stanton (2000) identified the dimensions of organizational climate as autonomy, cohesion, pressure, trust, recognition, support, fairness and innovation. The results of six climatic safety studies, based on various management factors, are summarized in Table 30.1. It is important to consider the workers' perceptions in developing a new system. The relationship between safety, quality, and environmental management will require similar considerations, and one can expect similar reactions to environmental issues as to safety, at least where local environment issues are concerned.

ASSESSMENT OF ORGANIZATIONAL CLIMATE

To assess organizational climate, Glendon proposes a Safety Climate Questionnaire (SCQ), shown in Table 30.2, that offers useful insights into developing the concept of best practice. Although this was developed for safety considerations, it is clear that these issues also apply to quality and environment.

Kennedy and Kirwan (1998) describe the relationship between safety management, climate and culture as follows:

> Safety culture is a sub-element of the overall organizational culture. It is an abstract concept which is underpinned by the amalgamation of individual and group perceptions, thought processes, feelings and behaviour which in turn gives rise to the particular way of doing things in an organization. The safety climate and the safety

Table 30.1 Six safety climate indicators

Factor	Examples
Management attitudes	Management attitudes towards safety Relationships Maintenance and management issues Management commitment to safety Employees' perception of management concern with their wellbeing Employee perception of management response to their concerns
Training	Importance and effectiveness of safety training Communication and training Training and management attitudes Personal authority Training and enforcement of policy
Procedures	Incident investigation and development of procedures Adequacy of procedures Policy/procedures Company policy
Risk perception	Level of risk at workplace Employee physical risk perception Work environment
Work pace	Work pressure Effects of work pace on safety
Workers' involvement	Status of committees Workers' involvement

Source: Glendon and Stanton (2000).

> management are at lower levels of abstraction (although not necessarily at the same lower level) and are considered to be a manifestation of the overall safety culture. The safety climate is, therefore, a more tangible expression of the safety culture in the form of symbolic and political aspects of the organization. These factors in turn will characterize and influence the deployment and effectiveness of the safety management resources, policies, practices and procedures.

This can equally well apply to quality and environment. A more straightforward definition centres on the 'Goal Setting Theory'. Cooper (2000) suggests that if one accepts the goal theory concepts, then the creation of a quality of safety culture becomes that of a superordinate goal. The concepts involved are:

- producing behavioural norms
- reductions in accidents and injuries (or defects and complaints in the case of quality)
- ensuring that issues receive the attention warranted by their significance
- ensuring that organizational members share the same ideas and beliefs about risks, accidents and ill health, defects, and so on
- increasing people's commitment

Table 30.2 Safety climate questionnaire

Factor	Description
Work pressure	Degree to which employees feel under pressure to complete work Amount of time to plan and carry out work Balance of workload
Incident investigation and development of procedures	Degree to which staff are involved in developing procedures Extent to which incident investigations get to underlying causes of incidents Effectiveness of procedures (also applies to corrective action for quality problems)
Adequacy of procedures	Accuracy Completeness and comprehensiveness Clarity Appropriateness of procedures Ease of selection and use of procedures
Communication and training	Degree of openness and extent to which communication reaches all levels in the organization Extent to which training incorporates all aspects of the job Relevance and effectiveness of training
Relationships	Degree of trust and support within the organization Confidence that people have in the organization's future Working relationships with others and general morale
Personal protective equipment (PPE)	Degree to which safety is a priority Extent to which people are consulted on safety Practicality of implementing safety policy and procedures

Source: Adopted from Glendon and Stanton (2000).

- determining the style and proficiency of an organization's health and safety and quality programmes.

ORGANIZATIONAL SUBCULTURES

A final consideration by McDonald et al. (2000) is the existence of subcultures. In their study of safety culture in aircraft maintenance organizations, their research suggested the existence of a professional subculture among aircraft maintenance technicians across four companies surveyed. The groups surveyed were: unqualified operators (29), aircraft technicians (336), licensed technicians (120), quality personnel/inspectors (29), graduate engineers/management (29), shift/crew management (34), planning (28), support personnel (17). There appeared to be a gap in 'job perception' between maintenance technicians and management. Technicians believed that they were solely responsible for aircraft safety, whereas management's belief was that the technicians' role was to follow procedures explicitly. This meant that the work was being done differently to the way management expected, since the technicians utilized their skill and professional values to carry out the tasks. If the tasks had been carried out exactly according to the procedures, then production would have been hugely delayed. This strong professional subculture appeared to be independent of the organization, as it was present in all four organizations.

This experience needs to be considered when developing 'current best practice'. It is a common finding in quality audits that there are three ways of doing a task. The first is the way described in the procedure. The second is the way that the workers actually do the work, and the third is the way that management think the task is done. The practice in this case is for the operators and the engineers to work together in developing and maintaining the procedures. It is management's role to approve their manufacturing and business processes, and they must ensure an appropriate approval process is in place. The problem of getting operator co-operation and involvement also requires work by management in motivating employees so that they participate.

Motivational theories

Kolarik (1995) presents various Management Leadership Motivation (MLM) models. Among the most frequently quoted models are these:

- Maslow's hierarchy of needs, which was mentioned earlier
- Frederick W. Taylor's scientific management concepts from the late 1800s which viewed the workplace as a system, and developed rules for work accordingly that were task-based
- Elton Mayo is credited with the development of the human relations concept, which focuses on interpersonal relations within an organization, and he is most famous for the Hawthorn experiments of the 1920s
- Kurt Lewin is credited with the development of the fundamental principle of participative management in the 1920s, which says that people are more likely to modify their behaviour when they participate in problem analysis and solution; he was also the first to identify and understand 'job satisfaction', and developed the 'force-field analysis' technique as a tool for change management
- Eric Trist and Fred Emery advocated the elimination of authoritarian management behaviour from the workplace in the 1950s, and proposed the development of worker teams for which management acted as a resource. This was the beginning of the 'quality of work-life' movement
- Douglas McGregor developed his Theory X/Theory Y model in the 1950s, which was based on the earlier work of Lewin
- Frederick Hertzberg developed his motivation hygiene factors model in the 1950s and 1960s. His 'hygiene factors' were those necessary to avoid dissatisfaction, such as supervision, salary, working conditions, interpersonal relations and so on.
- Rensis Likert, in the 1970s, developed a four-system model:
  - System 1 – an exploitative, authoritarian model (autocratic)
  - System 2 – a benevolent, authoritarian model (improves on System 1)
  - System 3 – a consultative model (improves on System 2)
  - System 4 – participative group models (the most democratic).
- Blake and Mouton developed the Managerial Grid Model in the early 1990s, which views leadership style as a function of, firstly, concern for people and relationships, and secondly, concern for production and tasks

- Helgesen describes the 'web' model that presents the organizational chart as a series of concentric rings with the leader located at the centre and the surrounding circles representing the levels in the organization; information flow is between any combination of people, and the emphasis is on sharing information, rather than a top-down flow of information.

An organization must adopt an approach to the motivation of employees if a truly integrated management system is to be developed. The web model, with its horizontal as well as vertical lines of communication, offers definite advantages in the area of communication and openness within an organization. The next challenge is to identify the current *modus operandi*, and then initiate a series of changes to develop a new approach to people motivation and change management.

Organizational change

A key question for managers relates to the size of the change required.

There is usually an overlap between old and new cultures, where opportunities exist in some areas to promote new cultures. The 'delta' concept (see Figure 30.2) requires an organization to identify these areas and use them as the foundation for the new culture. If the two circles are totally separated, then the task of moving to a new culture is much more difficult.

You can use organizational diagnosis to:

- assess the degree of change required
- discover what internal resources you have to help achieve it.

The reaction to change of an individual or group is predictable. Figure 30.3 shows the change in levels of energy or wellbeing for people involved in the change process during the various phases of the exercise.

CHANGING ORGANIZATIONAL CULTURE

The methods available for changing culture include the following:

- **Changing people** – recruitment, selection, redundancy
- **Changing roles** – reshuffle the pack, new locations

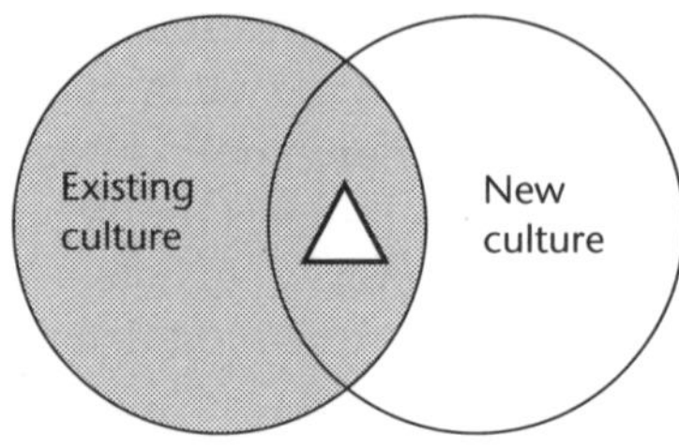

Figure 30.2 Change delta

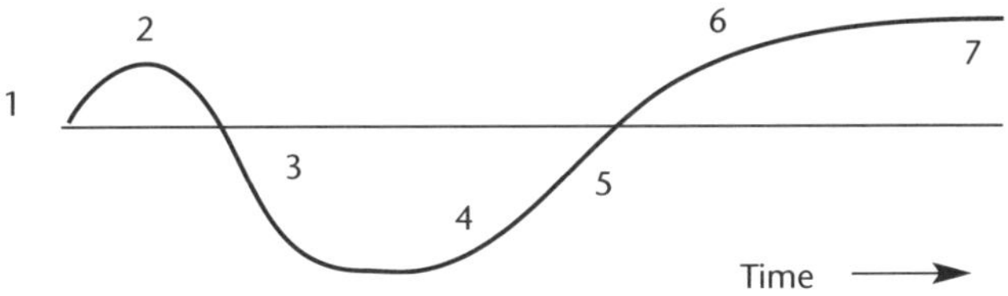

1. Immobilized
2. Denial/bargaining
3. Depression/anger
4. Letting go of old ways
5. Test/try new ways
6. Searching for meaning
7. Internalization of the new approach

Figure 30.3 Reaction to change (the 'grief' curve)
The vertical axis is a measure of the person's energy or wellbeing.

- **Changing people's beliefs, attitudes, behaviours** – group dynamics/teams, role models, learning organization
- **Changing the structures, systems and technology** – restructuring, reward/appraisal system, monitoring/scanning systems, budgeting systems, control systems
- **Through corporate image** – public relations/advertising.

Indicators of resistance to be aware of are:

- **Generalizing** – 'Everybody has this problem, and there's nothing one can do.'
- **Rigidity** – 'I have to do it this way. Anyway, it's always worked before.'
- **Redefining** – Individuals do not answer questions directly.
- **Self-interrupting** – When discussing the change, individuals will jump from one point to another without any apparent logic to their argument.
- **Minimizing** – 'It's not really a problem; we've been all right for the past 10 years.'
- **Over-dramatizing** – 'If I did that, it would be disastrous.'

Here are some counter-implementation games that are common in organizations:

- **Phoney purist** – 'I'm all for it, but let's be sure to get it absolutely right.'
- **Small print** – 'I think the overall concept is great, but does it cater for the small farmer specializing in goat's milk?'
- **Wise owl** – 'We must proceed with caution ...'
- **Bulldog** – 'No, we're still not happy ...'
- **Big print** – 'But what about the big picture and the long term ...?'
- **Peacekeeper** – 'We must make sure everyone is happy ...'
- **Technical showman** – 'Well, it's not as simple as it looks to the layman, actually ...'
- **Hand-off** – 'I think this is *our* job – we have a team working on it already'.
- **Friendly warning** – 'You can go ahead if you like, but don't blame me if ...'

RULES OF THE ROAD FOR CHANGE

Juran (1974) presented some 'rules of the road' for change:

- Provide participation, and enough time by starting small.
- Keep the proposals free of excess baggage.
- Work with the recognized leadership of the culture.
- Treat people with dignity; reverse the positions.
- Deal directly with resistance, using persuasion or quid pro quo deals, change proposals to meet objections, change the social climate, or abandon it as a last resort.

Juran further suggests conducting a 'barriers and aids analysis' to change, where all barriers and aids are brainstormed, ranked as high, medium or low, and any aids and barriers are matched up, identifying items needing team actions and developing an action plan accordingly. This will give the teams a starting point for improvement. Training programmes should focus on promoting awareness of team behaviour, the role of team members, and the need to monitor and measure team performance. Failure must be accepted as an option for some team projects, and management must guide the team to ensure that some project successes are achieved to motivate and develop momentum at the early stages of the team's development.

Organizations are learning to change, but still face the barriers outlined above. Hale (2001) summarizes various barriers to learning as:

- People are not surprised enough when things go wrong.
- Deviations are seen as normal, so they do not cause surprises and are not regarded as a problem. This tends to be a culture issue.
- Many people are afraid of blame or ridicule for reporting incidents or deviations. These should be rewarded, in order to promote higher reporting levels, since people learn from mistakes. In some jobs, like that of airline pilots, reporting is done on a confidential basis, thus leading to a level of trust between individuals and groups.
- Reporting should be made easy, with the minimum of paperwork and the use of online software systems with a range of pre-programming, if possible.
- Lessons learned should be reviewed and validated by teams, and the new preventive measures should be championed to promote the new learning requirements, so that, in time, these improvements become new norms for the team.
- The key to success is an organizational desire to learn. It must be organized, resourced, cherished and rewarded by top management.

Organization structures for quality

During a research project, the author visited a number of companies in Portugal, Spain and Ireland to assess the current organizational structures used to manage quality, safety and the environment.

PORTUGAL

The quality functions reported to the plant managers or the engineering/technical managers, and the main focus was on understanding and meeting customer needs.

SPAIN

The quality function reported to the plant manager in most cases. In one case, quality reported to the engineering function.

IRELAND

For quality, safety and environment, some of the larger organizations had integrated the systems at top management level but were still operating separate organizations at an operational level. The typical organization included a quality manager, who reported to plant managers in most cases. In smaller organizations, they tended to hold multiple responsibilities, usually engineering, maintenance and quality, with quality/manufacturing engineers as well.

Summary of organizational perspectives

In developing a quality organization one must take account of organizational culture and organizational climate. Resistance to change is a common organizational barrier to the development of quality management systems. One must understand the current cultural climate before embarking on new quality, safety or environmental programmes. Training, communication and consultation are common initiatives used in overcoming these barriers. The physical structures must allow for organizational responsibility as well as accountability. Very often, the responsibility for quality is placed on one person's shoulders, when in fact it is everybody's responsibility. This is the message that the organization must learn, and it must be reflected in the setting and meeting of its goals, objectives and targets at all levels of the company.

Further reading

Cooper, M.D., 'Towards a model of safety culture', *Safety Science*, No. 36, 2000, pp. 111–36.

Glendon, A.I. and Stanton, N.A., 'Perspectives on safety culture', *Safety Science*, No. 34, 2000, pp. 193–214.

Hale, A., *Organized Learning from Small Incidents*, Colloquio Internacional sobre Seguranca e Higiene do Trabalho, Porto, 2001.

ILO, 'IOHA Report on an International OHSMS', International Labour Organisation, Geneva, 1999. <www.ilo.org/public/english/protection/safework/cis/managmnt/ioha/chp_2.htm>.

Juran, J.M. (ed.) (1974), *Quality Control Handbook*, 4th edn, McGraw-Hill, London, 1974.

Kennedy, R. and Kirwan, B., 'Development of a Hazard and Operability-based Method for Identifying Safety Management Vulnerabilities in High Risk Systems', *Safety Science*, No. 30, 2000, pp. 249–74.

Kolarik, W., 'Creating Quality, Concepts, Systems, Strategies, and Tools', McGraw-Hill International Editions, London, 1995.

MacGregor Associates, *Study on Management System Standards*, British Standards Institute, London, 1996.

McDonald, N., Corrigan, S., Daly, C., Cromie, S., 'Safety management systems and safety culture in aircraft maintenance organizations', *Safety Science*, No. 34, 2000, pp. 151–76.

CHAPTER **31**

Total Quality Management

John Oakland

All companies compete on three main factors: quality, delivery and price. There can be few senior managers in the West who remain to be convinced that quality is the most important of these. Consumers now place a higher value on quality than on loyalty to their home-based producers. Price has been replaced by quality as the main determining factor in consumer choice in industrial, service, hospitality, and many other markets.

Quality

Quality is one of the most commonly misunderstood words in management. What is a high-quality pair of shoes or a high-quality bank account? It is meaningless to make statements about the degree of quality of a product or service without reference to its intended use or purpose. Ballet shoes would obviously have different requirements from those used in mountaineering, but both pairs of shoes may have the same level of quality – they are equally suitable for the purpose for which they were manufactured. Quality can therefore be defined as the extent to which a product or service meets the requirements of the customer.

Before any discussion on quality can take place, it is therefore necessary to be clear about the purpose of the product or service. In other words: what are the customer's requirements?

The quality of a product has two distinct but inter-related aspects:

1 **Quality of design** – This is a measure of how well the product or service is designed to achieve its stated purpose. If it is poor, the product will not work or the service will not meet the needs.

2 **Quality of conformance to design** – What the customer receives should conform to the design. This is concerned largely with the quality performance of the operations functions. The recording and analysis of data play a significant role in this aspect of quality, and it is here that the tools of statistical process control must be applied effectively (see Chapters 8 and 17–19).

It is vital to realize that the customer's perception of quality will change with time. The organization's attitude to quality must therefore change in tandem with this perception. The skills and attitudes of the producer are also likely to change. Failure to monitor such changes will lead to dissatisfied customers. Quality, like all other corporate matters, must be reviewed continually in the light of current circumstances.

A traditional misconception of quality management

Traditionally, quality has been regarded mainly as the responsibility of the quality control (QC) department.

There is a belief in some quarters that to achieve quality, we must check, test, inspect or measure – the ritual pouring on of quality at the end of the process. This is nonsense, but it is frequently practised. In the office, one finds staff checking other people's work before it goes out, validating computer input data, checking invoices, typing, and so on. There is also quite a lot of looking for things, checking why things are late, apologizing to customers for lateness and so forth. Waste, waste, waste!

Reliance on a high level of final or service inspection is often indicative of attempts to 'inspect in' quality. The traditional attempt at a remedy for poor quality was to employ more inspectors, tighten up standards and develop correction, repair and rework teams. But this approach promotes a *detection* approach to quality, rather than the more effective *prevention*.

THE FAILURE MULTIPLIER

Failures, in the form of poor quality and errors, have a way of multiplying so that one failure leads to more errors and problems elsewhere in the system. People in business then spend much of their time correcting errors, looking for things, checking why things are late, rectifying, chasing, reworking, apologizing to customers and so forth.

It is estimated that about one-third of all effort expended in businesses is wasted because of this failure multiplier effect, which means that the total cost to a nation's economy is enormous. Moreover, this is likely to be an underestimate because organizations rarely have a proper measure of how much profit they are losing through poor quality.

Competitiveness is seriously eroded by the costs associated with this organization-wide failure. The total cost to the organization is even higher when one considers the cost of all those things which could have been done in the time saved by getting it right first time.

The Total Quality Management approach

Many quality problems originate not in the manufacturing or operations areas of a company, but in the marketing, service, finance, personnel and administration functions. Quality cannot be 'inspected in' as a final, isolated function at the end of a process or sequence of processes. Quality – the quest for customer satisfaction – must be designed into all the organization's systems and instilled into all its employees.

Total Quality Management (TQM) is a way of managing to improve the effectiveness, efficiency, flexibility and competitiveness of a business as a whole. It involves whole companies getting organized and becoming committed to quality in each department, each activity and each person, at each level. TQM recognizes that for an organization to be truly effective, each of its parts must work smoothly with the other parts, because every person and every activity affects and in turn is affected by others.

TQM is also a method of removing waste, by involving everyone in improving the ways in which things are done. The techniques of TQM can be applied throughout a company, so that people from different departments, with different priorities and abilities, communicate with and help each other. The methods are equally useful in finance, sales, marketing, design, accounts, research, development, purchasing, personnel, computer services, distribution, stores and production.

TQM helps companies to:

- focus clearly on the needs of their markets
- achieve a top-quality performance in all areas, not just in product or service quality
- operate the simple procedures necessary for the achievement of a quality performance
- critically and continually examine all processes to remove non-productive activities and waste
- see the improvements required and develop measures of performance
- understand fully and in detail their competition, and develop an effective competitive strategy
- develop the team approach to problem-solving, develop good procedures for communication and acknowledgement of good work
- continually review the processes to develop the strategy of never-ending improvement.

TQM is not simply a cost-cutting or productivity improvement device, and it must not be used as such. Although the effects of a successful programme will certainly include these benefits, TQM is concerned chiefly with changing attitudes and skills so that the culture of the organization becomes one of preventing failure, and the norm that of operating right first time.

Systems and techniques are important in TQM, but they are not the primary requirement. It is more an attitude of mind, a culture based on pride in the job and requiring total commitment from management – commitment which must then be extended to all employees at all levels and in all departments.

THE QUALITY CHAINS

One of the most widely accepted definitions of quality is 'meeting the customer's requirements'. Perhaps 'delighting the customer' is a better objective. The ability to meet customers' requirements and then go on to delight them is vital. This is true not only between two separate organizations, but also between different parts within the organization itself. There exists in every department, every office, a series of suppliers and customers.

Throughout and beyond all organizations, whether they be manufacturing concerns, banks, retail stores, universities, hotels or other service suppliers, there is a series of quality chains (Figure 31.1). These chains can be broken at any point if one person or one piece of equipment fails to meet the requirements of the next immediate customer in the chain, internal or external. It is interesting to note that failure at any link in the chain often finds its way to the interface between the organization and its outside customers, and the people who operate at that interface usually suffer the ramifications.

A great deal is written and spoken about employee motivation as a separate issue. An important element of motivation, and the key to quality, is for everyone in the organization to have well-defined customers and suppliers. The demands of customers and the abilities of suppliers throughout the chain – internal and external – must be well defined. And it must be understood that customers and suppliers include anyone to whom an individual gives or receives a part, service or information.

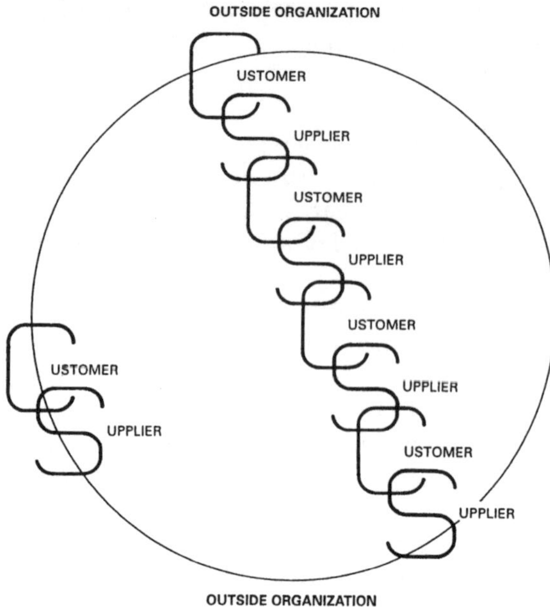

Figure 31.1 The quality chains

Some people in customer organizations never see, touch or experience the products or services that their companies buy, but they do see things like suppliers' invoices and other documents. If one of those invoices carries errors, what image of quality does that supplier transmit? Clearly, quality must involve everyone in the organization.

MEETING THE CUSTOMER'S REQUIREMENTS

Because the minimum quality standard is to meet the customer's requirements, quality management has wide implications. The requirements may include availability, delivery, reliability, maintainability and cost-effectiveness, among many other features. Whether customers are outside the organization or in another part of the same organization, their satisfaction must be the principal ingredient in any plan for success.

The first thing to do is to find out what the requirements are. When dealing with a supplier–customer relationship that crosses two organizations, the supplier must establish a 'marketing' activity charged with this task. The marketers must, of course, understand not only the needs of the customer, but also the ability of their own organization to meet those demands. Then, when all the specified requirements are met, steps can be taken towards delighting the customer by anticipating the requirements.

The transfer of information regarding requirements along the quality chains is frequently poor, particularly within organizations. Sometimes, it is totally absent.

To maintain a wave of interest in quality, and therefore to maintain quality itself, it is necessary to develop generations of managers who not only understand, but are dedicated to the pursuit of, never-ending improvement. This philosophy of continuous improvement requires that an organization should review continuously its customers' requirements (internal and external) and its ability to meet them.

PREVENTION, NOT DETECTION

Every day, in countless organizations, people examine the results of the day's work and start the ritual battle to determine whether or not the output is suitable for transfer to the 'customer'. They argue and debate the evidence before them, the rights and wrongs of their interpretation of the customer's requirements, and each tries to convince the other of the validity of their argument. This ritual is associated with trying to answer the question:

> Have we done the job correctly?

'Correctly', in this context, is often a flexible word. It can depend on the interpretation given to the customer's specification on that particular day.

The process just described is not quality control. It is detection – post-production, wasteful detection of bad product or service before it hits the customer.

To get away from the natural tendency to rush into the detection mode, it is necessary to ask different questions in the first place. We should not ask whether the job has been done correctly; we should ask first:

> Are we capable of doing the job correctly?

This question has wide implications, and TQM is devoted largely to the activities necessary to ensure that the answer is 'Yes.' We should realize straight away, however, that this answer will only be obtained using satisfactory methods, materials, equipment, skills and instruction, and a 'process' which is capable.

Process capability and control

A process is the transformation of a set of inputs – which can include actions, methods and operations – into desired outputs, in the form of products, information, services or, generally, results. There will be many processes taking place in each area or function of an organization. All work is done through a process in which inputs are transformed into outputs (Figure 31.2).

Once it has been established that processes are capable of meeting the requirements, the next question must be asked:

> Are we continuing to do the job correctly?

This requires that the process and the current control methods be monitored.

If the first question ('Have we done the job correctly?') is now re-examined, we can see that provided we have been able to answer the other two questions with a 'yes', we must have done the job correctly. No other outcome would be logical. By asking the questions in the right order, we have removed the need to ask the 'inspection' question, and replaced a strategy of detection with one of prevention. This concentrates attention on the front end of any process – the inputs and the process itself. It changes the emphasis of making sure that the inputs are capable of meeting the requirements of the process, and that the transformation process is understood and controlled. These ideas apply to every

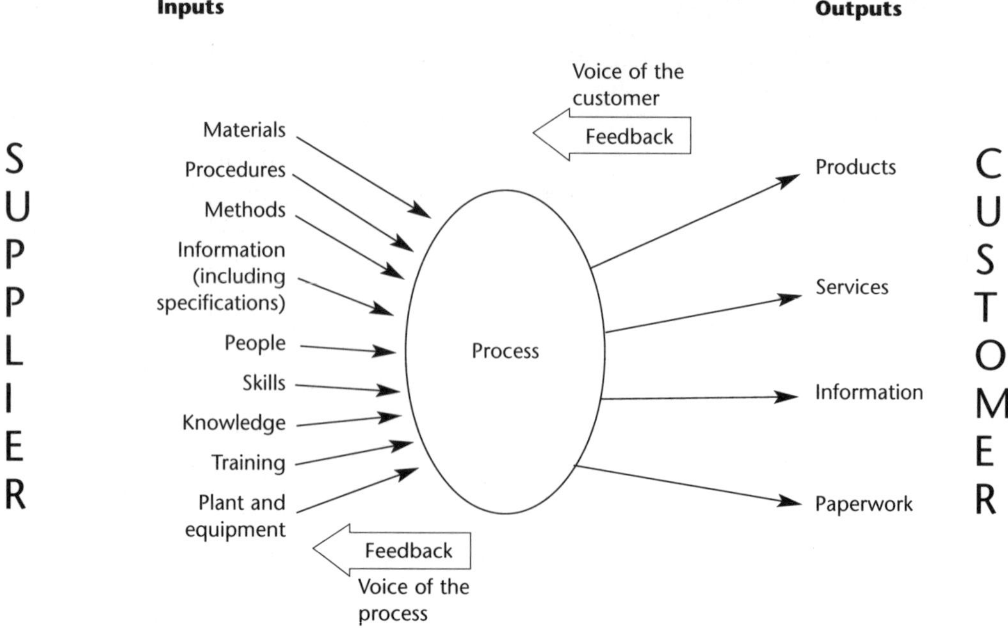

Figure 31.2 A process

transformation process, which must be subjected to the same scrutiny of the methods, the people, skills, equipment and so on, to make sure they are correct for the job.

QUALITY ASSURANCE

Clearly, the control of quality can take place only at the point of operation or production – where the letter is typed or the chemical made. The act of inspection is not quality control. When the answer to 'Have we done the job correctly?' is given indirectly by answering the questions on capability and control, then quality is assured. The activity of checking becomes one of quality assurance – making certain that the product or service represents the output from an effective system for ensuring capability and control. The unacceptable alternative is an organization in which barriers between departmental empires encourage testing and checking of products and services in isolation, without meaningful interaction with other departments.

The author has a vision of quality as a strategic business management function that will help organizations to change their cultures. To make this vision a reality, quality professionals must expand the application of quality concepts and techniques to all business processes and functions, and develop new forms of providing assurance of quality at every supplier–customer interface.

Commitment and attitude to quality

To succeed, TQM must be truly organization-wide. It must start at the top with the chief executive and the most senior directors and management, who must all demonstrate that they are serious about quality. Management's commitment must be obsessional, not just lip-service. Clear quality objectives must be set out in a quality policy statement.

If the chief executive of an organization accepts the responsibility for and commitment to a quality policy, understands what he or she is committed to, and articulates and demonstrates that commitment, the impact will be much greater than anything that the best quality manager could ever hope to achieve. This action by the chief executive in turn creates responsibilities for interaction between the marketing design, producing, purchasing, distribution, accounting and other service functions. These basic changes of attitude are required at all levels and in every department, starting at the top, to operate TQM. If the owners or directors of the organization do not recognize and accept their responsibilities for the initiation and operation of TQM, these essential changes will not happen.

Middle management have a particularly important role to play. They must not only grasp the principles of TQM; they must go on to explain them to the people for whom they are responsible and ensure that their own commitment is communicated. Only then will TQM spread effectively throughout the organization. Senior management must also ensure that the efforts and achievements of their subordinates obtain the recognition, attention and reward that they deserve. It cannot be said too often that TQM must involve everyone in all departments.

It is possible to detect real commitment – or the lack of it. It shows on the shop floor, in the offices – at the point of operation. One is quickly able to detect the falseness in those organizations where posters campaigning for quality are displayed but are not backed up by commitment. People are told not to worry if quality problems arise: 'Just do the best you can', 'That will be all right' or 'Let's hope the customer will not notice.'

In contrast, in a company where total quality means something, it can be seen, heard and felt. Things happen at each operating interface as a result of real commitment. Material problems are corrected with suppliers, equipment difficulties are put right by improved maintenance programmes or replacement, people are trained, change takes place.

TQM is concerned with moving the focus of control from outside the individual to within, the objective being to make everyone accountable for their own performance, and to get them committed to attaining quality in a highly motivated fashion. The assumptions a director or manager must make in order to move in this direction are simply that people do not need to be coerced to perform well, but that they want to achieve, accomplish, influence activity, and simply need to have their abilities challenged.

Total Quality Management is user-driven. It cannot be imposed from outside the organization, as perhaps a quality management system, standard or statistical process control can be. This means that the ideas for improvement must come from those with the knowledge and experience of the methods and techniques.

The shift in 'philosophy' will require considerable staff training in many organizations. Not only must people in other functions acquire quality-related skills, but quality personnel will need to change old attitudes and acquire new skills – replacing the inspection, calibration, specification-writing mentality with knowledge of defect prevention, wide-ranging quality management systems design, and audit. Clearly, the challenge for many quality professionals is not so much making changes in their organization, as recognizing the changes which are required in themselves. It is more than an overnight job to change the attitudes of an inspection police force into those of a consultative, team-oriented improvement force. This emphasis on prevention and improvement-based systems elevates the role of quality professionals from a technical one to that of general management. A narrow, departmental view of quality is totally out of place in an organization aspiring to TQM, and old-style quality managers will need to widen their perspective and increase their knowledge to encompass all facets of the organization.

Introducing the concepts of 'operator' self-inspection needed for TQM will require not only a determination to implement change, but also sensitivity and skills in managing human resources. Of course, this will depend very much on the climate within the organization. Those whose management is truly concerned with co-operation and concern for people will engage strong employee support for the quality manager or director in his or her catalytic role in the implementation process. Those with aggressive, confrontational management will create impossible difficulties for the quality professional in obtaining support from the 'rank and file'.

The basic building blocks of a TQM model are:

- the desire to achieve a TQM culture
- recognition of the need for excellent communications
- acceptance of the importance of total commitment
- core recognition of the supplier/customer chains and of the transforming processes which constitute all work.

While culture, communications and commitment are highly desirable, they are not immediately accessible to an organization. They represent the 'soft components' of the TQM model. Attention must now be turned to the 'hard parts' of the model: those necessities on which one can operate directly in order to achieve the less accessible soft outcomes.

The three hard components of TQM

In addition to the management commitment, the communications and the culture required, which have already been discussed at some length, there are three main hard components of TQM:

1 a documented quality management system
2 quality management tools and techniques
3 teamwork and people.

QUALITY MANAGEMENT SYSTEM

Consistency can only be achieved if it is ensured that for every product or each time a service is performed, the same materials, the same equipment, the same methods or procedures are used every time in the most effective and efficient way. This is the aim of a well-documented quality management system – to provide the 'operator' with consistency and satisfaction in terms of methods, materials and equipment.

The ISO 9000 series of standards sets out the methods by which a management system, incorporating all the activities associated with quality, can be implemented in an organization to ensure that all the specified performance requirements and needs of the customer are fully met.

Although this standard was originally directed towards manufacturing, it is equally applicable to non-manufacturing. Of course, seeking to delight customers with a product is not the same thing as seeking to delight with a service – not least because the customer's requirements of a service are often clarified only during the delivery of the service.

The quality management system must always be implemented in a way which meets the specific organizational and product or service requirements. The system then requires audit and review to ensure that:

1 the people involved are operating according to the documented system (a system audit)
2 the system still meets the requirements (a system review).

If during the system audits and reviews it is discovered that an even better product or less waste can be achieved by changing the method or one of the materials, then a change may be effected. To maintain consistency, the appropriate changes must be made to the documented system, and everyone concerned must be issued with and adhere to the revised procedures.

QUALITY TOOLS AND TECHNIQUES

All processes can be monitored and improved by gathering and using data more effectively. Statistical process control (SPC) methods, backed by management commitment and good organization, provide objective means of controlling quality in any transformation process, whether it is used in the manufacture of artefacts, the provision of services, or the transfer of information. The techniques of SPC are described in Chapters 8 and 17–19, but it is useful to say something here about SPC in the context of TQM.

SPC is not only a toolkit; it is a strategy for reducing variability, the cause of most quality problems: variation in products, in delivery times, in ways of doing things, in materials, in people's attitudes, in equipment and its use, in maintenance practices – in fact, in everything. Control by itself is not sufficient.

Incapable and inconsistent processes render the best design impotent, and make supplier quality assurance irrelevant. Whatever process is being operated, it must be reliable and consistent. SPC can be used to achieve this objective. Other tools may be required, for example to assist in defining the process, to develop quality costing, to design experiments, to study failure mode and effect, to manage design and development, and so on. These tools complement the SPC tools. The philosophy of never-ending improvement requires an attack on variability. SPC is a vital element in this attack.

Variability reduction is brought about by studying all aspects of the process using the basic question:

> Could we do this job more consistently and on target?

The answer to this question drives the search for improvements. This significant feature of SPC means that it is not constrained to measuring conformance, and that it is intended to lead to action to minimize variability, notwithstanding that the processes are already operating within their 'specified limits'.

Changing an organization's environment into one in which SPC and the other tools can operate properly may take several years, rather than months. For many companies, SPC will bring a new approach, a new 'philosophy', but the importance of the statistical techniques should not be disguised. Simple presentation of data using diagrams, graphs and charts should become the means of communication concerning the state of control of processes in all areas.

In the application of quality tools, there is often an emphasis on techniques rather than on the implied wider managerial strategies. It is worth repeating that SPC is not only about plotting charts on the walls of a plant or office; it must become part of the organization-wide adoption of TQM, and act as the focal point of never-ending improvement.

TEAMWORK AND PEOPLE

The complexity of most of the processes which are operated in industry, commerce and the services places them beyond the control of any one individual. The only way to tackle problems concerning such processes is through some form of teamwork. The use of the team approach to problem-solving has many advantages over allowing individuals or isolated departments to work separately on problems:

- The problems are exposed to a greater diversity of knowledge, skill and experience.
- The approach is more satisfying to team members, and boosts morale.
- The problems at cross-departmental or functional boundaries can be dealt with more easily.
- A greater variety of problems can be tackled, including those beyond the capability of any one individual or department.
- Recommendations by the team are more likely to be implemented than suggestions by individuals.

Most of these rely on the premise that people are willing to support an effort in which they have taken part or helped to develop.

When properly managed, teams improve the process of problem-solving, producing results quickly and economically. Teamwork throughout an organization is an essential component of the implementation of TQM, for it builds trust, improves communications and develops interdependence. Much of what has been taught previously in management has led to a culture of independence with little sharing of ideas and information. Teamwork devoted to quality improvement changes the independence to *interdependence* through improved communications, greater trust and the free exchange of ideas, data and knowledge.

Employees will not be motivated towards continual improvement in the absence of:

- commitment to quality from the management
- the organizational quality 'climate'
- a team approach to quality problems.

All these are focused essentially on enabling people to feel, accept and discharge responsibility. TQM organizations have made this a part of their quality strategy – to 'empower people to act'. Empowerment is very easy to express conceptually, but it requires effort and commitment on the part of all managers and supervisors to put it into practice. A good way to start is to recognize that only partially successful but good ideas or attempts are to be applauded, not criticized. Encouragement of ideas and suggestions from the workforce – particularly through their involvement in team or group activities – requires investment, but the rewards are total involvement, both inside the organization and outside through all the supplier and customer chains.

DEVELOPING THE HARD COMPONENTS OF TQM

The aim of TQM is to achieve the active involvement of everyone in quality improvement and satisfying customers' requirements. These requirements are constantly changing as customers' expectations increase over time. The components of TQM must develop, therefore, if this moving target is to be hit. Tools and techniques are not set in tablets of stone, and should themselves be subject to the process of never-ending improvement.

An example of this has been the lively debate in recent years about the role of quality management systems such as ISO 9000 in TQM. Unfortunately, many companies have sought approval to ISO 9000 for contractual reasons only – not because they have the essential commitment to TQM. Such organizations have missed an opportunity to lay a firm foundation for TQM.

The principles of quality systems can also be applied to safety, health and the environment. Forward-looking organizations now audit their procedures against the requirements of quality, safety, health and the environment.

The quality tools are also undergoing continuous development. New developments in the field of quality costing (process cost modelling), benchmarking and TQM performance-based measurement present exciting opportunities. Metrics need to be developed that measure the organization's non-achievement of quality.

Measurement of TQM progress is an important area. Many organizations are using criteria such as the Malcolm Baldrige National Quality Award Scheme, the European Excellence Award or the UK Business Excellence Award criteria (Figure 31.3) as an evaluative and diagnostic to measure TQM progress (see Chapter 26).

The concept of continuous improvement creates a need for the imaginative use and development of the components of TQM. The TQM model (Figure 31.4) incorporates many well-established tools, systems and techniques. The development and improvement of these are vital to the success of TQM.

Implementing TQM

Consider these quotations:

> Total quality management (TQM) is dead, long live business process re-engineering (BPR)!
>
> ISO 9000 is too costly/narrow focused, you should carry out self-assessment to the European Business Excellence or Baldrige Quality Award models.
>
> Statistical process control (SPC), failure mode and effect analysis (FMEA), design of experiments (DOE), and benchmarking – these are things you should be using.

And what about measurement, culture change, teamwork, quality circles, continuous improvement, and so on and so forth?

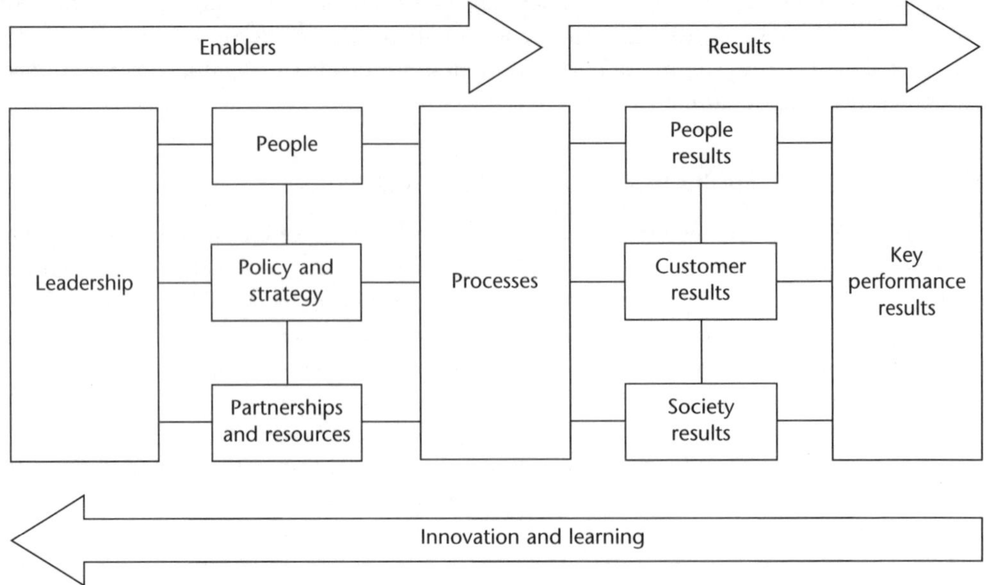

Figure 31.3 The EQFM excellence model

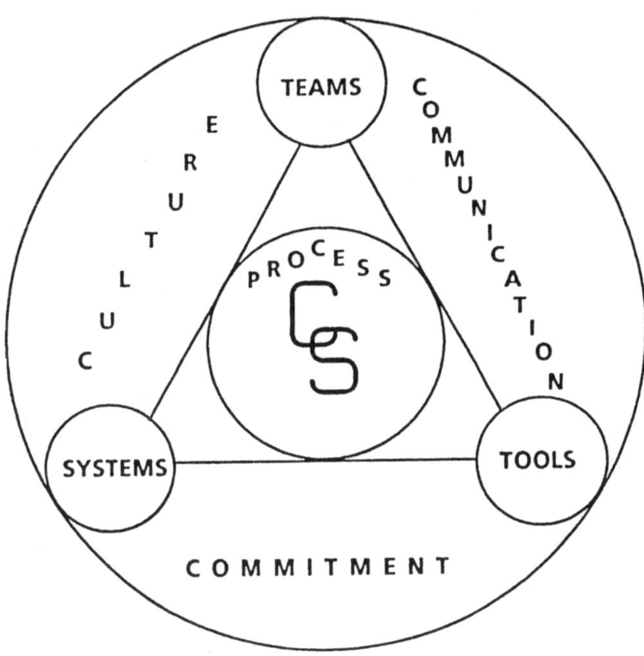

Figure 31.4 Total Quality Management model

No wonder people are confused and irritated by the conflicting messages (and combination of letters) they now receive from consultants, academics, business leaders and even politicians about what they should do to improve the performance of their organization.

To try to get some of these things into sensible proportions and shape, Oakland Consulting plc has carried out a great deal of research, teaching and advisory work. The people we speak to are often confused and in urgent need of a framework to pull this lot together, and it is probably no different in your organization. This section attempts to provide that framework – a blueprint for total organizational excellence.

Firstly, TQM is *not* dead, and is not the very narrow set of tools and techniques often associated with failed 'programmes' in organizations in various parts of the world. It is part of a broad-based approach used by world-class companies, such as Rank Xerox, Hewlett Packard, Milliken, ICL, TNT and Texas Instruments, to achieve organizational excellence, based on customer satisfaction, the highest weighted category of all the quality and business excellence awards. Total Quality Management embraces *all* of the areas mentioned so far. If used properly, and fully integrated into the business, this approach will help any organization deliver its goals, targets and strategy, including those in the public sector. This is because it is about people and their identifying, understanding, managing and improving processes – the things any organization has to do particularly well to achieve its objectives. Everything we do in any business or organization is a process.

The overall framework for total organizational excellence is shown in Figure 31.5. It all starts with the vision, goals, strategies and mission, which must be fully thought through, agreed and shared in the business. What follows determines whether these are achieved. The

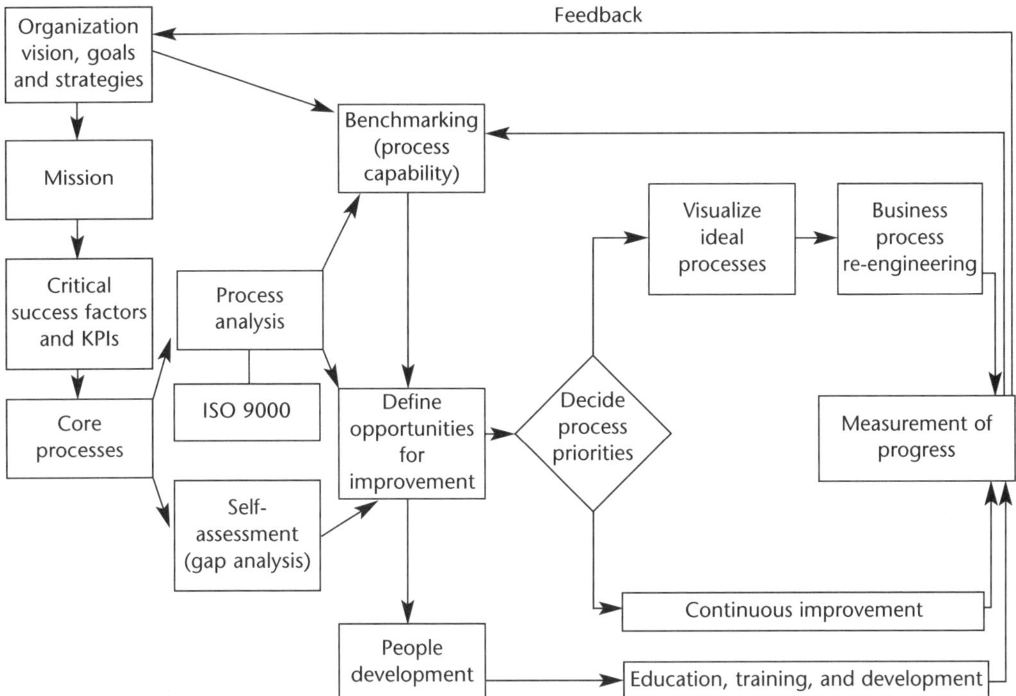

Figure 31.5 The framework for TQM implementation

factors which are critical to success, the CSFs – the building blocks of the mission – must then be identified. The key performance indicators (KPIs), the measures associated with the CSFs, tell us whether we are moving towards or away from the mission, or just standing still.

Having identified the CSFs and KPIs, the organization must know what are its *core processes*. This is an area of potential bottleneck for many organizations because, if the core processes are not understood, the rest of the framework is difficult to implement. If the processes are known, we can carry out process analysis, sometimes called mapping and flowcharting, to fully understand our business and identify opportunities for improvement. ISO 9000 standard-based systems should drop out at this stage, rather than needing a separate and huge effort and expense.

Self-assessment to the European/UK Business Excellence or Baldrige Quality models, and benchmarking, will identify further improvement opportunities. This will create a very long list of things to attend to, many of which require people development, training and education. What is clearly needed next is prioritization, to identify those processes which are run pretty well – they may be advertising/promoting the business or recruitment/selection processes – and subject them to a continuous improvement regime. Those processes which are identified as being poorly carried out, perhaps forecasting, training, or even financial management, may be subjected to a complete re-visioning and redesign activity. That is where business process re-engineering comes in. What must happen to all processes, of course, is performance measurement, the results of which feed back to our benchmarking and strategic planning activities.

World-class organizations, of which there need to be more in most countries, are doing *all* of these things. They have implemented their version of the TQM framework, and are achieving world-class performance and results. What this requires first, of course, is world-class leadership and commitment.

Conclusion

One of the greatest benefits of improved quality is the increased market share that results, rather than just the reduction in quality costs. The evidence for this can already be seen in some of the major consumer and industrial markets of the world. Superior quality can also be converted into premium prices. Quality thus clearly correlates with profit. The less tangible benefit of greater employee involvement in quality is equally – if not more – important in the longer term. The pursuit of continual improvement must become a way of life for everyone in an organization if it is to succeed in today's competitive environment.

TQM is an operational philosophy which is vital to the survival of most organizations throughout the world. European industries can learn from the Japanese experience and develop new ideas. Being second in applying new management techniques is not always a disadvantage. Later, fresh, well-informed and well-trained entries to the field can often outpace the existing players.

Further reading

BQF, *Guide to the Excellence Model*, London, 2000.
Deming, W.D., *The New Economics*, MIT Press, Cambridge, MA, 1993.

EFQM, *The European Excellence Model*, European Federation for Quality Managers, Brussels, 2000.

Oakland, J.S., *Statistical Process Control*, 4th edn, Butterworth-Heinemann, Oxford, 1999.

Oakland, J.S., *Total Organisational Excellence*, Butterworth-Heinemann, Oxford, 1999.

Oakland, J.S., *Total Quality Management: Text with Cases*, 2nd edn, Butterworth-Heinemann, Oxford, 2000.

CHAPTER **32**

Environmental Management Systems

I.C. Dean

The environmental issues

We can be certain that the environment will be a key issue for the world in the twenty-first century. Concerns about climate change, pollution, genetically modified organisms, use of resources and the general quality of life are increasing. Not only will all countries and organizations be affected, so will all of us as individuals. Concern about the environment is already a factor in legislation, the taxes we pay, the design of products, how we make and use them and how we organize work and leisure. The policies we adopt and the actions we take (or don't take) will affect our children's lives and the lives of their children to a degree which is only now becoming apparent.

As more research is conducted, we are being made increasingly aware that all human activities have impacts on the environment, and that these impacts may spread beyond the local environment to affect a region, or even the whole plant. As little as forty years ago it was possible to think of environmental impacts as being localized and pollution-based, and therefore a matter for localized action and control. Globalization has helped to change this thinking, but even before this term came into common use, the spread of certain technologies, the exploitation of natural resources and the pace of development were exerting a global impact on the environment.

In principle, a world-wide problem implies world-wide solutions. The record shows that such solutions are extremely difficult and time-consuming to agree, and even more difficult to implement. Individual governments fear that the competitiveness of their economies and the aspirations of their citizens may be compromised if they take action in isolation to limit environmental impacts. Individual companies similarly fear a loss of competitiveness, and lobby their governments accordingly. A world perspective can induce a feeling that individuals or individual organizations are powerless, and that only actions by governments and the largest international organizations can tackle the problem.

Sustainability

In the last fifteen to twenty years, the concept of sustainability has been developed. A report by the Bruntland Commission for the UN in 1987 defined sustainable development as that which:

> ensure[s] that it meets the needs of the present without compromising the ability of future generations to meet their own needs.

A succinct statement, to be sure. At a simple level, one can see that exploiting a renewable natural resource at greater than its natural recovery rate is unsustainable. The current rate of increase of atmospheric CO_2 is thought likely, on present evidence, to compromise the needs of future generations. For such examples, the Bruntland criterion seems unhelpful, but what about the use of non-renewable resources such as minerals? Any rate of usage will ultimately exhaust supplies. Do we stop using such resources? As yet, the concept of sustainability is not sufficiently developed to provide us with the answers to such questions.

Seen from the perspective of the twenty-first century, many developments in thinking in the past seem to have been very rapid, yet to the people who lived at the time, the changes were quite gradual. Mass changes in thinking take time, and sustainability certainly requires a huge shift in thinking, followed by changes in behaviour. The change in thinking is happening, but the necessary changes in behaviour are lagging behind. This does not mean that we should simply wait, but it does imply that there is no easy solution. On the positive side, the concept of sustainability can focus our research and analysis and provide direction, and this may be its greatest contribution.

It is worth examining what progress has been made in our thinking on environmental issues. There is a much greater awareness that our actions do have an effect on the environment. There is a general acceptance that climate change is occurring, although the rate of change is arguable. Chlorofluorocarbons (CFCs) are now seen as 'bad'. Recycling schemes have been started. Training is widely available. 'Green' politicians have been elected. The UK government has published some sustainability principles, and the UK Environment Agency publishes an annual 'state of the environment' report. The ISO 14001 standard has been accepted internationally as a model for environmental management systems. Some large corporations have started environmental reporting. In addition, schemes to rate the environmental risks to capital are available as a guide to investment decisionmaking.

Many environmental activists regard each and all of these as quite inadequate, but they are evidence that change is happening albeit slowly. We must build on this.

There are some obvious problems. One significant barrier to the change in thinking is the generally low level of awareness and understanding of environmental issues among the public. An example of this is the widespread belief that global warming is the cause of any unusual weather events. Too much of the debate is still at the 'four legs good, two legs bad' level. The definition of sustainability has been referred to above, and the UK government's proposals on sustainability also include 'high and consistent growth'. Environmental costs are not yet factored into the costs of materials, energy, production and distribution. Recycling capacity and markets for recycled materials fall well short of what is required. Sustainable sources of energy and materials cannot meet current needs. The tools for deciding what is the environmentally preferred option are still in the hands of experts, and the results can be counter-intuitive. Solving one problem may result in another which is no less environmentally significant. For instance, it is not so long ago that diesel was considered an environmentally better option than petrol, and the reduction of volatile organic solvents in paints may incur much greater energy usage for drying/curing.

Environmental strategy considerations

A business that plans on the assumption that tomorrow will be like today risks its very survival. Processes and plants may be rendered obsolete when they become incapable of meeting emissions standards economically. Products may be banned, as has happened with CFCs. Some raw materials may become unavailable or very expensive. Insurance cover may become unobtainable. Hard-won reputations may be destroyed. The ability to simply export such problems to areas with less rigorous controls has been reduced, and will reduce further in the years to come.

There is an old adage in business – 'Do not try to educate your customers.' Businesses are limited in their ability to persuade people to buy what they do not want – remember the Sinclair C5? Customers buy on value. What is the value to a customer of the environmental performance of what they buy, given that they have a choice? How many householders would pay a higher price for electricity because it came from a wind farm? Appealing to altruism does not seem to work. We are more likely to change our behaviour when we feel or fear the impact on our daily lives or the short-term future. The further away the effect is in time or space, the weaker our response, and this is certainly true for businesses. Businesses can be good at responding to immediate, well-defined pressures, but do less well on 'fuzzy', longer-term issues.

Businesses are now faced with some obvious pressures for changes in thinking and behaviour arising from existing environmental concerns:

- planning laws requiring environmental impact assessment for certain types of development
- emphasis on the use of 'brownfield' sites
- a growing body of environmental laws and regulations
- tougher emission limits, fines and liabilities for pollution incidents
- waste disposal regimes and taxes
- a growing awareness of the impacts of and the limits to the exploitation of natural resources
- the increasing cost of energy and materials as environmental costs are factored in
- increased insurance premiums for organizations with high-environmental-risk operations and a history of pollution incidents
- growing public awareness of environmental issues and the exercise of consumer choice
- powerful environmental lobby and interest groups
- 'quality of life' influencing people's decisionmaking
- the availability of environmental information and opinion on the Internet and elsewhere.

Most of these pressures are no different in principle from those which commercial organizations have always faced, and to which they have adapted. For most businesses, 'sustainability' means ensuring the continued viability of the business. Anything that is seen to imperil this continuity will engage their attention. The continued viability of a business in the very short term may simply involve operational responses – controls to meet emissions standards, cutting energy usage, reducing waste and limiting liabilities for fines and clean-up costs by 'end-of-pipe' solutions. If new technologies, designs and products are required for continued viability, the timescale will be much longer, and significant investment will be required.

The conclusions are clear. Short- and long-term environmental issues must be considered in formulating the policies and strategies for all businesses. Progress will be made when environmental sense is seen to make good business sense, and this is the key to eliciting environmental responsibility from commercial organizations.

The pressures listed above can be resolved into four main driving forces:

- compliance with legislation
- avoidance of liability
- managing costs
- preserving reputation.

Organizations can understand these forces and plan accordingly once they have the facts. A sensible first step, therefore, is for a business to gather and analyse the necessary information – but what happens afterwards?

Management systems

Organizations cannot achieve what they set out to do in a haphazard fashion, with people simply 'doing their best' or 'giving it their all'. Policies must be developed to provide direction. Some structure is essential. Capable people who understand what is required must be employed. Critical activities need to be planned and co-ordinated. Resources need to be provided. Feedback on what is being achieved must be available. A management system links these elements into a functioning whole. It enables the organization to achieve its objectives, and gives confidence to management that the objectives will be met. It should also give confidence to external parties such as customers and regulators that declared objectives will be met. A management system standard is a statement of the essential elements of an effective system for meeting a set of requirements based on experience. The ISO 9000 standard has been accepted around the world as the model for the management of quality. In spite of many well-publicized problems and criticisms, it is widely used by most large organizations in all sectors, and has led to acceptance of management systems standards and the management systems approach.

ISO 14001: 1996

BACKGROUND

In 1992, the British Standards Institute (BSI) published BS 7750 as an environmental management systems standard. It was firmly based on ISO 9001, and was tested extensively with pilot companies. This standard did not find international acceptance, partly because it was felt to be too prescriptive and too onerous in its requirements. The document was withdrawn soon after the acceptance of ISO 14001 as an International Standard in 1996. The UK and the other countries of the EU adopted ISO 14001 at this time. This standard caused a culture shock to those who were used to delving into the minutiae of ISO 9001 documentation requirements. Some environmentalists were disappointed because the concept of sustainability was missing, and at first sight it appeared that organizations could decide for themselves what constituted significant environmental aspects and impacts, and could factor in economic considerations. This, it was felt, would mean that organizations could decide to do very little, and still claim compliance with the standard and receive the third-party certification 'badge'.

Before considering this Standard in detail, it is worth looking at its declared purpose, because it is against this that it must be judged. The introduction to the Standard states:

> The overall aim of this International Standard is to support environmental protection and prevention of pollution in balance with socio-economic needs.

REQUIREMENTS

The Standard is based on a simple and well-tried model: Plan–Do–Check–Act. It starts with the establishment of an environmental policy, and goes through a four-stage cycle of Planning, Implementation, Checking/Corrective Action and Management Review to achieve continual improvement in environmental performance.

The Standard states a number of detailed requirements which an organization must meet:

- a documented environmental policy statement
- identification of the significant environmental aspects (causes) and their impacts (effects)
- identification of the legal and regulatory requirements applicable to the environmental aspects
- setting of environmental objectives and targets consistent with the policy
- establishing programmes to achieve the objectives and targets
- defining roles, responsibilities and authorities and providing essential resources
- appointing a management representative or representatives
- providing training and awareness and ensuring the competence of personnel whose work may create a significant impact on the environment
- ensuring internal communication and responding to communications from external interested parties and considering the need for external communication on environmental aspects
- documenting a management system
- controlling documents
- controlling operations associated with the significant environmental aspects
- establishing and testing emergency preparedness and response plans
- monitoring and measuring key characteristics of its operations
- investigating nonconformity and taking corrective action
- maintaining appropriate records
- auditing the system to a programme
- reviewing the system to ensure its continuing suitability, adequacy and effectiveness, and addressing any need for changes to policy and objectives.

There are many features that those familiar with the ISO 9000 series will recognize, and the correlation charts in Annexe B of ISO 14001 make this point.

The 'shall be documented' requirements are restricted to:

- policy
- environmental objectives and targets
- roles, responsibilities and authorities
- communications from external interested parties
- procedures where their absence could lead to deviations from the policy, objectives and targets
- procedures for monitoring and measuring
- procedure for evaluating compliance with legal and regulatory requirements
- management review.

There are, of course, requirements for records, which are, of necessity, documents. Elsewhere, the words 'establish and maintain' are used.

POLICY

Perhaps the most effective clause in the Standard deals with policy requirements (4.2). The organization must document a policy statement that:

- is appropriate to the nature, scale and environmental impacts of its activities, products or services
- includes commitments to comply with environmental legislation and regulations, continually improve environmental performance and prevent pollution
- provides the framework for setting and reviewing environmental objectives and targets
- must be implemented and maintained and communicated to all employees
- is made available to the public.

This is a more onerous set of requirements than that for quality contained in ISO 9001, and it is instructive that the ISO 9000: 2000 standard has borrowed heavily from this wording. The implications of this clause are far-reaching. Logically, the organization must know the nature, scale and impacts of its activities, products and services and the applicable legislative and regulatory requirements in order to set an appropriate policy. Commitments to compliance with legal and regulatory requirements and to the prevention of pollution can be tested objectively.

The Standard defines 'continual improvement' as:

> the process of enhancing the environmental management system to achieve improvements in overall environmental performance in line with the organisation's environmental policy.

The clause covering objectives and targets (4.3.3) makes it clear that the organization must consider legal requirements, its significant environmental aspects and the views of interested parties when setting and reviewing objectives and targets. It appears that continual improvement can be demonstrated by setting and achieving suitable objectives and targets within the framework of the policy, and thus can be assessed objectively.

Public access to the policy should cause organizations to think before publishing an anodyne 'feelgood' statement (all too common in quality policy statements) or making unrealistic claims for environmental performance or intentions.

SUPPORTING REQUIREMENTS

The remaining requirements in the Standard clearly support the achievement of the policy commitments. The requirements for communication internally and for the training, awareness and competence of personnel are a positive move to involve everyone whose work may create a significant effect on the environment. The requirements for the control and monitoring of operations with a significant effect on the environment and for a procedure for evaluating compliance with relevant environmental legislation support the policy commitments for legal compliance and the prevention of pollution. The audit requirements links the audit programme to the environmental importance of activities and to the results of previous audits. Policy commitments fall within the scope of audit.

Management review must consider the continued suitability, adequacy and effectiveness of the system for implementing the policy, and the need for changes to policy and objectives in the light of audit results, changing circumstances and the commitment to continual improvement.

EMAS

Although not a management system as such, the ECO Management and Audit Scheme (EMAS) requires the implementation of an environmental management system which meets certain specified criteria, and ISO 14001 does meet these requirements. EMAS is an EU initiative to promote environmental performance improvement. The scheme is voluntary, and the UK is piloting its application to local authority services. Registration is available on a site-by-site basis, rather than for the whole organization. In addition to a management system, EMAS goes further in requiring the publication of a quantified declaration of environmental impacts and the demonstration of progressive improvement. Such statements must be validated by independent verifiers. Each EU Member State has at least one body for accediting such verifiers. In the UK, this function is carried out by the United Kingdom Accreditation Service (UKAS), which also accredits third-party certification bodies for ISO 9001 and ISO 14001 certification.

The ISO 9000 experience

This Standard began as BS 5750 in 1979. In 1987, it was revised and accepted as an International Standard (the ISO 9000 series), and revised in 1994 and again in 2000. The third-party certification infrastructure began soon after the first release as a way of giving confidence to purchasers that an organization had the capability to meet the purchaser's requirements by implementing a quality management system which met the requirements of the Standard. It was intended that this independent verification would reduce the number of purchasers wishing to carry out audits on their suppliers. From its earliest days, the UK government believed that the adoption of such systems would drive up the quality levels of British manufacturing industry by linking the way organizations worked to meeting customers' requirements. It was strongly supported by the government, until the early 1990s, with several quite generous grant schemes. There is no doubt that there have been beneficial effects:

- In the hands of an organization committed to meeting customers' requirements, ISO 9001 has provided a framework for capturing and communicating best practice, and the system will be designed to support the achievement of business objectives.
- Organizations have formalized their ways of working, leading to greater consistency of actions and outcomes.
- Many organizations have been persuaded to address quality as an important management issue, rather than as an inspection activity.
- Audit has provided objective information about the management of activities – perhaps for the first time.
- Auditing for effectiveness by well-trained auditors has identified opportunities for improvement.
- The international acceptance of the ISO 9000 series has led to a common language of quality, and has reduced some barriers to trade.
- The best certification bodies have pointed out weaknesses in management awareness and control, which has led to improvement.

There have also been some well-publicized problems and justified criticisms that are instructive for ISO 14001 management systems:

- Purchasers demanding that their suppliers have certified quality management systems has led to a minimalist approach where the certification 'badge' is seen as more important than quality performance.
- In the UK, the government support scheme rules encouraged consultants to prepare one procedure for each clause in the Standard. The lack of process thinking and process analysis meant that interfaces between departments or functions were neglected. Such systems were not effective at driving improvement. The views of customers were not taken into account – unless they complained.
- Third-party certification bodies (and their auditors) became the arbiters of what was acceptable, and in some cases the bodies published additional requirements (although these were eventually withdrawn).
- The number of third-party bodies has exploded so that today there are more than seventy such bodies accredited by UKAS. *Caveat emptor!*
- Intense price competition has led to cost-cutting, which in essence means less time is spent on the certification audit process.
- The internal audit requirements in the standard quickly contracted into a compliance check rather than a test of the effectiveness of the system for meeting customers' requirements.
- The most trenchant critics of ISO 9000 believe that it enshrines a command and control ethos, which is both ineffective and inappropriate.

The net result is that there is a huge gulf between systems designed to drive quality improvement and support the achievement of business objectives, and those written simply to achieve certification. Many systems are now kept in being solely to gain entry to tender lists and because the loss of certification is seen as a black mark in the eyes of purchasers. It is not uncommon to find large organizations striving to improve quality performance quite independently of their quality systems.

Some of these problems arose directly from the nature of the earlier ISO 9000 series Standards – for example a procedure-driven approach, no requirement for continual improvement, and no emphasis on seeking the views of customers. There is no doubt, however, that many more problems arose from the certification process. The capabilities of certification auditors are highly variable, and the importance of quality policy and objectives has been underemphasized. Meeting the requirements of the Standard was the overriding concern of both the certifier and the certified, and did not guarantee quality – you do not have to have certification to manage quality, but you do not have to manage quality to achieve certification.

The latest revision of the Standard, ISO 9001: 2000, has attempted to address all of these perceived defects.

As well as the strengthened policy requirements, ISO 9001: 2000 includes requirements for identifying the organization's processes, continual improvement (which implies the establishment of a baseline) and customer feedback. All these features had already been present in ISO 14001: 1996.

What has been achieved?

It is clear that many of the criticisms of the ISO 9000 series have been recognized by the authors of ISO 14001. As we have seen, ISO 14001 places great emphasis on policy and commitments, which can be assessed objectively. The environmental field is subject to a growing body of legislation and regulation, and penalties and liabilities can arise independently of the market (which is generally not true for quality). The Standard explicitly requires compliance, and this too can be assessed objectively. There is a requirement for the identification of environmental aspects and impacts, and the most significant must be addressed. Prevention of pollution and continual improvement are required.

ISO 14001 does not enshrine documentation. Instead, the 'establish and maintain' wording allows the freedom to achieve compliance by a balance of communication, awareness, training and competence, as well as documentation. The task of auditors is more readily seen as that of testing effectiveness, rather than as checking documents.

By including 'products and services' within the scope of potentially significant environmental aspects, ISO 14001 causes an organization to think about the environmental performance of its supply chain, and the impacts associated with the distribution, use and ultimate disposal of its products. For many organizations, this demands new thinking, the gathering of new information, and the use of unfamiliar tools such as lifecycle analysis. Some major purchasers now evaluate the environmental performance of their key suppliers (B&Q, Blue Circle), and encourage them to address ISO 14001 (Ford).

One common thread to the reports from organizations with experience of implementing ISO 14001 requirements is the identification of actual or potential cost savings. Typically, these have come from rethinking the usage of energy and materials and the reduction and/or recycling of waste. These benefits may have come about because of increasing costs, but ISO 14001 does seem to be providing a framework for analysis and action.

Because the Standard does not set absolute performance criteria, it is quite possible for organizations carrying out similar activities in the same country to have quite different environmental performances and still meet the requirements of the Standard. Environmental legislation varies from country to country, thus similar organizations in different countries can have differing environmental performances and still achieve registration to ISO 14001. At first sight, this would seem to encourage global organizations to go where the regime of controls is less stringent. In fact, there is good evidence that some such organizations are working to operate all their plants to the standards of their home base (IBM, Ford, Hyundai Electronics) where these are higher than the local ones. Shareholder and stakeholder influence can be global too!

In formulating objectives and targets, the organization must consider not only the legal requirements and significant environmental aspects, but also its technological options and financial, operational and business requirements. This does not mean that an organization can simply declare 'no action' on significant environmental aspects because it would be costly or disruptive. In the UK, for operations subject to permits to operate, the existing law and the new Pollution Prevention and Control Act 1999 give the appropriate regulators considerable powers to impose conditions relating to best available techniques. There is no intention to force companies out of business, but dispensations for incapable processes will not be open-ended. For non-regulated organizations, the certifying body will need to be satisfied about commitment, and should not allow unjustified opt-outs. The position is broadly similar in other EU countries.

It is not clear what the uptake of ISO 14001 has been in the UK. The number of certifications awarded is significant, but in any case probably not a true measure of the use of the standard. Anecdotal evidence suggests that many more organizations have begun to address environmental issues but do not wish (or see the need) to go through the certification process. The experience with ISO 9001/2 certification may have caused some to question the added value of the certification process. Another factor may be a reluctance to open the organization to scrutiny where legal liability could be involved. Not surprisingly, the uptake of EMAS in the UK has been much lower than for ISO 14001 alone. There is an interesting contrast with Germany, which has far fewer organizations with ISO 9001 certificates, but far more with EMAS (UK 78, Germany 2523 registrations at the time of writing).

If an organization is committed to controlling and improving its environmental performance, ISO 14001 provides a coherent and powerful model for a management system applicable to any organization in any sector. It can be used across the whole organization, site by site or even product by product. The management system can be standalone, or it can be integrated with business management systems, quality management systems and health and safety management systems. The policy statement can be used as a set of audit criteria because the other requirements of the standard are logically designed to support the implementation of the policy. The 'establish and maintain' wording places the emphasis on outcomes rather than prescriptions. There is good evidence that organizations can save money, and the savings are likely to increase as environmental awareness grows, public sensitivity rises and environmental taxes increase.

For committed organizations, certification will be regarded as an external proof of commitment and/or as an internal milestone along an improvement route.

If an organization is not committed and has as its aim the 'badge' of certification, ISO 14001 requirements will be difficult to achieve and maintain. That is not to say that it will not be possible. The certification industry and the accreditation bodies will have failed the country (and possibly the planet) if certification to ISO 14001 does not avoid the problems of worthless certificates which have tarnished ISO 9001. Of particular note is the fact that the same third-party certification bodies dominate ISO 14001 certification and the same accreditation bodies act as the regulators. Only time will tell if the certification process is capable of meeting the challenge.

CHAPTER

33 Management System Integration

Pat Donnellan

Introduction

The integration of management systems for quality, safety and the environment has great attractions for organizations, but is something that poses a difficulty for many businesses. There are pressures from customers to implement quality systems such as ISO 9001, QS 9000, TS 16949 and current Good Manufacturing Practices (cGMP), depending on sector requirements. Environmental pressures are coming from legislation, customers and the community. Increasing numbers of businesses are required to hold pollution control licences due to the presence of high levels of hazardous materials in their processes. This in turn requires the company to implement an environmental management system (EMS). In the area of occupational health and safety, legislative pressures on hazardous industries such as chemicals require a safety management system under the Seveso II Directive (Council Directive 96/082/EEC). Other industries work on the basis of a safety management system or risk management in order to comply with health and safety legislation.

There are a number of accepted systems in use, the most popular being the ISO 9000 series or its derivatives for quality, ISO 14001 or EMAS for the environment, and a number of systems for safety that have been modelled on the ISO 9000 or ISO 14000 series of standards. Of these, OHSAS 18001 is the most recent, and is gaining popular acceptance due to its similarity to ISO 14001. Other approaches include ISA 2000, UNE 81901, Seveso II guidelines, and International Labour Organisation (ILO) guidelines. Many organizations have aligned the systems by developing single procedures for the common elements. Others have developed safety and environmental systems in parallel, due to the similarity of the systems and the common need for risk assessment and risk management. Others have added safety and environmental requirements on to their quality system, but have still kept the organizations separate. The difficulty with these approaches is that there is still a large duplication of work and resources.

In this chapter we look at various publications on integration, and review a new integrated model of management practice developed by the author at the National University of Ireland, Galway, that facilitates a very high degree of integration of these systems – almost 90 per cent of all activities.

The integration of quality, safety, and environmental management

What does 'integration' mean, as applied to quality, safety and environmental management systems? There are different perspectives on the issue. The Sharp Corporation wanted to have the best possible dealers in areas of quality, safety, environment, finance and personnel training (Corcoran, 1996). They required accreditation to ISO 9002 (as it then was) and BS 7750 for quality and environmental management. ISO 14001 was only issued in 1996, and BS 7750 was a popular choice for many organizations prior to that. This form of integration was based on the alignment of the various systems involved, and combining the best of the individual standards in one single standard, with an independent assessment by a recognized accreditation body. The benefit for the Sharp dealers lay in removing bureaucracy and using the same assessors and consultants, thus reducing cost. Since that time, ISO 14001 has been adopted as an environmental management system (EMS), and OHSAS 18001 as a safety management system (SMS), and ISO 9001 has been revised.

This link to standards requires a high level of synergy between the standards used and a new approach to interpreting and implementing the systems. Wilkinson and Dale (1999) carried out a literature review on the integrated management systems approach to quality, safety and environmental management in which they researched over eighty publications, most of which were written since 1996. They found a differentiation between the ideas of integration and alignment (MacGregor Associates, 1996). Integration was seen as having a top-level management 'core' with modular supporting standards that cover the specifics. Alignment, on the other hand, suggested a series of parallel systems with a high degree of commonality between them. These tend to be in the area of documentation, auditing or self-assessment, training of the workforce, reduction in individual external audits, and managerial responsibilities. The alignment of these standards can dramatically reduce the workload at the implementation phase. The extent to which integration can be applied depends on the specific company, the processes involved, and the organizational culture, to mention but a few factors.

Four different approaches to integration have been described (Wilkinson and Dale, 1998). The first approach involves the integration of the individual systems into every function in the organization, with a full organization-wide implementation of a QMS such as ISO 9001 as a start. The second approach is where integration is seen as combining the individual standards with a focus on the common elements as outlined earlier. The third approach involves the integration of the QMS, EMS and SMS with other systems such as Investors in People (IIP). In this case, the standards are linked through IIP, which can address training for the three other systems. The fourth approach is the one adopted by Sharp, where certified and uncertified systems are combined into one integrated system.

The approach taken by an organization deserves careful consideration. Strategic, cultural, business and flexibility considerations must be assessed. Integration has often led to a reduced flexibility, and that true, flexible integration must be planned, designed and implemented *by* the firm, *for* the firm (Crowe, 1992). This suggests that the approach to an integrated system is still a matter for the individual organization, taking all of its circumstances into account. An integrated system is seen as the linking of two systems in a way that results in a loss of independence to one or both systems (Karapetrovic and Willborn, 1998), and can involve the use of a conceptual model such as the European

Foundation for Quality Management's Model for Business Excellence, which spans the entire business. Hoyle (1996) supported continuous improvement, from the TQM philosophy, but also pointed out that a fully integrated system must cover all disciplines across the entire organization. He also suggested that the organization needed to be in the same 'culture mode'. Shillito (1995) wrote of the need to achieve 'unity of purpose', and advocated an approach based on assessment of risks and the effects on quality, safety and the environment, and continuous improvement.

Jonker and Klaver (1998) and Jonker (2000) suggested that 'integrating standards and systems offers a way to streamline improvement activities'. Integration lacks a methodology, and they propose integration at different levels: policy, conceptual, system, normative and pragmatic. A single policy based on a strategic plan to integrate is necessary, otherwise one ends up with a number of parallel policies for each new system. The EFQM model may be adapted as the conceptual model. The development of the model in a step-by-step way leads to integration. The system based on a model 'means that the requirements such as preparation, assessment, auditing, improvement and assurance are brought into one system'. Thus the model development, the method and the system form a cyclic development pattern. The normative approach involves taking into account the main standards and their norms and values, and handling the differences in an explicit manner. This makes integration easier. At the pragmatic level, integration is viewed from the employee's point of view. It makes sense to have one set of questionnaires, instructions and routines, as having separate documents for each system will only serve to confuse workers, who are likely to make mistakes, get confused and lose motivation. Employee training is therefore a key element in integration. Training on the standards and their philosophies, along with task-related training, is necessary if the system is to succeed.

The IOSH policy on integration

The Institution of Occupational Safety and Health (IOSH) policy statement on integration 'refers largely to matters such as organizational structures, strategic decision making, resource allocation, and the processes of auditing and reviewing performance'. The needs of each discipline should be taken into account without building islands of expertise in each system. This expertise should be applied to all system requirements, thus leading to a more efficient use of these experts. There are also philosophical differences in each system in areas such as quality standards for medical devices versus the more immediate risk from a manufacturing process. The philosophical focus must be maintained, as well as the basic system requirements. The organizations most likely to achieve integration are those that have good communication founded on trust, respect for the expertise of colleagues, and confidence in the change management process. These organizations are considered to have a positive culture, and are likely to introduce streamlined procedures and more effective decisionmaking.

Integration provides an opportunity for using the combined brainpower of all available specialists, which increases the possibility of arriving at an optimum solution. The momentum in one element may drive another element that in an independent system might get bogged down. Likewise, a positive culture in one system can transfer to another. On the other hand it is often argued that since the current systems work well, they should be left alone, or that the specialists will not embrace the new system, or that conceptual differences are difficult to reconcile. These same specialists may over-apply some elements from one discipline to another. There is the fear of building a newer, bigger, centralized, complex system with even more bureaucracy attached. The main reason for keeping existing systems separate is the period of organizational vulnerability while the new system is being implemented. This suggests that careful thought should be given to a parallel phase that leads to integration, assuming integration is the end strategy. The prerequisites for integration deal mainly with proper planning, education and training, metrics and the approach to handling the extra work at all levels of the organization. In general, an effective change management process is required to prepare the employees for the new systems. Once the preparations are in place, the integration process begins with the choice of an integrated management system model. This may involve using an existing system as a core, or shifting the core emphasis onto a new system. The strategy may involve a phased implementation, allowing time for the necessary training and organizational adjustments. The key maintenance work revolves around change management and responding to potentially significant events, and the changes that follow.

Tranmer (1996), in his analysis of integration problems, focused on the areas of structure, language and tools. His view of organizations trying to build the Tower of Babel on quicksand using a toothbrush conjures up a strange picture. The fact is that organizations often fail to set out a good foundation before building their management systems, and then lack a common language to ensure proper communication. Finally, they often use the wrong tools. He suggests a process focus that he breaks into core, supporting and assurance processes. Suitable tools are critical. In all organizations there are tools in daily use that could be applied to new systems. For example, simple flowcharting can be used to show decisionmaking processes as well as the more traditional process flow application.

Case study: The Tasman experience

The Tasman Pulp and Paper Company Ltd developed a single quality management programme incorporating quality, safety and environmental management in order to harness its team effort to maximum advantage (Massey, 1996). They used ISO 9000, ISO 14001 and a safety management system. They focused on the common elements of the various systems such as management responsibility, common audit, management review, nonconformity and corrective and preventive action, purchasing, calibration, design, document control, records, training, statistical techniques, and inspection and testing. These areas are the main focus of ISO 9001, and were extended to address environmental management. In areas such as a common audit, Tasman used employees with process knowledge and people living locally who therefore had a vested interest in the local environment. They also operated with an internal customer focus perspective, and teams sought to exceed these internal customer needs and minimize waste. The management focus was on planning, setting targets at process control level, and acting responsibly to the new culture of accountability created by new legislation. One of the main focus areas was changing behaviour at the levels of the group and the individual, as they believed that this would lead to a change in attitude towards quality, safety and environment.

An integrated model of management practice

An integrated model for quality, safety and environment that is based on management practice rather than on meeting elements of a particular standard was developed at the Department of Industrial Engineering, National University of Ireland, Galway. A total of 311 specific good management practices relating to quality, environment and safety were identified by groups of experts from academia, consultancy companies and practising business managers. Detailed analysis showed that only 13 per cent of these practices were unique to one of the three aspects (quality, safety and the environment), so it is clear that there is generally a real opportunity for developing fully integrated management systems. This is further supported by the fact that 105 practices are in areas which cover normal management activities across other functions.

The advantage of this model is that it addresses normal business programmes such as people development, strategic planning and partnerships alongside the requirements of quality, safety and the environment. This offers the opportunity to meet the organization's objectives without having to assign task forces or special committees to install systems, since the practices, when sustained, will do the job for the company.

The specific practices identified can be ranked in order of priority for an organization:

1 legal requirements
2 minimum business practices
3 certification requirements
4 total quality, safety and environmental (Q, S & E) practices
5 current best practice.

Detailed analysis showed the breakdown by ranking to be:

1 Legal requirements – 39 practices
2 Normal business practices – 38 practices
3 Certification requirements – 103 practices
4 Total Q, S & E practices – 92 practices
5 Current best practices – 39 practices.

By developing 77, or 25 per cent, of these practices, an organization will achieve a level of performance that is common to the approximately 95 per cent of organizations that do not pursue certification as a business requirement. This does not necessarily imply that these 95 per cent of companies practise only the 1s and 2s. Many of them will implement 3s, 4s and 5s, but choose not to have their systems certified.

Some features of the NUI Integrated Management System

Using appropriate software, it is possible to sort the practices by general topic and by area of responsibility. Table 33.1 relates the major elements of the system to the responsibility for each.

Table 31.1 Major elements and responsibilities contained in the model

System elements	*Responsibility/owner*
Business results	General Manager
Current best practice	Function Manager
Continuous improvement, benchmarking, teamwork	Management Systems Manager
Customer-related	Human Resources
Environment	Maintenance and Facilities Manager
Human-resource-, people- and organization-related	Operations Manager
Health and safety	Purchasing Manager
Process control	Area Supervisor
Partnerships	Safety Officer
Quality system	Environmental Officer
Strategic planning	Workers
Total Q, S & E	Engineer/technical resources
	Expert in a particular area
	Product design and development

Table 33.2 is an extract from the model, showing some of the human-resource-related practices that are required by various laws and regulations.

The model proposes that any organization must comply with 77 practices – all the practices ranked 1 and 2. Any organization that wishes to achieve certification must adopt 103 further practices, those ranked 3. This is in line with the general experience of certified organizations that certification does impose a large number of extra activities and procedures. Within this model, the additional practices address quality, safety and environmental requirements of ISO 9001: 2000, OHSAS 18001: 1999, and ISO 14001: 1996.

Table 33.2 Human-resource-related practices: Sample of level 1 practices

Focus	**Specific aspect**	**Specific activities, behaviour or practice or programmes**	**Rank**
Human Resources	Employee health	First aid supplies and competent persons are available on all shifts.	1
	Employee health	The health impact from processes is evaluated.	1
	Employee protection	Personal protective equipment requirements are defined and the equipment is provided.	1
	Non-employee safety	Specific safety guidelines are in place for visitors.	1

It should be noted that this model facilitates continuous improvement by incremental implementation of the practices starting with 1s, and progressing to certification, if required. Once these practices are integrated into the business, the organization can decide on an improvement path leading to best practice.

The model defines current best practices for an organization in terms of:

- continual improvement
- cultural aspects
- human resources
- knowledge transfer
- people participation
- training
- promoting innovation
- work with legislators
- management commitment to strategic issues
- concern for the future
- supplier development and partnerships
- new technology for safety, quality and environment
- close relationship with the community and public.

As a business priority, the organization should adopt the practices mentioned above, but it is also clear that some of the current best practices can be implemented at any time if the resources are deployed for these activities. An example of a best practice from the model is: 'There is a *Good Neighbour* scheme in place to share information and develop joint programmes.' This can be practised, but without positive results in waste management, emissions and pollution, this activity will not be successful, as it requires real programmes for co-operation, and positive results, in order to be regarded as a successful practice.

Implementing the model

The starting point for implementing the integration project is to carry out a self-assessment using the model, and then to develop the practices on a priority basis, subject to resource constraints. Legal compliance in the areas of product safety and the health and safety of employees are obvious priorities, followed by hazardous waste control. Within the law, one must do what is 'reasonably practicable' to assure health and safety, applying BATNEEC (Best Available Technology Not Entailing Excessive Cost) principles to environmental compliance. Investments in new technology for environmental compliance will, of course, also offer opportunities for improvements in safety and quality performance.

The initial step is to assess the current practices in the organization. This is best done by reviewing the list of practices in the model and assessing the degree to which they have been incorporated into the activities of the organization. To record the degree of compliance, a scale such as the following may be used:

A It is a normal practice with a defined owner.
B It is done infrequently – not practised on a regular basis.
C The practice has just begun, and resources have been allocated.

D It is not practised in the company.
0 It is not applicable to our business.

For all practices ranked 1, the required standard is full compliance with all relevant legal and regulatory practices – 100 per cent As. It is to be expected that in some cases not all of these practices will be fully integrated into the business, and may be at the B or C level of compliance. In that case, the organization must focus, initially, on compliance with these requirements, leaving the 2-ranked practices till later. The progress can thus be monitored in terms of the percentage of practices that are fully implemented.

Following the self-assessment audit, a plan of action can be put in place that prioritizes the work to be done based on perceived returns for the business by the management team.

The level of integration in the model

Examination of the complete list of management practices shows that they break down among the different disciplines as follows. Note that many practices meet more than one objective:

- Practices relating to quality management 104
- Practices relating to environmental management 100
- Practices relating to safety management 125
- Specific to quality practice 6
- Specific to environmental practice 10
- Specific to safety practice 26
- Practices relating to other management areas 125
- Practices related to safety, quality and environment 42

The specific breakdown of the 311 practices – (Q)37+(HS)76+(E)55+70+68+5=311 is shown in Figure 33.1.

The 42 practices that focus solely on quality, safety or environment are few, numbering 6, 26 and 10 respectively. There is a natural logic to this, in that the organization's first priority should be the immediate safety of its workers followed by concern for the local environment, and only when the business is up and running do the basic issues of quality arise. Beyond these unique practices, which account for 14 per cent of the practices, there is an overlapping focus on quality (104), safety (125) and environment (100), with the number of practices shown in brackets. These practices address areas right across the business, and their breakdown is shown in Figure 33.2.

From these practices, which usually constitute specific programmes in the business, one can develop the business in areas related to the core activities of quality, safety and the environment, and also in areas that are essential for the general management of the company. The main focus is on continuous improvement and human resource development. Note that there is an overlap in these practices, in that, for example, some practices for process control and continuous improvement may be the same. Excluding this overlap, there are 105, or 35 per cent, of the practices in these related business areas. This is the key to integration, as the focus of each practice has multifunctional objectives, with only 14 per cent being unique to quality, safety and the environment. It should be easier to

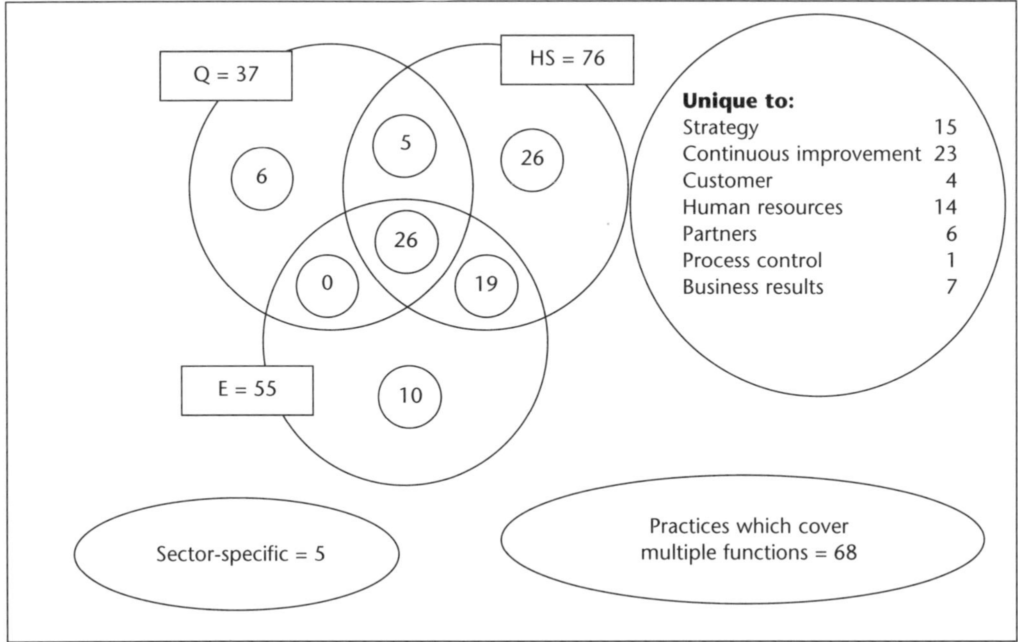

Figure 33.1 Practices by function

focus management attention on these unique aspects. Likewise, given the overlap between the practices in the three areas of safety, quality and the environment, the task of integration is easier, as many practices address at least two out of three of management's responsibilities. The key to integration is to ensure that management is performing its duties in a habitual way as part of its day-to-day activities. When a special effort is required to meet these responsibilities, they tend to be addressed in a less frequent manner, that is, it is not as a *practice.*

Attention is usually focused on safety and the environment in the aftermath of an accident or an incident, or following a visit from the authorities. The approach described here will allow management to promote safety and environmental practices at the same time as addressing quality and other business issues. It is a relatively small step to train people on the needs of all three disciplines, and to incorporate these practices into the normal daily routine. In this way, true integration is possible.

Conclusions

Examination of a comprehensive list of practices implemented in the areas of quality, safety and the environment suggests that the systems for managing these three aspects of the organization's activities can be almost completely integrated, with almost 90 per cent of practices focusing on general good management. Since smaller companies will have fewer resources to dedicate to individual management systems for the three areas of the business, the practice-based, integrated approach has obvious benefits. Given that about 96 per cent of companies in Europe are small or medium-sized enterprises (SMEs), there is wide scope for

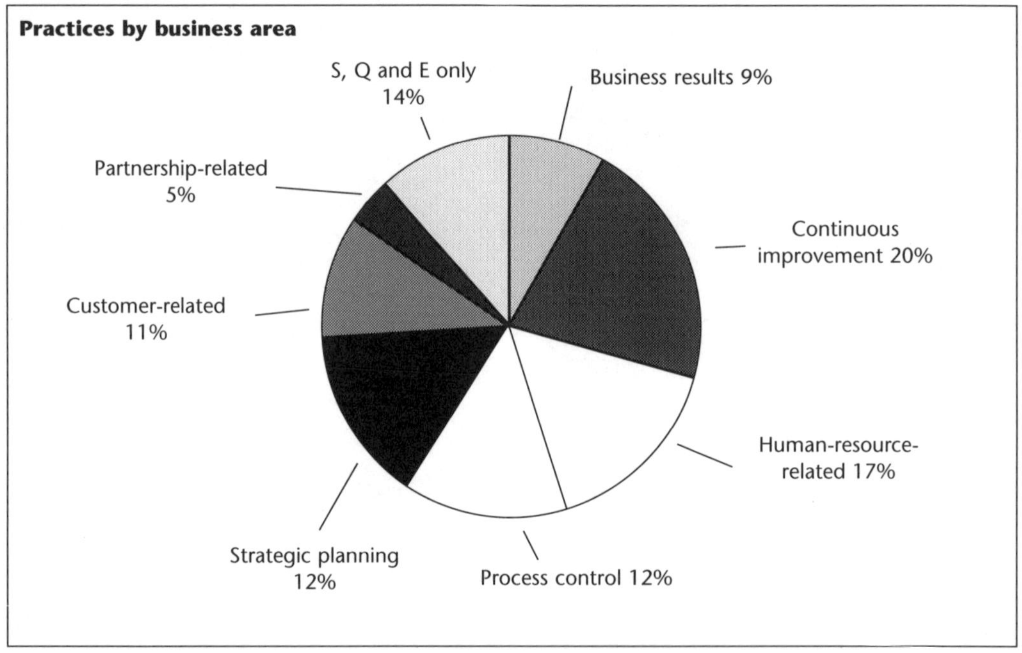

Figure 33.2 Breakdown of practices by function

the integrated practice-based approach to managing quality, safety and the environment.

Further information

Further information about the model used can be obtained from the author: <pat.donnellan@naigalway.ie>.

References

Corcoran, I., 'One goal, one standard', *Quality World*, Vol. 22, No. 10, 1996, pp. 724–6.

Crowe, T.J., 'Integration is not synonymous with flexibility', *International Journal of Operations and Production Management*, Vol. 12, No. 10, 1992, pp. 26–33.

Donnellan, P., Ares, E., Pérez, J. and González, B., *Integration of Quality, Environmental and Occupational Health & Safety Management Systems*, Irish Manufacturing Committee, Annual Conference, NUI, Galway, 2000.

ECBF CD, *Benchmarking FACTS – A European Perspective*, CD-ROM, DTI, UK and European Company Benchmarking Forum, 1998.

EN46001: 1997, *Quality systems: Medical Devices – Particular Requirements for the Application of EN ISO 9001*, National Standards Authority of Ireland, Dublin.

European Foundation for Quality Management, Brussels: <http://www.efqm.org>

EPA, *Integrated Pollution Control Licensing: Guide to Implementation Enforcement in Ireland*, EPA No. LC1, 1994.

Hoyle, D., 'Quality systems – a new perspective', *Quality World*, Vol. 22, No. 10, 1996, pp. 710–13.

Institution of Occupational Safety and Health, 'Integration of Management Systems for OSH,

Environmental Protection and Quality', <http://www.iosh.co.uk/about/condoc/>.

ISO/TS 16949: 1999, *Quality Systems: Automotive Suppliers – Particular Requirements for the Application of ISO 9001: 1994*, International Organization for Standardization, Geneva, 1999.

ISO 14001: 1996, *Environmental Management Systems – Specification with Guidance for Use*, International Organization for Standardization, Geneva, 1996.

ISO 9001: 2000, *Quality Management Systems – Requirements*, International Organization for Standardization, Geneva, 2000.

Jonker, J., 'Management Systems on the Move: A Comparison of Emerging Concepts and Standards in the Area of Quality, Sustainability and Accountability', *The 2000 Symposium of the International Research Network for Quality, Environment and Corporate Social Responsibility*, Manchester, June 2000, pp. 1–7.

Jonker, J. and Klaver, J., 'Integration: A Methodological Perspective', *Quality World*, Vol. 24, No. 8, 1998, pp. 22–3.

Karapetrovic, S. and Willborn, W., 'Integration of quality and environmental management systems', *The TQM Magazine*, Vol. 10, No. 3, 1998, pp. 204–13.

MacGregor Associates, *Study on Management System Standards*, British Standards Institute, London, 1996.

Massey, G., 'Tasman holds the combination to management systems', *Quality World*, October 1996, pp. 727–30.

OHSAS 18001: 1999, *Occupational Health and Safety Management Systems – Specification*, British Standards Institution, London, 1999.

Seaver, M. and O'Mahony, Liam, *ISA 2000: The System for Occupational Health and Safety Management*, Gower, Aldershot, 2000.

Seveso II Directive [96/082/EEC] of 9 December 1996, European Union.

Shillito, D., 'Grand unification theory – should safety, health, environment and quality be managed together or separately?', *Environment Protection Bulletin*, 039, Institution of Chemical Engineers, November 1995, pp. 28–37.

Tranmer, J., 'Overcoming the problems to integrated management systems', *Quality World*, Vol. 22, No. 10, 1996, pp. 714–18.

UNE 81901 EX, *Prevención de riesgos laborales*, AENOR, Madrid, Spain, 1996.

Wilkinson, G. and Dale, B.G., 'System integration: The views and activities of certification bodies', *The TQM Magazine*, Vol. 10, No. 4, 1998, pp. 288–92.

Wilkinson, G. and Dale, B.G., 'Integrated management systems: an examination of the concept and theory', *The TQM Magazine*, Vol. 11, No. 2, 1999, pp. 95–104.

Zwetsloot, G., *Joint Management of Working Conditions, Environment and Quality: In Search of Synergy and Organizational Learning*, Dutch Institute for the Working Environment, NIA, 1994.

Further reading

AICE, *Guidelines for Integrating Process Safety Management, Environment, Safety, Health, and Quality*, American Institute of Chemical Engineers, New York, 1996.

Andreas, M. and Gerfried, Z., 'Generic Management Systems as a Strategy for Lean and Integrated Quality: Environment and Safety Management in SMEs', *The 1999 Business Strategy and the Environment Conference Proceedings*, Leeds, September 2000, pp. 218–27.

Beechner, A. and Koch, J., 'Integrating ISO 9001 and ISO 14001', *Quality Progress*, February 1997, pp. 33–6.

Bititci, U.S., Carrie, A.S. and McDevitt, L., 'Integrated performance measurement systems: An audit and development guide', *The TQM Magazine*, Vol. 9, No. 1, 1997.

Block, M.R., *Integrating ISO 14001 into a Quality Management System*, ASQ Quality Press, Milwaukee, WI, 1999.

<http://www.bsi-global.com>, British Standards Institution.

<http://www.epa.ie>, Environmental Protection Agency, Wexford, Ireland.

Health and Safety Executive: <http://www.hse.gov.uk>.

Health and Safety Authority, Dublin: <http://ww.hsa.ie>.

Kozak, J.R. and Krafcisin, G., *Safety Management and ISO9000/QS9000: A Guide to Alignment and Integration*, Quality Resource, New York, 1997.

McCully, A., 'Why You Should Integrate ISO 9000 and ISO 14000 Systems', *Quality Digest*, 1997a, March.

McCully, A., 'Rockwell Leverages ISO 14000 and ISO 9000 Systems Management Systems', *Quality Digest*, 1997b, April.

Munn, S., 'Management System Integration: Doing Business in the 21st Century', <http://earthlink.net/~rpr-online/ITSMUNN3.htm>, 1996.

Renfrew, D. and Muir, G., 'QUENSHing the thirst for integration', *Quality World*, Vol. 24, No. 8, 1998, pp. 10–13.

Index

Implementing ISO 9000:2000

Matt Seaver

This book is a practical guide to setting up a broad-based quality management system that meets the requirements of ISO 9001:2000. It contains a detailed commentary on each of the clauses of the ISO 9004 standard, which is designed to facilitate best practice throughout the organization, and guidance on how the clauses can be implemented in a simple and practical manner.

The specific requirements of ISO 9001 are addressed in detail and practical advice is given on how to implement simple procedures that will be beneficial to the user as well as complying with the requirements. *Implementing ISO 9000:2000* covers the implications of ISO 9001 for small and medium companies and those in the service sector, as well as the larger manufacturing companies. A comprehensive set of procedures and record sheets for the various aspects of a quality management system, plus guidance on how to determine whether they are necessary in any given case, and how they can be modified to suit the circumstances, are also provided.

GOWER

Gower Handbook of Purchasing Management

Third Edition

Marc Day

Published in association with the Chartered Institute of Purchasing and Supply

The revised third edition of the *Gower Handbook of Purchasing Management* views procurement as standing on the boundary of the firm, looking outwards and scanning the environment for new opportunities and threats. In this respect, as in many others, the new edition is quite different from the previous two, reflecting the many changes that have taken place for businesses over the years. In particular this edition has been slimmed down and focused to assist the reader by working systematically outwards using a purchasing lens to view the wider business world. The aim is to show the potential contribution that purchasing can make as a driver for organizational efficiency and business development. It is this latter requirement, the need for purchasing to generate revenue, that has been identified as being ever more prominent as a demand on purchasing directors' time and effort.

The book is now split into three sections. Part I lays the foundations for building the organization of purchasing in a corporate environment. Part II overlays further applications on the foundations of purchasing organization. The assumption is made that the purchasing activities of a firm are proactive in outlook, gathering knowledge and measuring their current corporate purchasing performance, while also looking to generate revenues for the business. Finally Part III provides case studies which bring to life some of the learning achieved through the framework laid out in the previous parts.

Written by leading practitioners and academics, and published in association with the Chartered Institute of Purchasing and Supply, this book is destined to become a classic in the field.

GOWER

Gower Handbook of Supply Chain Management

Fifth Edition

John Gattorna

The ability to build and also maintain a world class logistics and distribution network is an essential ingredient in the success of the world's leading businesses, but keeping pace with changes in your sector and in others is hard to do. With the *Gower Handbook of Supply Chain Management* you will need to look no further. Written by a team of leading consultants with contributions from leading academic experts, this book will help you to keep pace with the latest global developments in supply chain management and logistics, and plan for the future.

This book has over thirty chapters with detailed accounts of key topics and the latest developments, from e-collaboration and CRM integration, to reverse logistics and strategic sourcing, and includes case studies from Asia, Europe, and North America. It looks at all aspects of operational excellence in logistics and supply chain management.

The *Gower Handbook of Supply Chain Management* will help managers to benchmark their operations against the best-of-breed supply chains across the world. It provides a unique single source of expert opinion and experience.

GOWER

Design for Six Sigma

Launching New Products and Services Without Failure

Geoff Tennant

The ability of Six Sigma as a corporate strategy for excellent customer quality has been clearly demonstrated in the growing number of organizations to adopt this approach. However, the real prize lies with 'advanced' Six Sigma applied directly to the design and implementation of new products and services and which fulfil customer needs and requirements from day one.

This book provides a detailed resource of guidance and inspiration covering all the aspects of business strategy, design, project management and execution necessary for the successful introduction of new products and services under the auspices of a customer-focused Six Sigma approach. With a clear discussion of all the aspects that contribute to the commercial design and launch of new products, services and supporting processes, this work lays the foundation for any organization to take on board *Design for Six Sigma*.

GOWER

Six Sigma: SPC and TQM in Manufacturing and Services

Geoff Tennant

This book comprehensively explores all of the underlying issues and elements which, together, constitute one of the most successful quality and management programmes upon which companies such as Motorola and GE base their success – Six Sigma.

The author was directly involved in implementing Six Sigma quality principles and practices into a European division of GE Capital, deploying this initiative in an entirely service-oriented business for the first time. Drawing from and reflecting on his experience, Geoff Tennant develops a reasoned exploration of the benefits that Six Sigma offers to any organization and what can be expected from start to finish. He investigates the relationship between Six Sigma and quality, customer satisfaction, business processes and organizational structure, statistics and analysis and process improvement methodologies. Aimed at quality professionals, senior management and directors, as well as practitioners and students of Six Sigma, *Six Sigma: SPC and TQM in Manufacturing and Services* provides an in-depth but highly readable insight into the quality initiative that is certain to sweep European companies as it has large and global American corporations.

GOWER